CONNIE MACK
AND THE
EARLY YEARS
OF BASEBALL

Sept 10th 1906

In Consideration of Edward T.
Collins signing for the season
of 1907. The American Base Ball
Club of Phili does hereby
agree not to farm or
loan him to any base
ball Club without his
Consent

       Connie Mack Mgr

NORMAN L. MACHT

CONNIE MACK

AND THE

EARLY YEARS
OF BASEBALL

With a foreword by Connie Mack III

UNIVERSITY OF NEBRASKA PRESS | LINCOLN AND LONDON

Library of Congress
Cataloging-in-Publication Data

Macht, Norman L. (Norman Lee), 1929–
Connie Mack and the early years of baseball
/ Norman L. Macht; with a foreword by
Connie Mack III.   p. cm.
Includes bibliographical references and
index.
ISBN 978-0-8032-3263-1 (cloth: alk. paper)
1. Mack, Connie, 1862–1956. 2. Baseball
players—Pennsylvania—Philadelphia
—Biography. 3. Philadelphia Athletics
(Baseball team)—History. 4. Baseball—
United States—History. I. Title.
GV865.M215M33 2007   796.357092—dc22
[B] 2006102532

Set in Minion. Designed by A. Shahan.

To L. Robert "Bob" Davids
founder of SABR, the Society for
American Baseball Research

CONTENTS

Foreword ix

Preface xi

Acknowledgments xv

Introduction 1
1. Growing up in East Brookfield 7
2. The Young Catcher 18
3. A Rookie in Meriden 29
4. The Bones Battery 39
5. From Hartford to Washington 44
6. Life in the Big Leagues 52
7. Mr. and Mrs. Connie Mack 60
8. Jumping with the Brotherhood 67
9. The Players' League 73
10. Uncertainties of Life and Baseball 84
11. Connie Mack, Manager 95
12. The Terrible-Tempered Mr. Mack 108
13. Fired 120
14. Milwaukee 131
15. Working the System 146
16. Learning How to Handle Men 159
17. Marching behind Ban Johnson 166
18. Launching the New American League 184
19. The City of Brotherly Love
    and "Uncle Ben" Shibe 194
20. Columbia Park and the "Athaletics" 204
21. Raiding the National League 209
22. The Bullfrogs 220
23. The Uniqueness of Napoleon Lajoie 227
24. Winning the Battle of Philadelphia 232

25. A Staggering Blow   259
26. Schreck and the Rube and
    the White Elephant   270
27. Connie Mack's First Pennant   282
28. Signing a Treaty   302
29. The Profits of Peace   308
30. The Macks of Philadelphia   325
31. The First "Official" World Series   336
32. Rebuilding Begins   359
33. "We Wuz Robbed"   378
34. Connie Mack's Baseball School   406
35. Shibe Park   421
36. Connie's Kids Graduate   434
37. World Champions   462
38. Mr. and Mrs. Connie Mack—Part II   492
39. The $100,000 Infield   498
40. The Home Run Baker World Series   517
41. Coasting Down to Third Place   545
42. Speaking of Money   564
43. Captain Hook   573
44. The Second Beating of John McGraw   586
45. Another Baseball War   603
46. The Athletics Win Another
    Pennant — Ho Hum   614
47. Swept   630
48. The End of the Beginning   649

    Epilogue   673
    Sources   675
    Index   677

ILLUSTRATIONS *following page 324*

Connie Mack's agreement with
Eddie Collins

Mary McKillop McGillicuddy
and Marguerite Mack

Rube Waddell as portrayed in a
1905 World Series souvenir booklet

Mack's children from his second marriage

Katherine Hallahan

Connie Mack, Ira Thomas,
and Stuffy McInnis

Connie Mack, Ira Thomas,
and James Isaminger

Bill Orr, Herb Pennock, Weldon Wyckoff,
Joe Bush, Bob Shawkey, and Amos Strunk

The 1902 pennant winners

Johnny Evers and Eddie Plank

Connie Mack

Albert "Chief" Bender

The $100,000 infield

Napoleon Lajoie

Frank "Home Run" Baker

Harry Davis

The Buffalo Players' League Bisons, 1890

Connie Mack

The 1901 Philadelphia Athletics

Cover of Mack's *How to Play Base-Ball*

Connie Mack, 1905

FOREWORD

CONNIE MACK III

I am most often asked with regard to my grandfather: did you know him? I respond that I was fifteen when he died in February 1956. When he visited us in Fort Myers, Florida, after he had retired, it was my job to go into his room at six o'clock each morning and sit there until he would awake. Then I would help him as he showered and shaved and got ready for the day. So, yes, I knew him. But now, having read this book, I can truly say I knew him.

He was born in 1862, just thirty-six years after the deaths of John Adams and Thomas Jefferson on July 4, 1826. It made me realize what an incredibly young nation we are. He was born during the Civil War. His life spanned the Civil War, Lincoln's assassination, the assassination of President McKinley, World War I, the Great Depression, World War II, and the Korean War. Dwight D. Eisenhower was president when he died. My grandfather was quoted as saying, "I was here before the telephone, before electric lights, the talking machine, the typewriter, the automobile, motion pictures, the airplane, and long before the radio. I came when railroads and the telegraph were new."

In his career as a catcher, he was among the earliest to move up right behind the plate for every pitch, when most catchers were still catching the ball on the bounce. While most pitchers in the early years pitched entire games, he was a pioneer in the use of relief pitchers. On one occasion, he used three pitchers in one game. Eventually, all three were elected to the Hall of Fame. He learned early on the value of spring training and the early conditioning of his players. He put together teams with players who thought for themselves. He valued educated players and ones who had baseball smarts. However, when he really needed to fill a position, he was willing to forgo those requirements. There is no better example of this than his signing of Rube Waddell. The stories about Rube Waddell and his catcher, Osee Schrecongost, are hilarious. Waddell, while being one of the funniest and most entertaining characters ever to play the game, was one of the greatest left-handed pitchers in the history of major league baseball.

ix

The 20-inning duel between Rube and Cy Young exemplifies the power and stamina of these early players.

I was intrigued by the process my grandfather developed in putting championship teams together. The network of people who would tip him off about a young player, the extent he would go to sign a player, the ability to spot talent, the willingness to give up good talent when he believed that the person wasn't the right fit for the team—all helped him to develop great teams and led to the great teams of 1928 through 1931. My grandfather said, during a 1941 radio interview, that the best team he managed was that of 1910–1914. Others say the 1929 A's were the best team in the history of the game.

The most fascinating history for me personally was the formation of the American League and my grandfather's role in it. In this context, this book is much more than a biography of my grandfather. It is a history of the beginning of modern baseball. At the age of thirty-eight, my grandfather, along with Ban Johnson and Charles Somers, established the American League. According to Mr. Macht, "These men were most responsible for the early success of the American League: Ban Johnson, with his vision, energy, management, and organizational skills; Charles Somers, with his unlimited faith and financial support; and Connie Mack, with his baseball acumen and willingness to work for the welfare of other clubs as well as his own."

I am in awe of the man and what he accomplished in his illustrious career. As a result of reading this book, I now have a much greater appreciation of why his name is so respected and remembered 50 years after his death—144 years after his birth. But I am just as impressed by and proud of the character of my grandfather. His determination, perseverance, persistence, and competitiveness, which jump from page after page, did not keep him from being the most caring, compassionate, and generous person. In fact, it is the sum of all of these qualities that made him the leader that he was, admired and revered by millions of people. One measure of a man can be made by observing how he treats others depending on their station in life. In the case of my grandfather, no matter how famous he became, he always treated every human being with respect and dignity. This book amply demonstrates that Connie Mack, my grandfather, was not only a great baseball man but also an authentically good human being.

I am so thankful for the time and effort, the detailed research, and the storytelling skill of Norman Macht. Not only does my family owe him a great deal of gratitude, but all of us who treasure our national pastime and its rich history must applaud this work.

PREFACE I met Connie Mack once, on the afternoon of April 13, 1948. He was eighty-five. I was eighteen, working for Ernie Harwell, then the broadcaster for the Atlanta Crackers of the Southern Association. My job included getting the lineups for him, so I had access to the field at Ponce de Leon Park. Atlanta was a regular stop for major league clubs barnstorming north from spring training. The Philadelphia Athletics were in town for two games.

Connie Mack was sitting on a park bench that had been carried out to left field for him, basking in the warm Georgia sun while his Athletics—Fain, Suder, Joost, Majeski, Chapman, McCosky, Valo—took batting practice. As I look back, it seems incongruous for a manager to be sitting on a bench in the outfield during BP. There must have been one or two players standing nearby in case a ball was hit that way. I don't remember. But that was where I went when I decided I'd like to meet this man I had read about in the baseball books that fed my youthful love affair with the game.

I introduced myself and shook hands—I remember bony but not gnarled fingers—and sat down beside him. I asked him something about some team that was in the news—it might have been a clubhouse fight or something of that nature. He answered politely, patiently, assuring me that whatever it was wouldn't affect the team's performance on the field. I asked him about this and that—an eighteen-year-old's questions, devoid of any great insight or import. After a few minutes I thanked him for the opportunity to talk with him and took my leave.

Over the years since then, I'd seen a steadily growing parade of books on John McGraw, Ty Cobb, Babe Ruth, Joe DiMaggio, Lou Gehrig, and Mickey Mantle, along with carloads of biographies and "as-told-tos" of lesser baseball figures. Nothing on Connie Mack. Here was a man who was born before professional baseball existed, whose life *was* the history of baseball. Nobody enjoyed a longer, more significant career, with more dramatic ups and downs. A grammar-school dropout, he created and built a business and ran it for fifty years, swimming his own race in his own way, pioneering management and human relations principles long before they were taught in business schools and "how-to" books.

Yet all that most people knew about him was an image of this tall, thin, saintly looking old man—as if he was born that way—and the conventional myth that Connie Mack was a tight-fisted skinflint who wrecked his teams to line his pockets.

Practically nothing was known about his early years and how he came to be the man he was. How much of what had been written and recycled as fact was really true? I decided to find out. That was twenty-two years ago.

Getting knowledge is the easy part. Getting understanding, the biographer's function, is harder. Understanding is, to a large extent, informed speculation. Nobody can truly know another person's inner life. Character is ultimately unfathomable. Ambiguity and inconsistency are part of human nature. Not everything can be explained.

In bringing Connie Mack's early years to life, we are visiting a time to which none of us was a witness. People think their thoughts and take their decisions in the light of their specific circumstances. Just as Connie Mack implored young reporters not to quote him as saying things he never said, I hear him whispering to me, "Please, heed my moment and the setting of my thoughts."

The attempt to understand someone in the context of his time and place asks that we temporarily suspend judgment. Understanding a man born in 1862 obliges the reader to make an effort, at least, to not judge him by the standards or mores or business practices of the twenty-first century, which themselves are far from universal. Some values are relative to time, not eternal.

While you research a man's life and the history he helped to create, the more you learn, the less you know, for what you learn puts into question what you thought you already knew.

All history is anecdotal. Much history is fiction, often beginning with a pinch of fact, seasoned with a handful of imagination, which produces a legend. Subsequent writers go along with what Stephen Jay Gould has called the "canonical legends." Handed down like family recipes from one generation to another, these legends become accepted as truth. That's why I have relied less on books and more on contemporary reports, game accounts, interviews—the unfiltered raw material of history.

My Quixotic quest has been for 100 percent accuracy. Experience prepares me for falling short. The researcher's path is fraught with booby traps and land mines and disappointments. I traced the files of the Philadelphia Athletics to Kansas City, then Oakland, where they were believed last seen collecting dust in filing cabinets in a disused closet before it was cleaned out and all the business records, correspondence, and other papers were thrown away.

Uncertainty rides with every baseball biographer or historian and never loosens its grip. There are no wholly reliable sources of statistics, especially for the early years of baseball. There are only varying degrees of unreliability. I use statistics sparingly. Those I use come from a variety of sources, including independent research.

Quotes are not put forth as verbatim accounts of what was said in conversations or interviews. They are used as related by participants or the press. Writers embellish, misquote, paraphrase, and invent. Players being interviewed or writing their own stories do the same. Where I quote dialogue, it comes from articles under Mack's or players' bylines; personal interviews—even if misrepresented by the interviewee—and reports of interviews or speeches or press conferences with Mr. Mack.

Memory is like skin. Age wrinkles it, causing it to stretch or sag. When a former player pens his recollections, by his own hand or that of a ghost, or spins yarns in his later years, the tale is told and retold with variations as time passes. Details change from one telling to the next, uncomfortable bits are deleted, personal roles exaggerated. As time ticks away and the years pass, memory becomes less an archive of facts and more an act of imagination. The longer we live, the more clearly we remember things that never happened.

Faced with different versions of the same incident, often from the same source, I have generally relied on the one that was told the closest in time to the events. Thus, if Eddie Collins or Connie Mack wrote or spoke about something within a year of its happening and touched or retouched on the same story years later, I usually went with the earlier version.

Memory is also absorbent. A player with no firsthand knowledge may have heard or read about someone's character or a particular incident so many times that he comes to believe it and relate it as fact. Rather than routinely repeating oft-told tales, I have tried to verify every anecdote or game account I came upon. Many good stories didn't make it into print because I couldn't find any evidence that they actually occurred.

John F. Kennedy once said, "The great enemy of the truth is very often not the lie, but the myth."

The myths you have heard about Connie Mack are the enemies of the truth. It has been said that all the biographer can hope for, if he is lucky, is to catch a fleeting glimpse of his subject. I hope this fleeting glimpse will illuminate some truth about Mr. Mack for you.

ACKNOWLEDGMENTS

This is the hardest part to write. I'd rather make a mistake on a fact of Connie Mack's life than leave out the name of someone who deserves thanks for invaluable help. And there are so many of them: librarians literally from coast to coast . . . church and university archivists . . . town clerks and historical societies . . . what seems like half the 7,000 members of the Society for American Baseball Research.

I am especially grateful:

for the cooperation and support of members of the McGillicuddy family: Connie Mack Jr., Senator Connie Mack III, Dennis McGillicuddy, Susie McGillicuddy, Ruth Mack Clark, Frank Clark, Betty Mack Nolen and Jim Nolen, Kathleen Mack Kelly, Tom McGillicuddy, Cornelius "Neil" McGillicuddy, Helen Mack Thomas, May, Helen, and Arthur Dempsey, Frank Cunningham; Connie McCambridge;

for their personal memories and access to the papers and scrapbooks of players Jack Barry (nephew John G. Deedy Jr. and niece Marion Roosevelt), Eddie Collins (Eddie Collins Jr.), Frank Baker (daughter-in-law Lois Baker), Clark Griffith (Natalie Griffith), and Rube Oldring (Rube Oldring Jr.);

for their critical reading and suggestions for parts or all of the drafts and redrafts of the manuscript: Bill Werber, John Bowman, John McCormack, Jerry Hanks, and Jim Smith;

for the indefatigable and relentless research and microcosmic fact-checking, without which this book would be riddled with factual misplays, of my go-to man, Jim "Snuffy" Smith;

for Emil Beck, who was there when Columbia Park was built in 1901;

for James "Shag" Thompson, the last of the 1914 Athletics;

for Fred Mossa, Dennis LeBeau, and the members of the East Brookfield Historical Society;

for Mike Scioscia's time and patience in sharing his insights into pitchers, catchers, managers, players, and the game of baseball;

for Ed "Dutch" Doyle, who knew more about Philadelphia baseball without looking it up than anybody I met;

for their voluntary contributions of clips and ideas they came upon in their own research and their ready responses to my innumerable queries and calls for help (and here's where I know I'm going to overlook somebody): Peter Baker, Rev. Gerald Beirne, Dick Beverage, Bob Buege, Bill Carle, John Carter, Joe Dittmar, Jack Kavanagh, Roger W. King, Dick Leyden, Bob McConnell, Joe McGillen, Jim Nitz, Dan O'Brien, Joe Overfield, Doug Pappas, John Pardon, Frank Phelps, Joe Puccio, Gabriel Schechter, Fred Schuld, Ron Selter, Max Silberman, Lyle Spatz, Steve Steinberg, A. D. Suehsdorf, Jeff Suntala, Tom Swift, Bob Tiemann, Dixie Tourangeau, Frank Vaccaro, Raymond C. Vaughan;

for copyeditor Bojana Ristich, a joy to work with, who smoothed out the bumps and made great catches.

CONNIE MACK

AND THE
EARLY YEARS
OF BASEBALL

INTRODUCTION

A little after four on the bone-chilling, damp afternoon of Friday, February 10, 1956, a small crowd began to gather outside Oliver H. Bair's funeral home at 1820 Chestnut Street in Philadelphia. Connie Mack had slipped peacefully into eternity on Wednesday afternoon. A public viewing was scheduled between seven and eight on Friday evening. The gray skies darkened quickly with winter's cruel impatience. To spare the early arrivals further discomfort, Bair's opened its doors at five.

Inside it resembled the Philadelphia flower show. There were flowers everywhere, lining the stairways and filling the huge rooms: roses, lilies, gladioli, orchids, carnations—120 floral pieces in all. Visitors carried still more sprays and bouquets; three young girls placed a cascade on the casket as they passed.

By seven Bair's was as crowded as dugouts in September, when late-season call-ups swell team rosters. Those who had come were Mr. Mack's kind of people: players from the greatest of his nine pennant winners, club owners and executives, scouts, umpires, politicians, priests and nuns, stadium workers, and youngsters, many wearing their team uniform shirts.

Although self-effacing, Connie Mack always enjoyed being the center of attention, feigning surprise whenever the spotlight found him after he had maneuvered to invite it. That was just one of the many seeming contradictions in his character. He had all the saintly virtues ascribed to him in his most saccharine profiles, but he could also be obstinate, profane, devious, and tough as a new catcher's mitt.

That morning many of the mourners had read the following description of him in the *Philadelphia Inquirer* by sports columnist Red Smith:

"Many people loved Mack, some feared him, everybody respected him, as far as I know nobody ever disliked him. Nobody ever won warmer or wider esteem and nobody ever relished it more. There may never have

1

been a more truly successful man. He was not the saint so often painted, no sanctimonious puritan. He was tough, human, clever, warmly wonderful, kind and stubborn and courtly and unreasonable, proud, humorous, demanding, unpredictable."

Born in Massachusetts, Mack could have been a model for Benjamin A. Botkin, whose *Treasury of New England Folklore* described the Yankee character as "sensible, self-dependent, God-fearing, freedom-loving, conservative, stubborn, practical, thrifty, industrious, inventive and acquisitive." Connie Mack was all of those except the last, unless you count twenty-game-winning pitchers and .300 hitters.

Ordinarily Mr. Mack would rather have been standing amid such a gathering as this, patiently signing autographs and posing for photographs with unfailing graciousness. But at ninety-three, frail in body and mind, with the team that he had created, owned, and managed for fifty years now gone from the family and moved a thousand miles away, he was ready to rest in peace.

As the early callers left to go home to their suppers, others arrived in a steady stream. At the scheduled closing time of eight, those waiting outside outnumbered those inside. And still they came.

Some of them stayed to visit, express their thoughts and feelings to the family, and swap favorite stories—tall tales and true—as baseball people love to do. Rube Walberg, Bing Miller, Jimmy Dykes, and Mule Haas, on crutches from a leg injury, had played on Mack's 1929–1931 pennant winners. They talked of the toughness, the gentleness, the sharpness and humor, the shrewdness and generosity of the "Old Man." But none of them, not even his children, the youngest of whom was born when Mack was fifty-seven, knew the entire man. Not that anyone can ever really know all the demons and delights that play at tug-of-war inside another person.

They laughed about their frustrating struggles to extract a raise from Mr. Mack, not understanding until years later that he resisted their pleas only because he didn't have it to give them and still remain in business. A surprising number of his "boys" came back to coach or scout for him, some for years, even decades. If they did it for love, not money, what did that say about the man most of them called Mr. Mack, even after he was gone?

Bing Miller was one who had returned as a coach. Recalling Mack's rawhide side, Miller spoke about getting into an argument one day with some teammates in the clubhouse. Connie Mack was then in his sixties.

"He had enough and said, 'Bing, shut up, or I'll whip you myself.' I took one look at Mr. Mack and said, 'Okay, Mr. Mack. I think you can.'"

Hans Lobert said he asked Mack for advice after being named manager of the Phillies in 1942. Mack told him, "You don't need any advice. Just learn players' ways and you'll be all right. But if you ever need any help, come around and see me."

Jimmy Dykes, another who came back to coach and eventually succeed Mack as the Athletics' manager in 1951, confirmed that Mack did indeed know his players' ways.

"One day Al Simmons and I were arguing on the bench in Chicago. It kept up until Mr. Mack couldn't stand it any longer. He jumped up off the bench and hit his head on the concrete roof. It must have hurt, but he didn't let on. All he said was, 'Dykes, keep your blankety-blank mouth shut.'

"When the inning was over, Simmons and I ran out on the field together, and Al said to me, 'Boy, you really stirred him up.' Back on the bench Mr. Mack turned to one of the other players and said, 'Look at those two. They're out there telling each other how mad they had me.'"

Frank "Home Run" Baker, the hero of the 1911 World Series, had had his differences with Mack in 1915 and never played for the A's again. But he drove up from his home in Trappe, Maryland, and called Mack "the finest man I ever knew."

Bobby Shantz and Joe Coleman, pitchers a generation later on Mack's last team, were there. Coleman had come down from Boston with his wife. "It's the least I could do," he said. "He did more for me than anyone will ever know."

Scoreboard operators, ticket sellers, and former batboys mingled with players, umpires, congressmen, priests, and nuns who had taught Mack's children and grandchildren at Melrose Academy. Nine-year-old Johnny McGinley was there with his mother, who recalled how Mr. Mack made "an awful fuss" over little Johnny when his late dad was a ticket seller at Shibe Park and brought Johnny to the ballpark with him.

Bernie Guest, a batboy when Eddie Collins of the $100,000 infield returned as a coach, described Mack's fun-loving side. "Collins was superstitious about the first step of the dugout. He would have that step shining, it was so clean. Every time he went out to the coaching box and turned around, one of the players would mess it up with dirt, water, or paper. Collins would come back and rave and threaten. Mr. Mack would put his scorecard up to his face to hide a chuckle."

The clock at Bair's passed nine, closed in on ten, but the knots of story-tellers remained. Longtime scout Harry O'Donnell countered the image of the miserly Connie Mack that had been created by some members of the press and sustained by the repetition that transforms myth into reality, fiction into fact.

One time Mr. Mack asked me to scout a team way out in the bushes and report back on its best player. When I saw him later I said, "That outfit ain't got anybody you could use, just nobody."

Mr. Mack said, "That's not what I sent you to do. Go back and get me a report on the best player they have."

So I went back. The guy was strictly Class C but I reported on him.

"Fine," said Mr. Mack, and paid the club owner, a widow who, I learned later, had to have the money to keep going, $5,000 for a useless prospect. He took that way to give her enough to keep the club.

Out in Chicago that morning, syndicated columnist Bob Considine had come upon Mickey Cochrane, Mack's greatest catcher, reading of Mack's death while sitting in the United Airlines waiting room at snow-flecked Midway Airport. Considine reported:

"The thing that will stick in my mind about Connie Mack is his dis-position," Mike recalled gently as he watched the snow outside. "I've never seen one like it. In his time he had to deal with just about every type of ballplayer there was. He had some real characters to handle, but they all ate out of his hand. . . .

"He was really something in a salary argument. Remember that old office he had high up in Shibe Park? You had to cross a walk to reach it. We used to call it the Bridge of Sighs. We'd go in like lions and come out like lambs.

"It was crazy and really sad in the old man's last days in action," he said. "We wouldn't know who we were working for from day to day. Lots of times Mr. Mack wasn't speaking to his oldest sons and vice versa. Mr. Mack stretched it a bit thin as manager, too. But when he had it they didn't come any smarter or shrewder."

The rosary was said. The crowd at Bair's began to thin. It was after ten thirty when the doors were closed. More than 3,400 people had come to pay their respects, more than sometimes showed up to watch the A's play in their last years in the city.

The next morning a cold, steady rain poured down as the funeral procession left Bair's and moved slowly toward St. Bridget's Church at 3869 Midvale Avenue. A policeman directing traffic murmured, "A century just went by."

Baseball people see the world through diamond-shaped glasses. One executive shook his head sadly and observed, "A rainout, and on his last day, too."

But it was a "sellout." More than 1,200 people filled the church, where a requiem High Mass was scheduled for eleven o'clock. There was a wedding in the church that morning, and it went overtime. The Mack family, the players and fans, league and club officials stood waiting in the rain. When the young newlyweds emerged, surrounded by smiling faces, they beheld a sea of wet and shivering mourners waiting to take their place.

The glow from six candles was reflected in the dark polished casket as Rev. John A. Cartin said, "It is not the custom in our church at requiem Mass to preach a sermon. Those who knew the greatness of this man can pay tribute to his greatness far better than I. His memory is held sacred in the lives of our people in general, whose inspiration he was. He will be missed by our American people, generations young and old."

After the service, as the crowd dispersed, an old man leaning on a cane stood beside a motorcycle policeman and said, "I don't know where Mr. Mack's going, but if they've got any baseball teams there, somebody's going to get the greatest manager who ever lived."

1 GROWING UP IN EAST BROOKFIELD

The Irish had a bad year in 1846, finishing last in the international league. For the third straight year, the potato crop had failed like a staff of sore-armed pitchers. Without potatoes, there was nothing to eat: no meat, no bread, no vegetables. They had no seeds or tools to grow anything else. There was no work, no money. It was human existence at its lowest level. Thousands died of fever and starvation-induced diseases. Over the next decade, a million members of the Ireland team declared themselves free agents and jumped to the new world. In one year alone, more than 37,000 of them arrived in Boston, swelling that city's population by one-third. They found no welcome mat. Boston considered itself the Hub of the Universe—The Hub became a widely used sportswriters' jargon for the city—the Athens of America. The Brahmins who ruled it deplored the influx of Irish immigrants. They hired a marshal to maintain civil order and protect property.

A study of the immigration records gives the impression that half of the new arrivals were McGillicuddys or MacGillycuddys or some other variation of the name. And of those, every other man appears to have been a Cornelius, with Dennis and Michael distant seconds. Among the women, there is an abundance of Marys, Margarets, and Ellens. For the researcher, this presents a thicket to hack through in the hope of finding the subjects of the search.

It is little wonder that during Connie Mack's long years of fame, many people with a McGillicuddy hanging from some branch of their family tree claimed to be related to him. One Boston McGillicuddy named Dennis told the newspapers he was Mack's long-lost brother. Mack complained to his real cousin, May Dempsey, "This fellow claims to be related to me. He picks me up in his car and takes up a lot of my time, but I don't know how he's related."

He wasn't. But Connie Mack never confronted a claimant to kinship with demands of proof before agreeing to leave a pair of Annie Oakleys at the pass gate.

Despite the knots of Old Country roots, a journey through the live leads and dead ends of town and church and military and census records, from Whitefield Parish in County Kerry to Massachusetts and Missouri, produces a substantial vine, if not a complete tree, of the family of Connie Mack. Its breadth suggests that there were and remain today legitimate cousins by the dozens, of first-, second-, and third-degree status. There could have been more; Connie Mack's uncle Thomas and his wife, Julia, had seven children, but five died before reaching the age of eight.

The McGillicuddys who crossed the ocean left behind a glorious past, filled with centuries of heroic military victories by their ancestral chiefs of the area around the McGillicuddy Reeks, Ireland's highest peaks, in southwest County Kerry. There is some evidence that they were a branch of the O'Sullivan More family, which might explain the family motto: "No hand is stronger in generosity than the hand of O'Sullivan."

Unfortunately for their descendants, the McGillicuddys forfeited most of their castles and vast landholdings as a result of being on the losing side in the playoffs against King James I, who seized land from Irish Catholics and gave it to English and Irish Protestants in the seventeenth century. Still, it might have been worse. Connie Mack's ancestors could have been among the thousands of Irish captives shipped off to the West Indies and sold into slavery by Oliver Cromwell during the Civil War that began in 1642. Mack might have wound up managing Fidel Castro and the Cuban All-Stars.

At any rate, there were enough McGillicuddys left for hundreds of them to pour into Boston and New York in the mid-nineteenth century. They came mostly as laborers or servant girls, on ships with names like *Moses Wheeler*, *Siberia*, *Cephalonia*, *Cambria*, and *Chariot of Fame*. Passage cost the equivalent of about twenty-three "New York dollars," a month's wages for many workers. The voyage took from six weeks to three months. More than four hundred steerage passengers were packed into overcrowded holds, subsisting on weekly rations of seven pounds of food per person, chronic shortages of potable water, and stifling air reeking from dysentery. Few of these "coffin ships" made the crossing without some passengers dying. But nothing they endured was worse than what they left behind, despite their immediate sense of loss and homesickness and the fear of the unknown that lay ahead. They had, at least, expectations, and that was a step up on the ladder of hope. For many of the women, unable to read or write, the future meant bearing children and heartaches with equal frequency.

So it was that the present was bleak and the future invisible in Ireland when, sometime in 1846, Cornelius and Ellen Joy McGillicuddy held their American Wake, as the mournful farewell gatherings were called, and said good-bye to at least six of their children they never expected to see again. Like millions of others of all ages, the children disappeared on ships bound for America. (Two of their cousins went to Argentina; a descendant of one of them, Eduardo McGillicuddy, became the Uruguayan ambassador to the United States.)

There is a gap in the passenger lists for ships arriving in Boston and New York around that time, so it is uncertain where the McGillicuddy children landed or whether they all arrived together. Davis Buckley, a Washington architect whose great-grandmother was one of them, believes that three of them arrived in New York on the same ship.

Those who can be identified with some degree of certainty include Thomas, age twenty or twenty-one; Patrick, nineteen; Michael, nine or ten; Cornelius, seven; and Mary Agnes, six. (Ages are best-efforts calculations; census, marriage, military, pension, and death records are like a shack built with no plumb walls—they seldom squared. A person could age nine years or twelve in the decade between census counts.) They made their way to the Worcester-Brookfield area in central Massachusetts. Mary Agnes met a man named David Roach in Connecticut, married him, and moved to Jersey County, Illinois, where they began a family of nine children. One of them, Cornelius, became a prominent politician and newspaper publisher in Missouri and a close friend of Connie Mack. Cornelius sired fourteen little Roaches, spreading the Midwestern branch of the family tree.

The rest remained in the Worcester area. The earliest record of Michael's residence in East Brookfield, fifteen miles west of Worcester, appears in 1853, when he was seventeen.

During these troubled 1840s, the children of Michael McKillop (or McKillup) were making plans to emigrate from the Catholic section of Belfast. Originally from Scotland, they traced their roots back to the McDonnell clan (of the red and black tartan and red lion), who were driven out of the highlands when their land was confiscated during the Reformation in the sixteenth century. They had fled to Ireland. Now they were fleeing poverty.

The McKillops included at least one boy, John, and three girls, Nancy, Sarah, and Mary. John and Nancy came first; family lore has it that Nancy became homesick as soon as she lost sight of land and prayed that the boat would turn back. A few years later, in early 1856, Nancy went to the docks in Boston expecting to greet her sister Sarah and was surprised when fifteen-year-old Mary got off the boat instead. (Sarah went to Australia.)

The sisters lived in Worcester, where Mary met Michael McGillicuddy. Michael stood about five-foot-seven; Mary barely reached five feet. Neither could read or write. Eventually Michael learned to write his name, signing it in a variety of spellings—Michel, Meichael, Michall—and sometimes simply making an X. Mary was about sixty before she could read or sign her name.

They were married on October 21, 1856, by Fr. J. Boyce in a Catholic church in Worcester. Michael gave his occupation as day laborer and his age as twenty-one; he was probably born September 27, 1836 or '37, and was no more than twenty. Mary said she was eighteen, but she was at most sixteen, probably born in June 1840.

The young couple rented a small frame house on the corner of Main and Maple Streets in East Brookfield, one block from the center of the village. Their landlords, Joseph and Mary McCarty, befriended the newlyweds and treated them as family. Main Street, designated by Postmaster General Benjamin Franklin as a Post Road in 1753, was a busy thoroughfare. Stagecoaches traveling through town churned up clouds of dust on the unpaved road. Every mile was marked by a milestone. One such stone, a reddish rock about four feet high and a foot wide, with "Miles from Boston 62" chiseled into it, stood by the road in front of the house. It stands there today.

East Brookfield, with a population of about three hundred, and three other villages—Brookfield, North Brookfield, and West Brookfield—made up the township of Brookfield. They were busy centers of potteries, boot and shoe factories, wool and cotton mills, and wagon manufacturers.

Mary was a city girl. She didn't like the isolation, the dust and mud, the swampland and algae-covered ponds that surrounded the village. She was seven months pregnant when she escaped for a day to attend her sister Nancy's wedding to Cornelius Sullivan in Worcester on June 6, 1857. (Nancy had three daughters, one of whom married a man named Dempsey. The Dempseys had ten children, whose undeniable status as Connie Mack's second cousins made them a close part of his widely extended family. He and the Dempseys visited often in each other's homes.)

When her time drew near, Mary dreaded the prospect of giving birth to her first child among strangers. She traveled to her brother John's home in Belchertown, twenty miles away, where his wife and daughters were eager to care for her. There Michael Jr. was born on August 23, 1857. Family tradition decreed that there must always be a Cornelius in the lineage, but a Junior could take precedence. Three years later a daughter, Ellen, whom they called Nellie, was born in the house in East Brookfield. Nellie was baptized on August 19; her sponsors were Joseph McCarty and her uncle Patrick's wife, Ellen.

Eight months after the Civil War began, Patrick was the first of the family to sign up, enlisting for three years on December 13, 1861. Listing his occupation as polisher, which could have been at one of the potteries or boot factories, he was mustered into the Twenty-second Massachusetts on January 26, 1862, and discharged three years later in New Orleans.

Michael was now a wheelwright, earning $2 a day. Mary was in her fifth month, carrying her third child, when the Fifty-first Massachusetts Volunteer Infantry came through the Brookfields, recruiting to fill its share of the state's quota of nine-month enlistees. The bounty of $150 must have looked as enticing as the opportunity to take off on a nine-month adventure; on August 30, 1862, Michael became a "Bounty," as the nine-month enlistees were called. Thirty days later he reported to Company B at nearby Camp Wool. After three weeks of rudimentary training, the company took a train to Boston, then boarded the transport ship *Merrimac*, bound for North Carolina.

Two other McGillicuddys, Daniel and James, had enlisted in September in Medford, Massachusetts. Daniel was in sick bay at the New Bern, North Carolina, barracks when Michael arrived on November 30 after a rough voyage. More men died from disease than in battle during the war, and Daniel was one of them. He died on December 1 from a hemorrhage of the lungs. The records show that his belongings were given to a cousin, who may have been Michael.

Company B was assigned to guard a wagon train during the battle of Goldsboro. Michael had just returned to the barracks on the Trent River, near New Bern, when Mary went into labor in the house on Main Street on the evening of Monday, December 22. Mary McCarty was with her. Between the mother's pain-filled screams and the newborn boy's crying, they did not notice when the town clock struck midnight. But five-year-old Michael Junior, shooed out of the house, had no doubts.

"It was definitely before twelve when I went around telling people I had a brother," he recalled.

The town clerk, Washington Tufts, entered the date as December 22 in the town records and on the birth certificate, which spells the name "McGillycuddy." But until he was past eighty, Connie Mack celebrated his birthday on December 23. When a relative sent him a copy of the records, Mack chuckled, "Well, it made me feel younger to believe it was the twenty-third."

On January 4, 1863, Mary, accompanied by Mary McCarty and Patrick McDonald as sponsors, brought her infant son to Our Lady of the Rosary Church in Spencer, three miles away, where he was baptized by Fr. Thomas Sheerin as "Cornelius son of Michael McGillichoddy & Mary McGillup his wife, born 22d Dec., 1862."

Contrary to every baseball reference book and numerous articles, profiles, and books in which he is mentioned, Connie Mack was not named Cornelius Alexander. His baptismal and marriage records contain no mention of "Alexander" or any other middle name or initial. It may have been a name he took at confirmation, but no confirmation record could be found. There are no legal documents, including his will, or certificates of incorporation, on which everyone else who is listed uses a middle initial, where Cornelius McGillicuddy ever used one.

Three of his daughters were certain there was a middle initial A, though they never saw it. One thought it stood for Alexander. Another was sure it was Andrew and named her son Cornelius Andrew for that reason. The third remembered giggling with her teenage girl friends because she had heard it was Aloysius and that sounded like such a funny name to them. (A son, Connie Jr., had no middle name when he was baptized. He took the name Alexander at his confirmation but never used it. That may be the reason historians retroactively grafted it onto his father's name.)

In January 1863 Michael McGillicuddy went on the sick list in New Bern. Suffering from what soldiers called "the southern malaria," chronic diarrhea, dyspepsia, rheumatism, and kidney and liver problems, he spent most of the rest of his enlistment in the hospital. About the only ailment he seemed to have escaped was the meningitis that devastated more than one regiment that winter.

The Fifty-first arrived back in Massachusetts on July 21, 1863. After a six-day furlough, it was reassembled and mustered out on July 27. Michael had last been paid on February 2; he had been advanced $43.59, in kind or cash, for clothing and had no money coming to him. When he reached home, he was expelling water from his lungs and suffering from "smothering spells" and stomach trouble. Dr. Fiske was called in to see him the next day and continued to treat him for years thereafter. Michael was twenty-six, broke and broken, and would never again be the man he had been when he had signed on as a Bounty nine months earlier.

When Connie was about four, the family moved a mile away into a tiny one-floor cottage they rented from John and Julia Stone for $6 a month. Located just above the bend where the road to North Brookfield curved off Main Street, the quarter-acre lot backed up to Mud Pond. A nearby Franklin milestone, still standing, reads "Boston 63 miles." Across the road was an open field, E. H. Stoddard's vegetable farm and stand, and the Forbes general store. In that cottage Dennis McGillicuddy was born in April 1867.

Almost from the day of his discharge, Michael began to draw a monthly disability pension that rose to $8 after twenty-three years. In 1879 the state created a pension for disabled soldiers, but there is no record of his collecting it until 1885. When his health permitted, Michael worked first at a cotton mill, then at the Forbes wheel and wagon shop.

Connie started school at the age of five in September 1868. He walked with Michael Jr. and Nellie to the large brick one-room schoolhouse. The first grade curriculum concentrated on reading, writing, spelling, and counting to one hundred. Michael was in the sixth grade, tackling arithmetic, U.S. geography, penmanship, and "object lessons," in addition to reading and spelling. In third grade, Nellie was doing a little primary arithmetic and sharing the daily ten-minute lesson from *Hooker's Child's Book of Nature* that the teacher read aloud to all the students.

There were three terms of ten weeks each, separated by long vacations. A high school had recently been built; it would be eight years before a class of one graduated from it.

Just off the schoolroom was a small, windowless closet, dark as moonless midnight—the dreaded punishment room. Connie once served a ten-minute sentence in the hole that "gave me the biggest scare that I had ever had, up to that time, in my life. I took good care I didn't go back a second time."

But others did. Despite the small enrollment—one year attendance varied between six and sixteen—it wasn't easy to keep order or do much teaching. The range in ages was formidable, from five to at least fifteen. When Connie was ten, they wore out three teachers, none lasting more than one term. Perhaps it was difficult to attract committed schoolmarms for $88 a term, $105.60 for the winter term. When enrollment went up unexpectedly one year, the teacher received an additional fifty cents a week for hazardous duty.

The school board's cautions against corporal punishment may have contributed to the discipline problems. "If resorted to by the teacher," it warned, "it should be for gross sins only. The system of pinching, hipping, slapping, pulling hair, springing whalebone on the lips, jerking, boxing, and a long catalog of brutal ways of punishment are condemned."

Other regulations posted in the classroom suggest that little learning was being accomplished:

"All standing, walking or running or playing on the seats or desks, or wrestling or scuffling in the schoolroom is positively forbidden. No person, while chewing tobacco, shall spit on the floor of said house or on the seats, desks or ceiling of the room."

(Nothing has changed in education: the school board's annual report noted, "Specialty has been made of reading, spelling and writing, studies heretofore too much neglected.")

Two houses away from Connie's home on the North Brookfield Road lived the Drake family. Young Connie sat by the hour, listening with fascination to the stories Eddie Drake told about his Civil War adventures. In June 1862, fourteen-year-old Eddie said he was seventeen and enlisted as a drummer boy. Wounded at Lynchburg, Virginia, he was taken prisoner in June 1864. In December, during a swap of one hundred Union prisoners for an equal number of Confederate captives, Eddie burrowed into the group unseen and was freed at Charleston, South Carolina. He came out of the war suffering from chemical dropsy and an enlarged spleen and was discharged on May 2, 1863. The older boy was a constant source of wonders for Connie, who was seven when he watched Eddie making a new product called soda pop in the Drakes' cellar, which had been turned into the home of the Aerated Works Company.

Another of Connie's earliest memories was of the large open field across the road, which served as the ball grounds for the kids in the area. An elderly Connie Mack said he could still hear the voice of one of his friends—Swats Mulligan or Will or Jack Hogan—calling, "Hey, Slats, come on over and play four-o-cat." Connie's tall-for-his-age and skinny build had quickly earned him that nickname. Whoever was calling, Connie always responded eagerly.

"We made two rings thirty feet apart, with a batter in each ring. A pitcher stood outside of the ring and lobbed the ball weakly in to the batter. He wasn't trying to make the batter miss it. That would spoil the fun. After hitting it, the batter would spring madly for the opposite ring. He was out if he was tagged with the ball between the circles. He could be put out by being hit with a thrown ball, or if the ball was caught on the fly he was out."

Nobody wore a glove. They used a flat bat and a ball made of cotton or rags covered with cloth or leather. "Later on when I grew a little older and taller, we began to play a game much nearer the game of baseball and less like cricket. We had a home plate and three bases and a big bat and a leather-covered ball."

Connie was nine when he began working summers in the Brookfield Manufacturing Company cotton mill. He operated a creaky old freight elevator, ran errands, and carried material from one part of the factory to another. He had an affable, polite disposition and was quick and bright. Everybody liked him. At the end of his first day of work, he was handed a small green pay slip for twenty-five cents. He never cashed it and carried it in his wallet for many years. His wages came to $6 a month. He turned the money over to his mother, proud to be contributing the rent money. "He always brought mother his pay envelope," Michael Jr. recalled. "He was always ready to give or share what he had."

Connie also earned ten cents a week picking vegetables for Mr. Stoddard. He spent that on himself.

At the cotton mill the workday lasted from 6:30 a.m. to 6:30 p.m., with an hour for lunch. Connie spent most of that hour playing ball after dashing home for a quick meal. Mornings and evenings there were chores to do. Connie chopped the wood for the kitchen stove. (His mother had a well-earned reputation as a baker of pies, cakes, cookies, and doughnuts. Like most women of the time, she tested the temperature of the oven by sticking her elbow into it.) When it snowed, Connie pushed the snow shovel. They had two cows and seven horses, the bulk of their household possessions, which were valued at $550 in the 1870 census. Michael Jr. milked the cows and fed the horses every morning before breakfast. Having quit school, he was learning to be a butcher. After breakfast he went to the slaughterhouse, picked up some cuts of meat, and sold them door to door.

Mary was expecting her fifth child in the spring of 1873, when twelve-year-old Nellie died of scarlet fever. In July another boy, Thomas, was born. Despite the ten-year difference in their ages, Connie and Tom became the closest of all the siblings. Another daughter, Mary, was born on Christmas

Day 1875 but died in infancy. Mary's fifth and last son, Eugene, was born on March 4, 1878.

On October 13, 1875, the Macks bought the cottage from John and Julia Stone for $625. They were helped by a $400 mortgage from George A. Sibley, one of the principal backers of the town baseball team, at 7 percent interest, paid semi-annually. The house was assessed at $500, the land at $100. Taxes for the first year were $11.75. Significantly, and unusual for the times, the deed was made out in the name of Mary J. McGillicuddy only. By this time Michael's health had deteriorated to the point where he could rarely do a day's work. But Michael Jr. was working as a butcher in Worcester and living at home, and Connie gave his mother whatever he earned. Between them, they paid off the mortgage in six months.

(In 1893 the deed to the house was transferred to Connie Mack, who paid the annual taxes on it. When his mother moved to Philadelphia in 1902, Mack turned it over to his brother Tom. On Tom's death it was sold to Emerson H. Stoddard for $750. The house burned down in the 1920s; the house that stands there today is built on the original foundation but is not the house the Macks lived in.)

The Boston and Albany Railroad stopped in East Brookfield on its route. Some of the land behind the cottage had been sold to a company building a branch line to North Brookfield, so the property line now ended at the railroad's right-of-way. Grading for the line had begun in July, and the tracks from the depot had reached the fork in the road when Mary Mack took ownership of the house. The trains began running on January 1, 1876; there were seven a day in each direction, and they shook the house as they went by between seven a.m. and seven p.m.

Connie Mack quit school in 1877 after the eighth grade. He had put on a spurt of growth that reached six feet and was still growing. He was now the tallest boy in the village and towered over the teacher. His knees were scraping the undersides of the little knife-scarred schoolroom desks. He never sat for the high school entrance exam, an ordeal held every June that most applicants failed. Connie Mack was always at ease yarning with visitors or writers in hotel lobbies or in one-on-one interviews. But no matter how many speeches he gave on the rubber chicken circuit, he always felt inadequate to give the kind of talk he wanted to make and regretted he had not had more education.

Watching his grandchildren playing one Sunday afternoon years later, he told his daughter Ruth, "I'm going to see to it that your boys go to college."

There were others, family and nonfamily, whose educations he paid for; how many cannot be counted.

But at the time he quit school, he had no qualms. He was ready to work full time. He did not quit because his father had died, "leaving the business of feeding a sizable and hollow-legged Irish family squarely on my hatrack shoulder blades," as some fanciful versions of his life, including a few under his own ghosted byline, have melodramatically told it. Michael McGillicuddy lived another fifteen years.

Perhaps in Connie Mack's mind his father had died as a major factor in his life by that time. His memory edited out the unpleasantness of his father's declining years, as he watched his mother put up with her husband's drinking, nurse him as his various ailments debilitated him, and raise five children while losing two others, all without complaining or losing her spirit. Whenever he talked to his children about his youth, Mack spoke fondly of his mother and her influence on him. He rarely mentioned his father, except to acknowledge that there was "a drinking problem."

Michael's working had become infrequent, but his visits to Stevens' Tavern were regular. Whenever his co-worker at the wheel shop, Simon Daley, half-carried him home, it was hard to tell if it was because of Michael's lameness or lack of sobriety. The tavern was only three hundred yards from the house, and as Dennis's wife, Annie, often said, "Michael McGillicuddy would go through six feet of snow to get to the pub." When his money ran out, Stevens put him on the tab.

Michael had plenty of convivial company. Temperance groups were active but, except for a brief period, largely ineffective. Those who didn't imbibe didn't need them, and those who did didn't heed them.

Mary's sister Nancy observed that Dennis and Eugene walked in their father's path; Connie, Michael, and Tom took after their mother.

No doubt about it: Connie Mack's optimism, patience, gentility, stoicism, dignity, faith, and antipathy to alcohol came from Mary McKillop.

2 | THE YOUNG CATCHER

When the fourteen-year-old Connie Mack became a working man in 1877, East Brookfield and its neighboring villages were recovering from the panic of 1873. The post–Civil War boom in railroad construction had climaxed in a speculative bubble in railroad stocks and bonds that was fueled by ordinary people who had never thought of taking financial risks. When the bubble burst in September, eighty-nine railroads were bankrupt; overextended banks and brokerage firms called in uncollectible loans and were forced to close their doors. National unemployment had reached 14 percent by 1876. Even congressmen took a pay cut from $7,500 to $5,000.

East Brookfield had the resources to bounce back. Abundant water power drove the mills. Plentiful supplies of clay kept the brick and pottery kilns busy. There were boot and shoe factories, wagon manufacturers, a foundry, and three general stores, one of which housed the post office. Soon a grain and feed store; hardware, furniture, and funeral accessories dealers; a sawmill; carpenter and machine shops; two blacksmiths; and an American Express office opened on Main Street or Depot Square.

The most prominent businessmen in town were members of the Forbes family and W. J. Vizard. The Forbeses were probably the wealthiest, but there were no ostentatious houses in East Brookfield. Most of the mill owners, who built fancier homes, lived in Spencer or North Brookfield. To some of the locals, George E. Forbes was the Mr. Potter—the villain in *It's a Wonderful Life*—of East Brookfield. Forbes owned a wagon factory, pottery, hotel, woolen mills, land along Seven Mile River that connected with Forbes Pond, and houses clear out to Podunk, a few miles out of town. Local lore accused Forbes of being mean to the widow Stevens and her daughter, who was "not right" according to a newspaper account, when he locked them out of the house they were renting from him. But the Macks had no animosity toward him. Forbes kept Michael on at the wheel shop despite his frequent absences. They traded at Eli Forbes's general store across the road from their home.

W. J. Vizard, born in England, arrived in town after completing a three-year enlistment in the Union Army. In 1870 he opened an oyster and refreshment room, then branched out into a pharmacy, boot shop, opera hall, summer resort and trotting track, and bowling alley/shooting gallery, where Connie Mack worked one winter. Vizard installed electric lights in the opera house in 1894, but the fire insurance company made him take them out.

The year Connie quit school he saw his first telephone in the Drake home. The streets were still unpaved in town and there were no sidewalks. Kerosene lamps lit Main Street except when the moon was full. The lamplighter earned about forty-two cents a night. Connie was not interested in that job.

In addition to the railroad, with its soot-spewing, tall-stacked engines, horse-drawn stagecoaches brought visitors and traveling salesmen to town and took them from the depot to the other villages or the East Brookfield Hotel on Main Street. In winter the coaches traveled on sleighs. Ox teams were also a familiar sight. A small steamer carried bricks across Quaboag Pond to a railroad siding.

The hottest political issue of the time involved secession. As part of the Town of Brookfield, the East Village residents didn't take kindly to paying taxes to help pay for projects over in Brookfield, three miles away. Their efforts to form a separate township were constantly thwarted by the legislature and the farmers in Podunk, who didn't want to be annexed into East Brookfield. It would take East Brookfield until 1920 to finally gain its independence, making it the youngest town in the state. (For its fiftieth anniversary in 1970, the town struck a medal showing a Franklin milestone on one side and a profile of Connie Mack on the other.)

This was the setting in April 1877, when Connie Mack applied for a full-time job across the road at Stoddard's farm and market, adjacent to the ball grounds. In a 1929 interview Stoddard said, "For three years he was in my employ, following out the principles of efficiency, integrity, and honesty, drilled into his mind as a youth. . . . He was tall for his age and witty and quick as a cat. He did his work well, honest and straightforward."

Some of those three years involved only summer work. There was more money and promotion opportunity in the shoe factories. When Connie was fifteen or sixteen, he went to work for Green and Twichell in Brookfield, cutting soles and heel lifts. From there he moved on to the George H. Burt Shoe Company, where he reached a salary of $10 a week, enough of a wage for many a man to support a large family at the time.

Life was not all work in the Brookfields, which were known as Showtown because so many traveling shows and locally produced entertainments appeared there. Connie Mack enjoyed them all: fairs, dances, parades, strawberry and oyster suppers, minstrel shows, circuses, acting troupes, concerts, political rallies and speeches, and historical commemorations. He began a lifelong love of the theater.

The most prominent local show business celebrities were the Cohans. George M. Cohan's grandmother and other relatives lived in North Brookfield, and the popular vaudevillians spent their summers there, before and after the fourth Cohan, George M., was born on July 3, 1878. Their presence stirred great excitement—and a little consternation when Georgie was old enough to terrorize the residents by riding his bike up and down muddy Main Street, causing havoc among the horses and pedestrians. Georgie hung out with the players on the town baseball team at Char Coughlin's soda and tobacco store. He and his pals, some of whom were considerably older than the brash youngster, formed their own team, called Coughlin's Disturbers. Never much of an athlete, George became an avid and studious fan of the game. His shows always fielded a team; sometimes the ability to pitch or play the infield had as much to do with an actor's being hired as did his acting ability. The theatrical highlight of every summer was a show put on at the town hall by the Cohans to raise the getaway money for their return to the vaudeville circuit in the fall.

Connie was five when the first Memorial Day was observed on May 30, 1868. That November they watched local Republicans fire a one-hundred-gun salute to mark the election of U. S. Grant as president. The Fourth of July was a time for Halloween-type pranks, picnics, speeches, and ball games. Every November husking parties ended with huge suppers and dancing that ended "I dare not tell at what hour in the morning," as the *Spencer Sun* said of an 1880 event in Podunk.

Fire-fighting competitions against companies from other towns always included a parade and banquet. The biggest social events of the year were the firemen's ball and a New Year's ball followed by an oyster supper. The social calendar was filled all year. The Macks were not high society, but Connie Mack was present at many of these occasions.

Not all the excitement was planned. About 6 p.m. on July 10, 1867, a seventy-five-foot passenger balloon, the *Hyperion*, floated over the village on its way to Worcester, bringing everyone out of their homes to gaze at the airship. On Saturday, May 11, 1872, the railroad depot burned to the ground. Connie probably watched the firemen manning the horse-drawn, hand-pumped engine in their futile efforts to stop the blaze. In November of that year the village was shocked when a fatal accident occurred. Two horses pulling wagons collided, killing both animals but leaving the drivers unharmed.

Sporting events included horse races, which coursed through the dusty town streets in summer and over the ice when Lake Lashaway froze. There was plenty of spirited wagering. The netting and trapping of passenger pigeons provided good sport and many a meal. At one time the migrating birds created as much traffic in the sky over Brookfield as today's Thanksgiving Day drivers on the Mass Turnpike. But by 1914 the birds would be extinct.

And, of course, there was baseball. Every village had at least one team. Rivalries were as fierce and games as hotly contested as they would ever be between any major league teams. Boot factories fielded department teams: clippers, sole cutters, bottomers, quicks, packers, finishers, treers. They played for pride and bragging rights and, as amateurs, truly for the love of the game, though they sometimes passed the hat and divvied up whatever they collected. Betting was lively among players and spectators.

Professional baseball was a shaky proposition that attracted little following in the Brookfields, even after the National League (NL) was created in 1876. It was so tarred with corruption and rowdyism that the *New York Times* in 1881 urged the nation to return to cricket as the national game:

"There is really reason to believe that baseball is gradually dying out in this country. . . . Probably the time is now ripe for the revival of cricket. . . . Our experience with the national game of baseball has been sufficiently thorough to convince us that it was in the beginning a sport unworthy of men and it is now, in its fully developed state, unworthy of gentlemen."

The *Times*'s disenchantment with baseball was not entirely groundless. Police in some cities posted signs at the entrance to ball grounds: "No game played between these two teams is to be trusted." The selling of betting pools and the "prearranged outcomes" of games had become so widespread that Henry Chadwick wrote in 1875, "If professional baseball died its tombstone would read, Died of Pool Selling."

Even the National League's staunchest supporters feared for its future.

In January 1881 Albert G. Spalding was quoted in the *Cincinnati Enquirer*: "Salaries must come down or the interest of the public must be increased in some way. If one or the other does not happen, bankruptcy stares every team in the face."

But nobody in the Brookfields cared about editorials in New York papers. Baseball was all the rage. The *Brookfield Times* gave the local teams front page coverage, at the same time cautioning managers to see that their men remained sober both before and after the games if they wanted to retain the financial backing of their sponsors. Another paper was "happy to note at Saturday's game the presence of some of the best families in town, among them three members of the clergy."

As four-o-cat evolved into baseball at Stoddard's grounds, Connie Mack showed an early aptitude for the game. He was full of ginger, took the game more seriously than the other boys, and began to take charge on the field. His abilities as a field general suited him for the catcher's position. In the summer of 1879 he made the East Brookfield town team. At sixteen, he was three or four years younger than most of his teammates, many of whom were volunteer firemen. Connie pitched occasionally but was the team's primary catcher from the start of the season. Despite his lanky build—fast approaching his ultimate height of six feet two and one-half inches—he was agile and had quick feet and a strong arm.

That summer he wore a glove for the first time. "It was made of buckskin and had no fingers," he recalled. "We chipped in and bought [it] for two dollars. It was used in turn by one player after another since it was common property." He still had no mask or chest protector.

The pitcher fired the ball sidearm or underhand from forty-five feet away (fifty feet beginning in 1881); the catcher stood ten or twelve feet behind home plate and took it on a bounce. It was a hazardous position for the hands and fingers. Rudimentary catcher's equipment and special baseball shoes were beginning to appear at Woodis's general store in North Brookfield.

One day Connie and a local pitcher named John Arthur Williams went to the home of National League pitcher Candy Cummings in the nearby town of Ware and paid him $10 to show them how to throw a curve (which Cummings is widely credited with inventing).

The stories that either Connie or the newspapers shortened his name to fit into box scores and lineups are fiction. As was true of many McGillicuddys, the family was commonly known as Mack, except in legal documents—deeds, military records, church records, and the like. Even in such cases, the names were used interchangeably. Voting records show both names, as well as variations like McGilacurdy, for the family between 1877 and 1899. Connie's name appeared in stories in the *Spencer Sun* as "Mack, catcher for the local amateur nine." Connie Mack later told the story that when he was managing the Pittsburgh Pirates, O. P. Caylor of the *New York Herald* learned that Mack's real name was McGillicuddy. Players and fans in every city razzed Mack about it for the rest of the season. Writers delighted in referring to the team as "McGillicuddy's Pirates." (Between 1892 and 1911 Pittsburgh was commonly spelled "Pittsburg," but for consistency I use "Pittsburgh" at all times.) Many of the children of the next generation who had nothing to do with baseball were unaware that the family name had ever been anything other than Mack. But the name was never legally changed.

Connie Mack bought the Worcester and Boston newspapers and DeWitt's and Spalding's annual baseball guides at the newsrooms on Main Street, but he was more interested in playing than following the major leagues. Worcester had a team in the National League for the years 1880–1882, but Mack never talked about going to their games.

His first action against major league players occurred on Tuesday, April 11, 1882, when the Worcester Ruby Legs came to East Brookfield for an exhibition game against the locals. A large crowd gathered at the grounds across the road from Connie's home. The Ruby Legs were a terrible team. Despite the presence of Harry Stovey and Arthur Irwin, who went on to long careers as players and managers, they won only 18 games and lost 66 that year. But they proved too much for the village team, winning 23-9. Connie had 3 hits off Frank Mountain, who was 2-16 for Worcester that year and later pitched a no-hitter.

Encouraged by the turnout for the Worcester game, Charles Sibley, the East Brookfield manager, aimed his sights higher. He wrote to Cap Anson, leader of the Chicago White Stockings, the greatest team in the nation, with two straight pennants behind them and a third on the way. Sibley asked Anson if he would stop in East Brookfield for a game in August on the way between Boston and New York. Anson replied that it would take a $100 guarantee to make it worth his while. Sibley said okay.

The prospect of playing against stars like Anson, the mighty Michael "King" Kelly, George Gore, and Silver Flint kept Connie and his mates buzzing with anticipation for weeks. Anson earned the unimaginable sum of $2,500 for playing baseball. King Kelly was rapidly becoming the most popular player in the land, the Babe Ruth of his time. The chance to bat against two of the National League's top pitchers, Larry Corcoran and Fred Goldsmith, excited more than daunted them. For days prior to the Saturday, August 26, game, Connie and his teammates worked to clear and rake their grassless grounds next to Stoddard's farm. They picked up the cans, tobacco tags, shoe scraps, and other "Irish confetti," as Mack dubbed it.

The crowd that turned out was bigger than the one for the Worcester game. Everybody was disappointed that King Kelly was not with the team—an umpire, John Kelly, was recruited to do the catching—but Anson played first base, and Corcoran and Goldsmith did the pitching. Chicago won 20–5, but that didn't matter. Everybody had a good time. At one point, Chicago right fielder Hugh Nicol crept up behind Anson at first base and crawled between his legs, Anson feigning great surprise. When the time came to pass the hat, they raised more than enough to cover the guarantee.

Connie's tall, thin physique caught Anson's eye. Every catcher in the National League or American Association (AA) was considerably shorter or heavier—or both. The first time Cap came up to bat, he turned to Connie and said, "I've looked at a lot of catchers and I don't think I ever saw one built as high as you."

Anson was also impressed by Connie's aggressive and spirited play behind the plate. Connie's brother Michael recalled, "Anson kept his eyes glued on Cornelius, and after the game was over remarked, 'There is one man who will make a ball player,' and singled out my brother, better known then as just plain Slats."

As a teenager, Connie was self-conscious about his unusual construction. Few men of that era reached six feet in height. His slimness accentuated his altitude. He towered fourteen inches over his mother. All of his brothers were shorter and stockier than he was. When his team rode in wagons to other towns, he was the primary target of the jeers and taunts of their rivals' followers.

Connie became very particular about the way he dressed. Throughout his adult life he was rarely seen in anything but a three-piece suit, high collar, and tie. When a St. Louis company that made his collars stopped producing them in 1908, he persuaded it to continue supplying him. Sometimes in hot weather he would take off the jacket and vest. That was as close to casual as he came. Even at home or when he was relaxing at his brother's lakeside vacation home, the shirt and tie were always there. When he played golf, the jacket might be replaced by a sweater, the tie by an ascot. Shorts or swimming trunks? Never. He had long, narrow feet, probably wore size 14 or 15 AA shoes. Later he would have all his suits and shoes custom made.

By the time he was nineteen Connie was wearing a low-crown derby in winter and a straw hat in summer. One day he was in a store in East Brookfield when a traveling salesman came in. Connie's eyes popped as he gazed at the drummer's getup: loud checked suit, high linen collar, and bright red tie. He stared with envy at the stranger's derby, which had a higher crown than any he had ever seen. It made the low-crown jobs worn by the local blades look like dumplings on a dish. If he wore one of those high crowns, Connie mused, he would be the fashion king of the Brookfields.

Connie had never been to Boston. He decided that was the only place he was likely to find such a hat, so he rode the train to the city. Gazing up at the tall buildings as he pushed through the crowded streets, he kept glancing down at the shops until he found one with a grand display of high-crown derbies in the window. In he went and asked to try one on. The hatter returned with an armful, picked one that looked the right size, placed it on Connie's head, and invited him to regard himself in the mirror.

"There I stood," Mack recalled, "a gangling of 6 feet 2 inches, all the taller because of the high crown. My trousers ended about six inches above the shoes, and I certainly looked like some character in a rube drama.

"Reason overcame style. I began to reflect that my appearance in front of the East Brookfield post office, with such a daring derby that accentuated my height, would draw the banter of the town wits.

"'I don't believe that suits,' I averred with all the dignity I could muster, 'and I wish you would show me something in a low crown.'"

The 1883 East Brookfield nine promised to be the best the town had ever fielded. Most of the players had been together for four years. Twenty-year-old Connie Mack was elected captain. He was the sharpest strategist and analyst of the game they'd ever seen. Coolly standing and peering at the scene before him, he would study the base runners' leads and movements, position his fielders, then give the sign to his pitcher, Will Hogan. Connie had caught all of Will's starts for five years; they knew each other like brothers.

The team was almost entirely Irish: two Hogans, Mack, Lynch, Murphy,

Manley, Fitzgerald, and Fitzpatrick, along with Clough, Lawrence, and Ensworth. In a team photo, five of the nine pictured and manager H. E. Langway sport full mustaches. Connie, sitting cross-legged with arms crossed in the front row center, is clean shaven. There is no evidence that he ever grew any upper lip adornment. Sitting between the broad-shouldered, hefty Hogan brothers, the boyishly slender Connie appears younger than twenty. His black hair parted over his left eye, he sported two roaches—swirls of hair dipping down over his forehead, a style worn also by Will Hogan and H. Ensworth.

During the winter the club held several dances at Fay's Hall to raise money for uniforms and equipment. The uniforms, featuring large block letters EB in the center of the shirt, black bow ties at the neck, and knickers to just below the knees, arrived in July. Connie's catcher's mask cost $3; wide-heeled shoes were $4.

The Central Massachusetts Amateur Base Ball Association put up a rosewood bat with an engraved silver plate as the championship trophy for the seven-team league. The season opened on May 19. Playing on Saturdays or Sundays, usually on Stoddard Field, East Brookfield went into July with a 5-0 record. It had defeated its closest rivals, North Brookfield, 10–5, and faced them in a return game on July 4. About one thousand spectators gathered at the North Brookfield commons for the holiday game. The home team batted first and took a quick 5–0 lead, but Mack's men fought back and tied the score in the eighth on 4 hits and an error. North Brookfield scored a run in the tenth to win 6–5.

That was the only loss of the season for East Brookfield, who had given the North nine their only defeat. The teams tied for first place, forcing a playoff for the championship. The big game was set for Wednesday, September 19, and never did any battle for a world championship cause more excitement or animated wagering among any two teams' supporters. The teams agreed on a neutral grounds at Oakland Gardens in Brookfield and imported a professional umpire, Otis Tilden, from a town outside Boston. North Brookfield bettors were confident their man, Pat Doyle, could outpitch Will Hogan and their Hibernian lineup would whip the East Village Irish. They generously offered 2-to-1 odds and found plenty of takers.

Long before Mr. Tilden called for the first pitch at 3:10 p.m., there was no room for another pair of feet to squeeze onto the grounds around the playing field. Youngsters slipped out of school to be there in time to secure a spot where they could see the action. The Hogans' sixteen-year-old sister

Margaret, Connie Mack's most ardent admirer, would not have missed it for anything.

East Brookfield won the toss and chose to bat last. The North took a 1–0 lead in the first, aided by a passed ball by Mack. In the third, it loaded the bases with nobody out. Things looked grim for the East boys.

"Here's where Hogan and Mack showed their metal," reported the *Brookfield Times*. "Daniels flew out to first base. Mack captured Gaul and Burke, one on strikes and the other on a perpendicular fly. The cheering was immense. Such a task would be performed scarcely once in a score of times before a score could have been made."

In the bottom of the fourth Fitzpatrick was safe on an error. After Clough forced him at second and Will Hogan grounded out, Mack, batting cleanup, shot a single to left that brought home Clough with the tying run. Mack stole second and raced home when Jack Hogan doubled.

Will Hogan nursed the 2–1 lead into the ninth. The East Brookfield rooters grew quiet and tense as the North put men on second and third with one out. Standing in front of the plate, Mack shouted encouragement to his pitcher. When the next batter struck out, the East followers roared. There were now two outs. One to go. The next batter struck out too, but Mack dropped the ball. The crowd held its breath while he picked it up and threw the batter out at first to end the game. Mack and his mates raced to embrace Hogan and swarmed all over each other with the boundless joy that surrounds the closing scene of every World Series. Their boisterous celebration was matched by the East Villagers, especially those whose pockets were now more prosperously lined.

The game had been a nail-biter to the last out. Doyle gave up 4 hits and Hogan 5. Mack had 11 putouts and 6 assists behind the plate. "I had some sizzling pitches to handle when he fanned the two final hitters," Mack reminisced, "but managed to hold onto them and they stuck in my glove like burrs."

Connie Mack always maintained that he felt "as much of a thrill recalling the details of this game as I ever did out of any World Series game." Reliving that triumphal day with writer Fred Lieb in his Shibe Park office sixty years later, he said, "I have enjoyed many victories—games which meant much to me and my Athletic club. But I don't think any other brought me greater joy than when East Brookfield won. At the time, it seemed to be the most important baseball game that ever was played."

The village went all out to celebrate. A nine-man committee of prominent citizens arranged a gala for Thursday, September 27, at Fay's Hall. Fans were invited to be present "with ladies" for the presentation of the prize bat. The souvenir invitations, printed on cream-colored satin mounted on gilt, beveled-edged cards and fastened with red silk bows, listed the officers and member teams of the Central Massachusetts Amateur Base Ball Association, the lineup of the championship team, and the score of each of its 11 wins and lone loss. The evening began with a brass band concert from seven to eight at Vizard's Park, "before a large and appreciative audience," reported the *Spencer Sun*. Then Prouty and Belcher's orchestra performed at Fay's Hall for an hour, the hall packed to capacity. After a galop, "Halloo, Halloo," closed the concert, and league president W. E. Parsons presented the prize bat to Charles A. Sibley, "The home nine had every reason to be satisfied by the generous ovation given them by the townspeople," the *Sun* noted. Then "an abundant collation was spread in the Baptist Vestry," and the dance lasted into the early morning hours.

The bat, with the results of the championship game engraved on its silver plate, hung in the Bay State Engine Company firehouse in East Brookfield until 1970, when it was moved to the museum in the East Brookfield library.

A few months after East Brookfield's victory, on Sunday, November 10, 1883, the country's time zones were standardized at the behest of the railroads. The residents of East Brookfield gained sixteen minutes. But they soon lost something more prized by them than a little extra time. Their star catcher and captain, Connie Mack, had played his last game for the home team.

After the championship game, the umpire had congratulated Mack on his game and asked if he intended to become a professional ballplayer. "If you do," Tilden said, "I will be pleased to recommend you."

"His kindly suggestion," Mack recalled, "caused me for the first time to want to go out and play professional ball. I decided right then and there that I would."

3 | A ROOKIE IN MERIDEN

In the spring of 1884 Connie Mack read in a Boston paper about six towns forming a Connecticut State League. He wrote to the managers of several of the teams, asking for a tryout, but received no replies. When the Burt shoe factory shut down for a few weeks in March, he decided to invest some shoe leather and make the rounds in person.

His first stop was Willimantic, a mill town about forty miles south of East Brookfield. "I told [the manager] I had my mitt with me and was prepared to show him what I could do in the loft of some big building. He laughed at my youthful enthusiasm but said it wasn't necessary and that he would consider my application and let me know by mail whether he could take me."

Mack went on to Hartford and New Britain with similar results. According to Fred Lieb, one of the managers said, "You ain't got enough flesh on your bones. They'd be knockin' you down."

To which Mack replied, "They haven't knocked me down so far, and if they do, I'll lose no time picking myself up."

The entire journey covered 150 miles, and he was soon back home. He wrote to Frank Selee, the manager of a club in Waltham, Massachusetts. Selee was only three years older than the twenty-one-year-old Mack, at the beginning of a long managing career that led to the Hall of Fame. He didn't answer Mack's letter either.

Discouraged, Connie went back to work when the boot factory reopened. Contrary to some versions of his life story, the factory did not go out of business and Mack was never unemployed.

Meanwhile, his best friend and battery mate, Will Hogan, received an offer from the Meriden club in the new Connecticut league. Connie said good-bye to him with a heavy heart. For the first time, he didn't look forward to catching for the East Brookfield nine in the fast-approaching new season.

While Connie sorted leather and cut inner soles, down in Meriden Will Hogan was having problems with his catcher, Bob Pettit. Pitchers were now allowed to use an overhand delivery. Even standing fifteen feet back of the plate, Pettit couldn't handle Hogan's speed. After practice on Thursday, April 17, Hogan went to Albert Boardman, the shoe merchant who managed the team. Hogan told Boardman he could pitch better if he had his hometown catcher, Connie Mack, behind the plate. Boardman agreed to give Mack a tryout.

Michael Jr. recalled, "Well do I remember the night [Connie] came home from the boot shop and mother handed him a letter from the Meriden team."

What Michael remembered was a telegram, not a letter, the first the family had ever seen. Nervously, Connie tore open the yellow envelope and read, "Come on at once. Boardman, Meriden B.B. Club."

"Cornelius opened it," Michael Jr. said, "read it and then passed it to his mother and father. 'That's what I want to do,' he said, 'play ball.'

"Father replied, 'Well, son, if that is what you want, do it.'"

It's doubtful that there was any more family discussion about it, and maybe not even that much. His father could not have talked him into or out of anything even if he tried, and Connie's future did not depend on his father's approval. Besides, snapped Connie's cousin May Dempsey a hundred years later, "Irish men didn't count for much in those days."

His mother was aware of the sordid reputation of baseball and its players. But she didn't have to extract any promises from her son to avoid evil ways and hard liquor. He was already the man he would be, and she was content with what she saw. She knew he was ready to leave home. His dreams and ambitions lay beyond the Brookfields. He knew what he wanted to do with his life, and he set out with confidence.

The family could manage without his factory earnings, at least for as long as it might take him to find out if he could earn a living playing baseball. His brother Michael worked as a butcher. Dennis, seventeen, was employed at a pottery. Tom, ten, and Eugene, six, were in school. Their father had gone for a physical in March that soon resulted in an increase in his pension to $4 a month. In January 1885 he would begin receiving $2 a month from the state. The family's needs were small. The house was paid for; taxes were $16.20 a year.

Friday morning Connie walked into the office of the foreman, George Burt, at the boot factory. "I'm giving my notice," he said. "I'm quitting Saturday night. I'm going to be a baseball player."

"You're making regular money here," Burt said. "There's no future in baseball."

Mack shook his head.

"Why not wait until next Saturday night?" Burt said. "I'd like you to stay on another week."

The season didn't open until May 3, but Mack said, "No, this Saturday is my last day. After that I'll never spend another day in the boot shop."

Sometimes, when retelling the story, Mack was apologetic. "Maybe I was too rude to him. I should have worked the extra week."

On Monday morning Mack stuck his buckskin glove in his pocket and walked to the depot, where he boarded a train to Meriden, eighty miles to the southwest. A prosperous, rapidly growing town of twenty thousand midway between Hartford and New Haven, Meriden was the center of the silverplate industry. Two days later Mack auditioned in a game against the Yale freshmen. That morning he received two telegrams, forwarded to him from East Brookfield. One came from Frank Selee, offering him $12 a week and board. The other was from New Britain with an offer of $60 a month. Mack said nothing about the wires. He put on a gray uniform with light blue trim and warmed up his pitcher, Will Hogan.

Mack batted third in the lineup and had 2 hits, but it was his work "at the points" that drew the most notice. Hogan struck out 17, allowed 1 hit, and walked 6, which accounted for half the Meridens' 12 errors (walks were charged to the pitcher as errors). The game, won by Meriden, 8–4, was called after 7 innings because the Yale catcher was too "broken up" to continue.

The next day's *Meriden Republican* enthused, "Hogan and Mack proved themselves to be first class men, and it was said by many that they were the best battery ever seen on the grounds. Mack and the Yale catcher received painful injuries, but pluckily kept on playing. If East Brookfield has any more players like Mack and Hogan, let's have 'em."

Albert Boardman wasted no time in sending for Will's brother Jack to play third base.

Will Hogan had worked up a sweat during the game. The chill evening air brought on a cold. For all his strong appearance, Will had inherited a disposition to lung disease that made him susceptible to colds that were difficult to shake off.

Emboldened by his performance and the two offers in his pocket, Connie Mack asked Boardman for $90 a month. Most players earned half that amount and held other jobs during the season; they played only twice a week. Will Hogan, at $100 and expenses, topped the team payroll. A surprised Mack got what he asked for without an argument.

Mack, the Hogans, Pettit, pitcher John Campana, and a first baseman from Brooklyn named Hyland (who didn't stick around long enough for his first name to be reported) shared rooms in a boarding house near the practice grounds in South Meriden. A bed and three meals a day cost Mack little enough to allow him to open a savings account at the City Savings Bank. Some months he was able to deposit his entire paycheck.

The 50-game season began with six teams: Meriden, Hartford, Waterbury, Rockville, Willimantic, and New Britain. Connie Mack would experience sixty-six more opening days as a player or manager, but none would compare with the excitement of his first. They opened at Hartford. Despite a chilly forty-eight degrees, after breakfast on that Saturday morning the six roommates went to the practice field and played "knock-up"—probably a game of fungo hitting—and catch. They ate lunch at the boarding house, then, to save the twenty-five-cent stage fare, walked the two and a quarter miles to the railroad station.

The station was a madhouse. The railroad rolled out new cars in honor of the season's inaugural and offered one hundred special round trip tickets at forty cents. By noon they were gone. Another 150 paid the full fare for the twenty-five mile journey. The mob included the ninety-four stockholders of the club, most of whom were well armed with cash to bet.

When the train pulled into Meriden at 1:48, the crowd parted to allow Boardman and his nine players to climb aboard first. Eager hands lifted the team's equipment up to the players before the boisterous rooters clambered aboard. Forty minutes later they arrived in Hartford, where Boardman hired carriages to transport the players to the grounds in style. More than 1,500 cranks (the term for baseball aficionados that was gradually being replaced by "fans") swarmed into the park. Since the uncovered grandstand behind home plate seated only 400, most of them stood along the foul lines. The ten-cent seats behind a wire fence in left field were filled. Youngsters perched in trees beyond the outfield fence, which was decorated with freshly painted advertisements, and the center field scoreboard, which posted out-of-town scores.

At three o'clock a fifteen-piece band began a one-hour concert—"a novel feature on the ball ground but becoming popular," said the *Republican*—while odds were agreed upon and wagers entered into widely but quietly, out of respect for the league rules banning betting in the stands.

The Meridens took the field in new gray breeches and caps trimmed with blue, short-sleeved white jersey shirts with an "M" on the front, blue stockings, and belts. Umpire Patrick Dutton called the game to start at four. Mack, chosen by Boardman to represent the visitors, won the coin toss and chose to bat last.

Two Hartford newspapers and the *Meriden Republican* covered the opener extensively, but their game accounts differ. None of the three box scores agree; none could be called accurate. Longtime Meriden resident Roger W. King, a member of the Society for American Baseball Research (SABR), reconciled them to provide the following account of Connie Mack's professional debut.

In the bottom of the first, both Jack Hogan and Connie Mack singled in their first at bats. Hogan scored on a passed ball; Mack was left at third.

In the third inning, Hogan had the second of his 4 hits. Mack walked and they pulled a double steal but failed to score.

It was not a good day for Will Hogan. Pitching in a gusty wind and sub-sixty-degree temperature, Hogan gave up 3 runs in the sixth, then switched positions with John Campana, going to right field, where he dropped a fly ball that let in Hartford's final run in its 4–1 win. There were numerous foul balls hit over the grandstand, but each time a boy recovered the ball and traded it for free admission, enabling the teams to play the entire game using one ball. The band played "Golden Chimes Scout" as the crowd filed out, the Meriden backers lighter of pocket as they headed for the 7:40 express that would take them home.

It was the practice for players to take turns in the coaching boxes when they weren't batting. Mack's work behind the plate and on the coaching lines quickly won over the *Republican*'s young baseball writer, Thomas Reilly, a future congressman, who wrote, "Connie Mack is nothing if not a hard worker. He coached the men excellently and it isn't his fault that they didn't run bases better."

When Hogan didn't pitch, Pettit caught and Mack played the outfield or first or third base. John Campana pitched the home opener against Willimantic at the field known as the trotting park. Mack started in left field, but after Pettit let three pitches get by him, Mack moved behind the plate. He had 2 hits and scored 2 runs in Meriden's 11–7 victory. (A granite marker at the site, put up by the American Legion Post 45 Club, commemorates Connie Mack's Meriden debut on May 10, 1884.)

At that time the manager's job was the equivalent of a general manager's today. The captain ran the team on the field. The *Republican* commented that "Mack is by long odds the best man for captain of the nine." After a few games Boardman agreed and gave the reins to the rookie catcher. Mack grasped them eagerly. He introduced a signal for a pick-off play involving the pitcher and shortstop. He showed the second baseman and shortstop how to move into position to take a sudden throw to second to catch a wayward runner by surprise. Mack and Hogan worked out a quick pitch scheme. Making a gesture as if to pick up his mask, Mack would spring into his catching position without it as Hogan threw to the unprepared batter.

Mack was also a chatterbox, distracting batters with a high-pitched needling or an innocent "How're you doing?" kind of patter. Nothing vicious or mean, but if he learned a hitter's weakness or vulnerability on some subject, he chirped away at it.

Moving close to the plate when they were within one strike of fanning a batter, Mack developed the art of bat-tipping, touching the bat just enough to throw off a hitter's swing. He then apologized with such sincerity that the batter was often fooled into believing it had been an accident. These tactics also amused the customers, who were close enough to the action to hear it all. Mack's hustle, lively banter, and willingness to play any position without complaint made him a favorite among Meriden cranks. One wrote to the *Republican* asking how much Connie Mack weighed. Tom Reilly replied, "With his hair combed, Mack weighs about 140 pounds."

Connie Mack observed and filed away everything that happened around him, as if creating the recipe for his own future as a manager. He studied strategy and the handling of men, as well as the economics of the game. And what an education his freshman year proved to be.

It was no secret which players were "sports." He saw the effects of whiskey and late hours on their performance on the field. Drinking, gambling, brawling, and whoring were ballplayers' primary evening activities. Throughout the major and minor leagues, alcoholism threatened to destroy the game. Club owners, players, and umpires traveled in a fog of whiskey. Hardly a day passed without an arrest or fight or shooting. In 1883 the Pittsburgh club of the American Association had been nicknamed Lusher's Rest.

The *Cincinnati Enquirer* once offered shaky players this advice:
"Whenever a ball looks like this: O

                               O

                       O take a chance on the middle one."

Mack also learned why hotels turned away the baseball trade. Pillow fights were a common diversion. They started with two players in a room and quickly spread into the hall, where others joined in until a blizzard of feathers filled the air. One night the Waterbury team stayed overnight in Rockville instead of returning home after a game. The players tore up the place, causing the innkeeper to demand double payment for the damage.

Mack disliked the manager, Albert Boardman, whom he remembered as "an outspoken, decidedly coarse fellow. The way he used to talk to us was fierce." He winced at the language Boardman used in tearing into players in front of the entire team. It wasn't the profanity that bothered Mack—his "goodness gracious" image was never realistic—but the unvarying vehemence with which Boardman attacked his players. It didn't matter if he was lashing them for carousing all night and sleeping all morning or dropping fly balls in the outfield—or the connection between the two. Mack might have accepted the methods and the language if they worked, but he saw that none of it had any effect on the guilty parties.

"I decided right then, there were matters relating to a player's habits which should be talked about between manager and player alone," Mack concluded.

Toward the end of May, Will Hogan, who had never regained his full health since the Yale game, went home to recuperate. The Meridens climbed to .500 in June, Mack enjoying his biggest day at bat on June 7. Playing left field, he was 5 for 5 and scored 3 runs in a 10–7 loss at Willimantic.

As the team continued to hover around .500 in third place, players came and went. Some simply quit; others were released to make room for new ones. And there were plenty to choose from, as many a player found himself far from home, broke, and out of a job when his team or league blew up. The Eastern League began with eight clubs and was down to five. The Northwestern opened with twelve and sputtered out of existence by August. The Union Association was too chaotic for anyone to calculate the final standings. Closer to home, the Massachusetts State Association disbanded in June.

The Meriden club was losing money. Attendance was falling; the five-cent scorecards weren't selling. At a stockholders' meeting on June 17, Boardman was forced out as manager, and George H. Lynn replaced him. The new management, hoping to turn the team into a pennant winner overnight, scurried after the "drops" like scavengers in an apple orchard after an autumn gale. They picked up two from Worcester—pitcher Frank

Nash and first baseman Matt Barry—and replaced Mack as captain with the more experienced Barry, paying him and a "change catcher," William Corrigan, $125 a month each. The club didn't get its money's worth. Corrigan played in 6 games; Barry hit .211 in 13 games.

Will Hogan returned but his strength didn't, so Meriden signed Jumping Jack Jones, a former Yale star locally renowned as a whistler in the Eli Glee Club. Jones had a year in the major leagues under his belt, winning 11 and losing 7 for Detroit in the National League and Philadelphia in the American Association in '83, but he was of little help to the Meridens and never pitched in the big leagues again.

By the end of the season, twenty-five players would appear in a Meriden uniform in at least three games and perhaps a dozen more in one or two. Of the opening day lineup, only Mack, Pettit, and Campana finished the season.

Facing high salaries and low income, the club called a general meeting, at which 150 people pledged to raise one-third of the $300 a month needed to supplement gate receipts and keep the team afloat. They urged the omnibus company to cut the one-way fare from fifteen to ten cents and pleaded for the public to stop watching games from the hillside outside the park, where stagecoach drivers parked, providing a vantage point for their passengers. The club suffered a financial blow when exhibition games against the New York Gothams were rained out three times. It did get one in against Harry Wright's Philadelphia nine on July 25.

A game against Waterbury at home on August 16 drew over three thousand, who saw Frank Nash shut out the league leaders, 2–0. But attendance averaged about five hundred. To spruce up the team, the manager ordered new uniforms: gray pants with blue jerseys, caps, belts, and stockings and an overshirt of gray with blue trim. It didn't help.

The Connecticut State League was crumbling. When Meriden played at Willimantic on August 30, the total receipts came to $20.70. The Meridens left town with $19.20, short of the $30 guarantee. The league gave Willimantic an ultimatum: come up with the rest of the guarantee or face expulsion. Willimantic said it didn't have the $10.80 and dropped out, leaving five teams to complete the schedule.

Mack earned the title "Old Reliable" for his clutch hitting and steady play behind the plate. But his hands were sore from the battering of the pitchers' fastballs. It was apparent that with the new shoulder-high delivery, catchers' gloves required more padding. He needed a rest and got it by playing all three outfield positions.

On September 15 Mack hit the only home run seen at the Meriden grounds that year, in a game against Hartford that ended in a forfeit. With Meriden leading 5–3 in the ninth, a foul ball was hit into a marshy area behind the backstop. Both teams searched in vain for the sunken sphere. League rules required the umpire to call for a new ball if five minutes of searching failed to turn up the old one. When Hartford called for a new ball, manager George Lynn took one from his pocket. The Hartford captain refused to use it, claiming it was illegal because it was not in a box sealed by the league secretary. The umpire said that was a National League rule not recognized in Connecticut. Hartford said nothing doing, and the ump forfeited the game to Meriden.

Will Hogan never regained his preseason form or health. At the end of July he went home again. In late August Mack received word that Will was seriously ill, his lungs hemorrhaging. He went to East Brookfield to see him and returned on Friday, September 19, to play in a benefit game for Will, who was failing fast. After the game he visited with his old friend for the last time, then returned to Meriden. Three days later Will Hogan died of consumption. He was twenty-three. Mack went home for the funeral.

More than two thousand turned out to see Mack catch Michael Walsh's 11–2 win over Waterbury on Saturday, September 20. Mack's 2 hits included his fourth triple of the year. That evening special buses ran from the Meriden House Hotel to Hemlock Grove, where a picnic to raise money for the club included music, square dancing, and a good deal of spending of Waterbury money won by local bettors. The highlight of the evening was a popularity contest. Paying ten cents a ballot, the voters elected Connie Mack most popular player and presented him a silver watch.

The season ended on October 8 at Waterbury, where Walsh, who had pitched almost every game for the last month, won, 8–2. Meriden collected $42 as its share of the gate. Waterbury won the league's silver bat in lieu of a pennant with a 34-13 record. Meriden finished second at 25-22. Official scorer Charles D. Goodwin showed Mack playing in 44 games, the most on the team, with 32 runs scored, 49 hits for a .277 average, and 26 of the team's 334 errors. (The rules still permitted the batter to call for a high or low pitch; anything not in the requested zone was a ball. Mack favored them high. On the banquet circuit in later years he admitted, "When the rules permitted the hitter to call for a high or low ball I was a pretty good hitter. Then they changed the rules [in 1887] and the pitchers could throw whatever they wanted to. If they kept the ball low on me I couldn't hit for sour apples.")

The Meriden club finished the season owing about $500, including play-
ers' salaries. The stockholders put on a three-day baseball fair at the Town
Hall to raise the money. The fair began with a Thursday night dance. On
Friday night Bob Pettit and John Campana fought to a draw in a boxing
match. On Saturday Meriden and Waterbury played an exhibition game.
In the first inning Mack hit a rattling three-bagger. A single brought him
home. At that point the game was stopped. Out strode Judge Levi L. Coe,
who delivered a ringing speech in which he compared the national game to
ancient Roman sports, commended honest ballplaying, and cited Connie
Mack as the embodiment of honesty in the game.

"His effective work and faithfulness to the club under all circumstances
led his friends to make him this present," said the judge, who then handed
the catcher a $75 gold Waltham watch with chain and charm.

Mack said a few words of thanks, then the crowd stood and delivered
three cheers for "Faithful Connie Mack." The watch was engraved, "To
Connie Mack from the Fans of Meriden." Mack carried it with him until it
was stolen from the Pittsburgh clubhouse about ten years later.

The fair culminated in a gathering in the park that evening that almost
turned into a donnybrook, as supporters of presidential candidates Grover
Cleveland and James G. Blaine waged spirited debates among the torch-
lights and banners. The three-day event turned a profit but not enough to
cover the club's deficit. On Monday the players were paid, thanks to manager George Lynn, who withdrew $350 from his personal bank account.

Connie Mack already knew he wasn't going to be back in a Meriden
uniform in 1885. The league had no reserve clause in its contracts, and he
had received offers from other teams during the last week of the season.
Weighing them, he considered Hartford to be the most financially secure,
and he signed for $125 a month.

Before boarding the train for East Brookfield, he deposited another $10
in his savings account, decided he didn't need two watches, and gave the
silver one to Michael Walsh.

In his first professional season, Connie Mack watched players pour their
careers down the hatch in saloons, teams and leagues go out of business,
his own team pay salaries it could not afford in a vain effort to field a winner and make it back at the ticket window, and a club manager dig into his
own pocket to make up the deficit and pay the bills.

None of this was lost on him.

4 | THE BONES BATTERY

For the first time since he was nine years old, Connie Mack did not work, nor was he in school, in the fall of 1884. "I decided to indulge myself in the luxury of a workless winter," he said in a 1930 newspaper series on his life. "I had full use of my money, and as my father had prospered in his small way, there was no necessity for me to send anything regularly home."

Here again his memory airbrushed out reality when it came to his father. Michael McGillicuddy was not prospering. It was now more than ten years since he had been able to work even half-time. He walked with a cane or crutches and was down to 130 pounds. He was still applying for an increase in his $4 monthly pension but without success.

But Connie's brothers, Michael and Dennis, were working, and if the family needed anything, Connie provided it. With the country in a recession, many of the shoe factories were shut down. In November a national reform movement resulted in the election of a Democrat, Grover Cleveland, to the presidency for the first time in twenty-eight years. Connie and Michael paid the $2 poll tax; voting for the first time, Connie cast his ballot for Cleveland. That didn't mean he was a Democrat; disenchanted Republicans who turned away from James G. Blaine carried Cleveland to a narrow victory. On the following Saturday evening Connie was one of the torchbearers who marched behind the East Brookfield band in celebration. "A bonfire and three cannons kept things lively all evening," reported the *Brookfield Times*.

Throughout his life Connie Mack would be politically interested, sometimes active, always bipartisan. He could endorse a Democrat for election without affecting his longtime friendship with his Philadelphia neighbor, Republican Judge Harry S. McDevitt. He had friends of both parties in the Republican-dominated state capital in Harrisburg, although it would take him thirty-three years to get a law passed permitting Sunday baseball.

Mack made a few trips to Boston that winter, skated on frozen Lake Lashaway, played whist, and escorted Margaret Hogan to dances and shows. He went with his little brother Eugene to pay the $2 license fee for their black setter, Prince. He spent time with Eddie Drake, who had set up a brewery in his basement and delivered the beer by wagon. He bought the latest *Spalding Guide* for ten cents and perused the ads for new, improved catchers' masks, gloves, and chest protectors. That made him restless. He couldn't wait for spring. When he read in a Boston paper that the Trinity College team had begun indoor workouts in Hartford, Connie packed his clothes, shoes, bat, and glove and took off.

Mixing with college students was a new experience for Connie Mack. Most of his friends had dropped out of school at an early age. He was acutely aware of his lack of education, but the student athletes' cordial welcome eased his discomfort. He was, after all, a professional ballplayer, and that carried more prestige among the college crowd than a high school diploma.

The students' conduct, intelligence, willingness to learn, and analytical approach to the game impressed him. "That was one reason," he said, "when I started to manage, I always gave a well-recommended collegian a chance, and most of all was patient and sympathetic with him after he reported."

Mack worked with Trinity's ace pitcher, Joseph Shannon, beginning a friendship that, like so many in Mack's life, lasted a lifetime. Shannon became a Philadelphia lawyer.

Some infielders began using a padded glove to handle hot line drives in 1883, but most continued to disdain such equipment. Reinforced full-fingered catchers' gloves were gaining favor, but a slab of round steak, though expensive, was still a handy piece of insulation. Mack began slipping a rubber pad inside his glove. A few catchers rejected all that "sissy stuff," but he realized that without more substantial protection, overhand pitching would chew up a catcher's hands and leave him with mangled fingers.

The Connecticut State League, renamed the Southern New England League, now included Hartford, Meriden, Bridgeport, Springfield, Waterbury, and New Britain. Hartford's manager and captain, Jack Remsen, had been an outfielder in the National League for six years. Bob Pettit from the '84 Meriden club had signed with Hartford, along with two collegians, pitcher Fred Tenney from Brown and first baseman Samuel Childs of Yale.

Hartford opened at Meriden, where Mack received a warm reception despite sporting the visitors' uniform. After wet grounds postponed their own home opener, the Hartfords made their debut at the Ward Street Grounds on a cold, raw May 5 before five hundred shivering fans scattered throughout the grandstand, side stands, and carriage enclosure, where ladies in bright dresses and picturesque hats livened the scene.

When he wasn't catching, Mack played right field, drawing good reviews at both positions. Hartford's pitching was poor. Tenney was released after one week. Jack Remsen was looking for new pitchers when Mack received a letter from a friend telling him of the exploits of Frank Gilmore, a pitcher for one of the Brookfield teams. Mack passed along the tip to Remsen, who dispatched him to Brookfield to bring Gilmore back for a trial.

The day after they returned Mack caught Gilmore in a 6–3 win over Meriden. A twenty-one-year-old right-hander, Frank Gilmore was as tall and thin as Connie Mack. He used a windup that distracted batters and delighted the fans. Gyrating his long arms and legs into pretzelian contortions, he looked as if he would never get them untangled. Out of this maze of limbs shot a fierce fastball or baffling curve. Mack earned as much praise for handling these pitches as Gilmore did for throwing them.

The sight of this pair of animated beanpoles walking side by side on the field drew good-natured hoots and exuberant ribbing as the patrons vied to tag them with the swiftest witticisms and nicknames. By June 1 Gilmore had won 5 and lost 1 for the first-place Hartfords, and the label "Bones Battery" had been pinned and stuck to them.

"But both have plenty of sinew in their work," observed the *Hartford Courant*.

Located midway between Boston and New York, Hartford was a convenient stop for big league teams to pick up some traveling money. In a game against Boston, Mack singled, stole second, and scored Hartford's only run in a 7–1 loss. On June 20 the Bones Battery defeated the New York Metropolitans of the American Association, 5–4, in 11 innings. Each time he did well against major league competition, it bolstered Connie Mack's belief that he had a future in the game.

When he wasn't catching or in the outfield, Mack played a few games at second base, covering the position "satisfactorily." But his catching, especially with Gilmore pitching, was invariably rated "first class." He had the ability to get inside a hitter's head and a feel for what a pitcher should throw in a given situation. Instincts, "baseball smarts," are not a matter of intelligence or schooling. They cannot be taught. A player has them or he doesn't. The great catchers, measured by their leadership on the field, their handling of pitchers, and their calling of a game, have them. Connie Mack had them.

The minor leagues were a haphazard business. Most clubs didn't own their own grandstands or playing fields. The quality and reliability of the umpires was erratic. "A lot of people like to hark back to the good old days," Connie Mack ruminated more than fifty years later. "But if baseball fans of today had a chance to see an old-fashioned game they'd give it a grand laugh. Clubs didn't own their own fields and many a time before we could play we had to get mowers and cut the grass ourselves. There were no regular umpires and those who acted as such were almost afraid to open their mouths. Gosh, how often have I seen the umpire chased off the field and in some cases beaten up."

Despite efforts to curb it, gambling was still rampant. When the management of the New Britain grounds decided to refuse admission to all reputed gamblers, attendance fell sharply and never recovered. Meriden didn't go that far. It just prohibited open betting in the grandstand. The gambling continued unabated but with restraint.

By the end of July the Southern New England League joined the list of baseball's faltering circuits. Bridgeport won 9 games in a row and climbed to second place, then kept on climbing clear out of the league and into the higher-class Eastern League, replacing one of its defunct franchises. A week later Springfield threw in the towel, which was practically its sole remaining asset.

The remaining four teams, calling themselves the Connecticut League, threw out all the records for the year and launched a new 24-game championship season. That didn't last long. Within ten days the New Britain club, rumored to be the victim of demon rum, could field only eight able-bodied players and disbanded. Meriden followed it out the door. When Norfolk dropped out of the Eastern League, Waterbury jumped in and took its place. That was the end of the Connecticut League, and Connie Mack witnessed another lesson in the fragility of professional baseball as a business and a career.

The Bones Battery's biggest game of the year was an exhibition at home against the New York Metropolitans two days after the short-lived "second season" ended. Gilmore pitched a 3-hitter and struck out 13 in a 6–0 win. Mack had 2 hits.

Their league having disappeared, Mack and Gilmore were free to accept an offer to work a September 17 Eastern League game for Newark against Waterbury. Mack's 2 hits put him in the 1885 record books with batting stats in three leagues: .188 in the Southern New England, .125 in four games in the Connecticut, and .500 in one Eastern League contest.

Pickup teams as well as major leaguers barnstormed until the snow fell. Based on their Newark performance, Gilmore and Mack were invited to join an independent team in Poughkeepsie, New York, for two games. "On Monday Gilmore struck out 17 Jersey Blues, and on Wednesday he fanned 14 of the Newburghs," reported the *Courant.* "Mack, as fine a catcher as there is in the country, played in fine form behind the bat as usual."

The New York Mets were also playing in the area. When one of their catchers was hurt, manager Jim Gifford remembered Mack. He sent him a telegram, and Mack took the next train for New York City. It was only exhibition games, but it was the big leagues.

On October 19 Mack had his first look at a future Hall of Fame battery: pitcher Tim Keefe and catcher Buck Ewing of the Giants. Mack was hit-less against Keefe in that game and was blanked again when Keefe beat the Mets, 6–5, four days later. But the *New York Times* devoted half its seven-line story to a favorable review of "Conley and Mack, the Mets' new battery, [who] filled their positions to good advantage."

The Mets rode the steam-powered elevated railway to the various grounds in the New York area. Fred Lieb described how one of the players plunked down the fare for all of them every time they rode the train. Mack felt embarrassed at being carried on the cuff. One day after a game he squared accounts by going into a saloon with the boys and laying a dollar on the bar. "This round is on me," he said. At a nickel a schooner, the buck did a thorough job of wetting down their dusty tonsils and soothing the rookie's conscience.

Mack's handling of Mets pitchers Jack Lynch and lefty Ed Cushman led one newspaper to comment, "The Mets' new catcher Mack showed up brilliantly, catching Cushman well and throwing to bases accurately." The New York pitchers agreed and asked Gifford to sign Mack. But Connie had to say no; before leaving Hartford, he had signed an 1886 contract for $165 a month. The Hartford management didn't know what league they'd be in, but they assured him they would field a team somewhere on opening day.

Connie Mack went home buoyed by an offer from a major league team, more confident than ever that he had made the right decision in departing the boot shop for baseball. His brief experience with the New York Mets made him a celebrity in the Brookfields. The first local native to play with a big league team, he was asked to speak at club meetings and socials. His friends at the news store and pharmacy peppered him with questions about the famous players he had seen in action. He found that he enjoyed being the center of attention.

Margaret Hogan was now a grown-up 19. Barely five feet tall, she was a dark-haired, bright-eyed colleen, a bubbly, outgoing magnet for a wide circle of friends. She and Connie were seen together at social events, and it was generally understood that a wedding was in their future. But there were two obstacles. The frequency with which baseball teams and leagues went out of business made Connie uneasy about depending on the game to support a family. And some friends advised him against marrying Miss Hogan because of the uncertain state of her health. Her vulnerability to the same disease that had carried off her brother Will at an early age seemed written in her pale face and frail body.

Responsible for providing his own equipment, Connie studied the Spalding ads displaying the new, improved gear. One featuring the latest in masks warned that "a broken-wire one will not stand the force of the ball without caving in and is liable to disfigure a player for life.... Our masks are made of the very best hard wire plated to prevent rusting, well-trimmed, well-padded with goat hair and padding faced with the best imported doe skin which is impervious to perspiration and retains its pliability and softness." It was priced at $3.50, as were an open-backed, full left-hand glove of Indian tanned buck and a fingerless right glove. Horsehide shoes cost

$6 (spikes fifty cents a pair extra); bats made from sun-dried ash, seventy-five cents. Spalding's $1.50 baseballs were warranted to "last a game of nine innings." As a proportion of his $825 annual salary, the cost of the gear Mack needed was about the same as that for a minor league player earning $12,000 today.

Despite his confidence in his ability, Connie Mack had good reason to be concerned about baseball as a business. For the 1886 season, his Hartford club had joined the Eastern League, now including Newark, Jersey City, Providence, Meriden, Waterbury, Bridgeport, and Long Island. Two weeks after the May 1 opening of the season, the Long Island club dropped out, followed shortly by Providence. The remaining clubs voted to wipe out all games played to that point and start over. With a nervous eye on other shaky franchises, they agreed to look no further than one month ahead in making a new schedule.

Hoping to avoid "vexatious delays" caused by searching for lost foul balls, league president George M. Ballard ordered that two balls be on hand for use in every game. Club owners grumbled; at $15 a dozen, balls were too expensive to use more than one a game, no matter how "punky" the ball became. The fiscal ice was so thin that when five balls were used in a game at Waterbury on June 14, club treasurers throughout the league trembled.

None of this deterred the Hartford backers from ordering new uniforms at a cost of $25 for an outfit of blue and white checked caps, pants and blouses, and blue stockings. Mack played first base on the day the new uniforms were introduced. In July he played a game at shortstop, the *Courant* noting, "Mack played a perfect game at short for the home club, showing himself a valuable man at anything he undertakes."

During the season Mack played every position except pitcher and batted anywhere from leadoff to seventh. His hustle and willingness to do whatever was asked of him kept him atop the fans' popularity rankings and earned him a midseason raise to $200 a month. Frank Gilmore was the team's most consistent pitcher, and the Bones Battery entertained audiences all around the circuit. On August 11, after a 12–1 win, an anonymous admirer sent Mack a large, silver-headed cane with a note: "To that most necessary appendage of the Hartford Base Ball club, plucky, energetic, reliable Mr. Mack."

But Mack's popularity and the spiffy new uniforms were not enough to draw sufficient customers to pay the bills. The club directors offered a season pass to anyone who bought a share of stock in the club for $6. They asked the cranks to pay double the usual admission to attend a benefit game and went so far as to ask all stockholders to leave their free passes at home and pay their way in. The fund-raising game was rained out. When it was finally played, only 600 paid their way in.

An emergency meeting raised pledges of $120 on the condition that a new, more competent manager be named. That savior turned out to be Charles F. Daniels, an umpire who had been an original member of the National League staff but was temporarily out of the game.

Meanwhile, other calamities besieged the league. Sometimes two umpires showed up for one game and none at another. When there was none, the visiting club had the right to choose a player to officiate. One day at Waterbury, when no umpire showed up, the opponents from Newark walked off the field and left town. The league fined Newark $200, which it refused to pay. The bickering threatened to blow up the entire league. But it was about to implode anyhow. Following the July 4 doubleheaders, Meriden quit. Results of all its games were eliminated from the standings. Calculating the records became so complicated that no final standings were ever compiled.

The confusion extended to the individual records. The *Spalding Guide* shows Mack fifteenth in batting with a .289 average in 46 games. The *Baseball Register* shows him batting .248 in 69 games. Mack probably got off to a slow start, then hit .289 in the 46 games after Providence and Meriden dropped out and the league started over. His fielding average for 46 games was a league-leading .942 for catchers. He caught one stretch of 10 consecutive games without a passed ball, a noteworthy feat for the time.

No won-lost or strikeout records were found for Frank Gilmore, but his opponents' batting average was reported as .200, fifth best in the league. Gilmore was an inept hitter by any standards, batting .100.

"He was a pitcher of the highest order," Mack said of Gilmore, "but there his value ended. He could not field his position and I think he was the most impossible hitter that ever lived, even among pitchers. He was actually applauded when he hit a foul."

Connie Mack saw black players for the first time that season. Meriden had a black pitcher named Grand, who faced Hartford once. On July 1 Hartford played an exhibition game against a black team from Trenton, the Cuban Giants. Mack umpired the game.

The remnants of the league soldiered on to the season's end. In August Connie Mack went on a hitting tear. On August 16 he had 3 hits and stole a base in a 12–2 win over Newark. Three days later he doubled and tripled in a 13–3 victory, then had a double and single the next day. On September 7 he had 2 hits as Gilmore shut out Jersey City, 2–0. The next day Mack had 2 more hits and Gilmore pitched another shutout, blanking Newark, 4–0.

Their hot streaks could not have come at a better time. Charles Daniels was determined to see Hartford play out the season, but the club was deeply in debt. There was no money to meet the payroll. Then Walter F. Hewett, son of a Washington grain merchant who owned the Washington club, came to town.

Washington had been briefly represented in the Union and American Associations, but the Nationals (or Statesmen, depending on what newspaper you read), owned by Robert C. Hewett, were now in their first year in the fast company of the ten-year-old National League. The team was unable to compete with the well-financed large market clubs. By August 11 it had won only 12 games and lost 60. Crowds at Capitol Park were rapidly shrinking into what might be more accurately called gatherings or groups.

Hewett was intent on revitalizing his team and boosting attendance by introducing some highly touted rookies, giving the fans reason to hope for better things next year. He had heard about Gilmore, who was said to have rung up 300 strikeouts already. He sent his son to Hartford to buy him and anyone else who looked promising.

After watching several Hartford games, Walter Hewett approached Daniels and made an offer for several players, including Gilmore. When word got out about the deal, Gilmore balked at going anywhere without his catcher, Connie Mack. According to Fred Lieb's 1945 biography of Mack, the Bones Battery had made a pact: if one was sold to the majors, he wouldn't go without the other. Gilmore went to Hewett's hotel room and announced that he wouldn't go anywhere without Mack. Hewett protested that Mack couldn't hit National League pitching.

Gilmore insisted that "we go together or I don't go to Washington."

Impressed with this show of loyalty, Walter Hewett studied the fidgety Gilmore, thought about his father's instructions, and decided that Gilmore probably wouldn't be much good without Mack's steadying presence. He went back to Daniels and added Mack to the package. The total price came to $3,500.

That's the way Fred Lieb told the story. Morris Bealle in *The Washington Senators* told it the same way. Connie Mack never told any version of it in the serialized stories of his life that appeared in newspapers from time to time. But in a 1948 interview with Ed Fitzgerald in *Sport* magazine, Mack said the story that Gilmore had refused to go to Washington without Mack was "absolutely wrong. It was the catcher they wanted. I've seen it so many times I wish you would correct it. If Frank Gilmore were alive he'd tell you he wouldn't even have been an ordinary pitcher without me."

Mack's assessment of Gilmore could explain why the pitcher might have been reluctant to leave Hartford without him. And if Fitzgerald quoted Mack accurately (which is by no means certain), Mack might have made his point clearer by saying, "It was *me* they wanted, not Gilmore," instead of "It was *the catcher* they wanted." It's also significant that the *Hartford Courant* first reported that three players—outfielder George Shoch, a .300 hitter who could play the infield as well; Bill Krieg, a .315-hitting catcher; and Gilmore—had been sold to Washington and the next day reported that "now five players" were involved, adding left-hander John Henry and Mack. This is consistent with Lieb's version of the events. Equally telling, when they all got to Washington, Connie Mack caught all 9 of Frank Gilmore's starts and only one game when another pitcher worked.

In any event, Hartford's best and most popular players had been sold before the season ended, provoking loud complaints from the club's followers. But, the *Courant* explained, "the baseball park company was in financial straits. What was done had to be done speedily. Fans can thank manager Daniels and Director Hall for doing the wisest thing possible under the circumstances."

The fans didn't thank the manager—fans will never thank a manager—for doing anything for financial rather than baseball reasons, no matter how "wise" or whatever the "circumstances."

Connie Mack had seen enough in his three years in professional baseball to understand this financial fact of life: if a club spent more than it took in, selling players was sometimes the only way to stay in business.

Prior to the start of Mack's farewell game on September 9, the umpire presented each Hartford player with a buttonhole bouquet from "a friend." The fans gave Mack a diamond stickpin and Gilmore a gold watch. Hewett wound up with slightly damaged goods as a result of the game. With Henry pitching and Krieg catching, both went for a pop fly and collided. Henry suffered a cut over one eye. Krieg had cuts on his lip and nose, a few loosened teeth, and a scraped shin. Gilmore, playing left field, came in to pitch. Mack was playing second base, so a new catcher went behind the plate.

Nobody on the train to Washington that evening could mistake the occupation of the five young men who climbed aboard in Hartford. Connie Mack used a long bat, which he tied to the outside of his trunk when he traveled.

The Washington manager, Honest John Gaffney, was no stranger to Mack, who had seen Gaffney umpire in New England. Mack called him "a perfect umpire. He would follow a ball all the way from the pitcher, and when he made his decision he would say, 'That was one-eighth of an inch outside' or 'That was one-eighth of an inch too low' and he was right." One of several umpires who billed themselves as "King of the Umpires," Gaffney was taking time off from umpiring in the National League to try his hand at managing. He had replaced Mike Scanlon on August 19 after the team had lost 12 in a row. When the rookies from Hartford arrived, the team's record was 15-78.

On a clear, eighty-degree Saturday, September 11, Gaffney threw four of his new players into action. Gilmore and Mack were at the points. Krieg played first base and Shoch right field. Under Mack's guidance and encouragement, Gilmore struck out 10 Phillies, walked 4, and gave up 7 hits. The Statesmen trailed, 3–1, in the bottom of the eighth when Mack, batting eighth, lined a one-out single over second base. Gilmore made contact with a slow curve and sent a shot right at shortstop Arthur Irwin, who couldn't handle it. Paul Hines then hit a triple that scored Mack and Gilmore. Hines scored when Cliff Carroll hit a bounder over first for a 4–3 lead.

In the ninth 2 hits put Phillies on second and third, but Gilmore got out of the jam as the crowd of 1,500 gave the home team a rousing hurrah.

The exuberant boys from Hartford were whooping it up in the tiny dressing room when a scowling Gaffney stuck his head in the doorway. "Here you new fellers," he hollered, "don't get swell-headed because you happened to win."

"That remark of his always stayed with me," Mack recalled. "He didn't know any of our personal habits and I always imagined he believed that we might all go out and paint the town red over this initial success."

Instead, Mack and Gilmore went back to the room and bed they shared in a nearby boarding house. The following Wednesday they began a road trip to New York, Boston—where they won 3 in a row for the first time all season—and Philadelphia. Mack cottoned to big league pitching, at least for 10 games, hitting .361 with 2 doubles and a triple and 5 runs batted in. With his lengthy strike zone, he drew few walks throughout his career, but he seldom struck out.

Mack's ginger and hustle made him an immediate favorite with the fans and sparked life into the spiritless Statesmen. The *Sporting Life* correspondent reported of the rookie catcher: "And what an impression he has made here. . . . He jumped into popular favor at once and people never seem to tire of singing the praises. . . . He and Gilmore have been dubbed the Shadow Battery and their work is beyond criticism."

With Mack's patient handling, Frank Gilmore pitched well. He started and completed 9 games, striking out 75 in 75 innings, for a 4-4 record with 1 tie. Erratic defense was responsible for most of the losses. On September 28 he struck out 16 St. Louis Maroons, tying the league's season high, in a 5–2 loss.

Near the end of the season Connie Mack learned firsthand that the major leagues were no more immune from the poison of corruption than the minors.

The Nationals were due to close the season at home against the seventh-place Kansas City Cowboys, beginning with a doubleheader on Thursday, October 7. On Wednesday night John Gaffney was roused from his sleep by a stranger who demanded to know "for a certainty" what battery Gaffney intended to use in the Saturday game. The suspicious manager fed him the names of two players he had no intention of using and went back to sleep. The next day the Cowboys failed to show up for the morning game and the Nationals claimed a forfeit. In the afternoon Connie Mack coaxed a 12–3 win out of Gilmore.

The Friday game ended in a 2–2 tie.

On Saturday morning Gaffney received three telegrams, all from St. Louis gamblers, all with the same warning:

CHANGE YOUR PITCHER AND CATCHER FOR TODAY'S GAMES. THERE IS SOMETHING CROOKED. A. G. Merwin.

USE CAUTION IN SELECTING PITCHER TODAY'S GAME. STRANGERS IN TOWN OFFERING ODDS ALTOGETHER OUT OF PROPORTION ON KANSAS CITY. C. D. Comfort.

LOOK OUT FOR SOMETHING CROOKED IN TODAY'S GAME. KANSAS CITY PEOPLE HERE BACKING THEIR CLUB AT RIDICULOUS ODDS. George Ehrlich.

Gaffney smelled something fishy. He had intended to use Gilmore and Mack that afternoon and had no doubts about the honesty of his two rookies. Neither, he reckoned, did the senders of the telegrams, who were trying to dupe him into benching them in favor of the battery the pool sellers had managed to reach with bribes. Gaffney ignored the wires and went with Gilmore and Mack.

The Shadow Battery turned in its best game of the year. Gilmore pitched a one-hitter and struck out 12. Mack's fourth-inning single drove in the first run in the home team's 3–0 victory.

After the game Gaffney said he was informed that he had accurately doped out the scheme, and the inquisitive stranger of Wednesday night was one of the St. Louis plungers on the Cowboys. "Never as long as I am manager of the National club," he said, "will I allow the nine to be used as tools of the pool sellers and these gentlemen will have to devise some less transparent scheme than the one set forth in the telegrams from St. Louis."

Only a half game separated Kansas City and Washington at the bottom of the standings. They agreed to play off the tie game on Monday. John Henry pitched; Mack did not play. The Cowboys won 7–5 and claimed seventh place.

Washington finished in the sub-basement, winning 28 and losing 92. But Hewett's new players had accomplished everything he wanted. The *Washington Evening Star* commented, "The increased attendance at Capitol Park since the Statesmen recently recovered from their lethargy and played with a little spirit shows how ready the Washington public is to support a team that will do its best."

During the next ten days the Nationals played exhibition games against the American Association Baltimores. Connie Mack managed a hit in two games off a twenty-year-old rookie left-hander, Matt Kilroy, from Philadelphia. Kilroy had pitched 583 innings, which didn't lead the league, striking out 513, which did. He still had enough stamina left to defeat the Washington club twice.

In gratitude for his work, Hewett gave Connie Mack $800 for his few weeks' work and an 1887 contract for $2,250. Despite its woeful record, the club actually showed a small profit.

For the first time, Connie Mack went home for the winter without worrying if his team or the league would disappear before spring. The National League was solid. It was the league of managers like Cap Anson, Harry Wright, and Jim Mutrie and his New York Giants. Club owners like Spalding in Chicago and Alfred J. Reach in Philadelphia had deep pockets and big stakes in the game's future success.

6 | LIFE IN THE BIG LEAGUES

Life in the big leagues in 1887 was far from luxurious. On the road players rolled up their uniforms, for which they were charged $30, and carried them with their shoes, bats, and other belongings. If they didn't have a suitcase, they wrapped their clothes in brown paper. Catchers lugged their masks and chest protectors. They changed at the third-rate hotels where they slept, two to a bed, and walked or rode in a horse-drawn omnibus to the ballpark. For these amenities they were charged fifty cents a day by their employer.

Farmers who lived near the railroad tracks could tell when a ball club was on the train by the sight of sweaty uniforms hung out the windows to dry. The uniforms might not match; there was no uniformity of apparel among the nine men on the field.

John Montgomery "Monte" Ward, star shortstop of the New York Giants, cited the questionable drinking water as one of the hazards of traveling:

"We would be in St. Louis drinking Missouri water one week—water so thick with mud that there would be thick settlings in the glass when you let it stand—and then we'd be drinking water out of Lake Michigan at Chicago. From there we would go to Cincinnati and drink Ohio River water, and then to Pittsburgh and sample the water of the Monongahela. We knew them all by color and taste."

The crude little dressing room at Capitol Park in Washington offered more facilities than most, such as they were. Connie Mack once described them:

"The locker room in the Washington ball park had no showers or bathing facilities other than a sort of barrel-like pool sunk in the ground filled with water. The water would stay there for a week without being changed. After a while they outgrew the barrel and put in little individual tin pans. On the other side of the locker room a sink was put in with three or four spigots from which we could fill our pans. I anticipated the shower bath by a number of years by filling my pan up at the sink and pouring its contents over my head and shoulders."

Every player was his own trainer, carrying his personal kit of iodine and arnica. Players debated the relative healing powers of whiskey versus tobacco juice for spike wounds and split fingers. Mack and Gilmore tended each other's aches and pains.

"Frank developed a sore arm, and I had a charley horse," Mack recalled. "Wintergreen was the only remedy for our aches, so we would spend half the night rubbing each other with wintergreen. I worked on his arm and he on my legs. Gosh, you could smell our room a block away."

When the wind was brisk and blowing from the north, the smell may have invaded the halls of Congress, a few blocks to the south. Set near a neighborhood of fine homes in a section called Swampoodle, Capitol Park was located at North Capitol Street between F and G Streets, where Union Station and the National Postal Museum now stand. The outfielders had a fine view of the Capitol dome. Beyond the left field fence, Baltimore and Ohio (B&O) railroad cars were shunted about on side tracks. A block away on the opposite side stood the Government Printing Office, whose upper floors afforded an unobstructed view of the action on the field.

The infield was well sodded, but grass was sparse in the outfield and foul areas. Outfield fences were decorated with advertisements for beer, tobacco, sporting goods, and public baths. The small, primitive grandstand, little more than bleacher boards, seated about 1,800; the bleachers, twice that number. The cranks were boisterous, sometimes riotous. When they took exception to a call by the lone umpire, the police often had to fire their revolvers in the air to restore order.

With a population approaching two hundred thousand, Washington was among the smaller cities in the league. It was also the hottest city Mack had ever known. In the heat of July and August, he recalled, "after a game I would get home utterly fogged out and I hardly ate any supper. All night I would lie in the vestibule trying to get cool. The next day would be the same thing over again."

Politicians and government employees formed the bulk of the team's following. One of them was John Heydler, a future president of the league, who went to work in the printing office in 1888. Heydler told Fred Lieb:

Everybody around the printing office knew and loved Connie Mack. He was one of our favorite players. There was a small butcher shop opposite the park on G Street, where Mack used to have a daily small steak cut to put in his left finger glove. Then we younger fellows would also buy steaks to put into our gloves. The butcher didn't know his baseball too well and expressed wonder that we should eat up all his steaks. Also he could never understand why Connie's daily steak didn't put more flesh on his bones.

In those days, which were prior to the big-glove period, it was no fun for the catcher to come up behind the bat, and the small steak that Connie stuck into his glove felt very good. Catchers, especially in one-sided games, then kept as far back as the stand would permit.

Another Statesmen fan was the young leader of the U. S. Marine Band, John Philip Sousa, whose passion for baseball was second only to his music.

Washington was fast becoming electrified in public areas; street lights brightened many sections of town. Horse-drawn streetcars were giving way to electric trolleys. A few hundred "electric speaking telephones" linked the White House and other government offices.

But there was nothing electrifying about the Statesmen's play in 1887. The April 28 opener was a harbinger. Led by the National Rifles Band, the Statesmen and Boston Beaneaters paraded in open carriages from the Willard Hotel to Capitol Park, where a downpour sent the 1,800 faithful scattering for cover and washed out the game. The next day the field was muddy, the skies threatening. But 1,500 returned to see the match between Grasshopper Jim Whitney and Old Hoss Radbourn, who at thirty-two would work only 425 innings that year, his lowest total in six seasons.

When Bill Krieg hit a home run in the third inning, "hats, umbrellas and canes were thrown into the air and the multitude shouted forth their joy in hilarious manner," was the Morning Republican's understated report. That was practically the high point of the season. The home team trailed, 9–4, when the rains came in the sixth inning.

Washington's 46-76 record for the year kept it out of the cellar only because a more inept Indianapolis team lost 89 games. Of the Hartford five, John Henry never started a game. Bill Krieg played in 23 games before losing the first base job to Billy O'Brien. George Shoch hit a disappointing .239. Frank Gilmore was erratic and wild all year, losing 20 of his 27 starts.

And Connie Mack? The praise he had earned during his brief year-end debut gave him no guarantee of making the team in the spring. Washington had two other veteran major league catchers, Pat Dealey and

Barney Gilligan. The five-foot-six Gilligan was small for a catcher and a lightweight at the plate, but he had been the team's regular catcher in '86.

So Mack had to prove himself. He knew that rookies who pushed themselves out front to be noticed usually got more opportunities than the ones who didn't. But, as he later told a writer, "Dern it, it's something I could never do."

He knew he wouldn't win the job with his bat. For the first time batters could no longer call for the pitch location. To help them adjust to the change, the rules makers decreed that it now took four strikes for a batter to be out, and walks would count as hits. (Both those rules were in effect for just one year.) They didn't help Mack, who batted .220 (subtract his 8 walks and it was .201). He had 26 stolen bases, not among the leaders, but evidence that he could run the bases.

In the end Mack's handling of pitchers and his defensive skills made his case for him. Base running and stealing were the crowd-pleasing offensive weapons of the time. The home run was considered, at least by the editor of the *Spalding Guide*, "a selfish display of brute strength that any soft-brained heavyweight could do." The double steal and squeeze play took brains and timing and teamwork. A strong, accurate arm, holding men on base, keeping pitchers focused, taking charge on the field, and calling pitches were what counted in a catcher. It didn't take long for Mack to demonstrate that these were his strong points.

Washington's ace pitchers were Jim Whitney and Hank O'Day. Whitney, described by a Boston writer as having "a head about the size of a wart, with a forehead slanting at an angle of 45 degrees," was called Grasshopper because of the way he walked. The twenty-nine-year-old, six-foot-two right-hander needed plenty of handling while winning 24 of the team's 46 victories. He never stopped griping at the umpire, whether he was pitching or at bat. Mack was so effective at calming him down that Whitney refused to pitch unless Mack caught him. Between them, they devised a sign for a pitchout, accounting for many of Mack's 119 assists that season.

Hank O'Day, one of a handful of players who became both umpires and managers, was that rarity among pitchers—a crafty right-hander. O'Day had a good fastball, but he relied on a variety of baffling change-ups that, for all their slowness, hit the catcher's glove like a cannonball.

"He threw the heaviest and hardest ball I ever caught," said Deacon McGuire, who had caught him in Toledo. "It was like lead."

Purchased from Savannah in the fall of 1886, O'Day was a hard-luck pitcher, whose 8-20 and 16-29 records in 1887–1888 belied his skill. He and Mack formed a brainy battery, but O'Day's personality was the antithesis of Mack's. He was a taciturn loner, possessed of a surliness that a perfect day in June might lighten only as far as grouchiness. He made W. C. Fields look like Shirley Temple. Once, when he was an umpire, he was sitting in a hotel lobby concealed behind a newspaper when a stranger sat down beside him and said, "Good umpiring job in the game today, Mr. O'Day."

The ump frowned as if he had just been handed a summons, then stood up, folded his newspaper, muttered, "What does one need to do to get any privacy in this hotel?" and walked away.

Connie Mack, on the other hand, welcomed all who approached him as if they were carrying a tip on a 20-game winner.

Yet Mack and O'Day remained friends until O'Day died in 1935, forty years after he became the only umpire ever to throw Connie Mack out of a game.

Catchers still stood as far back from the plate as they could and caught pitches on a bounce. They moved up only when there were men on base or the batter was within one strike of fanning. The conventional thinking was that with the catcher standing back from the plate, the pitcher could cut loose with his mightiest fastball. If the catcher moved up close, he couldn't handle the speed, and the pitcher would have to let up. Despite Gaffney's objections, Mack was among the earliest catchers to move up behind the plate at other times too. That enabled him to perform his newest trick: faking the sound of a foul tip. Under the rules, the batter was out if the catcher caught a foul tip, regardless of the count. If he saw a batter was going to swing, Mack would click his tongue or slap his glove or snap a piece of elastic webbing sewn to his mitt as the bat came around. If the batter missed the ball, the umpire, reacting to what he heard, called the puzzled, angry batter out. It must have been effective. John Heydler recalled "three men going out in one inning on foul tips to the long angular Mack."

(In 1891 the rule was changed; with fewer than two strikes, a batter was no longer out if a foul tip was caught. Mack may well have caused the rule change.)

For all his defensive skill, Connie Mack possessed one peculiar flaw: he could rifle the ball to second on the money, but he couldn't throw accurately to third. It's amazing that catchers were able to throw anybody out at any base in those days, considering that they were throwing a mushy ball that had been pounded out of shape after a few innings. Throws to second are made overhand from the shoulder, with the arm drawn slightly back. Throwing to third calls for more of a sidearm snap. Perhaps Mack's long arms were better suited to the overhand throw.

Modern catchers asked to explain this anomaly couldn't think of any catchers they had ever seen who could throw well to second but not to third. Some thought it might have been a mental quirk. Perhaps Mack had made a few bad throws to third, and that nagged at him. Charles Johnson, the best at throwing out base stealers in the National League a century later, said, "He could have had trouble with a right-handed batter at the plate, because then the catcher often has to step laterally instead of forward and throw more sidearm than overhand. Connie Mack's height and slim build might have made that a more awkward mechanics for him and that, combined with the shorter distance, may have caused him to be more erratic than throwing to second base."

Veteran Dodgers catcher Mike Scioscia said, "If a three-quarters arm angle was his natural throwing move, he could have had trouble with his accuracy to third as he would have to step back to throw and that might cause the throw to veer away from the base. Or he had to go overhand to throw over a right-hand batter, contrary to his natural arm angle."

Whatever the reason, Mack had no coaches to help him. He and Buck Ewing and Wilbert Robinson were inventing the modern catcher's position.

The problem worried Mack. He knew that at least two players, John M. Ward, captain of the Giants, and Boston star King Kelly, were on to his weakness and would steal third on him every chance they got. But "in those days," he said, "players didn't share what they learned, and nobody else caught on, sparing me from being run out of the league."

Baseball, like life, is a series of adjustments. To compensate for his weakness, Connie Mack came up with a play that, at the time, was a novel gambit. On a double steal attempt with men on first and second, he would go for the trailing runner. The first time he tried it was in Worcester on August 17. A Washington game in Boston had been rained out, and grounds in that city were not available to make it up. John Gaffney arranged for it to be played in Worcester, his home town. The return of major league baseball, if only for a day, five years after Worcester had lost its National League franchise to Philadelphia, was a gala event. Attracted by the presence of the great Kelly, more than four thousand fans paid fifty cents, and hundreds more climbed over the fence at the old Ruby Legs grounds.

The Shadow Battery of Gilmore and Mack started for Washington. Mack described what happened in the bottom of the third inning.

King Kelly, of "Slide, Kelly, Slide" fame, who in skill and audacity as a base runner never had a superior, was on second base. John Morrill, the Boston manager, who was very slow, perched on first base.

This was the copyrighted situation for the double steal, as base running was a big part of the attack in those days. Kelly pranced back and forth and got his usual jump on the pitcher and was almost within sliding distance of third base when the ball nested in my glove. In a flash it occurred to me that I could never get Kelly. So instead I pulled my arm back and hurled an accurate throw to the second baseman, who tagged the amazed Morrill standing up. Veteran Boston writers said it was never made before. During the remainder of the season I made the play frequently and many catchers since have adopted it.

Mack remained as noisy on the field as he had been in the minor leagues. When his team was at bat, Mack often coached third base and made plenty of noise there too. One day in May Chicago rookie left fielder Marty Sullivan hit 3 triples. The next day Mack, coaching at third base, made Sullivan his special target, riding him without letup. Sullivan made 5 errors.

Mack especially enjoyed matching wits with Cap Anson. On July 13 Grasshopper Whitney took a 3–0 lead over Chicago into the ninth inning. With one out, Anson hit a home run over the left field fence, but he stopped at third base.

"By remaining on the base," the *Washington Post* surmised, "Anson hoped to induce Mack to move up close behind the bat so Whitney could not speed the ball. . . . With the weakened delivery they might make enough hits to tie the game. Mack refused to play under the bat until Pfeffer had been thrown out at first for the second out. Whitney then struck out Williamson, and Anson was left on third. As a piece of strategy it was a dismal failure. As an exhibition of self-sacrifice it was a glorious success."

But perhaps Connie Mack's most valuable trait had nothing to do with how he played the game. Surrounded as he was by teammates who practiced little and drank much, he was devoted to analyzing and improving his game and was sober at all times. That was no small consideration when newspapers regularly carried reports like that of nine Boston players being fined at one time for "dissipation and carousing."

A profile in the *Washington Evening Star* said of Mack, "[He] is a Washington favorite. He is always willing to play and plays hard to win. The public would rather see any other man on the ball field make an error than catcher Mack. His success in his difficult position is due largely to the fact that he always keeps in good condition. His manager doesn't have to keep an eye on him for fear he will sneak off and get drunk. Whatever else may happen, he knows that Mack will play the same game week in and week out."

Connie Mack made his first appearance on a baseball card when Old Judge cigarettes issued a set of cards depicting all the Washington players. On the card Mack is standing erect, arm cocked ready to throw. Mack never smoked or chewed and tried to discourage his players and children from smoking, but he would appear on tobacco-sponsored cards in future years.

At the end of the 1887 season, Washington fans bought Connie Mack a silver tea service. National League president Nick Young, a resident of the city, made the presentation. With a full major league season behind him, a silver tea service, and a contract for $2,500 for 1888, Connie Mack was ready for marriage.

7 | MR. AND MRS. CONNIE MACK

Under "Social Notes," the *Spencer Sun* of Friday, October 28, 1887, reported, "Corney Mack, Catcher with the Washington ball club, arrived home Monday in good health and spirits. He has had a rather hard season's work, having caught some of the most erratic pitchers of the league, and during the last of the season caught every game the club played."

Mack found East Brookfield abuzz with activity. New sidewalks and lights lined both sides of Main Street and down to the railroad depot. The Women's Christian Temperance Union had succeeded in persuading the town to withdraw all liquor licenses; the amount of "medicine" sold at the pharmacies shot up dramatically.

"Sixty distressed people daily [on] average visit one drugstore-saloon for the medicine," wryly noted the *Brookfield Times.* "The proprietor is kind enough to keep open late at night to accommodate the working man."

When the short-lived ban was lifted, a dozen applicants sought licenses to sell liquor. Mack's first employer, E. H. Stoddard, was the Prohibition candidate for the state senate. Mack was no teetotaler—he later opposed national prohibition—but he might have voted for his old boss anyhow. Loyalty was more important to him than politics.

While the working man was getting lit up, the new street lights were not. "The lamplighter should use more oil," the *Times* complained. "The contract calls for lights to be lit until 12 midnight, but many are out by 10:30."

Connie Mack never talked on the record about when or how he proposed to Margaret Hogan. It might have been by letter or telegram during the season. He had played in a postseason series against Baltimore until October 19, and banns (a notice of their proposed marriage) had been posted on October 16. Anyone objecting to the marriage had two weeks to do so. Nobody did.

Margaret and her family were living in Spencer, three miles east of

East Brookfield. Spencer was 75 percent Catholic, evenly divided between Irish and French-Canadian. Hostility had grown between the two camps. The Irish wanted the church services to be held in Latin and English; the Canadians wanted French spoken. A priest who spoke both French and English was not an acceptable compromise. They finally resolved the problem by splitting the parish. The Irish built a second church across the street from the first, in which Connie Mack had been baptized.

The wedding of Connie Mack and Margaret Hogan on Wednesday, November 2, was the first in the new Irish Church of Our Lady of the Rosary, Fr. Thomas Beaven officiating. Mack was twenty-four, his bride twenty. Mack's brother Dennis and Margaret's friend Margaret Duff were the witnesses.

Where they went on their honeymoon was not reported. The *Spencer Sun*, sounding as if Mack had abandoned his bride, noted on November 11, "Connie Mack has arrived home from his wedding trip and will take up residence at his father's house."

Michael Jr. was now working in a hotel in Stafford Springs, Connecticut, where he met and married Ella Stebbins. But their father's condition—the house reeked from his chronic dysentery—and the presence of Connie's three brothers in the little cottage must have made it uncomfortable for the newlyweds. Connie had a winter job in East Brookfield managing Vizard's bowling alley and shooting gallery in the basement of the boot shop, and they put up with it for three months.

In February 1888 Mr. and Mrs. Mack left for Washington to set up housekeeping on their own for the first time. The club owner, Robert Hewett, was seriously ill, and the club had no manager. John Gaffney had had enough of trying to keep his players' minds on baseball and off their night life. He returned to the relatively peaceful life of an umpire. Hewett persuaded Ted Sullivan, who was slated to manage the Troy club in the International Association, to handle spring training chores for the team.

Sullivan, an impresario, promoter, innovator, scout, and acclaimed storyteller in a variety of dialects, remains one of baseball's most colorful and least known pioneers. Born in County Clare, Ireland, he had been active in organizing early minor leagues. He put together St. Louis's perennial American Association pennant winners, signing Charles Comiskey as captain, and later scouted for the Cubs and White Stockings.

In the spring of 1886 Cap Anson had taken his Chicago club to Hot Springs, Arkansas, while the Phillies had gone to Charleston, South Carolina.

The following spring Detroit went to Macon, Georgia, then barnstormed through the South and Midwest. Sullivan decided it was time to try training in Florida. The expedition provided Connie Mack with one of his favorite subjects for interviews and after-dinner speeches over the years.

On Thursday morning, March 1, the players gathered at the Washington railroad station to board the fast mail train to Jacksonville.

"Con Mack has not grown a pound heavier since he became a Benedict," reported the *Washington Post*. "Mrs. Mack's cheeks were a delicate flush of pride as she accompanied her husband into the station and observed the hearty greeting he received from his companions. Mrs. Schoch was also on hand to bid adieu to her husband and the two ladies said they had formed a compact to chaperone each other while their better halves are away."

The three-months pregnant Margaret Mack and her new friend were forced to rely on each other for help sooner than they expected. Eleven days later the great blizzard of '88 smothered Washington and the rest of the Northeast.

"There were fourteen members of the squad," Mack recalled of his first spring training jaunt, "four of them reasonably sober." They rode all day in coaches. At night they switched to Pullman cars—two to a berth—until daylight, when they were roused and ordered to move back into the lower-fare coaches, which ballplayers thereafter referred to as "Sullivan Sleepers."

In Jacksonville, Sullivan led them to a tract of woods out of town where a woman who owned two shacks put them up and provided three meals a day for a dollar per man per day.

The accommodations were "vile," Mack said, and the players quickly found a convenient source of booze among the nearby natives. "It was terrible—fights every night in front of those shacks. There was always at least one black eye in the crowd, and usually more."

They practiced in the sandy soil among the pine trees every morning and played against a handful of rookies that New York Giants manager Jim Mutrie had taken south. In a letter to the *Post*, Sullivan ballyhooed with the usual unfounded springtime optimism, "The men arrived here in good shape and surprised me by their excellent work in Sunday's game. Gilmore pitched in rattling form and Mack supported him in great style, his throwing to bases being particularly clever."

One of the rookies in camp was center fielder Ellsworth "Dummy" Hoy. Hoy was deaf and almost dumb or mute; he could make high-pitched squawking sounds. He was no dummy, despite the nickname that was attached to him. Between lip reading, sign language, and his squeaky sounds, Hoy and the players had no problems communicating.

Post columnist Shirley Povich later wrote that Hoy put up this statement on the first day in Jacksonville:

Being totally deaf, as you know, and some of my clubmates being unacquainted with my play, I think it is timely to bring about an understanding between myself, the left fielder, the shortstop, and the second baseman and right fielder.

The main point is to avoid possible collisions with any of these four who surround me when in the field going for a fly ball. Now whenever I take a fly ball I always yell, "I'll take it"—the same as I have been doing for many seasons and, of course, the other fielders will let me take it. Whenever you don't hear me yell, it is understood I am not after the ball and they govern themselves accordingly.

If a player hears the patter of my feet, pay no attention as I am only backing up. I watch both player and the ball, and never have I had a collision.

Traveling by coach all the way, the team went to New Orleans for two games, winning both, while enjoying the city's other pleasures. Mack avoided the night spots, but he accompanied the boys to the race track, where he enjoyed betting moderately on the bangtails.

They went to Birmingham and helped the local team open its new grounds, then on to Charleston, where they were refused entry to a few hotels before setting down in a decrepit joint where they were not allowed to eat in the dining room with the other guests. Shunted into a dirty side room, they ate at a long table, the food spread out family style.

Mack chuckled each time he described Ted Sullivan's tactic for seeing that his players were well fed. Sullivan took out a silver dollar, ostentatiously placed it on the table, and, with a wink to the waiters, implored them to "feed the boys well." Then, after a feast of double portions, he slipped the cartwheel back in his pocket and hurriedly made his exit, followed by the players, who never tipped in those days.

"This old pioneer of baseball died at a very advanced age [seventy-eight] during the season of 1929," the sixty-eight-year-old Mack said in 1930, "but for many years when we visited Washington he always came to our hotel to chat with me, and did so just a few weeks before he passed away. I never failed to ask him if he still possessed his unspendable silver dollar."

Despite his acknowledged skill as a catcher, Mack's light bat drew annual contenders for his job. There were two that spring: rookie Jeremiah Murray and Pat Deasley, a thirty-one-year-old veteran of three years with the Giants. When neither hit his weight, Mack's job was secure for another year.

Spring training did little to improve the Nationals' abilities on the field or intemperate ways off it. Sullivan left for Troy, and they opened the season with the owner's son, Walter Hewett, as the manager.

Before an opening day crowd of three thousand, Hank O'Day held New York to 7 hits, but errors gave the Giants a 6–0 win. For O'Day, nothing that year aided his dyspeptic disposition. The Nationals seemed to save their worst fielding for his starts and their scoring for other days. In his first 10 games, they scored a total of 9 runs. On April 23 he pitched a 12-inning 1–1 tie. The next day they scored 15 runs but still lost, 19–15. The day after that, with O'Day pitching again, they managed only 5 hits and lost 1–0 in 11 innings. For the year O'Day lost 29 and won 16.

Some newspapers began calling the team the Senators, while others used the Nationals. Both names gradually replaced the Statesmen. But a loser by any name is still a loser. They were even worse than the year before. The newspapers kept the headline "The Usual Defeat" set in hot type for frequent use. After just 2 victories in their first 14 games, the *Post* correspondent commented, "A pitcher and catcher and Mr. Hoy now constitute Washington's baseball club. The other six men who accompany them are put on the field for the purpose of making errors."

Fed up with his team's showing, Walter Hewett issued a public "No play–no pay" edict. Rejecting all "flimsy excuses," he decreed that players not in condition to play for whatever reason would not be paid. Fines of up to $100 would be imposed for drinking, and an eleven o'clock curfew on the road would be enforced. The Senators were not unique in this respect. Spalding's 1889 *Guide* editorialized:

> The two great obstacles in the way of success of the majority of professional ball players are wine and women. The saloon and the brothel are the evils of the baseball world at the present day; and we see it practically exemplified in the failure of noted players to play up to the standard they are capable of were they to avoid these gross evils. One day it is a noted pitcher who fails to serve his club at a critical period of the campaign. Anon, it is the disgraceful escapade of an equally noted umpire. And so it goes one season to another, at the cost of the

loss of thousands of dollars to clubs who blindly shut their eyes to the costly nature of intemperance and dissipation in their ranks.

Connie Mack didn't have to read it to know it; he saw it on the field in front of him almost every day. Hewett's threats didn't help. Only the equally feeble Indianapolis Hoosiers kept them from clinching last place by mid-June. Still, Washington fans kept hoping. Given a glimmer of encouragement, they turned out at Capitol Park. When the team returned from a successful trip in May, "Immense crowds welcomed the Statesmen home," trumpeted the *Morning Republican*, "where they took two games on Decoration Day from Anson's great Chicago White Sox, 8–1 and 5–3. Fourteen hundred attended the morning game and 3,200 the afternoon affair."

None of them got to enjoy the sight of Connie Mack in the patriotic red, white, and blue uniform of the day; he sat out both games. The next day reality returned. Chicago handed O'Day a 10–1 pasting and attendance quickly sank back to the 350 level.

As for the other half of the Shadow Battery, Frank Gilmore twisted his long right arm once too often, and no amount of snake oil or wintergreen could cure the soreness. Gilmore won 1 and lost 9 before he was released to Indianapolis on July 17. He and Mack would never again be teammates, but the Shadow Battery remained close friends.

The Senators had won 10 and lost 29 when Hewett induced Ted Sullivan to leave Troy and take over the reins. Sullivan brought with him a new shortstop and pitcher, but it was too late.

It rained all day on Monday, August 27, wiping out the day's game against the Phillies and enabling Connie Mack to be with Margaret when she gave birth to their first child, a boy they named Roy.

On Monday, October 1, a small group braved a dark, overcast sky to watch the Nationals and Indianapolis Hoosiers battle to see who would escape last place. Washington led, 2–1, in the top of the ninth. The Hoosiers scored twice to take the lead. As the clouds grew blacker and heavier by the minute, Connie Mack bent over in apparent pain behind the plate, ostensibly ministering to an injured finger, while another Hoosier base runner ambled across home plate without a play. Mack nursed his finger long enough for the umpire to have no choice but to call the game for darkness. Under the rules, the score reverted back to the last complete inning, and Washington escaped with a 2–1 win and a slippery grip on seventh place. The reprieve was temporary; in the end the Statesmen/Senators/Nationals finished a game and a half beneath Indianapolis.

Connie Mack caught 79 games, played the outfield in 4, and played first base and shortstop once each. He hit a meager .187 but muscled out 3 home runs, only 13 behind the league leader. One of them came off Chicago right-hander John K. Tener, a future National League president, Pennsylvania governor, and congressman, providing a source of good-natured banter between them whenever they shared a banquet speakers' table. Mack remained among the top fielding catchers, his 152 assists leading the league.

Connie Mack and his family didn't go home to Massachusetts that winter. Weakened by her pregnancy and childbirth, Margaret was not up to the cold blustery New England weather. They were not present on October 22 when Mack's brother Dennis married Annie Monahan, a tough, strong-willed woman whose father was a champion wrestler in western Massachusetts. Together with Grasshopper Jim Whitney and second baseman Al Myers, they were on their way to California, where Margaret rested in the sun while the players hooked up with barnstorming teams, jumping from one club to another on a pay-per-game basis. They ran into Albert Spalding's troupe playing exhibitions before embarking on a round-the-world expedition. Whitney and Mack were invited to join the voyagers but declined.

Whitney, Myers, and Mack earned enough to pay their expenses and return east with something in their pockets, a rare financial status for players heading to spring training. Margaret Mack returned to Washington in good health; soon after the 1889 season opened, she was expecting again.

8 JUMPING WITH THE BROTHERHOOD

The first cry of alarm that high salaries were threatening baseball's survival had come just three years after the National League was born. At a meeting in September 1879, the club owners recognized that the high salaries were attributable to competition among clubs for certain players. They vowed that at a certain level there would be no more "exorbitant" salary offers made to any players. The next day they came up with the reserve clause, which in effect gave the club an option on a player for the season after the one specified in his contract, at any salary the owner wished to offer. The player would have no option to sell his services to any other team. At first the reserve clause was limited to each team's designated five top players.

A year later, at a meeting in Pierce's Palace Hotel in Buffalo on September 20, league president William A. Hulbert declared, "It is ridiculous to pay ball players $2,000 a year, especially when $800 boys often do just as well."

At every meeting thereafter, the magnates complained about their high payrolls as routinely as they lit their expensive cigars. Finally, on October 17, 1885, they did something about it, setting a salary limit of $2,000 and a minimum of $1,000. The limits were essentially meaningless, as salaries were not stated in the contracts, and the cap was widely ignored. What hurt the players more was a ban on advances. Many players, unable to find jobs during the winter, relied on advances until the next season's first payday in April or May.

These actions by the owners prompted New York Giants shortstop John Montgomery Ward, who was also a lawyer, and several of his teammates to form the Brotherhood of Professional Base Ball Players. They elected Ward president. By uniting, Ward believed the players would have the clout to combat salary restrictions and the sale of players without their consent or a share of the selling price. The players didn't like the reserve clause and were convinced it was illegal. But in the absence of a practical alternative for preventing chaos and recognizing the owners' interest in protecting their investments, the players went along with it. They also pledged to raise the level of the game by discouraging players from drinking and gambling.

The ballplayers' restiveness was consistent with the national labor turmoil that had culminated in the 1886 Haymarket Square riots in Chicago between police and unionists. The players resented being treated as chattel in the same sense—but by no means under the same income or working conditions—as the rebellious meatpackers and steelworkers.

At first the Brotherhood was taken lightly by the National League. In November 1887 Ward asked that full salaries be written into contracts to eliminate the subterfuge of side deals. The league studied the proposal until the 1888 contracts had been signed, then turned it down. The owners' arrogance blinded them to the growing dissatisfaction among their employees.

The imposition of arbitrary fines chipped away at players' incomes and stoked the fires of discontent. Fines were levied for too much drinking and too little hustling, which the Brotherhood didn't disagree with, although the amounts were often considered excessive. Fines for losing equipment—or games—or for reasons never spelled out raised the Brotherhood's ire.

Connie Mack saw these pickpocket policies firsthand. Once in 1886 Washington outfielder Cliff Carroll, who took a pet monkey with him on the road, found his pay envelope $100 lighter for something either he or the monkey had done—he wasn't told which. He refused to sign his 1887 contract until the fine was returned. Hewett agreed to remit the fine and wrote out a check. Carroll signed; the check bounced. The Brotherhood took his case to the league and collected for him.

In 1887 Mack's Shadow Battery mate, Frank Gilmore, had picked a day he was not scheduled to pitch to be married. It proved to be an expensive wedding. John Gaffney, a bachelor, considered this insufficient reason to be absent and fined him $100.

Not content with their iron-fisted control over the players' professional lives, the owners on November 22, 1888, adopted a classification plan under which league president Nick Young would grade all players from A to E, based on their character and conduct off the field, as well as their performance on the field. Corresponding salaries would range from $2,500 down to $1,500. The new plan had no real effect on salaries, as side agreements were as plentiful as ever. In *Sporting Life* of April 5, 1890, Henry Chadwick estimated the 1889 salaries of some of the leading Brotherhood "Ingrates." Fred Dunlap and Buck Ewing topped the list at $5,000. Ward earned a reported $4,250. Connie Mack was down for $2,750 and Hank O'Day for $2,000, a ranking that must have rankled the terrible tempered O'Day.

The Brotherhood was incensed over the whole idea, which carried the threat of being blacklisted at the whim of an owner if players didn't behave or perform to his satisfaction. There was talk of a strike, but many players, including Mack, had already signed 1889 contracts and were reluctant to go back on them, fearing a public backlash.

In Washington, Walter Hewett was willing to spend to improve his team. In November 1888, he tried to buy Ward from the Giants for a reported $12,000 but was turned down.

Hewett had discerned no benefits from Ted Sullivan's jaunt to Florida in the spring of '88, so the Senators stayed in Washington to get ready for the 1889 season. They won a string of exhibition games, including one over a young pitcher for Yale, Amos Alonzo Stagg, who struck out 9 of the big leaguers and would have won if his catcher had been able to hold on to his fastball. Connie Mack did not play in that game.

Determined to find experienced leadership, Hewett searched until April before signing John Morrill for $600 a month. Morrill had led his home-town Boston Beaneaters for the past seven seasons. A lead-footed first baseman with a cold, dispassionate demeanor on and off the field, Morrill played as well as he led, producing a .185 batting average and a .250 winning percentage before Hewett fired him on July 6.

Perhaps it was living in a political climate that enabled Washington base-ball fanatics to slough off each year's losing team as routinely as a crab's monthly molting and greet the new season, like each new Congress, with hope and enthusiasm. When the players paraded through the city streets and arrived at Capitol Park, they were greeted by the largest opening day mob in the city's history. More than 3,800 paid their way in; the crowd in the bleaching boards (as the bleachers were then called) overflowed into the right fielder's territory. The visiting Phillies took the field first for a light fifteen-minute warmup, then the bell was rung to signal the start of play. The home team filed out of the clubhouse and across the field in new gray uniforms amid a hail of cheers.

Contrary to their usual custom, the Washingtons chose to bat last. It didn't help; they lost anyhow, 8–4.

Once again Connie Mack faced challengers for his job. The first was a twenty-nine-year-old rookie, Hi Ebright, who made 3 errors in the opening day loss and was advised to seek another line of work. In May another rookie, rifle-armed Spider Clark, arrived. He wound up playing more games at four other positions. Tom Daly, twenty-three, possessor of a more potent bat than Mack but so-so as a receiver, caught almost half the games. Daly went on to a sixteen-year career, mostly at second base.

Mack split his playing time catching and playing the outfield and first base. Now twenty-six, he had acquired something the other catchers lacked, and if nobody else appreciated it, the pitchers did. During his two years in the National League, he had studied hitters' strengths and weaknesses and compiled a mental book on them. It proved especially valuable for a rookie right-hander, twenty-two-year-old Alex Ferson from Philadelphia. Before each of his starts, Mack went over the lineup with Ferson, pointing out how to pitch to each batter. Mack coaxed 4 wins out of Ferson's first 5 starts. A lack of run support and periodic lapses in control resulted in a 17-17 record for the year. Except for one win in 1890, Ferson's lack of control prevented him from winning another major league game.

Hank O'Day was not so appreciative of Mack's efforts. Eager to play on a winner—and soon—O'Day yearned to play for the defending champion New York Giants. Hoping to impress their manager, Jim Mutrie, O'Day started against the Giants on April 29 in a game played on Staten Island. With Mack behind the plate, he lost, 4–2. He blamed Mack's 4 errors for the loss while ignoring the pair of ninth-inning home runs hit off him. O'Day finally got his wish in July. Hewett sold him to New York, where he was 9-1, helping the Giants finish first again by a 1-game margin over Boston.

Mack took part in his first triple play on June 20 at Indianapolis. In the days before the infield fly rule, infielders often dropped pop flies or line drives to try to turn them into multiple outs. In the eighth inning with the bases loaded, Paul Hines hit a pop-up to shortstop Arthur Irwin, who let it hit the ground, then picked it up and threw to Sweeney at third for the force out. Sweeney threw to Mack, who tagged the runner coming from third. Hines was legging it for second; Mack's throw to Al Myers beat him to the bag.

Despite playing a variety of positions, Mack had his best year at the plate. He batted .293—106 points over his 1888 average—with 42 runs batted in and 26 stolen bases. It was an aberration he could never explain, beyond observing that sometimes the balls fall safe and sometimes they don't. A more likely explanation is that he rose with the tide. After experimenting with a variety of ball and strike counts, the league finally settled on four balls for a walk instead of five; three strikes had been a strikeout since 1888. The league batting average soared 25 points, walks rose 80 percent, and strikeouts dropped as pitchers struggled to adjust to the more restrictive standard for bases on balls. The number of shutouts fell by half.

Shortstop Arthur Irwin, bought from the Phillies in June for $3,000, was the fifth field leader Mack played under in three years in Washington. This time the Nationals ran away with last place, finishing 13 games behind their nearest neighbor, the seventh-place Hoosiers.

The unrest among the players haunted the entire season. Every club held secret meetings, choosing two or three representatives to meet with other teams' reps as they traveled the circuit. Connie Mack was elected a Nationals representative. In June, Ward petitioned the league to repeal the detested classification system and ban the sale of players without their consent. His requests for meetings to air the players' grievances were ignored.

Strike talk revived. Some owners dared the players to walk out, vowing to use replacement players. The more militant players wanted to challenge the reserve clause in court, but Ward persuaded them to wait. He had something else in mind.

During the season Ward and a few trusted allies quietly sounded out potential financial backers among prominent businessmen. Ned Hanlon, player-manager of the Pittsburgh Alleghenys and a committed Brotherhood activist, found one in Cleveland streetcar magnate Albert L. Johnson. Johnson agreed to finance a team in Cleveland and became an avid recruiter of other investors, especially street railway operators looking for attractions adjacent to their trolley lines.

Confident of their backing, the Brotherhood met on November 4, 1889, at the Fifth Avenue Hotel in New York, and confirmed the rumors that had whirled for months. They announced the creation of their own league, the Players' National League of Base Ball Clubs.

In later years Connie Mack was ambivalent about his role in the uprising. Riding high after a world championship in 1929 and about to win another in 1930, he said of the 1890 revolt, "It has always been my belief that the majority of players were well satisfied with conditions under which they were working and that they would have preferred to stick to the safe and stable National League. Many, however, were won over by the unceasing importunities and threats of the malcontents. They left the National

League principally not to make enemies in their own profession. I will say for the Brotherhood leaders that I never doubted their sincerity or motive. After long consideration, I decided to throw my lot in with the players."

In fact, Connie Mack was not as reluctant to throw in his lot with the "malcontents" as this implies. He may have come to rue his radical days and rarely talked about them, but at eighty he admitted to Fred Lieb that being a longtime club owner naturally altered one's viewpoint.

The Connie Mack of 1889 was "an enthusiastic Brotherhood Players' League man," he confessed to Lieb. "I was younger then and things looked different to me. It seemed to me then that we had a good cause, and the Brotherhood intended to correct some of the inequalities and abuses which then existed in baseball. No doubt today, having some idea of the difficulties of operating a major league club, I would take a different view of such a movement."

This admission is borne out by Mack's actions in the fall and winter of 1889. He and just about the entire Washington team jumped to the Buffalo club in the Players' League, leaving the Statesmen so weakened that they were dropped by the National League, replaced by Cincinnati. On November 20, while his brother Dennis's first child, Hazel, was being born in East Brookfield, Mack took the train from Spencer to Hartford to meet Pittsburgh shortstop Jack Rowe, who, with his teammate Deacon White, had been an incorporator of the Buffalo club. Mack signed a three-year contract for $2,750 (all Players' League contracts were for three years with no reserve clauses). In December Mack seized the opportunity offered to all players to invest in their clubs. He took his entire savings of $500 out of the bank and purchased five of the club's two hundred shares. What Mrs. Mack, eight months pregnant with their second child, had to say about it—if anything—is not known.

9 | THE PLAYERS' LEAGUE

Connie Mack was a gambler at heart. Committing his life to a business whose foundation was still as wobbly as a newborn colt was an enormous gamble in itself. At twenty-seven, he had neither considered nor prepared for anything else. It was baseball or back to the boot shop at $15 a week.

As the owner of 2½ percent of the Buffalo club, Mack considered himself in honorable, savvy company, and with good reason. The five incorporators, including Deacon White and Jack Rowe, who had switched their holdings from the International franchise to the Brotherhood club and put up $1,000 each, were Moses Shire, a respected lawyer and real estate developer; former sheriff Frank Gilbert; and businessman Charles R. Fitzgerald.

Mack was undaunted by the hazards expressed in a *New York Sun* editorial: "The Brotherhood of Ball Players have one great difficulty to contend with: the trust or combination against them which they are seeking to overthrow is composed of eight or ten members. The one they would like to form is composed of nearly 150 members. That is much more difficult to handle than the other. They will need not only loyalty but enthusiasm all along the line."

Modern baseball fans' charming picture of the good old days is mostly myth. Since the first play-for-pay contract, baseball has been a business—show business. Fans and self-anointed experts of the twenty-first century who denounce the modern players' greed and yearn for the time when "they would play for nothing, just the love of the game," know not of what they speak. It was never that way.

Players never trusted owners, nor believed them when they "opened the books" to prove their losses. When five National League teams claimed to have lost money in 1889, Fred Pfeffer, Cap Anson's veteran second baseman in Chicago, asked the unanswerable question: "If National League owners are making such puny profits, why are they making such desperate efforts to continue in the game?"

The Players' League was a unique experiment in American labor relations. The players/employees shared in the administration and governing of the league. They were to share in any profits after expenses and fair returns on the owners' investments. Twenty thousand dollars in prize money, ranging from $6,250 to $400, was to be disbursed among the first seven teams in the standings.

The Brotherhood and the barons of baseball waged a war of words throughout the winter of 1889–1890. A National League committee of Spalding, Phillies owner Col. John I. Rogers, and the Giants' John Day launched a baseball tradition of issuing blustering statements and carrying unwinnable lawsuits into court. They warned that anyone jumping to the Players' League would never be allowed back on any club in "Organized Baseball" (those major and minor leagues and clubs subscribing to the National Agreement of 1883 to respect each other's contracts, reserve lists, and territories); at the same time they scrambled to acquire minor leaguers to fill their lineups. As in many divorces, the lawyers prospered the most amid the blizzard of charges, countercharges, and futile motions for injunctions. In the end, the players ignored the reserve clause with impunity; the National League failed to find a judge anywhere who would uphold it.

The dozens of newspapers in NL cities provided plenty of forums for both sides. Some ridiculed the Brotherhood's fur-coated, silk-hatted, diamond-studded delegates who met in New York for portraying themselves as "poor, miserable, overworked, underpaid, haggard, starving slaves of the League tyrants."

Henry Chadwick, an editor of the *Spalding Guide*, not surprisingly condemned the rebellion of the "ingrates." Others, like the *New York World*, gave their all-out backing to the players. The *Sporting News* and, after a change of heart, *Sporting Life*, did the same.

To most observers, the war was viewed as not so much between lords and peons as rival capitalists. As a lawyer, Monte Ward respected the sanctity of a contract. He was certainly no Bolshevik. Neither were player-owners White and Rowe, Ned Hanlon, or Washington captain Arthur Irwin, a prosperous manufacturer of fielders' gloves.

The players were not 100 percent united. Some who pledged allegiance to the Brotherhood changed their minds and returned to the safer hearth of the "seasoned" senior circuit. Others signed contracts with both leagues in case the rebels never saw an opening day. Later the Players' chief backer, Albert Johnson, admitted that there was a time "when we lost heart. Desertion seemed to follow desertion. I was considerably discouraged."

The *Buffalo Express* reported rumors that Connie Mack was about to break his Buffalo contract, then discounted the story, pointing out, "He owns $500 in stock."

The turning point came when King Kelly, the most popular player in the land, walked away from the bait of a large National League offer, allegedly saying, "I cannot turn my back on the boys," and signed as player-manager of the Boston Reds on November 24, 1889, vowing to "not touch a drop of liquor for a year."

The Players' League field captains now included Charlie Comiskey in Chicago, Ned Hanlon in Pittsburgh, Monte Ward in Brooklyn, King Kelly in Boston, and Buck Ewing in New York.

Commented the *St. Louis Republic*, "The National League has all the money and the Players' League has all the players."

The well-heeled National League was not the players' only enemy. The American Association had been a major league since 1882. All three leagues had teams in Brooklyn and Philadelphia. The Brotherhood would be going head to head with the National in Boston, Chicago, New York, Pittsburgh, and Cleveland. Only Buffalo faced no direct major league competition (an International Association club lasted only 24 games before moving to Grand Rapids).But the city had been a weak baseball town. In 1885 the Bisons had drawn so poorly in their last year in the National League that the entire team was sold to the Detroit Wolverines for $7,000. White and Rowe had lost $2,000 operating the International Association club there in 1889.

Baseball everywhere faced new competition from vaudeville for the entertainment dollar. Every city had at least one theater, which opened at noon and ran until midnight. A seat in the gallery cost ten cents; in most cities the best seat in the house went for fifty cents. To combat that, the Buffalo directors lobbied for twenty-five-cent admissions, but the Brotherhood insisted on a fifty-cent fare.

A split developed almost immediately when the new league abandoned its original plan to pool all income and divide it equally among the clubs. Instead, gate receipts would be split between the teams in each game, with the home team keeping its concessions revenue.

"The killing of the pooling of receipts idea means that teams in towns like Pittsburgh, Cleveland and Buffalo will get the skim milk, while the New Yorks and Bostons will take all the cream there is," foretold the *Cincinnati Times-Star*. As it turned out, that's what happened.

Not wishing to put a nickel into the pockets of Spalding and A. J. Reach, who made the baseballs used by the NL, the Players' League adopted a ball supplied by Ward's brother-in-law, ace hurler Tim Keefe. In a far-sighted move, it voted to use two umpires in each game. But it declined to adopt a new invention, a base made of rubber with an electrical attachment that rang a bell in the grandstand when a fielder or runner touched it.

The Buffalo Bisons were going nowhere for spring training, so Connie Mack rounded up some of his Brookfield buddies and worked out on his own. On Saturday, February 1, 1890, his second son was born in Spencer. Earle Thaddeus was baptized by Fr. Dolan on the sixteenth in the presence of his godparents, Margaret's brother John and her friend Margaret Duff.

At the end of March Mack wrote a letter to the Buffalo secretary, Charles Fitzgerald: "I hope to give a good account of myself this coming season behind the bat. I've been practicing for the last month and am in good condition."

Mack waited until his wife was hale enough to travel before taking the family to Buffalo in early April. They rented rooms in a house near a playground on Porter Avenue, a street that ended at a bathing beach where the Niagara River flows into Lake Erie. From there he could take a horse-drawn trolley or walk the mile to Olympic Park. The 1890 city directory listed him as "McGillicuddy, Cornelius, laborer." Domestically it was a pleasant summer for Connie Mack and his family. In a 1929 letter to the widow of Sam Wise, one of his Buffalo teammates, he wrote, "Have never forgotten [Sam] as so many things came up while we were together in Buffalo that always kept him in my mind" and "Well do I remember going to the market on Saturday night for our Sunday dinner."

Considering the Washington Nationals' poor showing in 1889, the fact that most of the Buffalo team consisted of Washington deserters made optimism a stretch. The *Cincinnati Enquirer* commented, "The Buffalo Players' League club is said to be incorporated under the title, 'Home for Respectable Old Men.' About one month after the season starts, the word 'respectable' will be changed to indigent."

In the annals of preseason predictions, it proved uncommonly accurate.

Two exceptions to the "old men" tag were Dummy Hoy, the popular center fielder, and the stringbean catcher Connie Mack, often the only right-handed batter in the lineup. Both were twenty-seven.

The weather was miserable, cold and wet, for the two weeks preceding the April 19 opener, so Mack worked out with other players at the Buffalo Armory. They managed to play only two practice games.

On opening day at Olympic Park the home team lined up in new white uniforms with brown trim and stockings. The newspapers listed Mack as six feet tall and 160 pounds, Dummy Hoy at five-foot-six and 155. (Over the years, Mack was variously described as anywhere from six feet to six-foot-four; he was actually just over six-foot-two. Hoy was probably shorter and lighter than his 1890 description.)

Olympic Park had been expanded to hold 5,000, including 2,000 bleaching boards seats at fifty cents. Grandstand seats cost fifteen cents extra; twenty-five cents bought an "opera chair." The Bisons stunned and delighted an opening day turnout of 3,500 by walloping Cleveland, 23–2, collecting 17 hits and 16 walks off lefty Henry Gruber, who went all the way. To prove it was no fluke, the next day the Bisons stampeded again, 15–8, and the day after that, 19–7. They did it again in the fourth game, 18–15, making a convincing case that the balls provided by Tim Keefe were, as charged, more tightly wound than those used by the National League and as hopped-up as a scalded cat.

According to Joe Overfield, the premier chronicler of Buffalo baseball history, "The only sour note to mar the general ecstasy in the Queen City emanated from the gentlemen of the press [who worked at field level behind home plate] who complained that while the field was being showered with base hits, they were being showered with cigar butts and tobacco juice by the excited fans in the stands above."

The euphoria quickly went as flat as yesterday's sarsaparilla, as Buffalo pitchers continued to surrender runs in more abundance than their teammates' bats could produce. Within two weeks the Bisons fell from the top to the bottom. The promising young George Washington Keefe, a southpaw who had been 8-18 for his hometown Washington Nationals in '89, publicly swore he had not touched a drop of whiskey since January 1 and would not do so all season. He probably should have. He won 6 and lost 16.

Charles "Lady" Baldwin, who had won 42 and lost 13—all complete games—for Detroit in 1886, absorbed all the punishment in a 30–12 loss to Philadelphia, giving up 28 hits, and decided to retire at the age of thirty-one.

The Bisons were in Brooklyn on July 12, when a local boy, whose last name was Lewis but whose first name remains mercifully unknown, said he was a pitcher and asked for a tryout. With little to lose, Jack Rowe started him. He worked 3 innings, giving up 20 runs on 13 hits and 7 walks, then switched with right fielder Ed Beecher. The Bisons tried to get him off the hook but fell short, losing 28–16. For both Lewis and Beecher, it was the only big league game they ever pitched.

George Haddock was smoked for 26 losses. Haddock won 34 in the American Association the next year, further evidence that the Brotherhood hitters were the true pioneers of the lively ball. The league batting average was 20 points higher and run production 20 percent greater than in the National League. "A hard hit ball in a Players' League game striking a fielder's hands feels like a ton of coal alongside of the Spalding ball," Mack observed.

Connie Mack continued to demonstrate that he was one step ahead of everybody else on the field, including the umpires. In a game against the Chicago Pirates at home, with Buffalo at bat and 2 outs, George Keefe was hit by a pitch. Before the ball was returned to the pitcher, Keefe picked up his speed as he reached first base and dashed for second. The catcher threw him out at second. As the Pirates raced off the field, Mack argued that Keefe could not be called out as the ball was not yet back in play after it hit the batter. The ump agreed and sent the Chicago players back onto the field.

On July 23 Jack Rowe was replaced as captain by first baseman Jay Faatz, who possessed an unlikely combination of traits: he was a volatile vegetarian. It was said that he could down fourteen varieties of vegetables at a meal, but an uncontrollable temper dwelt within him. Maybe if the Bisons were called the Turnips, he might have led them better.

By the end of August, Buffalo rested firmly in last place with a 29-73 record. The enthusiasm of the press wilted, as it reported on September 5: "The Buffalos made their first appearance at Olympic Park yesterday afternoon following a recent disastrous eastern trip. They were greeted by a small crowd of spectators [836] and received their usual drubbing at the hands of the Clevelands. . . . Connie Mack caught as well as ever and had one of the 5 hits."

The Bisons' slide took attendance with it. Late-season gatherings at Olympic Park hovered around seven hundred, occasionally topping a thousand when the league leaders came to town. Figures for all three leagues are suspect for that year. Newspapers routinely padded the numbers for the teams they favored and deflated those of the rival league. But the announced crowd of eighty at a game in Brooklyn was probably an actual head count. And in Pittsburgh one day the last-place NL Alleghenys played before seventeen spectators. According to business manager Al Pratt, only six of them—"traveling men"—actually bought tickets; the rest were locals who had passes.

When the Bisons demoted Jay Faatz on September 14, they appointed

Connie Mack captain for the rest of the season. At the time of his appointment, Mack was quoted as blaming the lack of pitching for the team's poor showing. Ever the optimist, he said that a speedy outfielder and reliable pitcher were all the team needed to improve, adding that he liked Buffalo and wanted to stay. The record books credit Jack Rowe with piloting the Bisons in their last 19 games, in which they were 5-14. But as the field captain, Connie Mack directed the team on the field and made the decisions during the game. This was Mack's major league managing debut.

Mack was surely aware of the dire financial condition, not only of the Bisons, but the entire league—indeed all three major leagues. Everybody was hurting. Both clubs in Cleveland were losing money. On July 15, Giants owner John Day told the other NL owners he needed $80,000 to finish the season or else he would sell out to the Players' League New York backers. Spalding and Anson led a rescue squad to prevent the loss of the New York franchise, which would have been a crushing defeat for the older circuit. The mortally wounded American Association struggled through one more season before giving up the big league ghost.

In September Moses Shire and Frank Gilbert, claiming they had lost all the money they had invested and didn't care to go in any deeper, threw in the sponge in Buffalo. The league took over the club and sent its secretary, Frank Brunell, to worry through the rest of the season. He relied on promises instead of paychecks to keep the team together.

Dummy Hoy, in a letter written to Joe Overfield in 1955, when Hoy was ninety-three, remembered the three principal owners as good people. He blamed the poor playing of the team for the poor attendance and described a last-gasp effort to raise more capital by passing the hat among the unpaid players:

"One day the leading members of the team, such as White, Rowe, Mack and others, called a meeting of the team. It was suggested that as the club was in financial difficulties, each player should be assessed a certain sum and share in the profits, if any. The majority, including myself, after our deliberation, decided to let the ship 'sink' and go home rather than throw good money after the bad."

Connie Mack knew what a hard sell it was to peddle a share of potential profits in a sinking ship. "There was such a feeling of unrest in the waning days of the season that many players openly expressed themselves as being anxious for the league to dissolve so they could go back to an organization operated on business principles."

It was obvious to even the greenest rookie that there would be no league profits to share. The players waived all claims to any prize money. Most of them were more concerned with just seeing their salaries. Deacon White said, "Rowe and I did not get a cent after the first of August, though the other players got a little something."

The Bisons finished with a 38-96 record, 20 games behind seventh-place Cleveland. Nobody worked harder in the vain campaign than Connie Mack. He caught 112 games, then the major league record, batted .266, and, aided by the rocket ball, hit a career-high 12 triples.

Final attendance estimates show the Brotherhood outdrawing the National League by about 100,000. According to the *New York Herald*, a booster of the Players' League, Buffalo's 60,138 was the lowest in the league, but it was more than the Giants, Alleghenys, or either Cleveland club drew. The *Herald* estimated the Bisons' expenses at $55,000, lowest in the league, with a loss of $14,285, also the lowest, which was no consolation to Mack and the other investors whose money it was. The New York, Boston, and Chicago Brotherhood clubs probably showed a profit.

The National League, which had been forced to use minor leaguers to replace its departed stars, reckoned its total costs of the war at $1.5 million.

At least a month's salary was owed to every member of the Bisons when the season ended. When ten of them, including Mack, were offered $100 each to go to Cincinnati to play a pair of exhibition games against the National Leaguers they didn't understand why, but they jumped at the offer. Later it came out that a group of Players' League backers had agreed to buy out the Cincinnati club for $40,000, a deal that required extraordinary efforts to scrape together the money. The news set the Brotherhood to howling. Ward considered the players' unpaid salaries a higher priority than investing in a weak NL franchise.

Connie Mack, sore over the loss of his savings and his delinquent salary, took a waspish swing at everybody involved:

> The trip to Cincinnati was unprofitable, as the Cincinnati club was not in it with the Players' League. We were tailenders but we had no trouble beating them. And that National League ball they use is fifty percent deader than ours. Beecher made a hit that would have been a homer easy here but got only two bases on it. . . . No wonder the National League scores were close. The ball must have been deadened since last year and the pitchers had a soft snap. I'm all the

more convinced our league made a mistake in paying $40,000 for the Cincinnati club. If the league has any money to spend they couldn't use it to better advantage than making Buffalo a fixture. Mark my word, that Cincinnati club won't be in it unless they're wonderfully strengthened. I don't think any more money is going to be spent on them.

Mack was right; the Reds fell from fourth to seventh in 1891. But he was whistling in the wind about Buffalo's future.

Back in Buffalo, most of the players, lacking the train fare home, hung around hoping to badger some cash out of the embattled Frank Brunell. On October 13 they cornered him in the Iroquois Hotel but extracted no money or promises from him.

"Buffalo players will whistle for their salaries now that the PBL is doomed," wrote the *Courier*. "The league might make up the salaries if they can figure out what shape the books are in."

A week later the league came to the rescue at a meeting in New York. Led by Frank Talcott, who was the first to come up with his personal check, the owners raised enough to pay the back salaries owed the Bisons.

The league was doomed, the victim of three mistakes, according to Brunell: raising only $20,000 instead of $50,000 per club to start; the lack of nonplaying business managers; and the lack of effort to reclaim National players who had joined them and then jumped back.

But the Brotherhood refused to go lightly. Ward and his allies tried to hold it together at the same time most of their backers were conducting peace talks with Spalding and his colleagues. On October 9, Spalding and John Day began two days of sessions with Brotherhood backers Johnson, Talcott, and W. Goodwin of Brooklyn in room 439 of the Fifth Avenue Hotel. All of them were dealing from weakness, trying to make the best deal they could. But Spalding was the shrewdest negotiator. Bluffing, he called for total surrender.

There were so many rumors of mergers and buyouts and assorted "understandings," all denied by Ward, Buffalo reporter C. F. Holcomb concluded, "I doubt if ever before so many contradictory statements were actually made by baseball leaders as during the present year. A person has become so fearful of placing trust in what he reads that the most safe way for him to cast his belief is to form his own opinion of matters and stick to it. If he is any way posted in the game he is liable to come out far more clearheaded and free from mental exhaustion than if he lets his ideas run on every passing rumor."

Ward, Hanlon, and Irwin sought a place at the table with the conferees, but Spalding, eager to split the players and their backers, persuaded the American Association to side with the National in shutting them out. The irate Brotherhood leaders denounced their "cowardly club owners" who panicked at the sight of red ink and were selling them out.

Eventually the New York, Brooklyn, and Pittsburgh clubs combined with their National League foes. Spalding bought out the Chicago Brotherhood club for $18,000, part of the money going to pay salaries and reimburse six players for half the money they had invested in the club.

Buffalo was out. The *Courier* traced its demise to "apathy and unbusinesslike methods among the stockholders. Had they come to the front and paid dollar for dollar and asserted their rights in the Players' organization, Buffalo would not have been dropped."

Even before the season ended, Pittsburgh Burghers manager Ned Hanlon was playing two hands. Still a leader of the Brotherhood, he sat in on secret meetings with the NL Alleghenys aimed at consolidating the two clubs. While league officials met in fancy boardrooms of Pittsburgh hotels, the Alleghenys' treasurer, William W. Kerr, toiled away in his tiny office beneath the warehouse of his Arbuckle's Coffee Company, calculating the liquidation value of the Burghers. Hanlon won assurance that he could return as the manager and a member of the board of directors of the Alleghenys. A few investors objected to the return of the manager who had deserted them for the Players' League, but they were outvoted.

Then, still in these dual roles, Hanlon prowled the halls of the New York hotel where confabs were taking place. He knew the rebel players were unfettered by reserve clauses, although their three-year contracts bound them to any team that stayed in business. He also knew that an agreement was in the works to return players to their 1889 teams, based on reserve lists submitted by National League and American Association teams. In the case of most of the Bisons, however, their former club, Washington, no longer existed in either league. Hanlon reckoned that they might be up for grabs. He wanted the rights to four of them: outfielders Ed Beecher and Dummy Hoy, infielder Sam Wise, and Connie Mack. He asked the Players' League directors for the right to negotiate with them.

"Since Pittsburgh put up none of the cash involved in the Cincinnati purchase," *Sporting Life* opined, "they may be deprived of these strong players. If Pittsburgh does get them it will be simply in recognition of Ned Hanlon's personal services and sacrifices for the Players' League and not for anything his club has done."

The Players' League's position was that it had gained control of the players when the league took over the club in August. But once the club disbanded, the league no longer had any right to the players' services. The Bisons were free agents. Hanlon went to Buffalo and met with the four players. Hoy turned him down and followed Charles Comiskey to St. Louis in the American Association. The other three expressed interest, but nobody was signing any contracts until things were finally settled.

That's the way it was left when Connie Mack and his family returned to his mother-in-law's house in Spencer for the winter. Mack was poorer but wiser about the business of baseball. You could lose a lot of ball games in a season; that he already knew. As a part owner of a club, you could lose a lot of money too. That was a new experience for him.

UNCERTAINTIES OF LIFE AND BASEBALL

The last Brotherhood backer to give up was George A. Prince in Boston. As late as December 1890 he was still hopeful of reorganizing the league with six clubs. But in case that didn't happen, he also applied for a franchise in the American Association. Sometime just before or after Christmas, he asked Connie Mack to meet him in Boston. At that meeting, Mack signed what was described as a "personal services" contract with Prince. It may have been an agreement to play for Prince in Boston if he succeeded in reviving the Players' League or receiving an American Association franchise.

During the following three weeks, Ned Hanlon, now officially manager of the Alleghenys, visited Mack, who signed a Pittsburgh contract for $2,400 and accepted an advance to bind it. Mack never talked about the exact terms of the contract with Prince, nor why he so readily walked away from it.

On January 14, 1891, Boston, Washington, and Philadelphia were admitted to the American Association. Prince blew up when he heard Mack had signed with Hanlon and informed Mack that he would hold him to their contract. American Association president Allen W. Thurman backed him. A deal was a deal.

Thus Mack, who has been erroneously described as "assigned to Pittsburgh" under the peace terms when the Players' League folded, became one of four cases of disputed claims to players to be decided by a newly created National Board of Control. Pittsburgh was also a party to the case of second baseman Lou Bierbauer. In an apparent oversight, the Philadelphia Athletics of the American Association had failed to list Bierbauer and outfielder Harry Stovey on their 1889 reserve lists. Considering them free agents, the Boston Beaneaters had signed Stovey, and Ned Hanlon had signed Bierbauer. In the fourth case, third baseman Denny Lyons was claimed by both the Chicago Colts and St. Louis of the AA.

The Board of Control, consisting of Allen Thurman, Phillies co-owner John I. Rogers, and L. C. Krauthoff of the Western Association, met at the Auditorium Hotel in Chicago on Friday, February 13. The *Pittsburgh Press* implored the board to be kind to the Alleghenys, who had won only 23 and lost 113 in 1890: "Some concessions should be made by the magnates of the stronger to the long-suffering cranks in Pittsburgh. Though they have been disappointed so often many of the patrons of the game are still willing to believe against their better judgment in the possibility of a club in this city that in a single season will win more games than it loses."

Pittsburgh president J. Palmer O'Neill made the case for his club's right to Bierbauer and Mack. Three AA spokesmen argued their side of the dispute. With a few short breaks, the board met long into the night, while two dozen baseball men, including O'Neill and Hanlon, dozed in the soft leather chairs in the lobby.

At three o'clock in the morning the board chairman, Thurman, appeared and invited the magnates into the smoke-filled room, where he read the verdicts. Philadelphia's claim to Bierbauer and Stovey was denied; Bierbauer was awarded to Pittsburgh and Stovey to Boston. The Colts' claim to Denny Lyons was denied; Lyons remained with St. Louis. In the case of Connie Mack, the board found that his agreement to sign with Prince's Boston club had been executed three weeks before the club had been admitted to the American Association. Therefore, it was not valid, since technically the club did not exist at the time it was signed. The Pittsburgh contract signed by Mack was an official league contract.

Thurman and Rogers had voted in favor of the Pittsburgh claims; Krauthoff dissented. O'Neill and Hanlon let out a whoop of delight. An angry Prince denounced Thurman for voting against his own league. The American Association, losers all around, mad at the board, the National League, and the world in general, sputtered through one more season and went out of business.

The *Chicago Tribune* took a swipe at the National League for knifing the AA on technicalities: "It was a trick to which a powerful body like the League should not have stooped."

In addition to a catcher and second baseman, Pittsburgh picked up a nickname that outlasted both players when the angry Athletics called its actions "piratical." The Alleghenys, also known as the Stogies or Troubadours, as well as other cognomens, proudly adopted the Jolly Roger as their emblem and have been the Pirates ever since.

(The next day the board created the first classifications of minor leagues as A, B, C, and D, based on salary levels, strength and numbers of teams, and populations of franchise cities. It also established the rules whereby higher leagues could draft players from lower leagues.)

Hanlon somehow snatched two more Players' League stars from their former American Association teams: slugger Pete Browning from Louisville and Silver King, a twenty-three-year-old sidearm pitcher who had won 45 games pitching 585 innings for the St. Louis Browns in 1888 and 32 games for Chicago in 1890. He also signed Louisville pitcher Scott Stratton, who had not deserted the AA club.

The merger of the two Pittsburgh clubs produced a fractious group of stockholders. Some of them tried to oust O'Neill as president. They opposed the return of the rebel Hanlon as manager, had doubts about O'Neill's knowledge of baseball, and objected to his free spending of their capital. They had some grounds for their concerns. The 1890 season had been a disaster. The Players' League Burghers' attendance had averaged 1,830, the Alleghenys' 411. Playing only 39 home dates, the Alleghenys' total attendance was 16,064, down from 117,338 the year before. There was obviously no padding of their figures.

O'Neill, who smoked nothing cheaper than a twenty-five-cent cigar, believed the appearance of prosperity would lead to the real thing. "Some people claim I am extravagant," he said. "The old management spent $64,000 buying players in the past four years. I haven't spent one-fifteenth as much and I have such players as Bierbauer and Mack."

The *Sporting Life* correspondent commented, "Five years ago J. Palmer O'Neill knew nothing about baseball. Al Pratt and Col. Beringer took him to his first game and when an outfielder dropped a fly ball, O'Neill yelled, 'Why didn't that fellow catch that ball?'"

Perhaps at Hanlon's request, somebody saw to it that the merger agreement limited the president's duties to prohibit him from interfering with the manager.

Over some investors' objections, O'Neill and Hanlon decided to go south for spring training, even if they couldn't afford it. Round-trip train fare for fourteen players—if they splurged on Pullman berths for the two-day journey—and fifty-cent meals would cost over $400. "There hasn't been a team that won in the last five years that didn't go south," O'Neill said. "I don't expect the club to make money on the trip. We might lose $1,200 to $1,500, but that is a mere bagatelle. I want my men to come here and open the season in good shape. To do that they must have some practice. The Chicago people went to Denver because they were guaranteed several thousand dollars. Manager Hanlon and I are in charge of the club and we will be responsible for its success or failure. . . . Manager Hanlon and I had a talk about the southern trip and we agreed it was the proper caper."

Mack appreciated this open-handed attitude toward spring training compared to Ted Sullivan's silver dollar yo-yo operation three years earlier. On March 20 the B&O Railroad took them to St. Augustine, Florida, where Hanlon had rented grounds owned by Cap Anson for $700.

Hanlon had a hard time keeping his players in line from the day they arrived. The team quickly divided into four cliques: the Brotherhood radicals—Connie Mack, first baseman Jake Beckley, and outfielder Fred Carroll; the loyalists (led by Doggie Miller), who had stayed with the Alleghenys and were out to scuttle Hanlon; the American Association transplants—King, Bierbauer, Browning, Stratton, and pitcher Mark Baldwin; and the defiant boozers of no particular ideology or agenda other than a good time.

Hanlon knew from experience he could not count on owners' backing when it came to disciplining dissolute stars. He tried gentle persuasion instead. They were not long in St. Augustine when six players ordered a keg of beer delivered to a pier for a sailing excursion. Hanlon spotted them and urged them to rethink their plans. They left the keg and put out to sea, but when Hanlon was out of sight they came back for it.

On April 3 the Pirates and Cleveland Spiders played the first spring training game in Florida between two major league teams. The Spiders, who won 6–3, trained at Jacksonville, and the two teams traveled north together a week later.

Full of optimism, the club secretary ordered fifty thousand scorecards printed, to be sold at a nickel each by a concessions partnership of Harry M. Stevens and Ed Barrow. For Mack, it was the start of a lifelong friendship with Stevens.

The Pirates leased Exposition Park, which had been used by the Players' League Burghers. Located on an island in—and sometimes under—the Allegheny River, its spring floods forced the occupants to open most seasons on the road. But only a brief pregame downpour marred the opening day parade from the Hotel Anderson through the city to the ball grounds, where the Pirates lost the opener, 7–6 in 10 innings to Chicago. After a month they were in second place with a 14-11 record. Then they went into a tailspin, losing 20 of the next 26.

The Pirates were a mutinous crew from the start. Pete Browning reported in good shape, but once the season began, he rode the waves of celebrity. He possessed too much social grace to refuse a drink when it was bought by an admiring fan, and there were many. Browning, who absolutely had to touch third base on his way from the outfield to the bench, had other quirks as well. They were overlooked when he was hitting, but he got off to a slow start and played a lackadaisical outfield. Hanlon had little patience for his peccadilloes. Browning swore he wasn't drinking and denied reports that "my lamps weren't true" as a result of too much whiskey. He blamed his problems on his sore feet and took the spikes off his shoes, for which Hanlon fined him $50. After 50 games Hanlon had had enough of Browning and released him. Pete signed with Cincinnati, where he gave the anti-Hanlon forces plenty of ammunition by hitting .343.

When Hanlon fined pitcher Mark Baldwin $50 for missing a game, Baldwin demanded his release. He didn't get it. Instead he was handed a heavier workload: 50 starts, 437 innings, and a 22-28 record.

Connie Mack got off to a slow start at the plate, which the *Press* correspondent blamed on the lack of meat on his bones. "Connie Mack was too light at the start of the season and lacked strength for some time. His trouble is not losing superfluous flesh in the spring; it's losing too much rather than too little which has a weakening tendency."

Mack stayed away from the factions and controversies and went about his business with his usual reliability. His long, lanky build continued to draw guying from the cranks. The *Press* commented on his intense demeanor and ability to keep his feelings under wraps, comparing him to Brooklyn's six-foot-two, 160-pound first baseman Dave Foutz.

"Dave Foutz and Con Mack when seen in the same game appeal to the humorous side of a person's disposition. Both take life very seriously and are fairly sensitive to the guying remarks of ribald cranks, but they do not show it to anyone."

Ban Johnson, then sports editor of the *Cincinnati Enquirer*, described his first impression of Mack: "In uniform he was the personification of thinness. When he walked you were afraid he might snap in two but he was hard as nails. Mack was one of the best catchers when a good backstop was rated for his brains in receiving and throwing rather than hitting."

The split among the players reached beyond them to the club's directors, who quarreled over Hanlon. Led by O'Neill, the anti-Hanlon faction prevailed. Hanlon was fired on July 30 but remained as center fielder. O'Neill hired Bill McGunnigle from the Providence Grays to replace him. At thirty-six, McGunnigle had already won three major and minor league pennants. A former catcher who also pitched, he was a teacher and strategist.

Of all the Pirates, Connie Mack was Hanlon's most avid student. Hanlon was already inventing many of the plays that John McGraw, Hughie Jennings, and Willie Keeler would become famous for in Baltimore, Hanlon's next managerial stop. He took credit for giving Mack "the groundwork that made him one of the greatest managers. . . . I took particular interest in drilling him in the finer points of the game. He assimilated and added to it."

Mack also learned from McGunnigle, the first manager Mack saw who moved his fielders by blowing a tin whistle and gesturing with a bat. McGunnigle slid from one end of the bench to the other to make it harder for the opposition to intercept his signals. But McGunnigle's semaphores couldn't lift the Bucs; they were last when he arrived and last when he departed at the end of the season. In five years in the major leagues, Mack had climbed out of the cellar only once, a seventh-place finish in 1887.

Connie Mack's 1891 uniform, given by him to Harry Howe of East Brookfield, is now in the town's Connie Mack museum. Made of wool, the white, short-sleeved shirt has button-on additions to convert it to long sleeves. There is quilted padding on the knees of the knickers and a red belt with leather trim. There are no letters or logos on the uniform. A label sewn into the shirt has a hand-printed "C. Mack."

The perennial springtime optimism had vanished rapidly. The war of 1890 left the customers indifferent to the fates of the survivors. Most teams lost money. When the American Association folded, four of its teams were taken into the National League, thus guaranteeing eleven also-rans instead of seven. To give the trailing teams a chance to start over, the league voted to split the 1892 season, with a playoff at the end if different teams won the halves.

The Pirates reorganized for 1892. O'Neill was ousted and William C. Temple was named president. But the treasurer, W. W. Kerr, who preferred to be addressed as "Captain," assumed greater power. Among the club's directors, it was Captain Kerr, the Coffee King, who was said to "know baseball." The club president might be prohibited from interfering with the manager, but not the treasurer.

The directors' first move was to hire Al Buckenberger as manager. Buck was a rarity for the time: a manager who had never played in the major leagues. A light-hitting infielder, he had been managing in the minors since 1884, before leading Columbus in the American Association for two years.

Before and during the season Temple and Kerr made deals that turned over the entire outfield and most of the infield and pitching staff. They put together one of the best outfields in the league: Patsy Donovan, Jake Stenzel, and Elmer Smith. The heavy-hitting Smith, a speedy base stealer, swung a 54-ounce bat. A native of Allegheny, he became Mack's closest friend on the team. They added pitchers William "Adonis" Terry and Red Ehret and acquired veteran Chicago third baseman Tommy Burns. They also let a good one get away, sending rookie Joe Kelley to Baltimore.

The demise of half the teams in the American Association produced a surplus of unemployed players. The Pirates received letters from many "who were used to hit you high and now were glad to take less," said Buckenberger. Some offered to sign for as little as $1,000 for the season.

Connie Mack was not willing to play for $1,000. He had not signed a new contract in the fall and saw no reason to take a pay cut. He spent little time in Spencer; his wife's health was not robust, so he took her to Florida. Buckenberger wrote to him several times but received no reply. Then, in April, he heard from a friend of Mack's in Spencer, advising him that Buck's latest letter had been forwarded to Mack in East Lake, Florida. In answer to a reporter's question about Mack's status, Buckenberger said, "Connie Mack has not been released. We are willing to sign him if he gives us reasonable terms. We won't pay him a big salary."

Later, when he became a club owner, Mack acknowledged that his view toward holdouts changed. But as a player he was as stubborn about what he thought he was worth as he would be in holding the salary line as an owner. He succeeded in signing for the same $2,400.

Margaret Mack was pregnant again. Before reporting to the Pirates, Mack took her and their two babies to Spencer, where she would stay in her mother's two-story frame house atop a steep hill on Brown Street.

Al Buckenberger was an easygoing fellow who didn't like carousers but didn't or couldn't do much about them. It wasn't his style to fine players. He preferred to look the other way. He made his strongest pitch for discipline in a preseason meeting, emphasizing heavier penalties for players deserting their posts "on the gate" than for less important matters like drunkenness. (On the road, a player, usually a pitcher who had worked the day before, was assigned to count the cash customers coming in to be sure the visiting club was given an honest tally. Since the 1890 war, turnstiles were suspected of having a certain flexibility.)

The rules Buckenberger laid down reflect both a timelessness and a uniqueness to their era:

When at home report to the grounds every day at 10:00 a.m. and 2:00 p.m. except Sundays. When abroad you will be called at 8:00 a.m. Be at your hotel at 2:00 p.m. every day of a game, unless you are on duty on the gate.

When doing duty at the gate you are expected to look after your club's interests. For leaving the gate without permission, a heavy fine will be assessed.

Retire no later than 11:30. Be a gentleman at all times. Look as neat as possible and do not let everybody in the hotel dining room know that you are a ball player. It is hardly a place for talking baseball.

Drinking of intoxicating liquors will not be tolerated at any time. Practical jokes will not be allowed. This kind of play leads to discord. Be careful as to whom you associate with. Avoid disreputable characters. If you have any grievance go to the manager. For failure to comply with these rules or obey instructions a fine of from $5 to $25 will be assessed for the first offense.

Though they played decent ball and were in the middle of the elongated standings, the Bucs were no match for Frank Selee's Boston Beaneaters, the Cleveland Spiders, or Brooklyn's Bridegrooms. Kerr was nettled by Buckenberger's light handling of the reins and lack of enforcement of his own rules. By June, Kerr persuaded Temple to move Buck into the front office and put Tommy Burns in charge. Burns had a reputation as a prankster and was no doubt one of Buckenberger's targets in his comments about practical jokes.

The Pirates were in sixth place when Burns took over and still sixth when Kerr released him and reinstated Buckenberger. One reason for firing Burns was to dump his $4,500 salary. But Burns had a three-year contract. He took Kerr to court and salvaged a $1,500 settlement. The league was struggling financially. Some clubs cut salaries; players who objected were released. In mid-June the magnates met and decided to cut rosters to thirteen, which reduced expenses and gave the weaker teams a chance to pick up some new players.

The Pirates fared better in the second half, finishing fourth. Looking back over the season, Connie Mack considered that his handling of the pitchers, his league-leading 143 assists, and a .243 batting average—only four Pirates outhit him—warranted a raise. His growing family was an added incentive to press his case.

He never had the chance. The day after the last game he and eleven other players were summoned to Kerr's office. "Boys," Kerr began, "you know what we have been up against for two years. You fellows did your part to wreck us during the Brotherhood fight, and most of the clubs are still in debt. Merging with the American Association hasn't ended our troubles. We haven't a dollar in the treasury and will have to go into our pockets to start the next season off. I have contracts here for all of you calling for $2,400 for 1893. Any player who does not sign for $2,400 before leaving for home will get one for $2,100 in the spring."

Mack said, "We twelve players realized that the statement did not depart from the truth, and accordingly made a dive to a desk for pens. I think a couple were knocked down in this football rush."

As it was, the Pirates' players fared better than most. All but three clubs released their players rather than pay them through the November 1 end of their contracts. But nobody considered them truly free; no other clubs attempted to sign them. The players soon learned that all twelve clubs had adopted the same salary cap. The National League now enjoyed a monopoly on big league baseball. There was a surplus of players. While $2,400 was not bad money—the average family lived well on one-fourth as much—they had less freedom to choose where they would work or to demand higher pay than Andrew Carnegie's steelworkers. Carnegie could tell his workers to take a pay cut or quit. Captain Kerr could do the same. But at least the steelworker could seek a job at another mill.

It irked Mack that the .400 hitter could earn no more than the .240 hitter, the best catcher no more than the rest. He considered this new clamp on salaries a step backward for the game and himself. He would soon be thirty years old, almost half a man's expected lifetime, and he was earning less than he had in Washington in 1889. Having survived the stormy seas of the minor leagues, with their frequent midseason shipwrecks, Mack had felt some sense of security on reaching the majors. Now it looked as if the game was a money-losing proposition at any level. The whole business could collapse at any time. When another player wrote him a letter saying he was thinking of quitting the game because of the cut in salary, Mack replied, "My only fear is that the game will quit us."

The bottom was about to drop out of Connie Mack's personal life too. Michael McGillicuddy had been unable to work for three years. He was getting thinner and weaker. By July 1 he had taken to his bed permanently. In a petition for a widow's pension, Mary McGillicuddy described her husband's last days. "[He] just wasted away and finally died, just dropped away. He was conscious until the time he died. His feet and legs welled badly during his last illness. His chronic diarrhea was something awful." Connie Mack was in Brooklyn with the Pirates on the morning of Saturday, September 10, when his brothers summoned him to come home. He left immediately, arriving in East Brookfield that night. His father died the next day. Michael was probably fifty-five.

Dr. David Hodgkins, using the common label applied to any of several forms of tuberculosis at the time, recorded the cause of death as consumption. All five sons were present when Fr. Dailey served solemn High Mass at the East Brookfield mission of St. John's Church. Interment followed at St. John's Cemetery in Worcester, where Michael had bought a four-space plot in 1873.

Connie Mack remained in Spencer with his wife and children for a week before rejoining the team in Pittsburgh.

Ten days after her husband's death, Mary went with her sons Dennis and Michael to Worcester and put her X mark on an application to have Michael's monthly $12 pension transferred to a widow's pension. She was awarded $8 a month. It would take her several lawyers, numerous depositions from friends and neighbors attesting to Michael's ailments, and eight years of petitioning the pension bureau in Washington to gain a full $12 pension. It was finally approved in 1900, retroactive to September 11, 1892, with an additional two dollars a month for Eugene until he reached the age of sixteen on March 3, 1894.

On Sunday, November 27, Margaret Mack gave birth to a daughter, Marguerite Veronica. Weakened by the birth, she remained poorly for two weeks, then began to strengthen. A little color returned to her cheeks on Monday, December 12, then quickly faded. She failed rapidly and breathed her last at 3:00 p.m. on Thursday, December 15.

Commented the *Spencer Leader*, "She was of a particularly sunny and vivacious disposition, and much loved by her circle of friends. She left three children: 4 years, 2 years, and 3 weeks."

The next day Connie Mack went back to St. John's Cemetery and bought a six-space plot.

In all subsequent accounts of Mack's life, there is scant reference to this tragedy. The biography by Fred Lieb says merely, "Mrs. McGillicuddy lived only five years after her marriage."

In "My Fifty Years in Baseball," a series that ran in the *Philadelphia*

Inquirer in 1930, Mack, after mentioning his marriage, said only, "Five years later Mrs. Mack died."

There's an old saying: "Pity the Irish, for they cannot show their emotions." Whatever its validity, it fit Connie Mack. He kept his feelings and emotions about his private life inside under lock and key. The memories, joys, or heartaches he sheltered were not for display—not to family and certainly not to the public. His children by a later marriage knew him as kind, generous, caring, and loving but not demonstrative. He never talked about Margaret Mack to them.

Only in *My 66 Years in the Big Leagues*, ghostwritten and possibly not even read by the eighty-eight-year-old Mack, do we get a brief glimpse behind the stoic veneer.

"We had five wonderful years together. Three children came to bless our union, and then Margaret died at the age of twenty-six. The loss was almost overwhelming. I was now a lone young father with three motherless babies, Marguerite, Roy, Earle."

The words were probably not his, but the feelings they expressed were true.

11 | CONNIE MACK, MANAGER

In the space of less than four months, Mary McGillicuddy, at fifty-two, went from being a full-time nurse for her bedridden husband to a widow with a fourteen-year-old son and then to a surrogate mother for three baby grandchildren.

On December 27, 1892, two neighbors, Frederick Bollard and John M. Howe, swore in affidavits in support of her pension petition that Mary "is a poor woman possessed of no property and is dependent on the daily labor of her hands for her support."

This wasn't true. She had plenty of help. Her aunt and sister and cousins all lent a hand. Connie hired a nursemaid for the newborn Marguerite. Tom, nineteen, worked as a bookkeeper while going to business school in Worcester and lived at home. Despite his complaints about the league's salary limit, Mack's income was more than ample for his own and his family's needs. For as long as he worked, Connie Mack would be a financial well from which immediate and extended family, friends, down-and-out ex-players, and needy strangers would draw generously, often without asking. He never denied his family anything, nor skimped on their support in any way.

Before Mack left for spring training in March 1893, the title to the little cottage was transferred to his name. The value of the house and half-acre lot was listed at $525. He paid the taxes—$9.03 in 1893—which would average about $14 a year, for the next twenty-five years.

Meanwhile, the custodians of baseball were wrestling with the rules again. Now that catchers wore pillow-size mitts, pitchers like Amos "Cannonball" Rusie were throwing fastballs that reached the plate in one-third of a second. To a batter, said Mack, "they looked like peas as they sailed by me. All I saw of them was what I heard when they went into the catcher's mitt."

Applications of mud, licorice, and tobacco juice made the ball so dark that the Baltimore Orioles painted their center-field wall white so they could pick up the ball in its flight toward the plate. It was time to do something to turn up the offense.

"Baseball has been too long in one rut," wrote a San Francisco pundit. Others who wanted the game left as it was were derided as reactionaries and "purists."

The most popular suggestion was to move the pitcher back from the line on which both feet were supposed to be when he started his delivery; it was now fifty-five feet, six inches from the plate. But how far back: fifty-eight feet, sixty-three feet, somewhere in between? Philadelphia baseball writer Francis C. Richter claimed he was the first to advocate in print a five-foot move, at the suggestion of William R. Lester, an editorial writer on the *Record*. It took until March for the National League to settle on moving the pitcher back five feet and replacing the line with a rubber plate four inches wide and twelve inches long.

The results: the league batting average jumped from .245 to .280; sixty-five players batted over .300, up from twelve.

The rules makers also banned flat bats, which had enhanced the bunting or "baby hit" game. Continuing their cost-cutting efforts, the owners adopted a 132-game schedule and pledged to work together to further reduce the high salaries.

Officially, betting on games was discouraged, but in reality it was so accepted and recognized by the league that President Nick Young felt comfortable in issuing this statement on betting guidelines, as reported in the *Pittsburgh Post*:

> For years in case of doubleheaders the second game was considered the regularly scheduled one and all bets had to be decided by its results. Game one was considered the makeup. This was based on regular games starting between 3:00 and 4:00 in all cities. When two games are played the first generally starts at 2:00 and the second at 4:00, the regularly scheduled hour. Pittsburgh sports fully understood this and for years made their bets accordingly. Now matters are different. The first game hereafter must be regarded as the regularly scheduled one and all bets must go with it.

To beef up the Pirates' pitching, Kerr and Buckenberger picked up 22-game winner Ad Gumbert from Chicago and lefty Frank Killen, who had won 29 for Washington. They also added rookie catcher Joe Sugden and veteran infielder Denny Lyons.

The Pirates didn't look much improved when they returned from spring training and lost their first three games around two rainouts. The muttering of "same old losers" began to rumble from the grandstand. Then they woke up and tore through the league, rarely losing in May and roaring into first place.

During that hot stretch a play took place that epitomizes Connie Mack the catcher and future manager. Before the infield fly rule entered the book in 1894, it was common for infielders to deliberately drop pop flies with a man on first to try to turn a double play. No triple play had ever been started by a catcher using this ploy.

On May 24 the St. Louis Browns played the last of a four-game series at Exposition Park. The next day the *Post* headline read:

CONNIE MACK'S GREAT HEAD
He Engineers a Triple Play and Saves the Day
Spectators Astounded and then Cheer with a Will
Win Four Straight from St. Louis

The account of the play, written in the days when newspapers provided prairie-sized spaces to fill, is worth reproducing, both as a portrait of Connie Mack the player and an example of the baseball writing of the time:

The fourth inning wound up with a climax that is still bothering the heads of 2,000 of the 2,430 spectators, causing them to ask for explanation as to how it was done.

In the inning Brodie reached first on one of those aggravating hits that slowly drop between the in and out field and always cause a post mortem to be held by two or three players. Peitz followed with just such another hit and Breitenstein got his base on balls. Here were the bases full with nobody out. The score was 3–2 in favor of the Pittsburghs. A hit meant two, three or possibly four runs for the pesky Browns, who are holy terrors once they get a lead.

There were faint cries of "take him out" though the majority of spectators were too much wrought up to even whisper. Captain Donovan came in from left field and had a few anxious words with [pitcher] Gastright. The short consultation seemed satisfactory to both. Nobody was paying particular attention to Connie Mack and nobody dreamt that he would pull his team out of the hole it was in. But Connie had his wits about him. Griffin came to the bat with determination to do or die in every movement. He boldly swung at the ball and sent it 160 feet straight up over his head. It went so high that Denny Lyons had plenty of time to run from third base to cover home plate, leaving his own corner uncovered. Mack got under the ball and to the horror of the spectators let it pass through his hands, giving it a good squeeze on its way down. Sly Connie knew what he was doing, and be it said he was the only player on the ground who was on to the trick. The moment the ball touched the ground there was commotion among the St. Louis baserunners. [Having held the ball long enough for umpire Tom Lynch to call the batter out before he let it drop, Mack was aware that the force was off and the base runners had to be tagged if they ran. Another game account said, "The three men on base were foolish enough to run on Mack's drop of a fly ball."] Brodie started on the dead run for home. Connie threw the ball to Lyons at the plate and shouted frantically, "Touch him. Touch him," as Lyons, after planting his foot on the plate, motioned to throw, the Lord knows where. It was easy to touch Brodie as he came thundering down the stretch, as he thought running away from danger, when in reality he was foolishly running right into the jaws of death. Then Connie swung his long arms toward [shortstop] Shugart, pointed to third base, and again shouted, "Touch him. Touch him." Peitz was running toward third base as he probably never ran before, scared almost to death. Shugart got there before him and neatly caught the ball thrown there by Lyons.

Mack stood in the middle of the diamond with his arms still stretched out like a general in a battle, until Shugart had dug the ball into the ribs of Peitz completing a triple play. Then he quickly turned and with a look of triumph stalked toward the bench. . . .

It took the other players and a great majority of the spectators two or three seconds before they realized the situation, and there was a spontaneous uprising of the multitude. A great shout went up, hats were waved enthusiastically. Cheers rang out that made the grandstand quiver, and frenzy reigned even after Connie had tipped his cap several times.

Mack capped the day by driving in the winning run in the eighth inning of the 8–7 victory.

These were the kinds of feats that earned Mack the reputation described by Hugh Fullerton Sr.: "Contrary to stats Connie Mack was a better hitter than credited and dangerous in the pinch. He was a perfect backstop: cool, unhurried, deadly in throwing. Experts of his day rated him the equal of Buck Ewing."

Ned Hanlon's Baltimore Orioles of the 1890s are generally rated the most notorious benders and twisters of the rules. They were not alone. It was a time when words like "shrewd," "smart," "wily," and "tricky" were applied to those teams and individuals who excelled at doing whatever it took—and whatever they could get away with—to win ball games. Those admirable traits were often attributed to Connie Mack. He also drew accusations of trying to inflict crippling injuries on players with his "blocking off trick" at the plate. Skinny as he was, Mack never backed away from a collision, but his blocking the plate was condemned as "dirty ball" by some out-of-town writers.

Since his minor league days, Connie Mack had continued to work on perfecting the arts of distracting chatter, quick pitches, and bat tipping. Baltimore catcher Wilbert Robinson said, "Don't let anyone kid you that Connie was a little tin god behind the plate. Mack never was mean like some of the catchers of the day. But he kept up a string of chatter behind the plate, and if you had any soft spot, Connie would find it. He could do and say things that got more under your skin than the cuss words used by other catchers."

Mack might coo, "Say, that was a beaut you hit last time. If you have any weakness, I don't know it."

He might soft soap an older player with, "You've had a great day. How can a man your age still hit so well? You hit that pitch so far, and when I called for it, I thought it would strike you out."

Sometimes his patter helped to set up his quick pitch. If the batter started to turn a little to reply, Mack signaled the pitcher to fire away, invariably catching the batter off balance.

One day Cap Anson came to bat with two outs and the bases loaded. Mack knew that Anson's style was to take two strikes before swinging. The pitcher threw two quick strikes. Anson took them. Mack then threw the ball back to the pitcher, put his glove on the ground, took off his mask and started removing his chest protector. Anson stared at him, confused. "What's the matter, Connie?" he asked. As Anson spoke, Mack gave a sign to the pitcher and jumped back behind the plate as the hurler threw a fastball by Anson.

"Strike three," yelled the umpire.

"We had a lot of success that way," Mack said. "Whenever the pitcher sneaked over a strike, I would invariably protest to the angry batter. 'That fellow,' I would say, 'has to stop that stuff or somebody is going to get hurt. I wasn't set for that pitch myself.'"

Mack was full of gosh-all-hemlock apologies whenever he tipped a bat to throw off a swing, feigning such sincere remorse over the "accident" that mollified batters just walked away.

Connie Mack never denied nor apologized for his use of these and other tricks. Sometimes he'd bring up the subject himself. In his later years, when he hosted his own annual birthday party for writers and friends, Mack enjoyed sprinkling a little vinegar on what had become his tooth-achingly sweet public image. One year he talked about a player who got even with him:

Farmer Weaver was a catcher-outfielder for Louisville. I tipped his bat several times when he had two strikes on him one year, and each time the umpire called him out. He got even, though. One time there were two strikes on him and he swung as the pitch was coming in. But he didn't swing at the ball. He swung right at my wrists. Sometimes I think I can still feel the pain. I'll tell you I didn't tip his bat again. No, sir, not until the last game of the season and Weaver was at bat for the last time. After he had two strikes, I tipped his bat again and got away with it.

To the delight of fans everywhere except New England, the traditional tailenders from Pittsburgh fought Frank Selee's defending champion Boston Beaneaters fiercely for the pennant.

Unaccustomed to such high altitude in the standings, Pirates rooters turned violent following a late September loss to Boston at home. Kid Nichols, who pitched the 7–2 win for the Beaneaters, later described the scene:

We were stoned as we left the grounds. Boston and Pittsburgh were fighting for the league lead and hometown fans were infuriated that we won the game. As we left the park they followed us carrying sticks and stones. Tom Tucker, our first baseman, and Hugh Duffy, outfielder, and I were in the last of the coupes in which we were driving away. The crowd let go at us with their missiles as we started down the street. I was hit on the head fully a dozen times and several of the sticks and stones hit Duffy and Tucker. I got out of the coupe and chased some of the rowdies and asked a policeman to arrest them. He didn't make a move so I climbed back into the carriage. The bombardment was renewed and we were called every vile name you can imagine. It was only by whipping the horses into a fast getaway that we escaped the mob.

But the Beaneaters pulled away, too far in front for the Pirates' season-ending 8-game winning streak to catch them. The Bucs finished second, 5 games back.

Despite his early season heroics, Connie Mack played only a minor part in the Pirates' great season. On June 13 in a game against Boston, the Beaneaters had men on first and third. The double steal was on. The man on first broke for second. When Mack threw to Bierbauer, Herman Long on third headed for home; Bierbauer's throw back to Mack was high and on the third base side. Mack reached for it as Long slid into him. Spikes ripped open Mack's left leg and cracked his ankle. Some writers, critical of his plate blocking, took a "serves-him-right" attitude toward Mack's injury. He was out for almost two months.

"I was never the same player after that," he told Fred Lieb. "I was slower on the bases and couldn't stoop as well behind the plate. It would catch me in the calf, where I had been spiked. Buckenberger and some of the players were kind enough to say that my injury cost the team the pennant."

In the 37 games he caught, Mack batted .286. For the first time he had been part of a team that had a chance to win. But he left for home disappointed that his injury had prevented him from making more of a difference and fearful that, at thirty-one, his playing days may have been cut short.

For all their complaints about pay cuts and salary limits, the players were lucky to have jobs. A Wall Street crash in May, a run on the banks to redeem paper money for gold, and a large railroad bankruptcy in August had touched off the worst financial crisis the nation had ever seen. More than 150 railroads, 15,000 companies, and 500 banks failed. Unemployment hit 18 percent, almost twice that in Detroit. Until the economy began to recover in 1896, the players had no leverage and no support from the public if they complained about their lot.

Buoyed by their strong second-place finish, the Pirates and their fans launched the '94 season with an early attack of pennant fever. But they stumbled out of the gate, limping along in seventh place until May, when they began to close in on the leaders.

Baseball on and off the field reached its peak of rowdyism in 1894. The Baltimore Orioles and Cleveland Spiders led the league in mayhem. "The Orioles," Mack said, "played the game like gladiators in ancient Roman arenas." They were clearly "not gentlemen."

The Spiders, led by manager Pat Tebeau, never let up on players or umpires, maintaining a steady barrage of invective. They kicked and quarreled through every game.

Club owners decried but did nothing to stem the rowdyism. Editorial writers warned that hooliganism and ripe language emanating from the playing field would drive away respectable customers. But John McGraw was probably closer to the truth when he said the fans preferred to see "aggressive players in action." Rather than repelling the customers, the reviled Orioles and Spiders drew large crowds of hostile fans on the road. They were the targets of insults and more tangible evidence of antagonism, hurled at them as they traveled between hotels and ballparks in open tally-hos.

The fans demonstrated that they could be as full of ginger and as rowdy as the players. Pittsburgh's fiercest rivals were the Cleveland Spiders. A series in the city by Lake Erie always drew train excursions of several hundred Pittsburgh fans armed with rattles, cowbells, wooden instruments, and other noisemakers. A three-game series that began on Thursday, May 24, ended in an eruption that led to a near riot and a forfeit.

The Friday 5–2 loss to the Spiders was one of Mack's worst days as a player. The Spiders stole at least 10 bases off him and left-hander Frank Killen. In the seventh, McAleer on third and Childs on first put on a double steal. Mack threw to second; Bierbauer threw back to the plate as McAleer barreled down the line. The throw was low. Mack bent to catch it. McAleer jumped toward the plate. His spikes caught Mack above the knee, slicing him open. To the Pittsburgh rooters, it looked like a deliberate maiming. They let McAleer know it with every bell and whistle they carried.

The Saturday game drew a record crowd, estimated at 8,000–9,000, to the four-year-old League Park. The fans spilled onto the field behind the foul lines. As the game progressed, those behind first base edged closer to the bag, heaping abuse on the visiting team relentlessly. In the fifth inning Pirates first baseman Jake Beckley went back for a pop fly. Someone in the crowd sicced a dog on him. Beckley caught the ball while shaking off the canine attacker. Two policemen stood nearby and watched as the dog disappeared into the mob.

In the ninth the Pirates led, 12–3, and the horns and rattles were loud enough to drown out a sawmill. As some fans on the field left, others leaped out of the bleachers and took their places. With Cleveland at bat and 1 out, Burkett reached base on an error. McKean forced him at second. Burkett playfully jabbed the pitcher, Red Ehret, in the ribs as he passed him to go to the bench. Ehret threw the ball at him and missed, the ball rolling into the crowd. When Ehret yelled for the ball, somebody threw a cushion at him. That touched off a salvo of cushions sailing out of the stands. The fans on the field picked them up and threw them back. The Pirates fans rang their bells and cracked their rattles as the Spiders beat a hasty retreat. Umpire Bob Emslie ordered the crowd to disperse and took a cushion in the face in reply. After fifteen minutes he declared the game forfeited, an announcement that inspired a new barrage.

That night a happy band of Pirates rooters went home rattling all the way.

On May 29 the Pirates defeated the Orioles, 3–2, and took over first place. It didn't last. Mack had a lame arm, which he doused with large doses of snake oil. He tried bowling to stretch the muscles. (Modern trainers, asked about the therapeutic value of bowling for sore arms, say, "It didn't hurt and probably helped.") His game left leg cut down his agility and speed.

The topers on the club stepped up their carousing, unchecked and undisciplined. Club owners generally preferred to go along with proven older players, who coasted on their reputations but still attracted the customers, rather than replacing them with young unknowns. A manager who benched too many of the regulars for being out of condition could expect no backing from the front office.

Within two weeks of reaching the top, the Pirates slid to fifth. Along the way they put on an offensive display that typified the season as pitchers continued to adjust to the lengthened pitching distance. On June 6 they defeated Boston, 27–11; the teams combined for 65 total bases and 8 home runs, 7 by the Pirates, whose 4 in the fifth inning set a record unbroken for exactly forty-five years. One of them was Mack's only homer of the year. A week earlier Boston and Cincinnati had run up 67 total bases. (The league batting average soared from .280 to .309, topped by four .400 hitters and one at .399.)

Games like these prompted league directors to consider restoring the fifty-foot pitching distance to end such "long drawn out and uninteresting contests." The 27–11 game had lasted two hours and twenty-four minutes.

In the midst of the Pirates' June fade, Captain Kerr, who had officially assumed the presidency in January, sent for Connie Mack. The conversation went something like this:

"You want to see me, Mr. Kerr?"

"Yes, Con. I want to ask you an important question. How would you like to manage the Pirates?"

"What's the matter with Buck?"

"What's the matter with him? He was second last year, and with a better club this year he's in the second division."

"But it's not his fault. Several of the players aren't in shape. I'm one of them. I think I've gone stale. Some of the other players have too. But we're coming around now."

"Don't you want the job?"

"Mr. Kerr, Buck and I are friends. He's a good manager. I don't know where you could get a better one. He had some hard luck. Why not wait a while and give him a chance?"

"All right, I'll wait, but not long if the club doesn't show some improvement."

The Pirates did improve, won some games, climbed a few rungs, then slid back into the second division. On July 26 Frank Killen, who had won 34 games in '93, was hit by a line drive that broke his pitching arm. He was finished for the year, with 14 wins. They were 2 games under .500, but that was only good enough for seventh place in the twelve-team league.

The other catchers, Bill Merritt and Joe Sugden, were better hitters than Mack, but the pitchers wanted him behind the plate calling the game, pulling them through the tight spots. Any pitcher would appreciate the qualities Mack displayed in a game in Baltimore on August 20. Jock Menefee was pitching. They had been kicking all day about the calls of the umpire, Mr. Betts, and several of them had been fined by the umpire as a result.

The Orioles loaded the bases after two batters walked on calls that so enraged the Pirates that first baseman Jake Beckley was ejected. Joe Kelley was the right-handed batter. Menefee threw two pitches over the heart of the plate. Betts called them wide. The count went to 3-0. Mack walked out to the box. "Use the curve ball," he told the rattled Menefee. "Start it in close. Kelley might bite."

Menefee threw a curve. Kelley, ignoring orders to take, swung and missed. Mack called time again and went out to Menefee. They could hear Ned Hanlon and the Orioles on the bench yelling at Kelley to take a pitch. "Try it again," Mack said.

Again Kelley swung at the slow bender and missed.

Another conference. "I have an idea," said Mack. "Send in a straight one and I'll tip his bat."

Menefee threw a fastball. Kelley swung just as Mack lightly tipped his bat, just enough to cause Kelley to pull it foul down the third base line.

The crowd noise was so loud by now that Mack and his pitcher had to stand close to hear each other. Menefee said, "What do we do now?"

Mack said, "Try the bender again. We may get him to swing at it and fan."

Menefee served up a roundhouse. Kelley swung and missed. The crowd noise gave way to groans and curses. The Pirates hung on to win, 7–5.

"Connie was one of those catchers managers nowadays would give dollars to get," Menefee recalled in relating the story thirteen years later.

On Saturday, September 1, more than three thousand turned out to see the Pirates and Washington split a doubleheader. Mack started the second game but had to leave when a foul tip hit him above the right eye. The following Monday morning the eye was still swollen almost shut. He was summoned to Kerr's office. This time he knew what was coming. On the way he rehearsed what he wanted to say, afraid he wouldn't have the nerve to say it.

Mack was confident he had the ability and experience to do the job. At thirty-one, he would be the second-youngest manager in the league, although seven others were in their thirties.

Kerr was not alone in his office. With him were former club president W. C. Temple and a director, Phil L. Auten.

> "Con," said Kerr, "we fired Buckenberger. I told him he's through. Now we're offering you the job as manager. If you don't take it, we'll have to give it to someone else. Do you want it?"
>
> "Yes, I want it," Mack said without hesitating, then added nervously, "if I can really be the manager and not have to do what someone else thinks."

*Kerr exchanged glances with his partners. "What do you mean by
that?" he asked.*

*"Well, I want to run the club, handle the players my way, make the
rules, and make all the trades."*

*"I promise you'll be the manager," Kerr said, "in fact as well as in name.
You can make the trades. I won't interfere."*

Connie Mack was either naive to believe that was how it would be, or
he chose to ignore the evidence around him. His ambition may have overruled his sense of the way things really were. He was aware that other managers had little control over their players or the trading of them. It wouldn't
surprise him when the *Spalding Guide* commented after the season:

> There is a class of club officials in the league who, for the life of them,
> cannot keep from interfering with the club's legitimate manager in his
> running of the team. Some of them have the cool effrontery of stating
> that "the manager of our team is never interfered with in any way."
> One costly result of this club official interference is that needed disci-
> pline of the players is out of the question, and in its absence cliqueism
> in the ranks of the team sets in—one set of players siding with the
> manager, and another with the "real boss of the team," with the costly
> penalty of discord in the ranks. It is all nonsense for a club to place a
> manager in the position with a merely nominal control of the players
> and then to hold him responsible for the non-success of the team in
> winning games.

Mack had to know that Captain Kerr was the very model of a modern
major meddler. The baseball writer for the *Post* commented on the firing,
"Buckenberger has this season been only manager in name. Players have
been signed and released without his knowledge, even against his wishes.
He cannot be blamed for the poor standing of the team at present. His
hands were tied, and he is heartily glad to get away, although he feels his
release keenly coming as it does just before the close of the season."

There was no public indication that Mack was to be anything but an
interim manager. In announcing the change, Kerr said, "Connie Mack will
have charge of the team until the close of the season and if the players do
not do better some of them will be sent to the bench." Mack needed no
more than the last part of that statement to realize that Kerr had no intention of letting him decide who would play and who would not.

The *Post* assumed that Mack was merely finishing out the season. "Who his successor will be, for Mack's appointment is but temporary, is not known and club officials refused to say a word on the subject. Indications point to the appointment of W. H. Watkins, present manager of Sioux City, who managed Detroit during their last years in the league."

But Mack had been signed through 1895.

Popular as he was as a player, Mack's promotion was greeted with indifference, even some resentment at his replacing the popular Buckenberger. "The club has made mistakes this season but its greatest is the release of Buckenberger," said the *Post*.

On the afternoon of Mack's appointment six hundred spectators showed up and watched the Pirates wallop Washington, 22–1. Then the team went to New York and lost, 14–13, after rallying with 4 in the top of the ninth to take the lead before giving it back when New York scored 3.

On September 25 Mack did something for the first time that he would do often over the years: he gave a local amateur pitcher a tryout by starting him in a big league game. Twenty-one-year-old Harry Jordan pitched a 10–7 win over Brooklyn at Exposition Park. He signed no contract and went back to the sandlots.

Another baseball war loomed in the fall of 1894. A group calling itself first the National Association, then the American Association, began offering National League players inflated salaries to jump. Al Buckenberger was seen at the Monongahela House recruiting visiting players for a new Pittsburgh team. The Pirates responded by giving raises of $200–$600 to several players. Other clubs handed the players a notice with their last paychecks, telling them their contracts had been renewed for next season "in accordance with the nineteenth paragraph of your contract"—the reserve clause—at the same salary. But the would-be rival major league promoters disappeared as quickly as they had appeared. The war clouds passed like a brief summer shower. As playing manager, Mack's contract remained at $2,400.

During the season, Connie Mack had seen the first of a new kind of baseball stadium. Following a fire, the Phillies replaced their wooden grandstand with a futuristic concrete and steel cantilever construction. They installed 1,500 "steel opera chairs" in place of the usual plain hard planks. It was too far ahead of its time for other magnates to see it as anything but economic madness and "delusions of grandeur."

12 | THE TERRIBLE-TEMPERED MR. MACK

Relying on the authority Captain Kerr had promised him, Connie Mack had enough confidence in his judgment to put it on the line. He named Monte Cross his shortstop in place of the aging Jack Glasscock. Mack had acquired him from Syracuse in September. In 13 games Cross had shown the kind of range that would rack up a lot of putouts, assists, and errors. He chose twenty-five-year-old rookie Billy Clingman over a couple of proven .300 hitters, Denny Lyons and Fred Hartman, to play third. He was satisfied with the rest of his infield and the outfield.

Mack believed that managing pitchers was his strongest point. He counted on a healthy Frank Killen as his ace; retained Tom Colcolough, an 8-game winner in '94; brought back the veteran Bill Hart from the minors; and added a nineteen-year-old Baltimore lefty, Brownie Foreman. He sent pitcher Red Ehret and cash to St. Louis for Emerson "Pink" Hawley, a nervous right-hander with rabbit ears and a rubber arm. Hawley had lost a league-leading 26 games while winning 19 in 1894. He was young—twenty-two in December—and durable, having worked almost 400 innings starting and relieving.

At seven thirty on the morning of Sunday, March 17, 1895, the Pirates boarded a train for Savannah and Mack's first spring training as a manager. The team stayed at the Haven Hotel, room and board $1.25 a day. They were in Savannah only a week before riding the rails to Charleston, Columbia, and Charlotte. Mack had played almost every position at one time or another, but he had never pitched. In Columbia, he started a game at first base with Frank Killen in the pitcher's box.

"[Killen] was not in good condition," Mack said, "and I transferred him to the first bag and went in to pitch myself. I started out in good shape and the first two men never felt the ball, and in fact could not see it until it was landed in the backstop's mitt. The third man then came to bat. I gave him a twister. The twister was punished with a hot line hit. . . . An incessant cannonade ensued and the last I can remember was that the ball went over the center field fence. Well, I didn't pitch another inning."

Mack played every day as they wended their way to Danville, Virginia, where they found only three players on the local team. Mack loaned them six players, and it became an intrasquad game, which was all right with him. He preferred to see his full squad practice every day. They worked out in Knoxville, then headed for Chattanooga for three days en route to opening day at Louisville on April 18.

As a reward for his boys' good play and flush with the gate receipts of the exhibition tour, Mack decided to treat them to better rooms in Chattanooga. He wrote to the proprietor of the Ship House, who responded with suspicious warmth and promptness, considering the reputation baseball teams carried. The proprietor even offered to provide a single bed for each man, an unheard of luxury.

Mack reminisced:

We arrived at Chattanooga at midnight, and the owner of the Ship House met us at the front door. He asked us all into the bar immediately. I was beginning to see then why he was willing to take in a bunch of social outcasts. . . . He was hoping to get all our money across the mahogany. When I told him my boys weren't allowed to drink, his whole manner changed. He stopped washing his hands in invisible water and suddenly discovered that he had such a crowd of guests he couldn't put us up.

My dander was up, and I marched the boys down the street to a hotel that I had thought was too rich for our blood. The night clerk was on the job, a callow youth whom no one had told that baseball players were unclean. I struck a bargain with him at the rate of $2 a day a man for food and lodging. He put me up in the bridal suite. When the owner showed up in the morning his horror was a sight to behold. But we were settled then and I don't think he could have moved us without calling in the militia. I had a happy crowd on that trip. The boys sat out in front on the porch, morning and evening, reared back in their canebottom chairs chewing tobacco and looking down from Olympian heights at the local citizenry.

They opened at Louisville before a sellout crowd of over eight thousand. Sporting new uniforms, they lined the field while the mayor walked to the pitcher's box and threw the first pitch. Mack should have given him a uniform and let him pitch. Frank Killen took an 11–2 pasting.

"I know the boys can play better ball than they put up here," a disappointed Mack said. "If I thought they could not do better . . . I would lie awake at night making plans to strengthen the team. One thing I am convinced of is the ability of Killen, Hawley, and Colclough to pitch good ball."

Mack's optimism was confirmed when they won their next 7 games and took a 7-2 record back to Pittsburgh for the May 1 home opener.

The team's strong start stoked civic pride in the city, which was now approaching a population of three hundred thousand, swelled by an influx of workers from southern and central Europe attracted by jobs in the rapidly growing steel and emerging aluminum industries. Immigrants eager to be accepted in their new world quickly realized that baseball was a surefire way to fit in. If you could talk baseball with other workers or the guys in the corner saloon, you were made to feel that you belonged.

Books of fifty grandstand tickets for $30, good for any game, sold briskly at Pratt's downtown store. Opening day tickets were in great demand at William A. McClurg, tobacconist, corner of Fifth Avenue and Wood Street.

Connie Mack took lodgings at 171 Federal Street, a short walk from Exposition Park in the city of Allegheny, now the north side of Pittsburgh. A prosperous center of business and industry, Allegheny was home to Andrew Carnegie's first public library, built in 1890. H. J. Heinz had a packing plant there among tanneries and slaughterhouses. Federal Street was lined with taverns and restaurants. Foods of all kinds were vended at the large brick Allegheny Market House. At Boggs and Buhl, an elegant department store, Mack could buy Arrow high stiff collars two for a quarter and low crown derbies for a dollar.

One section two blocks long in Allegheny West housed more millionaires than any other two blocks in the country. A short distance away, Mack's pal Elmer Smith lived amid a yard full of dogs, chickens, and ducks.

This was Connie Mack's Pittsburgh home for the rest of his time with the Pirates. It isn't there anymore. The new Pittsburgh ballpark now sits where he once resided.

Opening day festivities began with a parade from the Monongahela House Hotel at one thirty. Hundreds of newsboys led the procession to the park, followed by the Pirates and Cincinnati Reds, riding in open carriages. Every seat was filled at the park, and those who couldn't find a place to sit stood against the right-field fence. Ladies in brightly colored hats and dresses offset the low black clouds that hovered over the field but spilled no rain to spoil the occasion.

Baseball and theatrical stars were already a twosome. The first ball was thrown from the box seats by Rose Coghlan, a well-known but fading star of forty-four who was appearing on the vaudeville bill at the Alvin Theater. Captain Jake Beckley caught the ball, but instead of handing it back to the actress, he turned it over to umpire Bob Emslie. It was, after all, *the* game ball.

Bill Hart's curves were at their sharp-shooting best against the Reds. The home team, batting first, scored a 4–1 win. But the game was played in an odd shroud of stillness. The greatest racket came from the twenty-five-cent seats, where groups of restless newsboys rose from time to time and raced across the field to join those standing by the fence. Not a single kick or razzing was heard from the usually vocal Mack coaching third base. The players went about their business as if they were playing in a hospital ward. The reason: a new rule against "boisterous coaching," which made the game, as the *Post* writer put it, "too solemn and funereal." Fortunately, like other reform efforts that make things worse, the rule was soon forgotten.

Having turned over the regular catching job to Joe Sugden, Mack transferred his wiles to other tactics. He stored some baseballs in an icebox in the office. Before a game he gave some of them to a boy who patrolled the grandstand roof, retrieving foul balls that landed there. Mack kept some of the deadened balls with him on the bench. When visitors were at bat, the boy returned a frozen ball onto the field in place of the live one that had been hit his way. Mack slipped one into the game whenever he saw a favorable opportunity to do so. (In 1896 a new rule required the home team to give the umpire a dozen new balls before each game, nullifying the icebox strategy.)

Mack was certainly not alone in using such tactics, and he never talked as much about this one as his bat tipping or foul tip ploys. When Fred Lieb asked him fifty years later if the story was true, Lieb wrote that Mack smiled and said, "We had to use a lot of tricks to win games, and maybe that was one of them."

Connie Mack never believed in strict rules to govern the off-field behavior of his boys. He recalled the litany of regulations read by Al Buckenberger in 1892 and their lack of results. He was always reluctant to fine players, knowing that a wife and family were often dependent on that money to pay the rent and put food on the table. But sometimes that was the only effective threat or punishment.

Mack was not a teetotaler. He drank an occasional beer, never cared for whiskey, and later took a glass of wine now and then. He had seen alcohol's effects on players and found it difficult to understand why an athlete, especially one with a family, would jeopardize his career and impair his ability to succeed by excessive drinking and night-crawling.

But jeopardize they did. The principle of enlightened self-interest didn't sink in. "My notion was that ballplayers fit for the major leagues, the certainty of employment and real money assured them, would keep themselves in good physical condition as a matter of course," he said. "But I found they wouldn't, and I couldn't induce them to. Not those players."

Their escapades didn't escape the notice of the press. Mack's critics accused him of being too easygoing and lacking the firm disciplinary hand it took to control his team. There were frequent allusions to the "players' condition." More telling than the critical comments were the pointed references to their "never behaving better" or "tending to business" when they were winning.

Mack's pitching staff quickly turned erratic. Killen was batting over .300, but he was getting hit just as hard. The grandstand "cracks," as the experts were called, hollered to get rid of him. Mack stayed with him. Despite a sore thumb, he began catching Killen to try to steady him. Tom Colcolough was sidelined with arm problems after just one winning effort. Hawley and Hart were willing to work every day, but their arms were not.

Scrounging for pitching, Mack demonstrated traits that remained characteristic of him throughout his career. He seemed to know what was happening on ball fields all over the country. He wrote letters and gave amateurs a chance to show what they could do. At home or on the road, during spring training or winter vacations, even on the morning of an opening day, he always made time to sit and pen longhand letters to family, friends, fans, former players, scouts, job seekers—in vast numbers of each category. Everybody he knew became an informal scout for him or was pressed into service by him.

On May 27 he sat in his office and wrote on club stationery to Bill "Doc" Thompson, a resident of nearby Sharon, Pennsylvania, who had pitched 3 innings for the Pirates in 1892.

Dear Doc:

As you, Doc, no doubt are a little interested in the Pittsburghs, would like to ask a favor of you. Have heard such good reports of Gussie Gannon, the Sharon pitcher, that I would like to give him a trial. And if you will kindly speak to him in our favor, will be very thankful to you. Would like to hear from you on what you think of him.

"Address me at Willard Hotel, Washington. See you are having pretty good games. Remember me to Harry, and I hope you will meet with good success.

Sincerely, /s/ Connie Mack

Doc Thompson sent Gannon, a twenty-one-year-old left-hander, to Mack. He pitched in one game, giving up 1 run on 7 hits and 2 walks in 5 innings, then was farmed out to Syracuse. He never made it back. Gannon died at ninety-two with that one pitching line to immortalize him in the record books, thanks to Mack's letter. Gannon's son and nephew became Catholic priests, early members of an eventual army of ordained bird dogs for Connie Mack.

In the middle of a heat wave that caused twelve deaths, the Pirates went to Brooklyn on June 1 in first place, 2 games ahead of the Reds. At Eastern Park that afternoon Colcolough was pounded, but Mack demonstrated that he knew the rules better than the umpire and saved them from a loss. After Patsy Donovan doubled in the third inning, a brief shower delayed the game. When play resumed after fifteen minutes, Donovan left the bench and ran out to second base. As Brooklyn pitcher Brickyard Kennedy prepared to pitch to the next batter, center fielder Mike Griffin ran to the pitcher's box, took the ball from Kennedy, ran to second base and tagged Donovan. He claimed the runner was out for failing to retouch first base before returning to second. Umpire Jeremiah Murray agreed and called Donovan out. This precipitated a "lively tilt" around home plate. Mack argued in vain that the decision was contrary to the rules. He then announced that he was playing the game under protest. The league upheld the protest, Murray admitted his mistake, and the game was replayed.

But that didn't save Colcolough. He was shipped off to Syracuse, never to return to Pittsburgh.

Connie Mack was an aggressive player. He never avoided a confrontation at home plate and applied a firm tag in a collision. He encouraged his players to play the game the same way. They did, earning such notoriety for it that when they went a few weeks without sparking a single hot exchange, the *Post* found it appropriate to comment on June 3, "It is a noteworthy fact that not a cry of 'dirty ball' was used against the Pittsburghs on the eastern trip."

That soon changed. On Saturday, June 8, in New York, an incident resulted in what Mack later called the death knell of his season. Killen was pitching when the Giants loaded the bases in the fifth inning. Shorty Fuller popped up behind second base. Bierbauer dropped the ball.

New York Herald writer O. P. Caylor, who seemed to delight in looking for—or creating—openings to take a shot at Connie Mack, wrote this account:

"Farrell scored and Wilson reached the plate as the throw came in. [Catcher] Sugden muffed it. Killen, the pitcher, putting into practice Pittsburgh's 'dirty' system of play, ran up to the plate and threw himself at Wilson trying to block him until Sugden got the ball. Wilson slid feet first and Killen was spiked in the ankles. Killen turned and kicked Wilson as he lay upon the ground. As Wilson got to his feet the bully struck at him. The police came onto the field and stopped it."

In other descriptions of the play, the throw from Bierbauer was wild and rolled to the grandstand. When Sugden chased after it, Killen ran in to cover the plate. "Wilson could have walked in but slid instead," read one report. "In doing so he spiked Killen and pushed him aside."

Killen had to leave the game. He made one more start, on June 12 in Baltimore, winning 5–1. Then his wounds became infected. The dye in his socks got into his blood, causing blood poisoning, a common hazard in the days before white sanitary socks. He went into a hospital that night for what became a seven-week stay.

Strapped again for pitching, Mack was also dissatisfied with his catchers. Seeking a better hitter, he traded pitcher Ad Gumbert to Brooklyn for Tom Kinslow, a .300 hitter who batted 1.000 in the elbow-bending league. Mack knew what he was getting but hoped to bring about the catcher's reformation. It didn't work. When Kinslow missed a game and showed up the next day with a first-class hangover, Mack fined him $50. In late May Kinslow, whose home was in Washington, asked for a day off when the Pirates were in the capital. When he didn't show up the next day, Mack suspended him.

Connie Mack would try to effect a wayward player's reform for just so long. If it didn't happen, he'd give up. After he reinstated Kinslow, the Pirates were at home for a game against Louisville on Saturday, June 22. At game time Mack looked for Kinslow in the dressing room. There he found a messenger boy carrying a note from Kinslow for one of the players, asking that his uniform be packed and sent to him. Mack took the note and wrote on the back that Kinslow needn't worry about his uniform as the club did not intend to take him with it to Chicago that night. Kinslow showed up at the railroad station, contrite and promising to reform. Mack sent him packing, fined him $100, and suspended him again. (Kinslow drank himself out of the league and died at thirty-five.)

Mack paid the Reds $500 for Billy Merritt, a catcher who had been with the Pirates briefly in 1894. The five-foot-seven fireplug joined the Pirates in Chicago. "I now have a catcher," said Mack, "but where am I to get a pitcher?" With Killen out, Mack no longer went behind the plate. Sugden and Merritt split the duties the rest of the year.

Once again scouring the sandlots, Mack came up with a twenty-year-old law student, Jim Gardner, who agreed to pitch but refused to travel. Using him only at home, Mack wrung 8 wins out of his 10 starts.

His pitching staff still "shot to pieces," Mack turned again to Harry Jordan, the semipro pitcher he had used once at the end of the 1894 season. The Pittsburghs were about to depart on July 1 for a three-game series in Cleveland. Jordan became the main character in one of Connie Mack's favorite stories.

Going over on the train I began to realize what was in store for Jordan. I knew that Tebeau, O'Connor, and the others would ride him so unmercifully, in two innings he would be a wreck. I hit on a scheme. I called Jordan over to my seat in the car and told him that he must act as if he were deaf and dumb.

"When you get on the field, don't say a word to anybody, and don't pay any attention to anybody who talks to you. Be a deaf mute."

Then I informed my players of the plan and they agreed to cooperate. Tebeau knew I was short of pitchers and when Jordan started to warm up [on July 3], Tebeau came over to me and asked who he was. I quickly told him he was a semipro named Jordan who unfortunately was deaf and dumb, and that sad affliction would probably prevent him from ever making good in the majors. Pat swallowed my words and went back to the Cleveland bench and told his players that I was pitching a dummy that day.

One of the players did not hear Pat. In the first inning he started to yell at Jordan. Jack O'Connor was coaching and yelled to the razzer, "Don't waste your breath. That guy is deaf and dumb." After that not one word was hurled at Jordan for the rest of the game. I would like to say that Jordan won his game but he did not, but he gave a good performance. [Three errors cost him a 5–4 loss.] There was no rout and our prestige did not suffer. Had they known he could hear they would have razzed him out of the game in three innings.

Jordan lost his only other start, 10–7, before returning to the semipro ranks, where Connie Mack left him undisturbed thereafter.

Throughout June and July the Pirates commanded front page space in the Pittsburgh newspapers as they battled Boston and Baltimore for first place. The team's success didn't keep Captain Kerr from sticking in his two cents' worth of advice. Mack yearned for a team of clear-headed, quick-thinking, fleet-footed, innovative players who could take advantage of an opponent's mistakes and sometimes force them. He favored the use of deftly placed bunts, the hit and run, double steals, and squeeze plays. But he didn't have the horses.

One day Captain Kerr asked him why his team couldn't play like the Baltimore Orioles, the exemplars of Mack's kind of baseball. Mack replied, "We don't have the kind of players to do such things. We have only two fast men on our team and not many of them can bunt."

Kerr wasn't satisfied with that explanation, so Mack said, "All right, I will try it this afternoon."

Mack told his boys they were going to play that afternoon the way McGraw, Keeler, Jennings, and company played—lots of bunting and hit-and-run plays.

"They all laughed at me," he recalled, "and I couldn't help smiling myself. In the first inning we put on the hit and run. The batsman didn't get the sign from the man on first and the latter was caught ten feet at second. We kept on this way but never got anywhere. Some of our men couldn't bunt and popped up or were so slow that they were easily thrown out when they bunted correctly.

"President Kerr never made any suggestions about the Baltimore style of play after that wretched afternoon."

Pitching the arm off Pink Hawley, who worked 444 innings in 50 starts while batting .308, Mack kept his Pirates in or near first place. Every time they slipped to second or third, the knockers' voices rose with cries of "same old Pirates." They had seen so many failures, they knew that no matter how well the team was going, the good times would fade before the autumn leaves began to fall.

The Pirates awoke in first place for the last time on August 9. By the end of the month they had fallen to sixth, and on September 3 a 10–5 loss at Philadelphia bumped them into the second division.

It's difficult to reconcile the later image of Connie Mack that remains engraved in the public mind—the dignified, kind, soft-spoken, Grand Old Man of baseball, all of which he surely became—with the sharp-tongued, hot-headed young manager of the 1890s, which he just as surely was.

Despite revisionists' efforts to paint them otherwise, Mack's teams were never milquetoasts. He might urge them not to "get personal," but otherwise he tolerated far rougher language than he used himself. Over the years he employed some of the most celebrated and vocal bench jockeys in the business. Nor were his own volleys and fits of temper confined to the "gosh and golly" school of expression. His family finds it hard to believe, because he never swore in their presence, but he could rival any mule skinner or dockworker when his fuse was lit. Blowing off steam when the pressure built probably helped him stay healthy and aided his longevity in a job that could churn holes in a man's innards.

This seemingly dichotomous personality is common among athletes, coaches, and managers. Away from the field they might be the sweetest gentlemen, while on the field or diamond they could become raving maniacs.

From the coaching box or bench, Mack applied the needle as implacably as John McGraw. In a game on May 21, Mack rode Washington third baseman Bill Joyce and shortstop Danny Coogan so hard that Joyce booted all three balls hit to him and Coogan made three errors in Pittsburgh's 10–7 win. Only 4 of the 17 runs were scored as earned. To rattle a pitcher, Mack danced up and down the third base line, yelling, "He can't get 'em over. He can't get 'em over."

One day in a game against Washington, Mack was coaching at third base. The Senators' battery was McJames pitching and McCauley catching. Pat Donovan hit a high pop-up over McJames's head. As the pitcher waited for it to come down, Mack hollered, "McCauley's ball. McCauley's ball." McJames backed away, and the ball fell on the ground as Donovan crossed first base.

Mack was never an umpire baiter in the McGraw or Earl Weaver style, but he could explode when he thought a call was really bad. (The quality of umpiring in those days was uneven at best. Jeremiah Murray needed more postgame police escorts than a president and didn't return the next year, although he later worked in the league again. Another ump, William Betts, resigned in June after every club except the Pirates complained about him. He also returned.)

In September 1895, his team rapidly collapsing in the standings and frustrated by the poor umpiring, Connie Mack blew his cork high enough to be thrown out of a game for the only time in his long managing career. In later years he was not reluctant to talk about it. Each time he was asked if he was ever ejected from a game, he'd reply, "Yes, once"; admit that he had "raised an awful holler"; describe the incident; then add proudly, "And they had to call the cops to put me out."

It happened on Friday, September 6, at the Polo Grounds, where he often had troublesome encounters. The Pirates were winding up a disastrous road trip, in which they had fallen to eighth place. Disappointed over the shambles the season had become, Mack was tired, overworked, and sorely vexed. The umpire was Hank O'Day, Mack's erstwhile ill-tempered battery mate in Washington, who was once characterized by Tim Murnane of the *Boston Globe* as "honest but loses his head too easily."

The score was 3–3 in the last of the fifth. The Giants' George Davis led off with a drive to right field that Patsy Donovan ran down as Davis headed for second. Donovan had a strong arm and quick release. He fired the ball right to the bag where O'Day, the lone umpire, had hustled to make the call. O'Day signaled Davis safe.

The *New York Times* reported, "The ball and the runner both reached the bag within an infinitesimal fraction of a second of each other."

But the way Mack saw it, Davis was out by ten feet.

The writers, sitting at tables directly behind home plate in the first row, could see and hear everything that followed. The small crowd on hand didn't make enough noise to muffle Mack's high-pitched New England twang. O. P. Caylor of the *Herald* described it as he saw and heard it:

> From the stands it looked as if [Davis] was out, but O'Day was right at the base when the play was made and he declared Davis safe. This decision aroused the wrath of manager Connie Mack. . . . And he began to hurl all sorts of epithets at O'Day, calling the latter a dirty robber and names not quite so mild. This he kept up for some time,

until at last, as O'Day asserts, Mack applied a name to him which is unprintable. It must have been something unusually provoking, for O'Day turned a gray white in the face and walking toward the bench, said, "That will cost you a hundred, and it goes, too." Mack immediately got back in a vigorous manner. Then O'Day said, "Now you get off the field." Mack refused to go, whereupon O'Day summoned an officer and ordered Mack removed. The officer could do nothing with Mack and he refused to move. Two other patrolmen came up and the Pittsburgh manager was led by them as far as the diamond, where he agreed to go without further force. He did not go, however, until he walked up to O'Day and lashed him with language which could not be repeated in polite society.

"Mack retired from the field amid the jeers of the spectators," reported the *Times*.

When the game resumed, two singles, an error, and a passed ball produced 3 runs for a 6–3 New York lead. The Pirates tied it in the eighth, but another double by Davis drove in the winning run in the ninth.

The Pittsburghs finished seventh, just 2 games out of fourth and 17 behind the champion Orioles, with a respectable 71-61 record. "Had I won that pennant," Mack mused years later, "it would have made me a real big shot in Pittsburgh, for, with the exception of 1893, Pirate fans had known nothing but second-division baseball."

In the end it was the hitting, not the pitching, that hurt them. Their pitching was the third best, behind Baltimore and Cleveland, but their runs scored were the third lowest in the league. For Captain Kerr and his partners, the disappointment over the late-season slide was soothed by the harvest of the most profitable season in franchise history. Even the $5,000 annual rental they paid for Exposition Park was partially covered by renting it out to college football teams in the fall.

All of that put nothing in Connie Mack's heart or pocket. His reward was a hearty handshake. On October 8, before leaving for home, he signed another contract for $2,400, payable in monthly installments on the last day of each month beginning April 1, 1896, with the usual ten days' notice of release clause.

13 | FIRED

Connie Mack couldn't wait to begin planning for the 1896 season. Baseball was now his entire life. He was one of those people blessed by knowing exactly what he wanted to do with his life and being able to do it. He loved the cycle of the seasons: fall and winter meetings and scouting and dealing for players who might help him build a winner; spring training and the evaluation of his boys; the strategy involved in the playing of the games; even the season-long travel. He racked up more miles in Pullman compartments than anyone in the game and never tired of it.

His work was in Pittsburgh now. He spent two months in East Brookfield with his children, his brothers, and his mother and returned to the city shortly after Christmas, prompting the *Sporting Life* correspondent to comment, "I don't know how the young ladies in New England, especially one, will take the veteran's ruthless departure."

This offhand reference to a special romantic interest may have been a fanciful stab at gossip by the writer. If such a "special one" existed, the name never surfaced, and nothing came of it. Some current East Brookfield residents talk of hearing stories of ancestral females having "dated Connie Mack," but no evidence could be found to confirm any serious involvement.

Once, more than fifty years later, Connie Mack alluded to his love life—or lack of same—during those years. The Philadelphia Athletics were staying at the Del Prado Hotel in Chicago. Two young pitchers discovered that the way the hotel was built, they could look into other rooms from their own. One night these two Romeos saw a silhouette of a woman undressing behind a drawn curtain. They checked out the room number, picked up the phone, and invited the woman for "a party."

When they told her they were ballplayers with the Athletics, she said, "If my husband were alive he would come over there and shoot you both. But Mr. Mack will hear about this."

The woman, who was in her seventies, was true to her word. The next morning the team was summoned to a meeting in a mezzanine conference room. Mack, sputtering and fuming, his false teeth clacking, said, "There was a time when I was unmarried for eighteen years. In that whole time I never had anything to do with a woman. But you fellows—you fellows—the train isn't even out of the depot and you guys are off looking for something."

"And he was right," added Ferris Fain, Mack's first baseman at the time, as he related this story. "He knew what he was talking about."

Connie Mack was never a womanizer, but he was certainly no monk. He had been a dutiful and fertile husband and would be again. But during his thirties and early forties he was completely and happily immersed in being a baseball manager, which, for him, included the duties of a modern general manager, traveling secretary, and scouting director.

Though he gave a warm welcome to everyone who approached him, he was basically shy and reserved. His manner was dignified but not aloof. He was no back slapper or hugger, not demonstrative, but a gentleman at all times. He never saw himself as a matinee idol or magnet for women, even though ballplayers attracted as many female admirers then as they do today. Mack was sensitive about his long, skinny build and large feet. A *Milwaukee Journal* item in 1897 said, "Manager Mack states that the gentler sex have no attraction whatever for him. Furthermore, he often says, 'What if they did? It would do no good, for when ladies see me in a baseball suit it is all over with me.'"

But off the field Connie Mack made a handsome appearance, his thin frame erect; his face a little fuller, with a deep crease down his cheeks when he smiled; heavy, dark, straight eyebrows over his pale blue eyes; curly black hair neatly combed. An immaculate dresser, he was seldom seen in anything but a stiff-collared white shirt, tie, and three-piece suit, straw hat with dark band in summer, and derby after Labor Day.

Despite his disclaimers, Mack was by no means oblivious to women. He enjoyed the theater and vaudeville and always had an eye for a good looker. One day when he was close to ninety, he was riding in a car with his son-in-law, Jim Nolen. They stopped at a red light. Both men stared at a pretty girl standing on the corner. When Jim glanced at him, Mack smiled and said, "When you stop looking, you're dead." Near the end of his life a showgirl or chorus line would hold his attention as he peered at the small television screens of the 1950s. His favorite actress was Sheree North, a blonde bombshell on some early TV shows.

Mack was blessed with a natural metabolism that allowed him to eat whatever he wanted without gaining weight. He indulged his sweet tooth with candy, ice cream, blueberry pie. His eating habits were simple. He usually ate a big breakfast. A few crackers and a glass of milk would suffice for lunch. On the road he might enjoy a hearty dinner or settle for a bowl of corn flakes. As much or as little as he ate, he rarely varied from the 160 he weighed when he was thirty-three.

Back in Pittsburgh in January with nothing but baseball on his mind, Mack shored up his infield. His pitching had ranked third in the league in '95, but the team had been tenth in runs scored. The offense needed beefing up. Dealing with the St. Louis Browns' Teutonic trio of von der Ahe, Diddlebock, and Muckenfuss—owner, manager, and secretary—he sent them Monte Cross and pitcher Billy Hart for his former third baseman, Denny Lyons, a boozer he tried in vain to reform, and shortstop Bones Ely, who was almost as tall and thin—and as old—as Mack.

He wrote a letter to each of his twenty players, urging them to report in good condition at Hot Springs in March. Most of them did. Frank Killen, completely recovered from his 1895 injury, and four others went to the spa on their own in February.

While most first-class hotels still turned away baseball teams, a few were beginning to pursue the business. Mack received bids from several Hot Springs hostelries, which were accustomed to housing gamblers and criminal types taking the mineral waters, enjoying the racetrack and other games of chance, or just lying low. To the innkeepers, ballplayers were no lower on the social ladder. The completion of the Diamond Joe Railroad line to St. Louis had led to a construction boom, and there were plenty of rooms to be filled. But Mack was dismayed to learn that he would have to share the local park with the Cleveland Spiders.

On Wednesday evening, March 9, a crowd of enthusiastic Pirates' rooters gathered at the depot to bid farewell to Mack and nine players. The manager made a few remarks of an optimistic nature, as familiar and welcome a sign of spring as the robin's song, and they boarded the 8:50 train for St. Louis. There they were to be joined by pitchers Pink Hawley and Jim Hughey, an acquisition from the Western League. Only Hawley showed up. Hughey asked for a salary that Mack considered so unreasonable, he wired the hurler "an emphatic declination."

They arrived in Hot Springs on March 11 and planned to play their first practice game against the Spiders the next morning. But when they woke up, it was snowing. The ground was as white as the city they had left a few days earlier. Some of the players spent the day simmering in the baths. Others played whist.

They spent only a few days in Hot Springs before embarking on a two-week barnstorming trek in hopes of covering expenses. This was Captain Kerr's idea. Mack would have preferred to stay put and let all his men see some action every day. He sent no glowing reports to Kerr, considering it a worthless, premature exercise. Nor would he make any predictions for the coming season. "It will be settled on the diamond in due course," was his unsatisfying reply to reporters' prodding.

The Pirates' itinerary followed that of the Baltimore Orioles by a few days. Just before they were scheduled to play at Danville, Virginia, on April 6, Mack learned that the Orioles had drawn a large crowd but reaped small receipts. The bulk of the spectators watched from nearby housetops, sheds, trees, and wide gaps in the outfield fence. Mack was unperturbed, taking a view now long out of fashion that "people are not to be blamed for refusing to pay to see a league team practice."

They drew enough paying customers on the tour to show a spring training profit, the only time, Mack said later, that he could recall doing so. They enjoyed fine weather and good reviews, reporters commenting that the Pittsburgh players "are the most gentlemanly seen in the south this spring."

On paper, the 1896 Pirates were the strongest team ever seen in Pittsburgh. Cleveland manager Patsy Tebeau told writers that when he saw Mack's pitchers in Hot Springs, he was convinced they were all first-rank stars. But they started the season as though they were still working the winter kinks out of their systems. It didn't take long for the cranks to begin growling, especially the gamblers who expected them to perform up to their pre-season billing. The hitting and fielding were strong, but the pitching was sour, either inspiring or strengthening Mack's often cited contention that pitching was 70 percent of the game.

With Killen his only effective pitcher, Mack either persuaded Jim Hughey to come down in his demands or rescinded his "emphatic declination" of Hughey's terms. The big right-hander from Michigan arrived, but his debut was an unimpressive 8–0 drubbing by the Orioles.

Pink Hawley was especially inconsistent, except in the late innings, when he was consistently hit hard. On May 9 at home against Washington, he blew up under a blistering roasting from third base coach Scrappy Bill Joyce. "I knew I could twist Hawley," Joyce said. "I simply told him he was too pretty to pitch. His red silk sweater would match a pair of bloomers better than a pitcher's box. Hawley is a good fellow, but you can get his wheels working by joshing him."

Hawley hit 5 batters that afternoon, 2 of them in Washington's 11-run seventh inning. (The Senators' Win Mercer hit 3, including Hawley once.) Connie Mack had Frank Killen warming up and ready, but when Mack ordered Hawley to depart, Pink threw down the ball and refused to leave. "Come out of that box, Hawley," Mack yelled again as he ran out and led the steaming pitcher away.

The Pirates were in sixth place with an 18 14 record on the morning of June 1 when the *Post* reported the following:

> As far as manager Mack is concerned, he is just as popular now as he ever was, possesses the confidence of the patrons as well as the officials of the club. He said last night that he will continue to manage the club according to plans laid out by him at the beginning of the season. The unexpected weakening of the pitchers he had not bargained for, but is certain they will round to in a short time. The only worry he feels on account of the poor record of the team is because it has a tendency to keep the attendance down and cause the team to take in less at the gate than if the team was winning right along. As for the outcome of the race for the pennant he has no fears. The team is as strong as any in the league and is bound to be off in the leaders at the finish.

Connie Mack's players were not as rowdy a gang of umpire abusers as the Orioles, but they were close. And Mack was right there with them.

On June 3 at Baltimore the Pirates were riding home plate umpire George Weidman all afternoon. Frank Killen was pitching. He didn't agree with any of the ump's calls. Once Elmer Smith caught a fly ball in left field and threw it into the bleachers in protest of the ump's calls. These were the days when one ball often made it through an entire game. Players didn't nonchalantly throw them to the fans. When a new ball was put into play, Killen angrily ground it into the dirt.

"Weidman seemed unable to control the Pittsburgs at all," wrote the *Baltimore Sun* reporter.

In the fourth inning, when Weidman called ball four on the Baltimore batter, pitcher Bill Hoffer, the Pirates' infield stormed toward the plate. Third baseman Denny Lyons grabbed the umpire and shook him while Connie Mack and the other players berated him.

It was customary for the home plate umpire to use the mask of the catcher whose team was at bat. When the inning ended, Mack's catcher, Joe Sugden, started to hand his mask to Weidman. Mack ran out and snatched it out of the umpire's hands and carried it back to the bench while the crowd booed and hissed him. Baltimore catcher Wilbert Robinson provided the ump with a mask so the game could continue.

"This childish act was not characteristic of Connie Mack," the *Sun* commented. But it was. His temperament had not cooled completely. When it came to base-tossing and cap-kicking tantrums, once in a while he could still throw one with the best of them.

After a 5-7 eastern trip, the Pirates were only 4½ games out of first place but had slipped to seventh in the tight race. "Connie brought back with him that cunning smile and a carpetbag full of confidence and good cheer," the *Pittsburgh Press* noted. "He had no kick to make other than that the club had been up against some hard luck. He was honest enough to admit that on one or two occasions bad playing had something to do with the losses."

But the patrons were no longer laying off the manager. "The Pittsburgh team is at present in very bad odor among certain people in Pittsburgh," wrote J. H. Gruber in the *Post*, "especially among the gamblers. The 'knockers,' a term applied to those who blindly and ignorantly strike at the team, have their innings good and hard at present, but they are in the dark and blaze away without consideration. In seeking for a scapegoat they turn upon manager Mack. Of course where a team is successful a manager comes in for a large share of credit. Quite naturally, when a team loses, the manager is bound to take his share of the blame. How Mack can be blamed for losing six games last week is not very clear."

Mack was doing all he could, on and off the field, to help the team with his glove, bat, and head. He filled in at first base adeptly and caught occasionally. On July 3 his quick thinking led to a run. In the top of the eighth inning, the Reds had a man on first and Dummy Hoy at bat. As the runner headed for second, Hoy, thinking he would be thrown out, jumped in front of the catcher. He was called out for interference, but the runner was allowed to remain at second. (The rules did not require the runner to return to first.)

In the last of the eighth, the Pirates had Beckley on first. Mack was up.

Trying to sacrifice him to second, Mack fouled off two bunts. He then flashed Beckley the steal sign, jumped in front of the Reds' catcher, and walked off the field. He was out for interference, but it was as good as a sacrifice. Beckley was on second and scored the sixth run in the 6–3 win.

Off the field Mack looked for a second baseman to replace the injured Lou Bierbauer. More than a gloveman, he wanted somebody who could spark the team. He brought back some players he had farmed out, but they all proved to be wet flints. He scrambled to make deals wherever he could. One of those deals lit a fire, but not the kind Mack had in mind.

First he picked up second baseman Harry Truby from Chicago. Truby was a dud with the glove and the bat. On July 15 he made a deal with Al Buckenberger, now managing Toronto, trading Truby for twenty-five-year-old Dick Padden, who was hitting .275 but had never played in the majors. Mack knew Padden's reputation as a smart, quick, take-charge infielder with solid baseball instincts. From his first day on the scene other managers noticed how Padden picked up the entire infield. They congratulated Mack on his acquisition.

But Captain Kerr, who had not been consulted, was not impressed. Padden started out 4 for 18, then went 0 for the remaining 4 games of a home stand. When his horse collar grew to 0 for 21 in Chicago, Mack received a telegram from Kerr: "Do you consider the player you got as good as the one you gave up?"

Mack was infuriated. He considered the questioning of his trades as outright interference. It rankled him to have his baseball judgment second-guessed by a coffee roaster. He walked to the telegraph office and fired off a terse wire: "I told you so." Kerr would know what he meant.

When he cooled off, he realized he had made a mistake. The club president had every right to ask questions. But it was too late. Relations between the manager and president became frosty.

It's unknown if Mack said anything to Padden, but the second baseman immediately got hot, making 7 hits in his next 12 at bats.

Meanwhile Jake Beckley was in a slump. The twenty-nine-year-old first baseman, the team's most popular player, was batting only .253, fifty points below normal for him. Mack benched him for a while in July, playing first base himself. He assured Beckley that it was only temporary. At the same time, the upstairs experts were at work. One of the writers who had Kerr's ear persuaded the club president to get rid of Beckley before his hitting fell off so much that the club would get little in return for him. Without informing Mack, Kerr traded Beckley to the Giants for first baseman–out-fielder Harry Davis. New York sources said the Giants sweetened the deal with $1,000 cash, which seems likely, considering that Beckley was a career .300 hitter for nine years with the Pirates and Davis was a rookie.

The Giants were at Exposition Park for a doubleheader on Saturday, July 25. The first game was in the third inning when Mack was notified of the trade. When the inning ended, the six thousand spectators watched in confusion as Mack ran out on the field and met Davis coming in from left field. The two spoke briefly. Mack informed him of the trade, then returned to the bench, where he informed Beckley. The angry first base-man stormed into the dressing room, tore off his uniform, and changed into street clothes. Mack picked up a glove and went out to play first base.

The trade was then announced to the crowd. When Davis next came to bat for the Giants, he received a round of applause from the fans. (Davis has been credited, incorrectly, with being the first player to be traded during a doubleheader and play for both teams on the same day. Davis played both games for New York that day, then left for Chicago with his new team.)

Mack told reporters he had nothing to do with making the trade. He remained silent when people yelled at him from their windows, "Why did you trade Jake Beckley?" as he walked home from Exposition Park. Beckley, who played his way into the Hall of Fame during the next ten years in Cincinnati and St. Louis, made no bones about his displeasure at being uprooted from his home in Pittsburgh. He was no angrier over the deal than Connie Mack, who felt betrayed but should not have been surprised. He had seen Al Buckenberger and other managers treated the same way. Kerr may have been peeved at Mack for vetoing an earlier trade that would have brought second baseman John O'Brien from Louisville. He may have considered Mack's tele-gram impertinent and wanted to show him who was boss.

The bright side of the whole episode was that it introduced Mack to Harry Davis, one of the smartest players he would ever know. Davis became an immediate favorite with Pirates fans for his spectacular catches in the outfield and nimble handling of ground balls and wild throws when he played first base, though he batted only .190 in 44 games.

Connie Mack's disposition frayed as the season went along. On September 5 in New York, the express man bringing the bats was arrested for blocking a street. Mack learned about it two hours before game time. It was too late to hunt up the lost bag of bats, so Mack went out and bought a dozen new ones. Then the game was rained out.

Feeling peckish, he began refusing to name his next day's pitcher after each game, even though Killen, Hawley, and Charlie Hastings were the only ones starting regularly. Between injuries and poor play, by mid-August only three regulars except for pitchers remained in the lineup from the opening day roster: Patsy Donovan, Bones Ely, and Denny Lyons.

The newspapers generally continued to support Mack, but Kerr and some of his directors no longer shared their enthusiasm. Had they not held such great expectations in the spring, the looming sixth-place finish might not have been so disappointing. A more chilling factor was the prospect of a financial loss for the season.

Leaks from discontented directors reached the papers, prompting the *Press* to write a lengthy defense of the manager on September 17:

> The complaint has been made that manager Mack has been too lenient with his players. But this generally comes from those with little knowledge of the inside affairs of others' clubs, and who see visiting players only upon the diamond. Others in position to know can testify to the fact that Mack's men had a wholesome respect for his orders and the instances in which they were violated were remarkably scarce in comparison to other clubs. Another argument is that the best managers are those disliked by their players. This theory has been knocked out repeatedly. . . . Manager Mack understands the finer points of the game and more of these have been worked than ever before. When Mack took hold of the team, Donovan and Smith were supposed to be the only men who could bunt. Now every member of the club is likely to tap the ball gently. The club would never have reached the first division but for this teamwork.

Connie Mack was not surprised when Kerr called him into the office on Monday, September 21, and told him the club had decided to change managers. He turned down an offer to remain as a player-coach.

There are conflicting versions, some by Mack himself over the years, of whether he jumped or was pushed. It may be that he had anticipated a push and prepared a net to jump into. More than forty years later he confided to *Philadelphia Daily News* columnist Bob Paul that being fired "sort of jolted me. . . . It took a long time to forget how I felt when notified I was through."

Yet Mack had been negotiating for some time with a minor league club, Milwaukee of the Western League. The Pirates' official announcement of the change said that Mack had resigned to accept the management of the Milwaukee club. Mack admitted, "Several weeks ago the Milwaukee club wrote me to ask my terms to manage that team next season. I forwarded the terms and received word they would no doubt be accepted as soon as the president of the club returned from Europe. I received a telegram yesterday that my terms were satisfactory, so I accepted the offer."

It's likely that Ban Johnson, the ambitious, autocratic president of the Western League, was aware of Mack's problems in Pittsburgh and instigated Milwaukee's overtures. Mack had conferred with Johnson in the latter's office in Chicago when the Pirates were there right after the Beckley trade. Johnson told him the Milwaukee club was interested in him and assured him that the owners would give him a free hand to run the team as he saw fit. Mack said he wanted an ownership interest in the team. Johnson saw that as no obstacle.

Patsy Donovan replaced Mack, who laid no blame for his departure on the players and urged them to give Donovan their full support. While the team headed for St. Louis to close the season, Mack went to Chicago, where he met Henry Killilea at the Great Northern Hotel on the morning of September 23. A fellow Irishman, Killilea stood five-foot-ten and was a stocky, soft-spoken man with a full brush mustache. He and his brother and law partner, Matthew, controlled the Milwaukee club. The two men took an immediate liking to each other. Discussing the Milwaukee players, Mack suggested that some of them might do better in different positions from where they were playing, which surprised Killilea. "He knew each man's capabilities far better than I did," Killilea told reporters on his return home.

Mack assured Killilea that he was in good shape to share the catching chores. They agreed on a $3,000 salary and 25 percent ownership in the club. Killilea went back to Milwaukee, and Mack went to St. Louis to watch the final game of the season and wish his old team well. The players' respect for Mack was expressed when a group of them went to a jewelry store and bought a watch charm, which they presented to him at an exhibition game scheduled the day after the season ended.

Connie Mack was highly regarded around the National League and could have had another major league managing job. Half the clubs in the league would hire new managers for the 1897 season. A year later he was visiting in Pittsburgh and called in at the Pirates' office. Kerr greeted him warmly and admitted that he had made a mistake in letting Mack get away.

But Connie Mack considered himself a failure as a manager. He had been unable to control his men or his temper to his own satisfaction. As a player, he might shake his head in disgust or bewilderment at the self-destructive nocturnal habits of his teammates, but they had not been his responsibility. Now they were, and his attempts to change them had not worked, despite what friendly reporters said about his "gentlemanly" players. Tact and diplomacy did not come easily to him. His knockers among the club's directors drove him to a snappishness that those who later portrayed him as the saintly icon of baseball would have called "uncharacteristic." On the contrary, this was a basic part of his character that, tempered and less frequently displayed as the years passed, could still erupt in the form of scathing sarcasm or fury.

He was like fine wine: sharp in youth, mellowing with age, never losing piquancy.

At thirty-three, Connie Mack had reached half the life expectancy of white males his age. He was no longer young for baseball or any other occupation. But he didn't consider going to the minor leagues as a step backward in his career. He always took a long-range view and believed he needed the experience.

"I went to the minors on my own volition," he told writer Henry Beach Needham fifteen years later. "I wanted to learn how to handle men."

When Henry Killilea hired Connie Mack to manage the Milwaukee Brewers, he said, "You're in charge. Handle the club as if it belonged to you. Engage the players you think will strengthen the team without consulting me or any directors of the club."

After his experience in Pittsburgh, Mack would have been justified in feeling skeptical about these soothing words. This time they proved to be true.

When the 1896 National League season ended, Mack took a group of major leaguers, including some of the Pirates, barnstorming through Ohio. In Cambridge a semipro pitcher named Jack Taylor held them to three hits. Mack offered him a contract. According to a Pittsburgh writer, Taylor, twenty-two, was unaware that Mack was no longer the Pirates' manager. He signed what he thought was a Pittsburgh contract. When they parted, Mack said, "I'll look for you in Milwaukee about April 20."

"Milwaukee?" said the surprised Taylor.

Mack explained the situation to Taylor's satisfaction.

Back in East Brookfield he wrote letters to minor league free agents and National League teams who might have some surplus players. He followed up on every tip he received and every item he read in *Sporting Life* or New England newspapers citing some outstanding amateur prospect.

His sons, Roy and Earle, now nine and six, went to the same grammar school he had attended. Mack was there to celebrate Marguerite's fourth birthday in November and Earle's on February 1. These were big events. Mary Mack baked fancy cakes and invited their friends to the parties. Mack left the disciplining of his children to his mother, who ruled with a firm but kind hand and tried to keep them out of trouble.

"She never judged a person wrong in her life," Lieb quoted her grandson Earle. "When I was a kid I used to like to bring some of the gang home for dinner, maybe five or six of them. It always was all right with Grandmom. She used to sit and talk with us, but maybe two or three days later she would say, 'Earle, I wouldn't waste too much time on that one,' or, 'Earle, so-and-so is a mighty nice boy; he'll make a wonderful friend.' And every time she had them exactly right."

Mack's brother Dennis lived on the other side of town. He, more than any of them, had inherited their father's thirst. For the rest of his life he invested most of his income in liquid assets. When his wife Annie bemoaned her lot to her family, the Monahans told her simply, "You made your bed, now lie in it." And she did, with a capacity to endure misery that was rooted in a thousand years of Irish tears.

To help her financially, Mary Mack paid Annie to do her family's laundry. Annie, a solid five-foot-two and 160 pounds, scrubbed and ironed while raising her three children, who would soon number four and eventually six. Her eight-year-old daughter Hazel and Hazel's little brother Harold had the chore of carrying the wash basket up and down Main Street between the two houses, past the inquisitive eyes and wagging tongues of the whole town. The humiliation seared Hazel with a lifelong hatred of the place.

Roy and Earle played with their cousin Harold, swimming in the lakes and ponds that were rapidly becoming polluted by the surrounding factories and mills.

Connie Mack left for Milwaukee in early February and took up residence at the Republican House Hotel on the corner of North Third and West Cedar (now Kilbourn Street), two blocks from the Milwaukee River. Built in 1886 by Charles Kletzsch, who managed the bustling enterprise with his wife and four children, the four-story hotel featured ornate towers, balconies, fire escapes, and the extravagant gingerbread ornamentation of the Victorian era. One of the sons designed and installed the latest in-house electric lighting plant.

The ground floor public rooms included a plush, elegant ladies' parlor and a dining room and bar finished in dark wood paneling. Mrs. Kletzsch's German cooking drew many of the city's most prosperous burghers to the premises for her fifty-cent multicourse lunches and more elaborate dinners.

During his four years in Milwaukee, Connie Mack occupied room 183, which a visitor once described as containing "baseball lore and correspondence to a sufficient extent to fill a city library."

From the benches in front of the Republican House, where Mack often sat on a summer's evening, he could see Usinger's sausage factory up the block on Third Street and the City Hall with its greened copper bell tower roof. The bell that rang every hour is still in use today, though it no longer peals hourly. Whenever he appeared on a bench or in the hotel lobby, Mack attracted writers, fans, and players. As if holding court, he told stories, discussed inside baseball, and answered questions with unfailing courtesy and patience. But he refused all invitations to accompany his audience to the bar, partly because he agreed with Ban Johnson's belief that baseball was vulnerable to fans' perceptions. Be seen in a saloon one night, make an error on the field the next day, and you were pegged as a drunkard. There were more than enough players and managers who merited that label without anyone else innocently acquiring it.

One evening Mack was asked, "Are games ever thrown or sold? The home clubs seem to win most of the games. Is there an agreement to let the home club win?"

Mack said, "I know people have been inclined to believe such a theory this year, and in fact I believe that such a thing could have been done in years past, for financial reasons. But of course it is ridiculous to think that such a plan could be carried out. Supposing that the managers of two teams should stipulate that a game was to go to a certain one of the teams. The managers cannot win nor lose a game. That lies entirely with the players. Should we try to force the players into such a trickery, we would soon lose their respect and our authority over them as a manager, and baseball parks would become more degraded than a gambling dive."

"Don't you think that Baltimore threw games last year?" he was asked.

"No. Baltimore won every game it was possible to win. No professional ball team in any of the major leagues has ever sold a game. It would not be to their advantage to do so for the reason I have given."

Mack's baseball travels had never taken him to Milwaukee. The city had spent only one year, 1878, in the National League. It had hosted a nomadic club for two weeks in the short-lived Union Association in 1884 and pinch hit as a late-season replacement for the defunct Cincinnati club in the mortally ill American Association in 1891. Otherwise it had been represented in various minor leagues that operated beyond Mack's circles.

In Milwaukee he found a city not only strange to him but to the rest of the United States as well. Mack's Yankee youth had taken place in an environment predominantly Irish and French Canadian. Labeled the most foreign city in the country, Milwaukee's population, growing rapidly toward three hundred thousand, was almost 75 percent German. The rest were primarily Polish and Irish. There were fewer than one thousand black residents. At one time the city printed more German newspapers than English. The German newspapers had problems translating some of the game's idioms. Home plate was "Schlagger's stand," and the battery consisted of "Schleuderer und Fanger." The ethnic makeup of the city was reflected in its signs and advertisements: Meiselbach, Streisgutt, Zimmerman, Pabst, Schlitz.

Milwaukee's nickname of Cream City, by some accounts, came not from the abundant foam on the heads in the beer steins but from the cream-colored bricks made and used extensively in the city. It was a quiet city of artisans and home owners who, one booster boasted, "can find more comfort and enjoyment than in most major cities." By the mid-1890s breweries had surpassed meatpacking and tanning as the city's leading industry. In 1891 Pabst opened a pipeline from its cellar to its bottling operation, a project that required congressional approval. Pabst now exported one million barrels a year. The working man's social life and much of the city's business was conducted around the many beer taps. Beer money underwrote many of the city's cultural attractions, from beer gardens and theaters to public parks and the zoo. When the Stadt Theater dared to introduce English plays into its repertory, Fred Pabst built his own grandiose showplace, featuring electric chandeliers and a rooftop air-conditioning system, exclusively for German-language productions. Pabst also built a lakefront resort in Whitefish Bay, about eight miles north of downtown, which could be reached by bicycle, horse and buggy, or the *Bloomer Girl*, an excursion steamer on Lake Michigan. In 1888 the baseball team had been called the Schnits—short beers.

Mack had his choice of two trolley lines, which would take him for five cents to the ball grounds at Sixteenth and Lloyd Streets, or he could walk the mile and a half, an easy outing for his fast-paced long strides.

Located in a residential neighborhood, the Lloyd Street grounds had been built by the Killilea brothers in 1894. The pavilion was a handsome one-tier structure with rooftop press facilities. The long team benches, resembling park benches with slatted backs, sat about halfway between the grandstands and the foul lines in a vast expanse of foul territory. The bleachers were Balkanized. The Irish congregated back of first base and cheered enthusiastically whenever a fellow Hibernian came to bat. They reveled in having one of their own as the team's new manager. The Germans, wearing stovepipe hats and carrying large canes and umbrellas, sat behind third base and cheered for their landsmen. When the five-cent scorecards, which were printed in German and English, misspelled the name of the St. Paul manager, whose father was a County Cavan man, as Comiski, he drew cheers from the Poles in the bleachers while the Irish remained silent.

Connie Mack liked the city and the men with whom he was associated. Like Mack, Henry Killilea and his brother Matthew were sons of Irish immigrants. They were highly regarded corporate and criminal lawyers, leaders in the local Democratic Party. Henry was married; Matthew was single. A third major stockholder, meatpacker Fred C. Gross, was equally amicable.

Mack quickly discovered that when Henry Killilea assured him that he would be in charge of "everything," he meant everything. Mack was the field manager, business manager, general manager, scout, traveling secretary, public relations director, and purchasing agent. He negotiated all salaries and signed all contracts. He made the hotel and railroad arrangements, booked exhibition games before and during the season, collected the visitors' share of the gate on the road, and paid it out at home. He did all the buying and paid all the bills. He even had to choose the design for the new uniforms, spending almost as much time examining swatches of cloth from light green to black as anything else. It took him two months to decide on light gray road uniforms with black caps, belts, and stockings, and whites with blue trim for home use. He ordered fourteen of each. He drew the line at selling the scorecards and beer. Having met Harry Stevens in Pittsburgh, Mack asked him to come to Milwaukee and handle the concessions. Stevens sent his sixteen-year-old son Frank instead. He told Frank, "If you need any advice about anything, go to Connie Mack."

"I did," Frank said, "and never went wrong following the sound counsel Connie gave me."

Although he sometimes complained about the workload, Mack was learning every phase of operating a baseball team. It was a priceless education. "Countless problems arose and I taught myself how to meet them," he said. "It was a training that stood me in good stead when I organized the Athletics in Philadelphia a few years later. I have always figured that my decision to go to Milwaukee following my release in Pittsburgh was one of the best moves I ever made."

The Cream City club needed some positive public relations. The 1896 season had ended in chaos. On September 3 the Grand Rapids Gold Bugs failed to show up for a game at Milwaukee. When the gong sounded at 3:45 for the first batsman to take his place at the plate, nobody stood in. The pitcher threw three strikes, the umpire forfeited the game, and the disgusted customers went home.

The two teams were scheduled to play the next afternoon too. In the morning the large white flag with a patch of red in the center, signifying that a game was to be played that afternoon, flew from a staff atop the dome of the Pabst Building. But the Gold Bugs still hadn't arrived. About a hundred people had gathered at the Lloyd Street grounds by three-thirty. They found the gates padlocked. No players or club officials were in sight. The dispirited fans wandered away muttering and griping. Among them was a sportswriter for the *Milwaukee Sentinel*. Deprived of a few restful hours at the ball game, he returned to his office and wrote, "Experience of the past two days indicated a lack of system and a screw loose in the official makeup of the Brewers which cannot be remedied too soon, if the management expects to continue business at the old stand at a profit."

The club reported a loss of $2,500 for the year, in which they finished sixth, 16 games under .500. A bitter and unsuccessful strike in May by transit workers seeking a one-cent raise (to twenty cents an hour) was given as one cause of the red ink. Competition from foot races was cited as another factor. "But," concluded the *Milwaukee Journal*, "the truth is the fans became disgusted early in the season and remained that way most of the time since."

The Killilea brothers were counting on Connie Mack to restore the team's fortunes on the field and the good will of the baseball-crazy burghers.

Shortly after he arrived in Milwaukee, Mack was asked whether he had made any arrangements to take advantage of his Pittsburgh connections to obtain players on loan from the Pirates. The Western League constitution prohibited any team from accepting players farmed out from the National League unless the team kept the player for the entire season. The disruptive major league practice of recalling star players in midseason at its own discretion had long been a source of complaints by minor league operators. John T. Brush, who owned both the Cincinnati Reds and the Indianapolis club in the Western League, was notorious for shuffling players back and forth between his clubs, inspiring *Sporting Life* to call his teams "Cincinnapolis."

Mack, described as "a bitter opponent of the farming system," answered,

"President Kerr is in favor of such a plan, but I propose to have an honest team. Farming practice may be a good thing for some minor league clubs, but the National League manager usually gets the best of the minor pilot."

In the mornings after breakfast Mack wrote letters to prospects and veterans. He contacted National League teams, hoping for a first crack at their castoffs. Mack retained impressions of everybody he had played with or against during his thirteen years in professional baseball. He had formed definite opinions of players who might help him win and indefinite ideas of how he might reform those who partook too freely of the flowing bowl. Every day's mail brought requests for tryouts from sandlot players throughout Wisconsin. He rounded up more players than he could possibly use, intending to sort them out in the spring. He also heard from some of the 1896 Brewers, assuring him of their diligent conditioning activities. He seemed to be dickering for or actually signing enough men to field two or three clubs.

One player he enticed to leave his Kansas farm was Farmer Weaver, the man whose bat he had tipped once too often and earned a retaliatory crack on the wrist for it.

His correspondence done, he worked on creating new plays. "He has struck upon an excellent method of figuring out plays which is comparatively new," the *Journal* reported. "It consists of the use of cards. . . . Mack has been able to invent a number of deceiving tricks with which to fool the Brewers' opponents during the coming season."

How the cards entered into it was not explained. One of the new plays was a pick-off move with runners on second and third. The catcher would whip the ball to third; the third baseman would pay no attention to the runner there but quickly relay the ball to second, hoping to catch the runner off guard and too far off the bag.

In the evenings Mack enjoyed a full social life. He had his choice of entertainment in the lively theater district a block away at Third and Wells, from two-a-day vaudeville at the Alhambra to *King Lear* at the Davidson. The Academy of Music and Gaiety also presented plays in English. Mack bowled with a group calling itself the Quills. An ardent boxing fan, he was keenly interested in the upcoming championship bout between Gentleman Jim Corbett and Bob Fitzsimmons in Carson City, Nevada.

"If the fight lasts over 20 rounds," Mack predicted, "Corbett will be a sure winner. Corbett's tactics are to wear the man out gradually and if Fitz does anything, he will have to get in his work during the early stages of the game. However, I do not think that Fitzsimmons will be able to get a better decision than a draw under any circumstances. Jim knows what he is doing and would not enter a fight to lose."

Mack's ability to size up ballplayers was a little sharper; Fitzsimmons knocked out Corbett in the fourteenth round. We don't know if Mack put any money where his mouth was.

Given the battling factions in the National League—a "big five" of Boston, Brooklyn, Chicago, New York, and Philadelphia and a "little seven" of the rest—and the erratic administration of the league, disputes over the status of players were inevitable.

Mack hadn't been in Milwaukee two weeks when he created a sensation by announcing that he had paid about $1,000 for the contract of Duke Esper, a twenty-eight-year-old southpaw who had been 14-5 for the champion Baltimore Orioles.

"Even Connie Mack himself says he cannot understand how he managed to get Esper from Baltimore," reported the *Journal*. But the mystery of why Ned Hanlon would let Esper go or why the other National League clubs would waive any claim to him, as Hanlon assured Mack was the case, was of little interest to Cream City cranks. As far as they were concerned, Connie Mack was "big league," willing to spend what it took to give them a winning team.

Duke Esper never pitched for the Brewers. St. Louis declared it had claimed Esper on waivers. Mack discounted the announcement, displaying for writers a telegram he had received from Hanlon on February 16: "Have notified [NL president] Nick Young Esper released to Milwaukee."

However, two weeks later Young announced that Esper had signed with St. Louis, causing the *Pittsburgh Press* to comment, "President Young will have difficulty explaining why Esper belonged to Milwaukee on February 16 and St. Louis on February 28."

Young had no difficulty explaining it; he didn't bother. Hanlon returned Mack's check with a letter that offered no explanation.

"The loss of Esper," said the *Journal*, "well illustrates the great advantage the major league clubs have over the minor league teams."

Mack had other nettlesome negotiations. He traded third baseman Fred Hartman—the same Fred Hartman he'd had and didn't like at Pittsburgh—to the Browns for infielder Bert Myers. A clubhouse lawyer at twenty-two, Myers first claimed the deal was irregular. He tried to interest Washington in signing him, then held out for $1,500. Mack's highest offer was $1,200. For weeks Mack sent Myers contracts and instructions to meet the club in St. Louis in early April. Myers returned them unopened.

Refuting the romantic myth that the old time players played "for the love of the game, even if they had to pay their way in," Myers told the *Journal*, "It's a business with me, and I'm only asking what's due me."

Mack stopped wasting postage on Myers, who eventually accepted the reality that his hide belonged to Milwaukee, even if his heart didn't, and he had to play there or nowhere. He signed on Mack's terms. Disgruntled by being stuck in the minors, on the field he appeared to be going through the motions and "moves around like an alderman," said the *Journal*. Myers hit the bottle more than the ball. Mack tolerated it, fining and suspending him whenever he needed drying out. Then the repentant third baseman played well until he fell off the wagon again. Mack was still learning how long to be patient and when to give up.

Another headache for Mack concerned last year's center fielder, George Nicol. The speedy Nicol was popular in Milwaukee. He had been drafted after the 1896 season by Philadelphia, which immediately transferred him outright to Detroit in the Western League. When pressed for an explanation, Phillies president A. J. Reach admitted that he had drafted Nicol at the request and for the benefit of the Detroit club. Detroit president Vanderbeck denied the story, calling Reach "an old grandmother. He did me up to the queen's taster. It was at his suggestion that Nicol was drafted, not mine."

Nick Young said it was a common practice and not against the rules but conceded that it was not right to draft a player from one club and lend him to another in the same league. An arbitration board agreed and returned Nicol to Milwaukee.

One prospect who got away was Louis Sockalexis, a Penobscot Indian from Maine, who was attending Holy Cross College in Worcester. One of Mack's friends persuaded Sockalexis to play for Milwaukee, but Cleveland manager Pat Tebeau offered him a bonus and he signed with the Spiders.

At 7 a.m. on Wednesday, March 31, Mack arrived at Union Station. He and three players boarded a train for St. Louis, where the other players were to meet them. Hoping to play a practice game every day from April 2 to opening day, Mack had scheduled games against the Browns, Louisville, the black Chicago Unions and Page Fence Giants, and college and minor league teams. He worked out with the players, taking all the sprints, shagging flies in the outfield, and playing first base. He exercised his voice and practiced his razzing routines in the third base coaching box.

His first financial crisis occurred when most of the players showed up broke. Their salaries didn't begin until April 15, and the first payday wasn't until a month after that. Mack had to advance them money for ten-cent cigars and other necessities.

After a spell of rain, a warm, clear day greeted the season opener at Minneapolis. Nearly four thousand Milwaukeeans enjoyed a train excursion across the state, only to see the Brewers lose, 8–6. Two days later they lost their home opener, 11–4, to Minneapolis before ten thousand fans. (All attendance figures were based on estimates, there being no turnstile counts reported.)

To replace the lost Duke Esper, Mack signed Arthur "Dad" Clarkson. The thirty-year-old right-hander had pitched for the Browns and Orioles when Mack was in Pittsburgh. Dressed more like a banker than a ballplayer, Clarkson joined Mack for walks from the hotel to the ballpark. The two men in conservative three-piece suits would never have been taken for the baseball "tramps and loafers" denounced by blue-nosed preachers. Unfortunately, beneath the businessman's garb, Clarkson fit the preachers' concept of ballplayers. He never got into playing shape and was inconsistent except in his drinking. In a 5–2 loss to Indianapolis, the *Journal* said, he "grew weary of trotting terra firma in the seventh inning and took a balloon ascension of such an altitude that when he redescended four of the Farmers had crossed home plate."

Mack released him in mid-June.

Looking for pitching help, he took a train to Chicago and persuaded Colts manager Cap Anson to declare William "Adonis" Terry surplus. It cost him $1,000 and proved to be a bargain. Terry, the handsomest man in baseball, had won 20 games as a nineteen-year-old rookie with Brooklyn in the American Association in 1884. Mack had caught him for two years in Pittsburgh. Terry was Mack's last "drinking buddy," to stretch that term as far as possible: the last drop of beer Mack could recall downing was when he had drained a glass with his good-looking battery mate one night in Pittsburgh.

Terry became an instant winner and crowd favorite. Whenever the ex–big leaguers Terry and Mack were announced as being "in the points" for a game, the Cream City fans overflowed the stands and lined the outfield. As he piled up the victories, other teams in the league, anticipating that Chicago would recall him, issued a reminder that under the anti-farming rules, if Terry was recalled, all of his wins would be forfeited. Mack knew the rules. He had made sure that Terry belonged outright to the Brewers.

It's difficult for latter-day fans and historians to envision Connie Mack as anything but the tall, lean, eighty-something-year-old in the straw hat, high collar, and blue suit sitting in the dugout waving a scorecard. But in Milwaukee Mack was even more of a firebrand than he had been in Pittsburgh. He found the Western League umpiring even worse than it was in the National League, and he let them know it. The writers commended his umpire-jousting, and the fans loved it. They cheered his loud, animated coaching and were disappointed when he stayed on the bench, where, during tense moments in the action, he perched motionless on the edge, bent forward at a 45-degree angle.

Mack's belligerence began on opening day. The umpire, Daniel Lally, stopped the game several times to consult the rule book and reversed his decisions after one side or the other called him down. The *Journal* commented, "The feature of the contest was Mack's determination to dispute every point in regard to which there was the least doubt or unfairness. Heretofore, Milwaukee's managers have abided by unjust decisions by the umpire, but with Mack at the helm there will be no danger of the umpire overriding the Brewers."

In a game in May, the umpire ordered Mack off the coaching line because he had "crossed the line" in his comments. Mack refused to go. The ump drew his watch and gave Mack formal warning to scram. Mack ambled, smiling, to the bench.

One day, with Frank Graves umpiring, Mack was disgusted by the ball and strike calls from the first pitch. "What's the use of having a pitcher in the game?" he hollered. Graves suggested he would put Mack in the grandstand if he didn't shut up.

He was no calmer in exhibition games. He took the Brewers upstate to Manitowoc to play a local team. The locals were leading, 4–3, in the eighth inning, when Mack took such exception to the umpire's calls that he took his team off the field and went home.

He continued to be out in front of everybody else when it came to knowing the rules. On April 25 a Minneapolis base runner tried to steal second. The catcher's throw hit umpire Charles Reilly, who called the runner safe at second. Mack argued that the rules required the runner to return to first. When he lost his beef and the game, he protested. The league upheld his protest and ordered the game replayed.

"It is very seldom that one can get ahead of the ex-Pittsburgh player on baseball law," the *Journal* commented.

Mack's stubbornness also cost them an occasional game. When an umpire threw Bert Myers out of a game for arguing a close call at first base, Mack refused to let Myers leave the field. The ump forfeited the game.

Ban Johnson never stopped trying to improve his umpiring staff, just as Mack never stopped trying to improve his lineup. Although Johnson vowed to back his umpires, he wanted them to deserve his backing. By the end of the season he would go through thirty of them, an astounding number considering that he needed no more than four on any day.

Meanwhile, Mack seemed to claim every player who became available, coaxing some from National League clubs "on loan" for the rest of the season and farming out or releasing those who disappointed him. *Sporting Life* observed, "Connie Mack has his eagle eyes open all the time. Not a player is ever released by the National or Western clubs but that Milwaukee claims him."

One of his best pickups was Bill Reidy, a twenty-three-old right-hander cut loose in mid-June by Grand Rapids. Reidy won 16 for him the rest of the season.

Mack caught, played first base, and pinch hit. As a catcher, he was still as tough as the boot leather he had cut as a teenager. In a game at Kansas City, the home team, trailing 8–6, had 2 men on base in the top of the ninth. The batter hit a fly ball to left that fell beyond Weaver's reach. Weaver picked it up and threw to the shortstop, who wheeled and relayed it home to Mack. One run scored, but as the second base runner rounded third, the Cowboys' coach ran ahead of him and plowed into Mack, preventing him from making the tag. (There was no rule prohibiting the coach from running interference like a football blocker, as long as he stayed outside the foul line.) The score was now 8–8.

In the bottom of the ninth Mack was coaching at third. With two out and George Rettger on first, George Nicol doubled. Mack waved Rettger home. The throw beat him, but Mack, running down the line ahead of Rettger, collided with the catcher, Fred Lake, knocking the ball out of his hand. Umpire Graves signaled safe. The game was over. The Kansas City crowd, which had cheered the home team's tactics, descended onto the field in a howling mob to protest Mack's identical action. The police surrounded the umpire but not before Lake nailed him with a right to the jaw that cost the catcher $100.

Playing first base on a Sunday in July, Mack came closest to hitting for the cycle, rapping out a single, double, and triple in a 7–2 win. "The old boy's limbs were as limp as the branch of a willow," waxed a writer. "His hand clutched the bat as a turtle clutches to a stick, and his eye met the sphere with as much severity as a mother's lamp focuses upon the lassie who returns from church after 12 noon. It was a great treat to the crowd to see Connie in the game, a treat that should not be withheld from the enthusiasts for an extended time."

Connie Mack was once described as "apollonian," as in calm, poised, disciplined, undemonstrative. When he wasn't giving umpires a hard time, that's the way he was with the public and his players—most of the time. So the day second baseman Tom Daly hit a three-run double in the ninth inning to pull out a 7–6 victory, the sight of Mack embracing the rotund five-foot-seven Daly on the field amazed the onlookers.

"Imagine the tall Connie hugging the aldermanic Tom," the *Journal* noted. "Must have been a pretty contrast. Mack has the reputation of being bashful about such things, but there were no women present at the park."

Connie Mack's sense of humor often had a bite to it. That side of him was better known to his closest companions than the public. Bill Reidy, having tasted a big league demitasse with the Giants in 1896, made no secret of his yearning to return to the majors. He believed he had earned it with the Brewers and let everybody know it. His teammates guyed him with excessive and insincere assurances that he would surely be the top choice of any big league club.

Mack had already begun lining up exhibition games for the following spring as they sat on the bench during a September game at Kansas City. Suddenly a handful of telegrams was handed to him. Reidy, having heard rumors that several teams were after him, stared expectantly at Mack as the manager opened the envelopes.

"Yes, they're after you," Mack said to him. "Here are dispatches from three National League clubs that want you badly."

Reidy blushed and said, "Well, I won't leave you this year, anyway."

A messenger boy appeared and handed Mack two more dispatches. Mack opened them and looked at Reidy. "They have got to give bigger money than this," he said, "or I will not let you go."

Mack stood up and walked away, leaving the discarded telegrams on the ground. Reidy eagerly picked them up and read, "Will play those games at Milwaukee—Miller" and similar messages. (Except for a two-game trial with Brooklyn in 1899, Reidy finally made it to the major leagues with Milwaukee's 1901 club in the American League, winning 16 against 20 losses.)

Wearing his promoter's hat, Mack signed prizefighter Jim Corbett to play first base on Monday, September 20, in the next to last game of the year. The former heavyweight champ was earning a few hundred dollars a game for his appearances. Wearing his own gray uniform and black-and-gray checked cap, he had 2 hits and played an errorless first base. "Corbett handles himself with the quick, jerky motions of a prizefighter, but he plays a good game both at bat and in the field," the *Journal* reported. As an enthusiastic boxing fan, Mack must have enjoyed visiting with Corbett.

The Brewers hovered around the middle of the pack throughout the season, occasionally rising to second or falling to fifth. They won 85 games and finished third, 13 games behind pennant-winning Indianapolis. Adonis Terry won 21 and lost 5. Jack Taylor was 9-6 in his rookie year. Another youngster, Bert Jones, was 11-3. Farmer Weaver gave Mack a solid year, batting .339 and doing outstanding work in the outfield. Playing in about 30 games, Mack batted .288, according to one of several disparate sources.

The season was a success in other ways. Leading by example, Mack had given Milwaukee a team the *Grand Rapids Democrat* called "the most gentlemanly lot of ballplayers seen here this season."

Thanks to Sunday baseball and the sale of beer at the grounds, the Brewers turned a profit of almost $20,000. Salaries and expenses ran just under $20,000. Gate receipts at home topped $31,000, highest in the league, and $7,000 on the road. Mack sold Bert Jones to Cleveland for $1,000. Of the $6,000 guarantee the Brewers put up with the league, half of it was returned. No more than two other clubs in the league made money. Grand Rapids was the weakest. The league had to come up with the final paychecks for the Gold Bugs.

Without turnstile counts, reported attendance estimates of about 160,000 seem reasonable. Mack reckoned that half the total had shown up at Sunday games. Beginning in midseason ladies' days had become a regular feature. A gentleman could escort an unlimited number of women into the park free. As many as 1,000 were sometimes seen among the colorful crowds, cheering as loudly as the men. There was also a noticeable increase in the number of clergymen attending the games, most of them priests in the city that was more than 50 percent Catholic.

Connie Mack's 25 percent share of the Brewers' profits, added to his $3,000 salary, gave him the highest income he had ever earned. The *Sporting News* estimate that "he was $2,000 richer than he would have been if he had remained in the big league last season" was probably low.

Conceding that it takes good players to produce a winning team, the *Journal* lauded Mack for turning the Brewers around. "All one has to do is look at what the Brewers amounted to last season with poor management and then see what they have done this year by the hard and honest efforts of a man who devoted all his time and energy to building up a team that is a winner."

But Connie Mack wasn't satisfied with his performance. He had been unable to keep his temper in check, not just with umpires, but with his own players. He had blown up over bonehead plays and mental errors in the clubhouse after games.

"I then dressed with the players," Mack told Fred Lieb, "and there were the usual arguments after we lost a tough game. And in trying to fix the blame, hot words often were spoken on both sides.

"Then one day something came up that made me real sore. I was so mad I knew I couldn't talk calmly. So I waited around until all the players had dressed and gone home. Then I changed my clothes in the solitude of the clubhouse and was alone with my thoughts. I still was hot as I went home, but when I awoke the next morning it was just another ball game we had lost. It was a bonehead play, yes, but the ballplayers are human, and it was all part of baseball."

It was a turning point for Mack. He realized that calling a player down and arguing with him in front of the rest of the team bred ill will and resentment. He knew he could not control his temper. So he vowed to never again dress with the players. When a mistake was made, he would wait until the next day and calmly discuss it with the player in private, suggesting how the play should have been made. He learned to accept the inevitability of losing 50 to 60 games in the best of seasons, some of them tough losses, some caused by bonehead plays, careless base running, or missed chances.

He would never again take losing so hard. Well, hardly ever.

15 | WORKING THE SYSTEM

Baseball didn't stop for Connie Mack when the 1897 season ended. Back in East Brookfield he put together a team of local amateurs and major leaguers and scheduled games in Worcester and Meriden, but they were rained out. He went to games in Boston and Brooklyn, making the rounds like a salesman developing a territory, asking those clubs to keep him in mind when they had players to lend or sell.

His stop in Brooklyn led to the purchase of George Schoch, his old teammate from Hartford and Washington. Cream City cranks rejoiced over the return of the thirty-nine-year-old second baseman, one of their favorites from the American Association club of 1891.

On October 21 Mack attended the Western League meeting at the Great Northern Hotel in Chicago. The league approved a salary cap of $200 a month with a team limit of $2,000 a month. To enforce it, all player contracts had to be approved by Ban Johnson.

Said Johnson, "The gentlemen who have their money invested . . . do not intend to give all the profits to the ball players. We cannot afford to pay fancy salaries. When a man can make $200 a month for five or six months he is not doing poorly. When he develops and his services are worth more than our limit, he is ready for the National League where bigger salaries are paid."

Johnson's claim that $200 a month was good money to play minor league baseball was not without merit. At the time, Texas streetcar workers were striking for a raise to twenty cents an hour. Illinois quarrymen wanted an eight-hour day and $1.25 for it. St. Louis bricklayers were debating whether to demand fifty-five cents an hour. New York cabinetmakers marched to enforce an hourly minimum wage of thirty-two cents, about $20 for a six-day, sixty-hour work week. That would put them up there with painters, printers, and carpenters from New York to California in the top income bracket of skilled workmen. Young women working as clerks in the office of a New England dye manufacturer earned three cents an hour and didn't think about striking.

Throughout the winter Mack kept Matt Killilea and the Milwaukee newspapers informed of his activities. Under the league rules, if a team filed a claim on a player—like a claim on a gold mine—nobody else could sign him. Mack reported that he had signed or claimed a catcher named Alexander Langervine, who he had seen hit 3 home runs in an amateur game; a teacher from northern Wisconsin who asked for a tryout; and a catcher from Pittsburgh.

Mack realized that baseball's financial backers preferred to rely on older, experienced players with familiar names and reputations, even if those reputations included a proficiency in elbow bending. With rosters limited to fifteen or sixteen men, there was little inclination to carry young players with an eye to the future. Investors grew nervous if it looked like the club might lose money. Few such backers had deep pockets; they blanched at the sight of red ink, like a schoolgirl's first encounter with spilled blood. Mack had witnessed the rapid collapse of the Players' League when the backers cut their losses and ran. It was still an unstable business. Franchise transfers were frequent. Leagues seldom fielded the same teams from one year to the next.

None of that stopped Mack from prospecting. It was the part of the business he enjoyed the most. Like a forty-niner, he knew he might have to sift through hundreds of green rookies to find one gold nugget. But there were plenty of them: half the population was under twenty-three years old, almost all of them on farms and in small towns in the Northeast and Midwest. His seining activity was wryly noted by one newspaper: "Mack must be getting ready to free Cuba or start another Fenian raid. He has thirty men on the Milwaukee list."

(An interesting knock on a player was supplied by the *Milwaukee Journal* when Mack announced that he had claimed Walter Lyons, star third baseman for Youngstown in the Interstate League: "[Lyons's] only fault was his inclination toward fast life, swell hotels, and opera music." The fat lady sang before Lyons ever made it to the Big Opera.)

Mack's sweeps of the Wisconsin sandlots set up a howl from managers of state league teams. One complained, "Mack has listed nearly half a hundred players for the Milwaukee team next year. He kept his eye on the teams which played in the state last summer, and when he noted a man who looked like a comer, he listed him for next season. Every one of these men is confident in his own mind that Mack will retain him and so will not sign with any of the state teams. After Mack has given them a trial there will be plenty of material let loose."

According to a *Journal* story, Connie Mack's reputation as the Pied Piper of young ballplayers caused him to be the principal suspect when a Pittsburgh mother's ball-playing son disappeared. She appealed to Pirates manager Watty Watkins, who immediately fingered Mack as the most likely kidnapper.

One day in February a Pittsburgh detective showed up at the Republican House looking for Mack, who was not there. The sleuth went up Third Street to Matt Killilea's office. Killilea pleaded ignorance but pledged that if Mack had indeed lured the boy away from home, the club would see that the lad was returned to his mother.

Returning to the hotel, the cop staked out the lobby. Three hours later Mack walked in. After introducing himself, the detective said, "You have sixty players claimed for your club, and among them is a Pittsburgh lady's son whom you have enticed to come to Milwaukee. We demand the boy at once."

The astonished Mack replied, "If I have the woman's son, I do not know it. The fact is I won't be able to tell you who I have until I have a roundup. If you can wait until that time, maybe the boy will come out in the wash."

The detective left town empty-handed. The story may be the product of a newspaperman's imagination, but it points up the start of Mack's renown as every young hopeful's best chance to obtain a tryout.

From the beginning of his career as a manager, nothing annoyed Mack as much as wrangling with holdouts. In Milwaukee he had a league-imposed salary limit to obey. In later years his own sense of the need to balance income and expenses often put him against the wall when it came to making out a payroll. It infuriated him when players took their case to the press. He believed the details of salary disputes didn't belong in the papers. But when he reached his boiling point with a player, he didn't hesitate to let the world know it.

In 1898 his most irksome case was Bert Myers, the shortstop who had balked at signing the year before. When Myers squawked at being offered less than $200 a month, Mack exploded. "I can't understand this man at all. Last year we retained him on the team at times when he was in no condition to play, paying him a big salary all year. Now Myers, who is receiving more than many men who are his superiors on the team, comes back at us with a kick. All I can say is that I will not dabble with him at all. If he does not care to sign for the amount that is offered him, he can remain [at home] in Washington."

As much as he enjoyed writing letters, Mack was irritated by the need to spend day after day writing to holdouts. He was determined to see that it didn't become an annual ordeal. He sent his most stubborn cases an ultimatum: sign by April 1 or he would make up his lineup without them.

"I have decided to bring this useless writing of letters to an end," he announced with obvious annoyance. "If I keep up this incessant dickering with the men I will have the same troublesome experience to contend with next year." If his first baseman didn't want to accept the salary offered, Mack said he'd play first base himself. He counted on improving weather to prod his holdouts into line. "A warm day gives a ball player the fever. The thought, 'I wouldn't miss playing for a hundred' runs through their minds and then they pick up the pens and sign the contracts."

The prosperous '97 season inspired the Brewers' management to expand the bleachers and enclose the rooftop press box, which had been open to fans wandering in and out during games. They were encouraged by the interest in the game that ran so high that amateur teams played indoor games on winter nights. Another optimistic indicator was the bidding for the scorecard concession. A local man, Theodore Engel, outbid Harry Stevens, paying $2,000 for the rights and proposing to print photographs of the players on the cards.

Despite all his scouting, Mack went into the 1898 season with the kind of veteran club the owners welcomed. At the end of the '97 season he had used a common maneuver to protect players from the National League draft, a persistent bone of contention between the minor and major leagues. With the cooperation of Barney Dreyfuss, owner of the Louisville Colonels, he had sold shortstop Ed Lewee and first baseman Bob Stafford to Louisville before the drafting period began, then bought them back in the spring, "a dangerous practice . . . and an evil," wrote *Sporting Life* correspondent H. H. Cohn. "What if Louisville doesn't want to return a player, once the sale is announced?" The ploy depended on a trustworthy co-conspirator. Mack trusted Dreyfuss.

Farmer Weaver was back, as was Adonis Terry, who had a full-time job as manager of Milwaukee's Plankinton House Billiard Parlor and agreed to pitch at home only.

On March 21 Mack and five players held their first practice at the Lloyd

Street grounds. He was determined to have his men in top condition by opening day. He believed the first few weeks of the season would decide the Brewers' pennant chances more than the last few weeks. His plans to play practice games in Cincinnati were knocked for a loop when the Ohio River flooded, leaving the Reds' ballpark under water.

More than Mack's spring training plans had blown up. On February 15 the American battleship *Maine* blew up in Havana harbor. By opening day the United States was rattling its swords. On April 25 it formally declared war with Spain. For the next four months the war news overshadowed interest in baseball. On some days, when Mack passed the newspaper offices on his way to the ball grounds, he saw more people reading the war bulletins posted on the windows than he would see at the game.

The war dealt a setback to all of baseball. In May the Texas and Southern Leagues folded. Despite Ban Johnson's declaration that the Western was as solid as ever, there was sentiment among some club owners to cut their losses and shorten the season. The majority voted to play out the schedule. After the season Ban Johnson said, "I firmly believe that had we quit for the year, every league outside of the National would have quit. They were all ready to suspend." And the *Chicago Tribune*, calling it a "shaky, scary season," said, "At one time last season only the pluck and nerve of two men held the league in the business." It didn't name them; there were really three of them.

To keep the league intact, Mack and Comiskey, along with Tom Manning in Kansas City, had each put up $400 to bail out the Omaha franchise, which had replaced Grand Rapids, and move it to St. Joseph, Missouri, where the league operated it from mid-July.

The Brewers didn't fulfill Mack's hopes for a fast start. They were, to put it plainly, awful. Poor pitching, sloppy base running, and weak hitting lowered them into the basement. They bounced back as high as fourth but continued to play poorly.

Connie Mack's smooth sailing with Milwaukee fans hit its first reef in mid-July. Eighth-place Minneapolis came in trailing a 13-game losing streak behind it and piled up a 12–0 lead after three innings. The fans booed Mack for allowing pitcher George Rettger to come out for the third inning after he'd given up 5 runs in the second. They grew angrier when Rettger was hammered for 7 more in the third.

Of the 14–3 loss, H. H. Cohn wrote, "The Brewers quit like a lot of dunghills, and their playing was of a bright saffron hue. . . . A careless, I-do-not-care sort of a game was put up, and some of them ought to be minus some of the long green on next pay day."

That roasting marked the low point of the season for the Brewers. They began to win and climb in the standings. Their revival and a cooling of the war news inspired a rise in attendance. With the signing of an armistice on August 12, the fans flocked back to the games. Mack had learned not to worry about fans' reactions when his team was down. Patience, not panic, was his long suit. When the Brewers went 23-8 in August and climbed to within three percentage points of league-leading Kansas City, the *Sentinel* reported, "No happier or more excited lot of fans or rooters can be found anywhere . . . than in Milwaukee."

But after shooting to the top of the standings, the Brewers dropped like a stone, finishing third, 6 games out.

Jack Taylor had won 28 and lost 13. Mack wanted $2,500 cash for him. He offered Taylor to Louisville. The Colonels' secretary, Harry Pulliam, said he didn't have the money. (Louisville picked up Deacon Phillippe from Minneapolis for $1,200 instead.) Jim Hart of the Chicago Orphans met Mack's price. Taylor won another 5 games for Chicago that year.

The troublesome Bert Myers finally made it to the National League; Mack sold him for $1,000 to Washington. It took Mack longer to collect his money than Myers lasted. Myers was released after 31 games; Mack had to appeal to an arbitration board before receiving the sale money.

Connie Mack had no quarrel with H. H. Cohn's mid-July assessment of his nonchalant crew, despite the team's late-season rally. He was becoming more disenchanted with trying to build a winner out of recycled veterans who had little incentive, knowing they would never again see the major league scene, and were indifferent to staying in shape.

One day in early August he took his team to Waupun to play a semipro team. It was a meaningless exhibition game, but it proved to be a meaningful day for Mack. During an earlier visit to Waupun, he had been impressed by a young catcher named Clarence Beaumont. When Mack saw Beaumont run, he advised the twenty-one-year-old Beloit College student to switch to the outfield. Called Ginger because of his red hair and spirited play, Beaumont was now a left-handed-hitting outfielder. That day Beaumont covered more ground than all of Mack's outfielders combined. At the plate he sprayed hits in all directions. Mack invited him to join the Brewers for an exhibition series against the Chicago Unions, then signed him.

On August 23 Beaumont took an early train from Waupun and arrived in Milwaukee at ten o'clock. That afternoon he lined a single to center in his first at bat. In the fifth he hit an inside-the-park home run that helped defeat Kansas City, 5–3, and propel the Brewers into a first place tie with the Cowboys.

Beaumont brought speed, a strong arm, and crowd-pleasing hustle to the aging Brewers. He was the fastest in the league going from home to first. In 24 games he batted .354 and stole 11 bases. More than nine thousand cranks turned out to see the last home game of the season, a Monday doubleheader against Detroit. They came to cheer Ginger Beaumont more than the third-place Brewers.

Mack's experience with Beaumont reinforced his desire to create a team of young players. If they had the talent and the brains, he could teach them how to play the game to win. He knew it would take time and patience and the right kind of material. He couldn't do it with a club whose owners wanted a contender every year and familiar faces to attract the customers. Mack likened the baseball business to that of a merchant or manufacturer. To succeed, he had to plan three or four years ahead and develop his product slowly, until it was ready to market. Unlike other businesses, he'd have to do it out in the open, on the field, game after game, season after season, until the product was perfected. Given the opportunity, that's the way he would operate his baseball business.

Baseball's first exercise in nostalgia occurred with the retirement of Cap Anson in 1898. Mack was among those who noted with sadness the end of the line for the forty-five-year-old first baseman, who had played and managed his last game for the Chicago Colts in 1897, then managed the Giants briefly in '98.

An innovative manager with strict training rules and the temper and fists to enforce them, Anson was the first to emphasize teamwork. He had gone on a round-the-world voyage to promote baseball in 1888–1889. A hundred years later Anson would be pilloried by social historians imposing their moral standards retroactively on a society they never knew for his refusal to play against any team with a black player. But to his contemporaries, including Mack, he was hailed as an outstanding pioneer of the game. "The Napoleon of the Diamond," Mack called him, fondly recalling the appearance of Anson and his mighty Colts in East Brookfield in 1883.

At their fall meeting, Western League directors spent much of the time discussing the dissension in the National League and the likelihood of an eventual breakup of the unwieldy twelve-team circuit. The National's internal squabbling, interlocking ownerships, and on-field rowdyism were drawing increasing brickbats of ink, while the Western League was frequently lauded for businesslike methods, its cooperative spirit in helping its financially ailing franchises, and improving conduct on the field. While they had suffered through a losing season—only Minneapolis and Kansas City were reported to have shown a profit—the owners were happy with the way Ban Johnson ran the league. The 10 percent of the gate receipts remitted to the league was not all spent, and the surplus was returned to the clubs. "The league is strong," Johnson told the press. "We made money and have money in the treasury. We are not the bankrupt organization some of the jealous try to make out. We had a losing season, but not half so disastrous a year as the National suffered."

The need to replace the weakest links—Columbus and St. Joe—consumed a lot of discussion, but nothing was resolved. Tom Loftus was keen on moving his Columbus club to Denver, but it was too far away. Matt Killilea tried to persuade each club to put up $500 to buy the Toronto franchise in the Eastern League and give it to Loftus. That didn't go over. If the National League dropped Cleveland, Loftus was ready to move in. Alderman Franklin in Buffalo wanted the St. Joe franchise and all the players free. Comiskey, Mack, and Manning said okay if he would just reimburse them the $1,200 they had put up to save it. Franklin said no. Mack and the others said they'd just sell some St. Joe players to recoup their investment and he could have the rest. Franklin squawked and went home. After a few months of wrangling, they reached a compromise and Buffalo was admitted to the league.

The National League stayed with twelve teams for another year, and the Western was stuck with Columbus (until it moved the franchise back to Grand Rapids in the middle of the 1899 season).

It was no secret that Ban Johnson had been itching to put a team in south Chicago for more than a year. But he was respectful of National territory and was not ready to do any invading. He was even willing to give the franchise to the NL Orphans' owner, Jim Hart. But Hart said if he had it, he would use it as a "feeder" team for his Orphans, and Johnson had had enough of that with John T. Brush and his Indianapolis-Cincinnati player shuttle. Johnson didn't give up; he remained friendly with Hart, even moving his league office to a suite on the twelfth floor of the Fisher Building, three floors from Hart's office.

The efficient operation of the Western League stood in sharp contrast to the National, with its fractious magnates and weak president. Johnson's league also stood out among most private and public institutions of the time, where corruption was rampant and paper trails impossible to follow. Even where there was honesty, there was chaos. Corporate and municipal bookkeeping was sketchy at best. The idea of operating under a budget was still unknown in every city hall in the nation.

Johnson and his Western club owners realized that their customers considered baseball to be a form of show business—entertainment and nothing more. Professional baseball had little history at that point, certainly nothing that anyone could celebrate with pride. It had no stability, no traditions, and not enough of a loyal fan base to survive without broadening its appeal to women, the social set, and those who just thought it a "lark" to be at the ball grounds of an afternoon and would never think of keeping score. They understood that these potential customers were turned off by the brawls, physical attacks on umpires, and noisy gamblers in the stands.

The path to a favorable press, which Johnson considered vital to the game's success, was paved with pieces like the following year-end plaudits in the *Sentinel*:

"When Matt Killilea stated that baseball should be conducted as honestly as any other business without treating the public to buncombe, the eastern press applauded the sentiment and remarked how much different things would be in the National League if the same rule was followed there."

That path had potholes. Connie Mack's first personal encounter with baseball writers who have their own agenda and look for something—factual or not—to substantiate it began with a September 23 headline in the *Journal*:

DID CONNIE THROW GAMES

The paper accused Mack of "jockeying" on the team's last road trip to enable Kansas City to win the pennant over Indianapolis. Citing the anonymous "many" as accusing Mack of not caring to win, the *Journal* claimed that "for some reason he threw up his hands and did not try to take it."

Connie Mack didn't bother to respond.

Winding up a scouting trip through Ohio, Mack returned to Chicago on September 27 for a meeting with the Louisville club secretary, Harry Pulliam. That night Mack sent a telegram to the *Sentinel*: "Louisville gets Waldron and Beaumont." Irv Waldron was a young outfielder who had hit .260.

Mack never used the word "sold." But the Milwaukee papers called it a sale, though with none of the usual speculation about the selling price. Louisville was in no position to be aggressively buying players anyhow. The club was one of the weakest in the National League, expecting to be dropped from the circuit. The transaction wasn't considered important enough to be mentioned in the *Louisville Courier-Journal*. The two players' names appeared only in a list of ten players "picked up" by the Colonels, only three of whom reported, the rest "not being desired until next season."

Perhaps angered by being scooped, the *Journal* scorched Mack for selling Waldron and Beaumont. Subheads screamed:

MILWAUKEE PATRONS OF THE GAME SAY WORK WAS QUEER

THEY DEMAND EXPLANATION OF HIS ACTION IN
SELLING HIS BEST PLAYERS

The story went on:

> It certainly does seem a little extraordinary for Mr. Mack to come out with a statement one day that he will have a pennant-winning team in 1899 and the next day announce the sale to Louisville of his strongest players.
>
> What will be the Brewers' finish next year? Each day seems to bring the news that one of the star players of the Milwaukee team has been sold to a National League club. Today comes the news that Beaumont and Waldron have been sold to the Louisville team. At the present outlook the Milwaukee team will be made up of such men as "Texas pony" Burke and "$50-a-month" Rath, neither man having ability enough as a ball player to be on a team such as Milwaukee deserves. The fans are waiting with expectation to hear what Mack has to offer for the coming season.

The *Journal* sent a reporter out on the street to find and interview several carefully selected "well-informed patrons of the game" to back its contentions of "a general feeling of disgust."

Mack remained mum. He didn't think it necessary to explain or defend his actions. He knew what he was doing. So did the *Sentinel*, which pointed out (correctly) that had not Beaumont and Waldron been sold, both would have "undoubtedly been drafted next Saturday when the National Leaguers will be turned loose on minor league folds to seek whom they may devour." The National League had from October 1 until January 1 to draft minor leaguers for $500. Beaumont was said to be on the draft list of at least four National clubs.

It was a common practice for minor league owners to find a cooperative National League club who would "buy" or draft a player with the understanding that the player would be returned in the spring. Mack had done similar deals with the Colonels before. The *Sentinel* hinted that this might be the case with these two players:

"The Milwaukee club undoubtedly has other outfielders selected to fill the places left vacant by the sale of Waldron and Beaumont. But until the drafting season ends January 1 no announcements will be made of Mack's selections to fill the outer garden. Manager Mack will return to Milwaukee Saturday or Sunday after he makes another trip into Ohio and Kentucky. Perhaps he will then say the players have not been sold but only loaned for the winter."

The Sporting News did more than hint. Heading the story "PROBABLY A 'PHONY' DEAL—Milwaukee Club Puts Two Players under Louisville Protection," the unnamed writer likened the deal to "the case of Stafford and Lewee last season. The two players will probably be held by the Louisville Club until the opening of next season, when they will be returned to the local management. This notion on the part of Mack is a wise move, as at least one of the players would be drafted by the major league teams."

That was true of Waldron. Louisville returned him to the Brewers the following spring. But not Beaumont. On December 2 Mack sent a telegram to the *Sentinel* from East Brookfield: "Have made a deal with Pittsburgh trading Beaumont for Gray and Hart. C. Mack"

Mack had merely "parked Beaumont" with the Colonels, the *Sentinel* surmised, while he "secretly pursued a trade for him." But did he? Maybe Mack had intended to "buy back" Beaumont as well as Waldron.

According to the *Pittsburgh Press*, Pirates manager Watty Watkins had gone to Milwaukee in the fall to confer with Kansas City manager Tom Manning about the purchase of four KC players. While there, Watkins saw Beaumont play and told his boss, W. W. Kerr, about him, and "negotiations for his purchase started at once. Mack did not want to sell but was finally forced into doing so. What induced him to do so was not made public."

If this was true, what could have "forced" Mack into selling Beaumont? A threat from Louisville to return the player to Milwaukee, where he'd be subject to the draft? Possibly. Dreyfuss was trying to sell the Louisville club and buy into the Pirates, both of which happened eventually. It could have been that Pulliam told Mack the Colonels had decided to keep Beaumont and, rather than double-cross Mack, they would give him a chance to get some players in exchange by dealing with the Pirates now. But Beaumont was ostensibly the property of Louisville; any trade would have to be between Louisville and Pittsburgh (Dreyfuss did not yet control both clubs), not Milwaukee and Pittsburgh.

However it was accomplished, the whole episode points up the haphazard and disorganized state of the paperwork and administration of "organized baseball." Mack was apparently able to reclaim Beaumont from Louisville—or Louisville simply returned him—and trade him while the drafting period was still in effect. He presumably filed some kind of paperwork to remove both players from the Milwaukee roster before October 1—or maybe not. Maybe all he needed was an eraser to take them off his roster and a pen to put them back on. Or maybe he had simply "loaned" Beaumont to Louisville. Lending players to other teams, even in your own league, was done openly.

Was anybody breaking any rules? There didn't seem to be any. In October the *Sporting News* had acknowledged that it was a common practice and suggested a rule providing that any National League team buying minor league players merely to prevent their being drafted by other NL teams should be required to offer those players to all other NL clubs for $500 before sending them back to the minors. But this was the way the baseball world operated at that time, and Connie Mack went along with it. As irregular as it seems, nobody questioned it. None of the reported four teams who had been eager to draft Beaumont raised any objections. Nobody took it to the Board of Arbitration. Nobody could, with clean hands.

Eastern writers actually praised Connie Mack for pulling off a great trade. One went so far as to call it the "best stroke of policy executed in the history of the Western League."

Bill Grey (not Gray), twenty-seven, had played every position but pitcher for the Phils and Reds before becoming the Pirates' regular third baseman in 1898. Bill Hart had broken in with Sioux City, winning 25 games in 1891, and pitched for the Dodgers, Cardinals, and Pirates. In the spring of 1898 he had been hit by a line drive that fractured his skull. He missed four months of the season. Though he never had a winning record in the big leagues, he was considered a steady, brainy pitcher who could give a team 300 innings.

Mack's moves to strengthen the Brewers were all the response he needed to the *Journal*'s attacks on him. The reaction of the Killilea brothers and their partners, aware that Mack had received offers to manage from Brooklyn and the Phillies, was to sign their popular man-of-all-jobs for another year.

Connie Mack was content in Milwaukee. Between his salary and share of the profits when there were any, he was making more money than ever in baseball. At the league meeting in October he told reporters, "I am glad to keep out of the National League. The Western pays good profits and the speed of the teams compares favorably with that exhibited by the big leaguers. The Western League is a strong organization. The teams draw large crowds and the emoluments of service are entirely satisfactory to me. What more can any reasonable man ask?"

16 | LEARNING HOW TO HANDLE MEN

Connie Mack started the 1899 season with another edition of the Brewers that was old and rarely all sober at the same time. He was still searching for the most effective way to change players' behavior. Some he gave up on sooner than others. When pitcher Danny Friend got drunk in Columbus and was arrested for cutting a cab driver with a razor, Mack suspended him and made him sign a new contract with a temperance clause. Friend didn't believe in a temperance clause any more than he did in Santa Claus. Mack peddled him to Minneapolis for $400.

The league had no uniform dress code. Players often appeared on the field in different combinations of attire from their teammates. Mack had been trying to end that practice with the Brewers. "There will be no mixing of the uniforms on the field," he vowed, and ordered all new gray and white sets with dark blue trimmings from the Alfred J. Reach Company of Philadelphia.

Mack's hopes of getting his team in condition for a strong start were again set back, this time by a typical Wisconsin spring: snow and ice in the first week of April. Bundled up in bulky sweaters, the players worked out under the grandstand as best they could. Mack was struck by how big they looked, buried under layers of heavy outerwear. That evening in the Republican House lobby he jokingly suggested the team be called the Giants. "I like the sound of Giants," he said. "But not spelled and pronounced 'Joints' the way Scrappy Bill Joyce pronounced it in New York several years ago." The *Sentinel* used the name a few times, but it didn't stick.

Once the weather thawed, the Brewers played practice games against university teams from Wisconsin, Michigan, and Chicago. Mack played first base in intrasquad games but generally sat in the shade casting an appraising eye on his men.

Ever the optimist—in his business, he had to be—on the eve of the home opener against Minneapolis he said, "The team representing Milwaukee is the best I've ever had." Then he hedged, "I may not win the pennant, but I predict the boys will be strictly in the race."

In a replay of the Duke Esper fiasco of 1897, Mack purchased catcher Pat Crisham from Brooklyn and, on opening day, received a telegram from Brooklyn manager Ned Hanlon informing him that another National League club had claimed Crisham on waivers. The team claiming Crisham turned out to be the Baltimore Orioles, whose president happened to be the same Ned Hanlon. (Hanlon was also part owner of both teams; such was the state of the National League.)

At one o'clock on Thursday, April 27, the Brewers assembled at the Republican House and walked to the St. Charles Hotel, where the visiting Minneapolis Millers stayed. Climbing into carriages, they were led by Clouder's Military Band through the downtown streets and out to the ballpark, where Ban Johnson threw out the first ball. Then a fourth–inning downpour washed out the game. That evening both teams attended a production of *Trilby*, a popular melodrama of the time. Guests of the management, they watched from boxes decorated in baseball motifs.

In an early demonstration of how far ahead of the owners the fans were, Brewers patrons successfully petitioned the club to post the scores of other league games on bulletin boards on the grounds.

A social event of great moment occurred in Milwaukee on May 18, when a man named George Odenbrett was seen driving the first automobile in the city. Connie Mack was not impressed. He was never lured by the romance of the auto and didn't yearn to get behind the steering wheel and invite admiring onlookers to "watch my dust." He didn't learn to drive until he was in his sixties, tried it a few times, didn't like it, and didn't do it anymore.

By the end of May, the Brewers were out in front with a 3-game lead over St. Paul. But the race was so tight that when they slumped in mid-June, they tumbled from first to sixth in a hurry. They were shut out seven times in nineteen games, more than all the other teams combined. Attendance fell by 30 percent. The faithful howled for Connie Mack's scalp.

Looking for help, Mack combed four leagues and every college in the area but collected more dandruff than talent. He bought British-born catcher Harry Smith from Wilkes-Barre for $800 and signed a catcher from Purdue and a pitcher from Beloit. One collegian who showed promise was pitcher

Pete Husting, a law student at the University of Wisconsin, who joined the team in June and won 9 and lost 8.

Injuries sank any lingering hopes of the Brewers' finishing in the first division. On their last western trip three pitchers were sidelined with sore arms. Mack was also preoccupied by the illness of Matt Killilea and spent many evenings by the bachelor's bedside at the Republican House. Newly elected to the state legislature, Killilea was ill most of the summer and spent a month confined to his room.

The *Milwaukee Journal* continued to hammer away at Mack, giving him his first taste of being labeled a cheapskate. They blamed the club's poor performance and financial losses on the use of cheap players. "Manager Mack is a good judge of baseball players and a good manager," it said on September 14. "But good ballplayers cost money. Poor ballplayers come cheap. Clearly false economy."

Mack did not reply.

Connie Mack made his last appearance as a player in the seventh inning of a Labor Day morning game on September 4 at Grand Rapids. When right fielder Irv Waldron became ill and left the game, Mack moved first baseman Bob Stafford to right, sent catcher Kid Speer to first, and put on the mask and went behind the plate. Catching Charlie Chech, he was charged with one passed ball and was 0 for 1 in the Brewers' 14–6 loss. In the afternoon game Mack put Chech in right field and Speer caught.

The dark cloud of another baseball war hung over the Western League and all of baseball that year. Club owners who had been through the Brotherhood uprising and the American Association competition wanted no part of another battle. Whenever they fought, they saw the reserve clause ignored with impunity, salaries soar, and public interest decline. But they plunged ahead anyhow, like tribes bent on destroying each other long after they've forgotten why. In its attempts to maintain a monopoly on major league baseball, the twelve-team National League had swallowed more than it could digest. Syndicate baseball, with magnates owning pieces of several clubs and moving players among them to strengthen one at the expense of another, added to the public's disgust with the whole business. Baltimore had been plundered by Brooklyn. Denied Sunday baseball, the Cleveland owners had ransacked the Spiders to build up their St. Louis club. Attendance plummeted.

Throughout the 1899 season *Sporting Life*'s standard heading over its Western League roundup read: "Ban Johnson's Fine League Is Flourishing."

But it wasn't. At least five teams, including Milwaukee, lost money. The Columbus franchise moved to Grand Rapids, where it had died once before.

In mid-September Ban Johnson issued a rare—for him—pessimistic opinion that the game was losing its hold on the public. The outlook was so gloomy that Detroit manager and part-owner George Stallings considered quitting the game and opening a Detroit office for a Chicago brokerage firm.

There were rumors galore. Everybody was playing franchise chess, moving clubs about like pawns in speculative stories and fishing expeditions. The Western League would break away from the National Agreement and go head to head with the National. The American Association would be revived, invading both National and Western territory, including Milwaukee. Connie Mack downplayed their chances of success, pointing out that the Cream City wouldn't support two teams, and the proposed ball grounds were so far out of town nobody would be able to find them.

With Chris von der Ahe and Al Spink in St. Louis and Baltimore manager John McGraw in the vanguard, the American Association tried to persuade first Ban Johnson, then Cap Anson, to head the proposed resurrection of the league, which had expired in 1891. Both declined.

Stories of the Western League's imminent invasion of National League territories sprang up like mushrooms in a rain forest. Reports had Johnson sending Charles Comiskey to St. Louis, Connie Mack to Pittsburgh in one account and Washington in another, and Tom Loftus to Chicago. Jimmy Manning was set to move the Kansas City Cowboys to Boston. Everything that was said by somebody was denied by somebody else. Comiskey insisted that he knew nothing about anything. Connie Mack didn't bother issuing any denials.

National League magnates viewed the rumblings out of the west with amusement. President Nick Young declared that "nobody would dare challenge the National League." Ban Johnson said the Western League had no intention of fostering a rivalry with the National. Nobody believed him. Johnson had his own agenda and everybody knew it.

Management gurus say that behind every outstanding accomplishment you'll find a monomaniac with a mission. Ban Johnson was such a man.

A tall, well-upholstered, heavy-jowled, two-fisted drinker, he was the twenty-seven-year-old sports editor of the *Cincinnati Commercial-Gazette* in 1892 when Charles A. Comiskey was hired to manage the Reds. A man of strong opinions that he seldom kept to himself, Johnson had a favorite descriptive word for those he disdained—"stupid"—and a favorite target, John T. Brush. The fact that Brush happened to be Comiskey's boss at the time—he was the owner of the Reds—didn't deter Johnson from befriending the new manager. Brush also owned the Indianapolis club in the Western League. Johnson and Comiskey talked baseball and ideas and ambitions over many a schooner and shot in the saloons of Rhineland.

Comiskey saw a fertile potential for a league of small Midwestern cities. Born from the remains of an earlier organization, the Western League was formed in 1894. Johnson went to the first meeting as a reporter and, with Comiskey pushing him, emerged as the league's part-time president. Comiskey bought the Sioux City franchise and moved it to St. Paul. Over Brush's opposition, Johnson was reelected to the presidency in 1895. Now he presided over the most stable, respected circuit in the business. His uncompromising backing of his umpires had greatly reduced—but not eliminated—assaults on his staff. The league had gone until August before the first serious incident. Detroit shortstop Kid Elberfeld pummeled an umpire and was fined $100 and suspended for the rest of the year.

Ban Johnson's headquarters in Chicago was the most closely watched source of baseball news in the fall of 1899. There were no objective observers. The *Sporting News* supported its editor, Spink, in his efforts to revive the American Association. *Sporting Life*, backed by Al Reach, praised Johnson and his plans as long as they didn't conflict with the interests of the Phillies, of which Reach owned half. The paper's editor, Francis C. Richter, doubted that Philadelphians would back an AA team: "Proposals for a new club at this precarious time when teams in organized ball everywhere are struggling for existence would be a rash venture."

Ban Johnson showed up frequently in Milwaukee, conferring with Mack and Henry Killilea, who soon became his personal attorney and counsel to the league. Tom Andrews, a local boxing promoter, described one such meeting he attended at Killilea's home at 1616 Grand Avenue that fall. Charles Comiskey, Matt Killilea, and Fred C. Gross were also present.

"Unlike most meetings among baseball men of that time, our gathering had no refreshments," Andrews told Sam Levy of the *Milwaukee Journal*. "As Johnson said: 'Boys, we are here for business. Let us proceed.'

"'The only way to make our work a success is to go ahead as we plan: take the bull by the horns and don't give up until we are an admitted success. We have everything to gain, nothing to lose.'

"'Our idea of forming a new major league is to invade the larger eastern cities. Don't be discouraged if the National League tries to bluff us. Fight them with fire, gentlemen.'

"His middle name should have been Fighter!" Andrews said.

They discussed the likelihood of the National dropping four of its twelve teams before the 1900 season. Johnson was determined to be in position to catch them like an outfielder camped under a can of corn. Toward that end, they decided their regional identity was no longer appropriate for the expansion they had in mind. They should change the name to the American League. That would also undermine any potential American Association backers, denying them clear title to that patriotic-sounding emblem.

When the 1899 season ended, Connie Mack did some more business with Louisville. Barney Dreyfuss, anticipating that the Louisville club might be dropped by the National League, had sold his interests to a group led by Harry Pulliam and was trying to buy part or all of the Pittsburgh club. Mack prevailed upon Pulliam to draft infielder Wid Conroy from Utica of the New York League for spring delivery to the Brewers.

Mack went back to Massachusetts, but he didn't stay long. In October he was reported to be in Chicago, Cleveland, Philadelphia, New York, and California (he didn't get there) in pursuit of players. Accompanied by Matt Killilea and Fred Gross, he was in Chicago October 11 and 12 for the league meeting at the Northwestern Hotel.

After awarding the Indianapolis club $100 to buy itself a pennant for the 1899 championship, the directors distributed the remaining money in the league's sinking fund, from $900 for Minneapolis to $7.79 for St. Paul. Then, in a unanimous vote, they dissolved the Western League and immediately reorganized as the American League. In other business, they limited the number of players claimed to ten at any time and a total of twenty-five signed, claimed, or otherwise reserved prior to opening day. Johnson was authorized to draw up a 140-game schedule, arrange all railroad transportation, and choose either Spalding or Reach as the official supplier of baseballs. (The merger of the two companies in 1889 blunted the importance of this choice.)

Johnson was also instructed to apply to the Board of Arbitration for a change in the National Agreement, raising the draft price for American League players from $500 to $1,000 and making them subject to drafting after two years instead of one in the league. These changes were approved, placing the American in a higher classification than other minor leagues.

Johnson and Comiskey continued to negotiate with Chicago Orphans owner Jim Hart. Hoping to kill off the American Association and keep it out of his backyard, Hart had encouraged Johnson to usurp the "American" label for his league. Now Johnson pressed his desire to put one of his "minor league" teams in Chicago. Comiskey wanted the franchise.

Hart thought a minor league team in the city would further weaken the threat of a major league rival. He agreed, providing they rented his west side grounds to use when his team was on the road. Johnson nixed that idea and said the American League would build its own park on the south side of the city. Whereupon Hart denied that he had ever invited the nose of Johnson's camel into his Chicago tent.

It didn't matter what Hart denied. Ban Johnson was moving in.

Sporting Life warned that going into Chicago would be ruinous for the Western upstarts and doubted they had the capital to survive the impending war.

Mack was back in East Brookfield when Johnson and Comiskey went to Milwaukee in the last week of December to complete their plans for the 1900 season. From Henry Killilea's home Johnson announced that Comiskey would move the St. Paul club to Chicago "at any cost," with or without James Hart's consent, even if it meant breaking away from the National Agreement. What's more, Johnson added, if the National League dropped Cleveland, the Grand Rapids club would go there.

"We could eclipse the National League within three years," Johnson declared.

Connie Mack read these blustering statements with approval. He was ready to follow Ban Johnson into battle, wherever it led.

MARCHING BEHIND BAN JOHNSON

Connie Mack was at home in East Brookfield in January 1900 when tragedy struck the community. The Bergen brothers, Marty and Bill, both catchers, had followed Mack to the major leagues. Marty was the only catcher Mack had seen who could throw a man out at second from a squatting position behind the plate. Mack had once put in a claim for Bill, who signed with another club. On January 19 Marty Bergen went berserk, killing his wife and two young children with an ax before cutting his throat with a razor. Mack and Billy Hamilton, a Boston teammate of Bergen's, were the only baseball people with Bill Bergen at the funeral.

In March Mary Mack made her final appeal for an increase in her widow's pension. She was summoned to a hearing in Worcester by the pension bureau, but she pleaded that she was too ill to leave her home. A special examiner, Charles F. Nichols, agreed to come to her house. He found a tiny, white-haired woman of fifty-nine who appeared to be on her deathbed, attended by her sons Dennis and Eugene.

"She has been very ill," Nichols wrote in his report, "and is now in a very weak condition, and I am sure from her looks and what the family told me cannot live but a short time, unless she improves her present condition. She could not sit up and I took her testimony while she lay on a couch. The claimant is the mother of 'Connie Mack,' a ballplayer who is with the Washington league team for some years." (That's what Nichols wrote; the report didn't say who told him, and he was probably not a baseball fan.)

Two neighbors, Eddie Drake and Simon Daley, testified that Mary had been in feeble health for some time "and is liable to die most any time."

Nichols concluded that early action should be taken on the claim. He filed his eighteen-page report and depositions promptly. On March 26 Mary was awarded $12 a month retroactive to September 11, 1892. Her "present condition" improved, and she lived another twelve years.

Connie Mack didn't share the concerns for his mother's health. After celebrating his son Earle's tenth birthday with the family, he returned to Milwaukee in mid-February. *Sporting Life* correspondent H. H. Cohn jokingly described the thirty-seven-year-old, slender-as-ever Mack as "the same good natured, smiling, fat Connie of old." Mack lost a close friend when Cohn died the following September.

With Western players now protected from the draft for two years, Mack moved ahead with his plans to build an entirely new and, he hoped, younger team. He also looked forward to the fallout of players when and if the National League finally got around to lopping off four teams, a move that was expected any day. Meanwhile, baseball writers conjured up all sorts of imaginative scenarios for the 1900 season. There might even be four major leagues, they speculated.

It had been twenty-four years since the birth of major league baseball, but it was still acting like a teenager, hormones exploding with chaotic results. The game's physical growth was far ahead of its mental and emotional development. There were meetings going on everywhere, plots and counterplots, with more bones of contention than you'd find in a backyard full of hounds. John McGraw was scavenging in several cities for backers for a revived American Association. The Killilea brothers were reported huddling with Ban Johnson in New York, Chicago, and Milwaukee. A frantic week of train rides and confabs climaxed with a gathering in room 185 of the Republican House on the night of March 5. With Mack and Comiskey present, they put the last piece of the new American League in place, secretly incorporating Comiskey's Chicago White Stockings in Wisconsin to avoid a confrontation with James Hart and the National League until the National completed its club-cutting plans.

It took until March 8 for the National League to sever Cleveland, Baltimore, Washington, and Louisville from its ranks. (It also voted to redesign home plate from a square to the pentagon shape that is still used. This was done to eliminate the trouble over strike calls, with pitchers wanting the call when balls went over the corners. Now there would be no corners to kick about. Or so they thought.) Ban Johnson then made it public that the American League would field a team on a one-time cricket grounds at Thirty-ninth and Wentworth Avenue on Chicago's south side, with or without James Hart's approval.

After more bickering and barrages of statements and denials, the invasion of Chicago by the American League ended peacefully. James Hart extracted the right to claim up to two players from any American League team for $1,000 by August 15, and Ban Johnson agreed to keep his league in the National Agreement until the end of the year. Hart had one other condition: the "White Stockings" could not use Chicago as part of their name. He was not concerned about the competition. It would be located on the far south side of the city, downwind from the stockyards, an area lacking any attraction for the residents of the more densely populated north and west sides.

It was rumored that Ban Johnson had an interest in the new Chicago club, which he denied. He did have an interest in its success; if it failed, that would set back his plans immeasurably. Still, it seemed suspicious to some club owners that whenever they put in a claim for a player, they were informed that Chicago had made a prior claim.

While all this was going on, Mack showed up in Pittsburgh to complete the purchase of Pete Dowling, an effective southpaw for Louisville "when he avoids liquor." Barney Dreyfuss had bought control of the Pirates and was in the process of combining the Louisville and Pittsburgh rosters to create a powerhouse. Mack expressed confidence that neither the Brewers nor Pirates had anything to fear from John McGraw's efforts to put rival teams in their cities. "There isn't a ghost of a show for the project to ever get on its feet," he accurately predicted.

From Pittsburgh he went to Richmond, Indiana, to arrange for three weeks of spring practice beginning April 1. Then he was off to Cincinnati to try to sign two former teammates, outfielder Jake Stenzel, who had played for him in Pittsburgh, and Dummy Hoy, who was reported to have inherited property in Ireland, didn't need the money, and was not inclined to play in a minor league after twelve years in the National. Hoy changed his mind but signed with Comiskey's new Chicago club.

While the National owners couldn't stop feuding with each other, the American League remained a close-knit family, ruled by the patriarchal Ban Johnson. He had a hand in everything his family did, especially the weaker siblings. Anticipating the National's abandonment of Cleveland, he went to that city on February 28 to prospect for local backers. He struck a mother lode.

Charles W. Somers, a handsome man about town with a generous, adventurous spirit, had become wealthy with his father in the coal business. Jack Kilfoyl owned a successful men's furnishings store. Both were avid baseball cranks. Johnson left town with more than he had hoped for. Somers paid Tom Loftus $2,500 for the Grand Rapids franchise and opened his bankroll to fund Johnson's plans for the rest of the family. Loftus became the manager of Jim Hart's Chicago Orphans.

Comiskey was busy in Chicago fighting city hall for approval to build a wooden grandstand. So Johnson asked Connie Mack to go to Cleveland to help Somers and Kilfoyle get started. Mack had his hands full preparing for the new season in Milwaukee, but off he went.

Arriving around March 10, he found Somers and Kilfoyl with plenty of enthusiasm and money but no experience, no players, no manager, and no ballpark. "We want a first-class team and are willing to pay for it," Somers and his partner told Mack. The three of them went to Youngstown, where they called on retired outfielder Jimmy McAleer and talked him into signing to manage the team. They took some Grand Rapids players and, with Ban Johnson's help, signed some of the National League players who had been cut loose.

The National was asking $15,000 for the grounds it had abandoned in Cleveland. Somers had already paid for a lease on other grounds. After some negotiations with the National, Mack persuaded Somers to pay $10,000 for the League Park grounds and equipment.

Before going on to Chicago for more meetings, Mack was asked how he regarded Cleveland as a baseball city. "I visited the city in the National League and never saw a poor crowd here. We always drew well while I was with Pittsburgh, and even Washington brought out the crowds."

Asked if Kilfoyl and Somers were worried about the kind of team they would have, Mack said, "Well, a little, I guess. They told me that they wanted a first-class team and would not take anything else. I assured them that they can get it and they are the kind of men who know how to do it. They know what they want and will pay for it. That is the way to get first-class ball teams."

While stocking the Cleveland Blues' roster, Mack was also spending more money than the Brewers had ever put out for players. From Brooklyn he bought John Anderson, twenty-six, a six-foot-two switch-hitting first baseman called "the Terrible Swede," although he was born in Norway, and outfielder Dave Fultz, twenty-four. Heinie Reitz, the peppery second baseman of the Orioles' rowdy championship teams, and right-hander Tully Sparks came from Pittsburgh. He retrieved shortstop Wid Conroy, who had been stored in Louisville, and signed George Yeager, twenty-six, a light-hitting catcher with big league experience.

Clearly, Mack did not intend to rely wholly on green material. But he did fulfill his promise of an all-new team. Only three holdovers remained: Irv Waldron, Bill Reidy, and George Rettger.

Toward the end of March the following item appeared in a Milwaukee paper: "Connie Mack has a younger brother who is said to be a comer. Short of stature and stockily built, a third baseman, besides having a strong arm, he is said to be a good batter. Eugene Mack has received an offer from the Muncie team of the Indiana League."

The Indiana League opened in May and closed in June without Eugene showing up in any Muncie box scores, nor in the league records. There is no evidence that Connie Mack ever gave his brother a tryout. Eugene visited him in Milwaukee in late April before going back to work in a shoe factory in Spencer.

Mack arrived at the Arvinton Hotel in Richmond, Indiana, on March 31. Relaxing in the lobby, he read that Samuel Gompers of the American Federation of Labor was attempting to organize the ballplayers into a branch of the union. Gompers's timing was off. He had missed the Brotherhood boat and was too early for the next players' union sailing.

The Brewers were scheduled to inaugurate the new Chicago grounds on Thursday, April 19, but it rained all day. With no letup in sight, Comiskey suggested moving the opener to Milwaukee. The Brewers left Richmond and arrived in Chicago on Wednesday night, expecting to play the next day. Informed that they would open at home instead, they climbed back on the train and went to Milwaukee, only to learn that Comiskey had changed his mind. The opener was back on for Chicago on Saturday. They practiced at home on Friday, then took the morning train on a cold, overcast Saturday. Before a large, enthusiastic crowd Milwaukee won the first American League game in Chicago, 5–4, in ten innings. (When a Western Union operator tried to enter the grounds, Comiskey refused to let him in. He was concerned that if men could sit in saloons and restaurants and pool halls and read the play-by-play action, they wouldn't go to the games. Ban Johnson agreed and urged all his clubs to do the same.)

Despite the threatening weather and much to James Hart's dismay, the White Stockings were an immediate success. Comiskey claimed he took in more money in the first two days than he had seen all year in St. Paul.

Chicago, clad in intimidating new black road uniforms, opened the Brewers' home season on April 27. Innovations at the Lloyd Street grounds included a blackboard on which the lineups were written and a crier who walked about announcing changes in the lineup during the game. The Brewers won, 6–2, before a quiet crowd of about 5,000, who didn't know any of the players except Irv Waldron. Otherwise, the opening day lineup presented all new faces, as Mack had promised. Two days later the first Sunday game brought out a record crowd. The visiting Chicagos announced that they were paid on the basis of 15,847, by far the largest crowd the renamed league would entertain that season. Hundreds of brightly costumed ladies festooned the grandstand and stood among the overflow in the outfield.

The Brewers started fast, winning 11 of their first 15. Their spirited play and the unseasonably warm weather brought out big crowds. The *National Police Gazette* noted, "Connie Mack has given Milwaukee the best team that city has ever had."

Then things happened. Catcher Harry Smith was sidelined when he was hit on the shin by a foul ball. First baseman Bill Clarke broke an ankle and was out for the year. Heinie Reitz went to California, where his wife was ill, and never came back. Catcher George Yeager, batting a torrid .387 after 19 games, tore some knee ligaments. That finished him for the year. In July, Mack, fully expecting to be back in Milwaukee in 1901, offered to pay Yeager his entire salary for 1900 if the catcher would sign a 1901 contract. Yeager said no and wound up with Cleveland.

Wid Conroy had a bad ankle, then a split finger. Dave Fultz refused to play on Sundays. Pete Dowling missed a month with shoulder problems. Third baseman Jimmy Burke had arm problems. Mack put pitcher George Rettger on second and catcher Mama Diggins on first while he scoured the National League for infielders. He traded Charlie Chech to Cleveland for Lou Bierbauer, then sold Bierbauer to Buffalo in July and tried a Chicago City League shortstop named Schneider, who quickly disappeared. He bought Tommy Dowd from Chicago to play left field, then released him when Dowd wrenched his shoulder in some off-the-field adventure. Mack offered Cincinnati $1,000 for Sam Crawford, a twenty-year-old rookie outfielder from Wahoo, Nebraska, but was turned down. All summer he had players coming and going, aiding the railroad and telegraph companies more than his team.

There were a few bright spots. John Anderson was a consistent hitter and agile base stealer. Mack refused $1,000 from John T. Brush for him. Twice in June the Brewers played games in which neither team made an error, a rarity at a time when they could lead the league in fielding despite making 320 errors. Only four such games were played in the league all season.

An unpleasant confrontation touched off Connie Mack's first real tidal wave of criticism from the press and public. When Pete Dowling hurt his shoulder in June, Mack went hunting for pitching. Pete Husting, who had won 9 games for him in 1899, was coaching the University of Wisconsin team while finishing his term in law school. On June 15 Mack asked him to return to the Brewers for $150 a month. Husting wanted $175. "You've had no spring training," Mack reportedly told him. "Show me what you can do first." Husting agreed.

Husting won his first start on June 17 against Buffalo, graduated from law school three days later, then won again. After winning 4 of his first 5 decisions, Husting decided he had shown what he could do. He asked Mack for the raise. Mack said no.

Unlike most players, Husting had an alternative. He quit the team and went to work in his brother's law office while pitching for a semipro team in nearby Arcadia. Mack fined and suspended him, which didn't faze the pitcher. The fans took the player's side, criticizing Mack for not coming up with the additional $25 a month. They circulated a petition urging Mack to take Husting back and give him the raise, which didn't faze the manager.

A *Sentinel* editorial came down hard on Connie Mack and the entire baseball establishment:

> Husting joined the team a few weeks ago and pitched winning ball. He says he had an arrangement whereby he received $150 a month to begin with, and $175 if he did good work. He proved his value by winning games and reminded the manager of the agreement to raise his salary. He was informed he must continue to play at $150 a month or leave the club. He chose to leave, and was punished by being suspended and fined. This disregard of the rights of players is not uncommon in baseball. They are under the absolute control of the capitalists who organize baseball leagues. If one of them asserts the ordinary privileges exercised by citizens in other employments a fine and often suspension preventing the player from obtaining an engagement elsewhere is imposed. The real autocrats of the land seem to be the baseball managers.

In a decade Connie Mack had gone from being one of those players without rights to one of those "autocrats" he had rebelled against with the Brotherhood.

Later critics of Mack who have tagged him as stingy and miserly may see this as proof of their charge. But not every human motivation can be satisfactorily or conclusively explained. The truth often dodges and squirts like a globule of mercury when you try to grasp it.

The difference of $75 for the rest of the season was not coming entirely out of Mack's pocket, nor would it make a discernible difference in the club's bottom line. Mack had demonstrated that he would go high for good players in the open market. The Brewers' payroll was the second highest in the league, topped only by Chicago. He had been willing to carry the injured George Yeager on the payroll for the entire year just to secure him for next season. Over the years to come, Mack would pay voluntary bonuses and display many generous gestures toward players out of his own pocket—more of them unsung than sung.

How then to reconcile this seemingly contradictory tightness and generosity? It may not be necessary to reconcile them. Connie Mack was made of ambiguities and contradictions like everybody else. He could be tight and he could be generous, just as he could be kind and softhearted or sarcastic and tough as a whip. When he had the money, his payroll would be the highest in the league. When he didn't have it, he wouldn't pay even what he knew a player might be worth. Either way, whether his team was on top or on the bottom, he hated salary disputes.

There is another possible explanation.

As the *Sentinel* put it, "Husting says he had an arrangement." Connie Mack may not have taken the same understanding from their conversation that Husting did. He may have seen it as the pitcher asking for more money than they had agreed on. When a player agreed to a salary and then asked for a contract to be renegotiated, it wasn't miserliness that made Mack resist. It was an obstinacy that made him dig in and refuse to budge. The more the player tugged or the press pushed, the more unyielding he became.

More than anything, the incident illustrated one of Mack's prominent characteristics—a flint-hard Yankee stubbornness that manifested itself often throughout his life. He could be both mule and mule skinner. The case of Pete Husting would not be the last time this stubborn streak cost him, in public esteem or a needed player's services.

Still short of pitchers, Mack read that the Pittsburgh Pirates had suspended George Edward "Rube" Waddell. The talented but erratic twenty-three-year-old southpaw had been driving manager Fred Clarke nuts—in

Louisville and now Pittsburgh—for four years. Clarke had twice sent him down to the Western League, where Mack had seen him for the first time on May 6, 1898. Waddell had spent most of the '99 season with Columbus, which had moved to Grand Rapids in July. A favorite of the fans, he won 26 and lost 8, striking out 200. The Brewers dealt him four of his losses, hitting him freely in two of them. Waddell was a clumsy fielder who could be bunted on successfully. But Mack had seen enough to know that Waddell's raw ability more than matched these flaws and his outsized eccentricities. He threw harder than any pitcher Mack would ever see, had an off-the-table curve, and was completely devoid of nerves. He wasn't bright enough to be worried by anything.

With the Pirates to start the 1900 season, Waddell's pitching was as unpredictable as his behavior. When Rube was winning, the straitlaced, firm disciplinarian Clarke could tolerate him. But Waddell was not winning in June. Clarke suspended him for being "out of condition" and having injured a finger while playing catch with some kids or pitching in a sandlot game—nobody really knew.

Mack was aware that Waddell could—and did—jump a team whenever he took a notion, disappearing to Canada or a firehouse or a favorite fishing hole. This time, Mack read, Waddell had landed in Punxsutawney, a town about one hundred miles northeast of Pittsburgh, where he was pitching and playing outfield for the town's semipro team. His fun-loving, generous nature had made him the most popular gent in town with all the other kids, as well as the firehouse and saloon bunch. On the field he gabbed with other players, turned cartwheels whenever he felt like it, and threw lightning and jughandles, also when he felt like it.

But Waddell still belonged to the Pirates. Relying on his close relationship with Barney Dreyfuss, Mack took a train to Pittsburgh. Given the informality of the baseball business in those days, Mack simply asked Dreyfuss for permission to borrow Waddell. There was no deal, no trade, no money involved.

"Go ahead," Dreyfuss told him. "If you can handle him, you're welcome to him."

Hoping to go directly to Punxsutawney and bring Rube back with him, Mack immediately tracked him down at the Hotel Whitney and put in a call to him. He had never spoken to Waddell and doubted that Rube had any idea who he was. When he heard a voice come on the line, he said, "Hello, is that you, Rube?"

"Who in hell is this?" was the reply.

Something in his tone suggested to Mack that Waddell, though he'd been tagged "Rube" as far back as 1896, might be sensitive about his nickname, especially coming from a stranger. Mack switched smoothly to, "Eddie, this is Connie Mack of the Milwaukee club. I'd like you to do some pitching for me."

"Not interested," Eddie said.

Mack told him how eager the Milwaukee fans were to see him, how the Brewers could win the pennant with his help, how much money he could earn. Eddie wasn't buying any of it.

"I like it here," he insisted. "There is no money on earth that could make me leave Punxsutawney."

Disappointed, Mack returned to Milwaukee alone. The positive side of stubbornness is perseverance, and Connie Mack could exercise both sides. For the next two weeks he sent Waddell daily telegrams and followed them up with letters. How persuasive they were is unknown. It may just be that Waddell's cash, his credit, and his welcome in Punxsutawney had run out. Whatever it was, Mack's persistence was finally rewarded with a wire from Eddie: "Come and get me."

Baseball literature and legend are filled with stories of the deeds and misdeeds of Rube Waddell, the little boy in the six-foot-two, 200-pound body with a million-dollar arm and five-cent head. Some of the tales are true; all are plausible. Some of them will be recounted in this account of Connie Mack's life and times because the irrepressible southpaw became Connie Mack's first great pitcher, his most difficult challenge as a manager, and—out of the thousands of men who played for him—his favorite character. Through the years that followed, Mack's luncheon and banquet audiences, his children and grandchildren would hear him tell more anecdotes about the rounding up—but never taming—of George Edward "Rube" Waddell than of any other player. Despite memory's predilection for playing with details, Mack's version of his Punxsutawney expedition remained remarkably consistent with each telling.

On Wednesday, July 25, the Brewers lost their fifth straight to Buffalo, but Mack wasn't there to see it. He had left after the previous day's game to collect his new pitcher. He took a train to Pittsburgh and had to wait until three o'clock in the morning, he said, for a connection that stopped in Punxsutawney. He arrived around eight, roused Rube at the Whitney and bought him a breakfast of four eggs, pancakes, and appropriate side dishes.

Then Waddell announced that he had some business matters to clear up before leaving town. His business consisted of paying bills—or more precisely, of Connie Mack's paying the bills. Mack's hundred-dollar bankroll was rapidly depleted as they stopped at a gents' furnishings store, a saloon, a suit-pressing establishment, and a sporting goods store. Mack nervously peeled off the greenbacks, calculating as he went how much he would need to get them both back to Milwaukee.

"Eddie, I can't pay for much more," Mack said.

"Just one more stop," Rube said. They went to the Adams Express office, which was holding a hunting dog Waddell had ordered COD. Mack paid the $8 charge; what became of the dog never made it into any version of the story, but they didn't take it with them.

As they neared the hotel, Waddell added another "just one more stop," a pawn shop, where Mack shook as he shelled out $25 to rescue Rube's pocket watch.

Having covered all of Main Street during their settling-up spree, Mack was certain that word of their activities had spread. He knew how popular Waddell was in town. He was sure that someone must have recognized him as the former Pittsburgh player and manager. He was prepared for the local baseball fans to put up some resistance to his making off with their star player. Had he read the local paper that morning, Mack would have been even more nervous: the reason for his visit was no secret in the town.

They made it back to the Whitney about noon. Mack helped Waddell pack his grip, tipped a bellboy to carry it to the depot, ordered some sandwiches sent up, and kept out of sight until it was nearly time to catch the three o'clock train for Pittsburgh. Mack figured it would take them fifteen minutes to walk to the station, buy the tickets, and bail out Eddie's luggage.

Mack recalled:

We followed this plan to the letter, and everything was apparently going along smoothly, although every minute seemed an hour. Never did I inwardly root so hard for a train to appear as I did that afternoon in Punxsutawney.

Finally, about five minutes before train time, a group of important-appearing men approached us. My heart sank. As they neared me, unsmiling and determined-looking, I sensed there was trouble in the air. We had made some mistake and now the town knew what was up and sought to keep me from taking their attraction away.

Knowing Waddell's capacity for irregularity, I realized it would be comparatively easy for them to get out a fake warrant just to detain him, so they could talk him out of the Milwaukee project. . . . I steeled myself for the ordeal that was to follow.

One of the group stepped out and called me aside. He shook my hands and said, "You are Connie Mack?"

I admitted it.

"Well, my friends and I came down here to the station," he went on, to my astonishment, "to tell you that you have done us a great favor in taking Waddell out of this town." Then he called over his friends and introduced them to me. "Waddell is a wonderful pitcher," continued the spokesman, "but on account of his eccentricities the fans and ourselves believe that Punxsutawney would be better off without him. Nobody can control him."

In the meantime, the Rube had backed up against the curb of an iron fence at the station. He leaned over with his head on his hands like Rodin's Thinker. He imagined that the members of the delegation, whose glances he avoided, were giving me a battle to hold him. I did not disillusion him until we had safely boarded the train.

After another night of travel they arrived in Milwaukee on Thursday morning. Mack had advertised that Waddell would pitch for the Brewers that afternoon. About five hundred fans turned out to see him strike out 8 and give up 5 hits, but 2 wild pitches and an error in the first inning cost him a 3–2 loss. (In the *Sentinel*'s game account, the word "fans" appeared in quotes for the first time in that paper.)

Two days later Pete Dowling pitched a no-hitter against Cleveland, and on Sunday Rube threw a 2-hit shutout at the Blues, 4–0.

Waddell fulfilled all of Mack's hopes in Milwaukee. "He was sensational," Mack said. "He had everything, ability and color." He drew large, adoring crowds whenever he pitched. Ever the showman, Mack put on a glove and warmed him up. Standing in front of the grandstand, he sometimes stepped aside and let a fastball zip past his glove and crash against the boards. It never failed to get a rise from the crowd. "Kill 'em, Rube," they shouted.

Waddell had more fun than anybody. He pranced, he grinned, he bantered with the fans, he turned handsprings when he fanned the side or won a close game. And he was happy. There were plenty of good fishing spots—his favorite was Peewaukee Lake—and busy fire engines to ride.

The fans soon caught on to Rube's most visible superstition: before a game or after a few innings, he would go out to the bleachers and ask a fan to cut a sliver of material off the ends of his undershirt. It was, like many of his idiosyncrasies, unique to the Rube.

Starting and relieving, Waddell worked in 9 games in three weeks. He won 5 and lost 2 with 2 ties. On Sunday, August 19, at Chicago, a packed house of about ten thousand showed up for a doubleheader against the second-place Brewers, who were battling the White Stockings for the lead. (On the west side of town, the Orphans were playing the Giants before the smallest Sunday crowd—under three thousand—in their history.) Despite working twelve innings twice in the past week, Waddell went 17 innings in a 2–2 tie before he tripled and scored the winning run. According to the *Tribune*, Rube was firing "Chinese interrogation points" at the Sox. After he retired the last batter, he turned cartwheels of jubilation from the pitcher's box to the bench. The crowd's disappointment over the loss was dispelled by Rube's joyful antics.

The game lasted an inordinate three hours and seven minutes. It was now past six o'clock. Sox captain Dick Padden approached Mack and suggested the second game be cut to 5 innings. An idea sparked in Mack's mind. Waddell had finished so strong, shutting out Chicago over the last 8 innings, that he looked as if he could keep pitching until it was dark. Mack readily agreed to Padden's suggestion, then turned to Rube and said, "Eddie, if you will pitch this 5-inning second game, instead of going with us to Kansas City, you can go back to Milwaukee tonight and spend the next three days fishing at Peewaukee."

Mack knew his man; Waddell grabbed the ball and threw another 5 shutout innings, winning a 1–0 one-hitter.

Reports of the unusual iron-man performance appeared in newspapers all over the country, to Mack's ultimate dismay. Barney Dreyfuss read them and was reminded of his problem pitcher. The Pirates were in a tight pennant race with Brooklyn. If Waddell was pitching that well, they could certainly use him. Dreyfuss sent a telegram to Mack in Kansas City reclaiming his valuable property.

Mack doubted that Waddell and Fred Clarke would get along any better than they had before. He also realized that his own championship hopes would dim considerably if he lost his ace. But Waddell belonged to the Pirates. There was no getting around their right to him. Reluctantly, Mack telegraphed Waddell to report to Pittsburgh. He was not surprised when Rube wired back that he would quit before going back to the Pirates. Besides, he had become an overnight hero in Peewaukee and was in no hurry to desert his new circle of admirers.

On his first night at the lake a thunderstorm had come up. Lightning struck a dairy barn. The flames lit up the sky and Rube's eyes. According to the *Sentinel*, when Rube arrived at the scene, he found a group of farmers standing around watching the barn burn. Rube stirred them into action, shouting, "Why don't you try to save something?" as he dashed into the inferno. The others followed. They saved forty head of stock plus wagons, buggies, and machinery. Rube suffered a burn on one hand.

"I'm a peach at a fire," he told a local reporter. "There is nothing I like better than to fight fires. I was a fireman for seven years at Pittsburgh. I'm glad I was able to help the old farmer some."

Ignoring Dreyfuss's orders, Waddell rejoined the Brewers when they returned home and pitched 3 complete-game wins in a week. But Connie Mack didn't want to jeopardize his good standing with Dreyfuss. It might look like he was stalling Rube's return or abetting Rube's stubborn refusal to leave. He wrote the Pirates' owner a letter—no need for the speed of a telegram here—explaining that Waddell would never respond to letters or telegrams or threats of any kind. He advised Dreyfuss to send an emissary to corral Rube and bring him back. It wouldn't hurt that Rube might get in a few more starts in the meantime.

The Brewers were in Indianapolis when Pirates catcher Chief Zimmer showed up on Friday, August 31, with orders to escort Waddell to Boston in time for a Labor Day doubleheader. Rube told Zimmer he wasn't going, then pitched a 3–2 loss, called after 5 innings because of darkness, over Connie Mack's angry protests.

The veteran Zimmer was used to dealing with quiet, disciplined pitchers like Cy Young. Unable to cope with the adolescent Rube, he appealed to Mack for help. Mack advised him to take Rube shopping for a new wardrobe to win him over. The next morning Zimmer spent a few hours and unknown amounts of Barney Dreyfuss's money outfitting Rube with everything from suits to shoes, throwing in a new leather grip to carry it all. The happy Waddell was now willing to go anywhere with his new friend, and off to Boston they went.

Mack watched his chances for the American League pennant disappear down the converging railroad tracks. Without Rube they had to settle for second place, 4 games behind Chicago. The reunion of Rube Waddell and

Fred Clarke proved as rocky as Mack had predicted and did not bring the Pirates the pennant. They, too, finished second.

Before Waddell left town, Mack had been putting together a team to go barnstorming west to California and Mexico, starting in Chicago on September 22. Mack didn't intend to publicize it until everything was set, but the secret got out in a hurry. When Mack invited Waddell to go along, Rube immediately went shopping for appropriate arms for western-type hunting and told every gun shop owner about the trip. Each player put up a $100 deposit as a guarantee that he would stay until the end. It would be refunded if the gate receipts were sufficient. They weren't. The tour reached Denver, where cold weather caused Mack to abandon the idea and send everybody home. The venture cost him $400.

When *Sporting Life* reported Milwaukee's attendance for the year at 88,000, Mack scoffed. "We played to more than that on our sixteen Sundays at home," he said, adding that 150,000 was a more accurate estimate. Mack put the club's profits at $10,000. In Chicago, Comiskey claimed his club had drawn 250,000, more than Hart's Orphans.

Connie Mack put away his straw hat with its silk trolley, which fastened to his coat lapel to keep the hat from being blown away by Lake Michigan breezes. He took out his winter derby and headed for the battlefields of the conference room, where more significant actions had been taking place than on any diamond that summer.

On a Sunday in June that found every National club idle in the East, players from every club had met at the Sturtevant Hotel in New York. Alienated by the owners' actions and attitudes, they formed the Protective Association of Professional Baseball Players and elected Chief Zimmer president. A month later they met again, adopted a constitution, and hired a Buffalo attorney, ex-player Harry Taylor. Their primary objectives were to limit the reserve clause to five years and prohibit the farming out or selling of players without their consent and agreement to the terms.

Correctly reading the signs that the American League was intent on becoming another big league market for their services, the Players' Association wooed Ban Johnson, who welcomed their affections. Johnson promised to add provisions in his league's contracts limiting suspensions to ten days and the reserve clause to three years, paying doctor bills for game-related injuries, and allowing binding arbitration to settle disputes. The association also demanded the abolition of the practice of farming out players. Johnson was sympathetic but made no promises on that point. He had given them enough to earn the American League the public backing of the Players' Association.

American League expansion plans moved to the front burner as early as August. Henry Killilea and Connie Mack were among league owners and managers who met in Ban Johnson's office on August 23. They worked on the wording of the preamble to their declaration of independence from the National Agreement, making them equal in every way to the National. In order to gain the support of the minor leagues, they drew up a petition to do away with the drafting of players, a perennial grievance of the minors. Over dinner, they discussed possible invasion targets in the East.

"There is room for two leagues operating under an amicable agreement," Johnson told reporters, adding—naively? coyly? baitingly?—"we do not expect to find serious opposition to the request."

If Connie Mack had any inkling that his future lay somewhere other than Milwaukee, he gave no indication. On October 3 he told the press that he expected to have the same team back in Milwaukee in 1901. Before heading home for a brief visit, he had a long talk with Pete Husting and patched up his differences with the young attorney. Husting agreed to return to the Brewers in 1901.

Asked to comment on the rumors of changes in the works, Mack said he favored the admission of Baltimore and Washington to the American League. When speculation about Philadelphia popped up in various newspapers, there were hints that Milwaukee might be bounced from the league. Mack admitted that such a scheme was afoot, but Henry Killilea denied that Philadelphia was being considered. Ban Johnson issued a statement pledging to stay out of Philadelphia and St. Louis "unless the National League starts a war." But a few days later the league was reported to have formed a committee to search out playing fields in Baltimore, Washington, Philadelphia, and Buffalo.

Confusing? Contradictory? Smoke? It was all of these. In the midst of the hullabaloo, the *Sporting News* printed a cautionary headline:

IMMINENT DANGER

PROFESSIONAL BASEBALL IN A BAD WAY

Henry Killilea and Connie Mack had their own agenda when they went to Chicago for league meetings on October 29. They were determined to prevent the vacating of Milwaukee for an eastern city. Ban Johnson's first priority was to get rid of John T. Brush, who said he had sold his interest in the Indianapolis club but had merely transferred his stock to his wife's name. Mack and Killilea succeeded in retaining Milwaukee's place in the new order. Indianapolis and Buffalo were the most likely to be dropped.

Somers, Comiskey, and Mack were named to the league's circuit committee, but Ban Johnson was involved in everything. He went to Milwaukee on November 7, conferred with Matt Killilea and Mack, and left town with Mack. Two days later they showed up in Washington with Comiskey. They considered possible playing grounds in Baltimore and Washington, then, joined by Somers, moved on to Philadelphia. There Johnson issued a statement: "We have all the backing we want in Philadelphia and an option on the grounds."

It was not necessarily so. Branch Rickey once described Ban Johnson as "a tireless finder and maker of facts to preface every undertaking. . . . He never intentionally deceived. However, it can be said that he might let an adversary stumble along with less than all the facts."

The facts were they had some backing, from Charles Somers, but nowhere near all they wanted or needed. And they had no option on any grounds, nor any idea where suitable grounds might be available. They did have two local agents. Ban Johnson offered a 25 percent stake in the new franchise to Frank L. Hough, sporting editor of the *Inquirer*, and Samuel H. Jones, a sportswriter for the Associated Press (AP). Neither put up any money. It wouldn't hurt to have a few members of the press in on the ground floor with no risk. Both were highly regarded among their peers. Hough had been president of the Pennsylvania State League and Atlantic League. His column, "The Old Sport's Musings," was widely read. He became president of the Pen and Pencil Club and the sportswriters' association. Jones had been with AP since 1872.

The writers' names never appeared in the original shareholder records. The original 500 shares, issued in three certificates, were all in the joint names of Cornelius McGillicuddy and Charles W. Somers. They operated on nothing but faith and a handshake until March 10, 1902, when their agreement was first put in writing.

Nobody expressed any concern about conflicts of interest.

Hough and Jones took Mack on a walking tour of the city, wearing out his long legs as they looked at every empty lot from the pig farms on the south side to the north end. Unlike Boston, where the streets had evolved from a maze of cow paths, Philadelphia resembled a crossword puzzle pattern. William Penn had laid out the city in 1685 in straight streets and cross streets. The main north-south thoroughfare, Broad Street, was twelve miles long, then the longest straight street in the world. They walked past miles of brick row houses with white marble stoops that glowed from a daily scrubbing, down streets and alleys, past slums and houses of gambling and prostitution threading through the wealthier sections like long, thin genetic strands. Mack saw a piece of land he liked on Porter Street in South Philly. Jones and Hough preferred a location north of the city center at Twenty-sixth and Jefferson Streets. Used by the Athletics of the American Association in the 1880s, it was now a city-owned playground adjacent to a high school.

Comiskey and Somers were satisfied with the site. They persuaded Mack to go along with the local men, who knew the city better than they did. On November 19 Frank Hough appeared before the city's Common Council, seeking to lease the grounds. The request was referred to a committee on city properties.

Only six clubs—Cleveland, Baltimore, Washington, Milwaukee, Chicago, and Detroit—were represented when the league met at the Grand Pacific in Chicago on November 20. The league had dropped Kansas City and given the Washington franchise to Cowboys owner Jimmy Manning. Johnson had offered the Baltimore franchise to the two most popular members of the 1890s Orioles, John McGraw and Wilbert Robinson. McGraw represented Baltimore at the meeting, although the Orioles' franchise was not yet official.

They ratified a ten-year agreement and elected Ban Johnson president, secretary, and treasurer at a salary of $5,000. With an eye on Boston and Philadelphia, the six clubs established the procedure for admitting additional franchises.

Out of these meetings came the first acknowledgment of Connie Mack's possible departure from Milwaukee. Henry Killilea told a Milwaukee reporter, "I guess Connie Mack will be going to Philadelphia all right."

18 | LAUNCHING THE NEW AMERICAN LEAGUE

Three men were primarily responsible for the early success of the American League: Ban Johnson, with his vision, energy, management, and organizational skills; Charles Somers, with his unfettered faith and financial support; and Connie Mack, with his baseball acumen and willingness to work for the success of other clubs as well as his own.

In addition to putting up most of the money in Cleveland, Somers helped Comiskey with the building of his grandstand in Chicago and provided $7,500 startup money to go with Connie Mack's $2,500 stake in Philadelphia. When no local backers appeared in Washington or Boston, Somers financed the launching of those franchises, operating the Boston club himself. To avoid the appearance of syndicate baseball, he "parked" his interest in the Cleveland club in the names of Kilfoyle and Jimmy McAleer until he sold the Boston club to Henry Killilea in 1902.

Starting in December 1900, the pace was staggering for the next five months. Connie Mack, Ban Johnson, and Charles Somers spent more time with railroad porters and conductors than with their own families, slept in more beds than itinerant fleas, and signed scores of players—and lost dozens more—for American League teams. They were creating businesses: hunting for playing fields; ordering tickets printed; building grandstands; hiring managers, players, groundskeepers, office boys.

For Connie Mack, it began with a return to Milwaukee on December 2 "to clear up some pressing business matters," the *Journal* reported. Asked if he intended to return to Milwaukee for the 1901 season, Mack chose his words elusively. He had been cautioned by Johnson to say nothing that might annoy the prickly National owners and jeopardize any chance of a peace conference when the National League met next week. Johnson had publicly stated that the American League would not go into Philadelphia "unless the National League starts a war." But he knew war was inevitable. Mack said only that he "expected" to be back.

"He says he has not had any talk with any of the Philadelphia promoters," the reporter wrote, "in regard to assuming the management there. While in Philadelphia he stopped off to talk with some of the baseball promoters but he was never approached by anyone connected with the new team. . . . He said he has a number of excellent men in mind for Milwaukee next year but has not done anything to get them formally."

Mack's visits to Philadelphia were obviously for something more than the scrapple and pepperpot soup. To say he was not approached by anyone connected with the new team was literally true. Ban Johnson and Charles Somers had been with him. Hough and Jones had not approached him; it was the other way round. The newspapermen were the only baseball promoters with whom he talked, and they didn't talk about his assuming the management there because he was already slated by Johnson to be the management. His "I'll be back [in Milwaukee]" responses were contradicted by his actions. He sat in the Republican House while the Brewers' annual meeting on December 3 dealt with buying out his stock. He left town immediately after the meeting for a brief visit to East Brookfield before heading to Philadelphia.

Meanwhile the peripatetic Mr. Johnson met with Jim Hart in Chicago on December 4, skipped to Cleveland the next day, jumped back to Chicago on the sixth, trained to New York for a day, and, with Somers, "blew into Philadelphia with the snow" on Monday the tenth, the same day the National League opened its three–day meeting in New York. Mack met them, and the trio set up headquarters at the Lafayette Hotel on Arch Street, a block from City Hall.

During that week it had been all quiet on the baseball front. There was a break in the verbal volleys: no comments, no putdowns, no boasts, no threats. Ban Johnson was lying low, awaiting the call to the conference table. He and Somers were ready to board a train for the ninety–mile sprint to New York at any time. But the National left them cooling their heels. The invitation never came.

Rumors were more plentiful than roomers at the Fifth Avenue Hotel, where the National gathered. Despite Johnson's entreaties for peace and parity, Spalding and his followers were not prepared to accept, much less welcome, any challenge to their monopoly on major league baseball. They didn't want a fight, but they were not about to recognize the American

League as an equal. They were still paying off the debts from the 1890 Players' League settlement, but they believed they were financially stronger than Johnson's upstarts. They threatened to reclaim the four cities they had cut, forcing the American into a choice between head-on competition or quitting Baltimore, Washington, and Cleveland. They openly supported the resurrection of the American Association and tried to induce some cat's-paws to finance association teams in the eastern cities the American was invading.

The public was sick of the bickering. The feuds and fulminations of the magnates turned off their best customers. The professional game was still struggling to recover its popularity as a spectator sport. Attendance had slipped again in 1900. But it was thriving as a participant sport. That winter teams from regiments of the New York National Guard played a season of indoor baseball that drew extensive press coverage. The fans loved the game and hated the business, with its shams, deceptions, and manipulations, which were no better than the tactics employed by the robber barons of the steel, railroad, oil, and streetcar industries. The wealth and political influence of big business had given rise to the Populist Party, which cast all monopolies as enemies of the people. And the National League was a monopoly.

What Thomas W. Lofton wrote in *The Krank and His Language* in 1888 remained appropriate, as it does today:

"Kranks crawl into a shell and do not emerge until April. While in his shell his only article of food is gray newspaper articles on deals. During the krank's season from April to November he subsists on air and likes it strong. First characteristic is knowing it all and second is telling it all."

The only deals cranks wanted to read about involved players, not franchises and syndicates and arcane secret ownership arrangements. A. J. Reach was right when he commented, "The people are only interested in the contests on the diamond and the players who participate in them. The petty quarrels and wordy wars between club owners are annoying to them. I wonder why the newspapers sacrifice their space to record wars between men who own ball clubs."

But sacrifice they did, by the column inch and broadsheet. As a former newspaperman, Ban Johnson knew the power of the press. He won its support by selling his American League as a righteous cause, the "American Way," the unshackling of the workers from their eternal bondage to the rich National League monopolists, who were cast as no better than the mill and mine owners unleashing Pinkerton guards on striking underpaid workers.

The National said all the right things about sitting down with the Players' Protective Association to discuss the players' grievances and demands. But it was in no mood to give in on anything. A rumor that the players' leaders had gone to Philadelphia to meet with Johnson—which proved to be true—caused National League owners to "have something clearly resembling a fit," according to the *New York Times*. Johnson went further than he had before, granting the players a limited reserve or option clause and a ban on farming, trading, or selling players without their consent.

Clark Griffith was the Players' Association vice-president. Charles Comiskey had been Griffith's first major league manager in St. Louis in 1891. Now Comiskey hoped to induce Griffith to jump from Jim Hart's Orphans to his south side White Stockings as player-manager. He and Johnson counted on Griffith bringing other National League stars with him. Sometime in November the three of them met. Johnson asked Griffith what he thought their chances were of attracting National Leaguers who had not yet signed 1901 contracts.

"That depends," Griffith told them, "on what happens when [the players] meet with the National League in December. If the league agrees to raise the salary limit from $2,400 to $3,000, and a few other of our demands, it may be difficult for you to get players."

Although the salary limit was a grievance of the players, $2,400 contracts were actually rare and went only to the top stars.

On December 12, while Johnson, Mack, and Somers waited in Philadelphia, Griffith was the last person to enter the room for the players' showdown with the National League. League president Nick Young did not preside. Young, who had been secretary and then president since the league's beginning in 1876, was, in Griffith's words, "a fine character, getting old [Young was sixty], and too honest to sit in the chair." Albert Spalding was running things.

Sitting in the back of the room, Young tugged at Griffith's coat as he passed by and said, "They won't let me in on anything important anymore, but you won't get anything out of that bunch."

He was right. The National magnates rejected the players' entire wish list.

"One of them said he didn't give a damn about the ball players," Griffith said. "I told him he would be sorry for that remark."

The Players' Association released a statement to the newspapers urging all players not to sign National League contracts. An angry Griffith gave his own reaction to the press:

The National League is on the run and looking for highboard fences. They have not been doing the right thing with their players and by all appearances the American will put them on the defensive. I do not consider myself under contract to the Chicago National League club. If my terms are accepted I will sign with Comiskey. The National contracts are not worth the paper they are written on, now that there is a viable body ready and anxious to sign such players desiring to ignore those contracts.

The American League has a president who has complete authority and enforces every rule, while the National has practically no head and all rules are broken alike. In the American, the players have their hearts in the success of their teams; in the National, the players with few exceptions have never had their hearts in the success of the employers, and aside from trying to win games, their work has been heartless.

Griffith then sent a telegram to Comiskey and Johnson: "Go ahead, you can get all the players you want."

A week later a contentious session of the Philadelphia Common Council committee on city property took up the matter of a three-year lease on the Jefferson Street grounds at $1,000 a year. Frank Hough told the committee his company proposed to spend $30,000 in fixtures for "athletic purposes," not just baseball.

The local school board opposed the leasing of the playground. Councilman Edmonds said that when the grounds had been used by the American Association club, property owners had complained of damage to their property by frequenters of the games. Councilman Harris thought the price was too low. The motion to approve the lease was tabled. When the committee next met on January 3, they again put off a decision.

Commented the *Boston Globe*, "If the Philadelphia City Council makes a children's playground out of the grounds that Frank Hough and Samuel Jones have been after . . . it will be impossible for the American League to find satisfactory quarters for Connie Mack."

Still without a place of business in Philadelphia, Ban Johnson dispatched Mack to Boston to negotiate for a site there. If it couldn't find a place to play in Boston, the league was faced with retaining Buffalo as the eighth club. Mack stayed in East Brookfield and each morning put on his derby and overcoat, walked to the depot, and rode the train to Boston. Hugh

Duffy, the star center fielder for the Boston Beaneaters, met him in Boston every morning. A Rhode Island native, Duffy was four years younger than Mack. He had agreed to replace Mack as the Milwaukee manager.

In Boston Mack was dealing with veteran player and manager Arthur Irwin, who was also an astute businessman. Irwin had patented a fielder's glove that Reach was manufacturing. He held the rights to the Charles River Park, formerly used by an American Association team. The American League wanted to lease it. But the National League was still backing efforts to revive the American Association. Irwin had been promised a piece of the Boston club—if it happened.

On Wednesday morning, January 9, 1901, Mack arrived at Irwin's home to keep an appointment and was told to come back later. Irwin was in bed with the grippe. While Mack did some shopping in the overcast, 31-degree climate, Tim Murnane caught up with him. A former player and league president, Murnane was now a writer for the *Globe*. He asked Mack about his plans in Philadelphia. Mack bluffed. "I have several grounds picked out when the proper time comes." In his story, Murnane added that Mack said there was no truth to the story that the city government had refused to let the new club use the old Athletic grounds. Technically this was true. The city hadn't said yes, and it hadn't said no.

When Mack returned to Irwin's home, he found the sick man vague and indecisive, reluctant to make a deal until he knew whether the American Association might come back to life and want the field. He wanted no trouble with the National League. But maybe if he was given a piece of the new American League franchise, he might consider it. On the other hand, he had lost money as an investor in the Boston Brotherhood club and was leery of getting involved with another new venture. As Irwin rambled on between hedges and doubts, Mack grew more impatient. When he left, he relayed Irwin's views to Charles Somers in a long-distance telephone call. He returned to Irwin's home that evening, hoping to conclude the business. But Irwin remained undecided.

Exasperated and anxious to settle his own problems, Mack walked away from Irwin and began to look elsewhere. Hugh Duffy came to his rescue. He tipped him off to a piece of land on Huntington Avenue that had formerly been used by a carnival and circus. The land belonged to the Boston Elevated Railway Company, which was looking for a tenant that would promote traffic for the trains. "You'll find it better than the Charles River Park," Duffy assured Mack. "It'll need filling in, but it's within easy access of the business area."

One look at the site and Mack was ready to sign a lease. Acting for Somers, who posted two $25,000 bonds, Mack went to the office of the railway's attorney, Michael J. Moore, at 27 School Street in downtown Boston, on the afternoon of January 16 and signed a five-year lease.

"The American League people are pleased with the rent agreed," the *Globe* reported, "and are anxious to give Boston lively ball for 25 cents admission."

A relieved Mack dashed to the railroad station to catch the next train to Philadelphia. He told a reporter puffing to keep up with him that he was pleased to have Boston in the American League and suggested that the old Orioles' star Hugh Jennings might manage the team.

Boston Beaneaters president Arthur Soden was skeptical. "The day is past," he told Tim Murnane, "when good businessmen will put up money to fight an older organization like the National League."

Connie Mack still had to find a playing field for himself. Time was getting short. On January 17 the city again refused to act on Frank Hough's offer. Looking elsewhere, Mack found another site he liked, a large city block at Twenty-first and Lehigh. It was available for sale for $45,000 or for lease at $2,500 a year. But Hough and Jones said they had a better idea.

While Mack was out of town, Phillies president John I. Rogers and the National League may have inadvertently solved his problem for him. Philadelphia was one of the cities where they planned to install an American Association team to combat the American League. One of the backers was Francis C. Richter, editor of *Sporting Life* and the new *Reach Guide*. Richter had been in on the launching of both the original AA Athletics and the Phillies. He and one of his partners, Nevada silver king Hezekiah Niles, had taken an option on grounds at Columbia Avenue and Twenty-ninth Street, a city block owned by the Luther Martin estate.

Rogers was suspicious. He believed that Richter was a front for Cincinnati owner John T. Brush, and he didn't trust Brush. He suspected that Brush was trying to move into Philadelphia under the cover of an AA team, then maneuver him out of the Phillies. Rogers told his National colleagues if they wanted to put an association team in his city, they would have to rent his ballpark when the Phillies were out of town. When it came to political infighting, Rogers's voice was stronger than Brush's. Richter was told he'd have to use the Phillies grounds or it was no deal. So Richter and Niles dropped their option on the Columbia grounds.

Hough and Jones urged Mack and Somers to snap it up. Mack still preferred the Lehigh Avenue site. The newspapermen argued that the Columbia location was served by trolley lines from all sections of the city. The Pennsylvania Railroad's Engleside station was only two blocks away.

"Somers wanted me to follow Jones and Hough's advice," Mack said. "He figured they knew Philadelphia better than we did and we had to have the support of the newspapermen too, because we were a new club competing against the Phillies."

They didn't have to placate the writers to keep their support. In fact, the Philadelphia papers, even those that had no financial interest in the team, were solidly behind the American League. They were as fed up as the fans with Col. Rogers and his National cohorts' monopoly on the game.

But Mack gave in reluctantly—he still favored the Lehigh Avenue grounds—and on January 21 he signed a ten-year lease, an event that was overshadowed by the death of England's Queen Victoria, which captured all the front page headlines and hundreds of inches of ink for the next several days.

New York papers that echoed the National's line blamed Rogers for giving the invaders the break they needed. "He will get his when the war is over," predicted New York correspondent William F. H. Koelsch in *Sporting Life*.

Connie Mack had been working on the creation of the American League for the past two months. He had apparently been too busy, or just forgot, to notice that he had never formally applied for membership in the league for the Philadelphia franchise. Two days before the league's next meeting in Chicago, he hurriedly typed the following letter:

Philadelphia, Jan. 26, 1901

B. B. Johnson, Pres.
American League of Professional B. B. Clubs
Chicago IL

I herewith make application for the franchise for membership in your League for the city of Phil. Pa. And agree to comply with all conditions and requirements of the American League if granted such franchise.

/s/ C. McGillicuddy

Two days later Mack and Frank Hough were at the Grand Pacific Hotel in Chicago when the meeting convened at twelve-thirty. After the Baltimore franchise was approved as the sixth member, Ban Johnson read Mack's letter. Matt Killilea moved that the application be voted on. Comiskey seconded it, and the six voting members approved it unanimously. That's all there was to it. Philadelphia was now an official member of the American League. With Mack now eligible to vote, the seven then awarded the eighth franchise—Boston—to Charles Somers, who at that point also owned half the Cleveland club and three-fourths of the Philadelphia franchise.

Things were less complicated in those days.

In other business, the league constitution was read and ratified. Each club agreed to put up 51 percent of its stock and all ground leases to be held in trust by Johnson to ensure that they fulfilled their obligations as league members. This also gave Johnson effective control over the future sale or relocation of all teams. The league appointed Mack, John McGraw, and Charles Comiskey as a rules committee, approved a 140-game season, and agreed to limit rosters to fourteen players after the first two weeks of the season.

When the meeting reconvened at nine that evening, all members were "full of enthusiasm," said the *Sporting Life* correspondent.

To atone for the delayed ousting of Buffalo from the league, the eight clubs pledged not to raid the Bisons for players without permission from club president James Franklin. Ban Johnson was authorized to spend up to $60 a month for suitable offices, arrange all transportation needs, adopt an official ball, and negotiate terms with Western Union, whose presence at games was now deemed to be an asset.

Mr. McGillicuddy made one motion authorizing Ban Johnson to use his judgment in the issuing of season passes. This had been a controversial issue in earlier meetings. Some clubs expressed concerns over the number of passes being given out and questioned whether visiting clubs should be allowed to issue passes. Mack's motion to let Ban Johnson deal with it passed unanimously. (Johnson issued about two hundred league passes for 1901. One of them went to National League president Nick Young, who lived in Washington. It was accompanied by a note inviting Young to "go out and root for the new Senators." Young replied that he was sorry he was unable to reciprocate.)

Before adjourning, the league passed a resolution condemning "the evil of the farming and selling of ball players, as being unjust and unfair to the

ball player and against the best interests of the game of baseball." It vowed
to eliminate these practices.

Well, not all vows can be kept.

One last letter seeking peace had gone to the National League. There
was no reply. None was expected. Dreams of peaceful coexistence vanished.
The free enterprise system, with all its perils and risks, prevailed.

For Connie Mack, all that remained to be done was raise some money,
build a ballpark, put together a team, and open for business. He had three
months.

19 | THE CITY OF BROTHERLY LOVE AND "UNCLE BEN" SHIBE

It's likely that Ban Johnson awarded the Philadelphia franchise to Connie Mack for his services in helping to launch the new American League and because he believed that Mack, of all the Western League managers, was the best suited by temperament, tenacity, toughness, ability, dependability, and experience to succeed in the nation's third largest city.

The motto on the Great Seal of the City is "Philadelphia Maneto." "Maneto" comes from the Latin for "to continue or remain," appropriate for Mr. Mack, who remained there for the rest of his life.

He was going from the nation's most foreign city, Milwaukee, to its most American. Forty-seven percent of Philadelphia's population was second-generation American. Only New York and Chicago had more than its 1,293,697 residents, growing by 250,000 every decade. Philadelphia was the largest city in area in the country. There were vast open fields between some sections. Fairmount Park, a large forest preserve, stretched for twelve miles near the city center. To the northwest, Willow Grove Park was the site of fairs and band concerts.

The cold damp winters made it the national capital of catarrh and the postnasal drip. Newspapers carried full-page ads peddling remedies for the condition. Some of the wealthy residents fled the city during those months; others escaped the hot, humid summers that made it a fertile breeding ground for mosquitoes. In the early 1800s epidemics of yellow fever had killed thousands and sent as many as forty thousand residents fleeing the city.

In the eighteenth century Philadelphia had been the primary port of entry for immigrants. The Quaker City's Quakers were now outnumbered by East European Jewish, English, German, Irish, Scotch, and Italian families. The heavily Catholic city had seven hundred churches. Its streets and towns sang with Indian, Welsh, and English names: Wissahickon, Passyunk, Merion, Narberth, Bryn Mawr, Conshohocken, Chester.

The city had the patina of a sense of its history—a lengthy, proud, and honorable one. Some of its prestigious private clubs predated the Revolutionary War. Cricket clubs and soccer leagues were still active. Its reputation as a dull, priggish, nose-in-the-air place was promulgated by the nobs who wished it to be seen that way, the early Quaker influence, and such homegrown wits as W. C. Fields, who enjoyed castigating it with lines like, "Anyone found smiling there after curfew was liable to get arrested."

As is true of many jokes, there was a kernel of truth to Fields's jest. One disadvantage that Connie Mack faced was the statewide Blue Laws, forbidding almost everything on Sundays except breathing—and that not too heavily. There were many theaters, high- and low-brow—the city was the birthplace of vaudeville—and one of the nation's earliest movie houses, the Cineograph. But the sporting and theater crowds called the city Slowtown and deserted the place rather than be stuck there when everything was shut down for the Sabbath. Newspapers carried accounts of the proprietor of a sweets shop arrested for selling ice cream and soda water on Sunday. A Mr. Collison of Honesdale spent six days in jail on bread and water for refusing to pay the $4 fine for passing a Sunday working in his garden.

Beneath that haughty, austere crust, a lively bundle of neighborhoods—Pigtown, Swampoodle, Brewerytown—fought and drank and scrabbled to get ahead. For all its claims as a financial, cultural, and artistic center, Philadelphia was basically a blue-collar city with plenty of jobs and widespread middle-class prosperity. There was one home for every five inhabitants. It was surrounded by bountiful farmland, sliced by the Schuylkill and Delaware Rivers, and served by a busy seaport and the nation's largest railroad, the Pennsylvania. Fueled by extensive anthracite coal and iron mines to its immediate north and northwest, industrial plants produced everything from locomotives and ships to clothing, parasols, buttons, and the boxes that contained them.

During the Civil War Philadelphians' sentiments had been divided. It was now thoroughly Republican—and thoroughly corrupt. William Penn had founded the city on the principle of tolerance. More than anything, the citizens tolerated its corruption. There had not been a revolutionary moment since the gang of 1776 met there. The occasional perfunctory reform efforts had been bent to the political bosses' advantage. Lincoln Steffens, in *The Shame of the Cities*, found the muck the ripest for raking in Pennsylvania and labeled the Quaker City "corrupt but contented."

Fields called it the "City of Brotherly Graft."

Government was dominated by a ring whose power extended into the state legislature and the U.S. Congress and down into the schools, where teachers made cash payoffs to obtain jobs. New buildings and facilities were built at inflated, graft-padded costs. Most of the citizens didn't complain or bother to vote. Elections were rigged, the ring employing serial voters using names taken from tombstones, dead dogs, children, or people who had never existed. Mayor Samuel Ashbridge ran the city like a business—his own.

The Common Council was in the hands of the ring. One council member, William Vare, epitomized the political scene. He and his brothers held many city positions. As pioneer recyclers, they held the garbage collection franchise and fed the rich city slop to the pigs at their South Philly farm. They owned a large contracting firm that did work for the city and state, the Pennsylvania Railroad, Standard Oil, and the telephone company. The Vares also gave generously to church and charities and were obedient sons, very good to their mother. So nobody minded. They were local boys who had made good.

(Elected to the U. S. Senate in 1926, William Vare was never allowed into that chamber and was eventually barred by the Senate from taking his seat on charges of corruption and election fraud.)

Monopolies were formed or forming in utilities, oil, coal, steel, and street railways. John D. Rockefeller's Standard Oil Company was said to "do everything to the Pennsylvania legislature except refine it." J. P. Morgan was fighting Andrew Carnegie for control of the steel industry just as Ban Johnson was challenging the National League's monopoly on major league baseball. (In 1901 Morgan bought out Carnegie for $480 million.) The numerous trolley lines that crisscrossed the city were being consolidated into the hands of two ring members, while rival bosses fought to take them over for themselves.

Connie Mack would have to deal with these elements of local and state government. The council's decision on the use of the Jefferson Street grounds had probably been held up because the politicians were waiting for somebody to come up with what experienced businessmen called "the current price of doing business" in the city. But Mack was not interested in muckraking. He was not one of those described by Teddy Roosevelt as not knowing "when to stop raking the muck and look upward." Connie Mack was looking upward and forward.

Despite the competition from the Phillies, the Philadelphia American

League franchise was a plum. The city was five times the size of Milwaukee. It had a rich baseball history, going back to the organizing of a team in 1833. From 1871 to 1875 its baseball enthusiasts witnessed the rise and demise of three teams in the National Association: the Athletics, the Centennials, and the Whites. The Athletics lasted one year in the new National League in 1876, then waited six years before rejoining the National and fielding an entry in the new American Association.

Twice—in 1884 and 1890—the city's cranks enjoyed three major league teams scrambling for their support. But the peak of baseball frenzy occurred in 1883, when they celebrated their only American Association championship, won by the original Athletics.

Since 1892 the Phillies had been the only game in town. Despite the presence of baseball's only .400-hitting outfield of Sam Thompson, Billy Hamilton, and Ed Delahanty and such other stars as Elmer Flick, Napoleon Lajoie, and Dan Brouthers, they had never won a pennant. Attendance averaged just under 300,000, peaking at 475,000 in 1895.

Philadelphia—its name taken from the Greek word for City of Brotherly Love—was never known for brotherly love among its baseball cranks. Fed up with the National League's feuds, they were already—and would remain—among the loudest, most unforgiving, relentless hecklers and tormentors of players, home team as well as visitors, in baseball.

During their many meetings in November and December 1900, Ban Johnson had impressed on Connie Mack the need to find a prominent local backer, someone who would give them instant credibility and prestige as well as capital. Johnson had a suggestion: Benjamin F. Shibe. As far as Mack's future was concerned, it was the best advice Ban Johnson ever gave him.

"Uncle Ben" Shibe, as he was affectionately known in Philadelphia, was a short, stocky man of round face, thinning hair pomaded flat to his pate, and a graying bristly mustache. At sixty-two, he was old enough to be Connie Mack's father. Born in Philadelphia, he loved baseball but had never played the game. A childhood accident had left him with a gimpy leg. His father was an early manufacturer of baseball and other athletic supplies and equipment. As a young man, Ben made baseballs while working for the streetcar company. The expansion of baseball after the Civil War brought him enough customers to make it a full-time business.

In 1865 Philadelphia baseball enthusiasts hired London-born New Yorker

Al Reach for $25 a week to manage and play for the National Association Athletics. When his playing days were over, Reach started a company to manufacture baseballs and other sports equipment. In 1881 he proposed a partnership with Ben Shibe. From that union the A. J. Reach Company grew into the largest sporting goods manufacturer in the country. Much of its success was due to Shibe's inventions, primarily a machine to cut out the pieces of horsehide and punch holes for the stitches. A good cutter could maneuver thirty-two pieces from each hide. The covers were stitched by hand by women working as piece workers at home. Shibe's innovations made uniform quality possible. He also improved catchers' masks, chest protectors, shoes, and gloves.

In 1892 A. G. Spalding and Bros., a Chicago-based sporting goods manufacturer and retailer, merged with A. J. Reach, which then began producing the Spalding ball for the National League. The new company would be making the American League ball, stamped with the Reach name. The names and the color of the stitches were the only differences between the balls used by the two leagues.

Both Reach and Ben Shibe had been active in the formation and financing of Philadelphia baseball teams. As early as 1877, Shibe had backed a semipro team and was an investor in the American Association Athletics. Reach was one of the founders of the Phillies.

Ben Shibe had deep pockets, but he also possessed a far more valuable asset: a universal reputation for honesty, loyalty, and square dealing. His integrity was beyond question. His unassuming, down-to-earth demeanor won him legions of friends. Once he made them, he never lost them. You could walk from City Hall to Pigtown and call on every newspaper office in the city and find nobody who had a bad word to say about Uncle Ben Shibe.

Connie Mack and Ben Shibe met for the first time in early January at the Lafayette Hotel. Shibe was sympathetic to the American League. He believed that rival leagues were good for the game. But the meeting didn't go as Mack had hoped. There was no show of enthusiasm from Shibe, who listened but gave no sign of interest in investing in the new team.

There were complications. Shibe's wife of many years had recently died, leaving him in no mood to entertain new business ventures. He had cut down his involvement in the daily work of the business. He had all the wealth he could want.

Shibe's partner, Al Reach, was the president of the Phillies. Mack made no bones about his intention to raid that club for its best players. Shibe was also aware that his partner reaped more aggravation than pleasure from his association with the baseball business as it had evolved. John I. Rogers owned 51 percent of the Phillies. Reach's minority position left him powerless to do anything about the tactics Rogers employed that Reach found objectionable.

Ben Shibe had been involved with Rogers, too, in the original Athletics. At one time Rogers assessed the stockholders for more money. Shibe refused to pay unless Rogers let him see the club's books and list of stockholders. Rogers refused and threatened to take legal action to force Shibe to pony up. At this stage of his life, Ben Shibe didn't need that kind of headache.

Shibe had never made a dime out of his baseball investments. But that didn't bother him. The unpleasant memories of his former connections to the game, and Reach's current troubles with Rogers, made him wary of becoming involved again.

Mack left their meeting nervous and discouraged. He could go only so far with Somers's $7,500 and his own $2,500. He needed capital to prepare the field, build a grandstand, and sign players. He spent long days racing around the city trying to find new money and put the pieces together. Wherever he turned, he ran into pessimism and skeptics. The situation had him "guessing and worrying," he later told a *Sporting Life* correspondent. "There were times in those days when I almost thought I had undertaken an impossible task, for I met with many rebuffs from Philadelphians who told me frankly that a second club would never prosper in Philadelphia and even doubted if I could ever start the season."

At that point Mack's franchise existed only on paper in the minutes of the American League meeting, and this, he realized, would be null and void unless he could turn it into reality.

There were occasional rays of sunshine through the overcast outlook. Mack found a friend and ally in Billy Sharsig. The forty-five-year-old Sharsig had owned, managed, and operated teams in the area for twenty years. He had managed the Athletics in the American Association on and off for six seasons. But the Brotherhood war almost bankrupted him. He lost his entire capital of $18,000 and was forced to sell the team in 1891. Since then he had managed minor league teams in the state. Sharsig didn't have any money to invest, but he knew everybody in local baseball circles, and Mack needed that too. He hired Sharsig as the club's business manager. They hired a man who called himself Charles Goodfellow (his real name was Charles Erringer) to handle the duties of traveling secretary.

In mid-February Mack and Sharsig received an encouraging letter signed by forty employees of a large wholesale dry goods firm in the city:

Gentlemen:

We the undersigned by way of sending you words of encouragement in reference to your connection with the new American League of Base Ball Clubs, and representing the city of Philadelphia, look back with just pride to the halcyon days of the old Athletic club, and taking into consideration the actions of such men as Freedman of New York which is called "true sport," it is to laugh. And then our own celebrated Phillies, with their strong field glasses, buzzers, etc.[used to steal catchers' signs] how different the comparison. It is no wonder that our sport loving people are eager to grasp at anything that will give them good, clean baseball. . . . They tell us they do it for the benefit of the game, to get up a sideshow like the Association merely to keep someone else from managing similar organizations. But you will bear in mind that while they are doing the talking, the public is doing the thinking, and whenever the gong strikes for the season to open, you will find that not only this small testimonial of approval that represents 300 patrons of the game, but also that many missionaries to help the game along and to strike a blow at the Standard Oil and train-wrecking methods adopted by such people. This may seem strong language, but facts will not down. And all you have to do is play clean as well as good ball and the public will support you.

Beyond the ranks of the cranks, other interests were rooting for the Philadelphia franchise—and the entire American League—to succeed. The economic benefits were eagerly anticipated by streetcar companies, food vendors, railroads, hotels, printers, Western Union—down to the boys in the neighborhood who would sweep the stands and sell the cushions and peanuts.

Unknown to Connie Mack, other influences were at work. Ben Shibe had two sons, Tom and John, who worked for the Reach company. They were excited about the new team. Another major league would be good for business. They were impressed with the character, energy, and prudence of Connie Mack and believed their father would not have the problems with Mack that he'd had with Rogers. Most important, they had watched their father become withdrawn from his former activities following their mother's death. They felt that his becoming active in baseball again would be the best remedy to renew his zest for life.

Perhaps the most potent ingredient in the mix was that Ben Shibe had been a baseball fan from his youth. That virus may have been dormant, but there was no cure for it. Shibe discussed the idea with his partner. Al Reach didn't try to dissuade him, even though he knew the new team intended to sack the Phillies. But he cautioned Shibe to avoid being either a minority or majority owner.

"Take a 50 percent interest," Reach advised him, "no more and no less. That way, when he wants to do something, he'll have to convince you to go along with it, and when you want to do something, you'll have to convince him."

In a frequently told version of Ben Shibe's buying into the new team, he hesitates until opening day. When he stares wide-eyed at the crowd storming the gates to get into the park, he rushes into Mack's office crying, "Count me in! Count me in!"

But that wasn't Ben Shibe's style. He wasn't looking to get in on a "sure thing."

The story shows up in many accounts of Mack's life—although, to his credit, not in Fred Lieb's—and of Ban Johnson's as well. In a 1950 interview with Ed Pollock of the *Philadelphia Bulletin*, Mack is quoted, "It wasn't until the morning of opening day in 1901 that Mr. Shibe declared himself in. We were ready to go along without him."

Maybe Pollock made up the quote. Maybe Connie Mack had read it so often that after fifty years he had come to believe that must have been the way it happened. As the past recedes, the elapsed time between events shrinks, like the spaces between buildings as a train leaves a city in the distance, until it all blends together.

According to Frank L. Hough, writing in *Baseball Magazine* just ten years after the events, Charles Somers deposited the collateral for the ten-year lease on Columbia Park, which was signed on January 21. Hough placed Somers, Johnson, Mack, and Ben Shibe at a meeting that night at the Lafayette Hotel, where contractors Foster and Fry unrolled the ballpark plans. It was Shibe, wrote Hough, who insisted that the projected two-thousand-seat grandstand wouldn't be big enough, and they agreed to double the capacity.

There was no publicity about that meeting at the time. Shibe's connection with the new club remained a secret. But whose money were they spending? The seed money had been the $10,000, but the amount of fertilizer needed to make the plant grow was at least five times that much. The grandstand construction and field preparation would cost $35,000. Mack needed cash for advances to players he signed. He was traveling thousands of miles. There were uniforms to order, tickets to be printed, supplies to buy, people to hire.

In February Mack was reported as claiming to have $100,000 behind him. The money must have come from Ben Shibe, but Mack refused to identify his backers. Why was it kept a secret? Could it have been at Ben Shibe's request? Certainly the sooner Shibe's role was made public, the sooner the club could capitalize on his reputation to enhance its public support.

As always, secrecy bred speculation: the mysterious backer was said to be one of the Gimbel brothers of department store wealth; a prominent National League figure "whose identity must remain undisclosed"; A. J. Reach; "Pittsburgh money"; or National Leaguers out to ruin Col. Rogers.

Samuel Jones fanned the fires by assuring other writers that the new club was not wanting for money and had no interest in seeking local backers.

Shibe's official connection to the enterprise was finally made public on February 20, when the newspapers reported that a meeting of the stockholders had taken place the night before at the Lafayette and unanimously elected Benjamin F. Shibe president. Shibe reportedly accepted without the slightest hesitation.

The *Inquirer*, which might be considered a house organ for the club with Hough as its sports editor, was effusive but not alone in its praise of Shibe:

"The very fact that Mr. Shibe has accepted the presidency of the local club is a sufficient guarantee that it will be run on straightforward business principles of unquestioned and unquestionable honesty, with a profound contempt for anything and everything savoring of sharp practice. Under his direction the integrity of the club is assured.

"This will not be without its effect when the time comes for the signing of players. The older players know that Ben Shibe's word is as good as his bond and that when they enter into a contract with the American League, the spirit as well as the letter of their contracts will be observed."

In an obvious swipe at Col. Rogers and the Phillies, the *Inquirer* added, "There will be no drawbacks or pullbacks in the contract, no vague paragraphs susceptible to constructions by either of which the player may find himself skinned at the end of the season. With Ben Shibe as the head of the new club, everything will be clear and aboveboard."

Shibe, Mack, and Somers went into business together with no formal agreement. Shibe and Mack shared the power amicably without the need for multipage legal documentation. The American Base Ball Club of Philadelphia wasn't even incorporated until June 12, 1901, and then Charles Somers was not named among the five subscribers to its capital stock.

The corporation was capitalized at $50,000, divided into five hundred shares. The names of the subscribers, who were also the board of directors, and the number of shares for each were as follows:

Benjamin F. Shibe, 165
Cornelius McGillicuddy, 125
George W. Jackson, 200
William Y. C. Anderson, 5
John G. Hoffmeister, 5

The numbers don't mean anything. There may have been some legal requirements for outside members of the board of directors, accounting for Jackson, Hoffmeister, and Anderson, who was an attorney for the Athletics. The subscribers weren't actually buying the shares. The original five hundred shares were issued in the joint names of Mack and Somers. They remained on the books that way until November 12, 1901, when Ben Shibe's half-interest was first recorded in the form of two hundred thirty-five shares in his name and five each to Jackson, Hoffmeister, and Anderson. At that point, Somers and Mack each held one hundred twenty-five shares.

Nothing in the stock ledgers shows Ben Shibe buying out Charles Somers's interest at any time. Somers's shares were not transferred out of his name on the books until October 20, 1902, and then they were transferred to Connie Mack. It took another thirteen months for the two hundred fifty then in Mack's name to be transferred to the team attorney, William Jay Turner, in trust, presumably half for Mack and half for the two sportswriters, Hough and Jones. Meanwhile, Ben Shibe had signed over sixty-two shares to his son Tom and five to his son John, and Anderson and Jackson dropped out of the picture. (Hoffmeister eventually turned back his five shares to Ben Shibe on November 2, 1907.)

If all this seems incomprehensible in today's world of crossed t's and dotted i's, it was all in accordance with common practice at the time. Regardless of what the stock ledgers show—and they are open, just opaque to twenty-first century CPAS—Ben Shibe and Connie Mack were equal partners from the start, as harmonious as a barbershop quartet.

COLUMBIA PARK AND THE "ATHALETICS"

As he stood on the vacant field with Billy Sharsig on the windy, 30-degree morning of Saturday, January 26, 1901, Connie Mack didn't need any signs to tell him that he was in Brewerytown. He could smell it. The air was redolent with the aroma of fermenting mash and hops from the breweries a few blocks to the west. A goat of unknown pedigree or ownership grazed on the sparse vegetation that would soon be the outfield. They were pleased that little grading would be needed to level the grounds.

The field covered a city block 400 by 450 feet, bordered by Columbia Avenue on the north, Thirtieth Street to the west, Oxford and Twenty-ninth. Those dimensions would make it the smallest field in the league. Amid the swirling dust, the two men envisioned home plate at the corner of Thirtieth and Oxford, making right field the sun field. Depending on the depth of the grandstand and the space between the seats and home plate, the foul lines would extend 280–300 feet to right and 330–350 to left. In center field the fence would form a right angle about 440 feet from home plate.

The prosperous German neighborhood, separated from the Irish sections to the north and south by about five blocks, reminded Mack of Milwaukee. In the new gray stone St. Ludwig's Catholic Church three blocks away, the sermons at ten thirty High Mass were delivered in German. Connie Mack probably went at nine, when there was no sermon, and he could be on hand for morning practice. Every block had a Teutonic social or fraternal club. A community picnic in June was the biggest event of the year until the arrival of the new baseball team.

The area had everything the residents needed: a newspaper (the *Brewerytown Chronicle*), grocery stores, bakery, tailor shop, drugstore, taverns, and jobs. Trolley lines ran on Columbia and Twenty-ninth: open cars in summer with wood seats across the width of the cars and no center aisle and running boards for standing room. Eight cents would take you any-where in the city. Most of the men worked in the breweries or the ice house at Thirty-third and Columbia. Horse-drawn wagons filled with beer kegs or ice clattered over the Thirtieth Street cobblestones. A movie house would open within a few years. The ball grounds were described as being sur-rounded by a fence, then by saloons. Youngsters often waited by the swing-ing doors in hopes of being taken into the game by an emerging customer. Every taproom had a backdoor ladies' entrance into a room where there were tables. You could dine like a lord for thirty-five cents. A free sandwich and crackers came with a nickel beer, two with a ten-cent pitcher.

The biggest saloon, on the corner of Columbia and Hollywood, in back of left-center field, belonged to Matt Kilroy. As a rookie in 1886, the five-foot-nine left-hander had set a strikeout record of 513 and pitched a no-hitter for Baltimore in the American Association. Connie Mack had faced him in two postseason games that year. The next year he won 46 games, working 589 innings in his 69 starts. The workload proved too much; two years later he was down to 480 innings. Then his arm really fell off; he last pitched for Chicago in 1898. Kilroy became a regular at morning practices as an unofficial volunteer pitching coach and was always on hand at his place of business after a game. Many of the players who roomed in the neighborhood were frequent patrons of Kilroy's saloon.

Row houses lined the streets. Some were low, porch-front houses; others were brick with marble stoops instead of porches. Rooftops of the two- and three-story houses along Twenty-ninth and Columbia offered clear views of the entire playing field. Players could find room and board, including three meals a day, for up to $4 a week. A small hotel at Thirty-third and Ridge Avenue, run by Charles McDaniel, was also a popular residence for the young, unmarried players.

Connie Mack rented rooms for himself at 2932 Oxford in a three-story house with a porch eight steps up and a bay window on the second floor. He could walk across the street to his office beneath the first base grand-stand. Not that he was there much that winter.

Immediately after inspecting the grounds with Sharsig, he was off to Chicago for league meetings. On Monday morning, January 28, Billy Sharsig had the honor of turning the first spade of dirt before several hun-dred people, who raised a cheer that hung in a small fog of breath in the cold air. Billy then supervised the unloading of lumber, and the work of building a ballpark began.

There were no bureaucratic delays. The plans had been approved by Shibe and Mack almost simultaneously with the signing of the lease. Contractor James B. Foster, promising the job would be done by opening day, took the plans immediately to Jephan Hill of the building inspector's office, who handed them to his chief engineer. Ben Shibe deposited $20,000 in the bank for Foster to draw on. With fifty men working every day until dark, the fences went up in two weeks, and work on the grandstand began. Sign painters decorated the outfield planks with ads for beer, whiskey, and Cinco cigars. In center field a sign for the *Financial Bulletin*, a financial newspaper, used black letters on a yellow background. A new ball became as black as tobacco juice after a few turns around the infield and was difficult to see against the black letters. The sign was later painted over in green. The scoreboard was in right field. A small sign in center field said, "$25 will be paid to any player hitting this sign." Bill Bernhard became the first to collect the reward when he hit a triple off the sign on September 14.

In the midst of the construction, Ban Johnson sent Mack on another assignment. The Washington club had not yet found a suitable location. Johnson considered moving the franchise to Brooklyn. Despite two consecutive pennant-winning years, Brooklyn trailed most other National clubs in attendance. Johnson chalked that up to its fifty-cent general admission. He thought an American League team charging twenty-five cents would do well there. He sent Mack and John McGraw to Brooklyn to check out possible playing sites, but the situation was resolved when grounds were leased in Washington near a trolley line at Florida Avenue and H Street Northeast. Looking ahead, Johnson also took an option on the vacant Sportsman's Park in St. Louis.

On his return from Brooklyn, Mack hired a groundskeeper, Thomas Murphy, the artist who had doctored the field for the Baltimore Orioles during their championship years in the 1890s. Murphy had gone with John McGraw to St. Louis as groundskeeper in 1900.

During his stay in East Brookfield in January, Connie Mack decided to bring his brother Dennis and his family to Philadelphia and give him a job. He rented a house for them near Columbia Park and identified Dennis as a scout. That was for appearance only. Dennis worked for Murphy on the grounds crew and took tickets. The move to Philadelphia rescued his wife Annie and their four children from a life of dead-end drudgery. Annie's life was still hard, and her husband's thirst continued to soak up most of his income except for the pennies she could hide in the sugar jar. But the children's lives were immeasurably improved.

Foster estimated the single-tier grandstand, which extended from third base around to first, would be completed by March 15. The grandstand was not curved but cornered at a right angle behind home plate. Bleachers extended out to the fences on each side. Instead of dugouts, the teams occupied benches covered by an awning in front of the first row of the grandstand behind first and third base.

A ten-foot screen on wooden framing ran along the roof to keep foul balls in the park. A rooftop press box behind home plate was covered but not enclosed. It contained two rows of tables and a water cooler painted a "lovely heliotrope, embossed with silver leaf around the top and bottom," according to scribe Charles Dryden.

There were bleacher entrances behind first and third base, where portable turnstiles were used. A permanent turnstile was installed at the grandstand entrance behind home plate. During the season boys from St. Ludwig's School would gather around the bleacher entrances after school. One of them was Emil Beck. "After the fifth inning," he recalled, "if you were one of the kids chosen to help carry in the turnstiles, you could stay and watch the rest of the game."

On March 5, four thousand folding opera chairs arrived, and ten days later Foster met his goal. The grandstand was ready to be painted. Hoping to avoid labor problems, Mack hired union painters. An angry rival union, denied the work, boycotted the games. Once, during the season, with the team on the road, somebody hired a nonunion painter to adorn a sign with a portrait of a whiskey bottle. Mack had to pacify irate union leaders when he returned home.

Otherwise everything went smoothly. On April 1 the topsoil was spread as spring practice began. The players dodged mounds of dirt scattered about the outfield. Grass was sown but wouldn't grow in until after the season had begun. Infield grass was sparse. A dirt path went from the flat pitcher's box to home plate.

By some accounts, Connie Mack is credited with a canny public relations decision in reviving the old Athletics' name for his new team. He did it but without ever saying he was doing it. About eight years earlier, the name had been ruled a trademark in a lawsuit. Hezekiah Niles owned the American Association club's charter and the rights to the name. If the association club came back to life, said the experts, they would have the rightful claim to it. In late January, possibly to avoid any legal entanglements, Connie Mack distanced himself from the subject, expressing indifference.

"We haven't thought very much about a name for our club yet," he said. "I don't care much about a name anyway. So long as our team performs to suit the fans, I don't care what name they use."

Throughout February and into March the team was referred to as the Philadelphia American League club, occasionally as "Connie Mack's new Phillies." By February 28 the National League gave up trying to find suckers to back American Association teams in the East. That plot fizzled out, taking with it any threat of the resurrection of the old Athletics.

Mack still made no comments about a name for the team. Nobody polled the fans or sponsored a contest. Mack let it appear that, as was often the case, the newspapers would anoint the team with a nickname and through common usage it would stick. On March 28 the *North American* put forth the suggestion, "Columbia Park sounds all right, but if Connie Mack intends to call his team 'Athletics,' would it not be better to call the new grounds Athletic Park?"

Elsewhere the paper indicated its interest was more self-serving than sentimental. "It is to be hoped Connie Mack calls his club Athletics so as to avoid the necessity of adding American League or National League to the names of the local teams every time they are mentioned. That would save a whole lot of confusion and incidentally considerable newspaper space."

A week later the *North American* went ahead on its own and referred to "Mack's Athletics" in a headline. The field remained Columbia Park. Mack remained mum. But he had silently tapped into the sentiments of the writers and fans. When his new uniforms arrived on April 2—home white flannel with dark blue trim and striped pillbox caps, road gray with dark blue trim and coats to match—there was a letter "A" on the left breast of the shirts.

By opening day the team was, legally or illegally, officially or unofficially, universally and unequivocally the "Athaletics," as Connie Mack pronounced it.

Nobody sued.

Like Ben Franklin, another New Englander transplanted to Philadelphia, Connie Mack was a man of peace. But when a war started, he became a formidable front-line fighter for the cause. Mack, Ban Johnson, Jimmy McAleer, Jimmy Collins, and Charles Somers were the American League's principal raiders of the National ranks, signing players for other clubs as well as their own. They targeted only players who had not yet signed 1901 National contracts, ignoring the option or reserve clause.

Their objective was to capture the enemy's best players, whatever the cost. The strategy had two purposes: to weaken the National and stock the American clubs with faces familiar to the fans. They succeeded in signing fifty-seven National Leaguers that spring.

Every team was fair game except, it seemed, the Pittsburgh Pirates. Johnson believed that Barney Dreyfuss had no love for his NL colleagues after they dropped his Louisville club. He was confident that Dreyfuss would switch the Pirates to the American by 1902. (Johnson's hunch was well-founded. In 1909 Dreyfuss admitted that Harry Pulliam had stopped him from making the switch. "I had been humiliated by the board of directors of the National League," he said, "and I knew I would be better off financially as well in the American. But Mr. Pulliam said to me, 'If you drop out of the National it will mean the death of the old league. You have some good friends in the National who would be ruined now, if you desert them.' That settled it; I stuck, and I am glad now that I did.")

Only John McGraw ignored Johnson's hands-off policy, signing Pittsburgh infielder Jimmy Williams for Baltimore. Dreyfuss claimed Williams had already signed a Pirates contract and he would fight for him. He lost.

Ban Johnson was determined to direct his efforts toward strengthening the three teams that faced direct competition from established clubs: Boston,

Philadelphia, and Chicago. If his other club owners complained—and they did—he didn't care. Right or wrong, popular or pariah, Johnson was as immovable as Gibraltar.

Boston, Brooklyn, and the Phillies were the hardest-hit targets. Most of the Beaneaters' outfield decamped. Hugh Duffy went to Milwaukee as manager. Popular third baseman Jimmy Collins went across town to manage the American League team and took Chick Stahl, slugger Buck Freeman, and pitcher Nig Cuppy with him. Both of their catchers departed, Billy Sullivan to Chicago and Boileryard Clarke to Washington. Collins also snared baseball's best pitcher, Cy Young, and his catcher, Lou Criger, from the Cardinals. Facing disastrous losses, the Boston owners offered Charles Somers $100,000 in cash and a promise of a National League franchise next year if he would withdraw from the city and turn over the Huntington grounds lease to them. Somers turned them down.

Brooklyn lost Hugh Jennings, Fielder Jones, Joe McGinnity, and pitcher Handsome Harry Howell. Charles Ebbets was especially sore at Connie Mack for luring Lafayette Napoleon "Lave" Cross to Philadelphia. A man of all positions, the thirty-four-year-old Cross had played for three Philadelphia teams: the old Athletics, the Players' League club, and the Phillies. Mack and Shibe knew his return would be good news to Cross's many fans in the city. Cross was a favorite partly because he looked so unlike an athlete. The most bowlegged major leaguer in history, he made Honus Wagner's legs look as straight as clothes pins by comparison. At the time, Cross was bedridden with an injury that threatened to end his playing days, but Ben Shibe visited him and gave him a two-year contract.

In Chicago Comiskey signed Clark Griffith to manage his team. Griffith brought pitcher Nixey Callahan and outfielder Sam Mertes with him. The Orphans also lost pitcher Ned Garvin to Milwaukee and third baseman Bill Bradley to Cleveland.

Connie Mack's shopping list included just about everybody on the Phillies roster. He and his agents were rumored to be holding secret negotiations with so many of them at the same time that the beleaguered Phillies manager Bill Shettsline issued a press release on February 18, 1901, expressing his "indignation at the methods of Mr. Mack and another American League manager in inducing Phillies players to jump their contracts." He cited a case where, on the previous Saturday, Mack and Jimmy Manning of the Washington club had offered one of his best players more money than the National League limit. "They assured him that the renewal option had no legal effect and would guarantee him that no harm would come to him by reason of that clause." The player, Shettsline added, felt "morally bound" to stay with the Phils.

Mack didn't bother denying any of it. When a reporter asked him who the player was, Mack, accompanied by Johnson, Somers, and Manning, replied, "I really cannot say just which player Mr. Shettsline refers to. I have talked with a number of his men."

"All had a good laugh," the *Sporting Life* correspondent noted.

The player was probably Roy Thomas, who had starred at Penn and batted .325 as a rookie in 1899. Thomas turned down Mack's offer of a two-year contract at $3,250 and stayed with the Phillies.

Still, nobody was boasting about any conquests. Johnson wanted no publicity about specific signings. The raiders cautioned players they corralled to say nothing. Thus, in early March, when the *North American* sent telegrams to several of the top Phillies players, asking them where they intended to play in 1901, every one replied that he was undecided. None admitted to signing with the American League.

Johnson and his agents knew the National owners and managers were on the road too, following up every rumored capture in hopes of persuading, threatening, or intimidating the defectors into returning to the fold. All winter and spring the Midwest resembled a jungle full of explorers looking for King Solomon's mines. Mack crossed paths with his fellow hunters Duffy, McAleer, and Collins, as well as National League magnates trying to lure their jumpers back and hold on to those who were wavering. In some cases they succeeded, justifying Johnson's ban on claims of conquests that might prove embarrassingly premature. Once Mack found Hanlon and Ebbets on the same train with him going to Philadelphia, where they tried in vain to regain their wayward minions.

As far as the players were concerned, agreeing to terms was not the same as signing, as the hunters soon learned. They were determined to cash in on the collapse of the National's monopoly after ten years of "take it or leave it" since the demise of the Brotherhood. Playing one club or league against another was a game the players knew well. Speculative headlines proclaimed the signing of stars who later "unsigned" themselves or in fact had never signed with anybody.

The most celebrated jumping frog was Jimmy Sheckard. The Brooklyn outfielder signed with John McGraw in Baltimore in January for $2,250 and took a $200 advance. A month later he signed a similar contract with

Ned Hanlon in Brooklyn. In March he went back to McGraw and in April returned to Brooklyn, where he unpacked and spent the season.

Some magnates took a dim view of such players, considering any man who signed two contracts to be a "slow thinker" and thus not much of a player. As it turned out, though, that applied to some pretty good players.

Connie Mack didn't land every Phillies player he went after, but he bagged half of Shettsline's pitching staff: right-handers Bill Bernhard and Chick Fraser and lefty Wiley Piatt.

Fraser, thirty on March 17, had finished two years at Bryant-Stratton College of Business in Chicago and worked as a telephone installer. He broke in with Minneapolis in the Western League in 1894 and was durable but wild until he reached the Phillies, where he was 21-13 in 1899 and 16-10 in a 138-game 1900 season. Mack signed him for $3,000.

Bernhard, a day older than Fraser, was 15-10 in 1900, his second season with the Phillies.

Piatt, twenty-six, an Ohio State graduate, had won 47 in his first two years with the Phillies. Arm problems cut his work in half and his record to 9-10 in 1900.

By far the biggest prize snared by Connie Mack for the American League was Napoleon "Larry" Lajoie. Idolized by Philly fanatics, who called him "La-joy," Lajoie rivaled Honus Wagner as the greatest star in the game. He had averaged .345 since arriving in Philadelphia late in the 1896 season. Lajoie had come up as a first baseman and was switched to second in 1898 by Phils manager George Stallings. Wearing a small flat glove, he was as placid and nonchalant-looking in the field as at bat. He seemed careless and indifferent while catching the ball without trying to get in front of it. He had the instincts to read the ball off the bat—where it was headed and where it would bounce—and get a jump on it. And he came up with the balls, leading some experts to chalk up his effortless success to "lucky bounces." But Chicago writer Hugh Fullerton rated him the most graceful player of all time, making miraculous stops without any apparent effort.

A right-handed batter, Lajoie was impossible to pitch to. The term "bad ball hitter" could have been coined for him. He could break up a game hitting a so-called waste pitch, even a pitchout. An intentional walk was not always a safe option for a pitcher. Lajoie could hit brushback pitches off the left field fence or fling the bat at a pitchout and line it over first base. His eyes, judgment of distance, and reflexes worked together in perfect harmony. When he stepped into the batter's box, he drew a line in the dirt beside the plate. He didn't dig in but stood facing the pitcher, feet close together, ready to take a step or two to make contact wherever the ball was thrown. He gripped the bat loosely with a relaxed, almost inattentive attitude. Then, with a short, sharp swing, he sprayed line drives in all directions and over the distant fences.

"If you pitched inside to him," spitballer Ed Walsh said, "he'd tear a hand off the third baseman, and if you pitched outside he'd knock down the second baseman. . . . If he had a weakness it was a fastball right down the middle. He murdered breaking stuff."

The moody, untalkative Nap was as undisciplined off the field as he was at bat. He missed six weeks of the 1900 season because of a fight over a bat with teammate Elmer Flick in the clubhouse. Lajoie swung. Flick ducked. Lajoie's left fist smashed into the wall, breaking his thumb. Now labeled a "troublesome player," the truculent Frenchman from Rhode Island had a long list of grievances against the Phils' owners and was wide open to Connie Mack's siren song. Lajoie had signed a 1900 contract for $2,400, the league limit, plus $200 on the side. Told that he was the highest paid player on the team, he was peeved when he discovered that Ed Delahanty, the captain, was promised $600 over the limit. What's more, Lajoie claimed, he never saw the $200. He also said he had been charged for shoes and a uniform he never received and docked a day's pay on a day he had actually played.

On February 10 Mack denied that he was negotiating with Lajoie. That was true but misleading. Mack was relying on Frank Hough to make contact with some potential jumpers, who knew Hough as the *Inquirer*'s sports editor. Lajoie was one of them. On the night of February 14 Mack, Hough, and Lajoie met and worked out a two-year contract at $4,000 a year. King Larry had as shrewd an eye for finance as for breaking balls. No matter how the new club or the league might fare, he wasn't going to lose a penny. Mack agreed to his demand that a full year's salary be deposited up front in the Northwestern National Bank, in an account in the joint names of Lajoie's landlord, a Mr. Johnson, and Frank Hough. Every payday they would draw out a check. Lajoie signed. Mack put the contract in his safe.

Lajoie promised to say nothing about his signing. In reply to the *North American*'s March 10 survey, he wired the paper, "Have not decided on the club I shall play with. Will let you know as soon as I do."

After signing Lajoie, Mack headed to Cleveland and Cincinnati, where his prey included Elmer Flick, the Phillies outfielder who had not only ducked Lajoie's left hook but had outhit him by thirty points in 1900. In their first meeting Flick agreed to sign for $3,000. Then he began adding conditions: he was unsure of his legal status with the Phillies, whatever that meant; he wanted a guarantee against being blacklisted by the National League. When his hedgerow grew too high, Mack walked away from him. Flick remained with the Phillies.

Sometimes the raiders found themselves competing for the same player. Sam Crawford was wooed in Wahoo, Nebraska, by Mack and Jimmy Collins. Crawford, nineteen, had batted .267 for Cincinnati. At first Crawford accepted Mack's terms, but he was playing Mack and Collins against each other and both of them against Reds owner John T. Brush. He eventually persuaded Brush to match the American's best offer and signed with the Reds. Mack was angry.

"I have not yet decided what to do about Crawford," he said. "He had accepted my terms by wire and a contract which he promised to sign and return at once. . . . His acceptance of terms and agreement by wire to sign with me is as good at law as a signed contract, and if I went to court no doubt I could restrain him from playing with Cincinnati."

But he didn't. There were just so many players he could sign, so many negotiations he could handle, so many directions he could go at the same time, so many hours in the day and days in the week.

Returning to Philadelphia on March 6, Mack admitted that he had failed to sign the stars he had gone after and refused to name anybody he did sign. "I have an even dozen first-class players under contract now, but I cannot make known their names at present until I sign my full fourteen," was as far as he would go.

And with good reason. Although they were all beginning to sound like lawyers, nobody really knew what constituted a legally binding agreement. Everybody had an opinion on the legality of the option or reserve clause in the National League's contracts, but nobody really knew how the various judges in the various league cities might rule. Nobody could be sure which players would become rubberlegs and who would actually show up by opening day. Some of the dozen Mack thought he had under contract turned into bullfrogs. Others who had taken the bait on his line had not yet been reeled in.

With six weeks to go before opening day, poor bedeviled Bill Shettsline had no idea who, if anybody, would be wearing a Phillies uniform. On March 12 he wrote a plaintive appeal to Mack to call off the attack:

Cornelius McGillicuddy
Manager
Philadelphia American League Base Ball Club
Dear Sir:

It has been so frequently stated in the newspapers that it has become of public notoriety that you have been negotiating with certain players under contract with our club, that I thought it only proper to notify you formally that said players signed a regular contract with us for last year, including the well known nineteenth paragraph with its renewal option clause, which we exercised by sending written notice thereof prior to October 15, 1900. By said exercise of such option the players covenant to perform similar services and be subject to all the obligations, duties, and liabilities prescribed in said contract for the six months beginning April 1, 1901.

We are advised by distinguished authority that all such players thus duly notified are under contract with us as fully as if they had signed renewed contracts.

You will, therefore, please take this as a notice to discontinue further negotiations with said players and to annul any writings or agreements you have made with any of them, in violation of our prior contractual rights. I send this as a formal notice so that ignorance of our rights in the premises may not be hereafter pleaded.

I will thank you very much for a reply, either confirming or denying the statements as to such negotiations complained of.

I write this in no unfriendly spirit, but simply as a precautionary measure.

> Yours truly,
> /s/ William J. Shettsline

P.S. Will you also inform me whether your club has been incorporated, and if so, am I designating it by its proper name in this communication? wjs

This "just-for-the-record" document, obviously worded by the Phillies' lawyers, drew this public reply from Mack:

"I am going away in a few minutes to sign another star. So you see that letter hasn't frightened me a bit. Don't you suppose [Beaneaters' owner] Soden in Boston made sure the option clause was invalid before he offered

Collins $8,000 to stay with him? If they thought for a moment their contract was valid in law, why would they worry and go around offering their old players large increases in salary to re-sign with them this year?"

The war raged on throughout the spring, an economic battle waged with dollars in amounts that may have been no more than J. P. Morgan's monthly grocery bill but were unimaginable to the average six-day-a-week worker. According to a government report, ballplayers already earned more than the annual income of 85 percent of all artisans; 70 percent of doctors, lawyers, and newspaper writers; and 90 percent of theatrical performers. As it had been just a decade earlier, money was again as much a part of baseball reporting as runs, hits, and errors. Big numbers like $3,500 and $4,000 were tossed about, smashing the $1,200–$2,400 range for which most baseball "chattels" had been forced to work. Reports had as many as forty players signing for as much or more than Lajoie's $4,000. For the first time, some players earned more than their managers. Ned Hanlon's complaint to a Pittsburgh writer ten years earlier still reflected the attitude of owners, managers, and fans alike:

"There is nothing to my mind more demoralizing to the players than [the publishing of players' salaries]. It is misleading. Seldom are the figures right, and there isn't much use in trying to get them correctly, for one can't. Whose business is it how much salary a player gets? No man in any other business cares to have his salary published and it is not done. If you had any idea the trouble the practice caused you wouldn't keep it up."

Philadelphia writers speculated that Connie Mack's expenses could reach a staggering $31,000 in players' salaries alone. The total for all eight clubs in the American League could top a ruinous $200,000. Based on the 1900 season, Brooklyn president Ned Hanlon estimated the new eastern clubs' total expenses would be $65,000–$80,000, and they'd have to average four thousand customers a day at twenty-five cents to make it.

With everything else on his plate, Connie Mack was a member of the league's rules committee with Comiskey and McGraw. They immediately confronted a controversy. In 1900 foul balls did not count as strikes except for those tipped straight back at the catcher. Some players, notably McGraw, Willie Keeler, and Phillies slugger Roy Thomas, were experts at wearing down pitchers by deliberately fouling off pitch after pitch. Thomas claimed the record, fouling off twenty-seven in one at-bat against Bill Phillips of the Reds. Fans complained that the tactic slowed the action and prolonged the games.

Apparently Ned Hanlon, who hadn't objected when he was managing McGraw and Keeler in Baltimore, took a different view of the art now that he was in Brooklyn. The story goes that in a game in 1900, after Roy Thomas fouled off a dozen pitches against a tiring Brooklyn pitcher, Hanlon yelled at him, "Have your fun now, kid. We're going to take care of you next year."

That winter the National rules committee of Hanlon, A. J. Reach, and James Hart passed what was called the "foul strike rule," which said that "any foul ball not caught on the fly" was a strike until there were two strikes. Since 1894, a bunt that went foul had been called a strike, until there were two strikes.

Mack and McGraw were adamantly opposed to the new rule. "Calling foul balls strikes is an awful doggy rule," said Mack. They recommended the American League not adopt the rule.

The National proposed that a batter hit by a pitch should not be awarded first base; a ball should be called instead. Mack objected to that idea too: "The National League in legalizing the pitcher to soak a batter in the head any time will cause no end of trouble." The NL passed the rule but soon rescinded it. It also passed a rule requiring catchers to move up within ten feet of home plate for all pitches. No more wasting time putting on a mask to move up when there were two strikes on the batter. The American League did nothing in this regard until 1903.

There were reports that the American was thinking of eliminating or limiting the use of the bunt. Without using direct quotes, *Sporting Life* claimed, "Veterans like Connie Mack, Charles Comiskey and others say there will be added interest [if the bunt is eliminated]. They believe the cut and dried sacrifice hit cuts down stealing which is more interesting. . . . Baseball is for the spectators, who are losing interest for lack of action. Scientific baseball and inside tricks are often lost to the fans."

Considering that Mack's most successful teams would be built on "scientific baseball and inside tricks," the validity of attributing these sentiments to him seems doubtful. The bunt stayed.

The American League rules committee's report concluded:

"After careful consideration of the playing rules of 1900, we are of the opinion that no changes at present would be conducive to the furthering of the interest in the game, as the playing rules of 1900 as enforced by the umpires in the American League give fast, clean ball, entirely satisfactory to its patrons."

So the two major leagues began their antagonistic coexistence using different playing rules regarding catchers and foul strikes. Contrary to expectations, the foul strike rule did not result in shorter games in the National than the American. By midseason Athletics games were averaging one hour and thirty minutes; Phillies contests, over two hours. The fastest game of the year, a 4–3 Athletics win over Cleveland on June 19, took only seventy-two minutes.

The foul strike rule was criticized by some writers and fans. The *Inquirer's* account of the Phillies' opener included this comment:

"A lot of oldtimers and fans jeered at the new rule when Elmer Flick planted a ball against the right field screen about ten feet foul. The umpire called strike. The decision was greeted with alternate jeers and hisses. To call such a hit a foul is the height of asininity. If the National Leaguers are wise they will change the rule as they did regarding the base on being hit with a pitched ball, in deference to the express wishes of the public. Even the most obtuse magnate must have perceived that the sentiment of the spectators yesterday was against the innovations made by the rules dickerers."

But the new rule remained in the National's book.

The American League met at the Lafayette Hotel in Philadelphia on March 20. It approved a twenty-five-cent general admission, giving it an edge in every city where it faced National competition, as the National charged fifty cents—except in Philadelphia, where the Phillies charged a quarter. The schedule produced ten conflicting dates with the Phillies, including Mack's home opener on April 24 against Washington. The starting gong would sound at three thirty. There were practical reasons for beginning at that hour. Vaudeville houses opened at noon and ran until midnight, but the headliners did only two shows a day. Games could be completed between their appearances on stage. Businessmen, actors, and the stock market crowd could get to the ballpark and be home for supper or get to the theater in plenty of time for the evening performance.

During a break in the meetings, Mack revealed for the first time the names of some of the players he had signed—or believed he had signed. When he confirmed that Napoleon Lajoie was to be his team captain, he lit the fuse that led to the powder keg. Two days later, when Mack made public the signing of Phillies pitcher Bill Bernhard, the flame reached the powder.

"We're going to court," Col. Rogers declared.

"I am glad to hear it," Mack responded. "The sooner the better to put a stop to all further discussion and agitation upon the question of the validity of National League contracts, which would hold a player for a lifetime but deprive him of the right to hold a club longer than ten days. I repeat, the sooner the better, as it is not doing baseball any good to talk about lawsuits and making threats daily in the newspapers, and I wish this proposed lawsuit against Lajoie would come up tomorrow in the courts so as to have it settled immediately. As to the result, why that is a foregone conclusion. We will keep Lajoie and every other National League player signed by us."

On March 27 Rogers filed bill in equity number 789 in Common Pleas Court Number 5, seeking an injunction against Ben Shibe as president, Connie Mack as treasurer and manager, and Frank Hough as agent, to prevent them from employing Napoleon Lajoie, William Bernhard, and Charles A. Fraser. The Phillies were not interested in holding on to the sore-armed Wiley Piatt. The lengthy filing included a detailed history of the Phillies and their ballpark, as well as exhaustive legal language about the clauses in the standard NL contracts.

In their response, the Athletics listed eight reasons to deny the injunction. The first two claimed that the National contract in its entirety was illegal because it conflicted with some law enacted on June 2, 1874. The next two stated that there was no mutual obligation between the parties for the season of 1901. The last four referred to the constitutional rights of players as American freemen; club owners would deprive them of such rights if the validity of the National League contract was upheld. The option or reserve clause was inequitable and therefore illegal.

The hearing was set for April 20, four days before opening day.

In cities throughout both leagues, rumors of similar suits and countersuits sprang up like dandelions in the spring. Legions of lawyers contemplated a bonanza. But both sides realized that Lajoie et al. was a crucial test case. Ban Johnson believed the American's entire campaign against the National monopoly depended on its outcome. It was so important that when it was over, the league's directors agreed to reimburse the Athletics for half their $3,200 legal bills.

22 | THE BULLFROGS

With spring practice officially opening on April 1, 1901, Connie Mack couldn't wait three weeks until the Phillies' suit for an injunction was decided. If the court took Bernhard, Fraser, and Lajoie away from him, he'd deal with that when it happened. Meanwhile, he had to put together his team and plan his lineup on the assumption that the men he had to work with now would still be in his charge come opening day. If they all showed up, that is.

One of them, Minneapolis outfielder Al "Lefty" Davis, had accepted a $75 advance. He was asleep when his train from Tennessee stopped in Philadelphia, woke up in New York, and decided as long as he was there, he might as well sign with the Brooklyn Superbas. His excuse was that he was miffed because Connie Mack was paying bigger money to National Leaguers than to any of last year's American Leaguers.

"I signed Davis at his own terms," Mack said, "hence I fail to see where he has any fault to find. What is more to the point, after I sent him $75 additional advance money ten days ago I wired Davis to the effect that I would give him $100 as a present for expenses if he would report early this week instead of making me wait until next week. So you see his excuse for jumping a contract is a very lame one."

It was enough to tempt a baseball manager to scan the help wanted ads in search of another line of work. He never knew from day to day whose "agreement to terms" would hold, who would show up for spring practice, and who would not.

On the morning of April 1, the *North American* published the Athletics' fifteen-man roster. In addition to the three ex-Phillies, it included two pitchers: Mathewson and Willis.

Of all Connie Mack's contentious cases that spring, none were more indicative of the state of the game nor had a more significant impact on the future course of baseball history than those of Christy Mathewson and Vic Willis.

In the fall of 1900 Mathewson was best known as a football star at Bucknell: fullback, punter, drop kicker of field goals (worth five points). In one game his dropkicks had beaten Army. In 1899 he had kicked two against Penn, the first points Bucknell had ever scored against its powerful state rival.

Mathewson had also been the star pitcher for the college. After winning 20 games for Norfolk in the Virginia League in 1900, he was bought conditionally by the Giants and brought up in September. He lost three games and the Giants turned him back to Norfolk rather than part with $1,500 for his contract.

Matty went back to Bucknell for his junior—and last—year. Unknown to him, Giants owner Andrew Freedman asked John T. Brush, who owned a piece of the Giants as well as the Reds, to draft Mathewson for the Reds for the $100 fee. Brush then "traded" Mathewson to New York for sore-armed Amos Rusie, who hadn't pitched in two years. (Rusie appeared in three games for the Reds in 1901 and went home.) The trade, often cited as the most one-sided in history, was a sham from the start. Mathewson insisted that he was never notified of these transactions and assumed that he was a free agent.

To the American League, any player who had not signed a 1901 contract was fair and legal game. That included Matty. Connie Mack was aware of Mathewson's football and baseball records. While cognizant of the need to put a good product on the field in his inaugural season, he also saw this new beginning as an opportunity to fulfill his dream of taking young, intelligent athletes and teaching them, molding them into a perfect baseball machine. Christy Mathewson was the epitome of what Mack was looking for.

In January Mack wrote to Mathewson and offered him a contract for $1,200. Matty replied that he would not report until the school term was over in June. He would then play the balance of the season for $700. Mack agreed. On January 19 Mathewson signed the contract, witnessed, according to reports in the *North American*, by that paper's Bucknell correspondent, Lewis E. Theis, and C. J. Pearce, a resident of Lewisburg, where the school is located. In mid-March Mathewson, in debt and in need of books, asked Mack for a $50 advance. Mack promptly sent it to him.

When word got out sometime in March that Mathewson had signed a Philadelphia contract, an incensed Andrew Freedman fired off a letter to him. In a 1914 *Sporting Life* article, later reprinted in *Baseball Magazine*, Mathewson wrote:

> I received a red-hot communication from Andrew Freedman. It appeared I had committed some crime and must see him at once to straighten out the kinks in my reputation. Inasmuch as he offered to pay my expenses to New York and back, I thought I had better see what he had on his mind.
>
> I walked into his office unconscious of the weight of guilt I was carrying, but he speedily undeceived me. As soon as he saw me, he shut the office door, pulled up his chair, shook his finger at me and said, "See here, young man, what is this I hear about you and the American League? Don't you know that you belong to my club, and that you will either play in New York or you won't play at all?"
>
> I was completely taken aback and said, "Why, Mr. Freedman, I am already signed up with Connie Mack."
>
> "That don't make any difference," said Freedman, "the American League won't last three months, and then where will you be? Every player who goes with that league will be blacklisted. He won't be able to play anywhere else as long as he lives, and furthermore, you are the property of this club, and if you refuse to live up to your agreement, I will bring suit against you myself."
>
> This was a remarkable revelation to me. . . and taking full advantage of my childish ignorance [Matty was twenty at the time], he so wrought on my imagination that I didn't know where I was at. I naturally didn't want to forego my future career as a ball player, if such a career was a prospect, and I didn't want to go with a league that wouldn't last three months. But at the same time I didn't want to go back on my word to Connie Mack, so I explained to Mr. Freedman that I had already received $50 in advance money and asked him if he would return this money to Mack. He said he would and we left the matter in that way. I immediately wrote to Connie Mack, explained the situation, told him I was threatened with a suit by Mr. Freedman, and asked him if he would stand behind me in this suit. To this communication I received no reply. . . . Mack knew nothing of my ability as a player, except through hearsay, and no doubt thought if there was going to be so much trouble in getting possession of me, the game wasn't worth the candle.

In any case, I eventually returned to the fold of the National League, and the beginning of the season found me pitching for Andrew Freedman. Incidentally, he persistently forgot to return the $50 to Connie, so when I had received enough salary to enable me to do so, I refunded the money myself.

Written fourteen years after the events, this account illustrates the threats and pressure wielded against every National League player seeking to exercise his constitutional rights to freely sell his talents. It also differs somewhat from contemporary accounts. On March 25, 1901, the *North American* reported that Mathewson was in Philadelphia, and quoted him, "I have not yet signed with any club, and at present am undecided what to do. I have offers from the Philadelphia American League and New York National League clubs and will accept one or the other."

If he was there to discuss his dilemma with Mack, he received no relief. When he made this statement, he was either undecided whether to honor his contract with the Athletics or give in to Freedman's threats. He was dissembling about not having signed with anyone, but that may have been in line with the evasive tactics encouraged by Ban Johnson to preserve secrecy at the time he had signed.

Five days later, under the headline "Mathewson Belongs to Manager Mack," the *North American* said, "Reports to the contrary notwithstanding, Mathewson has signed with the Philadelphia American League club. If he has also signed with New York he has simply dishonored himself by signing two contracts."

On April 1 Connie Mack expected Mathewson to show up at Columbia Park, but that day Matty reported to the Giants. Three days later a different version of the return of the $50 advance appeared:

"Matty . . . yesterday tried to escape the legal responsibility for his acts by sending a check for $50 to the manager of the local club. But manager Mack, upon the advice of his lawyers, refused to accept the same, returning it uncashed with a letter ordering him to report here at once. If Matty refuses he will likely be made the defendant in two suits, one for breach of contract and the other for receiving money under false pretense."

The *North American* was not the only paper to condemn these "menaces to honest sport." Other Philadelphia papers, joined by the press in other cities, advocated the banishment of such jumpers from the game. In the end, Connie Mack took no action against Mathewson, who was lustily booed when he first appeared in the city against the Phillies. Almost fifty years later Mack told columnist Red Smith, "Another $500 would have kept him but I made no move because I just couldn't believe a college man would violate his word."

It's doubtful that another $500 would have been enough to counter Andrew Freedman's threats. And if such a demand was the reason for Mathewson's March 25 meeting with Mack, he was certainly rebuffed by Mack, who had Matty's signed contract in the office safe.

Mathewson was not the only bullfrogger who got away after Connie Mack had his signature on a contract. In January Mack had traveled forty miles south to Newark, Delaware, to see right-hander Vic Willis. After winning 52 games in his first two years with the Boston Beaneaters, Willis had reached the salary limit of $2,400 in 1900, when he slumped to a 10-17 record. Mack offered him $3,500 for 1901. That sounded good to Willis. To bind the deal, Mack gave him a $450 advance. Willis signed a receipt reading, "Paid on account of my salary for 1901."

Mack expected Willis to report on April 1. A week earlier Willis notified him that he wouldn't show up until Saturday, April 6. On April 2 the treasurer of the Boston club, J. B. Billings, arrived in Newark and went to Willis's home, where he promised to match Mack's offer. The next thing Connie Mack knew, Vic Willis was in the Beaneaters' spring training camp in Norfolk.

On hearing the news, Mack was incredulous. "If the report is true," he said, "our lawyers will deal with him the way contract jumpers should be dealt with. Of course, we can't stand for any such business and to keep baseball from falling into disrepute, we owe it to the public to make examples of these venal players and those disreputable club owners who are just as bad if not worse in tempting men to break contracts."

A few days later Mack received a check for $450 from Willis. He refused to cash it. Still, he took no legal action. Ban Johnson's club owners were under orders to stay out of the courts without first clearing any legal actions through the league's attorneys.

Let's pause for a moment to consider a "what if": what if the two future Hall of Famers, Christy Mathewson and Vic Willis, had honored their contracts with Connie Mack and been part of a pitching staff that later included Eddie Plank, Rube Waddell, Chief Bender, Jack Coombs, and Joe Bush? It's not inconceivable that they might have won every one of the American League's first fourteen pennants.

National League history might have been different too. The Giants were a sorry second division club. On some days the gatherings could be counted by the dozens, even for a doubleheader. The entire National League was in the fans' doghouse. Christy Mathewson has been credited with becoming an instant hero who singlehandedly saved the struggling league. As the league's biggest drawing card, at home and on the road, he would be the difference between survival and crushing losses for several clubs that year.

When spring training officially opened on April 1, the Boston American Leaguers went to Charlottesville, Virginia, but most teams stayed home. This was not spring training as we know it today. A half dozen players showed up that Monday morning at Columbia Park to do a little limbering up. Groundskeeper Tom Murphy and his crew were still spreading topsoil in the outfield. No grass would sprout until after the first home stand. The resident goat foraged the field for what scrubby greenery he could find.

Nap Lajoie reported in midseason condition after a month of playing handball. Catcher Harry Smith and pitcher Bill Milligan were ill with the grippe. First baseman Pat Crisham had a sick child at home and didn't report. Chick Fraser was in Hot Springs and wouldn't arrive for another three weeks. Lave Cross, a bigwig in the Democratic Party in Ohio, had been given leave to wait until after the election in Cleveland, in which his man, Tom Robinson, was elected mayor. He showed up on the fourth.

It was April cold and wet during the first week. Little practice took place. Connie Mack spent the mornings in his office, occupied with paperwork. In the afternoons he inspected the work being done, checking every detail: the chairs in the boxes and grandstand; the women's "retiring room," which would be staffed with attendants; the installation of a public telephone; the refreshment stands; the small open press box on the roof; the home team's dressing room, fitted with shower baths and "other conveniences"; the placement of the turnstile at the grandstand entrance.

On Friday, April 5, about six hundred desperate cranks, suffering from the diamond deprivations of winter, showed up to watch the now routinely tabbed "Athletics" work out. Except for the few players they recognized from the Phillies, it was difficult to identify anyone. The players wore an assortment of uniforms. One had a Milwaukee shirt, another a shirt with an "I" in the middle of it, probably from Indianapolis.

Mack was pleasantly surprised when more than nine hundred people paid their way in on a cold, wet Easter Monday to watch a practice game against a local pickup team, Moss's Professionals. Moss's included two forty-year-old former players, Arlie Latham and Cub Stricker. The neighborhood saloonkeeper, Matt Kilroy, did the pitching. The gates opened early to allow the customers to look over the new facilities. Ladies wearing furs admired the comforts and conveniences.

Latham was the first batter; Bill Bernhard threw the first pitch for the new Athletics, and the fans cheered lustily at the called strike. It was all very informal. Joe Sugden, a local resident who had played for Mack in Pittsburgh and jumped to the White Sox, caught a few innings. Wiley Piatt pitched the last three innings of the Athletics' 8–1 win and "struck out enough to keep fans from succumbing to coma preceding death from frostbite," quipped Charles Dryden of the *North American*. (Philadelphia fans had the pleasure of reading the wittiest, most inventive baseball writing east of Ring Lardner for the few years before Dryden joined Lardner in Chicago.)

The Yale University nine came to town on Thursday and attracted an unprecedented three thousand fans to a practice game. The Elis extended the rusty home team to 11 innings before losing, 4–3. The lively, enthusiastic crowd enjoyed every minute of the action and umpire Arlie Latham's clowning. The next day the A's picked on a local school team, scoring 21 runs in the third inning of a 41–1 romp. Lajoie hit 2 home runs over the left-field fence onto Oxford Street.

It was still cold and damp when the Phillies opened the National League schedule on April 18. Even so, the 4,500 who showed up were less than half what would normally be expected. Jimmy Sheckard, the renowned jumping frog, hit 3 triples for Brooklyn in its 12–7 victory. The sorry turnout was not due entirely to the weather or the fact that the Athletics were playing a practice game on the same day. It was the first sign that the city's baseball backers were choosing sides for the coming season.

An optimistic Connie Mack was ready to play ball. But first, it was the lawyers' turn at bat.

THE UNIQUENESS OF
NAPOLEON LAJOIE

Common Pleas courtroom Number 5 was packed on a cold Saturday morning, April 20, 1901, when presiding Judge Martin, flanked by Judges Stevenson and Ralston, convened the case of Phillies vs. Benjamin Shibe, Cornelius McGillicuddy, and Frank L. Hough. The Phillies were seeking a special injunction restraining Napoleon Lajoie, Chick Fraser, and Bill Bernhard from playing for any other club, but it was apparent from the start that Lajoie's uniqueness as a player made him the crucial test upon which the entire range of contract disputes would hinge. He was the star of the legal game as he was on the diamond. Pending the outcome, both leagues were keeping their hired guns in their holsters.

The basic issue was the presence in National League contracts of the reserve or option clause and the ten-day notice clause. The American League claimed it was inequitable to allow a club to release a player on ten days' notice, while the player could never give his notice unless he chose to retire from baseball. The National countered that part of a player's salary was "consideration" for that option and that the players understood that when signing a contract.

During the weeks leading to the hearing, lawyers for both sides and neutral observers offered curbside opinions. The dean of the Penn law school used the National contract in his classes. He declared the option clause legal but the rest of the contract unequal. "No court will uphold it," he predicted.

Phillies lawyer John G. Johnson, who had been Ben Shibe's attorney for many years, gave his client, Col. Rogers, a limited, guarded opinion that the option clause was probably legal.

Connie Mack reiterated his commonsense conclusion: "If they think the option clause will stand in court, why is it the National League magnates are scurrying around the country after the players said to have been signed by the American League?"

In the answers they had filed with the court, the three defendants denied everything except that they were alive: they were not nor had they ever been copartners in any business; no such thing as the Philadelphia American League Base Ball Club existed, either as a corporation or partnership of any kind; they had never persuaded Lajoie to sign a contract nor approached any other Phillies players "in the interest of the so-called Philadelphia American League Base Ball Club."

These denials may have tap-danced around the truth, but they were technically and legally correct. Perhaps as a result of some sagacious and farsighted counselor's advice, the Athletics did not yet exist as a legal entity on that date. Everything done until then—agreements between Shibe and Mack or between Ban Johnson and the two sportswriters, Hough and Jones, and Shibe's putting up the money to pay advances to players and build a stadium—appears to have been conducted entirely on handshakes and good faith. The club's earliest known certificate of incorporation is dated June 12, 1901; not until July would the articles of incorporation be filed with the state. If all this was planned in anticipation of lawsuits such as the one now at issue, some one or more of Ban Johnson's or the Athletics' legal team deserve the credit. Whether it would be believed or help the defense remained to be seen.

In a separate answer, Lajoie admitted that he had signed a 1900 Phillies contract that he "believed was only for 1900 with no options for subsequent seasons." Had he known it contained such a clause, he said, he would not have signed it. He denied that he had been persuaded by anyone to sign an Athletics contract but did not deny signing one.

The seats in the small courtroom were filled early by operators of other teams in various sports, curious lawyers, reporters, and a few players. For the fans who stood four deep around the seats, the main attraction was a chance to see the great Lajoie up close in the witness chair.

Col. Rogers and John G. Johnson sat at one table facing the judges' bench. At another table sat the Athletics' legal lineup: Richard Dale, William Y. C. Anderson, William Jay Turner, and Charles Higley, a Cleveland attorney representing the interests of Charles W. Somers. Both sides were fortified with stacks of law tomes and papers they leafed through while the court disposed of some routine matters involving the B&O Railroad and other parties of lesser importance than the main event.

Accounts vary as to the order of the proceedings. It's likely that Rogers delivered the opening statement for the plaintiffs, a ninety-minute oration that had the upright spectators shuffling restlessly from one foot to the other, like fans waiting through a pitching change before the star slugger steps into the batter's box. Rogers narrated the history of the option clause, which he had written as a substitute for the original reserve clause ten years earlier, after losing a similar case involving a player who had jumped to the Philadelphia Brotherhood club. In that case a Judge Thayer had ruled the reserve clause invalid.

The revised option clause now read: "the [club] shall have the option or right to renew this contract . . . for another period of six months beginning April 15 . . . and for a similar period in successive years thereafter, and the [player] agrees to perform similar services . . . for the period or periods of such renewals, provided only that written notice of the exercise of such option of renewal be served before the fifteenth of October."

Rogers maintained that his club had bought those option rights by paying "fabulous salaries" to the players. "Baseball players today receive more per hour of work than the learned judges on the bench," he said, then thundered a prophecy of doom if the game's operating methods were not upheld. "Every dollar of capital now invested in professional baseball will be withdrawn."

In defending the ten-day clause, Rogers shed revealing light on the attitude of National club owners toward their players at the time. He was also eerily presaging the arguments that would be voiced against guaranteed long-term contracts a century later.

"Ten days notice is required," he declared, "for the player to do his best. If the player were not confronted with the ten-days notice clause, he would play poor ball, perhaps becoming listless. The ten days notice is the club which compels him to do his best."

Nobody raised the implication of the other side of that coin: deliberately playing poor or listless ball to draw the supposedly dreaded ten days' notice of release might be seen by the players as a way to gain their freedom.

The defendants, citing Judge Thayer's decision, stated briefly that the National contracts were illegal because they deprived the players of the constitutional right to secure the best compensation possible for their services and skills as professional ballplayers.

After a recess for a conference at the bench, the questioning began at eleven thirty. John Johnson tried to elicit from Lajoie an admission that he was a rare and exceptional talent, a drawing card for the Phillies who could not be replaced. He got nowhere. Lajoie, cap in hand, said in effect, "Shucks, who, me? Why, I'm just a hack driver from Woonsocket."

"Larry Lajoie, in low tones and with a modest mien that paralyzed the fanatics, said that he had never heard of himself," wrote Charles Dryden.

The testimony revealed some interesting aspects of the way the business was conducted in those long-ago but far from innocent days. When Athletics attorney Richard Dale showed Lajoie his Phillies contract, dated April 18, 1900, and asked him if he had received a copy of it, Lajoie said, "No."

Phillies manager Billy Shettsline then testified that a player was not normally given a copy of his contract except "upon urgent request," and then not an executed copy, but an unsigned blank with the salary written in. No player received a copy that was signed by both parties. Shettsline added that Lajoie had signed his 1900 contract "at the grounds while in uniform and wrote his name with a lead pencil."

Asked by Johnson, "Was Lajoie a particular star at one position?" Shettsline replied, "Yes, we've played him at second base, but you can't hook him up wrong anywhere."

Johnson commented, "He can dodge foul balls as well as questions he does not like."

Richard Dale then cross-examined Shettsline.

DALE: "How much have you invested in the grounds?"

SHETTSLINE: "Two hundred thousand dollars."

DALE: "You have spoken about the expert playing of the different men. Can you mention any player on last year's team who was more expert than another?"

SHETTSLINE: "They were all experts. No, I mean, not so expert as Lajoie. I might say that Petey Childs [a reserve infielder who never played in a game with the Phillies] was not an expert."

To which attorney William Jay Turner interjected, "He was an expert with the buzzer, wasn't he?"

Turner was referring to an incident during the 1900 season in which a Cincinnati player coaching at third base uncovered a wire that ran to the scoreboard, where a Phillies reserve player sat watching the catcher's signs and relaying them to the coach who stood on a concealed buzzer when the Phils were at bat.

The crowd laughed; Judge Ralston rapped for order.

DALE: "Isn't Joseph Dolan, who is now playing second base for you, an expert?"

SHETTSLINE: "He's a good ballplayer, but not as good as five or six other second basemen in the league."

DALE: "Do you think Lajoie is?"

SHETTSLINE: "Yes, sir, I do. I think he's the best thing that ever happened."

Johnson was back on his feet to establish that the Phillies had lost the 1900 pennant solely because Lajoie had been out of action for five weeks following his fight with Elmer Flick on May 31. The Phillies were in first place at that time with a 27-10 record; they were 12-19 while he was out. Johnson asked Shettsline if that was not true.

SHETTSLINE: "Before Larry's injury the team was in first place and after that dropped off and never recovered its lost position."

This brought Richard Dale to his feet. "Isn't it a usual thing for the Philadelphia club to do," he asked Shettsline, "to lead for a while, then drop behind whether Lajoie plays or not?"

Another round of chuckles rippled through the crowd.

"How long has it been since the Philadelphia club won the pennant?" Dale asked the manager.

"Not once in nineteen years," Shettsline admitted.

With that the judges adjourned the hearing until the following Saturday morning. The consensus among the visiting attorneys in the room was that the court would deny the injunction. In the meantime, Connie Mack would be back on the bench managing in the big leagues again, all his prizes in the lineup while they awaited the judges' decision.

<table>
<tr><td>**24**</td><td>### WINNING THE BATTLE
OF PHILADELPHIA</td></tr>
</table>

An impressive lineup of managers led the American League in its 1901 inaugural major league season. Five of them made it to the Hall of Fame as players, managers, or both. Jimmy Manning in Washington was the oldest at thirty-nine; Mack was thirty-eight. John McGraw in Baltimore was the youngest, twenty-eight.

Connie Mack was the most experienced of the group, with two years at Pittsburgh and four in Milwaukee behind him. His reputation as a tactician and judge of players was established. His kicking and needling had diminished. He had learned to control—not conquer—his temper, sarcasm largely replacing profanity.

Washington was the weakest link. Manning, a light-hitting journeyman outfielder, had owned the Kansas City club in the Western League. In the expansion meetings, Manning bitterly opposed Ban Johnson's desire to desert Kansas City for Washington, but he found no support among his fellow magnates. Disagree with Ban Johnson, he learned, and you were a marked man, an outsider, banished from the inner circle. But Johnson had no local backers in the capital. And Manning deserved some consideration for the loss of his franchise. Charles Somers reportedly advanced him $15,000 to leave Kansas City and invest in the new club. Manning was essentially fronting for the league. Ban Johnson was the de facto president.

In Boston, Jimmy Collins was a handsome, swaggering third baseman, the best, Mack said in 1950, he ever saw. "He was one of the fastest men ever to step on a baseball diamond. He could hit to all fields and threw the ball like a jet-propelled rocket."

Hugh Duffy in Milwaukee had been the captain on four of Frank Selee's pennant winners in Boston. An advocate of the concept of teamwork pioneered by Ned Hanlon, Duffy went on to manage off and on for more than twenty years.

Clark Griffith was a shrewd five-foot-six pitcher with no fastball. He relied on guts and brains to win more than 20 games for six years with the Chicago Orphans. A tough, canny fighter, he taunted batters to make them overanxious, then threw soft stuff that had them tottering off balance. His eyes never lost the sparkle scouts look for in a prospect. He and Comiskey formed a foxy combination. Griff would win 24 games for the White Stockings in 1901.

In Cleveland, Jimmy McAleer, a stylish outfielder, came out of retirement after eight years of playing for the flamboyant, hot-tempered Patsy Tebeau and the Spiders.

George Stallings in Detroit was another hot-tempered, smart, fanatically superstitious, profane scrapper, no favorite of Ban Johnson. Stallings had been throwing tantrums and roughing up Johnson's umpires in the Western League.

And then there was John McGraw in Baltimore, no slouch when it came to mixing cleverness with rowdyism and mayhem on officials. Johnson was apprehensive about bringing McGraw and Stallings into his clean new clan. He doubted that they could contain themselves within the straits of prescribed conduct. He was right. In 1896 McGraw had announced that it would be his last season in the game. Ban Johnson and several umpires would be sorry McGraw hadn't meant it.

Johnson was also aware that Stallings and McGraw were colorful, aggressive personalities who drew customers at home and on the road. It didn't hurt to have a few managers that fans loved to hate. The crowds turned out as eagerly to hiss a villain as worship a hero. And profits were the pool on which Johnson's new venture would have to float.

But Johnson was determined to clean up the game, which was filled with characters who were not eager to be cleaned up. His crusade was akin to turning street gangs into choir boys. The principles Johnson enunciated were more than moralistic; he believed them essential to making ballparks safe and attractive places for women and families. The game had to broaden its appeal to survive.

"I made a fight against drunkenness, rowdyism, and profanity," he wrote in 1930, "suspending players right and left and even threatening managers with the loss of their franchises. Decent conduct was demanded not only on the field, but off the field as well. . . . Ball players were public characters and shamed the game when they shamed themselves. . . . The authority of umpires on the field was made absolute, rowdyism, bulldozing and vile language drew instant and severe penalties, and managers were ordered to drill it into their men that the game had passed beyond the beer-garden stage."

The new enterprise had been launched on a high wave of national prosperity. The nation's greatest economic expansion had begun in 1896 and would last until the next panic in 1907. During that time unemployment would average under 1 percent. Immigrants pouring into the country found baseball a way to fit in as Americans. There was plenty of factory work, and they worked plenty of hours—six days, ten hours a day, for $500 a year. The stock market was soaring, led by railroad stocks, some leaping hundreds of points a day. The six-month-old boom caused the board of a prominent Wall Street firm to declare, "The stock exchange is now only a gambling house."

Four days before opening day Connie Mack's lineup was still as unsettled as a seasick tourist's stomach. He had no guarantees which of his prizes captured from the National League would stick. National agents continued to trail them, using threats or cash to recapture them. The fate of Lajoie, Fraser, and Bernhard was in the hands of the judges.

First baseman Pat Crisham's little girl had died, and Crisham was abed with the same typhoid that had taken her. That left Mack with the untested Charlie Carr at first base. He was satisfied with the rest of his infielders—Dave Fultz, Lajoie, and Lave Cross—if he could keep them. He had two experienced catchers in Harry Smith of his 1900 Brewers and Doc Powers, a physician trained at Notre Dame who had impressed Mack with his work at Indianapolis last year.

The pitching looked solid, but it was stacked with ex-Phillies who might be swept away by the courts. They were all behind schedule in getting into shape after two days of rain had made the field too soggy to use.

Mack's outfield was full of question marks. Former Penn star Jack Hayden was a rookie. Phil Geier had big league experience but a light bat. Ralph "Socks" Seybold was a career minor leaguer, probably thirty, maybe older; nobody knew. He had failed in a brief trial with Cincinnati in 1899, but Mack had seen him in the Western League and liked what he saw: a smart place hitter, expert at hitting behind a runner at first, and an outfielder who studied his team's pitchers and opposing batters and positioned himself accordingly, making routine catches of line drives that seemed bound for extra bases when they left the bat. Standing five-foot-eleven and weighing something over 200, Seybold looked slow and cumbersome. He was deceptively fast, picking up extra money winning bets on races against unsuspecting speedsters on his own and other teams.

"We never knew his age or how much he weighed," Mack said. "Once his father came to town and we thought, now we'll get the goods on him for fair. But the old fellow wouldn't budge. . . . Once I went in the clubhouse and [Socks] was lying on the rubbing slab. That stomach of his was sagging way down to here. He saw me and grabbed it and pulled it up. I thought I'd die.

"Socks was so big the fans never credited him with all the good points that he showed to me in his daily work."

With the opener scheduled for Wednesday, April 24, against Washington, Mack fretted as the dampness rusted his men. Ban Johnson arrived in town about noon on Wednesday, but more rain arrived with him and washed out the new Athletics' debut. Only one of the league's inaugurals was played, the White Stockings defeating Cleveland, 8–2, in Chicago.

It rained on Thursday too, and a cold wind blew out of the north. When it stopped about noon, Mack and Billy Sharsig rounded up all the hands they could find to work on the field. About one thousand baseball-hungry fans showed up, but the grounds remained unplayable. (In Detroit, the Tigers started with a bang. Trailing Milwaukee, 13–4, they scored 10 runs in the ninth for a 14–13 win that remains the greatest opening day comeback in history.)

Mack was concerned that the postponements might take the edge off his grand opening. It was also considered bad luck to open on a Friday, but he was happy to see the skies clear. A steady wind blew the field dry enough to play.

The Phillies were hosting Boston a few miles away that afternoon, but you had to look hard in the newspapers to find any notice of it. Scattered throughout the sporting pages of the *Inquirer* was the enjoinder "FOLLOW THE CROWD," a reminder that Columbia Park was the place to be.

The Athletics sent out 4,000 invitations to local celebrities and politicians. The Union Traction Company promised plenty of cars on the tracks. They needed them.

When the gates opened at two o'clock, thousands of customers were waiting, pushing to be the first ones in to claim the best seats. The First Regiment Band was already seated. Bandleader Sam Kendle raised his baton, and a popular air rang out as the crowd poured in. It wasn't long before the whoops and cheers and chatter of the multitude drowned out the musicians. The grandstand and bleachers were filled an hour before the four o'clock game time. When the grandstand entrance was closed with another thousand people clamoring to get in, they rushed around to the bleacher entrances. Policemen frantically scurried about in search of stakes and ropes and sledgehammers to create a corral in the outfield.

"Then the right field bleachers overflowed and spilled a stampeded mob into the arena," Charles Dryden wrote in the *North American*. "Seldom have we seen such a popular demonstration."

Hundreds more were hoisted over the fence behind the bleachers by friends with ropes. One entrepreneur was reported doing brisk business selling "hauling tickets" on the Thirtieth Street sidewalk behind the left-field bleachers.

Some fans found their way to the roof and sat on the gravel surface. Others "draped themselves along the fence like herrings hung up to dry," wrote Dryden. "All fear that the delay in opening would blunt the enthusiasm vanished an hour or more before playing time came. The fanatics wanted something new, and they rallied nobly to the offering."

The paid attendance was reported at 10,594, with at least another 5,000 in the premises. At 3:55 the gong rang, and the players took their positions on the field. Umpire John Haskell appeared, dressed in a marine blue flannel shirt and dark blue suit. He walked toward the box seats where Ben Shibe and his party were seated. Shibe handed Mayor Samuel Ashbridge a box containing a new ball. Ashbridge wound up and threw the ball—box and all—to the umpire as the crowd cheered. Haskell dug the ball out of the box and tossed it to the starting pitcher, Chick Fraser. Then he turned to the rooftop press box and, introducing a new service, called out the batteries: "Carrick and Clarke" for Washington, "Fraser and Powers" for Philadelphia. Few could hear him; fewer still could understand him—the start of another tradition. (The use of a megaphone began later that season in Washington.)

Several of the Athletics were presented bouquets of flowers on their first time at bat, topped by an enormous horseshoe of lilies and roses for Captain Lajoie. Even the umpire was honored with a nosegay. The only damper to the day was the outcome on the field. The rust showed. The Athletics made 7 hits and 7 errors. Lajoie had 3 hits and scored the home team's only run in its 5–1 loss.

Across town, the Phillies entertained fewer than eight hundred as they lost to Boston, 4–2.

The next day was a busy one for the Athletics. In the morning their attorneys were in court for final arguments. That afternoon the A's lost again; Milligan was bombed by Washington, 11–5. They drew an encouraging second-day overflow crowd of about ten thousand. Mack allowed his fence advertisers rebates for two days because their signs had been blocked by the crowds standing in front of them.

That evening Shibe, Mack, and Charles Somers conferred about ways to strengthen the team. Mack put in a claim with the league for Hughie Jennings, who refused to sign with anybody until he completed his law school exams at Cornell on Saturday. Ban Johnson went to Ithaca to sign him for the Athletics. His exams over, Jennings "came to an understanding" with Johnson to play for Philadelphia for $3,500. He didn't sign a contract, but he notified Mack that he would join the team when it returned from its first western trip on June 6.

Connie Mack was uneasy. He had heard too many promises that weren't kept. Even some who actually signed, like Willis and Mathewson, had deserted him. He wouldn't count on Jennings until he was actually in uniform. Charlie Carr, who glittered in morning practice, then tarnished in front of a crowd, was released. Mack moved Socks Seybold to first base, sent Dave Fultz to the outfield, and purchased shortstop Harry Lochhead from Detroit. He started Fred Ketcham, who had played for him in Milwaukee, in place of Jack Hayden in the outfield.

Chick Fraser had an attack of rheumatism. The other pitchers suffered from a lack of work. But they won their first game on Monday, beating Boston, 8–5, behind Bernhard's pitching and Lajoie's 4 hits, including 2 triples.

Despite their early defeats, the Athletics were winning the competition at the gate against the Phillies. On May 1 they beat Boston, 14–1, before 2,023, while the Phillies played the Giants before 756 customers, the lowest attendance at a Philadelphia game in fifteen years.

Always hunting for pitchers, Mack found a local semipro star, Pete Loos, who was mowing them down for the Roxborough nine. He started Loos on May 2 against Boston. It was a disaster. Loos gave up 2 runs in the first, lost his compass, and walked 4 in a row in the second. A cold Bernhard was rushed in; Boston scored 9 in the second and 10 in the third. Final score: 23–12. Mack allowed Loos to rejoin the Roxboroughs.

The only bright spot in the first week's action was the hitting of Larry Lajoie. If the judges perused the box scores, all doubts about the captain's uniqueness must have been erased from their minds. He had 22 hits in 30 at bats, a .733 average.

The Columbia Park accommodations drew more praise than the players' performance. "Mack strives to please in an entirely new direction," the *North American* crooned, "and the innovation is one the public will certainly appreciate. Urbane and gentlemanly agents pass among the crowd calling attention to their 'clean' ham sandwiches. Mack's sandwiches do look tidy and are not sliced with a safety razor."

Vendors also sold peanuts, penny pretzels, and five-cent lemonade. The grandstand and bleachers were swept clean of the resulting debris before the next game.

Philadelphia's reputation for producing the loudest and prickliest leather-lunged fans began early. They were especially effective in the intimate ballparks of the time, where thunderous voices carried clear across the diamond to the seats on the other side. When a writer commented on May 1, "The very enthusiastic individual who made the afternoon hideous with his bawlings should be suppressed," he was probably describing the "Iceman," Michael Collins. Easy to spot in his pink striped shirt and straw hat, Collins sat at the end of the bleachers abutting the first base grandstand behind the visitors' bench. From four in the morning until early afternoon he roamed the neighborhoods hawking fish in the winter and strawberries in the summer. In the afternoon he was at a ball game, hollering constantly. Unlike future Philly foghorns, who flayed friend and foe alike, Collins rooted faithfully for the home team and aimed his barbs solely at the enemy. His voice, which overrode all other crowd noises, was described as "an asthmatic whistle of an oceangoing tug stuck in a railway tunnel."

The predominant ink and outsized praise heaped on the Athletics and Connie Mack irritated Col. Rogers, who accused the writers of being on the American League's payroll. The fact that the sporting editor of the *Inquirer* and the baseball writer for Associated Press were stockholders in the Athletics gave the charge some credence. But nobody owned Charles Dryden, who had made life miserable for Giants owner Andrew Freedman in New York before moving to Philadelphia. There were ten daily newspapers in the city, plus three German-language papers. Those that covered baseball agreed with the portrayal of Ban Johnson as the "liberator of the American baseball slaves." They had great respect for Ben Shibe, little respect for Rogers and his Phillies operation, and liked what they saw of Connie Mack. Despite his hectic schedule and the pressures of starting a new business in a new league in a new city, Mack was genial, approachable, always good for a quote. He was one of the few managers who routinely named his next day's pitcher for the writers.

Mack was just as congenial with young people. Once school was out, boys of ten or eleven manned the broom brigades, sweeping clean the bleachers and grandstand in exchange for a free bleacher ticket. Neighborhood youngsters vied for the job, showing up at seven thirty in the morning and working until noon. One morning a chubby eleven-year-old was wielding a broom when he spotted the rail-thin Mr. Mack walking toward him. Fifty years later the boy, LeRoy Shronk, recalled, "I never thought he'd notice me, but he stopped and put his hand on my shoulder. 'Son,' he smiled, 'I think you're carrying a little too much weight.' He was right, too. I was a butterball. But since he'd noticed, I was awfully proud."

Another youngster, who lived in the suburb of Germantown, was among the kids who idolized Connie Mack. "I used to wait outside the ballpark just to look at him when he walked out," recalled future manager Joe McCarthy. In McCarthy's later years an autographed photo of Connie Mack hung in the entranceway of his Buffalo home.

Philadelphia wasn't the only city where Ban Johnson's legions were thrashing the competition. The Athletics opened Boston's home season on May 8 before a crowd of twelve thousand, losing to Cy Young, 12–4. Jimmy Collins's Somersets were soon outdrawing the Beaneaters two to one when both were at home, causing the National club to flood the city with free passes, called "slows." When they began to play before cozy groups of fewer than two hundred, the Beaneaters cut their general admission to twenty-five cents.

While the Athletics were in Boston, the stock market suddenly crashed. Standard Oil fell 171 points in minutes; Northern Pacific Railroad, which had climbed from 170 to 1,000, lost half its value in one day. It was called the worst crash in the history of speculation. The collapse added to the National Leaguers' nervousness. The Wall Street crowd was among their best patrons.

Connie Mack was more concerned with his pitchers than with the stock market. It must have riled him to read that Christy Mathewson was 6-0 with 3 shutouts for the Giants. (For years Philadelphia writers continued to blacken Matty's reputation for his perfidious bullfrogging.)

There are several versions of who tipped off Connie Mack to Eddie Plank. They're all eligible for credibility. None can be proven. Nor are they contradictory.

Eddie Plank was a twenty-five-year-old left-handed pitcher for Gettysburg College. A local farmer, he had been enrolled for several years in the college's "Preparatory Department," the equivalent of a private high school, while pitching for the college team. He never attended the college, and the Preps had a team of their own, but Plank was too mature and too good for that level of competition. Varsity eligibility rules were lax to nonexistent. Pitching for the school and various town teams in the area, the six-foot, 175-pound southpaw had an unusual cross-fire delivery, what Plank called his "slant ball," that made him nearly invincible against other school and town teams. But the closest he had come to professional ball was an offer from the Richmond team of the Virginia League in June 1900. Two days after he arrived in Richmond the team folded, and he returned home without throwing a pitch. He reportedly had an offer from Hamilton, Ontario, but he didn't go. Scouts probably ignored him because he was twenty-five and still pitching against overmatched college students and local amateurs.

Maurice Musselman was a young pharmacist in Gettysburg who was active in the college athletic association and managed the business matters of the town team in 1900. He may have written to Mack about Plank, as some tales suggest. (He may have also told him about another college/town team pitcher, George Winter, who signed with the Boston Americans.)

Frank Foreman was a veteran major league pitcher. Connie Mack had batted against him in the National League and managed his brother Brownie at Pittsburgh. Foreman had coached the Gettysburg College team in 1900 and helped Plank develop his devastating sidearm delivery. Foreman also pitched for the town team that summer. The thirty-eight-year-old right-hander had gone to spring training with the new Orioles club but signed with the Boston Americans. His story is that while the A's were in Boston May 8 and 9, he called on Mack at his hotel and told him about Eddie Plank. Or maybe Mack had heard from Musselman and asked Foreman about Plank. The timing of their meeting in Boston is consistent with what happened next.

Connie Mack was interested—Mack was *always* interested—enough to send a telegram to Plank inviting him to join the Athletics for a trial at their next stop, Baltimore. Plank told a hometown reporter his "heart was almost leaping from behind [my] tongue" when he read the telegram. He packed and took the train to Baltimore, arriving on Sunday, May 12.

Two weeks earlier, a twenty-two-year-old Cleveland pitcher, Charles Baker, had been nicked for a record 23 singles in a 12–1 loss to Chicago.

Undeterred by that outing, Connie Mack paid the Spiders cash for Baker. Although Mack no longer wore a uniform during the games, he sometimes put one on and warmed up his new pitchers to see what they had on the ball. Monday morning he caught Baker, suffering a badly split finger for his efforts. With Bernhard, Milligan, and Piatt out of condition, he decided to start Baker that afternoon against the Orioles. Baker was wild, walking 6. So was his infield. Poor Socks Seybold, playing first, was digging throws out of the dirt and reaching in all directions. Trailing, 11–4, in the seventh, Mack sent Eddie Plank to the box to look him over. The final score was 14–5; Plank, said the *North American*, "although he could not entirely stop the Orioles' run-getting, made, on the whole, a good impression."

The bruised Baker was on his way to St. Joe, Missouri, the next day. Plank, apparently still unsigned but agreeable to Mack's offer (teams had ten days to sign a player who had agreed to terms and could play him in the meantime), went home and pitched for Gettysburg against Dickinson on Wednesday, winning, 4–2. On Friday, May 17, he rejoined the A's in Washington. The *Compiler*, a Gettysburg weekly, didn't report his signing until its May 21 issue.

Wiley Piatt started the Friday game in Washington. Mack was particularly perturbed when the Senators scored 2 in the ninth to pull out an 8–7 win that left the Athletics in seventh place with a 6-12 record. The next day he told his rookie left-hander, "Edward, you're pitching today."

When Eddie Plank made his first major league start, he immediately established himself as the most time-consuming pitcher in the big leagues, the fans' least favorite pitcher to watch. Between pitches he stood looking at the catcher, stooped to retie his shoelaces, tugged his cap, walked around, fussed with his belt, swiped at an airborne bug. With a man on first, he stared at him—not throwing over, just staring. Plank stood out there so long without moving that some batters called time and stepped out of the box—an uncommon practice at the time—to refocus their eyes.

The Washington fans began to get on him early, counting aloud until he threw each pitch. That didn't bother him. It made him worse. The *Washington Post* reported, "When the crowd started to count for Plank, he demonstrated his coolness by strolling around the pitcher's box several times before delivering the ball."

Except for a rocky sixth inning, when a few bases on balls and a key error by Cross helped the Senators to 4 runs, Eddie "kept his head in masterful style and made the Senators look like the proverbial thirty cents," said the

Philadelphia Times of his 11–6 victory, which took one hour and fifty-three minutes. "The way he twirled the ball, batted [he had 2 hits] and fielded speaks volumes for his future."

Five days later in Chicago, Plank's performance spoke a different volume for his future. The home team, choosing to bat first, teed off on him in a hurry. He lasted 2 innings, walked 3, uncorked 2 wild pitches, and gave up 6 of Chicago's 7 runs in the third. For Plank, this was a rarity; he would complete almost 80 percent of his starts.

Something else happened in that game that is still unique in American League history. Chicago lefty Ervin Harvey took an 11–5 lead into the last of the ninth. Joe Dolan led off with a single. Chick Fraser, who had relieved Plank, singled. Geier hit a fly ball that fell in for a hit. Harvey then walked Fultz and Cross, forcing in 2 runs. The score was now 11–7, bases loaded, nobody out, and Larry Lajoie at the plate.

Accounts of what happened next vary slightly. According to the *Philadelphia Public Ledger*, Chicago manager Clark Griffith went in to pitch and "purposely allowed the big Frenchman to walk," forcing in Geier with the eighth run. The *Chicago Tribune* reported that Harvey pitched one bad ball to Lajoie before Griffith came in. "The manager shortly opined it was better to have Lajoie on first . . . so he delivered three just outside the corner of the plate although he evidently tried to sneak the third one over."

W. A. Phelon of the *Chicago Daily Journal* has Griffith telling the catcher to stand away from the plate, then tossing deliberate wide ones to him. Phelon called it "the nerviest play ever turned on a local diamond and risky enough to scare an elephant." It worked; three ground balls ended the game with the score 11–9.

Regardless of how it happened, it's the only time an American League batter has been given the "supreme compliment" of an intentional base on balls with the bases loaded. (It has happened twice in the National, to Bill Nicholson in 1944 and Barry Bonds in 1999.)

It was still a loss for the Athletics. At the end of the day the White Sox were in first place at 18-8, the A's in seventh with a 7-15 record.

Connie Mack began to rival W. C. Fields as a master juggler. He installed a revolving door between second and third base and in the pitcher's box. Harry Lochhead was gone after 9 games. Mack moved Lajoie to short and Seybold to center field, put catcher Doc Powers on first base, and picked up a thirty-four-year-old Phillies castoff, Morg Murphy, to catch.

Then he received some good news for a change. The three-judge panel denied the Phillies' bid for an injunction against Lajoie, Fraser, and Bernhard. The judges were not fooled by Lajoie's modesty and recognized him as an "expert player." But they upheld the claim that the National contract was "lacking in mutuality."

A relieved Mack told reporters, "While I naturally feel pleased over the decision, it was only what I expected. The reserve rule, as interpreted by the magnates of the National League, is repugnant to all idea of fair play. It is essentially un-American and I never had an idea it would be upheld by any court of law. The decision will in no way affect our attitude toward the contract-jumping players.

"I shall make no move to secure Mathewson, Willis, and the others. If I had my way I would never permit any one of them to play in the American League. Let the National League magnates understand that and the jumpers will receive a punishment fitting their despicable crime."

Meanwhile, Mack continued to flare telegrams all over the country, asking his contacts to secure this player or that "at any cost."

"If Mack has signed half the players he dickered with, he would need an excursion train to bring them all back," quipped Dryden. Either it was all a public relations ploy to make it appear as if money was no object, or "at any cost" wasn't high enough. None of the rumored names wound up in an Athletics uniform.

Connie Mack's most important acquisition at that time cost him nothing, not even a telegram. Harry Davis was working as an accountant for the Lehigh Valley Railroad in Philadelphia, the same Harry Davis who had been traded to the Pirates for Jake Beckley in the middle of a game in 1896. Davis impressed Mack then with his timely hitting, intelligence, and clean living. Released by the Pirates in 1898 after a knee injury, Davis made brief stops in Louisville and Washington and quit baseball after the 1900 season in Providence.

Mack had tried to induce Davis to sign with the Athletics in the spring. Davis turned him down. Desperate for a first baseman, Mack went to his office and pleaded, "I need you."

Davis gave in, quit his job, and headed west with the team on May 21. Except for a year managing Cleveland, Davis would be associated with the Athletics as a player, coach, and scout for twenty-seven years. He was the first of Mack's "boys" who came to play and stayed, it seemed, forever, with a loyalty and devotion rarely found in professional sports.

"It was one of my best moves," Mack said, "and made possible my first three pennants."

The burghers of Milwaukee showed no resentment over Connie Mack's departure when Mack returned to Cream City for the first time on Sunday, May 26. More than ten thousand, the Brewers' biggest crowd of the entire season, turned out to welcome him. "Before the game began yesterday," said the *Sentinel*, "there were calls for Connie Mack, and the former popular manager of the Brewers was compelled to doff his hat in response to the applause of the spectators."

Mack had probably worn street clothes from time to time while piloting the Brewers, but his appearance now in a navy blue suit and straw hat was considered noteworthy enough for the reporter to comment, "Connie Mack does not don a uniform now that he is with the Philadelphias, and makes his appearance on the bench in the wearing apparel of the times." He was not the first to do so; Frank Selee and Ned Hanlon had begun managing in street clothes in the 1890s. On July 12, 1896, Brooklyn at Cincinnati, both managers, Dave Foutz and Buck Ewing, wore civvies.

After dropping the opener in Milwaukee, 6–5, the Athletics won the next 3. The modest winning streak climbed to 5 with a sweep of a morning-afternoon Decoration Day doubleheader in Cleveland. That day the club also picked up some extra income back in Philadelphia, renting out Columbia Park for the first auto races held in the country.

They went on to Detroit, where the winning streak reached 9, as Plank won his third since his debut. They had six .300 hitters in the lineup, led by Lajoie, who modestly predicted that his .500 batting average "will fall off." The streak ended with a 9–1 loss on June 4, but they had climbed to fifth place.

Connie Mack had a more mundane problem than sore-armed pitchers and scatter-armed infielders. Somebody was stealing baseballs from the clubhouse at Columbia Park. Only two people had a key in addition to Mack: head groundskeeper Tom Murphy and Dennis McGillicuddy. Before heading west, Mack asked his brother to conceal himself in the clubhouse at night from time to time to try to catch the thief.

On the night of Wednesday, June 5, Dennis was staked out in the dark clubhouse. Sometime during the night he heard someone entering. He turned on the light. It was Murphy. They began throwing punches and wrestling. Murphy picked up a bat and bashed Dennis in the forehead above the right eye. Dennis sagged to the floor, his skull shattered. Murphy left, locking the door behind him.

Versions of the incident vary widely. In the years to come, Dennis's wife, Annie, wove an imaginary tale for her children about how she awoke at two in the morning, saw her husband was not home, and knew that something had happened. Waking her ten-year-old son, Harold, she told him, "Find your father. He's been hurt." Harold went to the ballpark and found his father lying in a pool of blood. They took him to the hospital.

The first report printed by the *Inquirer* had Dennis staggering home about six in the morning and collapsing, his wife then calling a doctor. The next day the paper forgot that account and came up with a new one.

Probably the most accurate testimony was that of M. J. Smith, an assistant groundskeeper, as reported in the *North American*. Smith said he arrived at the ballpark at eight Thursday morning. A half hour later Murphy arrived and went into the clubhouse. At nine Smith went under the grandstand near the clubhouse to get a drink of water.

"The door was closed. As I approached it I heard groans coming from the inner room. As soon as I opened the door I saw McGillicuddy lying on three chairs in one corner. He seemed to be in great pain. His face was covered with blood, and I noticed that he was able to move with difficulty. Murphy was standing over the prostrate man, cursing and berating him. He had a baseball bat in his hand.

"When he saw me Murphy ran at me in a threatening manner and told me that if I did not leave the clubhouse at once he would beat my head in. I was badly frightened.

"A moment later Murphy came outside and informed me that if I told anyone what I had seen, he would give me a 'licking.'

"I did tell Nathan Stetson, who works on the grounds, and informed him of Murphy's threat. Stetson was as badly frightened as I was and for several hours we went about our business without saying anything to anyone.

"During all this time Murphy was standing guard over the clubhouse. No one attempted to enter. About noon he came out and locked the door and I saw him go to the manager's office at the southern end of the grounds."

Business manager Billy Sharsig was in the office. Murphy told him he was quitting and going to Baltimore to work. He asked for his pay, and Sharsig gave it to him. On his way out, Murphy commented that he had had some trouble with McGillicuddy.

About three in the afternoon Frank Hayes, a youngster who worked on the grounds crew, was walking by the clubhouse door when he heard groans coming from inside. The door was locked. Murphy was gone. Nobody else had a key. They found a policeman, who broke down the door. Finding the unconscious Dennis, they called Dr. C. J. Carron, who took one look and had Dennis removed to German Hospital.

Connie Mack heard the news when he arrived late that afternoon from Detroit. The Athletics had the day off. Mack went immediately to the hospital, where the doctors estimated that Dennis's wounds had been inflicted between midnight and three a.m.

"McGillicuddy's recovery is doubtful," the *North American* concluded.

In an unprecedented procedure, Dr. Deaver wired the broken skull together with silver wire. A week later Dennis was still "in precarious condition, with no hope for recovery."

The players immediately offered to play an exhibition game for the benefit of Dennis's family, but Connie Mack said no. "I'll take care of my own family," he told them.

Rain washed out the first game of the home stand the day after Dennis was attacked. That afternoon Tom Murphy called Connie Mack and made an appointment to meet him at the grounds at eight that evening to explain things. Mack agreed. Murphy didn't show up. It was a dodge to throw the police off his trail. Murphy was nabbed by a policeman at the B&O depot with a ticket to Cleveland in his pocket.

On Saturday another overflow crowd turned out to watch the rookie sensation, Eddie Plank, set down the Tigers with ease, 6–1. The Detroit players considered him the best left-hander they had ever seen. When he followed that five days later with a 2-hit shutout of Milwaukee, Eddie Plank was the toast of the city.

He didn't relish the spotlight. A long-jawed, solemn-faced loner with narrow, puffy eyes, Plank was so quiet and humorless that off-the-field anecdotes about him are scarce. He was not a lobby sitter, and he didn't go out with the boys for a beer. He had little to say except when conducting tours of the Gettysburg battlefield near his home. Even though fans complained that watching him pitch was like watching grass grow, they liked the results. He had won 6 of 7 starts.

"[Plank] has proven himself an expert," wrote the *Record*.

The *Evening Telegraph* waxed hyperbolic, while taking a poke at "rubber-legs" Mathewson:

There is no more use in smothering the truth than there is in trying to drown a cat in a tin cup. That man Plank is the greatest thing that ever happened and can shed a few rays of limelight on any of them, not excepting the great and only Mathewson, who set New York baseball daffy and started the journalists of that village on the Hudson to spouting hot air like Vesuvius shoots bricks. Mattie is all to the good all right but just part your eyebrows and gaze in rapture on the sweet boy that Connie Mack dug up from the battlefield at Gettysburg.

The secret of Plank's pitching is no secret at all. It is a good strong arm, a powerful constitution to back it, and neither drinks, smokes, chews nor swears, nor eats canned pickles, corn starch pudding and buttermilk in the same breath. Added to this, he used to work ten hours a day in a pretzel factory and knows how to twist things. There is no mayonnaise dressing on Plank and we'll be plankety-planked if he isn't the warmest baby that ever came down the Ridge road in a go-cart.

You get the idea.

The secret of Plank's pitching was more than what he did or didn't eat. He preceded his sidearm delivery with a confusing windup, circling his arm four times while shifting his feet and taking a step forward with each turn of the windmill. Umpire John Sheridan later claimed, "Plank got away with an illegal five-step windup for seventeen years."

In the box he talked to himself, especially in the late innings, when he would count down—"Nine to go . . . eight to go . . . "—in a distinctly nasal voice.

Nobody liked to face him, not even his own teammates in batting practice. He wasn't there to cater to the batters. To him, it was PP—pitching practice—not BP. He used it to work on his pitches. As the hitters popped up or swung and missed, the more they swore, the more he smiled. He was also rough on catchers' hands. Jack Lapp, who caught him in his later years with the A's, said Plank's pitches always dropped two inches lower at the plate than the catcher anticipated.

What Plank called a "let-up" on his curve ball was probably a slider. Some pitchers threw harder fastballs and sharper curves, but Plank had control and pitching smarts. Babe Ruth said he "could knock a bead of perspiration off your brow." Throughout his career he would average 2 walks per 9 innings. Plank was known for his pickoff move, which was more of a nonmove. "There are only so many pitches in this old arm," he said, "and I don't believe in wasting them throwing to first base."

Instead, Plank stood and stared at the runner, kept on staring at him till he leaned back toward the bag, then quickly threw a pitch. He was also a strategic fiddler, choosing his spots to throw a hitter off balance. Sometimes he would pitch without delay. Other times he wouldn't throw a pitch until the umpire warned him against further fiddling around.

Eddie Collins once described Plank's method:

"Plank's favorite situation was two men on and a slugger up. The better the hitter the better Eddie liked it. For, if a man had a reputation to uphold, the fans would egg him on, and he would be aching to hit. Plank would fuss and fuddle with the ball, with his shoes, and then try to talk with the umpire. . . . Then he'd dish up something the batter couldn't reach with two bats, would follow that with an equally wild pitch, inside. Probably the next would be a twister the batter could reach, but could not straighten out. A couple of fouls, and he would wink knowingly at me. Then he would attempt to pick off the base runners. Then, suddenly, Plank would turn his attention to the fretting batter again, who would, in all probability, pop up in disgust."

How Connie Mack kept his composure, much less his sanity, throughout 1901 is a tribute to his innate toughness. His native optimism went through a forge that would temper the hardest steel. If it wasn't one thing, it was two others. There were problems with the trolley lines to Columbia Park. Cars broke down mysteriously during the hours preceding the games, stranding thousands of potential customers. The transit company cut the number of cars, resulting in long waits. None of these things happened when the Phillies were home.

Mack's brother Dennis had barely moved from "no hope" to "some hope" status when another player wrangle erupted, this one a brannigan between two stubborn Irishmen, Connie Mack and John McGraw. Hughie Jennings was two weeks overdue. He still had not signed a contract with Mack or anyone else. At some point he may have promised his old Oriole teammate, McGraw, that he would play for Baltimore if he played for anybody. But Mack, not McGraw, had the American League rights to him.

Jennings finally showed up in Philadelphia on June 19. He ate breakfast with the visiting Cleveland Blues at the Bingham Hotel and reportedly told some of them he would be playing for the Athletics against them the next day. But first he was going down to Baltimore to "straighten out matters with McGraw."

That afternoon he went to the game at Baltimore, where he was recognized and cheered by the fans. He told McGraw he was going to play for Connie Mack if McGraw didn't object. McGraw objected. When Ban Johnson was asked about it, he said Jennings couldn't play for McGraw if Mack objected. Mack objected. Neither one blinked or budged.

McGraw persuaded Jennings to accompany the Orioles to Milwaukee, where the manager vowed to put Jennings in the Orioles' lineup. That spurred Ban Johnson to fire off telegrams to Jennings, Brewers president Matt Killilea, and umpire John Sheridan: if Jennings is in an Oriole uniform, do not start the game. McGraw said he'd play Jennings anyhow.

Gleefully watching this internecine melodrama, Col. Rogers of the Phillies swooped down and rescued Jennings from his dilemma, offering him an extravagant $1,000 a month for the rest of the season. For Jennings, now an aging first baseman with little future as a player, it was a bonanza. For Rogers, it was a flaming sword of revenge. Jennings had enough life in him to lead the Phillies, a .500 club in fifth place when he joined them, to a second-place finish.

The fact that Jennings, who had played for Brooklyn in 1900 and was still on its reserve list, could play for the Phillies in 1901 reflects the anger that Ban Johnson's raiders had ignited in National League bosoms. Brooklyn president Charles Ebbets had it in for Connie Mack for stealing Dave Fultz after Ebbets had drafted him from Milwaukee. He was also out the draft money. Mack told him his argument over the money was with "Milwaukee, not me." Mack further raised Ebbets's bile by signing away his third baseman, Lave Cross. Now, when Rogers saw a chance to get back at Mack, he found an eager ally in Ebbets. Once Jennings expressed a willingness to sign with the Phillies, Ebbets sold him to Rogers for $3,000.

"We could have secured more money from two other clubs for Jennings," Ebbets said, "but we let him go to the Phillies to get even with Connie Mack of the American League. Revenge is sweet. Mack did us several bad turns during the year and we simply took advantage of the chance to get even."

Ban Johnson blamed McGraw for the loss of Jennings to the enemy, giving McGraw more cause to believe the league father was treating his sons with unequal fairness. Despite their doubts about each other, Johnson and McGraw had worked together effectively during the organizing of the league. But the honeymoon cruise didn't last long. The ship hit the shoals on May 31 in Detroit when McGraw and his entire team came down on umpire John Sheridan over a call at home plate. When Mike Donlin threw a bat at Sheridan from behind the ump's back, Sheridan forfeited the game to Detroit.

McGraw thought Johnson's policies were aimed at him alone, and that's the way it seemed, because he ignored them more than anyone. Johnson's letters of reprimand and fines did nothing to change McGraw's behavior.

But McGraw and his players were not alone, not by a long shot. In the first week of the season, Clark Griffith touched off a near-riot in Chicago. The visiting Detroit Tigers scored 5 in the ninth to take a 7–5 lead as the twilight dimmed. Griffith stalled, hoping it would become too dark to continue. Failure to complete the inning would cause the score to revert back to the eighth, when Chicago had a 5–2 lead. Umpire Tom Connolly prodded Griffith's men to hustle. He refused to call the game. Griffith engaged the ump in a lengthy argument while the daylight disappeared. So Connolly forfeited the game to Detroit. Things turned ugly when the crowd made more than rhetorical noises about killing the umpire.

The more McGraw fretted, the more mayhem he visited on the umpires. The frayed tapestry of unity unraveled altogether when Johnson aired his suspicions that McGraw, encouraged by John T. Brush, was behind overtures to Jimmy Manning in Washington and George Stallings in Detroit to decamp with their teams to the National League. Brush hoped to restore the twelve-team league and destroy the American. McGraw denied everything and called Johnson a "Caesar" and "Tsar." Johnson called McGraw a Benedict Arnold. Charlie Comiskey backed Johnson, stating, "The sooner McGraw gets out of the league the better."

When a leg injury forced McGraw's limb to be encased in a plaster cast, one wag commented, "They should put another one on his jaw."

Tempers rose with the mercury, which turned the Northeast into a blast furnace throughout July and August. "Hot weather makes players ugly and spectators ugly," said umpire Bob Emslie. "It takes the life out of the umpires and they make miscues. The more the players quarrel the worse the umpires get. . . . Whenever there is a summer as hot as this the umpire gets curses from the first day to the last . . . because everybody is out of sorts."

Some of the heat exuded from under Connie Mack's high starched collar. His Athletics, mired in sixth place, were just plain awful.

When a team is going bad—worse than expected—it can affect a manager's appetite and sleep. He skips meals because he doesn't feel like eating.

He wakes up during the night and stares at the ceiling, playing with permutations of his lineup, thinking of what to say and who to say it to, trying to conjure up a trick play that might spark some enthusiasm in his dragging troops. In later years Connie Mack could sleep stretched out straight on his back, arms at his sides, and wake up eight hours later in the same position, regardless of how his team was doing. But in 1901 he was not yet immune to the frustrations that have assailed managers since the first base on balls was given up by a pitcher.

Mack's temper exploded midway through a 12-game losing streak, when the A's blew a 4–1 lead in the ninth, losing to Washington, 5–4, on June 26. "The Athletics left American Park this afternoon in a disturbed sort of condition," led the *North American*, "and manager Mack was belaboring his band with all the words of abuse he was capable of conjuring to suit the occasion. The A's today gave a woeful exhibition in the ninth when, victory almost a certainty, Lajoie and Hayden, by stupid and dumb plays, gave the game to Washington."

Everything sizzled in Washington on July 1, when the temperature hit a record 102. Eddie Plank had a 13–5 lead after 7 innings. He wilted, giving up 4 runs in the eighth. Then he melted, surrendering 4 more in the ninth. Both teams were so exhausted the game was stopped, a 13–13 tie.

They were banging out the hits: 23 in a 15–13 loss on June 29, 19 in the 13–13 tie. One day they set a record, racking up 41 total bases. But the pitching was poor and the defense even worse. Mack was booed by the home fans throughout a 16–0 rout for leaving Bill Bernhard in the box for the entire game. Plank was his only other pitcher able to work, and Mack couldn't see using him on a day they were doing nothing against Cy Young.

Slumps are never welcome, but this one came at a particularly inopportune time. The Phillies, sparked by Hugh Jennings, were winning. The city's attention turned toward them; their attendance rose as the A's faded.

Never one to stand pat, Mack began to deal. He sold Wiley Piatt to Chicago and released Milligan. He bought a thirty-two-year-old pitcher from the Penn State League who lasted 4 innings and was gone. He traded Phil Geier to Milwaukee for shortstop Tom Leahy, who didn't help; released the Penn phenom, Jack Hayden; and bought Matty McIntyre, a handsome, matinee idol outfielder with a shock of wavy black hair, from Augusta. Before he was finished, at least thirty-two players wore an A's uniform that year, more than any other in the league.

Then Mack caught two breaks from an unlikely source—Barney Dreyfuss.

Loaded with pitching, the Pirates were waltzing through the National League's weakened ranks. Mack had been waiting since April for Dreyfuss to decide which of his excess hurlers to peddle: Jesse Tannehill, Sam Leever, Deacon Phillippe, Rube Waddell, or Jack Chesbro. Mack would have taken any of them. One report had Waddell going to Boston, but it didn't happen. In May, he had been sold to James Hart's Chicago Orphans.

In July Dreyfuss decided that spot starter Snake Wiltse, a twenty-nine-year-old rookie southpaw, was expendable. Wiltse was 1-4 in 7 games. Dreyfuss considered it no particular aid to the enemy to relieve Connie Mack of some cash in exchange for Wiltse's services. Snake became a workhorse for Mack, averaging more than 8 innings per game, including two relief appearances, while winning 13 against 5 losses.

The second break came as a result of the American League's apparent prosperity. National Leaguers who had been hesitant about jumping into uncertain waters began to reconsider. Small groups of players were seen huddling in clubhouse corners, hotel lobbies, and train club cars, mumbling among themselves. Every clubhouse had its spies, agents, and double agents.

Dreyfuss knew what was going on. He started signing his best players to generous 1902 contracts, throwing in five-day vacations in Atlantic City as a bonus. But he didn't want to keep any of the ringleaders who were trying to lure his happy warriors into greener pastures. His suspicions centered on his shortstop, Bones Ely. At thirty-eight, batting only .208, Ely was clearly near the end of the line. The Pirates didn't need him. They had an outfielder named Wagner who could play shortstop. Dreyfuss released Ely.

The six-foot-one, 155-pound Bones had played for Mack in Pittsburgh. The A's snapped him up. Old bones make the best glue, and that's just what Bones Ely did for Mack's infield. From the day he joined the Athletics on July 28, the infield of Davis, Lajoie, Ely, and Cross was the tightest in the league. Ely didn't hit, but they didn't need his bat. They were already second in the league in scoring runs. They needed that key playmaker in the middle. The A's won 11 of the next 13, had the best record in the league—22-10—in August, and closed in on the fourth-place Tigers.

But it wasn't easy. On the morning of Sunday, August 4, they were in fifth place with a 36-43 record, 7 games behind Detroit and ½ game ahead of Washington. During the next ten days they played seven doubleheaders, 15 games in all, and won 10 of them, including 8 out of 10 from Washington. Fraser, Wiltse, and Plank pitched four games each, Bernhard three. One of Wiltse's starts went 13 innings. And nobody's arm fell off.

Catcher Harry Smith, who drew applause for hustling down the first base line ahead of batters to back up plays, was sidelined with appendicitis. Doc Powers did all the catching—every inning, every game, every double-header—while Mack scrambled for another catcher. It looked as if Powers might finally get a day off when a man named Morris "Farmer" Steelman walked into Mack's office on August 21 and said, "Mr. Mack, do you want to sign another catcher?"

"I certainly do," Mack replied.

Steelman had been playing for Hartford, sent there by the Brooklyn Superbas. Charles Ebbets cried foul when he heard Mack had signed him. Ban Johnson ruled that Steelman still belonged to Hartford. So Farmer went back and bought his own release, then returned to Philadelphia. Powers had to wait another week before being relieved of duty.

On August 23 the A's climbed into a tie with Detroit by beating the Tigers, 7–2, in a game featured by a Lajoie home run that cleared the fence and bounced into Kilroy's saloon. The team's surge reversed the tide of the fans. Crowds of five and six thousand returned. Connie Mack looked forward to an overflow turnout for a Saturday doubleheader against Detroit on August 24, but a steady downpour washed away the big gate.

The climb came with casualties. On August 14 George Winter, Plank's former teammate at Gettysburg, hit Plank in the head with a pitch in Boston. Plank, 14-7 at the time, was out for almost three weeks, leaving the other three pitchers to carry the load. Cross had a sprained ankle, Lajoie an abscess on the knee that led to blood poisoning. Doc Powers was worn out. Mack maneuvered, putting Fultz on second, Joe Dolan on third, and Bill Bernhard in the outfield when he wasn't pitching.

Connie Mack was shaken by more bad news when Billy Sharsig collapsed in the office and was taken home. He never came back; cancer took his life five months later. The popular business manager had been an invaluable aid to Mack during the groundbreaking work of creating the Philadelphia Athletics. Ben Shibe's sons, John and Tom, took on the business responsibilities. When the traveling secretary, Charles Erringer/Goodfellow, quit after one season, John Shibe took on that shepherding role.

Elsewhere on the hospital front, there was better news. Dennis Mack, who had hovered between life and death since June 5, went home from German Hospital on July 20. Connie Mack wanted Dennis to recuperate at their mother's home, but Dennis was in no condition to travel alone. So Mack sent for Eugene to come to Philadelphia and accompany Dennis to

East Brookfield. They returned on September 1 to testify at the arraignment of Thomas Murphy. Charged with assault with intent to kill, Murphy faced a possible seven years if convicted. Free on $600 bail, Murphy failed to show up at the hearing, jumped bail, and disappeared. A year later Connie Mack was walking in St. Louis when he saw Murphy. Mack called the police who arrested Murphy and sent him back to Philadelphia, where he was tried and convicted and sentenced to two years and nine months.

In the middle of the 1901 pennant race, early skirmishes in the battle of 1902 broke out. Ban Johnson publicly vowed to wreck the National League, while quietly seeking peace in meetings with Jim Hart in Chicago. Johnson was also angling to move a franchise, either Cleveland or Detroit, into Pittsburgh.

Players' fears that twenty-five-cent ticket prices wouldn't support the league's payrolls had dissipated. The wave of players now eager to cash in on the bonanza resembled the Cherokee Strip Oklahoma Land Rush of 1893. Suddenly baseball was seen as the quick road to riches for young athletes. Signed 1902 contracts were said to be piling up in the safe in Connie Mack's office. As usual, no captives were identified. Once again dollar signs made headlines as big as game results.

Had the "big money" cooled players' intensity and changed the game? At least one observer thought so. "Players don't play with as much interest as before," wrote a disenchanted John B. Foster, sports editor of the *New York Evening Telegram*.

That couldn't be said of Connie Mack's Athletics. They were now battling Detroit and Baltimore for third place. On September 5 they took two from the Tigers and trailed them by 4 percentage points. The next day they fell back, losing, 8–3, in a game called by umpire Joe Cantillon in the middle of the sixth inning when news of the shooting of President William McKinley reached the field.

The fates and weather combined to douse Mack's chances to overtake the Tigers. They played only one game of a five-game series at home against Detroit, rain canceling three and McKinley's funeral, which shut down the league, costing the fourth. Two rained-out doubleheaders meant at least twenty thousand ticket sales lost.

The A's finished strong, winning 11 of their last 13, but they were unable to improve on that .004 deficit and settled for fourth with a 74-62 record, 9 games out of first. Inconsistent pitching prevented them from keeping up with Chicago and Boston. There were too many times when Mack was shorthanded and had to reach into the bushes for help. Socks Seybold batted .333, Lave Cross .331, and Harry Davis .306 to produce plenty of runs, only 14 fewer than the pennant-winning White Stockings.

But it was Larry Lajoie's year. Rarely if ever has a player in either league had a bigger one. His batting average stayed above .400 from the first day to the last. His final figures, all league leaders, are staggering: .422, still the American League record; 229 hits (in only 131 games); .635 slugging average; 48 doubles, 14 home runs, 145 runs scored, and 125 batted in. Had there been Gold Glove and Most Valuable Player awards, he would have won them too.

For Connie Mack, it was his first opportunity to see Lajoie in daily action over an entire season. When it was over, he summed up his impressions of the King:

A mistake commonly made by people who follow the game of baseball is that when Lajoie makes an error, he is loafing on the ball. I have heard the fans in the grandstand many times pass remarks when he fumbled a ball, to the effect that if he had hustled after the ball he'd have had it. Any such criticism of Lajoie is unjust. He is a player in one respect like Bill Dahlen of the Brooklyn club. He plays ball so naturally and so easily that it looks as though he was not making any effort to make the plays. Lajoie is without doubt the greatest second baseman in the business. His reach is so long and he is as fast as lightning, and to throw to second is ideal. Any catcher who has played with him will tell you that he is the easiest man to throw to playing ball. He is sure of everything: high, low or wide of the bag, it's all the same to him. And his arm is as good as any of them. Combine all this with his batting power and there isn't a ballplayer in the business that compares with him.

Ban Johnson claimed that all of his clubs made money, but it's doubtful that this was true of Cleveland and Baltimore. Cleveland's attendance was the lowest in the league—131,380. Despite the presence of local favorites John McGraw and Wilbert Robinson and an aggressive team, the Orioles drew a disappointing 142,000, barely beating out the last-place Milwaukee Brewers' 139,000. For Ban Johnson, McGraw and the Orioles were becoming a hybrid of an albatross and a white elephant.

The American League won the battles in Boston and Chicago, almost doubling its competitor's figures in both cities. The Athletics, hurt by trolley-line sabotage and the loss of July 4 and seven Saturday dates to rain, drew 206,329 to the second-place Phillies' 234,937. On dates when both teams played at home, the A's outdrew their city rivals, sometimes two to one.

As early as July, Ban Johnson had made known his intention to move a team to St. Louis. But which one? St. Louis interests had bid $30,000 for the Milwaukee franchise, which Henry Killilea rejected. A weak club that won 48 games and languished in last place all season had subdued the burghers' enthusiasm. The Killilea brothers pleaded in vain to give Milwaukee a chance to prove itself. After their last home game, Johnson announced the removal of the Brewers to St. Louis.

There was talk of shifting Cleveland, which did not have Sunday baseball, to Cincinnati, which did; Detroit to Pittsburgh; somebody to New York. Johnson suspected that George Stallings was trying to move the Detroit club into the National League. But it was all empty speculation.

Ban Johnson's campaign to curb attacks on umpires must be counted a failure in its first year. McGraw, Griffith, and Stallings were not his only thorns. Within a three-week span in August he had suspended two players for taking punches at John Haskell, who didn't return in 1902; Hugh Duffy for landing a right to the jaw of Al Manassau, who also found other work; and Joe McGinnity for spitting in Tom Connolly's face. Connolly toweled himself off and stayed another thirty years.

If he ever took a minute to relax, Connie Mack might have heaved a sigh of relief, now that his first year in Philadelphia was behind him. He had started a business from scratch, raised the needed capital, built a plant, put together a team, and made it pay. He had survived a wave of trials, frustrations, physical blows to his personal and baseball families, rotten weather, and a hundred and one other distractions.

His achievements and grace under siege didn't go unheralded. In summing up the season, *Sporting Life* editor Francis C. Richter wrote:

Misfortunes of the team, desertions of Mathewson and Lefty Davis, half-season long weakness at short, first and left field, failure of Piatt and sickness of Smith all knocked manager Mack's plans sky high, proved disastrous to the team, and also for a time seriously affected the status of the club and the prestige of the American League. Fortunately,

Mack and Shibe proved equal to the emergency and their unremitting efforts to pull up the team resulted in success and restored the club to the good graces of the local public.

The acquisition of Harry Davis, pitchers Plank and Wiltse, Ely, McIntyre and Steelman all proved timely master strokes of judgment and execution. They put the team into the running at critical times and proved to the people the desire of the management to give the people of Philadelphia the best that could be had, regardless of expense.

With this good showing, the Athletics club will doubtless reap well next year. . . . They cleared a profit for the year and made the club a fixture among local institutions.

In conclusion I want to compliment manager Mack and his players for the uniform excellence of their work and the good impression they made upon the public. Manager Mack came to us a comparative stranger under adverse circumstances. Today he is one of us, with a host of friends and supporters. His unobtrusiveness, fairness and urbanity under all circumstances, his fortitude in the months of adversity, his moderation in prosperity, his perpetual prudence, all combined to make him the right man in the right place in the past crucial season. A less well-balanced man would have surely gone to pieces under the pressure of the fierce struggle for existence of an unfortunate first season.

Captain Lajoie and his players one and all deserve commendation for their earnest efforts despite discouragement, their uniformly steady playing, their abstention from rowdy ball, and their all-around behavior. No team representing this city was ever more harmonious, free from scandal or better behaved on or off the field. They have created for themselves a host of friends and patrons who hope to see them all back again to land the pennant next year.

But Connie Mack didn't take a minute to relax or bask in these accolades. The Monday after the season ended, the A's played an exhibition game against a black team, the Cuban X Giants, before a crowd of 1,670, many of them blacks, who saw a 4–4, 11-inning tie. Then they toured for a week, playing local teams throughout the state, without Lajoie and Davis, who were off with their own barnstorming team, and Dave Fultz, who had gone to captain a football team in Pittsburgh that had in its lineup the rubberlegged Christy Mathewson. Mack formed his own association football (soccer) team that played during the winter at Columbia Park.

There were meetings, secret strategy confabs with Ban Johnson, players to be pursued and signed. Mack still yearned for the irrepressible Eddie Waddell. The Rube had gone through an unimpressive, though not uneventful, season in Chicago: 13-15 after 2 losses in Pittsburgh. One night in July after pitching a 2–1 win in 113-degree heat in St. Louis, Rube was embroiled in a shouting match with pitcher Jack Taylor on the train to Chicago. Taylor declared that Waddell had to go.

Mack kept track of Rube's winter wanderings. He read that Rube had been in Chicago on November 18 and signed a 1902 contract. Next thing he knew, Rube was pitching out in California.

Richter commented on Mack's wooing of Waddell, "Has not Mack trouble enough already?"

Yes, Mack had trouble enough already. In November the Phillies confirmed what had been widely anticipated for months: they were filing an appeal of the district court's denial of an injunction in the case of Napoleon Lajoie.

25 | A STAGGERING BLOW

Connie Mack and Ben Shibe were all smiles at the American League meeting in Detroit in March 1902. They had plenty of reasons to be cheerful. Despite the rainout of lucrative holiday dates, their first year in business had been a grand success. Mack collected a dividend on his 25 percent share of the club; his salary was raised from $3,500 to $5,000 (still well below John McGraw's reported $8,000 in Baltimore). To compensate for those rainouts, the league granted them the home dates they wanted for the coming season: Decoration Day, July 4, and Labor Day.

The league office reported a net profit of $14,000 after expenses of just over $15,000. Suffused with gratitude and optimism, American League magnates boosted Ban Johnson's salary to $7,000.

Ban Johnson was always looking to strengthen the financial backing of his clubs. At almost every league meeting, he brought in some millionaire who had made his money in streetcar franchises or ice houses or breweries or hotels and introduced him as a prospective club owner. This riled the lifetime baseball men like Comiskey and Griffith. Griff believed that "the man who has learned the game on the field will fight to the finish, but the ones who regard the game as an investment are the first to pull out." These new capitalists who knew nothing about the game and didn't have a love of baseball in their blood would run when the red ink flowed. They were the sort who had deserted the Players' League ship in 1890 the instant A. G. Spalding fired the first shot across their bow.

"Bushwhackers," Griffith called them. Whenever Johnson presented one of them at a meeting, Griffith would mutter to Mack, "One more millionaire will ruin the league."

Connie Mack would smile and say nothing. His bitter experiences with the "bushwhackers" in Buffalo and Pittsburgh had been assuaged by his pleasant and profitable relationship with the Killilea brothers in Milwaukee. And he considered Ben Shibe a genuine baseball man.

Johnson brought three new well-heeled ownership groups into the league. He had found a way to rid himself of George Stallings in Detroit, where dissension among the owners and a weak team imperiled the future of the franchise. Samuel F. Angus was an insurance agent, railroad contractor, and hotel owner. Among his assets was a bookkeeper named Frank Navin, who later ruled the Tigers as president for thirty-two years. After less than a year as a club owner, Angus would cause the baseball veterans to cringe when he announced that he would go as high as a $50,000 payroll—for a fourteen-man roster—to give Detroit a winner. "[This] simply shows to what extreme a man will go who is not aware of all the little idiosyncrasies of base ball," commented *Sporting Life.* "How does Mr. Angus anticipate that he can make both ends meet in a city that even now is showing plenty of indication that it is becoming base ball stale again?"

In Washington, the last straw for Jimmy Manning had come in October, when he tried to tap the league's reserve fund to finance further raids on NL players. That was the fund's intended purpose, but Ban Johnson denied his request. Manning resigned and put his interest in the club up for sale. Johnson found a buyer in Michigan hotel operator Fred C. Postal, and he induced Tom Loftus, his former Columbus manager, to leave the Orphans and take over the capital club. But Johnson continued to pull the strings while he looked for local backers.

Over Henry Killilea's objections, the league approved the relocation of the Milwaukee Brewers to St. Louis. Choosing not to be part of the move, Killilea sold his interest for $40,000 to a group of millionaires headed by Robert L. Hedges, a Cincinnati businessman and bank director who owned the Columbia Carriage Company. Wealthy sportsman Max Ralph Orthwein became president. Matt Killilea and Fred C. Gross retained a piece of the club. Jimmy McAleer moved from Cleveland to manage the new Browns.

Charles Somers had run into problems with his other financial interests and sold the Boston club for $60,000 to a group headed by Henry Killilea. Somers remained a partner in the Cleveland club.

Connie Mack continued to resist efforts to adopt uniform rules. He refused to endorse the foul strike rule or a new NL rule making a foul bunt with two strikes a strikeout. The league went along with him. Reality overruled principle when an earlier "permanent" blacklisting of nine players—Christy Mathewson and Vic Willis among them—who had signed American contracts, then jumped back to the National, was repealed at the request of the new St. Louis Browns owners. One of the players on the list was outfielder Emmett Heidrick. Hedges had recently induced Heidrick to leave the Cardinals and sign with the Browns. Ticket prices were raised to seventy-five cents for covered grandstand seats and fifty cents for covered stands on the sides, except in Philadelphia, where prices remained unchanged to match those of the Phillies.

The league's celebratory mood continued into the evenings. One night the new members of the fraternity, Postal and Angus, hosted a banquet for sixty, including the press, at the Griswold House: oyster, fish, and beef courses—the works. The next evening the newcomers entertained them all at the Avenue Theater. Ban Johnson gave high priority to keeping the writers well fed and moist of gullet, along with serving plenty of column-filling quotes. Whenever his league met, he provided a press room stocked with writing material.

In a photo of a dozen of the magnates attending the meeting—eight wearing derbies, four in velvet-collared topcoats—taken on the sidewalk outside the hotel, Connie Mack stands in a three-piece suit and low crown derby, a heavy gold watch chain looped across his vest and linked to a buttonhole by a large fob. At thirty-nine, the youngest of the group, he looks prosperous and rested, his face full.

Convinced that the American League was here to stay, the wave of players eager to join it reached tidal proportions, practically wiping out the pre-1901 lineups of the Cardinals, Brooklyn, Chicago, and the Phillies. The Phillies were plucked and bled like kosher chickens; only one starter, Roy Thomas, and no pitchers remained from their 1900 team. In Pittsburgh, Barney Dreyfuss was still relatively untouched, having signed his players early with generous side deals. His payroll reached a reported $57,000, highest in the game. The Pirates would win the 1902 pennant by 27½ games.

One problem in signing new jumpers was that some of them had already signed 1902 National League contracts. Ban Johnson was adamantly opposed to signing contract breakers. Some of his club owners, in collusion with the players, got around that by predating their contracts. Counterattacking National clubs were then forced to backdate their contracts—at higher salaries—to reclaim their jumpers. These shenanigans prompted Ned Hanlon in Brooklyn to complain, "If things keep on at their present rate of signing and cross-signing, some of these players will be holding contracts dated years before their birth."

Connie Mack reaped his share of this 1902 spring harvest. He captured three more Phillies: outfielder Elmer Flick, a .336 hitter with some power; shortstop Monte Cross, a smart, far-ranging gloveman with a light bat who had played for Mack in Pittsburgh; and right-hander Bill Duggleby, a 19-game winner in 1901. Mack even hired away the Phillies' groundskeeper, Joseph Schroeder, who brought with him what proved to be an invaluable bonus. Schroeder's fourteen-year-old son Robert began by hawking peanuts from a basket and stayed for forty-eight years. Connie Mack sent him to business school; he became the club secretary and a member of the board of directors.

Quipped the *North American*, "What will Connie Mack do next [to the Phillies]? The peanut and sausage vendors are awaiting the word. The cantilevers remain and someone has removed the bases."

Mack also captured a prize from the Chicago Orphans, who were rapidly becoming known as the Cubs: outfielder Topsy Hartsel. The five-foot-five speedster gave Mack an ideal leadoff man, a perennial league leader in drawing walks, adept at stealing a base or an opponent's signs.

With these additions to the lineup that had finished strong in September, no wonder Ben Shibe, normally a conservative, matter-of-fact gentleman, waxed wildly enthusiastic about the league's and his team's prospects for the coming season. Connie Mack, described as "self-contained and imperturbable as usual," smiled but avoided predictions.

The American League's sunny disposition was in sharp contrast to the contentious, secretive National League. Compared to "the League," as the papers referred to the National at that time, the Middle East is a paradise of harmony and brotherly love. Half the owners, led by Andrew Freedman and John T. Brush, were conspiring to turn the league into the latest way of doing business—a trust. Almost two hundred multimillion dollar trusts now controlled practically everything Americans ate, drank, smoked, wore, rode, and burned to heat their homes and cook. Why shouldn't the national pastime enjoy this up-to-date efficiency—and the benefits of monopoly? The prospect of becoming as unpopular with the public as the Rockefellers and Morgans had become didn't enter the National conspirers' minds.

The plan leaked out at the National's circus-like meetings in December, sundering the sessions into chaos. Albert Spalding, who had a plan of his own to "combine" the American League out of existence, stepped in and tried to regain control. He was confident he could skin Ban Johnson and company in any bartering, as he had done with the Brotherhood a decade earlier. Disgusted by the actions of National club owners he considered blockheads, dismayed by the declining stature and plummeting attendance of the league he had helped create, and angered by the outgoing wave of players, the old warhorse succeeded only in deepening the split between the two factions. One night four of the club owners waited until the other four went to bed; then they elected Spalding president. The other four quickly went to court and quashed that maneuver. For a while there was no president. Whoever had the league records hidden in his room was considered to be in charge.

The Chicago correspondent for the *Sporting News* called the National "a pack of confidence and shortcard men whose word is no good unless there is a gun in front of them to make them keep it."

As the National owners fought back against the player raids, they made Napoleon Lajoie a primary target. An agent of the New York Giants went to Philadelphia armed, in one report, with a certified check for $15,000, in another with $7,000 in cash. Lajoie turned a deaf ear to the offers. Mack, with well-founded confidence, said, "I have absolutely no fears of his being tempted to break his contract. He has promised to keep faith with the club and to be loyal to me and his clubmates. . . . I have the assurance of every member of my team that they will live up to the terms of their contracts."

(The human pinball, Jimmy Sheckard, retained his jumping championship. He signed with Brooklyn, jumped to Baltimore, and, after four games, rebounded to Brooklyn.)

For the past few years Connie Mack's hopes of getting off to a fast start had been hampered by pitchers who were slow to round into shape. They needed warmer weather than hitters did, to strengthen their legs with long-distance running and stretch out their arms. So Mack made the travel arrangements for Duggleby, Plank, Wiltse, and Bernhard to go to Chapel Hill, North Carolina, with catcher Morris Steelman and infielder Clyde Robinson. "I always figured that pitchers are about four weeks behind the rest of the team at the start," Mack said, "so by going south they will have a chance to begin about on even terms with the rest when practice games begin here."

Mack remained in Philadelphia, supervising the expansion and rebuilding of the left-field bleachers, to double their capacity, and the resodding of the field, which raised the infield four inches and leveled the entire field. A cinder track encircled the grass. He ordered new uniforms with an old-fashioned script "A" on the blouse and leased Columbia Park to a black team, the Philadelphia Giants, when the A's were on the road. The Giants inaugurated night baseball in the city, using portable lights for a game on June 4 against the Cosmopolitans.

In North Carolina snow and cold winds forced the pitchers to move to Charlotte, where Eddie Plank was reported working on a slow curve and change-up. As a first-timer in spring training, Plank fell victim to a form of practical joke commonly played on newcomers, such as plebes at West Point. The prank consisted of blackening a man's face with shoe polish made of soot and tallow while the victim slept. One evening on the hotel veranda the talk turned to a recent hazing scandal at the military academy. Plank allowed as how nobody could black him without waking him. The next morning when he awoke and looked in the mirror, an ebony face looked back at him. Plank blamed his roommate, Bill Duggleby, who denied it was his doing. The culprit was never caught.

Spring practice began at Columbia Park on April 1, three weeks before the April 23 opener at Baltimore. Ten days later the A's played their first practice game, a 12–1 win over Bucknell, in which the A's used a one-armed pitcher identified only as Griffith. Mack didn't sign him. The next day almost 2,500 baseball-hungry fans showed up to watch them defeat Princeton, 21–4.

On Monday, April 21, two days before opening day, the Pennsylvania Supreme Court handed down its decision in the Phillies' suit against Napoleon Lajoie and the Athletics. It struck like a thunderbolt. The court reversed the lower court's ruling and upheld the mutuality of the National League's reserve or option clause. Lajoie belonged to the Phillies. He and, by implication, every other National runaway in the American camp might once again become the property of their former masters.

It is no exaggeration to say that if the National's interpretation of the decision were borne out and the ruling applied to every player, it would wreck the American League. Ban Johnson and his lawyers, of course, portrayed it as nothing more than a local disturbance that, in any event, they would fight all the way to the highest court. In fact, nobody knew where the shrapnel would fall, whether other courts would recognize or concur in the Pennsylvania decision, or how many players and teams might ultimately be affected.

In the eye of the storm stood Connie Mack. Faced with the possible loss of half his team, he must have felt as if the ten plagues were being visited upon him. He had taken a similar last-minute setback a year earlier when Vic Willis and Christy Mathewson had deserted him.

"The blow was a staggering one," he said. "To put it mildly, the verdict of the [Pennsylvania] Supreme Court threw us into a panic."

Phillies manager Bill Shettsline immediately sent telegrams to all his departed players, wherever they were:

"Supreme Court overrules court below in Lajoie case; decides our contracts absolutely binding on you. You are hereby ordered to report forthwith to me at Philadelphia Ball Park for performance of duties under your contract. Refusal to obey this will be at your peril."

Other National managers sent out similar wires. The players responded to them like teenagers told to clean up their rooms. They ignored them.

The decision was not the final act in the drama. It sent the case back to the Philadelphia judges for a hearing on granting a permanent injunction against Lajoie's playing for anyone other than the Phillies. Although Bernhard and Fraser were dropped from the original suit, the Athletics had agreed that they would also be bound by the court's decision. Now Flick, Duggleby, and Monte Cross were also in jeopardy.

On Tuesday morning Ben Shibe and Connie Mack met with their lawyers for two hours, trying to sort out the hidden meanings of the legal language. The Supreme Court's decision was unanimous. There was little doubt that it would be carried out by the lower court. In the meantime, they concluded, nothing had changed nor would change until the hearing on the permanent injunction, set for the following Monday.

So Connie Mack took his entire team to Baltimore on Wednesday morning. They arrived at 12:45 at the Eutaw House, ate dinner, changed into their uniforms, forced their way through the crowded lobby, and climbed into barouches for the parade to the ball grounds. An overflow crowd filled every seat and square inch of standing room behind the outfield ropes. Ladies in bright colored bonnets adorned every section of the stands beyond the special ladies' section. Peanut, lemonade, and sandwich vendors hawked their wares. The festive mood contrasted with the cloud of uncertainty that hovered over the league.

Mack put his regular lineup on the field, Lajoie batting fifth and playing second base, Bill Bernhard in the pitcher's box. Lajoie made one of his signature plays, ranging far to his left to cut off a hit and throw out the batter, to the admiring applause of the Orioles' fans. The A's held an 8–1 lead in the bottom of the eighth, when a telegram was handed to Connie Mack on the bench. It came from his attorney, William Jay Turner, notifying him that Col. Rogers and the Phillies had obtained a five-day temporary injunction against Lajoie's playing for the Athletics.

Mack didn't know what to do. Was the injunction effective in Baltimore? Might Lajoie's presence in the lineup result in a forfeit of the game? And what about Bernhard? The wire didn't mention him. Mack had received no legal notice from the Phillies. With the game safely in the win column, he took no chances. In the top of the ninth he sent Socks Seybold up to bat for Lajoie, then put Lou Castro in to play second for the last half inning. Bernhard finished the game.

Mack was soon on the telephone to his lawyers. They agreed that the most prudent course would be to bench Lajoie for the rest of the series in Baltimore and the games in Washington. The A's didn't open at home until May 2. Since the injunction named only Lajoie, the other ex-Phillies remained in the lineup.

Nobody moved in the packed courtroom on Monday morning, April 28. There was neither room nor sufficient fresh air for anyone to take a deep breath. Shibe and Mack were reconciled to the loss of Lajoie; his 1901 performance, when he led the league in everything except room service, had shattered any pretense that he was not unique. It was clear from the court's decision that the justices read the box scores as well as their law books. They wrote, "Lajoie may not be the sun in the base ball firmament, but he is certainly a bright, articular star. We feel, therefore, that the evidence in this case justifies the conclusion that the services of the defendant are of such a unique character and display such a special knowledge, skill and ability as renders them of peculiar value to the plaintiff and so difficult of substitution that their loss will produce irreparable injury . . . to the plaintiff."

On the point of mutuality, the court determined that the contract's terms were sufficiently mutual to make it binding.

It would take a nifty array of legal inshoots and fadeaways for the A's lawyers to strike out those heavy-hitting words. They concentrated instead on trying to salvage Fraser and Bernhard. To do this, they had to demonstrate that the two pitchers were just ordinary, no better than what could be found by the dozens on sandlots in any city. The Phillies had to argue that the two were exceptional talents, hard to come by, whose loss had severely injured their chances for success on the field and at the gate in 1901.

Of course, when the Phillies owned them, Fraser and Bernhard weren't worth being paid more than anyone else. Bernhard had squeezed $1,650 out of Col. Rogers in 1900, then won 15 games. Another of baseball's most honored traditions was already in place: denigrating players during contract talks, then lauding them to the skies once they'd signed.

As is true of most extreme positions, both sides had difficult cases to make, causing some embarrassing exchanges in the courtroom. Rogers and John Johnson again represented the Phillies.

Phillies manager Shettsline led off. Rogers asked him if Bernhard and Fraser were considered good pitchers.

"Yes, sir, they were A number one."

Rogers then asked, "Is the position of a pitcher a difficult one to fill?"

"Yes, sir, his position on the team is a very important one, and you need a pitcher of expert ability to win games. It don't matter how good the other players on a team might be, you cannot dispense with an expert pitcher."

ROGERS: "Since Bernhard and Fraser departed the team in 1900, have you ever been able to fill their places?"

SHETTSLINE: "No, not with pitchers of their ability and skill."

"What relation does the pitcher bear to the other players on a team as to skill, efficiency, and ability?"

"A most important one. A poor pitcher will demoralize the whole team back of him. A poor pitcher will lose games, no matter how many good men are back of him."

In a word-wrestling contest, Mack's attorney William Jay Turner tried to maneuver Shettsline into admitting that the Phillies had acquired the two pitchers from other teams. Shettsline conceded only that the Phillies had been "successful in negotiations to purchase a release from their contracts" for $1,000.

TURNER: "If Fraser had refused to play with the Philadelphia club, he could not have played with any club in the National League or in any other league under the National Agreement except the California League [a so-called outlaw or independent league]. Isn't that the only exception?"

SHETTSLINE: "I won't say anything about the exception—I think it is the California League."

"You had a team of expert players in 1900?"

"Yes, sir."

"Well, how did you come out in the race for the championship?"

"Third, close to second."

"During that season Bernhard and Fraser pitched and you had all the other great stars and finished third?"

(Reluctantly): "Yes."

"How did you finish last year?"

"Second."

"Well, how do you explain that?"

"You must remember we played against weaker teams last year."

"Was not the Pittsburgh team, which won the pennant last year, the same?"

"Yes, but it hadn't been playing together long in 1900."

"In 1900 the Pittsburgh team played better than your team?"

"Well, they finished ahead of us."

The best way to judge the club's loss, Shettsline added, was the fact that attendance was down by eighty-seven thousand from the year before. Shettsline concluded by assessing the two pitchers as first class, with no superiors, testimony that Fraser and Bernhard might have taken into subsequent contract talks.

When it came their turn, the Athletics' witnesses—Frank Hough, Ban Johnson, and Connie Mack—insisted there were fifteen to twenty-five pitchers who were better than Bernhard and Fraser. Pressed by Phillies attorney John Johnson to name them, Mack was forced to admit that all the known ones were under contract to other clubs or in the minor leagues, where their superiority was still more in the potential than the present. Mack then stretched reality a bit by testifying that it was very easy to get pitchers; the great trouble was that managers didn't give young pitchers a chance.

"If that is the case," Rogers asked Mack, "why did you employ these two pitchers at an increased salary?"

"They are very good pitchers," Mack said.

"The only game won by the Athletic club this season was pitched by Bernhard?"

"Yes, sir."

Mack's attorney then tried to salvage something with a final question to his client. "But Fraser pitched in the very next game and lost, didn't he?"

MACK: "No, sir. Fraser hasn't pitched a game yet."

The three judges were not fooled by any of the Athletics' pitches. They continued the injunction against Lajoie, slapped new ones on Bernhard and Fraser, and announced their intention to make the injunctions permanent once the necessary paperwork was completed. Rogers made it clear that he would immediately pursue the same legal recourse against his two most recent escapees, Bill Duggleby and Elmer Flick. Either by oversight or simply because he no longer wanted him, Rogers made no mention of Monte Cross, who that afternoon hit a pair of 3-run inside-the-park home runs in Washington, where the A's won, 12–9.

Ban Johnson called an emergency meeting of the league for Wednesday in Cleveland. He pledged to carry the fight to the next legal level, but nothing came of it. A heavy-hearted Connie Mack took the evening train to Washington, faced with the loss of three-fifths of his pitching staff, his star second baseman, and his best outfielder. The season had begun; no unsigned players were left to fill the holes.

"I felt as though they had swept my ball club right from under me."

Much has been written about *l'affaire Lajoie* in histories of baseball and the American League, team histories, and biographies of Ban Johnson and other leading actors in the drama.

They rarely got it right.

Contemporary reporting used such terms as "let go," "sent," "transferred," or "allowed to go" in reference to the dispersal of Lajoie and the four other players affected by the Pennsylvania Supreme Court's April 21 decision that eviscerated Connie Mack's 1902 team as the season opened. Mack is often depicted as sending Lajoie to Cleveland out of gratitude for Charles Somers's financial midwifery to four of the newborn league's franchises. Some accounts imply that Ban Johnson sidestepped the law in ordering Lajoie to Cleveland. But in fact there were no trades; no sales; no edicts sending, transferring, or allowing any of the players to go anywhere.

The court's ruling simply meant that the enjoined players must play for the Phillies and nobody else—in Pennsylvania. That's as far as the judges could go. There were enough precedents to raise doubts about other states honoring or following the Pennsylvania ruling. Courts elsewhere had previously found the National contract "lacking in mutuality." They didn't care if the Pennsylvania jurists disagreed.

In St. Louis a circuit court ignored the decision and ruled against the Cardinals' efforts to reclaim shortstop Bobby Wallace, outfielder Emmitt Heidrick, and pitcher Jack Harper from the Browns. A District of Columbia judge refused to extradite outfielder Ed Delahanty, third baseman Harry Wolverton, and pitcher Al Orth to the Phillies. And so it went.

As long as those ex-Phillies stayed out of Pennsylvania, they could remain with their higher-paying employers without the threat of arrest. That was also true of the Athletics' five, except that staying out of the state meant they could play only in the A's road games if they remained with Connie Mack. What's more, having jumped to another Pennsylvania team, their contracts with the Athletics had been nullified by the decision. In effect, that made them free agents. They could return to the Phillies if they wished, but they didn't have to. They were free to sign with any other team outside the state, with or without the approval of Connie Mack or Ban Johnson, as long as the state they went to didn't enforce the Pennsylvania decision.

This fact of life, sometimes forgotten in later reminiscences by Mack and others, is confirmed in a comment attributed to Ben Shibe and Connie Mack in *Sporting Life* of May 17, 1902. Told that Joseph McNamara, one of the Detroit club owners, was on his way to Philadelphia to discuss the purchase of Lajoie from the A's, Shibe and Mack "both declare that they have no intention of bartering off the services of the great second baseman, and they also add that they would have no right to do so, even if they were so disposed."

By that time, the A's had run out of legal maneuvers. On May 1 they announced their intention to appeal the permanent injunction to the state Supreme Court. Four days later they argued in court that the players should be allowed to continue playing for the A's while such an appeal was pending. Since an appeal could take until the following January to be decided; that would enable the five to play the entire season for Mack. When the A's struck out on that pitch, they gave up.

All five players—Lajoie, Flick, Bernhard, Fraser, and Duggleby—could have rejoined the Phillies if they wanted to. The first to crawl back on Col. Rogers's terms was Bill Duggleby. After splitting two decisions with the A's, Duggleby didn't even wait for the outcome of the final legal arguments. He signed with the Phillies on May 5 for $2,400.

Elmer Flick, pending the completion of the paperwork adding his name to the enjoined players, stayed in the A's lineup through May 6. Then, anticipating the legal ax and not wanting to go back to the Phillies, he made his own deal with the newly renamed Cleveland Bronchos and left Philadelphia on May 7. The Athletics had no say in Flick's going to Cleveland, and they were not entitled to any compensation for him.

Chick Fraser remained on the sidelines, uncertain of his next move. He may not have received any better offers from other teams, or he may have been haggling with Rogers, as he had done every year as a Phillies chattel. Two weeks passed after Flick's departure before Fraser signed a Phillies contract.

Bill Bernhard bided his time, sticking by Lajoie's side and following Napoleon's lead. Everybody, including Connie Mack, expected Lajoie and Bernhard to follow Fraser back into the forgiving arms of Rogers and Bill Shettsline. Lajoie collected his gear from Columbia Park soon after the May 5 hearing. It was no secret that he preferred to stay in the city, where he had a home and business interests and planned to be married soon. The Detroit Tigers offered to pick up his contract. The New York Giants offered him more money. The San Francisco club of the independent California League tried to lure him to the West Coast with a $3,000 salary and half interest in a saloon. He turned them all down.

Believing he held invincible high ground, Rogers counted on Lajoie's desire to stay in Philadelphia and hoped to reel in the star on the cheap. He maintained that the court's decision meant the players were legally bound by the terms of their last Phillies contracts. It was reported that Lajoie would sign for $4,000; Rogers offered him $3,000 plus a year-end $500 bonus. Lajoie held a grudge: he still hankered after the $400 he thought he had coming to him from 1900.

Meanwhile, the Philadelphia papers roasted Rogers for his niggling dilly-dallying. They reminded him of the difference Lajoie's bat might have made during a recent spell in which the Phillies had lost 9 one-run games.

By all accounts, Rogers and Lajoie were close to an agreement when Rogers added a condition: if Lajoie signed, he would be fined for the time he had missed with the Phillies. That was too much for Napoleon. He turned his back on the Phillies. "[Rogers] had the chance to do what was right," he told reporters, "and failed to take advantage of the opportunity."

Ban Johnson hoped to keep Lajoie and every National jumper in his domain. He also wanted to strengthen his weaker franchises, and Cleveland was the weakest, in last place with a 7-15 record. When Rogers and Lajoie fell out, Johnson couldn't order anything, but he probably urged Charles Somers to go as high as it took to sign the King.

Somers arrived in Philadelphia on Friday morning, May 23, and went to the Bingham Hotel, where his team was staying. That afternoon he met Lajoie and Bernhard at Columbia Park, watched Eddie Plank outpitch Oscar Streit, 6–2, then conferred with the players that evening in the room of manager Bill Armour. Everybody denied that any contracts had been signed before Somers boarded the 11:05 train to Cleveland. But Lajoie had $1,000 of Somers's money in his pocket.

It was variously reported that Somers offered Lajoie a four-year deal worth $25,000–$30,000 guaranteed, regardless of any future legal actions that might prevent Lajoie from playing for him, a condition entirely in keeping with Lajoie's record of caution, skepticism, and insistence on being protected.

The prospect of losing Lajoie and Bernhard propelled Rogers into apoplexy. He threatened to sue everybody who might have spoken to the ungrateful players about anything at any time. When the Bronchos opened a series the following Monday in Washington, he planted an agent in the grandstand, ready to swear to an affidavit if either player appeared in uniform. Lajoie and Bernhard went with the team to Washington, but they were still unsigned and neither was seen on the field. They returned to Philadelphia and took the night train to Cleveland. Arriving about noon the next day, they spent the afternoon and evening with Somers and Kilfoyle, while a parade of lawyers dropped by to offer advice about the legalities of their situation.

Assured that the Ohio courts would not honor the Pennsylvania decision but cautioned that they would have to stay out of the Keystone State or risk arrest, Lajoie and Bernhard signed Cleveland contracts. They bypassed Pennsylvania and relaxed in Atlantic City whenever the team played in Philadelphia.

When the Bronchos opened a home stand against Boston on Tuesday, June 3, Lajoie made a spectacular debut. Before a crowd estimated at ten thousand, far exceeding the team's usual audience, he doubled in the first run of their 4–3 win and was the pivot man on two "lightning double plays which shut off runs and saved the game," raved the *Sporting Life* correspondent.

Lajoie became an immediate hero. He wasted no time seeking business opportunities, opening a cigar store at a prominent downtown location in partnership with Bill Armour. For the next three months Cleveland had a 58-43 record and finished fifth. Lajoie batted .368. Bernhard won 17 and lost 5. Home attendance leaped to an average of almost five thousand. In 1903, the club was renamed the Naps in his honor. Two years later Lajoie would succeed Armour as manager.

From the day the legal blow fell on him, Connie Mack began scrambling for pitching. His friend, Boston manager Jimmy Collins, was the first to help, selling him right-handers Fred Mitchell and Pete Husting, the same Husting who had quit Mack's Milwaukee Brewers in 1900 over a salary dispute. Mack signed Ed Kenna, "the Pitching Poet," son of a Senator from

Virginia. Kenna, who wrote rhymes in the clubhouse, was released after a 14–6 loss to Baltimore on May 9. "[Kenna] may be long on meter but he pitches ragtime," wrote Charles Dryden. But Husting and Mitchell soaked up a lot of innings.

Having lost his captain, Lajoie, Mack gave the post to the veteran Lave Cross. But filling the hole at second base was daunting. He first tried Lou Castro, who turned more errors than double plays. When Cleveland had signed Lajoie, they released second baseman Frank Bonner, a washed-up toper described as "addicted to conviviality." Mack knew Bonner's reputation, but he was desperate. He signed Bonner when the A's were in Cleveland on June 11. Even when sober, Bonner was worse than Castro. Mack kept searching.

Replacing Nap's bat was more difficult than his glove. In just the second year of the American League's existence, Mack was looking back longingly to the "good old days." He was quoted in the *Sporting News*, "Good hard hitters are a scarcity this season. Six and seven years ago one could find from three to six on every team."

Cleveland backup catcher Osee Schrecongost, one of those characters who give baseball history more color than Joseph's coat, was a solid hitter. But Schreck carried a reputation of eccentric, unpredictable, flaky. Manager Bill Armour tried him at first base and didn't like what he saw. Schreck was picking up splinters on the bench for a week before he was released while the Bronchos were in Philadelphia.

Mack was looking to replace Morris Steelman, who couldn't buy a hit. Schreck was batting .338 at the time. His reputation didn't faze Mack. The next day Mack signed Schreck and put him in center field against Cleveland. He brought Dave Fultz in to play second base. The move put another big bat in the lineup, but it was not the answer. Schreck was too slow for the outfield.

Despite the chaos surrounding the team, the A's played well enough to stay among the leaders in the volatile early going. By May 25 they were 14-11, in fifth place, but only ½ game out of first. Fultz, Seybold, and Doc Powers were wielding the big bats.

Undeterred by the legal turmoil and the loss of their star second baseman, Philadelphia fans remained strong in their support of the Mackmen. More than five thousand showed up for the morning game on Memorial Day; in the afternoon over thirteen thousand overflowed into the outfield, while hundreds more perched on the fences and roof.

Mack's hunt for more pitching continued. The burden was being carried by Plank, Wiltse, and Husting. The overworked Plank was 3-7 by the end of May, including two losses in a week to Cy Young. When Plank and Husting became arm-weary, only Mitchell and Wiltse were available. In Chicago Mack brought in a twenty-five-year-old semipro, Odie Oscar Porter, started him against Clark Griffith, and sent him home after a 10–5 loss. Porter thus gained a line in the record books; he died a year later.

In a series opener at Detroit on June 7, Wiltse was pounded in a 9–1 loss. That evening Mack was singing his pitching blues to umpire Jack Sheridan. Sheridan said something along the lines of, "How about that fellow Waddell you had in Milwaukee? I hear he's going great out in Los Angeles."

Waddell, who had pitched for the Cubs in 1901 and had maybe—or maybe not—signed a 1902 contract, had won 12 games pitching for the Los Angeles Looloos in the California League, an independent loop operating outside the bounds of disorganized baseball. He appeared to be fair game.

Connie Mack needed no scouting reports. He knew how Eddie Waddell could pitch. Better than anyone, he also knew Rube's peculiarities. If the phrase "lefthanded all the way," referring to a southpaw pitcher of erratic mentality, was not coined for Rube Waddell, it was never more appropriate. Mack mulled. He had been able to handle unsteady Eddie's behavior in Milwaukee. But that was the minor leagues. Bringing Waddell to Philadelphia would shatter one of his basic principles of management: rules enforcing discipline allowed for no exceptions. Mack was certain Rube Waddell would break the rules. How could he permit that without risking the discipline and respect of the rest of his men? He prized harmony—what would later be called team chemistry—above all, and he knew Rube Waddell could be an unstable, combustible element.

Mack measured the makeup of his team. Fultz, Husting, and Powers were college men. Harry Davis and Lave Cross were veterans. They were not kickers and whiners. He could count on them to understand why the Rube had to be treated differently and why he would be worth it. They were the clubhouse leaders, getting on the malefactors and sluggards and keeping them in line. He would handle Waddell, letting the reins hang slack, acting as if he believed Eddie's excuses and wild tales whenever the pitcher disappeared or put the arm on him for a fiver. He didn't care how many gray hairs might result if each one was accompanied by a victory.

Then he considered his battered pitching staff. He recalled Waddell's devastating speed and unhittable assortment of curves that had won 10 games in five weeks in Milwaukee. No pitcher in the American League was his equal.

Mack also knew that Rube Waddell was a workhorse who loved to pitch, to strut the stage and entertain the crowds. Rube was willing to work every day, even twice a day, starting and relieving, if the right incentive was dangled before him. And Waddell would keep the turnstiles spinning. It was worth the gamble.

But first he had to corral his man. Recalling the trouble he had had extracting Waddell from Punxsutawney, Mack sent him a telegram asking if he would like to pitch for the Athletics. To his surprise, he received a quick reply: "Send me $100 and transportation."

It wasn't that easy. Mack wired the money and told him to meet the team in Chicago. The Rube didn't show.

Connie Mack seemed to have eyes and ears everywhere. Someone he knew told him he had seen Waddell board a train in Los Angeles followed by a group of men, probably teammates, who persuaded Rube to get off and go with them to San Francisco. When he heard this, Mack walked over to Ban Johnson's office. They decided to hire the Pinkerton Detective Agency, which put two of its West Coast operatives on the job. They found Waddell pitching in San Francisco on Thursday, June 19. Rube hit a home run to tie the game in the ninth but lost it, 5–4, in the tenth. Then, in the words of the *Los Angeles Times* correspondent, "The agent talked Waddell over, and loss of the game that he pitched in the afternoon did the rest."

Armed with Mack's handling instructions, the Pinkertons succeeded in bringing Waddell as far as Dodge City, Kansas. There the expedition stalled.

A pair of former featherweight champions, Young Corbett and Terry McGovern, were fighting in Dodge City, and Rube had to see it. Connie Mack could understand that; he would have liked to see it himself. After the fight Waddell hooked up with Corbett and his trainer, and they all went to Kansas City together. The Pinkertons wired Mack in St. Louis that this was as far as they would go. If he wanted his man, he would have to come and collect his prize himself.

That night Mack headed for Kansas City while his team, with Lave Cross in charge, took a train to Baltimore. Waddell, eager to show off before his new pals, arranged to pitch for a local minor league team. Mack arrived in time to talk him out of it, pack his cardboard suitcase for him, and shepherd him onto the eastbound express.

They reached Baltimore on June 24, while Plank was taking a 6–4 loss. The Athletics were now 25-24, 6½ games behind first-place Chicago.

Two days later Waddell made his first start for the A's. Baseball wisdom likens the relationship between a pitcher and catcher to that of a married couple attuned to each other's thoughts and moods. Pitchers are a breed apart from other players. Confidence can be shattered by a sudden loss of control or seeing a perfect pitch hit for a home run. The catcher must be the bracer, counselor, analyst, motivator, butt-patter, or kicker.

Doc Powers and Rube Waddell were from different planets. Powers could no more tune in to Waddell's mind than pick up signals from the moon. Catching Rube's debut with the A's, he made 3 errors and failed to throw out any of 4 base stealers. Waddell walked 3, hit 2 batters, and balked in a run in the 7–3 loss to the Orioles.

Recognizing the mismatch, Connie Mack decided to put Osee Schrecongost behind the plate for Rube's next start. This was a battery made in baseball heaven. Schreck was a capable catcher, among the first to receive every pitch one-handed using a big pillow mitt. "He used his glove hand like a shortstop," Mack said. He could also handle Rube Waddell as deftly as his overstuffed mitt. Schreck could prod him, scold him, cajole him, and get away with it. If Rube ran into a wild streak, Schreck might sit behind the plate and yell, "You big bum, pitch 'em over the plate or chase 'em yourself." Waddell was prone to not seeing or misreading or just ignoring Schreck's signs. No matter how many times Rube crossed him up, Schreck caught the ball somehow, preventing many a wild pitch or passed ball.

If there is beauty in symmetry, this was the start of a beautiful friendship. Rarely do two corkscrew minds travel such identical paths. They enjoyed plenty of escapades together, but they were not inseparable. After a game Waddell would go his own way more often than not. He had his own favorite haunts and coterie of hangers-on. Innocent and impulsive as children, for the next six years they provided baseball writers with more colorful copy than a stableful of Casey Stengels. Enough of it was true to make even the most ridiculous flights of fancy seem credible.

For example, did Waddell, after a night out with the boys, really jump out of a hotel window because he thought he could fly, ending up in the hospital? Probably not. But if he had, it's easy to believe that he asked Schreck, "Why didn't you stop me?" and that Schreck replied, "What, and lose the hundred dollars I bet that you could do it?"

They became roommates on the road and stayed at the same boarding house in Philadelphia. Their rooms must have resembled a fraternity house. A suit and tie was the accepted traveling attire of the time. When a suit became too dirty or wrinkled to wear, they would just as soon buy a new one as have it cleaned and pressed. Rube might pitch a long game on a hot, muggy day, then head for a saloon still wearing the same sweaty undershirt.

On one western trip, the A's were in Detroit, where Sunday ball was not yet legal. The two teams took a train to Toledo to play. At the station one of the players saw a heavy iron coupling pin lying near the tracks. He carried it on the train and slipped it into Schreck's grip. When they reached Toledo, Schreck could hardly lift his luggage. He opened it and found the coupling pin. Taking it out, he said, "Some guys have got a pretty far-fetched sense of humor, putting a dirty old coupling pin in with all my clean collars and shirts and stuff." The grip fell over, spilling out one empty cigar box and one soiled collar.

Schreck was a chatterer behind the plate. Branch Rickey recalled an incident in Philadelphia when he rejoined the St. Louis Browns after spending several days at home with his sick mother. His first time at bat against Bender, Schreck said, "When did you get back, Branch?"

"Just this morning."

The count reached 2 and 2. Schreck said, "You've been to see your mother, haven't you?"

"Yes, I have."

"How is she, Branch?"

Rickey turned to look at him. "She is better, thank you." When he looked up, Bender's pitch was on the way.

"I froze and took the strike dead through the middle," Rickey recalled. 'Ha ha,' said Schreck, "I struck you out.' You could have heard him in the outfield."

It was common for a writer to share a room with a player on the road. Hugh Fullerton Sr., a Chicago writer and prolific magazine contributor of the time, said, "I roomed with [Waddell] one season and we became great chums. I always called him Eddie. He would come to the room about midnight, take a dollar from my pocket, send a boy for two oranges, a lemon pie, and a bottle of beer, sit on the edge of the bed in his nightshirt while he consumed the supplies and then sleep as an infant. He had terrific speed, a fast-breaking curve and, when he was interested, he was unbeatable."

"When he was interested." The Rube was as easily distracted as a two-year-old. Fire engines, parades, buggy rides, marbles games, fishing holes, and Kilroy's saloon—anybody's saloon—all were irresistible off-field diversions. Rube Waddell would be Connie Mack's most challenging—and successful—feat of management.

"How Connie conceived the idea that Rube could be persuaded to pitch the kind of ball he is capable of pitching is a mystery known only to Mack," wrote Charles Dryden.

Rube's debut at Columbia Park brought out a Tuesday afternoon crowd of more than 2,500 on July 1. Mixing a deadly change of pace with his blinding speed and curves, he faced just 27 Orioles in a 2–0 win. The two who hit safely were erased on a pickoff and a caught stealing. He walked none and struck out 13. In the third, sixth, and ninth Waddell fanned the same three batters in a row. And he had a ball doing it.

"With two out in the ninth," Mack recalled to Fred Lieb, "he beamed at me and yelled, 'Send the crowd home; it's all over.' And sure enough, he struck out the last man."

Waddell had to fight his way through the adoring fans to the dressing room. He had conquered the city. And what a show he put on. Branch Rickey once described his pitching form: "He would give you that ridiculous windup, moving his arms all over the sky and then bringing the ball to a practical stop at his belt and all the windup had nothing to do with the pitch. It started from the belt. When he had control and some sleep, he was unbeatable."

On the Fourth of July, after a noisy, firecracker-armed mob of over 8,000 saw the A's beat Washington, 3–1, in the morning, another 14,462 jammed the grounds to watch Waddell perform again. They groaned as he gave up 5 runs in the first inning, but the A's pecked away, then exploded for 8 runs in the eighth to win, 12–9.

The Athletics were making money but no progress in the standings. They were still 7 games behind Chicago. With the addition of Waddell, Mack had three lefties—Waddell, Plank, and Wiltse—and right-handers Mitchell and Husting. He still had to do something about second base. He suspended Frank Bonner for two weeks and put Lou Castro back in the lineup.

Before the A's boarded the night train to Boston on Sunday, July 6, Mack confided to Samuel Jones, "I need a second baseman badly and I know where a good one is. I'm going to drop off at Norwich, Connecticut, and see if I can't get him. I won't tell anybody who he is until I have him signed."

Mack had been keeping track of twenty-five-year-old Danny Murphy, who was batting over .450 at Norwich in the Connecticut League. Murphy had been up with the Giants twice in the past two years but failed to stick due to illness, said one source, or a fondness for the red lights of the Tenderloin, said another. Mack bought the infielder's contract for maybe $600, maybe more, and directed Murphy to join the A's in Boston on Tuesday.

That afternoon, when the team dressed and left the hotel, there was no Danny Murphy in sight. Peeved, Mack penciled in Castro at second base. The gong sounded, the game began. Murphy arrived during the first inning, climbed into a uniform in time to bat for Castro in the second, and promptly spanked out a single to right. He followed that with a 3-run home run off Cy Young in the third and ended the day with 6 hits. The A's won, 22–9; their 12 hits in a 12-run sixth inning remained the record for fifty years. Connie Mack had found a second baseman.

Boston was not the only place where there were bombs bursting in air that day. John McGraw, after weeks of covert maneuvering and overt troublemaking on the field, which seemed calculated to provoke the wrath of Ban Johnson, obtained his release from the Orioles and signed to manage the New York Giants. There had been rumors that McGraw had his eye on New York, one way or another, even if it meant staying in the American League. The *New York Sun* reported that McGraw had been negotiating with political bigwig Frank Farrell to lease grounds in New York and move the Baltimore club there. Only when the grounds turned out to be unavailable, the report alleged, did McGraw turn to the Giants and accept their offer to jump. His assurances to the Baltimore stockholders that "I shall not tamper with any of the Baltimore club's players" proved hollow. Before selling his Orioles stock, McGraw plundered the team by releasing players who immediately signed with the Giants or with his ally, John T. Brush, in Cincinnati. In the following week he arranged the sale of control of the Orioles to Giants' owner Andrew Freedman, who then transferred all but five of the remaining Orioles to New York.

Ban Johnson moved quickly. On July 17 the St. Louis Browns took the field for a game in Baltimore. The Orioles did not. As soon as the umpire called the game a forfeit, Johnson declared the franchise forfeited to the league, which operated it for the rest of the season. It was a vital mistake by McGraw and his cohorts, who thus lost control of the franchise, paving the way for Ban Johnson to move it to New York that winter.

Johnson sent out a call for contributions of players to replenish the

Orioles' empty nest. Connie Mack donated Lou Castro and Snake Wiltse. The Orioles rejected Castro but took Wiltse. To replace him, Mack picked up twenty-three-year-old right-hander Howard "Highball" Wilson from Wilmington, who chipped in 7 wins for him.

McGraw's looting of the Orioles and forays to induce other former National players to desert the American League and join him set some of Ban Johnson's magnates atremble. Then a piece of good news broke in the midst of the uproar. Col. Rogers, still trying to regain Lajoie, Flick, and Bernhard, had taken his case to a federal court in Cleveland. On July 9 the judge dismissed the suit, ruling that the players had been freed by the Pennsylvania Supreme Court decision to sign with anybody they chose. The American owners' collective sigh of relief calmed the shock waves caused by McGraw's departure.

To the press, McGraw bitterly blasted "Czar" Johnson, branded the entire American League as a bunch of debt-ridden losers, and handed Connie Mack a symbol that has endured for more than a hundred years. Amid the flow of bile McGraw poured out to a Baltimore reporter, he said, "The Philadelphia Athletic club is not making any money. It has a big white elephant on its hands." McGraw added that Ben Shibe had not seen "a penny coming in at the gate" and wanted out. "No money was made last year and no money will be made this year."

Over the years Connie Mack and John McGraw remained respectful of each other's managing skills, but at this time Mack denounced McGraw, declaring that the deserter was all wet, was talking through his hat, and knew naught of what he spoke. With the jingle of his July Fourth receipts, which had set a league record, still fresh in his ears, Mack publicly bet McGraw $1,000 "that the Athletics did make money last year and are making money this year."

Beyond that, Mack said nothing to counter the derogatory "white elephant" tag. On the contrary, he cheerfully adopted it in all its ironic glory. He had a banner made with a white elephant on it and hoisted it at Columbia Park. It flew there at every game. The symbol was snapped up by newspaper cartoonists and writers and the public, and it is still displayed proudly by the Athletics' third incarnation, the Oakland Athletics.

27 | CONNIE MACK'S FIRST PENNANT

With the addition of Rube Waddell in June and Danny Murphy in July, Connie Mack believed his Athletics could do better than just finish in the first division. They could win the 1902 pennant. Mack now had the kind of team he had been trying to put together, without success, for the past five years: pitching, brains, speed, and power. The bunt, hit and run, and stolen base were the prevailing style of the game, and Mack fashioned his lineup accordingly.

Connie Mack considered the bunt an effective weapon for getting on base more than as a sacrifice. "If we were against a pitcher who was slow in bunts," he explained, "we dropped as many as we could into the infield. . . . When a ball was bunted the idea was not so much to advance the runner at the expense of being retired, but to advance the runner and reach base too."

Mack also believed in the bunt as a slump-breaker. "When a man struck a batting slump—and they will come to everybody—we made him bunt till he got his eye back. The result was that the team not only benefited by his times at bat, instead of having them wasted, but the player himself developed proficiency at one of the most valuable features of team play."

Mack carefully sculpted his batting order. He had two ideal leadoff men in Topsy Hartsel and Dave Fultz. Both were patient workers of walks, heady base runners, and excellent bunters. When Hartsel led off and reached first, Fultz seldom failed to advance him.

Harry Davis batted third and Lave Cross cleanup. They were line drive pull hitters, among the league leaders in doubles, and equally adept at the hit and run. When a play was on, they could be depended upon to poke the ball through the hole left by the man covering the base.

Slugger Socks Seybold batted fifth, followed by Murphy, Monte Cross, the catcher, and pitcher. Cross was one of those .230 hitters whose value is not reflected in the stats. Analysts with their formulae may not be able to prove or disprove the existence of the clutch hitter, but when the game was on the line, Connie Mack would as soon have Monte Cross at the plate as any of his heavier hitters.

Of the pitchers, Plank and Waddell were no easy outs, the Rube winning several of his own games with timely extra base hits.

Mack and Griffith and Comiskey and the other pioneers of the game were creating the strategies that are still in use. There was no "book"; they were writing it. Nor were there textbooks on management. The first study of business management, by Thorsten Veblen, wouldn't be published until 1904.

Each baseball manager had a staff of about fifteen players working for him. In Mack's case he was also responsible for the office, grounds, and concessions people. He had learned by observation, keeping or discarding things he had seen as a player that he liked or disliked in managers and club owners and adding his own intuition and character assessments.

Mack understood the need to handle each man as an individual. He studied the situation and adopted the method he thought would work. Some managers were by nature mild and easy-going, no matter what. Others were always gruff and pugnacious. Mack was Jekyll and Hyde, sometimes in the same bawling-out session. He might light into the object of his displeasure with a cutting tongue-lashing and when he saw the player's face bathed in remorse, quickly switch to a gentle hand on the shoulder and a paternal concern for the player's welfare and future.

As a field leader, he demonstrated his confidence in the players by giving them the freedom and responsibility to create ways to win. Many of his methods were similar to those that later brought great acclaim to Thomas Watson for his management innovations at IBM. In every office at IBM Watson would post a one-word sign: THINK. Connie Mack posted the same sign in the mind of each of his players. He didn't do their thinking for them. He focused on his objectives, told his men what he wanted to accomplish, and suggested ways they might succeed. He then left it to them to carry out the mission. He didn't signal their every move or call pitches from the bench. Led by Lave Cross and Harry Davis, they called their own infield defensive alignments and flashed their own hit and run, steal, and double steal signs. Sometimes the batter initiated the sign, sometimes the base runner. Hartsel and Davis were shrewd readers of opponents' signs. When it came to picking up pitchers' telltale habits, Harry Davis was the master, everybody else the pupils.

Mack knew his pitchers' strengths and opposing hitters' tendencies and put them together, using his scorecard to position the outfield. He also used it to keep score with a pencil and note where each batter hit the ball against each pitcher. The next time that pitcher was to face those hitters, he would refer to those notes in the pregame meeting.

This is the way they played the game. One day the A's had the bases loaded with Harry Davis on third. The count was 0-2 on the right-handed batter. Davis figured the pitcher would throw the next pitch outside. He flashed a sign to the other runners to start with the pitch. In those days pitchers took a full windup with a man on third. As the pitcher started his windup, Davis, a slow runner, drew scant attention, and they all took off. The pitch was wide and Davis slid across the plate safely.

On August 13 in the sixth inning against Detroit, Fultz was on third, Davis on first with 2 outs. Rookie George Mullin was pitching, Fritz Buelow catching. Davis signaled a double steal. On the first pitch he set out for second. Fultz started from third but dived back safely when the catcher faked a throw to second and threw to third.

"To the amazement of the spectators and even of the players," reported the *North American*, "Davis, who had reached second and touched the base, actually turned and ran back to first." He still thought a double steal would work if he could draw a throw to second. Before Mullin threw the next pitch, Davis broke for second again. Mullin threw to second baseman Kid Gleason. "And while the second baseman and [first baseman] LePine were trying to run down the agile Davis, Fultz gradually maneuvered toward the plate, finally making a break, and succeeded in beating LePine's throw. Although daring to a degree, the play was handled with admirable judgment by both men."

Davis regained second, making him the only man to steal the same base twice on one pitch. No other player ever successfully used this trick to produce a run on a double steal. (The rules were later changed, making the runner automatically out if he ran back toward first after reaching second safely.)

On September 4 Dave Fultz became the first in the league to steal second, third, and home in the same inning.

Connie Mack coached his catchers and middle infielders on defending against the double steal. "When a man went down to second our catchers always threw the ball hard and low," he explained. "The shortstop was the pivot of the play. He stood between the pitcher and second baseman. If

Monte saw that the man on third was not attempting to score, he let the ball go down to Murphy so that the putout could be made. But if a dash for home resulted he quickly intercepted the ball and shot it back to the plate ahead of the runner. In only a few instances did we fail to get away with it, and then not through any defect in the play, but because of some bungling in its execution."

Mack wanted his boys to lead happy lives and enjoy playing baseball for a living. To relax he sometimes took them to the theater or a boxing match. He wanted them to be married—if they weren't too young. He turned down teenage prospects who were already married as "not dedicated enough to the game." As a player in Washington, he had seen the erosion of players' morale when they were fined for taking a day off to get married, even if they weren't in the lineup that day. So when Danny Murphy asked for a few days off to go home to Norwich after a Saturday game, Mack readily agreed. Murphy returned a few days late, said he had been ill, and brought a young lady with him. He and Catherine Moriarty were married on the following Saturday morning; Murphy had 2 hits in the game that afternoon. Mack also gave Pete Husting leave to go home to Wisconsin to wed Agnes Sternberger.

Mack took pride in his players' acting like gentlemen at all times, on and off the field. He had learned to contain his own temper, and in any event he could no longer go out on the field to kick about an umpire's decision. "You don't gain anything by arguing with an umpire," the former firebrand preached, "and you don't help the team by being thrown out of a game." Not a single one of his players was tossed from a game that year.

There was another reason for his avoiding rowdy types and players with short fuses. Mack believed they were not quick thinkers. "Intelligent players know how to curb themselves when under fire," he told a *Sporting Life* correspondent. "For that excellent reason they seldom lose control of their think-tanks."

As for off-the-field behavior, Mack cited an example of his preferred method for dealing with night crawlers he wanted to keep. "I signed a man whose reputation had not been of the best," he said after the season. "Our boys talked to him, pointed out the absurdity of squandering his money and decreasing his earning capacity. This line of argument would have availed nothing from a manager, but coming from his teammates it had convincing force, and as a result the man in question now conducts himself in a manner above reproach."

Mack named no names; he might have been talking about Danny Murphy but certainly not about Schrecongost or Waddell, for whom no talk from anybody would have availed anything.

Mack's optimism about his team's chances was not borne out overnight. Danny Murphy's dazzling debut was quickly eclipsed by reality. Of course, the feet didn't exist that could fill Nap Lajoie's shoes. But Danny was just not a good second baseman. He had little range and his awkward footwork around the bag cost them some double plays. "He seemed afraid to risk making errors," Mack commented.

Murphy could hit, but he was slow and uncertain on the base paths. Mack bided his time. He didn't believe in doing or saying anything that might undermine the confidence of a new player. He would rather lose a game. When he thought the time was right for Murphy to accept instruction, he'd begin to correct the faults he saw. He never rebuked a player for fielding errors, but errors of judgment were something else. "I cannot excuse stupidity," he said. "A man should know what to do with a ball when he gets it or he shouldn't be in first class baseball."

A week after Murphy's arrival, the A's were still in fourth place, 7 games behind Chicago. When they made 9 errors in a 9–4 loss to the White Sox, they didn't look like championship material. Only Rube Waddell seemed unbeatable—and tireless. The rap on him may have been that he was "invincible . . . when he was interested," but somehow Connie Mack kept him interested. On Wednesday, July 9, Rube fanned 16 as he and Boston's Bill Dinneen went 17 innings, the A's winning on Monte Cross's home run. Three days later he outpitched Dinneen again, 3–2, before an overflow crowd. On the fifteenth he beat the White Sox, 9–3. Three days after that, he was not quite invincible; trailing Chicago 6–5 in the ninth, the A's staged a two-out rally. Murphy singled. Monte Cross walked. Schreck walloped the ball beyond anyone's reach in left field to bring them both home. Schreck and Rube were carried to the clubhouse on the shoulders of joyous bleacherites.

The excitement continued on the following Monday. Down 10–4 to Cleveland, the A's tied the score in the seventh. Schreck then drove in the winning run in the ninth. Waddell, pitching the last two innings in relief, was the winner. The next day he relieved Husting in the fourth with the A's trailing, 4–1. They came back to win, 9–4, and Rube had another of his 5 relief wins of the year.

At that point only 3½ games separated Chicago, St. Louis, Philadelphia, and Boston. The next day Eddie Plank beat the Tigers, 5–2, and the A's were in second place, 1 game back of Chicago.

The Philadelphia frenzy was cooled by two days of rain, on one of which Connie Mack needed police protection. Rain checks were not attached to tickets; they were separate slips of paper handed out at the gates. There was no threat of rain in sight at game time, so most of the fans threw them away. They played two innings before a sudden squall came out of nowhere and drenched the field. When the game was called, the paying customers, augmented by opportunists hanging around outside the park, stormed Connie Mack's office yelling for rain checks. Police armed with clubs guarded the door while Mack hastily removed rain checks from the safe and doled them out to people who produced their tickets.

When the rain abated on Saturday, July 26, more than thirteen thousand jammed the stands as Waddell won again, beating St. Louis, 3–1. He finally lost one the following Tuesday before the A's headed west. For the month of July he was 10–1 with 1 tie. His 10 wins in one month are still a modern major league record.

The Athletics went flat on the road. They booted away a few games. Mitchell and Wilson were hit hard. Waddell started four times in twelve days and had only one win to show for it, a 1–0, 13-inning thriller in Detroit, won by his own triple. They came home back in fourth place again, 3½ games out, and faced three doubleheaders in three days against Detroit.

They swept them all, the Rube coming back after his 13-inning outing on one day's rest to shut out the Tigers again, singlehandedly outhitting them, 3 hits to 2. Instead of scientists talking about studying his brain, somebody should have been trying to discover what his arm was made of.

On August 15 St. Louis lost two to Washington, and the A's edged into first place. "We are in the lead and we will stay there," Connie Mack announced. "That is a prediction, not a boast."

He was right. They won 10 in a row, lost 1, then swept St. Louis and led by 3 games. Mack had created his first well-oiled baseball machine. When the bunting and base running game was needed, they were the best at these arts. Involved in a slugfest, they could turn on the power. When the outfield was flooded with humanity, which was happening with profitable frequency, they altered their swings and their sights and shot ground rule doubles into the crowds like artillery shells.

They drew more than 100,000 paying customers for eleven games, more than the Phillies had attracted in forty-one home dates. A throng of 18,765, a record for the young league, turned out on Saturday, August 16, and saw Waddell fan 11 and defeat Clark Griffith, 2–1. A week later they packed more than 21,000 into the bulging facility and treated them to a 12–1 pummeling of Cleveland.

Writers milked the white elephant angle. "There is no hope for the white elephant," went an unsigned item in the *North American* that bore Dryden's satirical touch. "Securely tethered on the barren wastes of Columbia Park, and unable to escape to the rich pastures at Broad and Huntington streets [the Phillies' grounds], the poor beast is slowly starving to death. No vulgar excitement attends his passing. Only a corporal's guard of some 9,000 people daily have been going out to see the poor animal breathe his last. If the present neglect continues the grounds will have to be made twice as large to accommodate the floral offerings of the mourners."

While the pennant races were being fought on the field, the war between the leagues was still going on. But the tactics had shifted. The National League was now the aggressor, while the American clubs concentrated on holding on to their gains, quietly signing their stars to 1903 contracts. John McGraw, Charlie Ebbets, and Reds manager Joe Kelley prowled American League cities in quest of players. Billy Shettsline went to Cleveland in a vain attempt to bring Lajoie, Flick, and Bernhard back into the Phillies' fold. Other National clubs pursued them as well.

The first-place Athletics were a prime target for the National team wreckers. Mack credited Harry Davis with holding the team together and convincing the players to stay put. By early August Mack had all his players' names on 1903 agreements except for Dave Fultz and Rube Waddell, the National's principal targets among the A's. Charlie Ebbets eventually offered Fultz more than $5,000 a year on a two-year contract, a price Connie Mack regretfully told Fultz he could not match. But Fultz wound up with the newborn New York American League team in 1903.

Brooklyn agents offered Waddell a $1,000 bonus and $500 a month. There were other offers, too many for the Rube to handle. According to one of Dryden's "scoops," the A's were about to board a boat to cross Lake Erie from Detroit to Cleveland during a September trip, when Doc Powers commented that he hoped nobody would encounter *mal de mer* on the voyage. Rube said he had encountered just about every other National League agent but that one, and if he was on the boat, Rube would throw him overboard.

Rube Waddell was happy in Connie Mack's charge. He was the center of attention wherever he went, recipient of drinks on the house in saloons all over the city. Hordes of small boys flocked around him as though he was giving out free ice cream. He was the star attraction at a porch party given by Harry Davis's little niece that raised $80 for the Poor Children's Relief Fund. A cigar manufacturer came out with "the Rube Waddell Cigar." Soap and liquor companies hitched on to his comet. Had the Republican machine run Rube for mayor, he would have won easily. (Somebody may have thought of it; after the season Waddell applied for membership in the Fifteenth Ward Republican Club.)

The rest of the league had a vital interest in keeping Waddell in its ranks, even if it couldn't beat him. Mack carried a little black book in which he wrote each day's attendance and game details. His book showed that attendance jumped on days Rube pitched, at home and on the road. He drew crowds of ten thousand and more whenever he was advertised to start. They came to marvel at his assortment of fastballs, slow balls, and curves. They laughed at his cartwheels after he won a game. The sight of a twenty-five-year-old adolescent thoroughly enjoying himself lifted their spirits for a few hours, no small contribution to Thoreau's "mass of men" leading their "lives of quiet desperation." One day Rube was coaching at third base when Lave Cross hit a hot liner past his ear. Rube picked up two mitts and held them up to protect himself, while the crowd roared.

The American League was not entirely on the defensive. Connie Mack hinted that he had signed a few National Leaguers. Christy Mathewson and his catcher, Frank Bowerman, were reported to have signed with the St. Louis Browns and taken advance money. Mathewson denied it. Nobody believed him, and rightly so. He reneged on it, just as he had with Connie Mack, and went back to the Giants. This time "Grasshopper" Mathewson could not plead youthful naivete.

Convinced that Barney Dreyfuss had no intention of pulling out of the National League, Ban Johnson revoked his hands-off policy toward the Pirates. He enlisted the Pittsburgh catcher, Jack O'Connor, as an agent in the Pirates' clubhouse. On the night of August 20 Johnson and Charles Somers checked into the Lincoln Hotel in Pittsburgh under fake names. Early the next morning O'Connor led a parade of Pirates to the room, including third baseman Tommy Leach, shortstop Wid Conroy, outfielder Lefty Davis, and pitchers Jack Chesbro and Jesse Tannehill. Johnson and Somers left town before nightfall with a creel full of contracts. All but Leach would be in New York uniforms the next spring. They had gone as high as $8,000 to sign the 28-game winner, Chesbro, making him the highest paid pitcher in the game. One newspaper reported that Chesbro had once worked as an attendant at an asylum in Middletown, New York, earning less per year than he would earn per start in 1903.

Leach and Willie Keeler were reported to have signed with teams in both leagues. Kid Elberfeld and Sam Crawford were also generous with their autographs. To the players being pursued, it was an unprecedented opportunity to play one side against the other and squeeze as much money out of the situation as they could. The press gave plenty of ink to the circus.

"At the present rate," wrote a *Sporting Life* correspondent, "it will not be long before every star player in the country will carry a lawyer around with him, when the contract signing season is on. This business of a player changing his mind every day, a sort of case of 'Contracts—Fresh Every Hour,' is growing very ridiculous. It has passed the stage of being funny. It now begins to look as though no club can be certain of its team as a whole until reporting time comes, and even then some players may have two sets of bags in readiness to use in shipping their dry goods when the time to act arrives."

The A's began a western swing on August 27 and split 16 games in twelve days. Rube Waddell claimed 6 of their 8 wins, 2 of them on his own game-tying or winning triples. The Rube was so wound up, he wanted to pitch every day. When Mack told him he could work only every other day, he was disappointed. But he didn't disappear.

Not even a train wreck ruffled him. In the predawn hours of September 2, the A's train from St. Louis to Detroit collided with a Wabash Line freight. One engine wound up in a ditch. All the passengers were jolted out of their berths. None of the players was injured. They pulled into Detroit at four thirty in the afternoon and went to Bennett Field, where Waddell held the Tigers to 1 run, struck out 7, and doubled in a 5-run seventh.

Their lead dipped to ½ game at times during the trip, but they returned home with a 2-game margin over Boston and St. Louis. They were met at the station on a rainy Tuesday morning by a tumultuous mob, who idolized and cheered them as if they had conquered all the evils and half the diseases of the world.

The Athletics had captured the city and seemed headed for a monopoly on its baseball business. Though attendance figures cannot be considered precise, the A's lead over the Phillies was too enormous to be pecked at over details. Through August they had drawn more than 290,000, averaging about 5,700 to the Phillies' 2,100.

Al Reach and Col. Rogers were ready to concede defeat. Rogers had lost in every court in Ohio where he took his case against Lajoie and the others. They accepted that the Athletics were in the city to stay, and they had no wish to continue the war. They were also feuding among themselves. Following an angry quarrel in the Phillies' clubhouse one afternoon—Reach still blamed Rogers for the loss of Lajoie—a stockholders' meeting on September 3 resulted in Rogers's quietly surrendering responsibility for all future player signings to Reach and Shettsline. He also publicly surrendered to the Athletics.

"We do not oppose the presence of the American League in this city," he told the press. "We recognize that it has come to stay, and are satisfied that there is money to be made by two clubs. We have nothing to gain by this ruinous warfare; neither have they. Hence, both Mr. Reach and myself are ready to support and further any plan that will lead to an honorable peace."

Eager now to avoid conflicting playing dates, the Phillies agreed to postpone their game against the league-leading Pirates on Tuesday, September 9, and play a doubleheader the next day. But a steady rain prevented all action that day. On the tenth more than 17,000 saw Waddell win both games in relief against Baltimore at Columbia Park, while the seventh-place Phillies attracted only 172 customers a few blocks away. A week later a conclave of 158 accepted Rogers's invitation to pay to watch the Phillies, while the A's entertained 6,078.

Other National club owners were beginning to think peace too. Barney Dreyfuss, shaken by the raids on his team and the treachery of Jack O'Connor in his clubhouse and convinced that the American League intended to move a franchise into Pittsburgh, voiced his support for a truce. He had earlier challenged an American team to a postseason series against his powerful Bucs but withdrew that challenge following Ban Johnson's raid on his ranks.

On August 9 John T. Brush sold the Reds to a group headed by August A. "Garry" Herrmann and the Fleischmann brothers of yeast fortunes. They brought a cool-headed businessmen's view to the industry's turmoil and were eager for an end to it. Brush took control of the Giants.

It now seemed likely that Ban Johnson could overcome whatever political obstacles Brush and Andrew Freedman might throw in the way of his finding a playing grounds in New York. The nation's biggest market, which had the National's weakest team, was ripe for the taking. The Pirates had once played six games in three days at the Polo Grounds and scored more runs than their share of the gate: 96 runs to $94. John McGraw had been unable to raise the Giants out of the cellar and was not yet considered to be anything but a bully and a rowdy, a failure as a manager.

Even allowing for probable padding of the numbers released to the press, the American was winning the attendance battles in every city where the two leagues competed: Boston, Philadelphia, St. Louis, and Chicago. That these were the four teams fighting for the American League pennant may have been a factor.

The National had been forced to raise salaries to keep what players it had retained. It had been through this before, when it had competition from the American Association. But this was a far more expensive war. By 1902 the league payroll was double what it had been in 1900, while attendance was sharply lower in St. Louis, Boston, and Philadelphia and down slightly in Pittsburgh. A peace dividend of noncompetitive lower salaries was the most powerful incentive of all to end the war.

Ban Johnson trusted three of the National magnates: Garry Herrmann of Cincinnati, Frank Robison of St. Louis, and Jim Hart of Chicago. If there was going to be any truce, those three would have to be involved.

Connie Mack took scant notice of these faint cooings of the doves. He had a pennant to win. Beginning September 2 in Detroit, the A's won 20 and lost 5. They played to enormous crowds at home and away. In Boston on Monday, September 15, more than sixteen thousand covered the field, hemming in the players until there was little room for anyone to move. Eddie Plank beat Bill Dinneen in the first game. Between games the mob gathered within inches around Rube Waddell and Cy Young as the two aces warmed up, an experience unimaginable to today's fans. Rube won handily, 9–2, opening a 4-game lead over the Browns.

The following Saturday at "the White Elephant's Park," they broke all major league attendance records. "Exactly 23,897 Persons Saw the Athletics Win from the Bostons," the *North American* headlined with suspicious precision, "While Hundreds Sought in Vain to View the Game."

A doubleheader sweep of the Orioles on an overcast Wednesday, September 24, clinched the pennant, the city's first baseball championship in nineteen years. Connie Mack had survived the legal wrecking ball and rebuilt the shattered Athletics into champions. Their 56-17 record at home set the league record, which stood until the 1929 A's topped it. Despite the swollen payrolls of the baseball war, Mack had done it on a salary list, according to the *Washington Post*, of $32,000.

It rained almost without letup for the next five days. Nobody minded except the Washington manager, Tom Loftus, who was flooded out of one doubleheader against the champions before getting one in on the last day of the season, Saturday, September 27. He could have forced the A's to play a makeup doubleheader on the following Monday, but Connie Mack had arranged a game against a Wilmington club, with all the gate receipts to go to his players. Loftus accepted $500 from Ben Shibe to waive his claim on their appearance in Washington.

Connie Mack didn't plan to use Rube Waddell in the Saturday games. He gave Rube permission to pick up some extra cash pitching for the Camden, New Jersey, club against its rival, Gloucester, for the South Jersey championship. Waddell's crossing of the Delaware River carried more excitement if less significance than George Washington's crossing. Pitching against another hired gun, Cy Voorhees of Washington, Waddell gave up 2 hits, doubled, and scored the winning run in Camden's 2–1 victory. After the game it took a squad of police to separate Rube from his admirers, but not before somebody picked his pocket and separated Rube from a $165 gold watch that generous admirers had given him a week earlier.

The rain stopped long enough for the Wilmington game to be played, preceded by lengthy speeches and lavish gifts. No matter how ridiculous the stunt, Connie Mack was always willing to go along with it, long before photo ops became routine. Before a full house estimated at eleven thousand, the festivities began when a huge white trunk was carried out to home plate. Connie Mack, accompanied by the most rotund little boy they could find carrying a banner announcing the "White Elephant's Trunk," was escorted to home plate by the roundest pair of umpires available. Mack opened the trunk and removed a large bouquet of flowers, then perched atop the trunk beside the bench during the game.

In another game, Mack saved Rube Waddell for last, and the Rube finished his two-inning stint with a flourish. After striking out the first two batters in the ninth, he waved in all his fielders and directed them to the bench. Then, to the delight of the crowd, he fanned the last hitter. He would do this more than once but never in an official game. The trick backfired on him once, in a spring game in Memphis. Harry Davis was in charge of the team. In the ninth inning, Waddell shooed everybody off the field except the catcher, Doc Powers. He struck out three batters, but Powers let the last strike get away from him and the batter reached first. The next two men hit pop flies just out of Rube's reach. The puffing Waddell asked Davis to put the infielders back on the field. Davis refused. Rube then fanned the last batter.

As if putting an exclamation point to the year's competition between the Athletics and Phillies, only 101 fans chose to watch the Phillies that same day defeat the Boston Beaneaters.

Then the skies opened up again, and it poured until just before time for a giant parade to begin at 9 p.m. The parade, which seemed to go on for as long as an elephant's memory, blocked all traffic around City Hall. Every amateur team in the area and its attendant brass band marched down Broad Street, as did every politician who ever ran for office in the city. As the players rode by, Rube Waddell inspired the loudest huzzahs. And the white elephant was everywhere—on banners, transparencies, and floats. For now, the pale pachyderm was more venerated in the City of Brotherly Love than in India, Siam, or Ceylon.

The next night the Athletics threw a banquet for the players and writers. Each member of the champions received a watch fob designed with a gold baseball diamond and crossed bats. Connie Mack's was studded with a sparkling diamond at each player's position on the field. Everybody present made a few remarks, Osee Schrecongost drawing the biggest laughs. Monte Cross recalled how he had been a batboy for the 1883 champion Athletics and had dreamed of playing on a championship team. There were enough toasts hoisted to loosen Lou Castro's tonsils in a Spanish song—his swan song as a big league player—and for Castro to crown Rube Waddell "King of Pitchers" with a spray of flowers.

Dave Fultz was the only regular who missed it, having departed to begin his duties as football coach at Lafayette. Topsy Hartsel, Monte Cross, and Harry Davis joined a barnstorming team that headed west. Doc Powers began his post as house physician at St. Agnes Hospital. Connie Mack led the rest of the A's on the exhibition trail, including a game against the Colored Giants at Columbia Park on October 6, won by the A's, 13–5.

Mack received the first of many baseball mementoes from fans in the coal-mining regions north of the city. The Lansford Miners' Band gave him an inkstand and well carved from a single chunk of anthracite.

The Athletics led all major league clubs in attendance in 1902, topping 442,000. They had also rented Columbia Park to black teams, which often drew crowds of over 3,000. For the year they might have shown a profit of over $100,000. It was customary to declare a dividend for the stockholders following a profitable season, but Mack's 25 percent interest didn't necessarily put a quarter of the profits in his pocket. Most of the profits were reinvested in the team and its facilities. Whatever he earned, he had enough to open a bowling alley, a business he knew something about both as a bowler and as a manager at Henry Vizard's bowling emporium one winter in East Brookfield.

Despite missing more than one-third of the season, Rube Waddell had won 24 games and lost 7 and led the league with 210 strikeouts. After a rocky start, Eddie Plank won 12 of his last 14 to finish at 20-15. Pete Husting was 14-5. Dave Fultz and Topsy Hartsel topped the league in runs with 109; Hartsel's 47 stolen bases and Fultz's 44 were first and third. Lave Cross and Socks Seybold drove them in, Cross 108 times and Seybold 97. Seybold set the young league's home run record at 16, a mark that stood until Babe Ruth came along. Six A's batted over .300, led by Lave Cross at .342.

Rube Waddell became the first American League player enshrined in the original "Hall of Fame." In March 1903 the new National League president, Harry Pulliam, created a Players' Hall of Fame in the league's New York office, "to hand down to posterity men who were famous in their day as baseball leaders." A gold-framed portrait of Rube as the AL 1902 strikeout leader hung alongside NL batting champion Ginger Beaumont and the Pittsburgh championship club.

A puzzling incident occurred in October that bore some echoes of the Husting disagreement in Milwaukee. When Nap Lajoie had been lost in April, Mack had appointed Lave Cross captain. At the time no mention was made of extra compensation. The position usually carried an additional $500 stipend. According to F. C. Richter, writing in *Sporting Life* of October 25, at the end of the season Mack asked Cross how much he wanted for his captaincy. Cross said whatever the club decided was okay with him. Shibe and Mack decided on $500 and sent him a check. Cross wouldn't cash it and wouldn't say why, calling it "a difference between the Athletic management and myself." Mack said he didn't know what that difference was since Cross had given him no counterfigure. Cross may have thought he deserved a bigger bonus but wouldn't ask for it.

Cross had a record of quarrels over money. In 1897 he had claimed the Phillies owed him a $300 bonus. They traded him to St. Louis. He sued them and eventually lost the case.

"Why I don't want [the $500] is my own affair," said Cross, adding that he had no intention of quitting the team over the matter. There is no record that he and Mack ever talked it over and settled whatever differences there might have been. Mack didn't trade him; Cross remained the A's captain for another three years.

Connie Mack was the first pennant-winning manager to land a book deal. A local publisher, Drexel Biddle Press, brought out *How to Play Baseball*, by Connie Mack, the following spring. It included chapters on playing each position, base running, sliding, coaching, teamwork, the run-and-hit game, generalship, and "Brains a Primary Factor." The chapter on "The Art of Pitching" featured photos of Rube Waddell showing how he gripped his jump ball, drop ball, fast inshoot, underhanded raise, and slow ball. The names have changed, but there are no new pitches. His slow ball grip looks like a palm ball; his fast inshoot, which he described as "my best ball . . . which breaks when close to the batsman and is a very hard ball to judge," was probably a slider. His drop ball acted like a splitter.

Citing brains as the primary factor in a team's success, Mack considered base running the most important, most interesting, and most intellectual department of the game. A manager could flash all the signs he wanted, but once the ball was in play with a man on base, he couldn't do the thinking for the base runner.

"It requires the most skill," he wrote, "calls into play the quickest and keenest perceptions of judgment, demands agility as well as speed, daring courage and enthusiasm."

To steal a base, a quick start was more important than a long lead. He advocated standing close to the bag, lulling the pitcher into complacency.

The chapter on batting stressed confidence and courage. Mack was already lamenting the decline of players' bunting skills. "Many of the best players in the game cannot sacrifice when called upon to do so. This is especially true of a player who is known as a slugger."

The inclusion of a brief history of baseball in general and in Philadelphia specifically, biographies of both league presidents, and photos of Athletics and Phillies stars anticipated the imminent end of hostilities between the leagues.

In the second year of his partnership with Ben Shibe, Connie Mack felt comfortable and secure, free of the pall of potential second-guessing or interference in his judgment and handling of players. Between their profits and Shibe's willingness to spend from his own deep pockets, Mack had reached a position where he could begin to carry out his ideas on managing and building a business. He could look beyond the current season and plan two, three, four years ahead. In a manufacturing company, that involved developing and testing new and improved products. In the baseball business, it meant discovering, testing, and developing new young ballplayers. Regardless of its effects on the outcome of the pennant race, he had begun that process during the 1902 season.

Most of the lines he had out were trolling for young pitchers. Some he caught and threw back after a brief look. With others, he saw enough potential to mark them as keepers. Many were culled; few were chosen. Most of them he never saw before he bought them or invited them to try out in a game. Only when he saw them in action himself could he assess them. Mack's eye for judging talent in its rawest stages would be measured as much by what his rejects did elsewhere as by what the keepers produced for him. He never claimed infallibility and was always conscious of the gap between potential and ultimate productivity, especially among young pitchers.

For example, on Danny Murphy's recommendation, Mack gave nineteen-year-old Norwich pitcher Clarence Quinn a trial. Quinn started and lost the last game of the season. After a brief look in 1903, Mack gave up on him. Quinn never had another big league decision.

He bought Henry Schmidt, a 27-game winner in Oakland, but never used him. Schmidt signed with Brooklyn in 1903, won 21 games, then disappeared from the scene. Mack picked up and quickly discarded another Pacific Coast League star, John Hickey, who never won a big league game.

Other discoveries turned out better. Up in Worcester, Connie Mack's brother Tom kept tabs on New England prospects from his position at the Lincoln Hotel. Tom went to Holy Cross games, read the local sports pages, and listened to the baseball talk among the traveling salesmen and sporting crowd who frequented the hotel lobby and restaurant. He tipped his brother to a handsome, well-dressed Holy Cross Prep School student, Andy Coakley, who had shut out Harvard and Yale pitching for the varsity in the spring of 1902. Mack sent a scout to look him over and offered Coakley a contract in June, but the student turned him down. He was interested, but he didn't want to jeopardize his eligibility to pitch again for Holy Cross. Well, how about coming down to Philadelphia and pitching a few games using a different name?

It was common for college players to play in semipro circuits, even in the minor or major leagues, under assumed names to preserve their athletic scholarships and eligibility, while gaining experience and earning some money. Club owners went along with it; those who didn't give students game-action tryouts turned a blind eye to those who did. Often no contract was signed. Some colleges were sterner sticklers for the rules, although some of them didn't hesitate to allow nonstudents or alumni to play for the varsity team if they could hit or throw hard enough.

So it was that on September 17 a tall, thin right-hander identified as Jack McAllister started for the Athletics against Washington. It was Andy Coakley. His debut began on an unnerving note; in the first inning he hit third baseman Charlie Coughlin in the jaw with a pitch. Doc Powers, with help from a doctor called out of the stands, brought Coughlin around and saw him off to the hospital. Coakley went on to win, 6–5. He pitched 3 complete games in eight days, winning 2, and went back to school. But somebody had recognized him, and his Holy Cross playing days were over. The following February Connie Mack met him at Tom's hotel and signed him for 1903.

During the season Jesse Frysinger, manager of a Wilmington team that had played exhibition games against the A's, may have seen a game on June 17 between the Harrisburg Athletic Club and the Chicago Cubs in which the semipro club's pitcher, a recent graduate of the Carlisle Indian School pitching under the name of Albert, pitched well in a 3–0 loss. Frysinger is often credited with recommending the eighteen-year-old pitcher to Connie Mack. A Harrisburg physician and former Washington third baseman, Dr. Harvey F. Smith, also reportedly was instrumental in enabling Mack to sign Charles Albert Bender to a 1903 contract at $300 a month. Mack also sent $100 to the Harrisburg manager, who must have tipped him off too.

Even before the 1902 pennant race had been decided, Mack and John Shibe began putting together an Athletics professional football team. The Phillies had fielded a team in the fall of 1901, playing a few games at their Huntington Avenue grounds against college teams and pro teams from the Pittsburgh area, where the pro game had its strongest following. Adding to Col. Rogers's choler, the Athletics lured away many of the football Phillies' stars, including their captain, Charles "Blondy" Wallace, a 240-pound former Penn tackle.

A Pittsburgh promoter, David Berry, organized a team manned primarily by veterans of a powerful local team from Homestead, which had gone undefeated for four years before losing its financial backing from the Carnegie Steel Works. Berry had visions of a six-team league he would call the National Football League (NFL). He did not back down from that ambitious label when prospective entries from Boston, New York, and Chicago fell through, leaving a three-team league confined within the boundaries of Pennsylvania.

The three teams—Athletics, Phillies, and Pittsburgh Stars—had no problem lining up former college stars from all over the east and as far as California. The Stars featured Giants pitcher Christy Mathewson, a halfback reputed to be the best kicker in the country. Since punting and place kicking, plus running into and over each other en masse, made up the entire playbook, Pittsburgh was expected to win the championship, such as it was.

The Athletics featured a guard reputed to be the best pitcher in the country, Rube Waddell. Connie Mack figured this would be a good way to keep him out of trouble, between practices and two or three games a week. But after an incident on the first day of practice, Rube's pro football career ended.

"There was a little fellow from Wanamaker's [department store] who asked for the job of quarterback," Mack said. "I don't think he weighed more than 140. Well, the first practice Waddell tackled him and broke [the little fellow's] leg. It was the first inkling John and I had that players could be hurt badly in football. We got Rube out of there without delay. He was supposed to be pretty good, too, but we never really found out."

In addition to the league schedule, the Athletics played town teams in New York and Pennsylvania. Mack spent a few days in East Brookfield in November and left the week before Thanksgiving. On Friday, November 21, he was in Elmira, New York, where the Athletics played the first night game in professional football history. Mack provided the searchlights, set up along the sidelines and behind the goal posts.

"We turned them on the ball," he recalled. "The rest—crowd, players, and field—were pretty much in a shadow. It wasn't very satisfactory, but we tried to keep a searchlight trained on the ball. We had a big crowd. The grandstand was full. I stood in an aisle near the front and couldn't see the ball."

The Athletics won, 39–0. They were, said the *Elmira Daily Advertiser*, "big, fast and bad in the extreme. If a man played good ball against them, they soon put him out of business for the remainder of the game. . . . Philadelphia men worked with the speed of lightning and the precision of clockwork."

In "league" play, the Athletics split two with the Phillies. The games, one at each team's home grounds, drew upwards of five thousand spectators and spirited wagering. The Phillies and Pittsburgh Stars split a pair. The Athletics had beaten Pittsburgh once. If they won their final game against the Stars, they would take the first NFL championship. Dave Berry arranged the game for Thanksgiving Day in Pittsburgh. Counting on attracting a big holiday crowd, he booked the expensive Coliseum grounds, owned by William C. Temple, and guaranteed Mack $2,000. Berry counted wrong. That same day nearby Washington and Jefferson College played its big game and college football, not the raggedy pro game, was the rah-rah rage.

When the A's arrived in their carriages, a dismal sight awaited Connie Mack. Recent rains had left the field soggy. Only a few thousand people were present. Whatever they had paid for tickets had been attached by Temple to guarantee his rent money. Mack told his men to stay put; no pay, no play, he said.

While they were standing around, a stranger approached Mack and asked what was delaying the game. Mack told him. The stranger wrote a check for $2,000 and handed it to the dumbfounded Mack. A reporter assured Mack that the check was good—the man was William Corey, a Carnegie Steel executive and an avid football fan. Mack sent his men onto the field. The Stars and Athletics grunted and bashed and bruised their way to a scoreless tie.

Considering the championship still unsettled, the two teams agreed to a rematch on Saturday. This time there was no guarantee and slim pickings at the gate. A few thousand curious fans showed up and watched another scoreless deadlock until the Stars managed two touchdowns (at five points each) in the last three minutes and one extra point for an 11–0 victory. So nobody won the first NFL championship, as all three teams finished with 2-2 records.

Hoping for one last payday to recoup their losses, the A's and Phillies agreed to a playoff for city bragging rights on December 6. Both sides prepared for it with all the intensity of future World Series. A snowstorm that hit the city the day before the game swirled no more furiously than the rumors that Connie Mack had signed special players for the game, including one of the Phillies' linemen, who was bringing his team's signals with him. Maybe he did. The Athletics won, 17–6, before a hardy band of hundreds, huddled together in the cold wind.

Connie Mack and John Shibe found themselves with $4,000 in unpaid bills when their football venture ended. "There was just one thing to do to get out of debt," Mack recalled. "We went to John's dad, Mr. Ben Shibe, and he dug down. He didn't give much of a lecture, either, as I recall, merely suggesting, 'I think you two young men would do better sticking to baseball, a game you know something about.' It was good advice, and both of us took it."

28 | SIGNING A TREATY

While in Pittsburgh with his football team on the day after Thanksgiving, 1902, Connie Mack had gone to Schenley Park on Forbes Street to look over the grounds that had been optioned by local men eager for an American League franchise. There were stories that the Washington club was available. Other rumors had the Detroit Tigers moving. If suitable grounds couldn't be rented in New York, the Baltimore Orioles might wind up in Pittsburgh. With dust and soot from the Jones & Laughlin steel furnaces coating his derby, Mack pronounced the site ideal and said he favored the transfer of an American League franchise to the Smoky City. He didn't say which one.

Barney Dreyfuss followed these developments very closely. Publicly he discounted the threats to his monopoly on big league baseball in Pittsburgh, but behind the scenes he urged his National colleagues to end the war. League attendance had fallen more than 10 percent. The National was still paying off the debts from the buyouts of the four clubs it had cut two years earlier. Maybe it could effect a merger, creating a twelve-team league like the one it had given up on as a bad idea in 1900.

The strongest anti-peace faction was, of course, the players, who wanted to maintain the competition between the leagues. Only warring geese laid golden eggs; doves laid peanuts. The lessons of the disastrous three-way conflict of 1890 between the National, the Brotherhood, and the American Association, leading to the National's ten-year monopoly, were ignored by the players.

"Unfortunately for the players," wrote John B. Foster in Brooklyn, "they are such poor business men that they cannot foresee the terrifying collapse that must come in the future." Without a truce, Foster predicted, a slump would occur by 1904 "the like of which has never been seen in any professional sport."

The struggling National magnates could see it coming.

The last inflated straw for the club owners in both leagues may have been the $4,300 the Boston Beaneaters gave to Wiley Piatt, a sub-.500 pitcher for the past three years, to lure him from the White Stockings. If the Wiley Piatts of baseball were commanding that kind of money, what might the Mathewsons, Lajoies, and Waddells demand?

The dove of peace that had been circling for months flew into the dining room of the Criterion Hotel in New York on the evening of Wednesday, December 10, 1902, and landed at the table where Ban Johnson was dining. It came in the guise of three wise men from the Midwest: Garry Herrmann, James Hart, and Frank Robison. They came from a National League meeting at the Victoria Hotel, where they had been appointed as a peace committee. They handed Johnson a letter written that afternoon.

Recalling the scene, Johnson wrote, "The humor of the situation appealed to me, for both Colonel Robison and Mr. Hart had been loud in their declarations that they would drive me out of baseball, and so I blandly refused to discuss business at that time, but insisted that all sit down and join me in a bottle of wine." Johnson had no animosity toward Herrmann; they had been friends growing up in Cincinnati.

Johnson contained his excitement until he reached his room, where he tore open the envelope and read the request for a meeting between the leagues to settle their differences. Johnson arranged to meet the National peace committee in rooms 3 and 4 of the Criterion on the morning of the twelfth. In his recollections, he made no mention of the participation, if any, of Cleveland owners Somers and Kilfoyle, who were also staying at the Criterion at the time.

Satisfied that the National genuinely wanted peace, Johnson then called an American League meeting for Monday, December 22, at the Grand Pacific in Chicago. There he read the letter and subsequent correspondence between himself and Herrmann, in which Herrmann proposed a united twelve-team league.

"What do you say?" Johnson asked the fifteen men around the table.

All but one—Max Orthwein, one of the three St. Louis owners present—spoke in favor of two eight-club leagues peacefully coexisting. Orthwein did not think St. Louis could sustain two teams profitably. He thought one twelve-club league would be viable, but he agreed to go along with the rest. Authorized to proceed with the peace talks, Johnson appointed Charles Somers, Henry Killilea, and Charles Comiskey to his peace committee.

When Connie Mack expressed the belief that the greatest benefit of a peace agreement would be instilling better discipline among the players, he was thinking more of their contract-jumping activities than their nocturnal habits. Washington president Fred Postal put it more bluntly: if both leagues agreed on salary limits, every club could cut its payroll between $10,000 and $20,000.

The peace talks began in Cincinnati on January 9, 1903, the National group augmented by newly elected league president Harry Pulliam, a former newspaperman and associate of Barney Dreyfuss in Louisville and Pittsburgh. Long into the night the National pushed its twelve-team idea, under which the Athletics would buy out the Phillies and have the city to themselves. Johnson kept saying no, until the National finally gave up. Efforts to freeze the American League in its present territory were also rejected by Johnson. He was going to New York, and there was no stopping him. But he agreed to leave Pittsburgh to the Pirates.

The only item on the next day's agenda was what to do with the fifteen players identified as having signed contracts with teams in both leagues. Here things turned sticky. As the representatives tackled each case, there were frequent recesses while club owners were called for consultations. Nobody called the players involved. Thanks largely to the calming influence of Herrmann, Pulliam, and Somers, there was no belligerence. It was clear to both sides that civility, concessions, and compromises were necessary or the good ship Peace would sink—and salaries would continue to rise.

The biggest obstacle, the Jerusalem of the negotiations, involved Christy Mathewson and Frank Bowerman, especially Matty. The St. Louis Browns were clearly entitled to them; their contracts indisputably bore the earlier dates. But John T. Brush, now in control of the Giants, stubbornly refused to relinquish them. St. Louis president Robert Hedges, with Ban Johnson's backing, was equally adamant.

"Though Mathewson had not yet shown the brilliance that was to make him the great pitcher of the day," Johnson later wrote, "I recognized his ability and wanted him for the American League."

It looked as if the talks might collapse over the rights to the big right-hander. But Garry Herrmann was determined to resolve every dispute. He insisted they stay at the table until everything was settled, even if it took all night and all day Sunday. At the end of the day Hedges, "crazy for peace" in Johnson's words, gave in, issuing a statement in St. Louis surrendering Mathewson to the Giants.

Of the disputed players, the American League kept Ed Delahanty, Sam Crawford, Wid Conroy, Dave Fultz, George Davis, Kid Elberfeld, Bill Donovan, and Larry Lajoie. The National got Vic Willis, Tommy Leach, Harry Smith, Rudy Hulswitt, Sam Mertes, Bowerman, and Mathewson.

The agreements were typed. The delegates signed them, then held a "jollification meeting" and went home.

But not everything was settled. The two leagues, autonomous though they were, believed it was important to have unified playing rules. The American rules committee of Ben Shibe, Tom Loftus, and John E. Bruce, a St. Louis attorney who had no evident baseball background, met in Chicago with their National counterparts and a group representing the minor leagues. They tangled over the National's foul strike rule, under which foul balls counted as strikes until there were two strikes. The American still didn't like it. Shibe and Loftus expressed their league's opposition to the rule, but the National, led by James Hart, and the minor leaguers fervently defended it. The American was supported by the editor of *Sporting Life*, who called the rule "absurd, obnoxious, and unpopular," and by Henry Chadwick, who felt it was an inequity to the batter and gave the pitcher too much of an advantage. Unable to budge their National counterparts, Loftus, Shibe, and Bruce gave in. For the sake of uniformity in the rules, they agreed to recommend in their report that the American League owners accept it.

Historians have dubbed Chadwick the "Father of Baseball," but at this time his children didn't always think father knew best. The inequality of four balls for a walk and only three strikes for an out upset his sense of fairness and equilibrium in favor of the pitcher. He believed the numbers should be the same, either three of each or four. Nobody paid any attention. At the meeting Chadwick also proposed the adoption of a designated hitter for the pitcher, which Chicago writer W. A. Phelon called a "jackastic idea." James Hart told him, "We are here to harmonize rules, not to invent freak statutes."

There was another question that apparently resulted in a difference in the two leagues' rules, although the effects of this are difficult to document. Washington manager Tom Loftus had a gripe. Groundskeepers had long been diamond doctors, operating on their fields to create conditions that favored the home team. The Baltimore Orioles of the 1890s had raised the art almost to the level of classical sculpture. It was also a longstanding practice of minor leaguers working on skin infields to rake the dirt into a gradual, almost imperceptible, humpback in the middle of the diamond to promote drainage when it rained. As rain washed the dirt away, they would rebuild the hill. One effect was to elevate the pitcher's box, giving hurlers another advantage over the batters.

Loftus became irritated by these practices in the American League. Even with sodded infields, he claimed, "groundskeepers have been playing the game by putting the pitcher on a hill." Photographs of infields of the 1900–1910 era don't confirm when or where such a hill, distinctly higher than the grass around it, first appeared. Loftus also objected to the practice of "tilting the base paths to help or hinder batters."

The rules, as far as he was concerned, said the field had to be level. Loftus made his case to the committee. The members agreed that something should be done. What they did was approve a rule, not banning the practice, but limiting the height of the hill to fifteen inches above the baselines and home plate, with a "gradual slope." That still allowed for wide variations, which Ban Johnson declared he would not permit.

The American League next met on Friday, March 6, at the Fifth Avenue Hotel in New York. After a morning journey uptown to look over two possible playing fields—one near the Polo Grounds where Yankee Stadium now stands—the owners took up the rules committee's report. They were still unanimously opposed to the foul strike rule. Then someone suggested that since their own rules committee had, however reluctantly, agreed to go along with the National and minor league position for the sake of peace, they should support their delegates' actions and ratify the odious rule.

Hedges, Kilfoyle, Comiskey, and Killilea cried foul. A spirited argument consumed a few hours before Mr. Angus of Detroit, with Washington's Fred Postal seconding, moved that the rules committee's report be adopted. Killilea and Comiskey immediately tried to amend the motion to exclude the foul strike rule. On this vote they lost one of their allies, Hedges, who voted no, along with Ben Shibe, Angus, and Postal. The amendment was defeated.

When Ben Shibe, as a member of the rules committee, abstained from the vote to approve the committee's report, a 3–3 tie resulted. (The New York franchise had not yet been admitted to the league.) Ban Johnson then cast the deciding vote in favor. They all agreed to try the foul strike rule for a while, and if they didn't like it, they would throw it out next year. A year later they would vote to abolish the rule, but they couldn't persuade the National to go along with them and gave up. They also went along with the National's rule requiring the catcher to play up close behind home plate at all times, and a bunt foul with two strikes being a strikeout.

Where was Connie Mack during the meeting? He was with his team in spring training in Florida. Had he been present, he would have found himself in an uncomfortable position. He was unalterably opposed to the foul strike rule and fought it for another two years before abandoning the cause. But if he had cast the Athletics' vote against it, he would have been repudiating Ben Shibe's Chicago agreement. His strong feelings in the matter and his independence in baseball affairs would have clashed with his loyalty to his partner.

With the end of the conflict, the players' fears proved warranted. The peace dividend would come out of their pockets. The Players' Protective Association, now devoid of leverage, was another casualty. Excoriated by the *Sporting News* for exacting "every pound of flesh they could get" during the war, they were now the prisoners. The American League, having broken the National's monopoly, joined its vanquished foe in a duopoly, where the principle of profit prevailed.

A dozen years earlier, Connie Mack and Charles Comiskey had been among the Brotherhood ranks rebelling against the National's salary cap and arbitrary treatment of players. For the past two years courtrooms had rung with the oratory of Ban Johnson's forces proclaiming the rights of American workers to sell their services to the highest bidder and the inequities of the reserve or option clause. They had struck these clauses from their contracts and paid high, presumably deserved, salaries to hire away the National's best players.

Now, the ink barely dry on the treaty respecting each other's contracts, the American League unanimously passed a motion imposing a future salary limit of $2,400, except for captains and managers, with no side agreements. And the reserve clause became embedded in its contracts.

29 | THE PROFITS OF PEACE

A case can be made that Ban Johnson saved major league baseball. Certainly the game was now on its solidest footing in many years. Devoted fans looked forward to the 1903 season with the hope that the sporting pages would once more be filled with numbers preceded by a decimal point instead of a dollar sign. The war of the leagues had ended with two strong circuits sharing a sometimes querulous stew of competition and cooperation, where just three years earlier there had been a monopoly by the National League, whose repute had grown steadily more ill in the minds of the public.

Baseball writers agitated for uniform scoring rules, there being as many ways to score a game as there were official scorers, who were often the club secretaries. Fans castigated clubs for peddling scorecards with inaccurate lineups and outdated rosters. Still, these mere carpings over details were a welcome change from the constant denouncing of the sharks who controlled the national pastime.

Ban Johnson found two angels to back the American League's New York franchise, both "bushwhackers" by Clark Griffith's definition. But that didn't deter Griff from agreeing to manage the team. Frank Farrell was a former bartender who operated a gambling establishment. Big Bill Devery was a retired police chief. To put a sheen of respectability on the club, they installed as president Joseph W. Gordon, an elderly coal merchant in a velvet-collared jacket. Originally referred to as the Knickerbockers, the team became known as the Highlanders, partly an allusion to an elite British regiment, Gordon's Highlanders, and partly symbolic of the location and terrain of their playing grounds.

The American League directors stayed in New York after their March 7, 1903, meeting to consider several sites for a ballpark. Johnson was evasive about the sites they had in mind because whenever a location became known, Freedman and Brush of the Giants moved to prevent its use, usually by getting the appropriate political body to approve cutting streets through the property or refuse to abandon a street that ran through it.

On the evening of March 12 the American League formally awarded its eighth franchise to Farrell and Devery. The league's eight-city lineup would remain unchanged for the next fifty-one years.

For a playing grounds, the league decided on a piece of property "so mountainous," Johnson later wrote, "that it looked like a section of the Swiss Alps." It was uptown, way uptown, in Washington Heights, at 165th Street and Broadway, a few blocks from the Hudson River. James R. McNally, probably one of the backers of the new club, obtained a ten-year lease from the owner, the adjacent New York Institution for the Blind. On March 23 he assigned the lease to the Greater New York Baseball Association, effective April 1. The rent was $6,000 for the first year.

Ban Johnson stayed in New York to supervise the turning of this "gigantic rock pile" into a playable grounds in six weeks. He called in Mack's builder, James Foster, who had just finished tearing down the right-field stands at Columbia Park and expanding its capacity by five thousand seats. Johnson also borrowed Mack's groundskeeper, Joe Schroeder, to prepare the New York field.

As soon as the site became public knowledge, Freedman and Brush went into action. They stirred up opposition among property owners in the area, who petitioned the Local Board of Improvements to cut streets through the property. The controversy pitted the head of the Blind Institute, who favored a ballpark, against the superintendent of the nearby Deaf and Dumb Institute, who claimed a ballpark would have a demoralizing effect on the inmates in his care, as well as the pupils in a nearby public school. Nobody asked the inmates or pupils in any of these institutions how they felt about it.

Work on preparing the field went on during the hearings. It wasn't until April 9 that the Local Board of Improvements voted 4–3 to deny the petition to cut up the property. That's how close the American League came to being homeless in New York. When the Highlanders opened their home season on April 30, the grandstand and bleachers were still unpainted. Excavations had left parts of the outfield so far below the level of the infield that a center fielder playing deep couldn't see home plate. Right fielders were in danger of tumbling into a deep ravine if they charged after a ball too aggressively.

Connie Mack was not in New York for these meetings. He and his family spent Christmas and most of January together in East Brookfield. When he returned to Philadelphia, Mack was occupied with ordering new uniforms. Previously all uniform pants had come with built-in padding at the knees, hips, and legs. Now players sending their measurements to the manager often enclosed notes requesting that no padding be added. They preferred to arrange it themselves to suit their individual sliding styles and comfort.

Mack and the Athletics arrived in Jacksonville on the liner *Arapahoe* on February 28. Other teams went south in mid-March, but none to Florida. The A's were joined in the state only by Amos Alonzo Stagg and his University of Chicago nine, the first college team to go south for spring training.

On arriving, Mack expressed pleasure with the facilities at Phoenix Park, declaring that Jacksonville had every other southern city "wiped off the map." But it was just public relations talk. Conditions were crude. The park was nothing more than pine trees and ankle-deep mud. There was no baseball field. The only shower was a hot sulphur spring that flowed through a pipe and down on their heads in an endless stream. The players slept on cots in a large empty barn that had formerly housed a gambling casino.

Mack put them to work getting into shape. Most of them had sedentary winter jobs. Some loafed and gained weight. A few hunted and farmed. So getting into condition was the first priority. Batting practice could wait. Some players flushed the sludge of winter with daily doses of sulphur and molasses. After they ran and stretched and played catch, the most exhausting exercise was high-low. They gathered in a large circle. The player with the ball looked at one player and threw to another—a little too high or low or to one side. They kept this up at a rapid pace until all tongues were hanging out. To strengthen outfielders' arms, one player held a hoop a foot above home plate and the outfielders threw at it every time they caught a ball.

They concentrated more on headwork than footwork or batting practice. Mack considered the arts of sign stealing and anticipation to be key parts of a winning game. He wanted all his players to be alert to stealing catchers' signs and reading batters' body language and pitchers' tip-off quirks. He had them practice to perfection their own sign flashing between batters and base runners to set up double steals and hit-and-run plays without being detected. Harry Davis, Topsy Hartsel, and Monte Cross were the teachers.

"Connie Mack studies the moves of the other side closer than any manager I ever saw," Cross said after his playing days had ended. "At bat or in the field he can tell exactly what his opponents are planning and is often able to block them. . . . When you have tumbled to the system, signal the pitcher to waste a ball and you generally queer the play.

"One day in Philadelphia we made the Sox throw up their hands by simply working out their code of signals and meeting their every move. Fielder Jones threw his bat away after the third man in succession had been caught stealing on the hit-and-run play, because the pitcher sent the ball so wide the batter could not reach it. He and his players were outwitted."

Not everyone appreciated Mack's brand of baseball. George M. Graham of the *North American* decried what he considered the decline of the game:

"Base ball has steadily become more mechanical in the last few years. It is played more and more according to a system. Managers rely more on teamwork and less on individual effort. Outfielders no longer rush in and dive for low line hits. They are unwilling to take chances on losing the ball and having hits result in a triple or homer. Instead they wait for the bound and hold the runner at first base. . . . Probably this style of play is good policy and necessary evolution of the scientific game. That it makes base ball less exciting and spectacular no one can deny."

James Hart complained that catchers studying the situation and giving elaborate signals prolonged the games. "While these moves help win games they weary the crowd."

It would seem there has never been a time when the game was immune from disgruntled "traditionalists."

Rube Waddell didn't spend much time with the boys at Phoenix Park. He marched to a different drummer and sometimes *was* the different drummer. He and Osee Schrecongost had spent the winter soaking up the Florida sunshine and spirits. Whenever they went into a bar, Schreck sang out, "Give me a highball and make it so high it's a wild pitch." Rube immediately became the life of any party and was too much of a gentleman to refuse the free rounds that were thrust upon him. He found everybody so sociable that he declared he'd have to leave town to get in shape.

Waddell and Schreck enrolled at Rollins College in Winter Park to play for the college team. Rollins's opponents yelled foul. Alumni could play, but recruiting big leaguers was going too far. Osee and Rube sacrificed their academic pursuits and left the school.

Connie Mack had a hard time keeping track of Rube's whereabouts. One day he spotted his erratic star twirling a baton at the head of a parade promoting a visiting minstrel show. Mack tried to duck out of sight to avoid embarrassing Rube, but the unabashed Waddell saw him and waved. Following the parade to the theater, Mack found Rube assisting the bass drummer and brought him back to the barracks.

There was one part of Phoenix Park that attracted Rube like a fire engine: an alligator and ostrich farm, run by a man who charged admission to watch him wrestle the reptiles. Years later Connie Mack related to Arthur Daley of the *New York Times* what happened when the gator farmer showed up at the training camp with a complaint. "He was the dirtiest-looking man I ever saw, but I guess his complaint was justified. It seems that Rube Waddell broke into his act. One day this man was going to wrestle an alligator when the Rube jumped in ahead of him, wrestled the alligator and triumphantly hauled him up on shore. It wasn't too big an alligator, only about six or eight feet long, and not as big as those terrible, terrible alligators I saw later in San Antone."

With all his peccadilloes, Rube Waddell was what used to be called a "good soul." If he came upon a horse-drawn trolley stuck in the tracks, he added his broad shoulder to the beleaguered crew and helped push the car free. Rescuing people or animals from burning buildings was his specialty. Once he was reported as picking up a hot stove that threatened to ignite a store, carrying it outside, and dumping it in a snowbank.

As a humorist, Charles Dryden was the equal of Ring Lardner. He was an honest writer whose fictions interwoven with his reporting captured the true nature of his characters. He found rich material in Rube Waddell and once described a time when the team boarded its special car in Chicago and found it filled with other passengers by mistake:

There was no time to shift in the depot and the train pulled out with a double header raging in the special car. Among the passengers was a woman with much baggage and three small kids asleep on the open seats. When it came time to move to another car the woman was in a fix until Rube rescued her. No one else in the outfit gave her a thought.

With his hat on the back of his head and a cigarette hanging from the inner film of his upper lip, the giant athlete stowed a sleeping infant under each arm. Then he hung suitcases to the hands at the lower ends of these arms and said to the woman, in low, guttural accents, "Follow me." She took the other kid and followed, while Rube bucked the center through three crowded Pullmans. Dumping the sleeping babes and baggage where they belonged Rube bowed politely and said, "Cheer up, lady."

"That was the Rube for you," Mack would often chuckle. "By golly, but he'd do those things."

Did the Rube actually do those things—and more? Maybe. Could he have done them? Absolutely. It was all so typically Waddellian that Connie Mack was surprised at nothing he heard or saw. Sure, he grew exasperated and blew up at Rube now and then, but Mack loved George Edward Waddell like, well, like a child.

Rube could be on his best behavior, especially when in the presence of refined ladies, but Osee Schrecongost was another story. Even his best behavior was unpredictable to the point of lunacy. The first time the A's witnessed Osee's steak-nailing act was in a greasy spoon called Wolfe's Café, where they ate their meals in Jacksonville. Wolfe was also their landlord at the abandoned casino.

"When we ordered steak," Chief Bender related, "Wolfe would walk back to the kitchen and yell, 'One baseball steak.' Next thing we would hear was the sound of a mallet hitting the steak, a wood mallet with spikes in it."

If the steak was too tough to eat, Schreck's preferred means of protest was to ask for a hammer and ten-penny nail and nail it to the wall.

"It created quite a commotion," Bender said. "Wolfe was awfully sore, and for a while it looked as though we would lose our eating place, but Connie finally talked the proprietor into letting us stay."

This was not Schreck's debut as an interior decorator of dining rooms. He had performed the same rite in a swanky New Orleans hotel when he was with Cleveland in 1902, and he might have done it again when the A's visited that city. That he crucified steaks more than once seems sufficiently substantiated. That he did it in all the towns named in various tellings of the tale is debatable.

Connie Mack did more apologizing to hotel managers for Schreck's behavior than he ever had to do for Rube Waddell. The only property at risk from the Rube was Mack's sanity. But Mack shrewdly treated each of them differently as individuals. Once he fined Schreck $10 for some escapade they had both enjoyed. "But Mr. Mack," Osee complained, "Rube is just as guilty as I was and you didn't fine him at all."

"Now, lookit," said Mack, "if you want to be treated the same as George Edward, we shall do it."

Osee said no more.

Nobody—not Charles Dryden or Ring Lardner or Mark Twain—ever invented a pair of screwballs like the batty battery of Waddell and Schrecongost.

In Jacksonville, Connie Mack put his rookie pitcher, Albert Bender, in the charge of the veteran Harry Davis, whose first piece of advice was, "Kid, whenever you get two strikes and no balls on a batter, throw the next one at his bean. Don't be afraid. You'll never hit anyone when you throw at them. But don't throw behind them or you will surely hit them."

This was neither unusual nor mean-spirited counsel; it was an accepted part of the game. Bender heeded it, and throughout his career he kept a duster in his arsenal, even though it backfired the first time he tried it. In a game against the Phillies just before opening day, he hit Sherry Magee in the forehead. It didn't faze Bender; he won, 5–1.

Bender's father was of German ancestry. His mother was a Chippewa Indian. Bender had left the White Earth Reservation in Minnesota at the age of seven to go to a school for Indians in Philadelphia, then to the Carlisle Indian School. His interests grew over the years to include marksmanship, billiards, golf, jewelry design and appraisal, oil painting, and gardening. He excelled at all of them.

Usually cool and unflappable on the field, Bender took plenty of robust riding from players and fans. In the northern white-dominated society of the time, an Indian in a baseball uniform drew more unrestrained ragging than the occasional southerner. Whenever he appeared on the field, Bender was greeted with war dance whoops.

Bender's quick wit and even temperament kept him calm. When a young lady seeking autographs in a hotel lobby said to him, "I always thought Indians wore feathers," he allegedly replied, "Yes, miss, we do, but unfortunately this happens to be the molting season."

According to H. G. Salsinger of the *Detroit News*, "One day Bender was having a rough time, lacking his usual stuff and control. Fans were heckling him with Indian war whoops. Bender took it a while, walked over to the third base stands, cupped his hands and yelled, 'You ill-bred ignorant foreigners; if you don't like what I'm doing out here, why don't you go back where you came from?'"

Socks Seybold was said to have pinned the "Chief" label on Bender. The tag stuck. Connie Mack always called him Albert—the name Bender used to sign his contract—but Mack sometimes referred to him as "Chief" when talking about him.

Even before the peace treaty was signed, Col. Rogers and A. J. Reach had decided that after twenty years of owning the Phillies, they were ready to get out. Barney Dreyfuss, still untouched by competition, had advanced them money during the war. Rogers and Reach sold out to a group headed by James Potter, a Philadelphia socialite and onetime Penn athlete. But Barney Dreyfuss, Garry Herrmann, and the Fleischmanns owned almost half the 200,000 shares. (It would be another seven years before such conflicting interests were eliminated.) Dreyfuss effectively ran the club, installing his catcher, Chief Zimmer, as manager, and moving Billy Shettsline into the business office.

Profits are powerful peacemakers. With Rogers gone, the antagonism between the Athletics and Phillies went with him. They agreed to play a city series beginning April 4, alternating between the teams' home grounds. The players quickly picked up the scent of pelf. Led by Lave Cross, Mack's veterans demanded a 20 percent cut of the city series gate or they wouldn't play. These were not just practice games, they claimed, but city championship games, played before their paychecks began. Mack turned them down and was supported by a hastily called meeting of the club's directors. The standoff ended with a compromise: the players would share in the proceeds of exhibition games played during the season.

Mack took some heat for agreeing to let his American League champions play the seventh-place Phillies. His critics questioned how it would look if his team was beaten by tailenders. That possibility didn't bother Mack. The fans wanted it, his players would benefit by the practice games, and that was good enough for him. From the start he was always open to playing exhibition games against any National League team regardless of where either team had finished in the pennant races. And if they did lose the series to the Phillies?

"A defeat doesn't hurt anyone," Mack said, "and it sometimes does good."

After the Phillies won four of the five games, Mack met a disgruntled A's fan on the street. The man was peeved over the losses to the lowly Phillies and wanted to let Mack know it.

"I knew he was looking for an argument and a chance to roast me," Mack said, "so I just beat him to it.

"He said, 'Say, Connie, what do you think of a fellow who has a million dollars and plays cards with a fellow that has but fifty cents?'

"Never giving him a chance to go any further, I said, 'I think he is a pretty good sport. Goodbye.'"

When the courts cleared Lajoie, Flick, and Bernhard of their contempt charges, the Phillies didn't object. The three could now appear with the Cleveland club in Philadelphia without fear of being housed in the hoosegow.

The new amity brought other changes. Front office officials of one team were frequently seen at their neighbor's games when their own team was on the road. Nobody was nervous about spies or agents trying to kidnap players. The Phillies and A's posted each other's out-of-town scores on bulletin boards during their home games. When on Saturday, August 8, a section of the Phillies' left-field bleachers collapsed under the weight of a sudden rush of fans to the top, the park was closed for the rest of the season. The A's let them use Columbia Park for two September series.

A sign that had hung in the Phillies' park—"No Improper Language to Player or Umpire Will Be Tolerated"—was painted out by the new owners. They wanted to let their patrons know they were expected to behave like ladies and gentlemen without posted warnings. The patrons' behavior didn't change.

Except for the loss of Dave Fultz in center field, the A's lineup was unchanged. Fultz, considered the A's most valuable player by some writers, was a hard act to follow. To replace him, Mack bought thirty-two-year-old Ollie Pickering from Cleveland. Pickering was speedy enough to steal 40 bases, second in the league, but the writers rode him for "irremediable stupidity" on the bases. Pickering's only other distinction was a close resemblance to onetime St. Louis baseball impresario Chris von der Ahe.

To supplement his outfield, Mack paid $300 to Toledo for Danny Hoffman, who had led the Connecticut League at .338.

On the A's return from Florida, Connie Mack assayed his pitching riches and boldly predicted his Athletics would repeat as champions. He had a pair of lefties, Waddell and Plank, and two right-handed rookies, Bender and Weldon Henley. Henley, it turned out, had jumped an Atlanta contract and posed as a free agent. An electrical engineer out of Georgia Tech, he had not studied contract law. It cost him a $600 fine.

Andy Coakley was coaching the Holy Cross pitchers and working out with them and would be along in June. They were all healthy six-footers, except for Plank, a half-inch shy. In the days of a 140-game schedule, 85 percent of them complete games by starters, Mack was well fortified with strong arms.

Connie Mack had seen nothing in Rube Waddell's behavior so far to warn him that the strain of Rube's self-control since joining the A's might snap his mental garters. But before opening day there were omens that his celebrity might have gone to his head, where there were plenty of rooms to let. On their way to Boston for the April 20 opener, the A's stopped in Jersey City for two games. Mack allowed Waddell to skip the exhibitions. Rube remained in Philadelphia on Friday to be initiated into the Junior Order of American Mechanics, then went to Boston alone to attend a banquet in his honor.

The following Monday was a long day for the Rube. Pitching the opener before a record morning crowd of 8,376, he was run ragged by the Bostons, who picked on his one weakness—fielding bunts. His fastball was usually too overpowering to bunt, but this time it was room service for the hitters. Going after a slow roller in the fourth inning, Rube fell on his right shoulder and came up holding his left. He was ready to quit for the day. Harry Davis walked over from first base and not so gently persuaded him to stay in there and take it, which he did, a 9–4 licking.

That afternoon a throng of more than nineteen thousand turned out to watch Cy Young and Eddie Plank duel. Plank was no sharper than Waddell had been. The home team jumped on him for a quick 6–0 lead. After three innings Mack had seen enough.

"Albert," he said to Bender, "go in and pitch."

The rookie was not yet the cool Chief he would become. "I was scared," he admitted later.

Bender was wild but gave up only 1 run, a Buck Freeman homer. In the seventh the A's woke up against Young, banging out 3 singles and 3 triples for 6 runs. They scored 1 in the eighth and 3 in the ninth for a 10–7 win, Bender's first.

"Nice work, Albert," Mack said.

Forty years later Bender still regarded his major league debut as "my greatest thrill in baseball."

The pocket-size, leather-bound schedules distributed by the A's listed their home opener for Wednesday, April 22. Despite chilly temperatures, 13,578 fans crowded the stands and ringed the outfield. They cheered the unfolding of the 1902 pennant on the new flagpole and cheered some more as Rube tossed a nifty 4-hitter against Boston, 6–1. In his first three starts, Waddell struck out 30 but won only once.

Connie Mack cut the Rube and Osee plenty of slack because they were good at their jobs and they drew the crowds. Fans and players alike enjoyed the shows they put on. They roared with applause when Schreck played catch with three pitchers at the same time. With Plank, Bender, and Waddell throwing to him, Schreck caught each pitch with his mitt, shifted the ball to his tremendous right hand, then threw all three back at once, the balls separating on the way to their targets.

Crowds arrived early on days Waddell was announced to pitch. They never knew what they might see before or during a game. One day a pregame argument with Boston first baseman Candy LaChance led to a wrestling match on the field. Nobody moved to break it up. For thirty minutes they tangled before Rube pinned him. Then he got up and pitched a complete game.

Rube was scheduled to start on Friday, May 15, in St. Louis. Willie Sudhoff, a five-foot-seven Browns pitcher, tried to wear out Rube's arm before the game by betting Rube he couldn't throw the ball from deep center field to home plate. Rube stalked out to the fence and started throwing. Sudhoff kept needling him: "Bet you can't do it again." Rube kept throwing. After an hour, Sudhoff was confident that any normal human arm would be ready to fall off. Waddell fanned 13 that afternoon, including three pinch hitters in the ninth, and won, 4–2.

That was an eventful series for the Rube. According to Dryden, he went out one evening to Forest Park Highlands to enjoy the rides. The scenic railway sped down an incline with Rube aboard. It hit a post, the car stopped dead, but Rube didn't. He sailed through a clutter of wires, knocking the whole place out of business, and hit his head on a post. The management paid him $50 for his troubles and his silence. Rube pocketed the cash, combed his hair, and walked back to the Southern Hotel. (The Southern was the players' favorite stop. One of its amenities was a free pressing of the guests' suits. The players saved all their wrinkled clothes for the St. Louis stop.)

Before leaving town, Waddell signed a contract for $500 a week to appear after the season in a stage production of *The Stain of Guilt*, a melodrama that drew its title from the telltale nicotine stains on the villain's fingers.

The A's went on to Detroit, where Rube went fishing for a few days with some local anglers and returned in a condition delicately described as "not feeling well."

When Rube Waddell asked for a day off to get married, Mack readily consented, hoping the influence of a good woman might keep Rube in line.

Rube had been married once before; his wife had divorced him while he was pitching in California in 1902. On June 3 he wed May Wynne Skinner in Lynn, Massachusetts. But the marital knot failed to domesticate the twenty-six-year-old Waddell. The bride knew little about baseball and less about what she was getting into.

Connie Mack's game routine had settled into a pattern. He sat in the middle of the bench in suit and tie and high collar, keeping score, occasionally moving his outfielders with a wave of the scorecard, rarely moving except to squirm when things grew tense, talking to the young players seated on either side of him. He usually maintained a stoic calmness that gave no hint of his thoughts or feelings, except when a player's actions annoyed him and he shot a barbed remark or an umpire's call riled him.

Mack expected his players to maintain the same calm on the field. None of his players had been suspended since the league began. Not, that is, until June, when Topsy Hartsel was set down for three days for assaulting umpire Bobby Carruthers. (When Nap Lajoie suffered the same fate for a run-in with Carruthers, Ban Johnson decided it must be the umpire's fault and fired him.)

The A's continued to prosper at the gate, aided by a tight pennant race. As June began, only 3 games separated six teams. When Lajoie and Flick made their first appearance in Philadelphia since their forced departure, the three-game series drew more than thirty-seven thousand. Announced figures were subject to swelling, and visiting teams were often paid off on lower counts (turnstiles were not mandatory in every AL park until 1904). But there was no doubting the popularity of the American League brand of baseball. On Friday, June 12, Waddell and Addie Joss dueled for 14 innings before a Pickering home run won it for Rube, 2–1. That inspired a record throng of twenty-four thousand to ignore hovering rain clouds the next day, while thousands more banged on the locked gates in vain. Bender treated them to a 12–1 breeze.

Mack could only dream of how the turnstiles would whirl if Sunday baseball was legal in Pennsylvania. He had no hesitation about playing on Sundays. It didn't interfere with his attending early Mass, and he often used the day to scout semipro or minor league teams.

The Athletics were 9-2 on a home stand that sent them west in first place. An optimistic Connie Mack welcomed Andy Coakley in Chicago. But things went downhill in a hurry. Coakley and Henley were inconsistent. The workload fell on Plank and Bender. Waddell was now rarely in condition to pitch. He spent little time with his new bride and had nibbled away almost his entire year's salary in advances, despite Mack's efforts to control the flow. Whenever Rube hit the manager for a twenty, claiming family or friends were in town, Mack, who kept two dollar bills folded in his pocket, pulled out the pair of singles with a "Sorry, Eddie, that's all I've got on me," and handed them over. Or Rube would arrange for a bellboy to deliver a fake telegram to him in a hotel dining room, then inform Mack that it was a collect wire and he needed sixty cents for it. Or he needed money for a haircut. Or he had lost his 1902 championship watch fob. Once Mack put up a $10 reward for it. The next day a bartender showed up with it and picked up the tenner, which settled Rube's bar tab.

Mack tried everything, including hiring a private detective to keep his problem child out of trouble. "He lasted about two weeks," Bender recalled. "Harry Davis and I were sitting in front of the Euclid Hotel in Cleveland one night about eleven p.m. A hansom cab pulled up and Rube got out. He reached inside and pulled out the constable and threw him over his shoulder. The fellow weighed at least 230. Rube carried him into the hotel.

"'Getting in a bit early, aren't you, Rube?' Davis said.

"'As soon as I put down this drunk, I'm starting out for the evening,' Rube said. That was the last of the constable."

As the team slipped into second place, the players became fed up with Rube. They knew they could win if he did his job. But he was as wild in the pitcher's box as he was off the field. He lost three, four, five in a row. One day in mid-July Lave Cross let him have it in the clubhouse, dressing him down for his absences and failure to take care of himself. Rube cleaned out his locker, announcing that he was quitting and wouldn't be back.

He went across the river to Camden and tended bar. They loved him in Camden and welcomed him to pitch for a local team or hole up in the saloon whenever he felt like it. A few days later he was back. He went into Mack's office looking like a kid caught playing hooky. Mack sat at his desk, pretending not to notice him.

"I'm sorry I threw you down," Rube said. "I couldn't help it."

"What's that?" Mack looked up. "What are you talking about?"

Rube apologized for disappearing. Feigning great surprise, Mack said, "That's news to me. I didn't know you'd been away. But, you know, it's your turn to pitch today, and we need this game awful bad."

Waddell went out and shut out Chicago, 2–0. Pitching against the Browns three days later, he was the target of a constant harpooning from a coterie of gamblers. Andy Coakley, who had pitched six innings in relief the day before, was in the stands near the hecklers. (A pitcher who had worked the previous day didn't have to be in uniform, but he had to be available if needed in a pinch. More than once, Mack would send somebody to the nearest saloon to summon the Rube to put out a fire.)

By the end of the seventh, Rube was steaming. He was ready to charge into the stands and take a swipe at the snipers. He fired nothing but fastballs, whiffed the three batters, and leaped into the stands. His target was a ticket broker and gambler named Maurice Blau (a.k.a. Morris Blaw). Rube bashed him in the nose. The rest of the Athletics rushed to Rube's aid. Lave Cross picked up one of the hecklers and tossed him onto the field as Coakley sat astounded by the scene. The police broke it up and dragged Blau across the field to a paddy wagon.

Another interested spectator was Ban Johnson. He let Waddell finish the game, a 4–1 win with 12 strikeouts, then suspended him for five days. Ben Shibe vowed to clean out the gamblers. He banned Blau from Columbia Park and had four others arrested. Ban Johnson ordered the suppression of betting at all American League parks, a noble but futile gesture.

Waddell went three weeks without winning another game. The strikeouts piled up, but so did the walks. On August 1 he took a loss unique in league history: a no-hitter broken up by one batter who had 4 hits. Four singles by New York's Kid Elberfeld and 6 walks cost Rube a 3–2 loss. "If I would have walked him four times," Rube said, "I would have pitched a no-hitter."

After losing 3–0 to Boston at home on August 5, Waddell disappeared again. He was living in a saloon on Front Street, pitching for a Camden team, and tending bar in both cities. Mack sent word to him to rejoin the team at the Quincy House Hotel in Boston on Saturday, August 8. Rube didn't show up. He said he was through with the Athletics.

"I'm done so far as worrying over him is concerned," Connie Mack said. "If he wants to come back and do the right thing I'll give him one more chance. Of course, he must take the consequences, and he knows what that means."

Broke and about to be thrown out of her boarding house, Rube's wife pleaded with him to come home. He said he was through with her too. Mack suspended and fined him. Rube didn't care about that, but his wife did. Part of his salary was going directly to her. In a later Waddell divorce case, Mack may have been referring to this episode when he testified that "when his wife came around there wasn't as much for her as she had expected. She just simply bawled me out, and when [Ben] Shibe, owner of the club, started to explain to her she bawled him out, too."

They offered her the services of A's attorney Louis Hutt, who had Rube picked up by the police in a Haddon Street saloon. Booked for nonsupport and still facing charges of assault and battery filed by Maurice Blau, Rube spent the night in jail.

On Monday a repentant Waddell showed up at the Quincy House. But Connie Mack had run out of patience. His soft soap had hardened. No more jollying the Rube.

"I went after him strong," Mack said. "I was laying on the words thick and fast and I saw a nasty look come into Rube's eyes. Quick as a flash it dawned on me that I had gone too far. Breaking off in the middle of a scorching sentence, I reached out my hand and said, 'Say, Rube, I had you that time. All that time you thought I was in earnest.' And do you know that great big fellow who was ready a few seconds earlier to throw me through the door actually broke down and cried."

The Athletics bounced between second and fourth place, 4 or 5 games behind league-leading Boston. On Sunday, August 16, at St. Louis, Waddell and Bender lost a doubleheader. "We got a deadly crimp put in us today," Mack said. "This town always has been our hoodoo and always will be."

Both of Mack's catchers joined the casualty list that day. In the first inning of the first game, a foul tip split one of Schreck's fingers. Doc Powers wrapped it in rags and replaced him behind the plate. Schreck was on the bench in the third when Topsy Hartsel shot a foul bullet that hit him in the stomach and knocked him out. In the ninth Joe Sugden lifted a pop foul toward the Browns' bench. Powers dove for it. His knee struck a water keg and sent it spinning. Down he went in a shower of icy water. The iron rim of the keg cut his knee to the bone. Schreck had to catch the second game.

Then Hartsel went down with a charley horse. Harry Davis had a strained muscle in his side and rheumatism in his legs. Danny Murphy was still unable to turn a double play; the A's were last in the league in that department. And they weren't hitting, a condition blamed partly on the introduction of the hated foul strike rule, which resulted in the league's .300-hitting ranks thinning to eighteen from thirty the year before. "That foul strike rule raised Cain with my people all season," Mack lamented. He would try again that winter to repeal it. And would fail again.

After pitching a doubleheader in Detroit on August 21, Rube disappeared again. An offhand remark by Mack—"I'm done with Waddell"—was mistaken as a sign that the Rube was available, starting a feeding frenzy among other managers.

Mack continued to look for pitching. Hoping to find another Bender, he tried two more Indians. While Harry Davis was in Mt. Clemens, Michigan, seeking relief from his aches, he sent Mack Ed "Peanuts" Pinnance, who had worked his way through Michigan State as a calligrapher. Pinnance arrived carrying a huge suitcase made from the hide of an elk he had shot with a bow and arrow. Mack paid $1,500 to Ed Barrow in Toronto for Louis Bruce. Neither Pinnance nor Bruce ever won a big league game.

Losing 9 of their last 10 against Boston, the Athletics fell 15 games out. Mack considered using the last month of the season to try out new pitchers, then abandoned the idea when it looked as if a second-place finish was still possible. But he decided to finish the year without Rube Waddell, who was back bartending in Camden, swearing he would never pitch for Connie Mack again. A rumor that Waddell had been released by the A's was like chum dumped overboard into a school of barracuda. Teams began sending emissaries to sign him. They were disappointed; the rumor was false.

It rained all day on Saturday, August 29. Connie Mack was in his office when the door opened and in walked a contrite Rube Waddell. After a long talk, Rube signed a 1904 contract containing some disciplinary clauses, and Mack gave him permission to go to St. Louis to begin his theatrical engagement.

This was not Waddell's acting debut. Once when he was with Louisville, he had been invited to play a bit part in a local drama. When the villain began throttling the hero, Rube was to dash on stage and swat the villain. On cue he darted out, spied a pal in the front row, made a detour to the stage apron, and yelled, "Let's meet after the show," then attacked the villain.

When *The Stain of Guilt* opened at the Auditorium Theater in Philadelphia in mid-December, the management, hoping to cash in on Waddell's Quaker City popularity, billed him as the main attraction. On opening night Rube didn't show up until ten o'clock and missed his cue. At the next day's matinee, he arrived early with Schreck and a bunch of his Camden buddies and insisted on taking them all backstage with him. When they were asked to leave, a fight started. Rube was thrown out of the show, his trunk thrown out after him.

For all his zaniness and missed starts, Waddell finished with a 21-16 record and a league-leading 302 strikeouts. To put his performance in perspective, his strikeouts were just over 7 percent of the league total, a ratio he would match in 1904. Sandy Koufax and Nolan Ryan accounted for about 5 percent of league totals in their best years. In 1999 Randy Johnson's 364 were just 2 percent of his league's total.

Plank won 23 and lost 16; Bender was 17-15. The Athletics managed to edge Cleveland by ½ game to finish second.

Connie Mack's leadership, inspiration, and commitment to the welfare of his employees were rare attributes among the leaders of American industry at the time. Mack's players recognized and appreciated those qualities in their boss. They chipped in and bought him a large diamond ring. Before the morning Labor Day game, Socks Seybold made the presentation in the clubhouse. Harry Davis then spoke for the team, thanking Mack for his treatment of them.

"I hardly know what to say," Mack began.

"Go as far as you like," Seybold said, as laughter prevented any further sentimentality.

The Athletics' board of directors also appreciated their partner and manager, doubling his salary to $10,000.

In the spirit of peace and profits, postseason series were played in St. Louis, Chicago, and Philadelphia. Cincinnati and Cleveland played for Ohio bragging rights. John McGraw and John T. Brush spurned overtures of the Highlanders, who had finished a respectable fourth. Cold weather held down attendance in Philadelphia; the clubs lost money, but each player picked up an extra $200.

In early August Barney Dreyfuss had begun talking about a playoff between his pennant-bound Pirates and the American League winner. When the Boston Americans pulled away from the field in September, Dreyfuss and Henry Killilea arranged what became the first modern World Series. Ban Johnson was overjoyed when the Bostons won it, 5 games to 3. The American teams also won every fall series except Chicago's, which ended in a 3-3 tie. Johnson's American League upstarts were the kings of the hill.

With no football team to deal with that winter, Connie Mack went to the theater, enjoyed the boxing matches at the Washington Sporting Club, and went to dances and other social events. Later developments indicate that he was probably accompanied by a date sometimes, though no one woman gained any prominent mention as a frequent companion.

Sept 10th 1906

In consideration of Edward T.
Collins signing for the season
of 1907. The American Base Ball
Club of Phila does hereby
agree not to farm or
loan him to any base
ball club without his
consent
Connie Mack Mgr

Connie Mack's agreement not to farm out Eddie Collins without his consent.
Courtesy of the author.

ABOVE: Connie Mack's mother, Mary McKillop McGillicuddy, and Mack's daughter by his first marriage, Marguerite; taken about 1907. *Courtesy of Neil McGillicuddy.*

RIGHT: Rube Waddell as portrayed in a 1905 World Series souvenir booklet. *Courtesy of Robert Warrington.*

OPPOSITE: Three of Connie Mack's children from his second marriage (*left to right*): Mary, Ruth, and Connie Jr. *Courtesy of Connie Mack Jr.*

(ABOVE) Katherine Hallahan at the time of her marriage to Connie Mack in 1910. *Courtesy of Connie Mack Jr.*

(OPPOSITE TOP) Connie Mack, Ira Thomas, and Stuffy McInnis. *Courtesy of the Library of Congress, LCB-3260-7.*

(OPPOSITE BOTTOM) Connie Mack, Ira Thomas, and Philadelphia baseball writer James Isaminger (*far left*). *Courtesy of the Library of Congress, LCB 2-3260-6.*

ORR-PENNOCK-WYCKOFF-BUSH-SHAWKEY-STRUNK

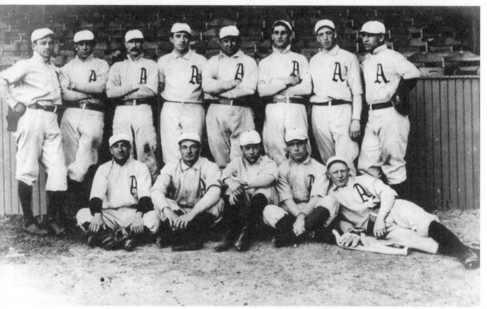

(OPPOSITE TOP) Bill Orr, Herb Pennock, Weldon Wyckoff, Joe Bush, Bob Shawkey, and Amos Strunk; 1913 or 1914. *Courtesy of the Library of Congress, LCUSZ62-133669.*

(OPPOSITE BOTTOM) The 1902 pennant winners. Top row (*left to right*): Highball Wilson, Bert Husting, Monte Cross, [unknown], Socks Seybold, Snake Wiltse, Eddie Plank, Dave Fultz. Bottom row: Luis Castro, Lave Cross, Harry Davis, Doc Powers, Topsy Hartsel. *Courtesy of the Library of Congress, LCUSZ62-122896.*

(ABOVE) Johnny Evers and Eddie Plank shake hands before the start of the 1914 World Series. *Courtesy of the Library of Congress, LCUSZ62-133667.*

(OPPOSITE TOP) Connie Mack in fall attire at the World Series.
Courtesy of the Library of Congress, LCB22315-4.

(OPPOSITE BOTTOM) Albert "Chief" Bender in one of his less
triumphant moments. *Courtesy of the Library of Congress, LCUSZ62-97857.*

(ABOVE) The $100,000 infield plus Danny Murphy (*left to right*):
Stuffy McInnis, Danny Murphy, Frank Baker, Jack Barry, Eddie Collins.
Courtesy of the Library of Congress LC DIG-GGBAIN-15514.

(BELOW) Napoleon Lajoie, who joined Mack's Athletics in 1901 and hit .422, still a league record. *Courtesy of the Library of Congress* LC DIG-GGBAIN-19545.

(OPPOSITE TOP) Frank "Home Run" Baker on a 1912 Miners Extra smoking tobacco card. *Courtesy of the Library of Congress, Lot 13163-32, No. 3.*

(OPPOSITE BOTTOM) Harry Davis, the American League home run leader 1904–1907. *Courtesy of the Library of Congress, Lot 13163-17, No. 4.*

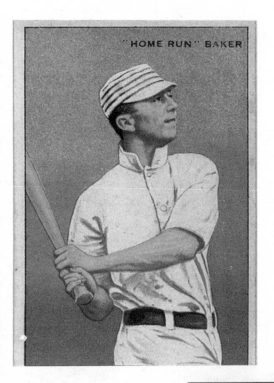

"HOME RUN" BAKER

DAVIS
First Base, Athletics A. L.

RAINEY, r. f.   IRWIN, 3d b.   CAR

The Buffalo Players'
League Bisons, 1890.
Courtesy of the Buffalo
and Erie County
Historical Society.

CLARK, C.   HADDOCK, p.   W
HOY, C.

BUFFALO BASEBALL CLUB I

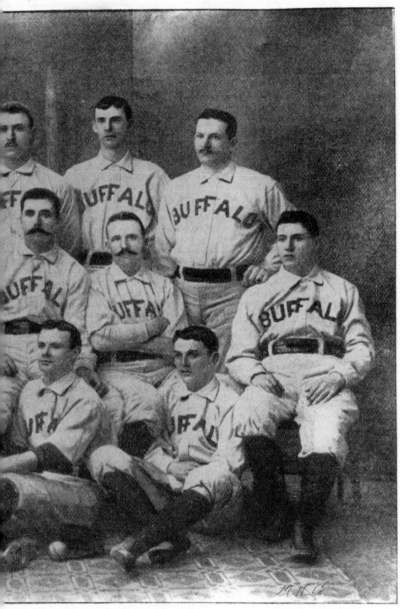

ROWE, S. S.   BEECHER, l. f.   HALLIGAN, C.
     FERSON, p.   KEEFE, p.

R'S LEAGUE ("BROTHERHOOD"), 1890.

Connie Mack in the A's dugout, ca. 1914.
Courtesy of the Cleveland Public Library,
Mears Collection.

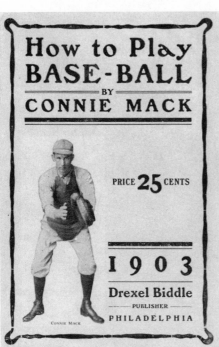

Connie Mack in 1905. *Courtesy of Robert D. Warrington.*

THE MACKS OF PHILADELPHIA

Going into the 1904 season, the major league magnates realized they needed some form of governing structure to settle the inevitable disputes that would arise between the leagues. They'd had enough of lawyers and courts. They believed that as baseball men, they could run their own affairs, settle their own disagreements, interpret their own rules. They created a National Commission, consisting of the two league presidents and a neutral chairman. Garry Herrmann of the Cincinnati Reds had impressed them with his mediation efforts during the peace talks. He was a respected political power in Republican circles and chairman of his city's water works commission. Despite his National League affiliation, he was considered objective and judicious enough to chair the National Commission.

Overall the American League was prospering. In appreciation of his leadership, the league directors raised Ban Johnson's salary to $10,000. Attendance had increased everywhere except in Washington and Chicago, where business was down 20 percent since the White Stockings had led the league in its inaugural season. There was a report that Comiskey, fearing he might have a losing venture on his hands, had tried to sell a half interest in the club to his manager, Nixey Callahan, and other investors for $12,000. Detroit was still shaky. Club owner Sam Angus tried to sell his colleagues on a limited form of revenue sharing. His proposal that receipts from holiday games be pooled and divided equally was voted down, 7–1. Angus gave up and sold out to lumber millionaire William Yawkey.

Still saddled with the weak Washington franchise, Ban Johnson's search for Washington businessmen to take over the club and pay off its debts landed two influential newspapermen, Thomas C. Noyes, city editor of the *Star*, and Scott C. Bone, managing editor of the *Post*. But it took until 1905 to completely extricate the league from the operation of the team.

The new owners mulled over an appropriate name for the club, something that would represent its presence in the nation's capital. Fans' suggestions ranged from "Diplomats" to "Grafters." A local committee of writers favored "Nationals," which they had been using, but the owners preferred to stay with "Senators." In March 1905 the owners would ditch the name and hold a contest among the Washington fans. The overwhelming winner was Nationals. Both names would be commonly used thereafter.

The Boston club also changed hands in the spring of 1904. Despite repeated statements by Henry Killilea that he didn't want to sell, he was badgered by former congressman John "Honey Fitz" Fitzgerald, who wanted to buy him out. When Fitzgerald's offer reached $100,000, Killilea gave in. But Ban Johnson didn't want Fitzgerald and vetoed the deal, claiming that the final terms were "not consistent with earlier understandings." Fitzgerald threatened to sue but never did. (Had the sale gone through, there might never have been a Harry Frazee in the Red Sox story, and Honey Fitz's grandson, John Fitzgerald Kennedy, might have become president of the Red Sox instead of the United States.)

Ban Johnson found another buyer more to his liking: John I. Taylor, son of the owner of the *Boston Globe*. There were now three teams in which newspapermen had an interest.

In an effort to field a contender and strengthen the league's standing in New York, the Highlanders' payroll soared to $60,000 for a sixteen-man roster, more than double that of most other clubs. Now a sideline observer, former Phillies owner John I. Rogers piped a familiar dirge: "One or two of the owners state plainly that to keep up with the tremendous increase in salaries would mean ultimate ruin."

With the expiration of long-term contracts at salaries inflated by the 1901–1902 competition for players, some clubs cut back for 1904. The Athletics had no extraordinary stars on their roster. They were a team, Tim Murnane commented, "of everyday players who give spectators a run for their money." Connie Mack was under no economic pressure to raise or cut payroll. The A's were making money; the players were not dissatisfied. Most of them saw themselves as farmers or businessmen, which indeed they were from October to March, as much as baseball players. And they knew they were lucky to be playing a game for a few hours a day and paid well for their efforts. The average working man earned a quarter to a half of a ballplayer's income and worked a six-day week for it—if he was lucky. Following the stock market panic of 1903, empty cars stood idle in railroad yards, workers in steel and cotton mills from coast to coast were hit with 10–20 percent pay cuts. Western Union messengers' wages fell from $3 to $1.50 for an all-night shift. Striking sausage cookers in the Chicago stockyards went on strike demanding $1.75 a day. From coal miners in Colorado to upholsterers in Boston, strikers sought shorter work weeks.

In January Connie Mack and John Shibe made their annual trek south in search of training grounds. Despite his public praise of Jacksonville, Mack had no desire to return. They settled on Spartanburg, South Carolina, where Wofford College offered a skin infield and a gym with real showers. The Spartan Inn promised more comfort and better food than Wolfe's old casino and tough baseball steaks.

With a holdover lineup, the A's spring training was uneventful. May Waddell arrived with Rube, probably at Connie Mack's invitation and expense, to keep a rein on her roaming husband. The wives of Monte and Lave Cross and Harry Davis were there if May needed any help. Mrs. Waddell cajoled Rube into going before a magistrate to raise his right hand and take the sobriety pledge for the next six months. Spartanburg held little of the social possibilities of Jacksonville, and Rube appears to have behaved himself.

The bushy handlebar mustache fashion of the 1890s had passed. Monte Cross was the only American Leaguer sporting any facial bristle. After batting a career low .189 in 1904, he would shave it off.

Missing from camp was Chief Bender, laid up with a severe case of mumps. Mack expressed his usual confidence in his pitching staff of Bender, Plank, Waddell, and Henley as they headed north. The Philadelphia spring turned in its normal cold, wet performance; the city series ended on April 13 with a shivering 714 faithful in attendance.

Mack awarded his groundskeeper, Joe Schroeder, the scorecard and refreshment concessions, where young Bob Schroeder also worked. To prevent a recurrence of the rain check riots of the past, the A's began the practice of attaching rain checks to the dated tickets instead of handing out separate pieces of cardboard on cloudy days.

They put up a 3-1 record on the road before their home opener on Thursday, April 21, against New York. Two umpires worked the game, a rarity at the time, but standard practice when breaking in a rookie umpire. For all his progressive ideas and insistence on curbing complaints on the field, Ban Johnson was unconvinced of the need for more than one umpire.

Yet it was impossible for one pair of eyes to see everything and call all the plays right.

"You did a lot of running," admitted umpire Billy Evans, "and—let's face it—a lot of guessing."

About fourteen thousand fans were rewarded for their six-month wait with a thrilling 12-inning battle, sent into extra innings by Danny Murphy's ninth-inning hit, and won by an RBI triple by Harry Davis, who also homered in the fourth. The new, abstemious Rube Waddell struck out 16 in the 3–2 victory.

The A's continued to struggle against their nemesis from Boston, losing 3 out of 4 at home, then suffering the same fate in a memorable series in early May in Boston. On Monday, May 2, Waddell pitched a 3–0 one-hitter before a ladies' day crowd of 6,500. Leading off the fourth, Pat Dougherty beat out a dribbler that Waddell failed to field cleanly. Boston's only hit could have been scored an error.

Among the spectators was the Boston strong boy, former heavyweight champ John L. Sullivan. After throwing out the first pitch, the great John L. visited with the players and sat on the A's bench during the game, to Connie Mack's delight. Sullivan took home 20 percent of the gate for his appearance. That evening both teams were guests at the Dudley Street Opera House minstrel show. For Mack, whose passions were baseball, boxing, and the theater, days didn't get much better than that.

Three days later Waddell faced Cy Young, the thirty-seven-year-old Ohio farmer who had won 400 games already. Young admired the pitching of the brash Waddell, ten years his junior, who had yet to win 100 games, but Rube ran his mouth more in a day than Young did in a year. When Rube boasted that he would trim Young the same way he had Jesse Tannehill on Monday, Young took it as "calling me out" and answered by pitching a perfect game.

"I had good speed and stuff," Young allowed after the game. "[Rube Waddell] and Connie Mack were the first to congratulate me."

Through May the A's kept winning, but so did Boston. Waddell was spectacular; as of May 23 he had lost only twice, both by shutouts. He had to be near perfect, for the team was still without Bender, whose mumps were followed by tonsillitis. In Chicago Rube pitched three days in a row, though he lasted only 2 innings on one of them.

Harry Davis and Socks Seybold were lame; Mack put the five-foot-five Indian, Lou Bruce, in the outfield. Ollie Pickering was suffering from a "torpid liver." Bender was in and out of action, plagued by appendicitis, which he put up with until December 15, when the annoying appendage was finally removed. When Davis came back, he broke a bone in his hand and missed another month. And they weren't hitting.

But nobody else was hitting much either. Henry Chadwick, complaining about the dominance of pitching and the numerous shutouts, continued to rail against the "obnoxious" foul strike rule. Another reason for the decline in offense was the growing use of the spitball. Difficult to control, the spitter was shunned by most pitchers. But for those who mastered it, it was a devastating weapon. Thrown with the same motion as a fastball, it was slower than a fastball but faster than a curve. It acted like a knuckler or splitfinger fastball, breaking in any one of several unpredictable directions before landing "like a brick" in the catcher's mitt.

The starting time of the games was another factor. The gong sounded at three thirty until mid-May, when some teams, the A's among them, moved the starting time to four o'clock. Batters were trying to hit a stained, beat-up fastball thrown by a Rube Waddell or Addie Joss or Cy Young in twilight. It's amazing they hit as well as they did.

Gathering dusk may have contributed to the beaning of Danny Hoffman. In the ninth inning of a game in Boston on July 1, left-hander Jesse Tannehill threw a fastball up and in to the left-hitting Hoffman. He ducked too late and it hit him in the head. Hoffman crumpled to the ground unconscious. Rube Waddell was the first off the bench. The players gathered around, uncertain what to do. Waddell picked him up, carried him out to the street, and flagged down a carriage to take them to the hospital. He stayed with Hoffman throughout the night.

"Nothing serious," the papers said. "Danny will be out for a week to ten days."

He was out for three months. His vision was affected. "The center of the field of vision was blank," Mack recalled in a 1920 *Bulletin* interview. "If Danny was looking at you he couldn't see you with his right eye. His field of vision was okay around the edges. He could see the second story of the building behind you and he could see your feet, but your face, at which his eye was pointed, would not register at all. Naturally he couldn't see a base-ball approaching."

The A's slumped. They lost a July 4 doubleheader at home during a 4-game sweep by New York. With the team hovering around .500 in fifth place, Mack perplexed a *Sporting News* correspondent by predicting that his A's would finish first. The writer portrayed Mack as reticent and conservative when asked similar questions in the past, but Mack usually expressed optimism at the start of each season in Philadelphia. During the season he was more likely to talk up his team's chances when they were trailing than when they were in the lead. It was part of his motivating technique.

Casting about for an incentive, Mack promised a new suit to any pitcher who won three games in a row and a suit for every player if the team won ten straight. It wasn't a high-risk offer; a new tuxedo went for $12.50. Eddie Plank and Rube Waddell were the first winners.

The pennant race was another humdinger. Through August, New York, Boston, and Chicago swapped the lead, with Cleveland and the Athletics not far behind. When the A's returned home on August 18 from a 10-2 western trip, in which Henley and Waddell won 7 of the games, more than a thousand fans greeted them at the station. The next day Waddell lost a heartbreaker—and another new suit—in the eleventh inning, when Monte Cross picked up a grounder hit by Lajoie and threw it over the first baseman's head. Lajoie circled the bases to give Cleveland a 2–1 win.

On Saturday more than eighteen thousand filled Columbia Park and saw Henley shut out the Naps, 2–0. Only 2 games separated the fourth-place A's from the league-leading Highlanders. That's as close as they came the rest of the way.

Detroit and Washington were the tailenders—Washington wound up losing 113 games—and Mack looked forward to gaining ground against them. He was bitterly disappointed when the Rube showed up on August 25 in one of his "not interested" moods and gave up 10 hits in a 7–2 loss to the Tigers. Angry and frustrated, Mack went into the clubhouse after the game and walked over to Rube, who sat on a stool unlacing his shoes. According to Edgar Wolfe of the *Inquirer*:

"Mack stopped in front of him and called him every name he could think of. Mack himself said he never knew so many hard names and personal insults as he hurled at the Rube could be called up at such short notice, and through it all Rube just sat with his head bowed soaking it up. As Mack stopped to get his breath and continue, Rube suddenly looked up and said, 'Connie, you ought to been down at the National Theater last night. I saw the best show I ever saw in my life.' Without another word, Mack turned and left him. As he afterward said in relating this incident, 'What's the use?'"

Boston-Philadelphia games were the league's biggest attraction in either city. (In ten dates at Columbia Park, Boston and the A's divided $67,000, enough to cover both teams' payrolls.) On Saturday, September 10, at Columbia Park, more than fourteen thousand watched a pitchers' duel between Plank and Cy Young, Plank winning, 1–0, in 13 innings. On Monday almost twenty thousand packed the park for a doubleheader. An indifferent Waddell was wild and lost the opener, 6–4. Andy Coakley won the second.

Only Plank and Coakley were consistent in September as the A's faded, finishing 12½ games out. With three weeks to go Waddell slipped trying to field a bunt and fell on his shoulder, putting him out of action for two weeks. Even so, he started 46 games, completed 39 of them, and worked 383 innings—all team records. His 349 strikeouts stood as the major league record for sixty-one years.

Mack cited the loss of Hoffman and the injuries to Harry Davis, even more than Bender's illnesses and Waddell's lapses, as the main blows to the team's pennant chances. Out of the race, he let Bender remain in Detroit to marry Marie Clement on October 3. The newlyweds, with three new shotguns, went on a hunting honeymoon to South Dakota.

Danny Hoffman came back and played in the last three games. He was gun-shy at the plate and would never again be the player Mack once described as "a world beater," second only to Cobb. But Connie Mack didn't give up on him right away. On October 10, in a game in Washington that fading light limited to five innings, the score was 3–3 in the top of the fourth. Hoffman was due up with the go-ahead run on base. Everybody on the bench, including Hoffman, expected Mack to pinch hit for him. Mack did nothing but call out words of encouragement to Hoffman, who flied out to end the inning. Later he explained his thinking to Wolfe:

"There was a valuable player that I had to help get his nerve back. If I had taken him out just to win that ball game he would have known that I didn't have confidence in his ability to produce, and this would have resulted in a further loss of confidence in himself. It would have ruined him forever. I would rather have lost that ball game than be the cause of a player further losing confidence in himself. Because he is getting his confidence back, he will win a lot of games for me even though he lost that one."

New York and Boston took the pennant race down to the last day, when Jack Chesbro, seeking his forty-second win of the year for New York, took his twelfth loss instead, as a result of what manager Clark Griffith always maintained was catcher Red Kleinow's passed ball, not a wild pitch by Chesbro. The National League race had been over since the Fourth of July, after the Giants won 18 in a row. McGraw and Brush refused to play any postseason games against an American League team.

Putting a stronger team in New York had doubled that club's attendance over 1903. Even without Sunday games, Boston and Philadelphia went over a half million, almost matching Chicago, which had a Sunday advantage.

Beginning in September, Connie Mack signed or was reported signing enough players who never made it to man an entire league. Some were conditional purchases with a thirty-day return option. He was thwarted in attempting to draft outfielder Otis Clymer from Buffalo when the Pirates announced that they had bought him before the draft window opened. Mack launched a blistering attack on the practice of major league teams protecting a minor league club from losing a player by buying the player, then selling him back after the draft closed. Once again Mack's views were influenced by where he sat. As a minor league operator in Milwaukee, he had regularly made similar arrangements with Louisville and been chided by the newspapers for it.

Connie Mack's relations with the press were almost always cordial, respectful on both sides, warming over the years into fondness, approaching awe among younger writers, reverence among those who grew old with him. He was always good for a story to help fill a columnist's needs. The older he became, the greater his inventory of stories grew. But beginning in Pittsburgh and intensifying in Milwaukee, he built up a deep dislike for being misquoted and was particularly peevish when he saw himself saying things in print that he had never said. Premature or unconfirmed reports of trades or player signings irked him. He hated it when holdouts negotiated through the newspapers and writers threw speculative salary figures around as if they knew what they were talking about.

During the 1904 season reports that he had purchased a shortstop named Pastor from Nashua touched off this snappish response: "You never have heard me say that we had Pastor. Wait until I say that we have signed Pastor before you claim that he is an Athletic."

Pastor never was signed.

At the league meetings in December in Chicago, Mack was interviewed by a reporter who quoted him as being critical of the Phillies' out-of-town ownership. The Phillies had lost 100 games, finished last, averaged about two thousand customers per home date, and filed for bankruptcy. In November the sheriff moved to auction off their assets, equipment, and lease on the grounds at Broad and Huntingdon. When Mack saw his alleged remarks in print, he fired off a wire to the paper vehemently denying he had said any such thing.

F. C. Richter backed him, doubting that Mack had said what was attributed to him. "Mack minds his own business about as well as anybody in baseball," he wrote in *Sporting Life*.

In the fall of 1904 Connie Mack decided to move the rest of his family from East Brookfield to Philadelphia. He had earlier moved to larger quarters on the other side of Columbia Park, at 2937 Columbia Avenue, and brought his younger brother Eugene to live with him and manage his bowling alleys. He was now in a position to provide his mother with a life of ease, with no housework or cooking chores. On October 21 he was in Worcester to attend the funeral of his Uncle Patrick's wife Ellen. While there, he discussed his idea with his mother.

Mary McGillicuddy was now sixty-three, small, spry, showing no signs of her earlier "near-death" condition. She had a full round face, a high forehead crowned by a nimbus of white hair. Her old-country brogue had disappeared. She was undaunted by the prospect of managing her son's household. A city girl at heart, she welcomed the change and became a regular at the games, sitting behind the home team's bench, wearing a green cap with a visor shading her eyes, scorecard in hand, watching the action with no show of emotion. Whenever she returned to East Brookfield to visit her old friends, she spoke of how much she enjoyed living in the city and how proud she was of her son Connie.

Tom's daughter Helen, who was eight when her grandmother died, remembered her fondly. "Grandma Mack was like all the rest of us Macks. She had a lovely disposition, but was somewhat of a disciplinarian in that she was honest beyond belief and expected her family to be the same. Liquor and smoking were not tolerated.

"I felt a real warm loving grandmother feeling about her. Once I caught the whooping cough while I was [visiting] there and every time I coughed, she said, 'God bless you.' You can imagine how many times I was blessed."

Mack's sons Roy, sixteen, and Earle, fourteen, had probably gone no farther than the eighth grade. There was nothing for them in the Brookfields. Earle, shorter and stockier than his father, caught for the town team and showed some potential as a ballplayer. Roy, the smaller of the two, was an infielder. Mack's daughter, Marguerite, was twelve.

Returning to Philadelphia, Mack looked for a larger home to accommodate the family. He bought a three-story house at 2930 Oxford Street, opposite the home plate entrance to Columbia Park, and had it renovated from top to bottom. When the family moved in February, Mack transferred the title to the East Brookfield house to his brother Tom.

No school records could be found, but gleanings from sports pages of the time indicate that Roy and Earle attended Central High School, one of the most prestigious schools in the city. A 1906 school team roster shows a shortstop Mack, class of '09. If this was Roy, he was a freshman at seventeen. It may have been Earle, who was an all-scholastic catcher in 1907–1908. Mack asked the Shibes to make a small duplicate of Osee Schrecongost's mitt for Earle. At sixteen he was warming up Rube Waddell at Columbia Park and being tutored by Schreck. Roy reportedly transferred to Central Manual, where he played second base. They both played for a semipro team in Atlantic City in the summer of 1908. In February 1909 Mack sent Earle to a prep school connected with Niagara University, then to Notre Dame, where he didn't stay long. By the spring of 1910 Earle would leave the academic world and begin a career as a baseball lifer.

Connie Mack's brother Dennis remained a problem. Mack gave him a job taking tickets at the games. Dennis also worked the gate at shows and circuses. Once Connie set him up in a tobacco shop, but little of his income made it home. Dennis's pledges to the parish priest to lay off the booze might last three months. Then he'd go off on a toot. The elephants he saw were not white but pink. They drove him into an institution at least once. A convivial fellow, Dennis was friendly with some of Connie's players, to Connie's chagrin. An expert with a pool cue, Dennis would go with Danny Murphy and Chief Bender to pool rooms, where they'd bet on him against some mark. Then they'd finish the night at Joe Armstrong's saloon.

Dennis's son Cornelius, who went by the name of Neil, remembered how, as a five-year-old, he would sit on the stairs watching Bender and Murphy deposit his father in the front room "and he had the DTS and said he saw rats all over the place.

"When we were at the supper table and he'd come in, my mother would tell me to 'watch the cup' where her household money was kept. He would drink away the whole household. One day my sister Mary told my father he should stop drinking. He said, 'Mary, you're a pretty little thing but you got a big mouth.'"

An exasperated Connie threatened to send the whole family back to East

Brookfield. Annie got down on her knees and begged him not to do that. He relented and continued to subsidize the family, which now included four girls and a boy. Annie would give birth to another boy in 1906. Every month two checks arrived at the house, one for the rent and one for food.

Despite their enduring portrayals as penny-pinchers, Connie Mack and Clark Griffith supported vast arrays of relatives of more than one generation throughout their working lives. And no down-on-his-luck former player ever left their offices empty-handed. When Mack learned that his old Shadow Battery mate, Frank Gilmore, was "not in the best of circumstances" in 1921—thirty-three years after they had last played together—Mack took his team to Hartford to play an exhibition game, the A's share of the receipts going to Gilmore.

One day in 1904 Al Maul, a Philadelphian whose fifteen-year pitching career had ended in 1901, came looking for a job. Mack had caught the journeyman right-hander in a few games in Pittsburgh in 1891. He hired Maul to guard the entrance to the upper pavilion at Columbia Park and to help out at the bowling alleys during the winter. Maul later scouted for him and remained on the payroll for forty years.

31 | THE FIRST "OFFICIAL" WORLD SERIES

"Was there ever a manager more serene in defeat under aggravating circumstances than Connie Mack?" wrote F. C. Richter. "In that particular he resembles the late Harry Wright more than any managers we have known."

At forty-two, with ten years as a manager behind him, Connie Mack may not have achieved serenity in defeat, but he had subdued his temper. Subdued, but never mastered. When the circumstances were aggravating enough or when he believed he had been wronged, he could fire off a barrage of sarcasm, no less sharp for being softly delivered. With maturity had come the difficult art of maintaining emotional equilibrium, an attribute essential to the health and longevity of all baseball managers—the capacity to savor good times without getting too high and endure the bad times without getting too low. He had learned to accept the inevitable losses, as often as 40 percent of the time for the best teams, 60 percent or more for the worst. He had acquired patience with players' mistakes, especially those of youngsters who needed time to develop.

Something old and something new were discussed at length at the American League meeting in Chicago in December 1904. The old was a renewed effort to get rid of the foul strike rule. Two old allies, Comiskey and Mack, were on opposite sides of the issue. Comiskey argued that the league was doing well and the fans seemed satisfied with the way the game was being played, so why change anything. Mack still didn't like it and tried once more to kill it. Although there was sentiment to do something to boost offense in the game, Mack failed to gain enough support and never brought it up again.

A letter from Garry Herrmann suggested something new: interleague play. Herrmann proposed that each league adopt a 112-game schedule, followed by home-and-home series between the clubs of the two leagues. The idea drew a unanimous thumbs down around the table. They all agreed, however, to a proposed championship series between the two pennant winners, administered by the National Commission.

When the meeting adjourned, Mack and John Shibe went in search of a new training site. They went first to Mobile, Alabama, where Mack had made a tentative deal to use the city's Monroe Park. When they saw it, they didn't like it and moved on. They headed for Texas, stopped in Shreveport, liked what they found, and went no farther. A few weeks later Mack received an invitation from a wealthy Cuban to train in Havana, all expenses paid. He was tempted; spring training was no moneymaker. But it was too late. He had signed a lease in Shreveport.

Philadelphia writer Ed Pollock placed the oft-told crackers-in-bed story as occurring that winter. Mack, he related, tried to get Rube Waddell's signature on a 1905 contract for weeks without success. One day the Rube showed up at Mack's office. Asked what was bothering him, Waddell squirmed and didn't answer.

"Is it money?" Mack asked.

No, it wasn't about money.

Well, what was it, Mack coaxed.

"It's Schreck," Rube blurted out. "You shouldn't let him eat animal crackers in bed. You should put that in his contract."

Roommates still shared one bed on the road, and the crumbs had apparently been rubbing Rube the wrong way.

Mack assured him he would take care of the problem. Rube signed. Mack sighed and put the contract in the safe. In other versions of the story as told by Mack, it was Schreck who made the complaint about Rube. Maybe they were both guilty. Charles Dryden wrote that Waddell complained about Schreck's "pizzazz" sandwiches—Limburger cheese and raw onions on rye bread—but they probably both enjoyed them. Anything was possible with that pair.

On January 25, 1905, a blizzard hit Philadelphia, the temperature dropped near zero, and Mack was felled by the grippe, as the flu bug was then called. A letter from Chief Bender didn't aid his recovery. Bender had been separated from his appendix in December. There were complications. He would miss spring training.

Mack climbed out of his sickbed to attend the first baseball writers' dinner, a gala event in the Bellevue-Stratford's elegant Clover Club dining room, on February 13. Invitations were limited to 150. The room was decorated with the 1902 pennant and a huge white elephant banner. Ben Shibe provided souvenir baseballs with the names of the honored guests, Connie Mack and Billy Shettsline, stamped on them, and small bats that made a clatter when used to applaud a speaker. The legal scraps and differences of the past were forgotten as Shibe, Al Reach, and Col. Rogers dined together on caviar, gumbo, planked sirloin steak, rum omelets, champagne, and imported beer. Every writer present made a brief speech as the room filled with cigar smoke.

When Mack's turn came, he made no mention of his own team. He graciously lauded Billy Shettsline's efforts to restore the Phillies to health, wished them well in 1905, and sat down.

On March 1 the Athletics boarded the L&N express for New Orleans. They were accompanied by Sam Erwin, a liquor distributor who lived two houses from Mack at 2934 Oxford. Erwin was seventy-two, a one-time handball champion, and an old friend of Ben Shibe's. An investor in the Philadelphia Players' League and American Association teams, he was one of the first baseball men Mack had met in Philadelphia. While filling in as manager of an Athletics' reserves team barnstorming through Pennsylvania in 1888, he had heard pitcher Mike Mattimore refer to the players as "Yannigans." Erwin picked it up and applied it to the rookie or second-string teams he would manage for Mack every spring. There are accounts of earlier uses of the term, but not much earlier.

Another newcomer on the train was Frank Newhouse, ostensibly a trainer but whose duties were more those of a watchdog over Rube Waddell. A former boxer, Newhouse trained several prominent pugilists of Mack's acquaintance.

The A's arrived at the height of Mardi Gras week in New Orleans. Mack figured on stopping there to work out for a day, then get in a few lucrative practice games before moving on to Shreveport. Through newspaper and magazine stories, Rube Waddell had become a national celebrity. The March 2 New Orleans *Daily States* noted, "Rube Waddell has never visited New Orleans; everybody is anxious to see him in action. His performances on and off the diamond have made his name a celebrated one all over the country."

Due to arrive on the morning of Friday, March 3, the train was delayed for eight hours by a freight train wreck that left the players no time to limber up before the weekend exhibitions. On Saturday President Teddy Roosevelt's inauguration went better than Rube's New Orleans debut, the

A's losing, 7–2, to a local nine. The team stayed at the St. Charles Hotel, an immense step up from the fleabag facilities baseball had been consigned to just a few years earlier. One of the nation's largest and grandest hotels, the six-story St. Charles housed more than a thousand guests. It featured a promenade, palm garden, billiard room, Turkish baths, and barber shop. The dining room, furnished with Queen Anne chairs and white linen tablecloths, offered the best dinner in the city for fifty cents. It was also said to be the scene of one of Osee Schrecongost's earlier hammer-and-nails tough steak protests, requiring Mr. Mack to turn on his best Gaelic charm to persuade the management to permit his team to stop there.

The Young Men's Gymnastic Club made its facilities available for the players to shower and change before and after the games at nearby Sportsman's Park. All in all, it was the ultimate in spring training comfort and luxury.

Looking ahead to the 1905 season, Connie Mack hoped to lower the age of his lineup. At the December league meeting in Chicago, he tried to trade thirty-five-year-old Monte Cross to Washington for shortstop Joe Cassidy, a former high school star in nearby Chester. The deal fell through. Mack then offered $7,000 for Cassidy and was turned down.

But for all Mack's signing of young players, his veteran squad included only three rookies who would make the team. When Harry Davis was sidelined with a broken hand in 1904, Mack had sent him scouting. Davis came up with a recent graduate of Central High in Philadelphia, a shortstop and third baseman, Jack Knight. Mack signed him. On the recommendation of Harrisburg Athletic Club manager Jesse Frysinger, he signed two Pennsylvanians, outfielder Bris Lord, twenty-one, and catcher Harry Barton, twenty.

Barton received a thorough look, as Schreck missed most of the camp. First his father's death called him home. When he returned, he learned of his sister's death and had to go back to Pennsylvania again. But the five-foot-six Barton was too light on the scale and with the bat and didn't last.

Bris Lord quickly demonstrated the strongest arm among Mack's outfielders, but his inexperience showed at the plate.

Mack was impressed with the rangy, six-foot-two Knight's fielding and baseball instincts, but he had his doubts whether Knight would hit enough to stick. The schoolboy enjoyed a memorable St. Patrick's Day, hitting a 3-run home run in the first inning off Rube Waddell for the Yannigans. That evening they all enjoyed a local production of *A Rollicking Irish Lad*.

For the past three years, Andy Coakley had joined the team after the season started. This was his first training camp. Fifty years later, in an interview pocked with a few memory lapses, Coakley recalled the calm, businesslike atmosphere:

"Nobody on our club gave me the business. I was treated the way any ballplayer would want to be treated . . . and the funny part was that the two toughest men on the club, by reputation, Waddell and Schreck, were probably our best friends." In fact, Coakley said, Rube wanted to be his roommate, "but I balked when I found the Rube sitting at the foot of the bed one night with two revolvers pointing at his reflection in the mirror and talking about his control."

Commenting on the game's earlier reputation for being populated by drunken rowdies, Coakley estimated that no more than a half dozen of the twenty-five players in camp were tipplers.

Charles Comiskey also spoke of the changes in the game that spring.

There was a time back in the '80s when any ballplayer who was anything of a star was made a hero of. The female following simply went wild over their pets. They spoiled the players and behaved in all kinds of foolish ways. The ballplayer was head and shoulders more popular than the matinee idol. Now the cities in the major leagues have grown bigger and the crowds do not go crazy over ballplayers. Now fully ninety percent of the ballplayers save their money. It has become a legitimate business and the men are of a higher class. Many are college men and almost all are gentlemen. . . . Managers of the big leagues find that in recent years they get few calls for advance money. A player will be ordered to report by a certain date and he will get on a train and ride to the point of reporting. He never bothers about asking for car fare. He has saved it from the year previous.

Of course there were exceptions, and Rube Waddell was one of them. But Rube was an exception to just about all the rules of grownup behavior. Rube behaved himself most of the time in Shreveport. He seemed to be on friendly terms with all of the town's thirty thousand inhabitants. There were no parades to distract him, though he did work a stint as the trumpet player on a local tramway. And he did fall off the wagon at least once, according to Andy Coakley:

"Waddell went out on the town one night and wound up in the hoosegow. Some of the older players got in touch with the sheriff. Next morning he told Rube he'd been sentenced to the chain gang and proceeded to put the irons on him. Rube roared like a gored bull. The sheriff let him go on for a while before breaking the news it was a put-up job."

Each player came to camp with one uniform and wore it for every work-out and practice game. "You can imagine what they looked like after we'd played a few exhibitions on the way north in the red-clay whistle stops," Coakley said, " but who cared? We were ballplayers, not clothes horses."

One thing about the uniform irritated Coakley: the standup collar that chafed his neck. "In desperation one day I turned the collar inside my shirt and Lave Cross said to me, 'Andy, you know, one of these days they'll make 'em like that.'"

Anticipating capacity crowds once the season began, city building inspectors had ordered new joists installed under the bleachers at Columbia Park. The playing field was raised six inches and resodded, the grandstand painted, folding chairs renovated. Nearly fifteen thousand baseball-starved addicts showed up for the April 1 opener of the city series. Chief Bender, despite his lack of conditioning, seemed in midseason form, blanking the Phillies, 4–0.

Connie Mack opened the season with his usual optimism. Asked about the likely effects of an increased use of the spitball, following Jack Chesbro's success with it in 1904, he allowed as how it was not really a new pitch and expected that "every team will have its Chesbro." His lack of concern proved justified. Many pitchers tried it, but few could control it. Those who couldn't quickly abandoned it. Besides, managers had taken to smearing balls with various peppery or sticky substances before giving them to the umpire when a spitballer was pitching for the visitors.

The home opener against Boston on Friday, April 14, had the capacity crowd of fifteen thousand gnawing their fingernails at the end. Bender out-pitched Cy Young and took a 3–0 two-hitter into the ninth. Boston scored twice and had the bases loaded with 2 outs before Bender struck out pinch hitter Bob Unglaub. Early in the game Monte Cross suffered a broken hand when he was hit by a pitch while trying to bunt. This thrust young Jack Knight into action long before Mack wanted to use him. Knight hit better than expected for a while—he was actually leading the league at .407 on May 1.

In the second game Boston jumped on Andy Coakley for an early 5–1 lead. Mack sent Waddell in to relieve him in the fourth; the A's came back and won it in the ninth. This began a new pattern for Mack. He displayed less patience with a pitcher's wobbly start and used a quicker hook than most managers of the time. Except for a weak New York staff, the A's would have the fewest complete games in the league that year. Mack didn't hesitate to call on Bender and Waddell for double duty, using each out of the bullpen twelve times in 1905. And it worked. Bender was 7-1 in relief, Waddell 8-0. In six years with the A's, Waddell never lost a game in relief.

This was a departure from the way the game had been played. "Old school" pitchers like Cy Young didn't like the new strategy. They favored keeping the starter on the slab and giving him a chance to "pull himself together."

Mack also disdained using his pitchers in a fixed rotation, preferring to match them against certain teams. "I do not use them in turn," he said, "but when I think they're best."

On April 21 the A's helped attract a record 18,344 to Boston's home opener. Shut out on 1 hit until the eighth, they scored 5 runs for a 5–4 win. Waddell, relieving Coakley, fanned 5 in the last 2 innings. The A's early success against their 1904 nemesis boosted Mack's morale. He probably celebrated by going to see his friend George M. Cohan starring in *Little Johnny Jones* at the Hollis Street Theater that night. Three nights later both teams occupied box seats as guests of the management for the musical *Floradora* at the Majestic. The lively theater scene and the chance to see family and old friends in the area made Boston Mack's favorite stop in the circuit. He invariably left passes for delegations from East Brookfield, relatives, and pseudo-relatives. He was especially attentive to groups of youngsters from his birthplace, sometimes inviting them to join him for lunch before the game or dinner afterwards.

Nobody pulled away from the pack in the first month, six teams taking turns in first place. From then to August 1 Cleveland and Chicago swapped the lead back and forth, the A's trailing by a few games in third.

Connie Mack's following among the priesthood sometimes seemed to pay him a greater reward than a tip on a player. One day in May they were scheduled to board the Western Express to start a road trip. Hours before their departure, Fr. McCarty, a priest at St. Peter's in Reading, asked Mack if the A's could stop off and play an exhibition game for the church building fund. Fr. McCarty's parents had been neighbors of the Macks in East Brookfield and owned the house the Macks rented. The priest's mother had been at Mary Mack's bedside when Connie was born. Mack couldn't turn him down. He notified the players of the change in plans. They grumbled about the extra game, but it saved them from a fiery train wreck when the Express hit another train near Harrisburg and exploded.

Rube Waddell stayed behind to have a small tumor removed from his chin. It didn't slow him down. He won 10 in a row, taking his first loss on June 9, 3–2, in 14 innings to Chicago. He was giving up fewer than 7 hits per 9 innings. When he lost it was usually walks and his own fielding mishaps that beat him. And when he blew up, it was Vesuvian. In a game in Washington on June 28, he turned a 2–0 lead into a 6–3 loss in a 6-run eighth, the last run forced in on 3 straight walks. A *Washington Post* writer commented that Rube was "a great quitter when things are breaking badly."

Coakley and Weldon Henley were inconsistent. A no-hitter on July 22 was the highlight of Henley's season; he won only 4 games all year. Bender now suffered off and on with a kidney ailment. That left Waddell and Plank to do most of the pitching. The A's were last in hitting and fielding in the early going. Mack platooned Bris Lord in place of Danny Hoffman against left-handers. Schreck and Harry Davis carried the team. Schreck caught almost every game, especially when Doc Powers split a finger. In mid-July the New York Highlanders were short-handed from injuries. They had no catcher. Nobody in the league objected when Mack loaned Doc Powers to Clark Griffith. It was not an uncommon courtesy. There may have been some "sale" paperwork to cover the transaction, but everybody knew it for what it was. With Powers, the Highlanders won 12 in a row.

The A's pitching began to improve in July. On Tuesday, July 4, in Boston, Plank started the morning game with almost nine thousand early birds on hand. He felt ill after the third inning. Mack rushed in Coakley, who took a 5–2 lead into the ninth. With 2 on and 1 out, Mack called on Waddell to close it out. The Rube, who was scheduled to start the afternoon game, retired the last two batters. The use of three pitchers in a game was rare enough for writers to credit "Connie Mack's brainwork" for the A's triumph.

That afternoon Waddell started against Cy Young. Boston scored 2 in the first. The A's tied it in the sixth when Lord singled and Davis hit one of his league-leading 8 home runs. None of the 12,666 spectators went home as the two pitchers matched zeroes from the seventh through the nineteenth inning. In the top of the twentieth the A's scored twice on 2 errors, a hit batter, and a single by Hoffman. Waddell held on for the 4–2 win. He had walked 4 and struck out 11. Young had not walked a man. Game time was three hours and thirty-one minutes.

Waddell guessed he'd thrown 250 fastballs, shoots, raises, and drops. (It's not unlikely; Hugh Fullerton claimed he once counted 211 pitches thrown by Waddell in a game.) Years later Young recalled:

[Rube] was at his best that day and had all our many left-hand batters swinging like so many old women. On the other hand, the Athletics were always threatening to put me off watch. . . . How did I feel when the scrap was over? Well, I thought it was all right until I hit the club-house. Then I all but keeled over.

When I sat down and tried to get up it was as if there was a pain in every bone in my body. Then, when I tried to take off my shoes I hardly had strength to untie the laces. And what do you think the Rube was doing?

There he was on the other side of the clubhouse turning flip-flops and smoking a cigarette.

The hit batter in the twentieth inning was Jack Knight, whose hand was broken by the pitch. Monte Cross, downed on opening day by an identical injury, was now ready to go back into action. Mack was happy he had been unable to trade away the veteran.

Men were men and arms were arms in those days. Schreck caught all 29 innings that day, still the major league record. Three days later both pitchers were on the slab again in Philadelphia. This time the game went only 10 innings, the A's winning, 2–1, on a Hoffman single. Mack's careful cultivation of Hoffman's confidence following his beaning was bearing fruit. Rube would have gone all the way, but he hurt his hand trying to stop a ground ball in the seventh. The hand swelled up; after giving up a leadoff single in the eighth, he had to come out. Bender finished it.

This run of exciting action and the closeness of the pennant race—1½ games separating three teams—must have inspired every baseball fan in the city to be at Columbia Park for the following Saturday's doubleheader against Boston. Hours before the two o'clock game time, more than twenty-five thousand tickets had been sold. Thousands of frustrated fans banged on the locked gates, while more adventurous hordes clambered over the outfield fences. The nervous head cashier scooped up all the receipts, stuffed them into bags, called for a police escort, and took them across the street to Sam Erwin's house for safekeeping.

Joe Schroeder's grounds crew circled the entire field with ropes, leaving thirty feet of open space behind the infield and three feet along both foul lines and behind home plate. Foul balls drilled into the crowd knocked off hats and bruised limbs. At least four dozen balls were pocketed, as little effort was made to retrieve them.

Eddie Plank started the first game. Bender relieved him in the fourth. Both were hit hard, but no stats for the day should be counted against the pitchers. The confined playing area resulted in a total of 63 hits in the two games. It was not responsible for one hit, Harry Davis's long home run that landed on Columbia Avenue.

The crowd behind the ropes kept jostling for a better view. Fights broke out amid the pushing and trodding on neighbors' feet. Like an incoming tide, the mob knocked down the ropes and gradually crept toward the infield, forcing the outfielders toward the bases. With 2 out in the bottom of the fourth, Schreck doubled. Bender walked. Hartsel hit a fly ball into the crowd that by now had reached the edge of the infield dirt. At that point umpire Silk O'Loughlin stopped the game, climbed to the rooftop press box, called for police reinforcements, and in his trademark orotund delivery ordered the crowd to move back so the game could continue. It took thirty minutes to push everybody back and put up the ropes again.

The game ended, an 11–8 Boston win, on an appropriately bizarre note. Bender, the last batter in the ninth, was ejected while at bat for throwing dirt on the umpire. Harry Barton completed his at bat.

Because of the delay in the action, no time out was taken between games. They managed to play eight innings before darkness ended the A's 11–4 victory. The week's events—the A's winning 5 of 7 from Boston before huge crowds in both cities—were followed by a letdown. They played raggedly on the next western trip but bounced back swiftly from each brief slump. Henley had his only effective stretch of pitching during the trip, but Waddell turned wild and erratic, throwing away games in Detroit and St. Louis.

Chicago, Cleveland, and Philadelphia were virtually tied for the lead when the A's launched a stretch of 9 straight games against the White Sox, 5 at the end of the western trip and 4 at home beginning July 29. Plank launched the series in Chicago with a 2-hit 1–0 masterpiece, his thirteenth win. After winning 4 with 1 tie in the first 8 games, the A's were in position to take the lead on Wednesday, August 2. A good weekday crowd of nine thousand groaned when the erratic version of the Rube showed up and staked the White Sox to a first-inning 3-run lead with 4 walks, a bunt single, and a hit batter, while he struck out the side. Then the real Rube emerged and shut them down the rest of the way on 3 hits, striking out a total of 14. The A's got 2 back in the first on a Danny Hoffman home run and 3 singles, took a 4–3 lead in the third on Socks Seybold's 2-run homer, and ended the day at the top of the standings.

Throughout his life Connie Mack kept in close touch with his old friends in East Brookfield. Shortly after the A's went into first place, Mack received a letter from four of his 1883 teammates:

"We're watching your ball score every day. We wish you the best success and sincerely hope you will succeed in your masterly efforts to win the championship."

It was signed William A. Fitzpatrick, George H. Ensworth, John D. Morgan, and Fred Mann.

It was also a lifelong characteristic of Connie Mack to answer his personal mail as promptly as his most urgent business correspondence. He immediately replied.

Friend Tick:

Your letter at hand. Am more than pleased to hear from my old friends. It seems good to be remembered by those with whom you have been associated in years gone by and to know that they are with you in spirit if nothing more.

I would like to win this year as the honor of playing for the world's championship comes but once in a lifetime. Our boys are confident of winning and we have at this stage the best chance.

With very best wishes,
I remain, your old pal,
Connie Mack

Connie Mack was not envisioning dynasties. Playing once for a world's championship seemed a sufficient goal in itself.

The Athletics opened a lead that stayed at 4 or 5 games through August. Rube Waddell stayed sober and racked up the strikeouts. On August 15 he fanned 9 in a 5-inning no-hitter. Three days later he relieved Henley in the ninth of a 3–3 game and worked 7 scoreless innings, striking out 12. He pitched two games in three days in Cleveland and ran up 43 consecutive scoreless innings before an error let in a run on September 5 in Boston, a game he lost, 3–2, in 13 innings, despite another 17 strikeouts.

Eddie Plank was another workhorse, winning 25 of his league-leading 41 starts and 36 complete games. Andy Coakley had settled down and was on his way to a 20-win season. But Chief Bender was still afflicted with recurring physical problems.

Jimmy Dygert joined the club on August 31. Bought from Utica in 1904 and farmed out to New Orleans, the five-foot-ten right-hander led the Southern League with a 20-4 record. He escaped the yellow fever epidemic that hit New Orleans and forced the team to play most of its late-season games on the road. Dygert was an adept fielder who could throw several pitches, including the spitter, for strikes.

Andy Coakley pitched a 13-inning, 3–2 win on Thursday, September 7, in Boston and was given the next day off to visit his family in Providence. Waddell started on Friday and quickly gave up 2 runs. A nervous Mack gave Rube an early hook, pinch hitting for him in the third. He sent in Dygert, who earned his first big league win, 5–3.

The A's left Boston with a 4½-game lead. Their train stopped in Providence, where Coakley waited on the platform, natty as usual in his straw hat, his rollbag of uniform and spikes under his arm. Labor Day had passed, the last day for wearing straw hats according to the rules of fashion. It was traditional for men attending a Labor Day doubleheader to skim their straw hats onto the field after the last out was made. Those who didn't risked having their skimmer grabbed and smashed. This ritual was religiously observed among ballplayers until well into the 1930s. Rube and the boys were in high spirits when they boarded the train at Back Bay station. They had trashed every straw hat they spied by the time they reached Providence. Rube saw his next target atop Coakley's cranium.

What happened next varies in some details according to who's telling the story. The action probably took place on the train, not the platform. Waddell may have gotten off the train to greet Coakley on the platform while some of his teammates watched from the open door, which tipped Coakley that something was up. He put his hat under his jacket and dashed for the door with Rube in hot pursuit. Rube lunged for the hat. Coakley swerved and the spikes protruding from his uniform roll caught Rube on the chin. Coakley dropped the roll. Rube rushed at him again and tripped over it. He fell, hitting his left shoulder against a seat corner. At that point, Connie Mack, who was in another car, came in and stopped the horseplay. The players settled down. The card games began.

According to Coakley, somebody said, "Rube, Andy's your friend. Shake hands and kiss and make up."

Rube replied, "I'll shake hands but I'll be damned if I'll kiss him."

Neither Mack nor Coakley considered Rube's fall the cause of his subsequent arm trouble.

"It was a hot night," Mack said, "and the Rube discarded his tie and collar, rolled up his shirt sleeves and sat next to an open window. The next morning when we reached the North Philadelphia station, the Rube came up and told me he could not raise his left arm. It was as stiff as a pine board.

"This genuinely alarmed me, for the Rube always had boasted that he never had a sore arm in his life and always was quick to twit any pitcher who complained on that score.

"I firmly believe that the Rube contracted his ailment more from exposing his arm to an open window than from the fall against the car seat."

For the next few weeks Philadelphia papers were filled with speculation: was Rube Waddell shamming or really hurting? Some reports claimed that neither the trainer nor the doctors could find anything wrong with his shoulder. Rube readily agreed to try every kind of treatment suggested by the experts, which wasn't much at the time.

As if the pennant was already in the bag, rumors began that New York gamblers had gotten to the Rube to lay off the World Series. New York writer Joe Vila either started or gave credence to the story in his *Morning Sun* column, an early example of baseless rumor mongering. Not only were the tales premature, but there was still a month to go in the pennant race. It didn't make sense for gamblers to promise Waddell a big payoff if he didn't pitch in the World Series and then have him jeopardize his team's chances of even getting into the Series by not pitching for the final month. There was no evidence to support the rumors, and they were completely contrary to the nature of the man. Rube Waddell loved center stage, playing to the audience; the bigger the crowd, the more he reveled in it. He would not have missed a chance to strut upon the World Series stage, facing the great Christy Mathewson, for all the money gambled on the Series. Matty would have inspired Waddell's mightiest efforts, just as the venerable Cy Young always did.

"Waddell is childishly tricky, but not crooked," wrote F. C. Richter in *Sporting Life*.

Connie Mack adamantly rejected the idea. "Knowing the Rube as I do,

I'm positive that he would have shed his life's blood to be in the Series and duel with Mathewson. The Rube had his faults, but he was never a coward, and all the gold in Christendom could never buy him. These ungrounded and undeserved rumors of scandal mongers were a rank injustice to the great lefthander."

Certainly nobody knew Rube Waddell better than Connie Mack and his teammates. None of them believed it. Besides, Mack was too concerned with winning the pennant to worry about who might pitch in a World Series.

During the next few weeks the White Sox chipped away at the A's lead, and it looked as if the phantom New York bribers would have done better trying to buy off Chicago's aces, Frank Owen and Nick Altrock. Beginning September 21, the White Sox won 9 of 11 in Boston and New York and came into Philadelphia for a three-game series just .003 percentage points behind the A's.

On Wednesday, September 27, the day before the Chicago series began, Henley started against Detroit and was quickly routed. Mack sent Waddell in to pitch. He threw a half dozen pitches and had nothing. It was obvious this was not the normal Rube Waddell. Mack replaced him with Bender, who was not much better.

Still the papers refused to let up on the Rube. Mack continued to defend him. "Some people have been roasting Waddell, but I can't do so when I feel certain he is not faking the extent of his lameness. I'm convinced the trouble is rheumatism in his shoulder."

The city was wired with "crucial series" electricity when the White Sox arrived. The three games would draw 64,620. Every newspaper in town gave them front page coverage, prompting the *Record* to remind the club that it wouldn't be drawing sellout crowds were it not for the prominent free publicity from the papers. Both Mack and Billy Shettsline readily acknowledged the importance of the press's support to the success of their businesses. (They were too polite to point out that baseball news sold papers.) Maintaining good relations with the writers was a high priority for them. Connie Mack had a keen innate sense of public relations and was a master of its arts. Probably no other city had as close a relationship between its teams and the press. The Philly writers had hosted the first baseball dinner in February, and Mack would return the favor many times. Nor did the presence of the *Inquirer* and AP sports editors among the A's ownership cool or sour the coverage of rival papers and services.

The ticket windows and gates were closed at Columbia Park hours before the first pitch on Thursday, September 28. The crowd behind the outfield ropes was more orderly than usual. Eddie Plank was at his best, tossing a 3-hitter, two of the hits ordinary fly balls that went beyond the ropes. But he was locked in a 2–2 tie until the seventh. With Topsy Hartsel on second, Harry Davis hit a line drive to left. The ball hit Hartsel's glove, left on the outfield grass as was the custom, which slowed it enough for Hartsel to beat Nixey Callahan's strong throw to the plate. The A's won, 3–2.

On Friday Bender cruised to an 11–1 win before another overflow crowd.

Mack longed to have a healthy Rube Waddell to put away the White Sox, and Rube was itching to pitch. On Saturday morning he rushed up to Mack and excitedly declared that he had been swinging his arms about to loosen up when he suddenly felt something snap in his shoulder. Mack was skeptical.

"Put on a mitt and catch me," Rube begged.

Mack borrowed a mitt and crouched down. Rube appeared to be throwing smoothly and without pain, but his fastballs were coming in with something less than the usual mustard on them. Unconvinced, Mack called on Plank again. Before an announced crowd of 25,446, Eddie was wild. He walked 4, hit 2 batters, gave up 11 hits. The A's lost, 4–3. They led by 1 game with a week to go.

Both teams faced seventh- and eighth-place Washington and St. Louis in the final week. The A's won 3 in a row from the Browns, while Chicago was taking 2 out of 3 in Washington. The lead was up to 2 games.

While the White Sox rode the train to St. Louis on Thursday, the A's played a doubleheader in Washington. It was the Chief Bender show. He shut out the Nationals, 8–0, in the first game. Andy Coakley started the second and gave up 3 runs in the first 2 innings. Mack had seen enough. He sent Bender up to pinch hit for Coakley in the third. Bender hit a triple, then pitched the rest of the game. It was getting dark while the A's, trailing 7–6, batted in the eighth with 2 out and the bases empty. One more out and the game would be called because of darkness. They rallied for 3 runs. Bender then disposed of the Nats in the last of the eighth, and the A's lead was up to 3 games. For the day, Bender pitched 15 innings, striking out 14. He also made 5 hits, including 2 triples and a double, and drove in 7 runs.

The crowded lobby of the Riggs House Hotel swarmed with Philadelphians who had taken the short train ride to Washington to celebrate the pennant clinching. One more A's win or Chicago loss would do it. Several players' wives were there, along with Schreck's mother, an avid rooter. Joe Schroeder puffed on a big cigar and passed out lapel pins of white elephants attached to blue and white ribbons. Sam Erwin carried a large banner reading "Champions of 1905" and smaller flags with "Athletics" in white letters on blue material.

Chief Bender escaped the tumult long enough to take the steam lift to the top of the Washington Monument for a look around. When he returned, he was mobbed by admirers. Somebody handed him a twenty-five-cent cigar. Another fan presented him with two pointer pups.

Mack started Andy Coakley the next day, hoping to make all the celebrating official, but the collegian was worn out. He had never started more than 8 games in his three previous seasons. This was his thirty-first. He had won 20 and lost 7, good enough to lead the league, but he was out of gas. The home team teed off on him for 5 hits and 4 runs in the first 2 innings. At that point Mack decided to take another look at Rube Waddell. Rube's fastball had some snap to it, but he was obviously rusty. In the next 3 innings he walked 5 and threw 2 wild pitches, but kept the Nats from scoring while the A's tied it, 4–4.

In the fifth a huge cheer went up from the folks seated behind the visitors' bench when the scoreboard showed that St. Louis had scored 5 runs against Chicago. The Washington pitcher, Cy Falkenberg, was holding the Athletics in check while the Rube ran into trouble. Walks, a wild pitch, and errors sent 2 Nats over the plate in the sixth and 1 in the seventh. In the eighth Waddell was rocked for 4 hits and threw another wild heave. The Nationals led, 10–4.

Convinced that their own game was lost but the Browns' 6–1 lead over Chicago would prevail (the Browns won, 6–2), the A's rooters contained their exuberance no longer. To the bewilderment of the Ladies' Day crowd, while the Rube was being roughed up in the eighth, the visiting fans broke out the banners and flags and began whooping it up. Schreck's mother draped the championship banner over the railing. They didn't care if they had backed into it.

The team's arrival in Philadelphia at ten thirty that night was greeted by an immense crowd, so thick it was almost impossible to get through it to the street. Most of the players went through the baggage room to escape the throng. Bender and Waddell, aided by a police escort, pushed through the mob to the streetcars.

Connie Mack took one more look at Waddell the next day. One inning was enough; the Rube had nothing on the ball. He was through for the year.

When some of the A's played a warmup exhibition game in Brooklyn on the Sunday before the World Series, Waddell played right field and, according to the *Times*, "was very careful about handling and throwing balls."

In winning the 1905 pennant, Connie Mack may have done his best managing job, measured by getting the most out of what he had to work with. This was recognized by one Boston writer who commented, "Connie Mack does not hesitate to change pitchers and use pinch hitters. . . . He has a fair team but gets the most out of them."

Tim Murnane saluted Mack in the *Boston Globe*. "Connie Mack is regarded as the ablest and most diplomatic manager in baseball. He never has an unkind word for his players and should any of them have an off day he knows just what to say that will make them feel better over it. No other manager could handle Rube Waddell, and Connie has tamed the Rube down to such a point that he had but little trouble with him any more. In the science of the game Mack has no equal. Watch the teamwork of the Athletics and one can see the master hand of Connie Mack."

The A's had beaten the teams they had to: 12-9 against Chicago, 15-7 over Boston (reversing their 9-14 record of 1904), 15-7 against Cleveland.

Their offensive numbers seem modest today. They had no .300 hitters, but they led the league in runs scored, doubles, and slugging average. The infield was old but smart. At thirty-two, a healthy Harry Davis played in 143 games, led the league in doubles, home runs, scoring, and RBI. He would have won the MVP Award had there been one. The thirty-nine-year-old Lave Cross played almost every game at third base, and Mack called his ability to execute the hit and run as responsible for the pennant as any other individual efforts. Monte Cross, thirty-six, made up for a lack of range with experience, positioning himself according to the hitter and pitcher. Danny Murphy was an average second baseman of the time, still learning the game and the position, made better by those around him. Jack Knight had borne out Mack's appraisal of his fielding ability and hitting inability.

Osee Schrecongost caught a league-leading 112 games, for which Mack rewarded him with a $600 bonus, paid, at Schreck's request, in $50 installments to make it last through the winter.

Including Joe Myers, a young pitcher Mack tried out in the last game of the season, he had used only 19 players, the fewest he would ever use.

Mack had kept Rube Waddell in line most of the time. There were no week-long defections to tend bar or go fishing. His toots were one-nighters. He was a robust twenty-eight and recovered quickly. His stinginess in allowing baserunners was at its peak. Occasionally his interest waned but never his willingness to work. He led the league with 26 wins, 46 games, and 287 strikeouts. He and Plank carried the pitching load when Bender was ailing. The Chief was strong at the finish, when Coakley tired, Henley failed, and the Rube's rheumatism sidelined him in September.

In the National League, the New York Giants coasted to a 9-game margin over the Pirates. They outhit, outran, and outscored every team in either league and had all the pitching they needed. They stole 291 bases and led the league with 39 home runs. Mathewson won 31 and lost 8, his third 30-win season. Joe McGinnity slipped to 21-15 after two 30-win years. Red Ames provided a surprising 22 wins against 8 losses.

Of all his teams, John McGraw later called this one his favorite, his best and smartest. "We did not have a really slow-thinking player on the team."

Nothing destroys the notion that only one set of qualities defines a successful manager as persuasively as a look at the two most successful skippers of the Deadball Era. Sons of Irish immigrants, growing up in poor families in small towns, Connie Mack and John McGraw each would win six pennants between 1902 and World War I. Yet no two men could be more unalike as leaders.

They had played against each other in the 1890s, Mack at Pittsburgh and McGraw with Baltimore. Both had used whatever tricks they could get away with. McGraw tripped, held, and bumped baserunners at third base. Mack tipped bats, faked foul tips, and chattered to distract batters behind the plate.

Each wound up where he belonged. McGraw was made for a city that offered the company of actors, gamblers, pool sharks, and Wall Street manipulators in large numbers. He invested in pool rooms and race tracks and paid off cops for protection. He drank and brawled and saw the inside of more than one precinct headquarters and courtroom.

The only fisticuffs associated with Connie Mack were the boxing matches he enjoyed. He seemed to epitomize both the gentility that the Quaker City aspired to and its blue-collar toughness.

The moniker "Muggsy" befitted McGraw, although he hated the name. Nothing more intimate than Mr. Mack seemed appropriate for the tall, soft-spoken gentleman in the high starched collar, and that is how he was most often addressed by the public and many of his players.

McGraw's language could turn the air around him blue and sulphurous.

Mack's expressions of anger and irritation were not limited to "goodness gracious," but he had come to rely more on the needle to make his point.

The two men had some similarities. Both were excellent, but admittedly not perfect, judges of players. Neither would criticize a player for making a fielding error. But they handled mental errors differently. McGraw's style was like being whacked with a birch rod before the entire class in a Dickensian orphanage. Mack's approach was more like being summoned to the headmaster's office in an upper-class prep school.

"Mental lapses, missed signs, and disobeyed orders drove him crazy," Travis Jackson, captain of McGraw's later pennant winners, said. When those things cost them a game, the Giants sat glumly on their three-legged stools until McGraw finished his tirade. He didn't hesitate to tear into a player in the dugout with the entire team looking on.

Connie Mack preferred to sleep his anger away and seldom went into the clubhouse after a game. The next day he would impart his lessons privately to a player whose mistakes had cost them the game.

Both managers valued brains over brawn, although McGraw called most of the pitches and preferred to do the thinking himself. Christy Mathewson wrote that the 1904 pennant had been won by McGraw's ordering every play from the bench. Mack encouraged his men to be more innovative on their own. Branch Rickey summed him up: "I understood why [Mack] was so different from McGraw yet equally masterful in handling men. He was a pedagogue, a kindly instructor. It was his desire that his players should learn from him and then think for themselves on the field of play."

Both were considered by their players to be the best in the business, and each routinely nominated the other as tops in their industry.

McGraw appeared in three games for the Giants that season; thus every National League team had a playing manager to some extent, the only time that would be true in the twentieth century. There were never eight in the American League.

This first "official" World Series was widely followed. Thirty-eight special wires were installed for national newspaper coverage. Streets in New York and Philadelphia were filled with fans outside newspaper buildings, where megaphone men announced every pitch and play from a platform in front of a scoreboard or an elaborate mechanical or electrical recreation of the action. All across the country fans watched bulletin boards and thousands of tickers chattering out the play-by-play. Stricter standards for roping off the outfield limited attendance to under eighteen thousand in Philadelphia. The Phillies offered the use of their larger facilities to the A's, who turned them down. Betting was heavy but not one-sided; the odds stayed around even money.

The *Inquirer* offered to put $1,000 in gold into the players' pool if the Athletics won the world championship. The *North American* installed a victory gong at Fifteenth and Market Streets. It was to sound once for a double, twice for a triple, three times for a home run. It rarely rang. The Athletics were a potent late-inning threat, so Mack and Shibe asked Ban Johnson to start the games at three instead of three thirty to avoid having games shortened by the early autumn darkness. The National Commission agreed.

Before the Series began, most of the players from both teams agreed among themselves to split the players' pool shares, regardless of who won. (This practice went on for several years until the National Commission banned it.) Mathewson and his catcher, Roger Bresnahan, were two who didn't go along with it. Three of the A's also rejected the deal. After the Series some of the Giants refused to pay up. But the disgruntled A's were in no position to squawk. They had nobody to appeal to.

The Giants' arrival in Philadelphia on the morning of Monday, October 9, equaled the entrance of Roman legions into a conquered city. Led by a brass band and surrounded by three hundred loyal rooters, they left Broad Street station in open barouches adorned with small blue and white pennants announcing "New York Champions 1905." The band led them right into the lobby of the Continental Hotel, where a crowd of curious local fans, including many women and children, surged around the players.

When the Giants walked onto the Columbia Park diamond that afternoon, they looked and acted like world beaters, dressed in new, all-black uniforms with white lettering and stockings, a startling contrast to the Athletics' season-worn, worse-for-wear garb. The Giants believed they were unbeatable, and it was Christy Mathewson, twice a jumper to the American League, twice a reneger on AL contracts, who made them feel that way.

Captain Lave Cross met McGraw and the umpires at home plate to confer on the ground rules before the first pitch. Before they parted, Cross handed McGraw a small metal white elephant. McGraw took it in good humor.

Mack's guests on the home team's bench during the game included New York manager Clark Griffith, Washington manager Jake Stahl, and Phillies second baseman Kid Gleason, a longtime friend whose NL career went back to Mack's first full year in Washington.

Connie Mack would have savored a Waddell-Mathewson duel, but he admitted that it probably wouldn't have changed the outcome. The Athletics didn't look like they could score off Mathewson if they had played till Christmas. In three games in six days Matty threw 27 shutout innings, struck out 18, gave up 14 hits and 1 base on balls. After the first game, Mack said hopefully, "I don't think Matty can pitch another such game in such a short time." But McGraw had sized up every Athletics batter perfectly. His analysis and Mathewson's ability to carry it out made him even more dominant in his next two starts.

Plank and Bender were almost as good. Bender gave up a total of 6 hits in two starts, a 3–0 win over McGinnity and a 2–0 loss to Mathewson. Plank's losses were by 3–0 and 1–0.

In the only game that wasn't close, Coakley's 9–0 loss in Game 3, the A's looked as ragged and weary as they felt, making 5 errors.

A rainout of the Wednesday game in Philadelphia gave the players time to become upset over newspaper reports of 36,000 attendance at the Tuesday game in New York. The Giants' official count was 24,992. The players appointed reps from each team to lodge a complaint, but the sun came out the next day and dried up the grumbling.

The five-game Series ended on Saturday, October 14, in New York. On the following Monday the Athletics gathered at Columbia Park, where Connie Mack announced that the club's share of the gate—$8,131.49—would be divided among the players as a bonus. For those who had agreed to the pooling with the Giants, their $451.75 bonus from the Athletics plus their $765 from the shared players' pot netted them more than the winners' shares of $1,142 kept by Mathewson and Bresnahan. The Athletics also divided $1,000 from the sale of 10,000 souvenir books of player profiles, written by Charles Dryden and published by the *North American*.

The city was not finished celebrating. As Connie Mack had written to his friends, the honor was in playing for the world championship, win or lose. A half dozen newspapers sponsored a huge parade on Monday, October 23. They invited the Giants to be part of it, and McGraw accepted. The New Yorkers arrived on the train, enjoyed a festive dinner, and mounted floats and automobiles for the ride down Broad Street. The parade stepped off at eight o'clock; the last of the bands reached the end of the line after midnight. The way was lit by flaming torches. Bicycles, floats, and automobiles carried players, prize fighters, football and basketball teams. An elephant covered with a white sheet drew the biggest applause. The strollers included 150 Columbia Park employees, led by Joe Schroeder, mascot Jack Taylor, and a seven-year-old batboy named Jan Garber, who went on to become a headline orchestra leader for forty years.

Two nights later the Athletics hosted a banquet for two hundred players, writers, and guests at the Bingham House—a typical nine-course feast of the time, from oysters to dessert and cigars. Everybody was called upon to speak. Rube Waddell was reportedly moved to tears as he expressed his sorrow at not being able to pitch in the World Series.

The toasts were lengthy, but Connie Mack, allotted fifteen minutes, took less than two, concluding with, "Gentlemen, I am proud of all those flattering remarks, but at that I had not much to do with it at all. We worked hard, all of us, and were well-supported by the press and the public. They spurred us on. As for the winning of the pennant, it was the players that won that, not me."

John Shibe presented gold watch fobs to the players, who then gave Mr. Mack a $900 Cunningham self-playing piano. Spokesman Harry Davis said, "Mr. Mack has treated us like members of his own family. At home or abroad he always looked after our comfort."

To which Mack replied, "You can now see why we win pennants."

The players picked up some additional money barnstorming around the area for a week, drawing as many as two thousand to some games.

Doc Powers used his World Series share to buy a $4,500 house and resumed his duties at St. Agnes Hospital.

Osee Schrecongost, looking very big league in flashing diamonds and a fur-lined overcoat, visited friends with his wife and baby in Youngstown, where he had played nine years earlier.

Rube Waddell did some vaudeville turns demonstrating the art of pitching, accompanied by a Great Dane borrowed from former heavyweight champion Bob Fitzsimmons. He played handball and kept his doctor appointments and stayed out of trouble.

On the eve of the November 22 league meeting in Chicago, an interview with Charles Comiskey appeared in the Chicago papers. Comiskey was still fuming over Johnson's earlier suspension of White Sox outfielder Ducky Holmes for "bullyragging" umpires, leaving his team short-handed. Comiskey blasted Ban Johnson's leadership and accused him of plotting to merge the league with the National. Johnson angrily denied the accusation. Comiskey said he was misquoted, and he wouldn't have said anything if rumors of such a merger had been promptly denied by Johnson. No other magnates backed him, and when the club owners passed a resolution reaffirming their support of Johnson and their intention to remain independent of the National, Comiskey heartily made it unanimous. Still, it marked the beginning of a decline in the friendship between the two men.

Six clubs and Johnson favored a 140-game schedule for 1906 if the National went along with it. The National didn't, so the course remained 154 games.

Johnson polled the owners for opinions on changes in the rules. Five advocated doing something to increase batting. Although scoring had increased, team batting and slugging averages had fallen for the fourth straight year. There was sentiment for moving the pitcher a foot or two farther back, a suggestion that always came up whenever a lack of offense was bemoaned. Others suggested three balls for a walk or shrinking home plate or the strike zone. Connie Mack expressed his satisfaction with the rules as they were, but after the meeting he boosted Henry Chadwick's "jackastic" idea of a designated hitter. The public, he said, would rather watch a superior batsman than a pitcher whose time at bat is a farce. Mack didn't see it as a way to prolong the careers of veterans whose legs were gone. He saw it as an opportunity to give young players a chance to gain hitting experience rather than just sitting on the bench. It would give managers more chances to look over prospects, and nobody looked over prospects more than Connie Mack. He had an additional reason in mind. On hot days, he preferred to see his pitchers stay off the bases to conserve their energy for pitching. Sometimes he ordered them not to swing at any pitches.

Dissenters claimed that Mack's idea would prevent pitchers from developing their hitting if they ever wanted to switch to another position. Besides, these early purists maintained, baseball was supposed to be played by a nine-man team, not ten. Teach the pitchers how to hit, they said. When the rules committee met in February, Connie Mack didn't raise the issue. The idea resurfaced from time to time but was always turned down as too drastic a change in the game. The prevailing sentiment was, "Leave well enough alone."

The Athletics had drawn bigger crowds than any team in the city's history. Business was good; the future looked bright. Columbia Park would have to be expanded again to accommodate the customers. The Phillies, under Mack's former ally, Hugh Duffy, were also improving, having climbed to fourth. They would offer more competition at the gate next year.

And the A's were another year older.

32 | REBUILDING BEGINS

Age was not the only problem with Connie Mack's infield. There was discord. Lave Cross was Mack's captain, but Harry Davis was the manager's primary counsel. That irked Cross and may have been behind the fuss he had made over accepting the $500 captain's bonus in 1902. When Davis had been injured and gone scouting for Mack in 1904, Cross asked him one day if he'd found anybody. "Yes," Davis replied, ribbing Cross. "I found a man [Jack Knight] to take your place at third." Cross took it in fun at the time, but it had him looking over his shoulder at his likely replacement while Knight subbed for Monte Cross at shortstop in 1905. Danny Murphy's clumsy efforts at second base irked the captain too, and he was not diplomatic in letting Murphy know it.

Connie Mack respected and appreciated Lave Cross's contributions to the Athletics' success. Lave had been with him from the start, had played hurt, missing only four games (all in 1905) in the last four years. But he would be forty in May. Washington Nationals manager Jake Stahl knew that Cross was unhappy. He approached Mack, who told him he would not take any money for Cross nor trade him to any team unless Cross was satisfied with the terms. Cross agreed to play for Washington. Mack was still interested in the Nationals' young shortstop, Joe Cassidy, but Jake Stahl wouldn't give him up. (Two months later Cassidy died at twenty-three from malaria.) So Mack let Lave Cross go to Washington and received nothing in exchange. There was no bitterness in the parting; when friends of Lave's held a planked shad testimonial dinner for him on April 10, all the Athletics were there. Cross had lost his championship gold watch fob, and the players presented him a new one.

Unlike today, when few teams even bother with a captain, the position was an important one at the time. Soon after Mack named Harry Davis to replace Lave Cross, Davis described the duties in the *North American*:

Placing players in the field correctly according to the batter and the pitcher. The captain calls the player who is to take a fly ball. Must watch his pitcher closely to see when the time is ripe for a change, or when the twirler needs a moment or two to collect himself. He should create opportunities for the men to pull themselves together when they have become confused. He must be able to anticipate the wishes of the manager in order that valuable time not be lost and valuable points given to his opponents by his running to the bench to receive information. The captain must also watch the play of his opponents in the field in order to impart to his players any weakness he may discover or to the umpire any infringement of the rules by opposing players. The captain should be on the coaching lines as much as possible to give his players the benefit of his knowledge and observation.

When he wasn't batting, the captain often coached at first base. With the A's, the third base coach was chosen more for his ability to read pitchers and pick up catchers' signs than for directing base-running traffic.

Some managers acted as their own captains, but Connie Mack relied on his captain in all the ways that Davis described. Mack ordered the pitching changes, but Davis presided over them.

Monte Cross was thirty-six. He had also given Mack steady service, playing in all but two games in 1902–1904. Mack planned to move Jack Knight to third base. He had another prospective shortstop in twenty-one-year-old Rube Oldring.

The circumstances surrounding the major league debut of Oldring are another example of the chaotic conditions of the business. Oldring was an outfielder and shortstop at Montgomery in the Southern Association in 1905. The manager, an old National Leaguer named Tom O'Brien, recommended him to Mack, who apparently bought him in August to report in the spring. But nothing about the deal was reported in the papers. Perhaps Mack didn't want to upset either of the Crosses with another reminder of their baseball mortality during the fight for the pennant. The Southern season ended on September 22. The next day Oldring reported to Mack in Philadelphia.

"He told me I was not eligible for the World Series so I might as well go home and play some semipro games and earn some money," Oldring said in a 1936 interview. He went home to New York City. On September 30 in a game at New York, Highlanders' shortstop Kid Elberfeld and outfielder Dave Fultz collided going after a fly ball. Both were out for the rest of the year. The next day was Sunday. The Highlanders played a game against a semipro team, the Manhattans, at Olympia Field in the Bronx. Oldring had often played there before turning pro and was well known to the Manhattans' manager, Jess McMahon. When Oldring showed up to watch the game, McMahon spotted him and offered him $25 to play third base that day. Oldring agreed. He had a few hits, stole a base, and hit a 3-run inside-the-park home run that capped the semipros' 7–5 win over the Highlanders' makeshift lineup, in which Clark Griffith played left field and Hal Chase shortstop.

After the game Griffith, unaware that Oldring was the property of the Athletics, asked Oldring how much he would take to sign a contract. "I said $40 a game," Oldring recalled. "We agreed on $200 for the rest of the season. I got a big kick out of Clark Griffith's not knowing what I did. I knew Connie Mack would get a good laugh at the idea that another major league club was helping develop one of his own recruits."

The draft period began that day for major league clubs. Clark Griffith, who knew of Oldring's record in Montgomery, apparently drafted him. Nothing more certain than "apparently" can be applied to these transactions as the records and contemporary reporting are sketchy. We don't know just when Mack filed the paperwork on his purchase of Oldring with the National Commission or when Griffith attempted to draft Oldring. It wasn't unusual for the names of minor league players purchased by major league teams during the season to show up on the postseason reserve lists of both teams. We do know that Mack must have reported the transaction at some point; when Griffith attempted to draft Oldring, the commission notified him that the Athletics had a prior claim to him.

It is a fact that Oldring started at shortstop for New York the next day and every day for the rest of the season. The *New York Times* said of his debut, "Manager Griffith presented another new aspirant for major league honors in Oldring, who played so well at third base for the Manhattans on Sunday. Oldring is an old Olympia Field player. During the recent Southern League season he was a member of the Montgomery team. His work in the first game yesterday was excellent. He proved himself an unusually capable infielder."

So there was no secret, no "assumed-name" subterfuge. Connie Mack was well aware that his new infielder was playing for the New Yorkers. He didn't object. That all of this was accepted and treated as nothing out of the ordinary comes through in the references to Oldring in the spring of 1906. The *Washington Post* casually mentioned that "Mack also has Oldring who was with the New York Americans last fall," without saying how Mack acquired him. The *Atlanta Constitution* quoted Mack, "Oldring is a good all around man as he proved in the games that he played with the New York Americans in the last few weeks of last season."

Mack's plans to remodel his infield were set back when Rube Oldring broke his ankle sliding in a practice game. He would be out until July.

Mack also bought Montgomery third baseman Art Brouthers, who, he said "is a fast fielder, covers plenty of ground and goes after everything. I am told also that he can hit a bit, being a big powerful fellow."

Perhaps the deals with the Montgomery club included a promise to bring the A's to the Alabama capital for spring training in 1906. That's where Connie Mack went in February to await the arrival of his troops.

Mack knew his chances to repeat in 1906 rode on Rube Waddell's arm and head. He kept a close watch on Waddell all winter, engaging an unidentified agent to report to him weekly on Rube's activities and condition. Waddell assured him that his arm was fine again. Before boarding the train in Philadelphia, Rube told the crowd gathered to see the team off, "I am in great shape and I want you to watch my work this season. I owe it to myself and to the good friends who stuck by me to get even for the roasting I got last fall when I met with an accident. You can bet I will pitch my arm off to make good for Connie Mack and the Athletics."

After a few days of limbering up, Mack took the veterans to New Orleans for a week of profitable practice games. The only poor weather they ran into was on Thursday, March 8, which Mack and the boys spent at the race track.

The Young Men's Athletic Club invited the team to use its clubhouse and baths. Mack accepted the offer, which the Young Men soon regretted. Back in Montgomery, Mack was shown a telegram sent to the *Inquirer* stating that the players' roughhousing had torn up the facilities and the A's would no longer be welcome. Mack was as concerned with his team's conduct off the field as on it. He heatedly denied the charges and was backed up by the *Inquirer*'s on-the-scene correspondent.

It was cold and wet for a week in Montgomery. The idleness was hardest on Rube Waddell. His arm may have been sound, but his head wasn't. His early promises to behave quickly dissolved. The departure of his keeper, Frank Newhouse, who left to become the Washington groundskeeper, was coincident, not contributory, to Rube's return to carousing. He became a local hero when he helped to put out a small fire and was soon enjoying the company of every sport in town. Returning from an outing one night in Birmingham, he was hit on the head and robbed of $40. The only thing Connie Mack said to him was, "If you'd stay away from alleys and back streets, you wouldn't have that bump on your head."

The wheels fell off Osee Schrecongost's wagon too. His gold watch fob and diamond stickpin advertised that Schreck had arrived. He'd worked hard last year, helped the A's win a pennant. He deserved to relax and enjoy it. Mack had less patience with Schreck than with the Rube. He had plenty of other catchers. They couldn't swing a bat like Schreck, but at least they were smart and sober.

Harry Davis volunteered to work on Schreck. He thought he had succeeded in straightening him out when he learned that Schreck had developed a thirst for milkshakes. One day Davis went into the drug store alone and ordered a shake. "You want the kind Mr. Schreck gets?" asked the soda jerk. Harry said yes and watched the boy pull out a bottle of sherry and half fill the glass with it.

Schreck never straightened out all year. He and Waddell had a falling out, and Rube moved out of the house where they had been boarding.

Snow and ice covered the fields in Philadelphia as the A's began their trek north through Nashville and Knoxville. Ben Shibe was supervising the $15,000 improvements to Columbia Park. The outfield was banked along the fence to give standees a better view. The third base bleachers were enlarged by two thousand seats and realigned. Instead of running straight to the fence, the yellow pine boards now curved across the foul line to face the infield.

Rube Waddell was "in old form," reported the papers after he threw a 3-hitter in a 7–2 preseason win over the Phillies. Rube was also in old form after dark, drinking more, sleeping less. Some nights on the road Schreck had the bed all to himself, when he wasn't out too. Rube ignored his wife, leaving her penniless. She went to Desertion Court, where the A's lawyer displayed Rube's $2,400 contract and promised to send half of each paycheck directly to Mrs. Waddell. From then on, she saw some money more regularly than she saw her husband.

After winning their first two games in Washington, the A's played their home opener before an overflow crowd in overcoat weather. Harry Davis hoisted the 1905 pennant and Chief Bender defeated the Nationals, 4–2.

When Danny Hoffman was beaned in 1904, he was among the top out-fielders in the league. Only Keeler and Flick were outhitting him at the time. In 1905 he had led the league with 46 stolen bases and come through with some key hits, but to Mack he never looked comfortable at the plate. Treated by an eye doctor all winter, Hoffman believed that his sight was as good as ever when the 1906 season started. But Mack could see that it wasn't. He benched Hoffman after seven games. Danny complained. He aired his gripes to the rest of the players, seeking their sympathy and support against the manager. Connie Mack wouldn't put up with that. To him, harmony and winning went together. He looked for a way to deal Hoffman.

In the aftermath of the devastating earthquake that hit San Francisco on April 18, 1906, Mack agreed to take his team to New York for an exhibi-tion game for the relief fund. The game was played on Sunday, April 29, and raised over $5,600. That afternoon Mack huddled with Clark Griffith and swapped Hoffman for the rights to negotiate with his former center fielder, Dave Fultz. After three years with New York, Fultz, only thirty, had become a Wall Street lawyer. Mack was unable to persuade Fultz to come back. He received nothing in return for Hoffman and brought up Harry Armbruster from Newark to replace him. Armbruster proved to be only a temporary patch.

Early in the season Connie Mack triggered the enforcement of a new league rule. Teams were now using an average of nine balls a game, a significant increase over a few years earlier, when two or three would suffice. At $18 a dozen, this was an expenditure of more than $1,000 a year, enough to pay a rookie's salary. One reason for the need to use more balls was the increas-ing resistance from fans, who were expected to throw back foul balls. In the eyes of the clubs and much of the public, keeping a foul ball was tan-tamount to stealing. Charles Dryden observed, "A fan in the grandstand catching a foul ball stands up and throws back the $1.50 ball. A ball hit into the bleachers is quickly concealed under a shirt or jacket and like money loaned to relatives stands a poor show of coming back. The man who wins a scramble for it conceals it and ignores pleas of outfielders through the wire netting for its return."

Foul balls that were returned found their way to the home team's bench. The manager was responsible for supplying the umpire with replacements when needed. Since his managing days in Pittsburgh, Connie Mack had been among the practitioners of selective ball use. When the visitors were at bat and a ball was needed, he would pick out the softest, most scuffed one in his cache of retrievals and put it into play. When his team was in the lead, he would try to keep a doctored or lopsided ball in play as long as possible.

On Friday, April 20, the A's built an 11–3 lead over New York. Mack kept feeding mushy balls to his pitcher, Andy Coakley, frustrating the New York batters. Clark Griffith protested to Ban Johnson, who ordered that henceforth the home team must furnish the umpire with a dozen new balls and a dozen used ones at the start of each game. The umpire would supply all the replacement balls needed. Foul balls returned to the bench could not be used again in that game.

The A's were hitting over .300 in the early going, but the pitching ranks suddenly thinned. Coakley, never in robust health, came down with the grippe and went home. Eddie Plank had a cold. Weldon Henley was roughed up for 9 runs in 3 innings in the April 29 exhibition game at New York and received a ticket to Rochester. Bender and Waddell were left to carry the load.

Bender had added a talcum pitch to his arsenal. He kept a bag of talcum powder in his pocket and rubbed one side of the ball against it. This gave the ball, he said, an unusual and unexpected drop, similar to a spitter, which he said he threw only once. On April 30 against Washington at home, he had a 6–0 lead in the ninth with 2 out. Three doubles and a single made it 6–3. Bender then walked 2 to load the bases. On a 3-2 count, he decided to throw a spitter. The batter, Mal Kittridge, took it; the umpire—to Bender's amazement—called it strike three. "And that," he said, "was the last time I ever threw a spitter."

On May 4 in New York, Bender, who had gained a reputation as a chronic kicker, was ejected by umpire Tim Hurst in the fifth inning. Waddell finished the inning, then Plank finished the game and took the 6–2 loss. It was noteworthy only as a rare instance of three future Hall of Fame pitchers working in one game for the same team.

An 11-game winning streak put the A's into the battle for the lead with Cleveland and New York. Waddell may have been going without sleep, but it didn't slow him down in the box. On May 12 he shut out Chicago on 5 hits, 4–0. Five days later leadoff man Ty Cobb, starting his first full season with the Tigers, beat out a bunt down the third base line. Neither Cobb nor any other Detroit batter had a hit after that. Four days later Rube left for a pinch hitter, down 1–0 in the ninth to Cleveland. The A's tied it. Bender came in and gave up 1 hit, but it was a game-winning home run in the thirteenth.

Bender started the next day. He was wild, but third baseman Art Brouthers was wilder. His 3 errors gave the game to the Naps. When leaky fielding cost the A's a 9–7 loss two days later, the Philadelphia hecklers got on Brouthers and rode him right out of the lineup. Mack put Jack Knight on third. Before the season was over, he tried four third basemen. None of them came close to filling Lave Cross's shoes. This may have been the root of the lesson Mack learned and later passed along to Branch Rickey one night in a Pullman compartment as they traveled north together from spring training: "Now, lookit," he told Rickey, "don't let go of your older player until you have something just as good or better to take his place."

The last game of the home stand on May 28 was rained out, but the A's lost more than gate receipts that day. Waddell took a notion to rent a carriage and team at a livery stable. He drove them at a gallop down Columbia Avenue and collided with a delivery wagon. His only injury was to his left thumb—a sprain, they thought. He started on June 5 in Chicago; in 3 innings he walked 7 and threw a wild pitch. They discovered his thumb was broken. He also had rheumatism in his right hip. Mack sent him to the Mt. Clemens spa to be boiled out and stay out of trouble.

The A's struggled for three weeks on the road. The hitting disappeared; the fielding was atrocious. The usually reliable Harry Davis dropped three throws to first base in one game. The pitching was a shambles. Andy Coakley returned weak and underweight. Within two weeks he would depart again, this time to recuperate in the mountains of Vermont. Before leaving Philadelphia, he secretly married Hattie Gray on July 16 and headed for the hills on his honeymoon. While there he would do Connie Mack a far greater service than if he had pitched and won a few games.

Chief Bender lost twenty-five pounds, "debilitated by bowel troubles," according to the *Sporting News*; suffering from chronic cholera, said another report. Only an 11-2 stretch by Eddie Plank and the failure of any other team to pull away kept the A's in the race. The first half of the season ended on July 14 with New York and Philadelphia tied for first place.

Back in 1903 Connie Mack's brother Tom had tipped him off to a freshman athlete at Colby College in Waterville, Maine. John Wesley Coombs was a six-foot, 185-pound football, baseball, basketball, and track star. He ran the 100-yard dash in 10.2, put the shot, threw the hammer, and pole vaulted. As a right-handed pitcher, he threw a fastball that college kids couldn't catch up with and a curve that outcurled most big league hooks. Mack sent scout Sam Kennedy to look him over and may have watched him pitch during a trip to Boston.

That winter Connie Mack tried to sign Coombs at Tom's Franklin Hotel in Worcester. But Coombs was set on finishing his studies. He was going to be a chemist. Each summer Coombs pitched in the New England resort town circuits. Tom kept an eye on him. A lot of other scouts did too. In December 1905 Tom persuaded Coombs to meet Connie Mack at the Franklin. Mack offered him a 1906 contract for $2,400 and agreed that Coombs could join the A's after graduation.

"It looked like a million dollars to me," Coombs said. Mack put the signed contract in his safe.

On Monday, July 2, while the A's were practicing before a game at home, Jack Coombs was riding street cars all around the city looking for Columbia Park. When he finally arrived, Connie Mack greeted the nervous rookie and told him to go into the clubhouse and get a uniform. He then asked Coombs to do some throwing in front of the bench. Years later Coombs recalled:

I was out there tossing a few to a rookie catcher and in a few minutes a big elephant with arms like a gorilla's came lumbering up. He had a big quid of tobacco in his jaw and when he spit it was like a shower bath if you were to the windward. Well, I thought I'd give the big scoundrel a show and I drew back and let my fast ball fly. The big gorilla waved one of the catchers over and he drew back and let a fast one fly. Well, sir, when I tried to see that ball go in there, I was amazed. Why, it threw out steam. But, I thought, maybe I can show him up with my curve. I threw it, and if I do say so myself, it had a right good hop on it. Then he let his go and, by the gollies, I've never seen anything like it in my life. It curved in, out and sideways.

With that exhibition of how they pitched them in the majors, I was all ready to pack up and go back to dad's farm at Kennebunk.

At that point Connie Mack told Eddie Waddell to quit showing off and sit down. Then he assured John—"You call him Jack," Mack told a reporter, "but he was always 'Jawn' to me"—that he had what it took to be a successful big league pitcher.

Harry Davis recalled his first impression of Coombs. "He resembled anything but a pitcher. He had the small-town mark hanging all over him. His long arms flapped at his sides; he wore a look of bewildered amazement for weeks. He never had traveled far from Maine. He was entering a new world."

Coombs made his debut on July 5 against Washington. He was nervous, walking 5 and giving up 4 hits in the first 3 innings. But a base runner caught stealing and 2 double plays bailed him out. Doc Powers and Harry Davis calmed him down. Davis told him, "These guys are bums. They couldn't hit the ball if you carried it to the plate."

After the A's scored 2 in the third, Coombs gave up no more walks and only 3 singles and won, 3–0.

Despite shoddy defense—Monte Cross made 9 errors in six games, Rube Oldring at third base was throwing souvenirs over Harry Davis's head into the stands—and only three healthy pitchers, the Athletics won 16 and lost 7 on their July home stand, including 5 out of 6 from Chicago. They headed west with a 1½-game lead over New York, 9 over the fourth-place White Sox. The indefatigable Eddie Plank was 19-5. Then, on the train to St. Louis, he caught a cold that settled in his left shoulder. Plank didn't start again for five weeks. Rube Waddell reinjured his thumb, either in a sandlot game with a bunch of kids or a wrestling match in a saloon, and missed a few more weeks.

The A's lost 8 in a row, while the White Sox were launching a home stand that led to 19 consecutive victories. On August 12 they moved past the A's into first place. The experts didn't expect the White Sox to stay on top for long. One *Sporting News* correspondent sniffed, "Chicago leading by a slight margin this evening looks out of place. A team with a lot of bum hitters, not one in the .300 class, certainly should not head the procession of so strong a league as the American." Only 10 games separated Chicago from sixth-place Detroit.

On Saturday, September 1, in Boston, "Colby Jack" Coombs and rookie Joe Harris started the first game of a doubleheader. The next day's headlines called it "the greatest game in the annals of baseball." After 6 innings the score was 1–1. After 23 innings it was still 1–1. Both teams told umpire Tim Hurst it was too dark to continue. Hurst ordered them to play one more. In the twenty-fourth Hartsel singled and stole second as Lord struck out. Schreck singled him in. Seybold and Murphy hit ground rule triples into the crowd on the field. With a 3-run lead, Monte Cross got himself out in a hurry before it became too dark to allow Boston to bat. Coombs then finished them off quickly in the bottom of the twenty-fourth. Coombs struck out 18 and walked 6, 5 intentionally. The game remains the longest played on one day in AL history. Since it lasted four hours and forty-seven minutes, the second game was postponed.

Coombs may have wrenched some ligaments in his arm that day. But he certainly didn't suffer any immediate effects. Four days later he asked Connie Mack, as was his habit, "Who's going to do the chucking today?" To which Mack replied, "I guess I'll let you do the chucking today, Jawn."

The Highlanders swept five doubleheaders in six days as part of a 15-game winning streak that carried them into first place. On Labor Day, September 3, the Athletics contributed to one of those sweeps. But umpire Silk O'Loughlin had an even worse day. In the first game New York shortstop Kid Elberfeld took exception to a call and tried to stomp on Silk's feet with his spikes, then attempted to beat him up before the cops escorted the hot Kid off the field. The A's led 3–0 in the ninth of the second game. New York tied it, scoring 2 runs when Willie Keeler ran into second baseman Jack Knight as Knight was poised to field a ground ball. O'Loughlin refused to call interference. Harry Davis hollered for eight minutes while the A's retired to their bench. When Davis was ejected, Connie Mack refused to put his team back on the field. O'Loughlin forfeited the game to New York.

"In all my baseball experience," Mack said, "I never saw an exhibition of incompetence and abject cowardice such as displayed by O'Loughlin on this occasion."

The A's rapidly tumbled to fourth place, and Mack conceded that his team was out of the running. His hopes were down, but his spirits were up. He began to look ahead a month earlier than usual. For the Athletics, 1907 spring tryouts were about to begin.

While Andy Coakley was in Rutland, Vermont, for his health and honeymoon, he did what any ballplayer would do: he went to baseball games. Rutland had a team in the Northern League, a popular semipro circuit for college players. Coakley had pitched there in 1904. He was impressed by a nineteen-year-old shortstop named Collins and recommended him to Connie Mack.

Edward Trowbridge Collins had finished his junior year at Columbia University, where he was more interested in playing football than baseball. Despite his five-foot-nine, 145-pound build, he was a star quarterback and punt returner. He was not really much of a baseball fan. Although he lived just outside New York City in Tarrytown, the first major league game he had ever seen was Game 2 of the 1905 World Series when he was eighteen. He had given little thought to a baseball career. But there was money to be made on the resort town teams—when the players were paid.

Virtually all college stars played in the summer leagues. Some used fake names; some didn't. Many colleges turned a blind eye and didn't penalize their student athletes, who often needed the money for tuition. Collins and two Fordham men, second baseman Dave Shean (also recommended by Coakley and signed by Mack) and pitcher Dick Rudolph were playing for Rutland under their own names. Jack Coombs had dominated the league pitching for Barre-Montpelier in 1905. Nobody at Fordham or Colby objected or took away their college eligibility.

Collins arrived in Rutland in a roundabout way. Yale baseball coach Billy Lush operated a team in Plattsburgh in upstate New York. He invited Collins to play for him. Collins played a few games for a team in Red Hook, New Jersey, then went to Plattsburgh. After winning 2 and losing 13, the team ran out of money. Unpaid for several weeks, Collins left and joined the Rutland club just as Coakley and his bride arrived.

Lush moved on to Rockville, Connecticut, and put together a team. In late August Collins followed him there, the local paper identifying him as "a U. of Vermont man said to be a star." Connie Mack, who knew Lush as an outfielder in the National League in 1896 and the American in 1904–1905, had kept track of Collins since receiving Coakley's letter. He sent his catcher/scout Jimmy Byrnes to Rockville to take a look at Collins. Back came the report: "Get him quick. He's got the makings."

Collins was no secret. Plenty of scouts had seen him. Dave Fultz, Mack's former center fielder, called him the best college player he'd ever seen. Other former players who saw him at Columbia called him the equal of Chase, Lajoie, and Wagner already. In a practice game against the Giants, he hit a double off Joe McGinnity. John McGraw considered it a fluke and ignored him. When a friend urged Clark Griffith to sign Collins, Griffith said, "Tell him to come around some morning and I'll look him over." Collins never went.

While other teams waited, Connie Mack acted. As soon as he heard from Byrnes, Mack telephoned Billy Lush and asked him to bring Collins to see him when the A's were in New York. Lush told him the Rockville season ended on the Friday after Labor Day. They had a pickup game scheduled on Saturday. That suited Connie Mack just fine. The Athletics were playing in New York that Friday and Saturday. He would stay over and meet them at the Fifth Avenue Hotel on Sunday morning, September 9.

Thirty years later Mack recalled their first meeting. "[Lush] walked in accompanied by a frail, excited-looking youth, dressed in the Kollege Kut Klothes of the day. . . . He was modest, but not timid. He believed in himself, and before long I believed in him, too."

This was Mack's recollection after Collins's playing days were over. At the time, Collins didn't think he was good enough to play professional ball. He had no idea what occupation he might pursue. Maybe he'd go to law school. Mack assured the youngster that he had a bright future in baseball. Collins remained dubious. But spurred by Mack's words of encouragement, he decided to give the game a chance.

At the same time, Collins didn't like the possibility of being relegated to the minor leagues, a helpless pawn who could be transferred from one team to another at the whim of various managers. He'd rather find something else to do with his life and get started on it. Collins voiced his concerns to Mack. "If I sign," he said, "I'd like a guarantee that I won't be sent out to another club unless I agree to it."

Connie Mack nodded. That was all right with him. He preferred to educate his boys himself rather than trust them to other teachers anyhow. He reached for a blank piece of paper, picked up a pen and wrote:

In consideration of Edward T. Collins signing for the season of 1907, The American Base Ball Club of Phili does hereby agree not to farm or loan him to any base ball club without his consent.

Connie Mack Mgr

Rather than date it on a Sunday, Mack wrote "Sept 10th 1906."

Collins signed a 1907 contract for $400 a month and went home. Mack went to Philadelphia for series against Washington and Boston before heading west on September 15.

Either Mack invited Collins to join the A's for their last western trip, or he was surprised when Collins showed up at Columbia Park. Recollections differed over the years. The earliest account indicates that the invitation was offered by Mack. It was common practice, even into the 1930s, to invite recruits to experience a late-season stay with the big league club. Giving them a little playing time, even without a current contract, happened too.

Either way, Collins showed up at Columbia Park on Thursday or Friday morning. Heading south on the train, he had worried about whether he was making a mistake. He was captain-elect of the Columbia baseball team (the school dropped football as too dangerous after 1905). He hadn't been concerned about playing in the Northern League, but recalling it nine years later to *Baseball Magazine* editor F. C. Lane, Collins said, "I was anxious not to jeopardize my athletic activities at Columbia by appearing openly with a major league club."

Connie Mack was sensitive to that risk as well. A man was fanning the breeze with Mack in the manager's office when Collins appeared in the doorway. Mack sprang up, said, "Hello, Sullivan, glad to see you," while pushing Collins into the hallway. "Go down to the clubhouse and I'll see you a little later."

A few minutes later Mack told the puzzled Collins, "That was Tim Murnane of the *Boston Globe* in my office. I was afraid he might recognize you."

Thus was Eddie Sullivan christened. Collins always insisted it had not been prearranged between them. Mack asked him to work out in the mornings with the team, then disappear lest one of the Boston writers recognize him, since Collins had played against Yale and Harvard. Philadelphia writers were less likely to know him.

In the end it didn't matter. His play at Rutland and Rockville, not his brief pseudonymous sojourn with the Athletics, cost him his eligibility. Perhaps a 1905 two-part article in *McClure's* (the most influential magazine of the time), "The College Athlete—How Commercialism Is Making Him a Professional," contributed to the change in academic attitudes that sidelined Collins at Columbia the following spring. He was paid to coach the 1907 Columbia nine instead.

On his first day with the Athletics, in a uniform too big and baggy for him, the self-conscious rookie walked onto the field. Rube Waddell was the first to speak to him. "Hey, kid," Rube called. "Get a bat. I'll throw you some."

Collins picked up a bat and stepped into the left-handed batter's box. "He threw three curve balls that looked like they dropped off a table," Collins recalled. "I missed all three. I looked—and was—pretty discouraged as I walked away. Rube came over and patted me on the back. 'Don't mind that, kid,' he said. 'I do that to 'em all.'"

Harry Davis and Connie Mack were watching. They waved Collins over and told him that Rube did in fact do that to 'em all, in games as well as practice. "You won't see that kind of pitching often," Mack assured him.

Sometimes Connie Mack lost a star prospect he thought he had. On August 27 he announced the purchase of two pitchers from Augusta, a twenty-one-year-old left-hander out of Crabapple, Georgia, named Nap Rucker, who had won 27 games, and Jim Holmes, twenty-four, a 26-game winner. Between the two, they had appeared in 98 games for the pennant winners of the "Sallie" League, as the *Augusta Chronicle* spelled it.

The major league drafting period began September 1. Under the National Agreement, no minor league club could sell a player to another minor league club after August 25. But it could sell him to a major league club after that date. Newspapers in late August reported minor league clubs working on imminent sales of prospects who would bring more than the $500 draft price. Charles Ebbets, who had been scouting in the south and saw Nap Rucker pitch, and Garry Herrmann were the only big league magnates in Cincinnati for the draft meeting on September 1. Ebbets claimed three pitchers. Rucker was one of them.

Connie Mack said Rucker and Holmes were already his property. The National Commission rejected Mack's claim to both pitchers, ruling that he hadn't filed the contract of sale prior to the August 25 deadline.

A different reason for the commission's denying Mack's claim appeared in a story about Rucker in the 1913 *Reach Guide*. Dodgers manager Patsy Donovan was said to be the one who saw Rucker pitch that year. "President Ebbets attended the drafting meeting in the Fall and learned that Rucker was bound by a contract to be sold to Connie Mack. But as Mack had put up no money to bind the bargain, the National Commission annulled the contract. Then Ebbets slipped in a draft for $500 on the spot, being the only major league magnate, except Garry Herrmann, at the meeting, and Rucker was awarded to him. All major league magnates have attended the draft meetings since then."

But that wasn't the reason given at the time. The commission just said Mack failed to submit the paperwork before August 25. It appeared that Mack had gotten a raw deal, but there is no record of his making a fuss about it. He probably went along with it rather than start a fight with the new governing structure of the game. But the Augusta club howled. It contended that the sale was legal since the August 25 deadline applied only to sales to other minor league clubs, not big league buyers. Further, it said, the sale had been approved by the Sallie League president, who knew the rules. The Augusta club was right. But it didn't do any good. It was out whatever amount Connie Mack was willing to pay for Rucker above the $500 draft price. And Connie Mack lost Nap Rucker.

The ruling applied to Jim Holmes too, but since only one player could be drafted from a club, Holmes was still available. He reported to the A's and appeared in three games with little success. Rucker won 134 games in Brooklyn.

One day in early September a man named Henry Beach Needham walked into Mack's office under the first base stands. He carried a letter of introduction from a former player. Needham was a writer of short stories and magazine articles, including the 1905 *McClure's* series criticizing semipro college athletes.

The letter explained that Needham wished to accompany the Athletics on their last western trip of the season and write a series of articles based on his observations. Normally eager for publicity, Mack hesitated. "I was in something of a pinch on account of the request," he wrote later, "mainly because I wasn't caring much about having the team written up at the time. It was a team of green youngsters, material the rawest, that I had in charge, and which Mr. Needham was to see perform."

Needham pleaded. Mack gave in and allowed him to make the trip. As often happened with Connie Mack, the encounter developed into a long, close friendship. In the years that followed, Needham sometimes sat on the A's bench during games and was a frequent visitor to Mack's home.

"He proved to be the sort you like to travel with," Mack wrote. "In the hotels he and I had adjoining, usually connected rooms. We ate together, we spent our evenings together. More than that, he sat on the bench with me. In this way he began to learn inside baseball. He soon had what we hear so much about: baseball brains.

"His magazine articles printed after the trip were the first of the kind printed in America . . . in magazines of general interest."

So a troop of raw, green Athletics and a magazine writer headed for Chicago on September 15. Left at home were Plank, Bender, Coakley, Cross, Knight, Doc Powers, Socks Seybold, and Danny Murphy, who had taken his lumbago-sore bones home without telling anybody. Led by John Shibe and augmented by a few college players, they toured the area playing exhibition games against black teams.

Needham's education began on the train. He spent some time in the company of Schreck in the smoker car and afterward told Mack, "I've been all around, but I've heard things tonight I have never heard before."

On Monday, September 17, Sullivan broke in at shortstop with Dave Shean playing second. His debut was a memorable 11-inning duel between Rube Waddell and Ed Walsh, who combined for 23 strikeouts. Soon after the lineups went out over the wires, sporting editors in Philadelphia began inquiring, "Who's Sullivan?" Nobody in the press box knew. In his first at bat he beat out a swinging bunt for a hit, then stole second but didn't score. He sacrificed once and struck out twice in the 5–4 loss. In the field he handled 2 putouts and 4 assists flawlessly. The writers eventually discovered his identity, but he played out the season as Sullivan. Mack played him at third and shortstop and used him to pinch hit once. The early report in the press was, "Sullivan appears to be a fine fielder but weak hitter."

For the next two weeks Mack treated a parade of players to their big league cups of coffee: pitcher Mody Cunningham, who won his only start; Carl Schumann, who lost his only two starts; Bill Bartley, who relieved three times; Willy Fetzer, who pinch hit once. Dave Shean hung around long enough to play for six teams and appear in the 1918 World Series with the Red Sox. During one stretch Mack's green boys went 48 innings without scoring a run. The A's wound up using a total of thirty-one players during the season; the league average was twenty-five. The Browns got by with nineteen.

One night Mack took them all to the Columbia Theater, where George M. Cohan was starring in *George Washington Jr*, a patriotic pageant in which Cohan introduced the song "You're a Grand Old Flag" while marching up and down the stage waving a large American flag. All the players and writers signed a ball, and when Cohan made his first appearance on stage, Rube Waddell stood up and tossed it to him from the box seats.

They went on to St. Louis, where Schreck stayed out all night. When he showed up at the Planter's Hotel the next morning, an exasperated Connie Mack didn't wait to hear his explanation. "Pack up and go home," he said.

Mack had known from the early weeks that he didn't have a championship team. But nobody else in the league did either. The White Sox scored more runs with fewer hits than any team ever would and won the pennant with the lowest batting average in the league.

Even so, the Athletics could have won if not for the illnesses and injuries that sidelined Murphy, Plank, Waddell, Bender, and Coakley for so long.

Waddell and Osee Schrecongost had been on a season-long toot. "You can see [Waddell] every night at his usual bars all night," wrote a *Sporting News* correspondent in late August. He also reported that "the team has quit on Connie Mack because he persists in letting Waddell do as he pleases." But the Rube never begged off. When he was fit, he worked whenever he was called upon and never complained. Despite his injuries, he appeared in 43 games and led the league in strikeouts.

One day years later Connie Mack was telling Cleveland manager Lou Boudreau about the way things were done in the old days and Rube's readiness to answer the call at all times. "Teams used to use a talley-ho to get from the park to the hotel. One day I went into the ninth leading by three runs. Players not in the game were already in the talley-ho. With two out they got the bases filled. I called time and sent someone for the Rube. I'll never forget him coming in from left field, stopping behind third base to put on one shoe, walking to the box before he put on the other. At that time a relieving pitcher wasn't allowed to warm up, not even one practice pitch. Rube just flexed his arm a bit, fired three straight strikes, and the man at the plate never got the bat off his shoulder."

Mack may have added some dramatic effects to the story, but it was true that Waddell was always ready to come in and close out a game regardless of how soon it was after he'd pitched a complete game or how little sleep he'd had.

And it was true that Connie Mack treated Waddell differently. He knew he'd be going against his principles of management when he signed the Rube. He took that risk, and it had paid off. He knew all of Rube's faults. He knew, too, that his pitching staff was anchored by Waddell. So Mack coddled, cajoled, and coaxed his best out of him. And when they were winning, nobody complained. When the season was over, he defended Rube, sort of, saying at least Rube was honest, not given to making excuses or trouble with other players:

I treated Waddell as I would be treated myself. I do not have the trouble with Waddell as some people think I have. . . . Rube of course is a peculiar fellow. He has his whims just as other players do, but Waddell is all in the open, does his peculiar stunts in full sight of the baseball public. If you consider that this big fellow has been pampered and spoiled by the newspapers in every city in the circuit, it will not be hard for you to see how it happens that he is spoiled. But Waddell is far easier to get along with than some other players. When he wants to do something he goes and does it, and offers no explanation either before or after the act. I would rather have a player of the Waddell type than one who sulks. Now there's one good feature in the Rube's makeup; he never sulks, and he does not instill trouble in the ranks as some other star players do.

Henry Beach Needham wrote a series of short stories that first appeared in *Collier's* magazine in 1914, then in book form as *The Double Squeeze* in 1915. The characters are transparently based on Athletics players and Connie Mack. Game details reflect the team's strategies and style of play. In an introduction to the book, Mack praised Needham for accurately summing up his philosophy of a baseball manager's job in the story "A Tree Full of Owls":

"Tris Ford, although the ablest tactician in baseball, was at bottom a business man. Like the best merchants and manufacturers, they never fail to look ahead. He planned two, three, often four years in advance, and he went after players."

Nobody went after players like Connie Mack did. He had earned a reputation as the most aggressive talent hunter in the business. Most teams had one full-time scout; some had two or three. Mack had six. He was said to have strings on more than a hundred minor leaguers. Some managers, on hearing about a promising youngster, might invite him for a workout and a lookover. Connie Mack's method, as Clark Griffith described it in a 1910 interview, was, "Sign you now and try you out later."

33 | "WE WUZ ROBBED"

In the six years since his arrival in Philadelphia, Connie Mack had prospered. He was nowhere near the category of the Morgans, Vanderbilts, or Carnegies. But by the standards of the time he was considered well-to-do. In addition to his salary, now $15,000, Mack's one-fourth interest in the Athletics had earned him dividends.

Unlike his friend John Shibe, who owned a yacht and went in for speedboat racing, Mack's tastes were simple and basic. He lived comfortably but not ostentatiously. He enjoyed the theater and boxing matches. He dressed well, his clothes and shoes made to order. He provided generously for his extended family. One writer estimated that Mack's entire household—his mother, three children, and his brother Eugene—could manage very comfortably on $3,000 a year.

Mack branched out as a businessman and investor. He sold his bowling alleys at a good profit and bought a building at 44 North Eleventh Street, a two-story structure with a bar downstairs and an apartment upstairs, a half block from the busy Reading Railroad terminal. He set Eugene up in business there and called it the White Elephant Saloon. Their brother Michael and Dennis's son Harold worked there; Michael and his wife, Ella, lived in the apartment. From its gala opening on Wednesday, March 21, 1906, the saloon prospered. Tradesmen and travelers frequented it for the nickel beer, free lunch, and the latest sporting news on the chattering ticker.

Mack and John Shibe went into land development. They bought five acres in Bala, a fashionable suburb adjoining Fairmount Park, where Ben Shibe resided, divided it into seventy-two lots, and began putting up houses. They were negotiating to buy a city block in West Philadelphia for $70,000, a deal the *Philadelphia Record* initially reported as intended for a new stadium for the Athletics. But the A's had no intention of locating in West Philadelphia. The *Record* acknowledged that the bulk of the team's patrons was drawn from the northwestern section of the city, "together with Kensington and Manayunk, and these people could not be induced to travel to West Philadelphia to patronize the Athletics."

It was no secret that the A's were shopping for a site for a new stadium. So any negotiations involving Mack or one of the Shibes was routinely assumed to be for that purpose. They tried to buy the Columbia Park grounds, where their lease had two years to go, but it was not for sale. They were said to be looking at land near abandoned railroad stations or one block from Columbia Park or Twenty-eighth and Montgomery.

Meanwhile, Ben Shibe was quietly covertly buying up property lot by lot not far from the Phillies' grounds.

The Athletics' success story was not unique in the American League. The "baseball craze is here to stay," declared the *New York Telegraph*. The need to replace the old wooden grandstands with larger, more comfortable, fireproof stadiums was evident, not only in the major leagues. Though not in the class of the steel, oil, railroad, and mining industries, baseball had become a multimillion dollar business.

The Cleveland Naps were the first to insure their players against injury in train accidents for $100,000.

"The six million admissions last year in the National and American Leagues are a drop in the bucket," said the *Telegraph*. "The 30 minor leagues and nearly 5,000 professional players are still a small percentage of the baseball world. Every town has at least one amateur club. The aggregate millions spent on baseballs and equipment is stupendous."

Commenting on earlier predictions that the craze would soon end, the *Telegraph* described the eternal essence of the baseball fan. "The youth of today playing in vacant lots, parks and streets . . . is the fan of tomorrow. . . . Love of the game never leaves the devotees. He may grow fat and he may no longer be able to handle the bat himself, but there is nothing that carries him back to the happiest days of his life like a good game of ball between good players."

The *Philadelphia Telegraph* estimated that it now cost $100,000 or more to operate each of the sixteen major league teams, broken down as follows:

Player salaries: $50,000–$60,000 (An undocumented range of American League salaries published in a Brockton paper in March went from the Athletics' $44,000 to Cleveland's $80,000.)

Other employees: $10,000

Rent and interest: $10,000–$20,000

Spring training: $2,500–$5,000

Hotels and railroads: $15,000 (Railroad costs would go up in 1907, when new regulations banned the 25–50 percent discounts the teams had negotiated.)

Balls, bats, advertising, etc.: $5,000

Ten percent of gate receipts went to the league; twelve and a half cents from every ticket went to the visiting team.

This cost estimate did not include things like meal money. Barney Dreyfuss experimented with giving the Pirates $2 a day on the road. The big eaters complained; the skimpers patronized the dime soup kitchens and pocketed the difference. Dreyfuss went back to picking up the checks in the hotel dining rooms.

At the 1906 winter meetings the National League passed a rule requiring all teams to provide adequate dressing rooms for visiting clubs. This enabled clubs to stay at the better hotels, which didn't like ballplayers in dirty, sweaty uniforms mixing with other guests in the corridors and lobby before and after games. The American League took no such action.

The AL wanted to go to a 140-game schedule, but it couldn't persuade the National to abandon the 154-game slate. One club owner chided the National for adopting a "can't to can't" policy: a season lasting "from when you can't play in the spring until you can't play in the fall."

Baseball had become a respectable business, suitable for women and for businessmen to entertain clients. The Pirates had installed thirteen luxury boxes on top of the grandstand roof. Leased for $60 a year, they were quickly snapped up by a who's who of industrial magnates, while others went on a waiting list. When the cost went up to $75 in 1907, only one failed to renew.

In Philadelphia the coziness between the newspapermen and the two clubs continued. The writers, who organized the Philadelphia Sporting Writers Association, threw a banquet honoring Mack and new Phillies manager Billy Murray at the Majestic on February 28. The teams reciprocated by entertaining twenty scribes one week later.

After one spring training in Montgomery, the restless Mack and Shibe headed west again and settled on Marlin, Texas. Along with his new recruits and veterans, Mack brought a new trainer to Marlin. Martin P. Lawler was a cut above the rudimentary muscle-pounders of the time. A student of Swedish massage and gymnastics, he would earn his salary just keeping Eddie Plank's overworked left arm going through the season.

In Marlin, Connie Mack made a new friend. For all their diversity, the friends of Connie Mack shared one thing in common: they lasted a lifetime. There are trails of correspondence spanning forty years, some longer. The previous spring, a wholesale grocer from Palestine, Texas, had been in New Orleans on business. The twenty-eight-year-old Hyman Pearlstone was a baseball nut, one of the earliest subscribers to the young *Sporting News*. Pearlstone was delighted to find the Athletics were also stopping at the Hotel Roosevelt. One evening he struck up a conversation with a player, who noticed that Pearlstone was wearing an Elks pin. The player commented that Doc Powers was an Elk. Pearlstone introduced himself to Powers and invited him to the theater. When he learned that the A's would be training in Marlin, Texas—just down the road from Palestine—in 1907, he invited Powers to visit him for a few weeks before camp opened. Jack Coombs was another visitor to Palestine, where he met his future wife and later owned a home.

When Pearlstone approached Mack at the hotel in Marlin, Mack could have politely tolerated or brushed off the small-town Texas fan. But he didn't. They must have enjoyed each other's company immensely. After the season started, Mack sent him a package containing an Athletics uniform, shoes, a ball and glove, and a letter inviting Pearlstone to spend his vacation traveling with the team.

"My wife thought I was crazy, but I decided to go," he told a *Dallas News* reporter.

For the next forty-four years, Hyman Pearlstone took one month-long road trip with the Athletics every season. In the early years he was considered a good luck charm by the players, who greeted him with "On the road with the winning club" whenever he joined them. Pearlstone warmed up pitchers in morning practice and sat to the left of Connie Mack on the bench. He paid his own way, at the team's rates. "The club secretary paid all my bills and I settled with him at the end of the trip." In 1913 the total tab for a thirty-one-day trip came to $142.

In the 1930s Pearlstone would sometimes take his grandson, Larry Budner, with him. Budner remembers a 1938 trip to Chicago, when he was eight. The A's were staying at the Del Prado Hotel. When Budner and his grandfather saw Mack eating lunch alone in the dining room, they sat at another table. Pearlstone said, "We won't speak to him now. He always lunches alone so he can think about the day's game."

Over the years the families visited in each other's homes. Pearlstone moved to Dallas, where he prospered in the wholesale grocery and hardware business and as a banker. He advised Mack on investments, including some oil and gas fields that never produced any gushers during Connie Mack's lifetime. He also became an active bird dog for Mack, keeping an eye on Texas college players.

Connie Mack introduced another innovation to baseball in 1907. At the time teams used young boys to round up balls that got by the catcher during batting practice. A man named Wellington Titus invented a portable batting cage in Hopewell, New Jersey. One day Mack sent a scout to look over a player in that town. The scout turned down the player but told Mack about the cage. According to Titus biographers, Mack bought the first one used in professional baseball.

It didn't take Connie Mack long to realize that he would have to go into the season with a carryover lineup. The new players didn't impress him. He couldn't even muster up the ritual spring enthusiasm over them, except for one: Si Nicholls, an infielder purchased from Memphis, who had been called up in September. "If this man doesn't make good I'll quit picking young players," Mack hyped. Nicholls and Jack Knight would compete for the third base job. Davis, Murphy, and Cross completed the infield. Topsy Hartsel and Socks Seybold were fixtures in left and right field. Mack had given up on Rube Oldring as an infielder and told him, "From now on you are my center fielder." Watching Bris Lord and Oldring, Mack wished he could combine the best of each into one complete player. Oldring was the better hitter and had more speed; Lord had the better arm. In one exhibition game he threw out two runners at home and one at third. But Lord lacked baseball smarts, the instincts that Mack valued but couldn't teach.

Mack counted on Schreck and Doc Powers to do the catching. He could only hope that Schreck had shed his "big shot" strutting and was ready to do his best again.

The pitching was set: Plank, Bender, Dygert, Coombs, and possibly Waddell. Mack put a question mark after Rube, no matter how fervently he promised to behave. Waddell arrived carrying over 200 pounds but was said to be "hard as nails, no fat." One night Mack was standing in front of the hotel when a fire engine raced by carrying the Rube in full fire-fighting regalia. Otherwise, Rube couldn't find much trouble to get into in Marlin.

Andy Coakley's health had been a concern. Mack didn't know if he could count on him and sold him to Cincinnati, on the condition that he was physically able to pitch. Coakley gave the Reds two solid seasons, retired for two years, and tried a brief comeback; then a thumb injury ended his playing days. He became the coach at Columbia for thirty-seven years.

The only new pitcher who impressed Mack was a burly right-hander purchased from Seattle. Harry "Rube" Vickers was twenty-eight. He had been up briefly with the Reds and Dodgers a few years back and toiled in the minors ever since. His fastball reminded Mack of Amos Rusie. His quirky, deceptive delivery was unique. But Mack was dubious about his attitude and willingness to apply himself. Last year in the lengthy Pacific Coast League season, he had pitched 517 innings, winning 39 games and losing 20. But, Mack said, "to hear him tell it, he had won 65."

Mack once called Vickers "the greatest liar I ever managed. He could fib faster, smoother and better than any ball player I ever had. Why, once when I caught him red-handed in a lie, I got real mad and said, 'Vickers, if I ever catch you lying to me again, you're through, fired, done for. I won't have you around.' But before I walked away from that fellow's locker, he was spinning me the biggest lie of all—and, what's more, he knew that I knew what he was doing."

Hoping to cover the costs of spring training and linger longer in the sunny south, Mack arranged a five-game series in New Orleans with the New York Giants, beginning on the Wednesday before Easter. He and John McGraw, whose Giants practiced in Los Angeles before traveling to San Antonio and New Orleans, agreed to a Waddell-Mathewson matchup on Good Friday, March 29. Promoted by the host New Orleans Pelicans as the 1905 World Series match that never happened, it was sure to attract a sellout crowd. The weekend games also promised record receipts for the city. The lengthy stay meant the city series against the Phillies had to be cut short. Mack figured it would be cold in the north anyhow, and the A's would draw bigger crowds against the Giants. He turned out to be wrong on all counts. The weather was warmer in Philadelphia that week, and the Giants series was a financial disaster. Mack wasn't there to see it. He knew what his regulars could do. He put Harry Davis in charge of them while he and Sam Erwin went north with the Yannigans.

Chief Zimmer, a veteran catcher who had umpired in the National

League for two years and was now a Southern Association ump, was agreed upon by the A's and Giants to work the games, although McGraw later denied it. The Giants won the Wednesday game, 4–3, before about three thousand fans. Either McGraw was dyspeptic or he was brooding over some past run-in with Zimmer; whatever it was, he rode the ump throughout the game.

About two thousand turned out the next day, a reported one-third of them women. The Giants batted first against Plank. With 2 outs, Art Devlin singled. Cy Seymour singled him to third, and took second when Oldring threw to third. With Frank Bowerman at bat, Plank stepped off the rubber and faked a throw to third. All the Giants yelled "Balk" and charged the umpire. The air turned blue in the center of the diamond as McGraw and his men poured on the brimstone. Zimmer insisted that Plank's foot had been off the slab. McGraw called him an embroidered liar. The nine New York and Philadelphia writers on hand had begun to send their game accounts and suddenly found they had a fight to cover.

Zimmer threw McGraw and Bresnahan out of the game. They refused to leave. Zimmer called for a police escort. Bresnahan left; McGraw didn't. He ordered his team off the field. Zimmer gave the Giants five minutes to come back, then forfeited the game. That made the New Orleans manager, Charlie Frank, madder than anybody. He had to give out rain checks and send everybody home.

That night McGraw said he wouldn't show up if Zimmer was the umpire on Friday. "Zimmer couldn't umpire a dog fight after the yellow streak he showed," were his reported sentiments.

On not-so-good Friday, a capacity crowd arrived expecting to see a duel between Mathewson and Waddell. McGraw stayed away and put Bresnahan in charge with orders for the Giants to stay off the field if Zimmer was the umpire. He was, and they did. Five minutes after game time Zimmer declared the game forfeited to the Athletics. The crowd was mutinous. Harry Davis, hoping to avert a riot and give his players some practice, conferred with Bresnahan. They agreed to find an umpire and play the game and settled on Pelicans outfielder Joe Rickert. The fans got to see Mathewson pitch 5 innings in the A's 7–0 win, but not Rube Waddell.

The Giants abruptly left town but not before a fracas, involving heated exchanges and some pushing and shoving, broke out between the two clubs. Charlie Frank brought his Pelicans back from nearby Alexander City to finish the series, vowing the Giants would never be allowed back in Athletic Park. He filed a complaint with the National Association, which eventually ordered the Giants to reimburse him $1,000.

A hint that the thirty-year-old Waddell might not be the Rube of old appeared in an exhibition game on the way home. In the ninth inning he told his teammates to leave the field, all but first baseman Harry Davis. Davis went along with the stunt. But the Rube was unable to zip his fastball past the batters. Each time somebody connected with one, Rube had to chase it down. He was fast getting fagged out. He pleaded with Davis to put the rest of the boys back on the field. Davis refused. Rube was all in by the time he got the third out.

Some of the veteran Athletics had less confidence than their manager in Jack Coombs. To put it bluntly, they considered him yellow. Twice in the late stages of the 1906 pennant race they had seen him blow leads of 4 and 5 runs. On September 13 he had relieved in the tenth inning, walked the first batter, and gave up the game-winning hit after a sacrifice. He seemed to go to pieces under pressure. They shuddered when they saw him come into a game and let him know how they felt in subtle and not so subtle ways.

But Connie Mack chalked it up to inexperience. He saw what some of his players didn't: the collegian's eagerness to learn and ability to absorb what he was taught. In those respects, Coombs exemplified the reason Mack favored college men. His decision to hand "Jawn" the ball on opening day 1907 may have been Mack's way of showing his confidence in Coombs as much as protecting the older arms from the cold weather.

The tantalizing warm spell of early April was blown away by wintry gales that greeted the A's and Boston on Thursday, April 11. One of the league's early anomalies was the extraordinary number of long games between those two teams, many of them involving Coombs or the Boston starter, Cy Young. This one went 14 innings. After a brass band and the two teams marched to the flagpole—the Athletics led by writer/partner Sam Jones and Tom Shibe—the band played "The Star Spangled Banner." Newly elected mayor John E. Rayburn, a onetime semipro player, threw out the first ball, then a reported fifteen thousand frigid fans watched Young throw 6 no-hit innings before the A's scored 2 in the seventh. Both teams scored in the ninth to send the 4–4 tie into extra innings. Buck Freeman's 3-run home run capped Boston's 8–4 win.

It was too cold for anybody in the league to play the next day, prompting Ban Johnson to assert that he wouldn't start a season before April 18 in the future, no matter what the National League chose to do.

Saturday wasn't much better. Mack started Rube Vickers, but Vickers quit after one inning, claiming he couldn't control his pitches in the strong wind. Mack soon came to realize, "Before a game Vickers will spend hours telling how easily he will win his game. Five minutes after the game starts he will begin explaining why he can't win it."

Mack sent in Waddell. After Hartsel's home run in the eighth gave the A's a 4–2 lead, Rube reverted to his juvenile antics in the ninth, giving Connie Mack and the four thousand frozen fans something more than the icy wind to shiver about. With 2 outs and 2 strikes on Armbruster, Waddell began to bait him around the edges of the plate. Armbruster didn't bite and walked. Unable to throw his fastball past anybody at this point, Rube tried to dance around the banjo-hitting pinch hitter Al Shaw and walked him too. Then he plunked the left-handed leadoff man, Denny Sullivan, in the back with his first pitch. That was enough for the agitated Mack. He signaled his captain, Harry Davis, to take the ball from Rube. Davis tried, but Rube pleaded for a chance to get the next batter, Jimmy Collins. Davis said no and took the ball from the pouting Waddell. Bender came off the bench and threw three fastballs past Collins to end the game.

Connie Mack adopted the quickest hook in the league. He didn't hesitate to pull a starter after one inning, a reliever after a few batters. Of the four pennant contenders in 1907, the Athletics had the fewest complete games. It was not so much a change of philosophy on Mack's part as a realization that his pitching was not as reliable as he had expected it to be.

"We're beaten before we go into any game simply because our slabmen are not in any form," he lamented. Mack's last straw with Rube Vickers came on the first western trip. They arrived in Chicago on Wednesday, May 8, restless after two days of rain and a day on the train. They spent another idle day when it poured all day. Watching the still hitless-wonder White Sox world champions on Thursday, Vickers said to Mack, "I'll be darned if I can understand how they got to be world champions."

"You want to work against 'em?" Mack asked.

"Sure," said Vickers.

"You'll pitch tomorrow."

The first six batters Vickers faced produced a walk, triple, double, and 3 singles for 5 runs. When the carnage finally ended, Vickers headed for the far end of the bench away from the manager. Mack called to him. Vickers pretended he didn't hear. Mack called again. No response. A player seated beside Vickers poked him. "Connie wants you." Vickers got up and walked over to Mack.

"All I want to tell you," Mack said, "is that's how they come to be world champions."

Three weeks later Rube Vickers was in Williamsport.

Cold weather, rainouts, and illnesses kept the pitching rotation messed up through May. Mack suspended Rube Waddell for thirty days for carousing. But it didn't last thirty days. Mack needed him, unsteady and unpredictable as he was. Mack didn't get a complete game out of anybody in a three-game series against a weak New York team. On Saturday, May 4, Dygert's spitter dried up. The Highlanders scored 6 in the first on 6 hits, 2 walks, a wild pitch, and an error. The error came after Waddell relieved Dygert. With men on first and second, the ball was hit back to Rube. He turned and threw to third, but Jack Knight was dozing off the bag. Mack yanked Knight and put Si Nicholls on third.

The infield was unsettled. Nicholls didn't have the arm for a third baseman. Knight covered a lot of ground but wasn't hitting. Monte Cross's old bones were aching. Danny Murphy suffered from rheumatism. The only solid fixture was Captain Harry Davis. At thirty-three, Jasper, as the players called him, was as good as ever, digging low throws out of the dirt with the best of them. Said the *Boston Herald*, "Taken all in all, there are few first baseman who have anything on Harry Davis for all-around ability." Davis would lead the league in doubles and, for the fourth year in a row, in home runs, with 8. One of them, on April 24 in Boston, was the first ever to clear the right-field fence by a visiting player. Admiring one's long drives is not just a modern trait. One paper reported, "Harry stood at the rubber after he hit the ball and watched it go over and as soon as he satisfied himself that the ball was fair he started on his jaunt around the bases." (SABR researcher Ron Selter calculated its distance at 350 feet, a shot worth admiring in the mushy-ball era.)

Mack's outfield was in poor shape too. Rube Oldring sprained an ankle. Bris Lord wasn't hitting and ran them out of a few wins with some blockheaded base running. His batting average had gone down each year; he was batting .182 when Mack gave up on him and sold him outright to New Orleans.

Rube Waddell was like the little girl with a curl right in the middle of her forehead: when he was good, he was very, very good, and when he was bad, he was horrid. In Chicago he threw a 3-hitter; in his next start in St. Louis he and Vickers were bombed for 17 hits. They lost three in Cleveland, two by shutouts. Rube started the third game. In the midst of a 4-run first inning, he tried to pick up a bunt and fell on his right shoulder. Nothing unusual about that for the clumsy Waddell. But he sat on the grass and held his left arm—also not unusual for him—while grimacing in apparent pain. The trainer helped him up, and they started for the clubhouse. Connie Mack stopped them and suggested that since all the grass stains were on the right side of Rube's uniform, perhaps his left arm was still sound enough to continue pitching. Rube stayed in and gave up 1 more run in the 5–2 loss.

They came home in fifth place, 7½ games behind the White Sox, and won 4 out of 5 from Boston. A Memorial Day doubleheader drew a total of twenty-three thousand to the morning and afternoon games. But they gained nothing on Chicago.

By early June the pitching was beginning to round into shape, except for Bender, who seemed to be plagued by what one writer called "chronic organic troubles." By June 6 he had won only 2 games.

The infield was still a shambles. Murphy sprained an ankle. Cross strained his back. Then in walked the cocky twenty-year-old Eddie Collins, a.k.a. Sullivan, fresh from graduation at Columbia. Collins had everything Connie Mack looked for in a youngster. He was intelligent and eager to think, talk, and learn the game above all other interests. Mack didn't believe in rushing newcomers into action if he could avoid it. He preferred to have them sit beside him through one or two full seasons, where he could teach and they could ask questions. The morning practices gave them a chance to work on the physical part of the game. He urged them to study the veterans, how they went about their business, and arranged for Collins to board with Harry Davis and his family.

The White Sox were at Columbia Park to open a long home stand on Tuesday, June 4. Mack agonized over his lineup. With Cross limited to coaching third base—where he was an eagle at spotting catchers' signs and pitchers' tip-off traits—and Murphy sidelined, he had no choice. He put Nicholls at second, Knight at third, and Collins at short. They were terrible. Collins made an error. Knight made an error. Even steady Eddie Plank caught the jitters and made a wild throw. The errors led to 7 runs in the 10–6 loss.

In the eighth inning the Athletics had loaded the bases with Collins, hitless so far, due up. Mack sent Bender in to pinch hit for him. In the ninth, Nicholls moved to short and Bender played second, handling one ground ball flawlessly. After the game a dejected Connie Mack sat in his office, "a picture of misery and despair," wrote Sporting News correspondent Horace Fogel, "in the most dejected mood I have ever seen him."

The fans had roasted Knight and Collins after each misplay. The next day the newspapers amplified the chorus of boos. Connie Mack was not concerned about Collins; he'd be fine. But he had given up on Jack Knight for not applying himself seriously enough to improve either with the glove or the bat. Errors were part of the game, but so was attitude, and Mack didn't see what he wanted from Knight in that department.

It rained all the next day. Mack was busy on the telephone. He asked for waivers on Knight. Cleveland and Washington claimed him. Then he received a call from Boston. Jimmy Collins was available. Mack took the next train to Boston.

Jimmy Collins had been a Boston favorite since 1896, first with the Beaneaters, then as player-manager of the new American Leaguers (or Americans, as the team was nicknamed at the time) beginning in 1901. He had led them to pennants in 1903 and 1904 and to victory in the 1903 World Series. But a 20-game losing streak in May 1906 had started them downhill, and they plummeted to the cellar. When Collins tried to bring in new players to turn the team around, the owner stopped him and did his own recruiting and importing. Collins, unable to shake off a knee injury that limited him to 37 games, began staying away from the ballpark and was suspended on August 28. He was fired as the manager but kept on as a player. It was an uncomfortable situation for him and the club. Besides, he was the team's highest paid player at $8,500.

A steady hitter and smooth fielder, Collins had long been admired by Mack, who consistently named him to his all-time All-Star team. "Jimmy was another Lajoie," Mack once said, "slick and fast. He had a great knack of coming up with the ball between hops. He was also a great base runner and a timely hitter."

Collins was thirty-seven, but he looked to Mack as though he had not lost a step in the field. On Thursday Mack watched him handle 7 chances, including 2 hit-robbing snares of line drives off the bats of Cobb and Jones that brought the cheering crowd to its feet.

Collins was expensive, but Mack wanted him. In addition to a two-year contract at $8,500, Collins, who had married Sadie Murphy of Roxbury during the winter and preferred to stay in Boston, wanted a $3,000 bonus to go to Philadelphia. Mack agreed. He gave the Red Sox Jack Knight and $7,500, and Mack and his new third baseman left for Philadelphia.

The Athletics recouped some of their investment in Collins on Saturday, when a crowd of almost fifteen thousand greeted him at Columbia Park with a huge ovation. He rewarded them with 2 hits in the 4–2 win over St. Louis. The transformation of the A's was dramatic. Monte Cross was ready to return to action at shortstop. Si Nicholls moved to second. Mack could keep Eddie Collins beside him on the bench and use him to pinch hit. (In August Mack received a call from Newark asking if it could borrow Collins for a big series against Jersey City. Collins agreed to go. In four games he was 8 for 16 but did almost as much damage with his glove, making 3 errors in his first game at shortstop. Newark asked him to finish out the season there, but Collins refused and returned to Philadelphia. He never played another minor league game.)

For the first time all year, Mack's outfield of Seybold, Hartsel, and Oldring was in top form. Even Schreck was sober, twenty-five pounds lighter than a year ago, his agile footwork enabling him to nab would-be thieves on the base paths. He and Nicholls were the team's top hitters.

The biggest turnout of the season, almost twenty thousand, filled the seats and outfield on Saturday, June 15, with Larry Lajoie and the Naps in town. Cleveland's spitball artist, Glenn Liebhardt, started against Eddie Plank. In 1906 Liebhardt had pitched five doubleheaders in the Southern Association and won 9 of the 10 games. When the A's pounded him for 7 runs in the second inning, the Naps claimed the ball had been "glucosed" to nullify the effects of his wet fingers. Having played for Connie Mack, Lajoie was sure he knew how the ball happened to be so sticky.

Then the third-place Tigers came to town for the first time. Hughie Jennings was in the first year of his fourteen-year run as the Detroit manager. The old Baltimore Oriole had turned Ban Johnson's conservative circuit upside down with his antics in the third base coaching box. With only two playing managers in the league—Fielder Jones at Chicago and Lajoie—managers frequently manned the coaching lines. None of them caused the sensation that Jennings did. Plucking grass and flinging it in the air, dancing around with his arms waving, he was never still and never silent. He mixed unintelligible screeches and piercing "ee-yahs" with a steady patter of encouragement: "That ol' boy's up there for a purpose. . . . Make up your mind you can hit and you will. . . . Now just watch him, he's never failed yet."

Philadelphia fans hooted him. Writers claimed he was breaking six different rules governing coaches' conduct. Once when he lost his voice, he took a train conductor's whistle with him and blew it constantly until Silk

O'Loughlin threw him out of the game. Back came Hughie with the whistle the next day and drew a ten-day suspension. There were no rules against whistles, but Ban Johnson didn't like them, and that was enough to earn a suspension.

Asked to comment on Jennings's style, Connie Mack said he didn't think the hijinks contributed anything to winning. But he understood why Jennings made so much noise. "Bellowing and monkeyshines in the coaching box have the single object of rattling the other team. Lively coaching is the kind that keeps your own men awake and encouraged."

The newspapers condemned the umpires for not stopping Jennings from "carrying on like a lunatic," as Fogel put it, "chasing up and down the coaching lines like a hyena. Why not build a cage for him at each ballpark in the circuit? If he must have a policeman's whistle and toy sirens to blow, why not give him bells to ring and pistols to shoot off?"

But Hugh Jennings wasn't only about bells and whistles. He brought the 1890s Orioles' scrappy approach to the game to the previously tame sixth-place Tigers. He installed the twenty-year-old Ty Cobb in right field and turned him loose on the bases, a display of confidence that Cobb credited with launching his spectacular career. The Tigers were playing the fastest, most scientific "inside game" of any of the western clubs.

The renewed Athletics split the Detroit series, Rube Waddell taking both their losses. In the opener on June 18 he blew up in a 5-run fifth. In the fourth game his clumsiness fielding bunts cost them the game.

After going 9-5 against the west, the A's took 5 in a row from the league doormats, the Nationals, and edged past Detroit into third place. They didn't stay long; in Boston they lost 3 out of 4—and Jack Coombs. On June 27 the right-hander tore a tendon that threatened to put him on the sidelines for the rest of the year. Jimmy Dygert went in cold from the bench and gave up a run-scoring hit in the 1–0 loss. With Coombs out and Bender nursing a lame arm, Mack recalled right-hander Bill Bartley. Plank and Dygert were his only reliable pitchers. Mack was fed up with Rube Waddell, but he had to use him when Rube wasn't off on a binge.

On July 4 the standings were:

Chicago 43–23
Cleveland 42–26
Philadelphia 37–29
Detroit 35–28

The A's had an unusual one-day stop in Detroit on July 5. Dygert was knocked out in the sixth. Mack sent in Waddell, who acted as if he wished he was someplace else. He pitched the last 3 innings like batting practice. Mack sat on the bench and lit into him every time Rube came off the field. Waddell ignored him. That night on the train to Chicago Mack said he was ready to peddle the Rube. But the writers were skeptical. Connie had been talking that way since April. And every time he did, the good, even the great, Rube showed up. Maybe that's why Mack said it. On July 11 in St. Louis, Rube relieved Dygert in the seventh and picked up the win. Two days later he pitched a 5-hitter.

When Bender said he felt better, he began a streak of 11 wins, never giving up more than 2 runs in a game. When he finally lost one, to Chicago on August 21, it was by a 1–0 score.

Mack was desperately looking for pitching help. He sent Al Maul scouting in New England and Jack Coombs to look over the American Association. They turned up nobody. Back home John Shibe signed a young southpaw, George Craig, off the sandlots.

Before returning home, the A's lost 3 in Detroit. In one game Mack used three pitchers in 3 innings, Bartley and Craig among them. (Bartley pitched 2 complete games without a decision; they were both ties.) Mack picked up pitcher Sam Hope from Newark. Hope faced 4 batters, retired 1. That was the end of Hope.

Then they came home and won 13 of 16 against the west. Two of the losses came on successive Saturdays, when the erratic Rube Waddell showed up and threw away a game to Chicago and another to the crippled Naps. In between he went on a week-long spree to Atlantic City. The writers were making jokes about him. The fans began to boo him. The Rube didn't read the papers, but the fans' hostility hurt him. He had already turned over more leaves than an October nor'easter, but he vowed to turn over another new one.

His teammates were fed up with him too. It's doubtful that they let down in their play when he pitched, as has been written. They were in a pennant race and were out to win every game. But the turmoil was a distraction. They took their concerns to Connie Mack and asked him to get rid of the Rube.

Mack wasn't ready to let Waddell go. He knew that the left-hander was healthy and unbeatable on his good days. His pitching staff was thin, with Coombs sidelined and Bender on and off the sick list. But he didn't use that approach with his boys.

He appealed to their pocketbooks. At home and on the road Waddell was still a big attraction. Attendance was higher whenever he was expected to pitch. "The Rube is a great drawing card," Mack told them. "Without him, the gate will fall off. If the gate falls off, I won't be able to keep up my present salary list. If you boys are willing to take a cut in your salaries, I'll let him go."

They decided to put up with Rube and his shenanigans for now.

Connie Mack was awake early as usual on Labor Day morning, September 2. He didn't have to look out the window to hear that it was raining hard, something else that was all too usual in this cold, wet summer. It didn't matter that the tail-end Washington Nationals were the opposition that day. The Athletics were in a tight battle for the pennant. The Tigers held a 1-game lead over them, with Chicago another ½ game back and Cleveland 2½ behind Detroit. So with a break in the weather, A's rooters might fill the seats and half the outfield for both the morning and afternoon games.

After breakfast Mack walked to his office. The rain had eased by then; it gradually let up until, at ten o'clock, the grounds crew set to work making the field playable. Mack took a chance on Coombs, who wasn't yet fully recovered from his torn tendon. Jawn gave it everything he had for 6 innings but lost, 3–1. That afternoon any doubts that the Athletics needed a bigger place of business were demonstrably dispelled. They had to close the gates an hour before game time, leaving at least five thousand disappointed customers scrambling to find a way in or over the fences. The rookie "Idaho Wonder" Walter Johnson took a 2–1 lead over Eddie Plank into the ninth, when Collins and Oldring singled. Cross, pinch hitting for Powers, put down a bunt that Johnson picked up and threw into right field. The winning runs scored amid the joyous bedlam of the huge crowd.

The sun shone and the A's made hay for the rest of the week. They regained first place and pulled in just shy of one hundred thousand fans, culminating in a Saturday mob with an estimated fifteen thousand left in the streets around the park when the entrances were pushed shut.

Connie Mack was mindful of his experience down the stretch in 1905, when his pitchers had been overworked and worn out. But he had a rusty Jack Coombs, who said he was ready to work again; an unreliable Rube Waddell; an inexperienced Bill Bartley; and a Bender whose arm or innards could go bad at any time. Plank and Dygert couldn't do it all.

Sturdy as he looked, Eddie Plank was vulnerable. Martin Lawler ministered to his arm and shoulder and gave him more attention than any other pitcher. But there was nothing the trainer could do to alleviate Plank's mental exhaustion. Nobody expended more mental and emotional energy in a game than the fidgeting, concentrating, conniving Gettysburg Eddie. His time-consuming puttering before throwing a pitch, his mind calculating the whole time, was as wearing on him as on the impatient batter, umpire, and fans. Silk O'Loughlin asked Ban Johnson to do something to curb the dilatory tactics of pitchers like Plank who were causing games to drag on past two hours.

Doubleheaders loomed. The A's would be pitching by committee. Everybody who was healthy might be called on to start or relieve on any day.

They spent the week of September 9 playing eight games against Boston. Two of them went 13 innings: a classic Waddell-Young 0–0 tie when the very, very good Rube showed up, and four days later a 6–6 tie in which the horrid Rube was gone by the fourth, and Coombs, Bartley, and Plank worked the rest of the game.

In one of their two losses that week, Jack Knight came back to bite them with a game-winning home run off Bender. Meanwhile, the Browns took 3 out of 4 from Detroit while Cleveland was beating Chicago. By Sunday night the A's led both Chicago and Detroit by 3. Except for four games in Washington, they were home for the rest of the season. They were a great home club—50-20—while breaking even on the road. Connie Mack exuded confidence. The players were spending their World Series money. "The pennant is won," declared Horace Fogel. Ed Bang of the *Cleveland News* conceded the flag to Connie Mack. Philadelphia papers began to speculate on pitching matchups against the National League runaway winners, the Cubs.

Then the most calamitous week in the Athletics' seven-year history fell upon them. Jimmy Collins was limping with a bum knee. Bender's arm went lame again. Harry Davis had a sore hip, could hardly run, and couldn't slide at all. Trying to give Plank and Dygert a rest, Mack started Coombs. He was kayoed in the first by New York. Mack used Bartley and Craig to mop up in the 17-hit assault. The A's lost 2 while Detroit was taking 2 from Chicago.

And it rained on Wednesday and Thursday and Monday, a total of three games washed away. The only two they played, they split with St. Louis. An earlier strategic move by Connie Mack now backfired on him. The scheduling of makeup games was up to the home team. At times when his pitching was thin, Mack had deliberately not rescheduled rainouts to avoid doubleheaders. Two games against New York had been rained out in May. Mack could have made them up then but didn't, to save his pitchers. A July 29 rainout with St. Louis could have been played on any of the next three days or in September, but it wasn't. An August 9 rainout with Detroit could have been played the next day but wasn't. When it rained in late September, there were no more opportunities to reschedule those games. As a result, nine rainouts and ties were never made up. Detroit had four games cancelled; the A's would finish the season with five fewer decisions than the Tigers. (Another consequence was a rule change requiring rainouts and ties to be made up at the earliest possible dates beginning in 1908.)

Connie Mack had hoped to clinch the pennant by Friday, September 27, giving him more than a week to rest his pitchers. But on that Friday morning, with the Tigers in town for three games, the A's lead was onion-skin thin: .6058 to .6056.

Two umpires worked the series, "Messrs. O'Loughlin and Connolly," as the box scores identified umpires. The British-born Tommy Connolly, five-foot-six and weighing maybe 130, was undemonstrative, shouting his ball and strike calls in a loud clear voice without gestures. Silk O'Loughlin played to the grandstand, thrusting his right thumb back over his shoulder while yelling "Strrrriiiike" and his trademark "Tuh" for strike two in a tenor that rivaled Irish troubadour John McCormack. Players making fun of his vocal histrionics faced an early shower. "Silk was fierce and fiery on the ball field when the occasion demanded," said umpire George Moriarty. "Physically, Silk couldn't open a can of peas, but his moral courage made him a giant in a tight spot during a ball game."

Connie Mack respected O'Loughlin's honesty, but he had cast doubts on Silk's "moral courage" following an incident in 1906 that led to the forfeiture of a Labor Day game in New York. Mack never lodged an official protest, but, significantly, O'Loughlin hadn't been assigned to Philadelphia for a year.

The A's lost the game and the lead to Detroit on Friday, 5–4. Plank outpitched Bill Donovan, but outstanding fielding and timely hitting by Germany Schaefer and Sam Crawford and a costly error by Jimmy Collins beat them. The A's had 13 hits but left 12 on base.

Saturday it rained. Sunday they rested. Monday morning people began gathering around Columbia Park hours before the showdown doubleheader would begin at two o'clock. And they never stopped gathering, first by the hundreds, then the thousands. The last ticket was sold and the gates pushed shut shortly before noon. The more agile who were left outside scrambled over the beer ads on the outside of the right-field fence and spilled onto the field. A human battering ram massed behind center field on Columbia Avenue and broke down the fence. Thousands more perched on rooftops along Twenty-ninth Street. Not a blade of grass was visible beneath the throng behind the outfield ropes.

The official attendance of 24,127 was a record for a major league game. In the years to come, when those who were there spun tales to their children and grandchildren about baseball in the good old days, this would be the day most often remembered. Ty Cobb called it the greatest game he ever played in.

Great doesn't equate with well played. The A's made 6 errors; Detroit made 7. But for excitement, drama, and controversy in the crucible of a fierce pennant race, this game rates as great.

Connie Mack needed two wins that day. Anything less would enable the Tigers to begin the final week with at least a 1-game lead and only the second division Nationals and Browns as opposition. The A's faced three tough games with Cleveland before ending the season in Washington.

Whatever stirred inside him, Connie Mack showed nothing but his customary calm as he took his usual seat in the middle of the bench, scorecard and pencil in his right hand, left elbow on his knee, his chin resting in his left hand. However long the game might last, he wouldn't budge from that spot. Nobody had ever seen him go to the water bucket for a drink during a game, even on the hottest days. He might use a little body English to coax a ball fair or foul or into an outfielder's glove. If he became nervous or excited, his bony rear end might shift back and forth on the bench; the seat of his trousers wore out long before the cuffs frayed.

Wild Bill Donovan, who was 6–1 against the A's so far this year, and Jimmy Dygert were the pitchers. Both were considered well rested; Dygert hadn't pitched since Thursday, Donovan since Friday. The Athletics knew that Donovan often grew stronger as a game went along. Before the game, Connie Mack reminded them, "Go to it, boys. Bang away."

Mack's expression was probably the only one in Columbia Park that didn't change while the A's scored 3 runs off Donovan in the first.

Pitching with an early lead seemed to unnerve Dygert. After Rossman led off the second with a single, Coughlin hit a comebacker to Dygert, who made a bad throw to second. Everybody was safe. Schmidt sacrificed them to second and third. O'Leary hit another tapper to the pitcher. Instead of going for the out at first, Dygert went after Rossman, who was halfway home. Dygert chased him toward the plate, then fired the ball to Schreck at the last instant. The ball bounced off Schreck's chest protector, and Rossman scored. The rattled pitcher then walked Donovan on four pitches.

Mack could see disaster coming. He had to get Dygert out of there. But who to bring in? He needed Plank for the second game. Coombs had been too erratic to trust in this spot. There was nobody but Rube. Mack could only hope the good Waddell would show up. He sent him in and stopped squirming when Rube struck out Jones and Schaefer to end the inning.

The A's continued to pound Donovan, scoring 2 in the third, while Waddell stifled the Tigers. In the fifth, Harry Davis hit a home run over the right-field fence. The fans' cheering and foot-stomping rocked the wooden grandstand. Jimmy Collins hit a fly deep into the crowd, then Oldring hit one to the edge of the crowd in left. Davy Jones backed up to the ropes but stopped short of reaching over them. The ball dropped at the feet of the first rank of standees, well within his reach. Collins scored. It was now 7–1.

Ty Cobb said, "When [Jones] came back to the bench our players were so mad they practically tore the uniform off his back."

Later there was speculation over why Jennings left Donovan in so long. He had plenty of able pitchers. Connie Mack offered a sentimental explanation to Fred Lieb. "We hit Donovan hard enough in the early innings to drive two pitchers out of the box. But Bill was a Philadelphian, and whenever he worked at Columbia Park, his father, brothers, a lot of relatives and friends came out to see him pitch. And if we had made twenty runs off him that day, Hughie wouldn't have taken Bill out; he wouldn't hurt Donovan's feelings before his people."

Maybe. It's doubtful that Jennings would have risked a pennant for Donovan's feelings. He may have figured that the way Waddell was throwing, the game was lost, so why use another pitcher. Donovan was the gamest pitcher he had and may have refused to come out if he was asked. The most likely explanation came from Donovan himself. He had been hit hard in Friday's game but won because none of the hits came at the right time to beat him. All during that game he suspected that one or both of the Athletics' coaches were reading his catcher's signs. They were experts at that. Down 7–1 now, he was convinced that they were still reading them. He may have told Jennings, who replaced his catcher, Schmidt, with Fred

Payne after the fifth inning. Payne was a .166 hitter, but he had a better arm and head than Schmidt. Payne and Donovan huddled and changed their entire sign system. That's when Donovan "suddenly braced," "suddenly settled," as various writers reported it.

The Tigers got to Waddell for 4 runs in the seventh, but it wasn't the Rube who blew up. He gave up a hit and a walk and should have been out of the inning without a run scoring. Donovan led off and hit an easy fly ball that Oldring dropped. Jones walked. Schaefer hit a double play ball right at Nicholls at short. He booted it. Crawford walloped a double into the crowd. Cobb's groundout scored Schaefer. Rossman's groundout scored Crawford. The A's led, 7–5. They scored a run in the bottom of the seventh; Detroit scored 1 in the eighth. It was now 8–6.

Given Connie Mack's pattern of using his pitchers, he would have likely brought in Bender at this point, as he had done so often that year. But Bender had an ailing wing. Waddell had been effective for 7 innings. He wasn't clowning. And the Tigers had three left-handers coming up to bat. One of them, Crawford, was killing them, but Cobb was hitless.

Crawford singled to center to start the ninth. Cobb stood in, leaning over the plate. Waddell shot a fastball up over the inside corner. Cobb took it. Afterwards, Rube said he guessed Cobb would be looking for the next one outside, so he threw another one up and in. Cobb outguessed Rube and was looking for the same pitch again. He stepped back from the plate and whacked it over the right-field fence to tie the game. The impact hit Connie Mack like an earthquake. He slid so far on the bench that he tumbled into the bats lined up on the ground in front of him.

Mr. Mack picked himself up and nodded to Eddie Plank to go in to pitch. If he held them here and the A's could score in the last of the ninth, Eddie could still start the second game. If this one went longer, there probably wouldn't be enough daylight to play a second game. Mack sent Doc Powers in to replace Schreck behind the plate. Plank ended the inning with no more damage.

But the Detroit battery's change of signs had quieted the A's attack. Donovan's speed never slowed nor his curves dulled. Both teams scored a run in the eleventh. Plank pitched out of a 3 on, 2 out spot in the twelfth. Nobody threatened in the thirteenth.

In the bottom of the fourteenth, Harry Davis lifted a high fly into left-center field. Sam Crawford raced along the ropes directly toward a blue-uniformed policeman sitting on an upturned soda crate. The cop jumped up to get out of his way just as Crawford and the ball arrived. The ball fell into the crowd just beyond the ropes and Crawford's glove. Davis stood on second. The crowd roared.

So did the Tigers. They swarmed around Silk O'Loughlin at home plate, demanding that interference be called. As the chief umpire, O'Loughlin had to make the call, even though he was far from the action and probably had a worse view than the players on the bench. All the A's were on the field, claiming the policeman had been trying to get out of Crawford's way. Topsy Hartsel reported to Mack that O'Loughlin told him he had seen no interference. Mack remained calm, satisfied that that was the way it would stand. But the Tigers kept arguing. Thousands of feet stomped on the floorboards of the grandstand. The noise was deafening.

O'Loughlin made no sign, no gesture, indicating a decision. Meanwhile, out near second base, little Tommy Connolly stood quietly. Why O'Loughlin waited so long—or maybe it just seemed so long—is a mystery, but he finally walked out to Connolly at second base and asked, "Was there interference, Tommy?"

"There was," replied Connolly without hesitating.

Only then did O'Loughlin raise his right hand and declare Davis out. Well. That really set the flint to the fuse. Somebody said something to somebody, and fists began flying on the field. Monte Cross and Claude Rossman squared off. That brought more police and some spectators into the melee. Somebody reportedly called Connolly "You Irish immigrant." That was mild compared to what Connie Mack was yelling at Silk O'Loughlin. He hadn't been so mad since the day he cussed out Hank O'Day and was ejected back in 1895.

When the field was finally cleared, with Cross and Rossman banished, Danny Hoffman hit a long single that would have scored Davis easily with the winning run. It went for naught except to rub a little salt into Connie Mack's wounded heart.

After 17 innings it was almost six o'clock and almost dark. Silk O'Loughlin called the game. Connie Mack was still seething. In a rage he invaded the umpires' dressing room looking for O'Loughlin, not Connolly.

"Poking one of those bony fingers at O'Loughlin," Fred Lieb wrote, "he said, 'Silk, if you will tell me why you told Hartsel you saw no interference, and then changed your mind, I will take back everything I said.'

"Silk made no reply."

In retrospect, it seems obvious why O'Loughlin made the call as he did after conferring with the umpire who was closest to the play. But it isn't clear why he didn't say so at the time. Whether that exchange between manager and umpire actually took place as Lieb described, the incident shook O'Loughlin. When O'Loughlin died in 1918, the manager of the Philadelphia hotel where he had stayed revealed that he had called on the umpire in his room that evening to hear his version of the play. "Silk told his story, and at the finish broke down and fell to his knees. Making a gesture upward, he said, 'Before God, I was right.'"

Connie Mack went home that day believing he had been the victim of a felony. He obtained affidavits from the policeman and spectators in the vicinity of the alleged crime. He publicly called O'Loughlin a "robber" and was publicly rebuked for it.

The *Detroit News-Tribune* expressed surprise at the vehemence of Mack's outburst. "If Connie Mack has made his statement blindly and in the heat of anger he should be the one made to suffer. This is the first time a magnate has deliberately impeached the integrity of an umpire. Mack probably spoke too hastily. . . . Mack is the last man in the league thought to make such an attack on an umpire. No matter what decisions are rendered Connie takes them philosophically as a rule and never makes a kick."

Francis C. Richter, usually a stolid Mack booster, defended O'Loughlin as "honest, courageous, and called it as he saw it."

O'Loughlin was in Chicago during the World Series that fall and told the *Chicago American*, "I have been accused of being crooked by Mack and I will allow no man to get away with that no matter if I never umpire another game of ball as long as I live. I put it up to Mr. Johnson to look into the matter and I feel sure that I shall get justice."

The matter came up at the league meeting in December. Ban Johnson disposed of it by suggesting that managers be more careful in what they say in the future.

The Athletics never forgot it. Thereafter they would draw a thumb for slipping in a reference to it while arguing with O'Loughlin over a call they didn't like. A deep frost set in between Connie Mack and Silk O'Loughlin. The two stubborn Irishmen never spoke to each other again. According to George Moriarty,

In the summer of 1918, just prior to a game one day, Connie Mack invited me to umpire a benefit game which the Athletics were to play at the shipyards in Philadelphia. Connie also asked me to persuade Silk, with whom I was teamed at the time, to officiate in this game with me. Connie stated he would have extended a personal invitation to Silk, but presumed Silk would frown upon it. After the game I conveyed Connie's request to Silk, but the latter appeared stunned and surprised. A full minute seemed to pass before Silk answered, and in those fleeting seconds I thought I saw a great change in his expression. He was spanning the events that led back to that hectic afternoon in 1907, and was dropping a gigantic burden he had been carrying for those eleven years. Silk, the great little gentleman-warrior, accepted the invitation, and seemed willing to bridge the chasm of bitterness that intervened.

The following day, Silk asked my opinion of the estrangement between himself and Connie. He told me he had suffered untold agonies and remorse over the affair. . . . I realized the American League deplored the break between these two men and felt the moment of reconciliation was imminent. . . . I explained it to Silk in that manner. At first he was inclined to be adamant, but he finally became acquiescent to a point where he said at the start of next season he would shake hands with Connie, and let bygones be bygones.

The handshake never took place. That winter the influenza epidemic took Silk O'Loughlin.

In the last week of the 1907 season, Jimmy Dygert pitched 3 shutouts in four days, giving him 21 wins for the year, but the A's were unable to catch up with Detroit. Plank lost twice; the Tigers won 5 of their last 7 and finished 1½ games in front.

Connie Mack always maintained the disputed decision had cost him the game and the 1907 pennant. But other factors cost the A's that game: 6 errors, Topsy Hartsel being picked off second after a lead-off double, Ty Cobb outguessing Rube Waddell. As for the pennant, the loss of Bender for the last three weeks, the injury to Coombs, Rube Waddell's consistent inconsistency, the nine games that were never made up—any one of these factors was enough to make the difference. That the Athletics were able to hang on so close to the leaders to the end was a tribute to Mack and his players, who never gave up. "Keep plugging; we'll get 'em yet," Mack exhorted his men, and they had responded.

In a 1943 *Atlantic Monthly* article, Connie Mack said, "The worst mistake I ever made was back in 1907, running nip-and-tuck with Detroit. I had a pitcher named Jimmy Dygert who could beat anyone for seven innings, then he was finished. If I had found this out in time I could have won the pennant. I didn't realize it until after the season."

It's difficult to reconcile this statement with Dygert's 21-8 record and strong finish. But Dygert had completed only 18 of his 28 starts—64 percent, about the same as Waddell and well below the league average of 74 percent. Bender completed 20 of 24 starts, Plank 33 of 40, so Mack may have been using them as his standard for Dygert, a standard few pitchers could meet.

At the end of that hectic, frustrating, disappointing final week of the season, Connie Mack was exhausted. And it showed. "He is a hard worker," said a Detroit writer, "and the work tells on him."

Even the local writers, who did nothing but watch and report what they saw, were worn out. "I never put in such a season of hard labor before," moaned Horace Fogel. "To tell the truth I was all but down and out before the end came and could scarcely hold myself together till the finish, when I had to hie myself out to the country for a brief rest."

But Philadelphia newspapers no longer presented a solid corps of support. The Record charged that baseball's pennant races had been rigged to boost attendance for the past two years. Ben Shibe angrily denounced the charges. Philadelphia fans had no problem putting Ben Shibe's reputation for honesty above that of the Record's writers, Ray Ziegler and A. M. Gilliam.

Despite the rains and cancelled games, the Athletics had enjoyed another prosperous season. Attendance was up 130,000 to 625,581—almost 10,000 a game—a record for the city.

After ending the season in Washington on Saturday, October 5, Connie Mack left for Worcester on Tuesday to visit Tom, his wife Alice, and their three-year-old daughter Helen. They lived in the Franklin Hotel. Helen's favorite uncle, Connie was always a welcome visitor, but this was not just a social visit.

The Franklin was about a mile from the Holy Cross campus, where the Crusaders' ball field was located. For three years Tom had been watching the school's shortstop, Jack Barry, and sending his brother reports on him.

Born in Meriden, Connecticut, where Connie Mack had begun his professional career, Barry was the epitome of Mack's kind of ballplayer. "In the critical stages of the game is where Barry would shine," recalled his college coach, Pat Carney, "both at bat and in the field: cool, a quick thinker and game as a pebble. Barry seldom failed to save a close game for us with an exhibition of some of the finest fielding I have ever seen, or to win a close game for us with one of his timely hits.

"Barry had a wonderful arm, could throw from any position, and fielded his position in great shape. He was equally good going to his right or left for ground balls, could go in fast for slow hit balls, go back well for fly balls, and in taking a throw at second base for a double play, could complete it quicker than any ball player I have ever seen. He was a marvel of speed even at that time."

Barry was a leader, captain-elect of the 1908 team. Of course, a star like Barry didn't go unnoticed. Other scouts saw him too and were ready to sign him after graduation.

Connie Mack didn't wait that long. The practice of signing college players before their final collegiate season was common. A letter he wrote in April 1908 to third baseman Larry Gardner at the University of Vermont illustrates Mack's approach. In it he offered Gardner a contract for $300 a month, with one month paid in advance, to join the Athletics after graduation. Mack assured Gardner that his senior year of baseball would not be jeopardized because "it will not be necessary for anyone but you and I to know that you have signed." (Gardner eventually signed with the Red Sox.)

Tom invited Jack Barry to meet his brother at the hotel. It helped that Coach Carney was a former outfielder for the Boston Nationals and knew Connie Mack's reputation as a manager and teacher. Carney urged Barry to talk to Mack, "for I knew that Connie was a great manager for a young player to sign up with," Carney wrote.

At the meeting Barry threw Connie Mack a curve. He wanted a bonus to sign. "It's not my policy to pay bonuses," Mack said. Barry said he wanted $500. Mack knew other teams would gladly pay it. He agreed but requested of Barry, "Don't say anything about it." (Barry never did; long after all the participants were deceased, Jack Barry's nephew revealed the story to the author.)

Barry agreed to report after the 1908 Holy Cross season and graduation. Connie Mack put the signed contract in his safe and headed for California for three months to rest and look for another reliable left-hander.

Stopping for a few days in Chicago, Mack gave no hint that Rube Waddell's days in an Athletics uniform were numbered. "One thing is certain," he told a reporter, "we will not let Rube Waddell go yet. The big southpaw is too valuable a man to dispose of and his arm is too good for a long time yet if it remains as good as it was for the best part of last summer. I must admit that Waddell is not the easiest man in the world to get along with. He needs constant attention and watching. He is far from being foolish, however, for he knows how far he can go at any time and still be within bounds. When he's working well, he needs the most watching. When he is not in good form he is on his good behavior. We may get some youngsters for next season but no change will be made in the regular team."

Meanwhile, some of the Athletics had organized a week's barnstorming tour in Pennsylvania and New Jersey. Led by Harry Davis, they invited Rube Waddell to join them. It wasn't unanimous. Fairly or not, some of them blamed Rube for costing them the pennant with his unreliability during the season and for that ninth-inning home run of Cobb's. But Rube was the magnet that would draw the crowds, so they took him along.

Before they started, everybody agreed that no money would be divided until the tour ended and all expenses had been paid. Everything went smoothly until they reached Williamsport, the next to last stop, on Friday, October 11. There, as Mack put it, "Schreck was seized with a thirst." Osee talked Rube into demanding their share of the money then and there.

Thirty years later Mack related the story to John Kieran of the *New York Times*. "They had a meeting and by George it was pretty serious. Harry Davis was the one who was taking care of the money and he wouldn't give it up. Rube, egged on by Schreck, was ready to fight for it. There were a lot of big strong fellows—Bender and Davis and Murphy and Rube and Schreck—and for a time it looked like half my team would be killed off."

Davis and the rest held their ground. Waddell left the team and went home.

Winning bred tolerance for Rube's peccadilloes; losing dissolved it. As much as he valued harmony, Connie Mack knew that arguments, fights, and temper tantrums were bound to occur during a long season. He also knew that a talented team could overcome cliques, jealousies, even animosities, and still win. But he believed that a team could win just as handily and a lot more happily without those distractions. When he learned about the Williamsport blowup, he realized that the hostility felt by his players and the public toward Rube Waddell had become too deeply rooted to ignore. The Rube had to go.

Mack was certain there were a lot more strikeouts in the thirty-one-year-old Waddell's amazing left arm "when he was right." Other managers believed it too. But they were also aware of what they'd have to put up with if they acquired Waddell. So when Mack tried to trade him, nobody offered an acceptable player in exchange. In the end he had to settle for cash, which he needed less than a dependable arm. On February 6 the St. Louis Browns paid $7,500 for Waddell, confident that they would get it back at the gate whenever he pitched. They were right.

Connie Mack was genuinely sorry to see Rube depart. He always maintained that "Waddell had more on the ball than any man that ever lived." But it was more than that. For all the gray hairs Waddell gave him, Mack missed him like a father misses a favorite child who gave him the most joy as well as the most trouble. "I never had a dull moment while he was on my payroll," Mack said, "but I always liked him for all that."

In 1914, when Rube Waddell lay dying of tuberculosis in a San Antonio sanitarium, Connie Mack saw to it that Rube had the best medical care and the A's paid all the bills. Rube's sister, whose husband was a Western Union manager, kept Mack informed of Rube's condition.

Mack was in Raleigh when he learned of Rube's death on April 1, 1914. He told reporters, "Waddell was the greatest pitcher in the game, and although widely known for his eccentricities, was more sinned against than sinned. He was the best hearted man on the team and every man whom he came in contact with will verify my statement. If a teammate was sick, Rube was the first man to see him and the last to leave. If he had money it went to some gift or offering for the sick man. He made my team, and every follower of the White Elephant banner in this city knows this in his heart. He came to Philadelphia a stranger but entered into the spirit of the city and tried with all his heart to bring pennants there. He may have failed us at times, but to him I and the other owners of the Philadelphia ball club owe much. The pennants of 1902 and 1905 were won for us mainly through the efforts of the Rube, and if he had not been injured in that straw hat incident at the close of the latter season we would have won that world championship from the Giants in a walk. He was badly injured, too. I cannot say how sorry I am to hear this news."

Three months later Waddell's battery mate and playmate, Osee Schrecengost, died in Philadelphia.

In 1923, when John McGraw advised Mack that Rube's grave in San Antonio had no suitable marker, they raised the money to install a granite monument.

While scouting in California in November 1907, Connie Mack confronted a mother who didn't want her son to be a ballplayer. As he did wherever he went, Mack had won many friends on his previous trips to San Francisco. One of them, Chief Deputy Coroner Peter McCormack, thought of Mack while watching a local left-hander, Harry Krause, pitch for playground teams and then for St. Mary's College, where he was now a senior. Mack had also been tipped off to Krause by another Irishman, Josh Reilly, a San Franciscan who had played briefly in the National League when Mack was managing the Pirates. Reilly, a third baseman with the San Jose club, wrote to Mack advising him to sign Krause, who wanted $400 a month. Mack sent Reilly a 1908 contract for that amount and a $200 check in advance to bind the deal and asked Reilly to get Krause's signature. He received no reply.

Soon after he arrived, Mack saw Krause pitch for St. Mary's against a team from Honolulu. After the game he asked the pitcher why he had not signed the contract. Krause told him his mother wanted him to finish college before he even thought about becoming a ballplayer. Mack visited Mrs. Krause and assured her that Harry's studies would not be interrupted. He wouldn't have to report to the Athletics until after graduation. With that promise, Harry signed. Mack also signed an outfielder from the University of California, Heinie Heitmuller, and acquired catcher Syd Smith from Atlanta and right-handers Nick Carter and Vic Schlitzer from the Class B New York State League, where Schlitzer had won 27 for Utica. Between draft fees and purchases, he spent almost $12,000 on minor leaguers.

Mack was back in Philadelphia in time for the writers' banquet on February 24, 1908, honoring Monte Cross, who was leaving to manage Kansas City. Two days later the A's left Broad Street station at 3:55 for New Orleans, where they would stay for two weeks. Among the group was Joseph

C. Ohl, the new traveling secretary. Ohl fit right in with the Athletics. He was a talkative, good-natured optimist who fielded complaints as smoothly as Nap Lajoie handled line drives. Ohl's sideline made him even more interesting to Connie Mack: he managed two prize fighters.

Among the missing was Eddie Collins, down with pneumonia in Tarrytown.

They arrived in New Orleans on Friday, worked out on Saturday, and played their first practice game on Sunday. Jimmy Collins, after a winter of rigorous training at home in Buffalo, reported twenty-five pounds lighter, his bum knee completely healed, and displayed all his old agility. Without Rube Waddell, it was a calm, uneventful spring. The weather was good, but the water was bad. When Mack and Rube Oldring took sick from it, the club brought in bottled water. Doc Powers picked up an ear infection while swimming in the salt water pool at the Young Men's Gymnastic Club and went home to recover. Then Socks Seybold tore up a knee sliding and went home on crutches.

Mack considered his options. He could move Danny Murphy to right field and put Si Nicholls on second and Collins, when he recovered, at short. Coombs could play the outfield until his sore arm healed.

Then they went on the road for two weeks, heading north. Sizing up the pennant race, Mack considered the Tigers the team to beat. They were young, fast, and powerful, with a proven pitching staff. The emergence of Ty Cobb as the most dynamic force in the league gave them a dimension no other team could match. Starting only his third season, Cobb was already the nonpareil of baseball, against whom future phenoms would be measured and hyped as the next Cobb.

"Cobb twisted the American League into knots with his audacious batting and baserunning," Mack said. "His fire on the ball field was amazing, his spirit undaunted. He was never beaten."

Mack knew the youngsters he was bringing along were nowhere near ready. His only chance to be in the race was to get off to a fast start, open a big lead, and hope it held up when the inevitable late-season wilting occurred.

They opened the season with eleven games against New York and Boston. As usual, it was cold and wet. As usual, Bender was sick, this time with a heavy cold. Plank needed warmer weather to pitch at his best. Mack decided to use his veterans sparingly until May. His opening day pitcher in New York was Nick Carter. Rube Vickers, back for another chance after posting a 25-9 record at Williamsport, started the second game, and Vic Schlitzer the third. They lost 2 of the 3 but pitched well. Carter lost, 1–0, in 12 innings. Vickers lost a 4-hitter, 2–1. Schlitzer won, 8–2. In those first eleven games, they were 6-5.

Mack placed his hopes for a fast getaway on those three arms plus Jimmy Dygert. They worked just about every day, often two or three of them in a game. Vickers took over the workhorse role; starting and relieving he appeared in 53 games, second to Ed Walsh's 66. Vickers gave Mack 300 innings of work.

"If the pitching doesn't break down, nothing can stop us," Mack declared. It didn't turn out that way. The hitting broke down first, then the fielding and base running, although the A's pulled off the club's first triple steal, led by Harry Davis, on April 27, and the next day turned a nifty triple play. But generally they played ragged ball. Mistakes on the bases cost them some games; errors cost others. Game after game they had 3 hits, 2 hits, 6 hits. Even when they won, they might do it with only 3 hits. The pitchers began to believe they had to throw a shutout to have a chance to win, and even then they might earn nothing but a draw. It was only a matter of time before they collapsed under the strain.

The outfield was never settled. A still wobbly Eddie Collins played right and center, as did Jack Coombs. Mack bought Jack Fox from Memphis, tried five-foot-five Herbie Moran, signed Frank Shaughnessy when the short-lived independent Union League folded in May. Sometimes Danny Murphy patrolled the outfield.

The infield didn't come together either. Collins and Nicholls shifted between second and shortstop. Mack dipped down to Monroe in the Cotton States League to buy Frank Manush, older (by eighteen years) brother of Heinie Manush. And it was still only May. By the end of the year thirty-seven players would wear an Athletics uniform, nineteen of them making their major league debuts.

The A's won against the tail-end Highlanders and Nationals but couldn't beat the western teams, at home or on the road. On the Browns' first visit to Columbia Park, Rube Waddell's return drew more than twenty thousand on a Tuesday afternoon. He had a grand time beating his old teammates, 5–2. On July 29 he struck out 16 of them, tying the league record. It took the A's until August 14 to win one from him.

By mid-June the Athletics' team batting average was .206, last in the league. Yet they stayed in the pennant race. All hopes of sprinting out of the gate to a commanding lead had vanished. But nobody else was sprinting either. The A's were in the pack with the four western clubs in a race so close you could cover the first six teams with a one-cent stamp. They were actually in first place on Sunday morning, June 7. They dipped to second that afternoon, when they had only 2 hits in a typical 1–0 loss. The next day Waddell blanked them, 10–0, and they tumbled all the way to fifth, only ½ game from the top. They lost 7 in a row, 4 by shutouts, and fell to sixth, still only 5½ games out of first. The White Sox jumped from seventh to first in four days as the start of a 13-game winning streak put them into the lead despite their being just 3 games over .500.

The slim margins between the teams didn't delude Connie Mack. He knew his Athletics couldn't keep pace with the younger, more aggressive western clubs. And they didn't. By the end of June they fell 6 games behind the league-leading Browns. It was time to concentrate on the future.

Connie Mack's baseball school was now in session. The headmaster, whose boys esteemed him as a paternal influence as much as an employer, was now forty-five years old, the oldest manager in the league except for Joe Cantillon, forty-six, in Washington. He had been a manager for fourteen years. Creating champions out of raw young talent was still his favorite part of the business. He had the backing of his partner and enough resources to absorb the nearly 30 percent drop in attendance that 1908 would bring. He had the patience to endure the mistakes and errors that green players make while they learn. At the same time Mack understood one of baseball's enduring truths: nobody could ever know beforehand how a rookie would adapt to the major leagues.

The morning practices belonged to the youngsters. That was their time to take instructions and experiment. The afternoon games were lesson time on the bench for the newest students. Mack taught them to concentrate on what was happening on the field and learn the secrets of inside baseball. He told them he wouldn't be giving them orders, telling them what to do all the time. They would learn how to fish for themselves, to call their own signs, design plays, and execute them. Connie Mack was not afraid to make a mistake, and he created an atmosphere in which his boys would not be afraid to try plays that failed, then go back and work to perfect them or try something else.

"Players should be drilled to think for themselves," he told a writer. "If they are bright and capable they soon learn to pull together. All coaching should be done in practice. When the men are on the field lined up for the game, like actors, they should know their parts, without help from the manager on the bench. It is necessary to occasionally give advice and instructions. This is especially true when the players are at bat. On the field, any necessary help should come from the team captain."

On the bench he might say, "Watch this base runner. See if you can find out anything. Watch his hands, his feet. See if you can discover his signals for a hit and run play."

Sometimes he'd say to one rookie sitting beside him, "Watch the second baseman," and to another, "Watch the shortstop. See if you can tell which one will cover the base on a steal attempt. If you're the hitter, then you'll know where to poke the ball."

Harry Davis gave them tips on reading pitchers. Frank Smith of the White Sox was a tough spitball artist for them. One day Davis told them he noticed that every time Smith threw a spitter, he looked at the ball when he rubbed it. If he just rubbed it without looking at it, a fastball was coming. Eddie Collins picked up the knack and soon didn't need a tipster. He developed the ability to read what kind of pitch was coming by the pitcher's wrist or hand position when the ball was thrown. Pitchers who threw every ball the same way gave him the most trouble. Tip-offs didn't always help. Ed Walsh raised his eyebrows and the peak of his cap went up when he applied the slippery elm to the ball. He knew it and everybody in the league knew it, but they still couldn't hit it.

Soon the youngsters were watching everybody on the field. One of them discovered that a certain infielder had a habit of shifting a little to his right when his catcher called for a curve and to the left when a fast one was called for. All a batter had to do was glance at the infielder to know what was coming.

A sign on the left-field fence at Bennett Park in Detroit advertised the Penobscot Inn. The ad featured a large painting of an Indian's face. The eyes were made from flat pieces of tin. One day the A's pitcher was being hit hard in the first inning. As the bombardment continued, a rookie sitting beside Mr. Mack said, "I may be crazy, but it looks to me like that Indian's eyes are moving." He was right. The eyes moved to the left when a fastball was called, to the right for a curve. The A's changed their signs; the Tigers didn't score again the rest of the game. The next morning they went behind the sign and found ropes and pulleys used to move the eyes and reported it to the league. Connie Mack had taught them well.

Mack advised them to watch their own teammates too, to spot what the other team might pick up. Fidgety Eddie Plank was enough to make an alabaster bust nervous. When he first broke in, Mack and his catchers had noticed he was tipping his curve by moistening his fingers, then wiping them dry. He cured himself of the habit—most of the time. Mack taught his boys to be alert to it; whenever Plank lapsed they were to holler a reminder to him.

Hundreds of young athletes could run, throw, and hit. But if they didn't instinctively know what to do—how to play the game to win, to pick up on Mack's points and pursue them on their own—he'd let them go. Mack looked for "born" ballplayers. It only took one. He believed he could build a winning team around that one star. It didn't take him long to realize that Eddie Collins could be that kind of star.

The young Eddie Collins was all legs, "split to the navel," Branch Rickey described him. He could fly—home to first on a bunt in 3.4 seconds—but he was an awkward runner. His sliding made Connie Mack wince. The teacher didn't tell the pupil how bad he was at running the bases. He waited for the right opportunity. Then, one day when Ty Cobb was on first base, Mack said to Collins, "Eddie, did you ever notice how Cobb slides? Very nice, isn't it?"

Mack never mentioned it to Collins again. He didn't have to. He relied on Eddie's intelligence and determination to improve. And it worked. The next spring Collins spent more time in the sliding pit than anyone else. He became as elusive a base runner as Cobb.

But Collins was still a man without a position. They needed his bat in the lineup; he and Murphy were the two leading hitters, which wasn't saying much. Collins was batting around .250 at the time. Any idea of playing him in the outfield ended abruptly one day.

"It was a mean sun field," Collins recalled, "and the sun glasses hooked to my ears kept sliding down my nose. Then a high fly ball came soaring over near the line and I went for it. The glasses slipped. I stumbled, fell, and the ball whizzed past my ear to smack the earth. When I came in, Mack said, 'You better stay away from the outfield or you'll get killed.'"

Francis C. Richter, editor of *Sporting Life*, described Collins as "not at home as a second baseman; [he] loses many plays." Collins had big hands and heavy fingers, but he didn't have the arm for a shortstop or third baseman. Mack watched and thought and concluded: Danny Murphy is a better outfielder than Collins will ever be; Collins might one day become a better second baseman than Murphy will ever be. He moved Murphy to right field. Under the tutoring of Mack, Murphy, and Harry Davis, the making of a second baseman began.

Jack Barry played his last game for Holy Cross on June 16, the Crusaders defeating Williams, 5–0. The *Worcester Evening Gazette* reported that Barry had "turned down at least four other clubs and decided to cast his lot with Connie Mack, and will sign after today's game." That signing had taken place months earlier, which explains why Barry "turned down" the other clubs.

When Barry reported to Connie Mack in Philadelphia, "You'll sit on the bench and observe," Mack told him.

On the afternoon of July 4, Cy Young had a 4–2 lead over Plank. With 2 out in the last of the ninth, A's catcher Syd Smith singled. Mack motioned for Barry to run for Smith. Socks Seybold pinch hit for Plank and singled to right. Barry tore around to third, earning a word of praise for his base running from one writer. He then scored his first big league run when Topsy Hartsel hit a line drive to left.

On Monday, July 13, Mack sent him out to play second base after Nicholls was lifted for a pinch hitter in the seventh. Barry handled one chance cleanly.

Two days later Mack squirmed watching Nicholls at second and Collins at short butchering plays that cost them the first game of a doubleheader against Chicago. For the second game Mack moved Collins to second and started Barry at short. It was the debut of this keystone combination. Barry had 2 hits; the A's won, 7–2.

Not devoid of superstition, Connie Mack stayed with them the next day and they won again, 5–3. It didn't last. On Friday the Tigers handed them their worst shellacking in the club's young history, 21–3. Cobb had 5 hits. Jack Barry made 2 errors. Vickers, Schlitzer, and Maxwell, the latter drummed for 16 hits and 7 walks, took the punishment. For the rest of the season, Mack tried Barry at second, third, and short before putting him down as his future shortstop.

In the fishing port of Gloucester, Massachusetts, where only haddock and cod were caught more often than baseballs, there lived the McInnis family. The five sons were all athletes. The middle one, John, was the best. Mrs. McInnis rented out rooms to fishermen. When John was about eight, the boarders began to play ball with him. "That's the stuff, Johnny," they called out to the youngster when he made a good catch or hit.

So they began to call him Stuffy, and soon everybody was calling him Stuffy. When he was fifteen, the five-foot-eight Stuffy was the star shortstop on his high school team. A year later he played for a semipro team managed by Billy Madden, one of Connie Mack's bird dogs who seemed to be everywhere, especially in New England. Now, at seventeen, still in high school, Stuffy was playing weekdays for Haverhill in the New England League and batting .301 and weekends for an independent team in nearby Beverly. Tom Mack saw McInnis when Haverhill played at Worcester and wrote Connie about him.

Somehow Connie Mack learned that McInnis, though being paid regularly by Haverhill, had never signed the contract sent to him by the club. Mack thus considered him a free agent. He bypassed Haverhill and contacted McInnis directly. McInnis, or his father for him, signed a Philadelphia contract for 1909. When Denver tried to draft McInnis, Mack revealed that Stuffy belonged to the Athletics. Haverhill squawked, claiming that McInnis belonged to him. The club owner couldn't produce a signed contract, but he said he had written a reserve clause in Stuffy's receipt for payment.

The controversy went to the National Commission, which censured Haverhill for its conduct in using an unsigned player for more than ten days, then not placing him on its ineligible list. The commission ruled that the Philadelphia club "was clearly within its rights when it signed this player." Connie Mack's record with the National Commission, counting his loss of Nap Rucker, was now 1-1.

Much fiction posing as fact has been told or written about Joe Jackson, especially by Jackson himself, who was once described by F. C. Lane of *Baseball Magazine* as "a warm fervid imagination, which looks upon facts as hurdles to be surmounted by brief but frequent flights of fancy."

Jackson's Greenville manager, Tommy Stouch, told one story; biographers of Jackson have spun others, with varying degrees of reliability. The account that follows is based primarily on contemporary reports and recollections that seem compatible with those reports.

Early in the season, Connie Mack had heard about a nineteen-year-old outfielder who was hitting everything pitchers threw in the Carolina Association. He sent Al Maul down to Greenville, South Carolina, to look him over. Maul spotted Joe Jackson as a natural. He had a perfect swing from the left side, with an inborn sense of timing. Jackson couldn't read or write, but there wasn't anything anybody could teach him about hitting.

Swinging a 48-ounce black bat—his Black Betsy—the six-foot-one Jackson hit any pitch he could reach, wherever it was, "so hard," Larry Lajoie said, "it sounded like a bullet whizzing by."

Mill towns produced ballplayers as abundantly as textiles. When the cotton mills were in New England, every town that had a mill or a courthouse square had a team. When the mills moved south, the Carolinas became the incubators. Born and raised in South Carolina, Jackson was wearing shoes when Al Maul saw him, but everybody called him "Shoeless Joe."

In one game Jackson had 6 hits: 2 home runs, 3 triples, and a double. He was fast on the baselines and ran down fly balls all over the outfield. Maul called him "a jewel." But he was a rough-cut jewel. Three times that year he stole a base that was already occupied.

Maul also liked a Greenville pitcher, twenty-one-year-old Hyder Barr, a recent Davidson College graduate. Barr, a versatile .299 hitter, could play in the infield or outfield and had a 12-6 record as a pitcher.

In mid-July, on his scout's recommendation, Connie Mack paid $900 for Jackson and $600 for Barr; they were to report after the Carolina season ended. A Greenville correspondent for *Sporting Life* called Mack's new prize another Ty Cobb.

Jackson turned twenty on July 16. Three days later he married Katie Wynn.

Jackson and Barr arrived in Philadelphia late on the morning of Monday, August 17. They checked their bags at the station and made their way to Columbia Park. Neither one played that day. A ninth inning triple by Eddie Collins and single by Danny Murphy sent the game into extra innings. It remained tied until darkness ended it.

Barr, a "ladies' man," according to Jackson, "had taken up with some girl" and asked Joe to go back to the station and get their bags. At the station Jackson heard an "all aboard" for a train headed south. "I couldn't stand it," he said. "I went up to the window and bought a ticket to Greenville and caught that train."

When Jackson didn't show up with the luggage, Barr went to the station, found his bags, and guessed what his absent teammate had done. He told Mack, who sent one of his scouts, Sam Kennedy, to fetch Shoeless Joe. Kennedy brought him back.

Connie Mack penciled Joe in the lineup in center field for a game against Cleveland on August 24. Jackson didn't show up. On his way to the grounds, he told a writer, "I took a notion I'd like to see a show. So I hopped off the car without a word to anybody and spent the afternoon watching a burlesque performance." It looked like Connie Mack had another Rube Waddell on his hands.

Mack finally got his new prize into a game on Tuesday, August 25. Jackson dropped a fly ball in center field but made some far-ranging catches and strong throws and had a single in 4 at bats against right-handed spitballer Charles Berger. Connie Mack enthused about him to the press.

It rained for the next two days. Sitting alone in a hotel room looking out at the weeping gray sky and thinking about his bride of five weeks was too much for Joe. He got on a train and went home.

This time Mack sent the disabled Socks Seybold after him. In a story that must have reminded Mack of his travails in bringing Rube Waddell east from Los Angeles in 1902, he told Fred Lieb, "Socks got him on the train, bought Jackson's dinner for him, spent the early evening with him, saw Joe was in his berth, and then retired. But when Socks got up in the morning there was no Joe. During the night he had slipped out of his berth, got off the train at one of the stops, and worked his way down to Greenville."

A week passed before both Seybold and Jackson were back with the Athletics. Jackson played against New York on September 8 and 9, going 1 for 5 in each game. After a day off they went to Washington for a Friday doubleheader. Jackson was 0 for 4 against Walter Johnson in the first game and 0 for 5 facing Tom Hughes in the second. He was clearly an unhappy young man. The only meal he could order on his own was breakfast. Jack Coombs recalled, "He knew he wanted ham and eggs for breakfast but he couldn't read the menus for the other meals and had to have someone with him whenever he went into a dining room."

There are stories that some of the Athletics made fun of Jackson and didn't like him. It's true that he was unlike anyone most of them had ever known. There were very few southerners in all of major league baseball at the time. And as Ty Cobb had quickly learned, in a nation just one generation removed from the Civil War, a southern accent inspired plenty of cruel as well as good-natured ribbing. If any of the A's played any of the usual rookie-initiation pranks on Joe Jackson, there is no evidence pointing to any particular players or pranks. Nor did Jackson need any taunting to feel awkward and out of place in the unfamiliar surroundings of a large northern city and the company of older, educated teammates.

It may be that Jackson felt offended when, according to Coombs, Mack asked several of the players to give Joe a "good talking to," explaining how he couldn't help the team if he kept disappearing for a week or two at a time. Whatever they said to him may have done more harm than good. It certainly had no positive results. Jackson sought solace in whiskey that wasn't as good as the white lightning back home.

Connie Mack realized he had a lovesick, unhappy "jewel" on his hands. He told Joe to go home and enjoy a proper honeymoon with his Katie, and they'd see him in the spring. Jackson broke for home like Ty Cobb intent on stealing the base.

Nobody had to tip Connie Mack to Amos Strunk. Fast as a jackrabbit, the eighteen-year-old outfielder had been a Philadelphia high school star. He was playing for the Shamokin club in the independent Atlantic League, managed by Mack's old third baseman Lave Cross. Mack signed him and tried him in a dozen games. He was green and needed plenty of schooling, but that's what the Connie Mack baseball academy was all about.

In the spring Mack had sent outfielders Jack Lelivelt and Frank Shaughnessy outright to Reading in the Tri-State League. In exchange Reading manager Jacob Weitzel gave him first choice from the Reading roster. Mack selected third baseman John Franklin Baker. A muscular, thick-wristed, twenty-two-year-old farm boy from the tiny hamlet of Trappe, Maryland, Baker could lift a hundred-pound sack of corn and put it on the back of a truck with one hand. He was a hard, tough, taciturn gentleman. Baker was a sandlot pitcher when Buck Herzog, managing a semipro team in nearby Ridgely, signed him for $5 a week and board. Herzog, later a longtime third baseman for the Giants, made a third baseman out of Baker. In 1908 Baker batted .299 at Reading.

Frank Baker joined the Athletics in Chicago on Sunday morning, September 20. Striding into the Lexington Hotel dining room, Baker saw Mr. Mack eating breakfast. He walked to the table and announced, "I'm here, Mr. Mack."

Mack looked up from his orange juice, bacon and eggs, and tea, and said, "I see you are."

That afternoon the A's were shut out without a hit by Frank Smith. Eddie Plank took the 1–0 loss. The next day Baker started at third base and had 1 of the team's 3 hits off Ed Walsh. Two days later the left-handed swinger, batting third, hit 2 doubles off Smith in a 3–2 loss.

Mack saw at once that Baker needed no bench time. He was ready. He was not fast, but he got a quick start racing in to pick up a bunt or slow roller and firing the ball to first. During the next few weeks, he showed

Mack he was not afraid to risk an error, ranging far off the bag to make plays and making them flawlessly.

Assessing his pitching, Mack was reluctant to count on Rube Vickers. Although Vickers was giving him 300 innings of work, the erratic Canadian still gave Mack the willies. One day he started in Cleveland. In the first inning a walk and an error put Naps on second and third with 1 out. Mack ordered Lajoie walked intentionally. Vickers threw three wide ones, then one not wide enough. Lajoie held the bat at the knob with one hand, reached out, and lined it down the right-field line for a double. The fuming Mack immediately waved Vickers to the dugout and sent Jimmy Dygert in to pitch. When a player really made him angry during a game, Mack sometimes let his long bony index finger do the talking for him, rather than spew language he would later regret. While Vickers tried to stammer out an alibi, Mack pointed a dagger-like finger at him, then pointed to the locker room, stabbing the air like a woodpecker.

Harry Krause reported after graduating from St. Mary's in May. He made his first start on May 27, a 5–4 win over Detroit, then lost to Chicago, 5–1, two weeks later. Mack then sent him to Harrisburg, where he won 17 and lost 4. Mack believed that Krause was now ready.

But the most important boost to his pitching came when Jack Coombs regained a healthy arm. Coombs pitched his first complete game of the season on August 1, a 4–3 win in St. Louis. The more he pitched, the stronger he grew, chalking up 4 shutouts, while continuing to fill in in the outfield. Mack figured if he could somehow coax a full season out of the fragile Chief Bender and not have to overwork Eddie Plank, his pitching would be strong for 1909.

Mack's greatest concern was his catching. Osee Schrecongost had moped through a miserable season. He missed Rube Waddell. He was off the wagon, but without his old pal, it wasn't fun anymore. The Limburger and onion sandwiches had lost their pungency. His hitting fell off. Five times Mack put him on waivers. Nobody claimed him. In St. Louis on September 17, Mack tried to sell Browns manager Jimmy McAleer on the idea that reuniting Schreck with Waddell would revive the catcher. McAleer didn't think he could handle both Schreck and the Rube and said no thanks.

Mack asked waivers again. The White Sox, in the thick of the pennant race, claimed Schreck for $1,500. He appeared in six games for Chicago, and that was the end of the big league line for Osee Schrecongost, the most colorful catcher of them all.

Doc Powers was still Mack's smartest catcher, but his arm had lost its strength. Disenchanted with Syd Smith's attitude and social life, Mack traded him to St. Louis before a game between the two clubs on August 2 for a veteran backup catcher, Bird Blue, who was not part of his rebuilding plan. A wag at a Lancaster paper suggested that Mack acquire a local pitcher named Red White to pitch to Blue, giving the A's "the only star spangled battery in the business."

In August Mack bought Jack Lapp, a local boy, from Hazelton in the Atlantic League. He saw Lapp, twenty-three, as a dependable number two catcher and pinch hitter. Deciding to go with three catchers, none of them number one, in December Mack paid $4,000 to the Tigers for their twenty-seven-year-old backup catcher, Ira Thomas. The six-foot-two Thomas became another of Connie Mack's lifers, as coach, minor league manager, head scout, and close friend for as long as the Athletics remained in Philadelphia.

Some later writers, notably Wilfrid Sheed, delighted in throwing mud at the often sugar-coated hagiographic portrayals of Connie Mack, charging deferential writers with fraudulent coverups of a conniving, mendacious, stingy club owner. But the lengthy roll of players who stayed on with Mack or returned to work for him in various capacities speaks more to the basic truths. Connie Mack was no saint. He was a kind, patient, generous, loyal, understanding, gentle man, "a true gentleman," pitcher Rube Bressler called him, "in every sense of the word." As the manager of a business, he cared about his players and employees as people, treated them with dignity and respect, and showed a genuine interest in them and their problems. These principles of management were innate, not the product of any business school education. And they were not particularly prevalent among business tycoons of the time. Employees stayed with the Athletics for decades, often for life. Mack's harmonious twenty-one-year partnership with Ben Shibe, whose probity was beyond question, is sufficient testimony to support the paeans that would come Connie Mack's way in later years.

But now, in the fall of 1908, none of the other American League magnates had such kind words for Connie Mack. He was drawing brickbats from the managers of the four western clubs who were battling for the championship. Every game was important to them. When the A's embarked on their final western trip, Mack left most of his veterans at home. Harry Davis, Collins, and Barry were sidelined with minor injuries. Mack's experimental lineups might include an infield of people named Barr, Manush, Nicholls, and Baker. He paid $750 for a "can't miss" first-year catcher from the New York State League named Ben Egan and put him behind the plate to catch pitchers called Flatter and Kellogg and Files and Martin and Gus Salva. (Egan missed, failing to hit his 195-pound weight in stints with the A's and Cleveland.) On some days there were only two players in the lineup anybody had ever heard of. In a game in Chicago, only Murphy and Seybold were left from the 1905 champions.

The teams that had to face a Coombs or Plank claimed Mack was playing favorites by using unknown hurlers against other contenders. Some club owners went so far as to demand that Mack forfeit his franchise for putting such raw teams on the field.

Unperturbed by the complaints, Connie Mack sat and studied his boys. "He's not saying much," noted Frank Hough in the *Inquirer*. "He never does. But he's doing a lot of thinking, the result of which will be made manifest later."

Back home the fans had no interest in these unknowns. Only 1,281 showed up for the last games at Columbia Park, a doubleheader on Saturday, October 3, against Boston. The A's won the first, 8–7, and lost the second, 5–0, when darkness added to the gloom after six innings.

The Athletics finished sixth, 22 games behind the champion Detroit Tigers.

Both pennant races, each involving three teams, went down to the last day. The nation's interest in baseball so overshadowed the presidential campaigns of Taft and Bryan that Norman Mack, chairman of the Democratic National Committee, asked one club owner to hurry up and get it over with so they could stir up some interest in the election. Detroit edged Cleveland by ½ game; in the National the Cubs finished 1 game ahead of New York and Pittsburgh.

The fall rumor mill ground out all sorts of trades: Mack was after Davy Jones of the Tigers, Tubby Spencer, and (not *the*) Albert Schweitzer of the Browns. The writers had nothing else to deal in except rumors and speculation as, in the words of Horace Fogel, "You can never get Connie Mack to divulge his plans until after the deals he has been working on have been put through."

On June 24, with his club in Philadelphia, Clark Griffith had resigned as the New York Highlanders' manager after months of bickering with the club owners, Frank Farrell and Bill Devery. Kid Elberfeld replaced him for the balance of the season. The New Yorkers were lodged in the cellar. Attendance had frittered to such a low state that *Globe* writer Mark Roth quipped, "If it gets any smaller, they'll have to put fractions on the turnstiles."

While the Athletics were in New York for a four-day series in early September, Frank Farrell approached Connie Mack. "If you are tired of managing the Athletics, Connie," he said, "I'll make you an offer."

Mack had nothing to lose by listening. "What is it?"

Farrell offered him a five-year contract at $25,000 a year and a piece of the team. Mack knew why his friend Clark Griffith had resigned. It reminded him of the interference he had taken from Captain Kerr in Pittsburgh. There was no way he would leave the company of Ben Shibe to go into business with the two New York ex-bartenders. He preferred to stay where he was and rebuild the Athletics, not the Highlanders/Hilltoppers/Yankees.

35 | SHIBE PARK

For two years rumors and real estate transaction reports had the Athletics buying this grounds or that in various sections of the city. But Connie Mack and Ben Shibe had already picked out their future business location: an undeveloped area northeast of Columbia Park, bordered by Twentieth and Twenty-first Streets between Lehigh and Somerset. The neighborhoods immediately surrounding it were or had at times been known as Goosetown, Swampoodle, Gillietown, and Irishtown.

The land was mostly vacant, ungraded hillocks pocked with puddles that seemed never to drain or dry up. Two unpaved streets, Woodstock and Lambert, ran through it, parallel to the north-south Twentieth and Twenty-first. A city dog pound had once occupied the area. The kennels left behind now belonged to the Women's Society for the Prevention of Cruelty to Animals.

A line of three-story rowhouses filled the other side of Twentieth Street. Saloons and stores dotted the other perimeter streets. A block away on Twenty-second stood the City Hospital for Contagious Disease, primarily smallpox. The hospital was a rundown Victorian pile of bricks that could have been a setting for a Dickens novel. Between the hospital and the dog kennels, there was little interest in developing the area. So it figured to be cheaper than any similar acreage that might be available closer to City Hall to the south. (When the intended use of the land for a stadium became known, the uninformed wondered why anybody would build it in such a location. The informed knew that the hospital was scheduled to be closed by the summer of 1909.)

The site was adjacent to the grounds that Connie Mack had favored during his first search for a place to play in 1901, when his partners talked him out of it. "It was available [in 1901]," Mack said, "on a ten-year lease for $1,500 a year, or $45,000 to buy." The C. S. Bromley textile mill now occupied that city block.

In addition to its lower cost, the land was in a favorable spot on the city's transit map. The North Philadelphia (Broad Street) Station of the Pennsylvania Railroad was six blocks away. Visiting teams could get off the train there and walk to the ball yard. The rudiments of a subway system had been laid out; the first section was due to open in 1909. Trolley lines ran from the center of the city up Broad Street. Fans could transfer to the Lehigh line or walk the seven blocks. Other lines passed within four blocks and were fed by transfers from outlying trolley tributaries. The Phillies were in business five blocks away at Broad and Lehigh.

Shibe and Mack knew that if their plans became public too soon, land prices would soar. So they arranged for Joseph M. Steele to front for them. Steele was one of the sons of William Steele & Sons, architects and contractors, who would build the stadium. Joe Steele set out to buy up the lots from the individual owners.

The secret was well kept. The property owners could not imagine a structure of any importance being built as a result of the sale of their small individual holdings. The existence of the two streets cutting through the lots seemed to rule out any scheme to unite the disparate parcels and put up a substantial building.

By the end of 1907 all the land had been acquired by Steele at a cost of $128,000, of which $60,500 was mortgaged. The total cost, including taxes and interest and settlement of the mortgages, came to $141,918.92.

There remained the obstacle of the two streets crossing the land. With John Shibe's backing, attorney Louis Hutt, who represented the Athletics (and, occasionally, Rube Waddell in his domestic tribulations), had been elected to the Common Council from the Twenty-ninth Ward. Once the real estate purchases were completed, Hutt introduced an ordinance "to strike from the City plan and vacate Woodstock and Lambert Streets, between Lehigh and Somerset Streets."

The ordinance was referred to the Committee on Surveys. Hutt was a member of that committee. On February 8, 1908, the committee recommended approval of the plan. Without specifying the use, its report simply stated that "it is the intention to use the block of ground . . . in one piece and Lambert and Woodstock Streets would interfere with the development."

The Select and Common Councils approved the ordinance on Tuesday afternoon, February 24. When the mayor signed it, construction of Shibe Park became possible.

As predicted, once the news was out, property values and rents in the area took off. New home construction picked up. Matt Kilroy, proprietor of a saloon on Columbia Avenue since 1901, immediately leased another one on the corner of Twentieth and Lehigh, across from the right-field corner. He remained in business there until 1935, when Kilroy's became Charley Quinn's Deep Right Field Café. Trainer Martin Lawler opened a cigar store two doors away at 1933 Lehigh.

From the start, Ben Shibe was determined to build the largest and finest baseball stadium in the world, a fireproof showplace of concrete and steel—the first of its kind—with walls sixty feet high, stores under the pavilion on Lehigh, broad promenades, twenty-one turnstile entrances and fourteen exits, a restaurant, public telephones, a completely outfitted first aid room, men's rooms in the grandstands and at each end of the bleachers, and ladies' rooms staffed with matrons on each level of the grandstand and pavilion. There was room under the left- and right-field bleachers for vast storage areas and parking garages and service stations for players' and patrons' automobiles. When the writers climbed the 147 steps to the press box, they would find pencil sharpening machines at their service.

"Nothing is too good for Philadelphians," Ben Shibe told the *Inquirer*, "for Philadelphians have certainly been good to us."

The home clubhouse was larger than the visitors', with three shower stalls to two for the visiting club. Each had room for twenty lockers. A tunnel led from the dressing rooms to the field. The umpires had their own dressing room and walkway.

No detail was overlooked. Water plugs throughout the grandstand enabled one man to hose down the stands and seats in one hour after every game. Shibe consulted builders and concrete experts to learn if wood or concrete bleachers would be hotter in the summer sun. They told him concrete was cooler. "Wood will retain the heat from a hot sun," Shibe reported. "Concrete will not, because it's so hard the sun cannot penetrate it. ... I am assured that [concrete] bleachers will be many degrees cooler than if they were constructed of wood."

Connie Mack hired Jim Fitzgerald, the renowned grounds and tennis courts caretaker of the Germantown Cricket Club, to lay out and supervise the installation of the new ballpark's playing surface.

Descriptions of the edifice as it would look from the outside promised cathedral-like grandeur. "The pavilion, the main entrance of which will be at Twenty-first Street and Lehigh Avenue," wrote Connie Mack in the October 1908 *Baseball Magazine*, "will be of French Renaissance style of architecture, with the walls of brick and terra cotta trimmings. The mansard roof will be of green slate.

"This structure surpasses the old Greek amphitheaters both in size and in beauty. So big and wonderful is the new ballstand that it alone is worth the price of admission to one game."

Terra cotta casts of Ben Shibe and Connie Mack adorned the space above the main entrance, with SHIBE PARK carved between them. A fancy script "A" was inscribed over the other entranceways. Parades of alternating Ionic columns and high, arched windows lined the grandstands along Twenty-first and Lehigh. Rising above the main entrance was a five-story octagonal tower, twenty-four feet in diameter, housing the business offices. Connie Mack's office, reached by an elevator or a catwalk from the grandstand, filled the top floor.

The double-decked grandstand, from first around to third base, held 10,000, using 5,500 steel folding chairs in the lower deck. Twenty-five-cent bleachers for 13,000 were turned toward the infield along both foul lines to the fences. Wide promenades in back of the grandstand and behind the bleachers could hold 7,000 people standing. Another 10,000 might squeeze onto the outfield, which was banked to improve the view. Why, it might even be possible to jam 40,000 people into the place, making it the largest ballpark in the major leagues. For accurate attendance counts, an electrical device would be installed in Ben Shibe's office to register every turn of the turnstiles.

On April 3, 1908, William Steele &Sons received a permit to build the $250,000 structure. (The total cost came to $315,248.69, including fixtures and equipment ranging from cuspidors to lawn mowers.) On Thursday morning, April 16, Ben Shibe turned the first spadeful of dirt.

It took several months just to clean and grade the land, a fleet of horse-drawn wagons carrying away the debris. On the morning of Saturday, October 3, Ben Shibe put in place the cornerstone at Twenty-first and Lehigh. Into it went copies of every Philadelphia newspaper, *Sporting Life*, photos of Shibe and Mack, the latest A. J. Reach *Baseball Guide*, an official American League baseball, and a newly minted quarter. The small gathering included some of the A's veteran players, John and Tom Shibe, head groundskeeper and concessionaire Joe Schroeder, and the A's most faithful fan, Hughie Dougherty. The stone was inscribed:

American Base Ball Club, Philadelphia, 1908
William Steele & Sons Company
Architects and Builders

A week later Joe Schroeder began supervising the digging up and removal of the Columbia Park sod to the new grounds.

Connie Mack and Ben Shibe were at the site every day, supervising, inspecting, monitoring the on-schedule progress. Out-of-town visitors included Albert Spalding, Cleveland Naps owners Kilfoyle and Somers, and a New York architect who was designing a new Pittsburgh plant, Forbes Field, scheduled to open in June 1909. (These new edifices served as models for a young Birmingham, Alabama, businessman, Rick Woodward, to build the first concrete and steel ballpark in the minor leagues. Woodward asked Connie Mack to help lay out his field's dimensions. Rickwood Field opened in 1910 and is still standing.)

Charles Murphy, owner of the Chicago Cubs, viewed the construction with unguarded admiration for Ben Shibe's great gamble. "Just thinking of building a half-million dollar baseball plant is enough to make a man gasp," he said. "Even the young magnates in those cities which charge much higher prices than Philadelphia haven't the nerve to risk such a venture."

Community vest buttons popped with pride when Governor Bunn dropped by one Sunday and declared, "Philadelphia will have in Shibe Park and the new Philadelphia opera house just built by Hammerstein two more institutions unrivaled anywhere in the world."

Not bad for the city the out-of-town writers called "Slowtown."

It was all a far cry from the wooden grandstands and bleachers and rickety fences of the ramshackle orchards that had sufficed for the game's infancy. In less than a decade baseball had come from a low level of society inhabited by bums, drunkards, brawlers, and gamblers to being mentioned in the same sentence with an opera house.

The most persuasive evidence that baseball had graduated into the class of big business was the federal government's sudden interest in it as a source of significant tax revenue. Congress proposed a tax of five cents per ticket.

The price tag for the new stadium—the equivalent of $10 million today—seems modest by modern standards. It's easy to look back from today's skyboxes and luxury suites and television rights and $2 million average player salaries and smile at the trepidation raised by such a gamble. The reader of history must overcome the handicap of knowing how the story ends. It's almost impossible to put yourself in the minds of the participants, who knew only the beginning of their journey and not how it would turn out. At the time, spending that much to erect a "baseball plant" was an enormous leap of faith into the unknown future of the game. There is no way to comprehend the uncertainty, the complete unknowability of the outcome of the huge investment they were making.

During all this time, title to the grounds remained with Joseph M. Steele. On August 26, 1908, the three Shibes, Mack, Samuel Jones, and Frank Hough met and formed the Athletics Grounds Company, a separate corporation, capitalized at 100 shares of $50 par value, "to hold, lease and sell real estate." Their individual interests in the company corresponded to their holdings in the baseball club. The plan called for Joe Steele to transfer title to the property to Ben Shibe at cost, with the new corporation buying the property from Shibe at the same price.

They met next on Saturday morning, October 17, to approve the bylaws and elect officers: Ben Shibe, president; Connie Mack, treasurer. The handwritten minutes of these meetings were not penned by Connie Mack, but they were signed by him as the designated secretary.

The legalities were not completed until the morning of Thursday, December 31, at the Athletics' office in the Girard Building. The stockholders resolved to purchase the grounds from Ben Shibe for $141,918.92. They then voted to increase indebtedness from "nothing to $350,000" and asked Shibe to take the purchase price in the form of a $150,000 mortgage at 6 percent interest for five years, with a company option to extend it for another five years. Ben Shibe agreed. Next they voted to issue $200,000 in ten-year bonds at 6 percent interest, payable "in gold coin," constituting a second mortgage on the grounds and stadium. Only $112,000 of the bonds were sold by November 1909.

The actual construction costs were borne by the Athletics baseball club—$191,387.03 through September 30, 1909—and the proceeds from the sale of the bonds, which were eventually redeemed by the club. In lieu of rent to the Athletics Grounds Company, the club paid the taxes on the property, the $15,720 interest on the debt, and the annual $20,000 deposit into the sinking fund to redeem the bonds.

The Athletics launched the first wave of modern stadium construction. For all of Shibe Park's splendor, Connie Mack accurately predicted that "in another year some other city will outdistance Philadelphia." Charles Comiskey purchased a lot at Thirty-fifth and Shields Avenue on which Comiskey Park would open in July 1910. Club owners in Boston, Brooklyn, and Detroit followed the A's trailblazing path in the next few years. Magnates in Cleveland, New York, and St. Louis launched extensive remodeling projects.

On another political front, some of Connie Mack's friends in the legislature introduced a bill authorizing Sunday baseball. It was opposed by the Phillies' owners and went nowhere.

Successful businessmen in other industries, always on the lookout for profitable and ego-enhancing enterprises, watched the construction of these magnificent new plants, which bespoke prosperity and had the added fillip of serving as prominent monuments to their builders. They saw the names of Shibe and Ebbets and Comiskey carved in stone for all to see and admire, and they were envious. They watched and waited to see if the return on these extravagant investments in amusement grounds would prove to be justified or folly.

The construction of Shibe Park sparked the development of a bustling community of businesses, banks, shops, restaurants, and saloons. A new St. Columba's Roman Catholic Church and School opened three blocks away while the stadium was going up. The middle-class, blue-collar neighborhood, with its spotless sidewalks and three-step marble stoops, became the seasonal home for many players who rented rooms. Jack Barry and his wife rented an apartment in a house on Twentieth Street owned by a couple named Kratz. In the evenings Barry sat on the porch smoking a few cigars before bedtime. Jack Coombs became a tenant of Monte Cross, who lived nearby. Chief Bender bought a house in the 1900 block of Tioga, seven blocks north. Eddie Collins and Eddie Plank boarded with the Harry Davis family at 2405 West Ontario Street, a few blocks from the park.

Mack's Oxford Street residence was now too far from his new place of business to suit him. He purchased a porch-front rowhouse on a 16 by 120 foot lot at 2119 Ontario for "a nominal consideration." The move made it easier for Mack to drop in in the evenings on players who lived in the neighborhood to make suggestions or discuss plans or check on an injury. His brother Eugene moved to 1529 North Twenty-ninth Street. Michael still lived upstairs over the White Elephant on North Eleventh Street.

Mack's children, Roy and Earle, would be playing ball in Atlantic City that summer. Then Earle went off to Notre Dame prep school in the fall. Roy went to work for the American Thread Company. Sixteen-year-old Marguerite was still at home. Grandma Mary Mack had learned to read and sign her name. She, not Connie Mack, signed the report cards that Marguerite brought home from school. Mack's niece Helen recalled visiting the family in Philadelphia and her grandmother reading stories to her.

With all that was going on, Connie Mack still found time to travel. In

November he spent two weeks on Maryland's Eastern Shore, where he called on his new third baseman, Frank Baker, at his farm in Trappe. Baker was an expert hunter of ducks and geese. Mack was not. His idea of a pleasant outing was not sitting in a cold duck blind at dawn. From there Mack was off to the league meetings in New York.

On February 1, 1909, the steam heat up and running, the Athletics moved into their new offices in the tower of Shibe Park. Mack took some time to put his office in order before going to Atlantic City for a week. While there, he refereed a charity basketball game between the Knights of Columbus and Eagles at the Million Dollar Pier. Next came the rules committee meeting in Chicago, where he gave his support to the sentiments to abolish the spitball, saying, "By eliminating the spitball, baseball will be an ideal game."

The only significant change in the rules required relief pitchers to face at least one batter. This resulted from complaints aimed at Washington manager Joe Cantillon, who occasionally brought in a parade of three or four pitchers, each one allowed five warmup tosses, giving the man he really wanted to pitch more time to warm up.

Meanwhile, Connie Mack and Chief Bender were negotiating through the newspapers. Bender wasn't exactly a holdout; he hadn't been sent a contract yet. The keen-eyed marksman was busy entering shooting matches and winning most of them. Just about every week in the Philadelphia area there was a purse up for grabs, sometimes as high as $500. Bender talked about quitting baseball and making a living on the trapshooting circuit.

Asked to comment, Mack said, "That's just talk because he knows he's due for a cut in pay." Anyhow, Mack added, "I'm not counting on him for an important part of the team."

Much as he disliked newspaper conjecture over salaries, Mack didn't hesitate to put his case before the public:

Bender has been receiving the best of treatment from the Athletic club and in return has not given the services he should have rendered. Last year, for instance, he got what he wanted, and what did he give in return. The record shows 17 games of which he won 8 and lost 9. During the last two months of the season he didn't work at all for us. But I want this made clear: if Bender signs at my figure, no matter how small, and then turns around and takes his regular turn next season, and pitches as well as he is capable of doing, and renders first class service, I am willing to pay him the same salary next fall as I paid him last year.

Bender signed a contract with incentive clauses just before the team left Broad Street station for New Orleans at 11:05 on the night of March 8. Mack dispatched Joe Ohl to Greenville, South Carolina, to escort Joe Jackson to New Orleans.

The baseball business had come a long way from the days when Connie Mack had to go door to door begging innkeepers to rent him rooms for his troops. In New Orleans they checked into the elegant Hotel Dechenaud. The players no longer carried their own rolled-up uniforms. Equipment trunks now traveled with the team.

The weather was warm but wet. Mack was determined to work his pitchers into shape gradually, not trying to bring them to midseason form by opening day. He put an extra burden on young southpaw Harry Krause by tagging him as another Rube Waddell, but Krause shook it off, showing as much poise and composure as if he'd been in the big leagues for years.

The practice fields swarmed with eager young prospects, to Connie Mack's delight. Like a sculptor visualizing the form that lay within a block of marble, Mack believed in his ability to size up a player in the raw state, peering into a gawky rookie's head and heart and forecasting his future. He wasn't perfect, never claimed to be, any more than McGraw or Griffith or Jennings or anybody else in the business. (Mack and John McGraw pursued Eddie Collins's teammate at Columbia, third baseman Frank Nohowel, who was touted as a better athlete than Collins but was reluctant to play pro ball. When McGraw finally signed him in 1912, the *New York Times* headlined, "McGraw Outwits Mack." Nohowel never played an inning in the major leagues.)

The possibility that the "next Ty Cobb" might turn out to be the next nobody didn't faze Mack. "I'm not much of a trader," he told a St. Louis writer. "I would rather develop a new man myself. You know, every manager has a different idea about what characteristics denote greatness in a developing player. What I may see in a man other managers might pass up. It's sort of intuition, I suppose you would call it. Sometimes I am right, sometimes I'm wrong."

Visiting experts saw only a gang of unfamiliar, untried names and washed-up veterans on the field. Out-of-town writers observed these green grasshoppers enthusiastically booting ground balls, running into each other, and heaving wild throws—and consigned the A's to the deepest part of the second division for the coming season. Most of them.

Among those who had learned not to write off any Mack-led team was J. Edward Grillo of the *Washington Post*. "Though no one seems to think that Connie Mack's team will have a chance in the American League race next season," he wrote, "it would not be surprising to find the Athletics factors in the race. Mack has never had a team which was impressive on paper, and yet he has captured two pennants and been in several of the other races, right to the finish. Next year Mack will have more youngsters on his team than ever before. He has got rid of most of the veterans, and starts out with a bunch of what might be termed untried material. On the face of it the team does not promise much. But one should not overlook the ability of the man in charge. He can do wonders with a lot of ballplayers and it must not be forgotten that he has retained a pitching staff which is sure to be troublesome."

Connie Mack was delighted at the hustle, the enthusiasm, the eagerness to learn that he saw among his young colts. Fumbled grounders and wild throws didn't bother him. He preferred to see a player try his best and fail rather than shy away from a play in fear of making an error. And he let them know it.

"Don't be afraid to throw," he told Barry and Collins and McInnis and Baker. "Let it go. I'd rather see you heave it a mile than to hold it back and the throw either fall short or the runner beat it. In either case the base runner is going to be safe, so give 'em all you've got every time."

When two players collided going after a pop-up or fly ball, Mack didn't wince. That was better than seeing them both stop and let the ball drop between them. "I'd rather see both men anxious and fighting to make the play," he told them, "instead of one being afraid of making an error and the other scared of getting hurt."

Stuffy McInnis had quit school in the middle of his senior year rather than miss spring training. Everybody expected him to be farmed out, but Mack had no such plans. He didn't know where he'd play McInnis, but he didn't want young Jack under anybody else's tutelage. Mack assigned Ira Thomas to look after him. A sociable fellow with a booming voice, Thomas didn't smoke or drink. He preached abstinence to the rookies and advised them to avoid hanging around with players whose habits differed from theirs. "I waited to see which way [those] players went after a game," he said, "and then I'd go the other way." Thomas steered McInnis to the ice cream parlors in the evenings, then tucked him in bed early.

As delighted as Connie Mack was with his "second team," Sam Erwin was downright ecstatic over it. Now seventy-five, Erwin looked forward eagerly to managing his Yannigans in their games against the first-string team. Their spirit and enthusiasm made him feel as young as they were. This year's youngsters seemed driven to prove themselves, to show that they belonged and were ready to take over. Erwin tapped into that eagerness by holding meetings in his room, where he suggested signs they could flash to each other and plays they might try to execute.

Eddie Collins was strong and healthy and hitting a ton. So were Jackson, Strunk, and Heitmuller. While the veterans looked on practice games as tune-ups, the Yannigans went at them as if they were the World Series. Sam Erwin was having the time of his life watching his boys give the regulars a shellacking day after day. The stung veterans fought back, and a rivalry developed between the two sides of the camp that has rarely been equaled in spring training competition.

After two weeks in New Orleans, Mack asked Harry Davis to take the regulars home by way of Mobile and Atlanta to begin the spring series with the Phillies. There was something about his B team that intrigued the skipper. He wanted to see more of these young men, to concentrate on watching them without the distraction of managing the veterans. He decided to lead them through the hinterlands this time, miss the city series, and arrive just before the season opened.

When they started north, the youngsters kept up the evening meetings on their own. They told nobody about the sessions, not Sam Erwin, not Connie Mack. "As a result," Eddie Collins recalled, "we got to know one another better and, furthermore, we came to understand why one player did this, another did that, etc., and what, among our own accomplishments, spelled success."

Mack and his boys arrived in Louisville on March 29 and were greeted with complaints from Cap O'Neill, the local baseball promoter, for bringing the second-stringers to town instead of the regulars. Nobody in town knew who any of these players were. They wouldn't draw a crowd, and they wouldn't provide much of a workout for the local nine.

That afternoon at Eclipse Field, Joe Jackson strode to the plate, walked between the umpire and the catcher into the batter's box, drew a line in the dirt three inches from the plate, put his left toes against the line in the deepest part of the box, and stood erect, his right shoulder aimed squarely at the pitcher. The pitcher threw. Jackson took a twenty-inch stride and fired his perfect swing. The ball soared over the right-field fence, where only three balls had been hit in the past five years. Connie Mack could still picture it thirty-seven years later as he told Arthur Daley of the *New York Times* that it was "the longest hit I ever saw in my life. Goodness me, it went a terrible distance."

Mack's boys demolished O'Neill's team in two games, and Cap was happy to see them leave town. Everywhere they went, they whipped the local teams. On the trains, on the buses to ballparks, and in their rooms they held their secret meetings.

Or were they really still a secret?

Generations of players swore that nothing ever got by Mr. Mack. He knew all their tricks, their habits, their subterfuges to cover up their late-night activities, who was hitting the bottle, who was disgruntled. It certainly seemed that way. It's hard to say exactly when he caught on to the Yannigans' secret meetings. Eddie Collins thought that Mack was on to them when they reached Terra Haute, Indiana. The players dressed at the hotel as usual and boarded the bus to the ballpark. Normally, the manager never rode with them. He took a trolley or bus by himself. So they were surprised when Mack got on their bus and sat down. "Just thought I'd see how you boys acted," he explained to his startled charges.

The players put their heads together as usual, murmuring about some plays they might try that afternoon. Mack gazed out the window, giving no indication that he heard any of it, and said nothing.

Their last stop was Reading on Saturday, April 10. The story of Joe Jackson and the milk cans varies in its timing and setting. If it happened, it was probably at the Reading depot that the homesick Jackson saw the cans with their red tags waiting for the milk train and said something like, "I wish Connie would put a tag on me and send me south."

Five days later Mack optioned Jackson to Savannah in exchange for the right to select one player from the Savannah club.

Mack sent Frank Baker and Jack Barry ahead to Philadelphia to play in the city series and regretted it. In the April 7 game, as Sherry Magee slid into third, Baker caught his foot on the bag and sprained his ankle. He had to be carried off the field and driven to a hospital. He might be out for two weeks. Jack Barry came up lame and would miss opening day.

But Connie Mack was looking beyond the first few games or weeks. He was thinking in terms of years. For the first time, he believed he had an entire lineup of those smart young players he had dreamed of. They were, in Ira Thomas's judgment, "the brightest bunch of ballplayers I've ever met in one team."

At seven o'clock on the morning of Monday, April 12, 1909, a man named George McFadden approached the corner of Lehigh Avenue and Twenty-first Street. Elated to find the corner deserted, he walked to the main grandstand entrance of Shibe Park, leaned against the door, and did not move from the spot for the next five hours and fifteen minutes. Soon he was joined by a few other men, only slightly disappointed to find that they were too late to buy the first ticket to the Athletics' opening day in their magnificent new stadium.

From then until noon, as the packed trolley cars unloaded their passengers, the small party grew. Lines at the grandstand and bleacher entrances thickened and lengthened at a constantly quickening pace, like a snowball rolling down a mountainside. Men, women, boys, and girls jostled and elbowed and trod on each other's toes to be sure they were not left out. They were formally dressed for the most part, but not just because this was a historic occasion. Everyday wear for men consisted of two- or three-piece dark suits, shirts with detachable stiff paper collars and cuffs, and hats, derbies at this time of year. Most of the boys wore caps. Many of the women wore their Easter outfits, with large "peachbasket" hats that drew good-natured teasing from the men. Skirt hems were a few inches from the ground. Wealthier women wore silk stockings; working girls, black or white cotton hose.

They were favored by mild temperatures with no sign of rain, although a few wore overcoats against the early morning chill. Instead of the smell of the breweries around Columbia Park, the breezes spread the warm aroma of freshly baked bread from Freidhofer's Bakery.

Rather than wait in line for hours, hundreds of men preferred to take their chances and pass the time over foaming five-cent steins at Kilroy's. Some of them eventually crashed through the center field gate and spilled into the outfield crowd. Late arrivals waved $5 and $10 bills in the air hoping to buy a place in line. Finding no takers, they began to ring doorbells at the houses along Twentieth Street, where rooftops commanded a view of the field from beyond right field. The sun would be in their eyes, but by the time the first pitch was thrown at three o'clock, it would soon disappear behind the sixty-foot-high grandstand. The residents leaned ladders up to the openings to the roofs, set up crates and makeshift bleachers, and charged $2–$5 a head. The economic impact on the neighborhood was immediate.

For those in line, twenty-five cents bought a general admission ticket for a seat in the bleachers or a place to stand in the outfield. The more agile among them could climb atop the twelve-foot concrete outfield wall and the scoreboard in right field, which displayed both teams' batting orders and batteries, the batter, outs, balls, strikes, the umpires, next game information, and scores by innings of National and American League games. There was another one in the left field corner, marked "SCORE BOARD" for the benefit of newcomers to the game.

As always, Connie Mack was an early riser. The stadium was empty and quiet when he arrived, the fresh bright green paint still unmarked, the steel folding chairs still unscratched, the vast sea of seats still unoccupied. The white elephant banner flapped proudly in the breeze.

"Fool's Park," some skeptics called it; only a fool would think it could be filled often enough to pay for itself. Connie Mack and the Shibes were gamblers but not fools. Still, "We wondered if we could ever fill those long rows of seats," Mack said later.

Mack may have paused to remember George W. Uber, the manager of the A's telegraph office since the club opened for business in 1901. Mack considered his park employees as much a part of the Athletics family as his players. Uber had died the past September.

The players arrived early too, for morning practice. Home teams' morning workouts would be more important this year, as a new rule curtailed their pregame warmups. In the past, pregame practice consisted of both teams on the field at the same time amid a chaos of balls being hit and thrown in all directions. From now on, the visiting team would have exclusive use of the field for thirty minutes before a game, followed by ten minutes for the home team.

The A's regulars had been in the city since April 1, enabling them to inspect their new workplace and stake out their locker locations in the clubhouse. Mack's band of Yannigans had not arrived until Saturday night. They were getting their first look at their new baseball home. The sight lines, the winds, the backgrounds, sun fields, rebounding foibles of the fences and scoreboard, the infield dirt and outfield grass—all that had to be learned.

At ten o'clock all the Athletics were on the field. The trainer, Martin Lawler, came out of the runway into the third base dugout and announced that Connie Mack wanted to see them in the dressing room. Quietly the players filed in: from thirty-eight-year-old Doc Powers, the oldest and the only one who had been with the Athletics since their first opening day in 1901, to the youngest, Stuffy McInnis. Most of them were in their twenties. They were all curious. The older ones couldn't remember Mr. Mack ever holding a meeting like this on the morning of a game.

Mack's comments were aimed primarily at the youngsters he had shepherded north. For the first time, they realized the impact of their own meetings, which they thought had gone unnoticed. They heard their first big league manager telling them how impressed he was with their preparation and discipline, their initiative in trying to find ways to play the game to win.

"Play together," he stressed, "as a team." He expressed his confidence in them and their future if they played together with emotion and spirit and harmony. He reminded them not to get into heated arguments with the umpires. "I don't pay you to kick and be suspended. I want you to keep away from the umpires and play ball for all you are worth. Hits and runs win games, not protests."

Reluctantly, for he preferred not to play his rookies so soon, he told them that McInnis was starting at shortstop and Amos Strunk in center field. And, he added, henceforth there would be a meeting like this at ten or ten thirty every morning, at home and on the road.

His young players' spring training huddles had inspired Connie Mack to introduce the daily skull session to baseball.

When the great doors to Shibe Park swung open at 12:15, George McFadden put down his quarter and led the throng that pressed at his back.

The green walls unmarred by advertisements, the shining seats, and the vast manicured grounds drew gasps of admiration from the fans getting their first look at this unprecedented palatial setting for a baseball game. A special souvenir program was on sale for ten cents, but the Athletics offered their customers another innovation: free scorecards. As a patron of the theater, Connie Mack was used to being handed a free program listing the cast and other information about the play. He believed his patrons were entitled to the same service. The idea was applauded by newspapers in several cities, the *New York Sun* commenting, "Free score cards . . . will mean that a great many persons who do not know how to keep score will learn how. That is one point in favor of the plan."

But the Philadelphia newspapers didn't cheer. They were trying to sell papers with lineups in them outside the stadium.

The scorecards were not a losing proposition for the A's. Advertisers, including Dr. Pepper, Hires Root Beer, Schmidt Beer, and Eugene Mack's White Elephant Saloon, covered the cost. The club paid young boys a quarter to hand them out, fifty cents to the supervisors. Connie Mack's nephew, Dennis's son Neil, was a supervisor. "I had the upper stands and I brought in six other guys," Neil said. "We bought yellow pencils, two for a penny, with erasers on them, sharpened them up and when I'd hand a guy a scorecard and he asked how much, I'd say 'Free' but made it sound like 'three' and stick a pencil in their pocket and they'd give us a nickel and wouldn't think about the change. After the second inning we could watch the game.

"Whatever money I made I gave to my mother."

The First and Third Regiment fifty-piece bands began to play at one. Soon every seat was taken, and the outfield embankment was covered. Progress was not without its dissenters. Fans in the upper pavilion complained that it was too high. Bleacherites griped that they were too far from the action on the diamond. When the gates were closed, leaving the streets filled with frustrated fans, 30,162 tickets had been sold. Thousands of invited guests and uninvited crashers swelled the crowd.

The Athletics appeared in their new uniforms: white with a black stripe midway up the stockings, black belt, white cap with black cords across the crown and sides, topped by a black button. Some wore their navy blue military coat-sweaters with rolled gray collars and a six-inch white "A" on the left breast.

At two-thirty a pair of local singers, Fred C. Yoekel and James McCool, led the crowd in singing "America." The Red Sox and A's, followed by dignitaries and bands, marched to the center-field flagpole, where the bands played "The Star-Spangled Banner" as Ban Johnson and Ben Shibe raised the flag.

The murmurs of curiosity about the unfamiliar names in the A's line-up—Strunk? McInnis?—were soon supplanted by cheers when old favorite Danny Murphy drove in a first-inning run. Murphy had 4 hits and Eddie Plank breezed to an 8–1 win, sending everyone home happy.

Almost everyone.

Along about the seventh inning, Doc Powers felt a sharp pain in his gut. He said nothing, batted in the eighth, and was safe at first when the short-stop fumbled his grounder. A few minutes later he scored when Collins drew a bases-loaded walk. The pain grew sharper. Powers finished the game, then collapsed in the clubhouse. An ambulance took him to Northwest General Hospital, where doctors diagnosed "acute gastritis . . . something he ate . . . be back in uniform in a few days."

Martin Lawler blamed it on the wide belts and big buckles that bound a catcher's abdominal muscles through all that crouching. One doctor theorized that the effort to catch difficult foul flies had resulted in internal injuries.

It was none of these things. What happened was a fluke in an adult, an intestinal twist that occurred in male infants more than anyone—intussus-ception, a telescoping of the small or lower intestine up into the large intestine above it, causing a blockage. Whatever Powers may have eaten before the game was long past that part of his anatomy.

Powers showed no improvement the next day, but the doctors remained unconcerned until the pain became unbearable that night. They operated at 1 a.m. Wednesday and found extensive gangrene. They removed twelve to fifteen inches of his bowel. The "no need to worry" outlook suddenly turned grim. On the following Monday Powers was stricken with perito-nitis. A second operation left him weakened, unable to take nourishment. Surgeons opened him again, but there was nothing they could do. On Sunday, April 25, a priest administered the last rites, with Powers's wife, Florence, at his side. Doc Powers died at 9:14 the next morning.

The Athletics were in Washington. Connie Mack took the train to Philadelphia to do what he could for Florence Powers and her three little girls. The next morning Mack helped with the funeral arrangements before taking the noon train back to Washington. He felt as if he had lost a son. Powers was the model of the kind, intelligent gentleman that Mack wished all his players to be.

Testifying to Mike Powers's popularity, thousands of people filed by the body on view at the home of a friend, press gate guardian George Flood, and lined the route of the funeral on April 29. The game in Washington was postponed so that both teams could attend the service. The Phillies and visiting Brooklyn Dodgers, other players, and umpires joined the procession to the cemetery, followed by vans filled with flowers. The entire city wept; the skies rained for the next two days.

Connie Mack said, "Doc Powers' loss will be severely felt by the team." Hardest hit was Eddie Plank. Powers had caught 205 of Plank's 282 starts since 1901. No more would he hear Doc's "Work hard, old boy, work hard" words of encouragement. It took more than a month for his concentration to return.

Connie Mack arranged and promoted a Doc Powers Day on June 30, 1910, to raise money for his widow. Players from the other eastern American League clubs came to Shibe Park for an afternoon of field events and an exhibition game against the A's. Mack sent out letters and post cards to friends and fans, urging them to buy tickets for the day. Everyone, including Mr. Mack, paid to get in. The event raised almost $8,000.

For as long as there have been press boxes, there have been second guessers in them. When the Highlanders followed Boston into Shibe Park, Jack Knight was their shortstop, the same jittery Jack Knight, Philadelphia schoolboy star, who had been traded to Boston for Jimmy Collins in 1907. After a year in the minor leagues, Knight had been purchased by New York.

With Jack Barry still out, McInnis was the A's shortstop. In the first game of the series, Knight made some outstanding plays. McInnis made 2 errors in the fifth inning that gave the visitors a 1–0 win over Vic Schlitzer. Francis C. Richter, who had razzed Knight and lavishly cheered the trade for Collins at the time, now wrote, "Jack Knight's work with the Highlanders bears the mark of a finished shortstop, a position in which the Athletic club is now experimenting. In all ways the Jimmy Collins deal turned out a losing one, only designed as a temporary makeshift."

Some fans joined the press knockers. One wrote to Mack, "What a great thing it is to build such a grand building with such spacious accommodation and so much thought for the comfort of the public. But we fans would rather sit on a barbed-wire fence than to be looking at our present team."

The young players understood the spot they were on. They knew their mistakes were plainly visible to the public as well as their manager. But thanks to Connie Mack's patience and forbearance from criticizing them, they weren't afraid of the consequences. Everything he did was aimed at helping them grow in poise and confidence and mental toughness, so they wouldn't shatter under the strain. How he did that is illustrated by an incident described by umpire Billy Evans.

In a game at Detroit, one of Mack's young outfielders was out of position from where he had been told to play a certain hitter. "As a result," Evans wrote, "he muffed a fly ball, after a hard run, that would have been an easy out had he played properly for the batter. As the inning closed, I walked over to the Philadelphia bench to get a drink. While I was there the player who made the error arrived at the bench. Before he had a chance to utter a word, Mack said, 'No outfielder could have got that ball. Nothing but your speed enabled you to get your hands on it. At that you would have held it, had not that high wind been blowing.'

"All of this was true, but Mack said nothing to the player about being away out of his position. The next day he told him about it, when the two met in the hotel lobby."

While his boys were taking the heat from the press and fans, Connie Mack gave them daily confidence shots. "I know I've got a good ball team here," he told them. "The only team we have to beat is Detroit. You can whip all the other teams as soon as you get into the proper stride. Just keep on trying. You may be licked in today's game. Never mind. And don't worry if you lose tomorrow, As soon as you strike the proper gait, you'll go to the top rapidly."

Mack benched Stuffy McInnis and put Si Nicholls at short until Jack Barry was ready to play again. Baker took his first swings as a pinch hitter on April 19 and was in the lineup after that. On April 24 he hit a grand slam in the first inning in Boston, the drive clearing the distant right-field wall. That was all Plank needed for a 4–1 win.

With the loss of Powers, Mack bought Paddy Livingston, a light-hitting catcher who had been with the Reds in 1906, from Indianapolis. Livingston was available because he was a holdout. The American Association had imposed a salary cap of $300 a month, and he refused to take a cut. Thomas and Jack Lapp were slowly learning the pitchers. Thomas, though slow to get the ball away, had recovered from his sore arm of 1908. He wouldn't hit much, nor would Livingston, but Mack preferred a good brain over a good bat behind the plate any day, and they both had that.

Wearing a knot of black crepe on their shirts in memory of Doc Powers, the Athletics began to come together in early May. Mack was sold on Baker at third and Barry at shortstop. A strong, frisky Eddie Collins was rapidly becoming recognized as the equal of Cobb in many observers' view. The stalwart Harry Davis was playing with the agility of a teenage ballet dancer, leaning, bending, twisting, leaping to spear and scoop errant throws from his young infield. Davis served as pitching coach, infield coach, bench coach, tutor, mentor, and captain. During spring training he had worked with Plank, Coombs, and Schlitzer on the art of throwing a changeup that broke sharply, perhaps a forkball. When a pitcher needed calming down, Davis did the calming and sometimes signaled to Mack if he thought a pitcher should come out. When a pitching change took place, he officiated in the box.

The outfield, except for Danny Murphy, remained unsettled. Rube Oldring, who had all the tools but lacked the spark and confidence to be great, continued to disappoint Mack. Heitmuller was slow; Hyder Barr was fast and a good judge of fly balls, but he wasn't hitting. At thirty-five, Topsy Hartsel was slowing down. This was where the juggling and platooning had to be done until somebody won the jobs in center and left.

The pitching was strong. Bender, Coombs, and Krause were almost invincible. In a series against Washington, after Plank lost, 4–3, Bender won, 2–1; Coombs edged Walter Johnson, 1–0, on Murphy's ninth-inning home run; and Harry Krause tossed an impressive 1–0 five-hitter in his first start of the year. Baker, Collins, and Murphy were on fire with the bat. They started their first western trip winning 2 out of 3 in St. Louis, handing Rube Waddell a 5–1 loss; they would beat the Rube four times this year. Then they whitewashed the White Sox three times, Coombs and Walsh battling 13 innings to a 1–0 A's win; Krause going 12 for another 1–0 result; Jimmy Dygert tossing a 5–0 victory.

Commented the *St. Louis Globe-Democrat*, "Connie Mack has been robbing the kindergartens. With the exception of Davis, Plank, and Murphy, his team looks like the freshman nine from Hackwater College. But they only look that way."

When they arrived in Detroit, Ira Thomas told them about first baseman Claude Rossman's weakness: he had a psychological block, couldn't throw the ball. On anything other than a routine play, Rossman physically stuttered and sometimes froze altogether rather than taking a chance on throwing the ball away. And when he unfroze, he was as likely as not to throw wild. They decided to take long leads off first, try to draw a throw from the pitcher or catcher, then take off for second. This also forced the middle infielders to play closer to second base.

On May 22 Thomas demonstrated what he'd told them. The slow-footed Thomas was on first. He took a long lead, started for second, then deliberately fell in the dirt. The pitcher threw to Rossman, who held the ball while Thomas got up and scrambled to second. A disgusted Hughie Jennings pulled Rossman out of the game. The A's stole 4 bases in their 7–1 win, took 3 out of 4 from the defending champs, and moved into first place for a day. Suddenly those April experts who had called the Athletics an experimental team, doomed to seventh place at best, were now claiming they had predicted from the start that Connie Mack had another contender.

"The game has never had a man who could dig up as many good ballplayers from the most remote sources as Connie Mack," wrote a *Washington Post* reporter. "All winter long Mack was being sympathized with. No better than seventh place was picked for him and there seemed to be some doubt about that. But Mack seems to have another ball team. He tore his old one all to pieces and here he bobs up again with a winner."

They won 12 out of 14, prompting the *New York World* to admit, "It looks like Connie Mack is going to come through with another champion team, as he did in 1902 and 1905 when, with a team that looked weak, he grabbed off the American League pennant."

Baseball had changed since 1901, and Mack was adapting. In that inaugural year there had been 229 home runs hit in the American League. In 1909 there would be 109, most of them inside the park. Run production would be down by 30 percent. The foul strike rule, widespread use of the spitter since 1904, bigger gloves, and faster outfielders all led to changes in batters' approaches to hitting. A brief spurt of slugging had been replaced by players' studying pitchers and defenses in order to poke the ball safely. John McGraw said, "Batters now go to the plate less with the idea of punishing the ball than with studying and scheming to hit safely rather than hit far."

The 1906 White Sox had demonstrated that a team could win a world championship with the lowest batting average and slugging percentage in the league. The bunt, hit and run, sacrifice, squeeze play, and stolen base were the game of the day. And Connie Mack's Athletics were built to play that game.

Every morning, in the clubhouse or sitting in the bleachers at home, in Mack's room or a hotel meeting room on the road, they held their meetings. From the start, Mack made it clear that the sessions, lasting anywhere from ten minutes to a half hour or more, would not be lectures. Every player was encouraged to speak up, suggest plays, ask questions.

"Don't feel that anyone is going to laugh at your suggestions," he said. "We are all going to talk. They say that if you let a fool talk long enough he will say something smart. So we're all going to be fools and talk."

If they came up with something that he already knew or had planned, he let them think it was their idea.

Ira Thomas recalled, "It was amazing how many beneficial plays were dreamed up during these meetings."

Mack wanted his players to know each other so well that each could anticipate how the others would make a play, whether in fact they were capable of making such a play, and how they were likely to hit against a given pitcher. What were the chances of the man at the plate being able to put down a safe bunt or execute a hit and run against the pitcher in the box at the time? They had to know. They'd be giving their own signs: hit and run or sacrifice or squeeze or double steal.

They learned, for example, that Jack Barry was the best at bunting and executing the double squeeze, and if he signaled it, the men on second and third could take off with the pitch, confident that Barry would put down a bunt that would enable them both to score. When a man was on second with less than two out and Barry at bat, the base runner learned to watch the jittery third baseman. If he played in for a bunt or took a step or two in with the pitch, the opportunity to steal third was there. If he played back, Barry could beat out a bunt with ease. A man on third with Eddie Collins at bat had to stay alert; Collins wouldn't hesitate to put on a suicide squeeze play even with two strikes on him—and succeed. He was relaxed at the plate, varying the way he held the bat, but it was always still, giving no clues to what he might do before lashing out at the ball or dropping a bunt.

Collins batted third in the lineup, Harry Davis sixth. After he saw how aggressively Collins ran the bases, Davis said to him, "Any time you're on base and I'm at bat, I don't need any signs from you. Just run. Never mind me. I will see you going."

They weren't always left on their own. If he saw that what they were doing wasn't working, Mack didn't hesitate to step in. For example, midway through a game where Ed Walsh's near-balk move to first had foiled a few hit-and-run efforts, Mack said, "No more. If you want to hit and run, try that game from second."

He was more likely to get on them about mental errors made in a game they won than a poorly played loss. They felt bad enough when they threw one away and were more receptive to learning after a win.

Mack urged them to know their opponents as well as their teammates. This was the essence of baseball brains; longtime manager Lee Fohl later described it as "the ability to study opposing batters and pitchers, to see the defects in the opposing team and profit by them." Each morning they discussed the team and pitcher they were due to face that afternoon, how to pitch to the batters, what the pitcher's weaknesses were. Was he clumsy fielding bunts? Should they wait him out or attack first pitches? They analyzed plays and players, mentioned habits and foibles they'd noticed. They argued about the best way to break up a double steal or foil a squeeze play, what to do in a pickle or a pickoff. Then they went out and experimented in practice, discarding what didn't work, perfecting what did.

On their own, the pitchers studied the box scores of every game in the league. They knew who was hitting and who was in a slump, what kind of pitchers held them hitless, and which ones were "cousins." Using the only resources they had, they were their own advance scouts.

Connie Mack was not a fiery, inspiring orator. His credo was simple: teamwork. Think. Create. Experiment. And stay in shape. He told them they owed it to themselves, their families, their teammates, the customers who paid to watch them perform, and their employer to take care of themselves, get plenty of rest, and be prepared mentally and physically to do their best each day.

His father's drinking and its effects on his mother and their life in East Brookfield were etched in his memory like the rings in an old tree. He never spoke of it, but it was there when he brought up the subject to his players.

"I take every opportunity to discuss drinking," Mack told Henry Beech Needham. "My angle of approach is maybe one thing, maybe another. Perhaps we've heard about certain members of the opposing team. Perhaps we know some of the players have been making a night of it. Then I tell our boys it may not show today, maybe not tomorrow, but it's sure to show the day after.

"Of course I don't single a man out and aim my remarks at him personally in the morning talk. I talk generally, vaguely as far as the object of my remarks is concerned, but straight to the point."

What shone through to his boys was his honesty and sincerity; he meant what he said, believed it, and acted consistently with it. When he had to straighten out one of his players, Mack could do it either calmly and peacefully or really lay it on, but it was usually done privately.

At first other managers ridiculed the idea of Mack's morning meetings. You couldn't talk a guy out of a slump with a skull session, they said. It's a waste of time to tell a pitcher how to pitch to a batter; most of them couldn't carry out the instructions, even if they could remember them. Their scoffing inspired jokes like the one about Mack going over an opposing team's batting weaknesses in a meeting. When he finishes, a rookie says, "Mr. Mack, there's one fellow you forgot, this man Totals. I looked at the box score and seen that he got four hits yesterday."

Never mind. The mocking and the jokes didn't bother Connie Mack. He had his methods. He had his boys. He would take his chances with both.

Mack was still dissatisfied with his outfield, except for Danny Murphy. The Washington captain, Bob Ganley, was available. Ganley didn't appear to be Mack's kind of player. He was thirty-four and had a stronger thirst than arm. The only thing going for him was some speed and experience. Nationals manager Joe Cantillon wanted some of Mack's youngsters in exchange. Mack said no; Ganley wasn't worth it. He'd pay cash only. Cantillon let Ganley go for the waiver price of $1,500.

At the end of May the A's played three doubleheaders against Boston to make up rainouts. Four were 1-run games; two were shutouts. On Saturday, May 29, in the first inning Frank Baker hit the first home run out of Shibe Park, a clout that cleared the right-field wall and bounced off a house on Twentieth Street. John Shibe ran out and retrieved the ball, had it gilded, and displayed it in his office. The A's swept the pair behind Krause and Plank.

On Decoration Day morning Bender took his first loss, 3–2 to Ed Cicotte. Coombs lost the afternoon game, 2–1, to Cy Morgan, who seemed to be able to beat the A's just by showing up. The thirty-year-old right-hander was now 2-6; both his wins were against the Athletics. Mack figured if they couldn't beat him, they might as well trade for him. A sub-.500 pitcher with control problems—mental and physical—Morgan had a devastating assortment of curves. But whenever he walked a few batters, he lost confidence in his hooks and started grooving pitches. He was working on a spitter to go with the inshoot he threw with the same motion. The Red Sox weren't happy about his experimenting or his attitude on defense. When a ball was hit to the first baseman, Morgan stood and watched instead of covering first base.

During the long train rides, Morgan might entertain his teammates with song and dance routines, but he woke up mean and grouchy. One morning in a Chicago hotel he thought the service was too slow. He picked up all the silverware on the table and threw it into an electric fan. That brought him quick attention from the hotel manager as well as the waiter.

So the Red Sox decided they'd had enough of Cy Morgan and were ready to trade him. On June 5 Mack sent Vic Schlitzer and $3,500 to Boston for Morgan. Schlitzer won 8 games for Boston in the next two years. Morgan won 49 in three years with the A's.

The going turned choppy in June. Plank and Coombs went through a period where one bad inning cost them game after game. Dygert was inconsistent. Vickers was ineffective. Morgan gave them a brief respite, beating St. Louis, 3–1, in his first Philadelphia start.

And they stopped hitting. When they won, this is how they did it: on Friday, June 11, Rube Waddell had them down 1–0 in the seventh. Bender pinch-hit for Plank and singled. Ganley singled him to third. With 2 outs and 2 strikes, Collins put down a perfect bunt to squeeze in the tying run. They won it in the eleventh when Collins beat out an infield roller, Murphy bunted him to second, and Davis singled.

Addie Joss, said by Collins to throw the best change of pace "that ever floated under my bat," almost no-hit them on June 8. The only hit came when Danny Murphy hit a double one pitch after claiming, unsuccessfully, that the previous pitch had brushed his shirt.

Ganley wasn't hitting. Mack put Rube Oldring back in center field and tried everybody in left. To add to their woes, a week-long trolley strike and two days of rain cost the club at least $35,000 in lost revenue.

The Tigers came to Shibe Park for the first time on June 16. Veteran right-hander George Mullin, 11-0, was due to start the first game. That morning the Athletics discussed how to attack him. Somebody mentioned that Mullin took pride in his hitting and enjoyed talking about it. A career .263 hitter, he was often used as a pinch hitter. Somebody else said he noticed that Mullin didn't pitch as well when he wasn't hitting. Keep him off the bases and he might let down in the box in the later innings. Another player asked which of the A's pitchers was most effective pitching to Mullin. Mack said Bender. It was Plank's turn, but Bender was rested. Bender pitched, held Mullin hitless, and the A's handed him his first loss, 5–4.

As June ended, the A's bats woke up, but they couldn't gain on the first-place Tigers, who led on July 4 by 5½ games. The Red Sox stayed in the race despite weak pitching. For the first time in league history, a pitching staff would complete fewer than half their starts, prompting a *Boston Herald* writer to observe, "With the number of pitchers used in games these days, it would take a Philadelphia lawyer most times to select the pitcher entitled to the victories or to be charged with the defeats."

On June 29 the A's began their longest trip of the season, encompassing 20 percent of the entire schedule and taking them to every city in the league. They started in grand style, winning 4 of 5 in Boston and 5 in a row in New York before heading west. Collins was the first in the league to reach 100 hits. He and Davis and Baker each hit game-winning home runs in one week. Detroit lost 3 in a row, and the lead was down to 2½ games when the Athletics arrived in Detroit on July 8.

The Athletics and Tigers were the fiercest rivals in the league. Any game in which Ty Cobb played had the potential for fireworks, but that potential seemed to become reality more often than not when these two teams clashed. Whenever the A's won in Detroit, they huddled in the middle of the horse-drawn bus that took them back to the hotel, out of the range of the garbage and missiles fired at them. Connie Mack was still angry over Silk O'Loughlin's call in the 17-inning tie with Detroit that he believed had cost him the 1907 pennant. The A's had faded out of the three-way race in 1908, but that did nothing to lighten the animosity between the clubs.

And here they were again, the Athletics fighting, surprisingly in the eyes of most observers, to knock off the two-time champions. The big story was Harry Krause—the new Rube Waddell—on the field. Krause, who turned twenty-two on July 12, had run his record to 8-0 by shutting out Boston twice; then he beat Detroit, 3–1, on July 8 and 7–1 three days later. Six of his 10 wins were shutouts; he was scored on in only 5 of 97 innings pitched.

Running on Rossman and the Detroit catchers, the A's stole 7 bases in one game, took 3 out of 4, and headed for Cleveland within .002 percentage points of first place. And then, just like that, they stopped hitting again. Danny Murphy couldn't buy or beg a hit. They lost 3 of 4 one-run games in Cleveland for want of a Murphy clutch hit. Harry Davis was hurting. Mack put Hyder Barr on first. Barr made 3 errors in a 6–5 loss. Mack gave up on him as Davis's future replacement and sold him to Atlanta.

They lost 3 in a row in St. Louis, where Krause's winning streak came to an end—two weeks later. On Sunday, July 18, the A's took a 4–3 lead in the eleventh. The Browns loaded the bases with no outs in the bottom of the inning. Bender relieved Krause and gave up a 2-run single to Dode Criss. The official scorer listed Bender as the losing pitcher. A few weeks later Ban Johnson overruled the scorer and charged Krause with the loss. (There were no rules determining winning and losing pitchers until 1950. Ban Johnson had the final say in such matters in the American League.)

After losing 4 in a row in Chicago, they ended the thirty-day, thirty-one-game trek by salvaging a sweep of 4 at Washington. But the Tigers had pulled away again, and Boston was closing in on them from behind.

Connie Mack continued to back his players. He did no large-scale lineup shuffling. In the meetings he remained attentive to their suggestions. During a game he sat on the bench looking as calm as a spectator without a bet on the outcome. At least that's the way it looked to the average fan in the stands.

"Mack apparently is a stoic," wrote Grillo in the *Washington Post*, "but in reality is anything but that. He assumes this attitude for effect and results seem to indicate that it is a success. Mack's teams always hustle and that without being driven. There is something about the Mack method that makes his players put forth every effort for him. They like him, too, and yet he has little to say one way or the other."

Mack's composure was deliberately put on to infuse an atmosphere of calm confidence in the dugout. But he wasn't silent. He wanted his boys to be alert, hustling mentally as well as physically, their minds focused on the game. "Come on, a little life, boys," he might say, or "Wake it up down there." His own emotions seemed strapped inside, churning away, imperceptible except to the keenest observer. Eddie Collins was a keen observer.

"From the stands he looks motionless," Collins wrote. "However he is under a terrific mental strain. He is one of the nerviest men in the world when the game is being contested. He seems to be just a bundle of nerves, installed on the edge of the bench and ready to collapse if something out of the ordinary happens. But he never collapses. It has always been a wonder to me how the man can restrain himself from giving vent to some hysterical outburst."

Once in 1908 another keen observer, a *Cleveland Press* writer, had focused on Mack sitting in the dugout during a game,

putting on a performance which had the show in the center ring beaten to a whipped cream froth.

Mack gave a combination exhibition of a facial extortionist and a first-class case of fidgets . . . and his gyrations made a regular army signal service man at wigwag practice seem as immobile as a cigar store Indian.

He began when his team took the field, by moving Shaughnessy and Fox in positions where they might better get a drive from Josh Clarke's bat. Then when Josh singled to left center and reached second when the ball escaped Shaughnessy, his knees danced impatiently, and he scribbled a reference on a pad. With Bradley at bat, a wave of Mack's right hand pulled in the fielders. He smiled and nodded vigorous approval when Stovall flied to Nicholls, but gave a fair imitation of a Wounded Knee ghost dancer when the shortstop threw poorly to Powers and Clarke loped home. More copious notes.

During the play Mack telegraphed messages to somebody, somewhere, with long prehensile fingers on one knee . . . then he kept time with his impatience by doing a breakdown with one foot; he leaned forward, watching each play intently, straightened his long back, frowned, looked solemn, and finally in the fourth, when Murphy's single dribbled through Hickman's understandings, he smiled a smile of sweet content.

It's good to watch the Naps and Athletics put up a game . . . but it's a lot more fun to keep an eye on C. Mack and his three-in-one circus that makes him the shrewdest manager base ball ever produced. And there is no extra charge for the grand added attraction.

Thirty-five years later Mack's grandson, Frank Cunningham, was an A's batboy. He was struck by "Pop-Pop's" outward composure. "I was impressed with how calm he was during every game," Cunningham said. "I was sitting next to him once during a close game and the other team had men on base and we could lose the game and it was tense. I could feel it. I remember looking at him and wondering, 'How could he live this long with all this excitement? How come his heart didn't stop?'"

In his later years, Mack would sometimes go home after the first game of a Sunday doubleheader and listen to the second game on the radio. In the privacy of his living room, the cover of composure came off. "He never sat down," Cunningham said. "He would walk back and forth and jingle the change in his pocket until the game was over. You were in the room with him but he wasn't really aware of your being there because he was so engrossed in the game."

The western teams came east on July 29, the Tigers riding a 6½-game lead. Paced by Collins, who was now leading the league in batting, .351 to Cobb's .332, the A's took 4 out of 5 from Cleveland and 3 of 4 from Chicago, cutting the lead to 2 games.

On Tuesday, August 3, the uproarious umpiring career of Tim Hurst came to an end in Philadelphia. The A's won the first of two against Chicago, 2–1. In the second game, with O'Loughlin behind the plate and Hurst on the bases, the A's were in the midst of a 4-run eighth inning when Hurst called Collins out on a play at second base. Everybody else on the field had seen second baseman Jake Atz juggle the throw. Collins protested vehemently. The diminutive Hurst had been in hot water before for swinging a mask or fist at a player or manager. This time he spat in Collins's face. When the game ended, many of the sixteen thousand fans stormed onto the field intent on raining moisture, bottled and unbottled, on Hurst. A wall of police and players surrounded the umpire and escorted him off the field. Hurst refused to apologize or even file a report on the incident. Ban Johnson fired him.

(When Tim Hurst died in 1915, Connie Mack said of the pugnacious Irishman, "Hurst lost his head at times, and this was eventually his undoing, but he did more to stamp out rowdyism than any other official I have known. He was fearless and one of the gamest men who ever handled an indicator. In the old days, when an umpire had a harder class of men to deal with, Hurst used force when necessary, and I never saw him get the worst of an encounter with a player. And at the same time he was always a friend of the player and I have seen him go to the aid of a player more than once. I can remember an instance in particular where he took an awful licking from a gang of bleacherites to protect a player.")

The Tigers came in for four games beginning Friday, August 6. Mack told his team he intended to pitch only the left-handers Plank and Krause against the Tigers' lefty-heavy lineup of Cobb, Crawford, McIntyre, Rossman, and Jones. That afternoon, before a crowd of 12,749 that ignored heavy, overcast skies, the strategy worked against everybody but Cobb. He led off the second against Krause with an inside the park home run. In the fourth he walked, stole second and third, and scored on a wild pitch. It's easy to say that Cobb was a nemesis to the A's, but he was the same to every team. Detroit/Cobb won, 3–1.

On Saturday it was Plank vs. Mullin, two fidgeters whose delaying tactics created overanxious batters and impatient spectators. But even the prospect of a tedious two-hour game didn't stop more than twenty-six thousand people, many of whom overflowed into the outfield. In the first inning, catcher Oscar Stanage knocked Collins for a loop as Collins tried to score. The burly catcher threw an elbow into Eddie and sent him sprawling, senseless for about five minutes. No fight started; the benches didn't empty. It was just part of the game. The only argument came after the umpire called interference on the catcher and the run counted. Collins woke up and drove in 3 runs and scored the other 2 in Plank's 5–3 win. When Stanage left the game in the sixth with a split finger, the Philly fans gave him a stout jeering.

Krause came back on Monday, aided by a Baker home run and 8 Detroit errors for a 7–1 win. The next day Eddie Plank made everybody nervous, not just the Detroit batters. Connie Mack's outward calm concealed plenty of inner agitation. Three times the Tigers loaded the bases and failed to score. The more pinches he got into, the more Eddie fidgeted, posed, changed positions, held the ball. Plank's home run and some aggressive base running gave the A's a 3–1 lead. In the ninth, the Tigers had runners on second and third with 2 outs and Ty Cobb at the plate. Plank called catcher Paddy Livingston out for a conference. The infielders joined them, expecting a discussion of whether to walk Cobb and pitch to Wade Killefer. Instead, Plank said, "If I get two strikes on Ty, I'm going to throw a spitter." Livingston didn't know whether to laugh or argue. Plank didn't throw spitters; the inexperienced catcher had rarely caught one. But Plank was serious, so all Paddy said was, "I will be looking for it."

Eddie Collins wrote:

The first two pitches were balls with Ty tense and anxious. Then, after stalling around extra long, Plank shot over a strike catching Cobb off guard. Cobb was vexed. Next, a nice tantalizing curve, and the ball was slammed down the right field line, foul by inches. The next pitch was a ball, making the count three and two.

As Livingston returned the ball on that pitch Plank moistened his fingers and no one saw him. He fiddled around, changed his pose, then changed back, but at last he pitched. That spitter sure broke. It would have been a credit to Walsh and it went over the pan for a perfect strike.

Though Livingston had given the sign he had not anticipated the terrific break and the ball knocked him over as he blocked it.

Cobb, however, was paralyzed and Paddy pounced on the ball and touched him out. The game was over. It was Plank's first and last spitter.

The A's then took 3 out of 4 from St. Louis, and when the sun set on Saturday and the western teams headed home, they held a ½-game lead over the Tigers. Mack deflected the praise some writers handed him for turning his raw material into winners virtually overnight. "The boys themselves have done the work and they should receive the praise. I felt confident all through even when the outlook was the darkest that they would make good. They have done so. Now they must hold on to what they have got. Detroit and Boston are mighty dangerous propositions."

The young Athletics rolled on. They knocked out Walter Johnson in the first inning on Monday, but Johnson came back the next day and beat them, 1–0, in 12 innings, giving Collins some sore ribs from an inside fastball. Plank won the third game; then they began their last invasion of the west, leading Boston by 1 game and Detroit by 1½.

Dodging Addie Joss, who was sidelined with a pulled muscle, they took 4 from Cleveland, Cy Morgan winning 3 of them. Mack was platooning his outfield, replacing Hartsel and Ganley with Oldring and Heitmuller against left-handers. It was mid-August and two outfield slots were still unsettled.

Before the A's reached Detroit, the Tigers made two significant trades. They sent Claude Rossman to St. Louis for Tom Jones, and second baseman Germany Schaefer to Washington for Jim Delahanty. Jones and Delahanty were right-handed batters who might be less vulnerable to Plank and Krause. Jones was not the hitter Rossman was, but he had no mental throwing impediments. (The twenty-eight-year-old Rossman's big league career ended that year, prompting writer Frank Hough to comment, "The A's are sorry to see him go. When Claude was compelled to make a throw, it made no difference in which direction the throw went. Large happenings were sure to follow.")

The Athletics came into Detroit on Tuesday, August 24, with a 1-game lead over the Tigers, 2½ over Boston, Krause and Plank ready, and loaded with confidence. In the opener Krause cruised until the seventh, when the Tigers scored 4 runs and beat him, 7–6. But that was not the story.

Ty Cobb and Donie Bush were on a tear. They never stopped running, rolling into and over infielders guarding the bases. On a play at third base, Cobb slid into the bag with his left foot, his right foot about ten inches in the air. Baker had the ball in his right hand and tried to tag the elusive Cobb. He missed, but Cobb's spikes didn't miss Baker. They grazed the third baseman's forearm, opening a gash that spewed blood over his arm.

Martin Lawler came out and wrapped it and Baker stayed in the game. Afterward, it took ten stitches to close the cut.

Connie Mack was furious. He may have been a stoic on the bench, but when he was sore, he could blow up like an overheated Stanley Steamer. The frustrating late-inning loss may have stoked his boiler; had the A's won, there might have been less steam to release. Maybe. Mack charged:

[Cobb] boasted before the game that he would get some of the Athletics. He made good by spiking Baker and all but cutting the legs off Collins. Actions against Cobb should be taken by the league officials. I would not have him on my team if he played for nothing. Personally I am not very well acquainted with the young man. I think it's just his second nature to act mean on the ball field. He probably gets up in the morning with a grouch on and it sticks on him all day. Then when the game is on he gives vent to this feeling by making trouble. Such tactics ought to be looked into by the American League and I intend to see to it that the matter is taken up. Other players have rights as well as Cobb. He should not be permitted to vent his spite upon them. He may be a great player, but he is a pinhead in this respect. Organized baseball ought not to permit such a malefactor to disgrace it.

Cobb returned the fire, chiding Mack for running to the newspapers to knock him:

Mack knows that I never spiked a man deliberately. And he also knows that the runner is entitled to the line. If the baseman gets in the way he is taking his own chances. When I slid I made for the bag. If the man with the ball is in the way he is apt to get hurt. But that is his lookout. He has no business on the line. It is a plain case of squeal with Mack. . . . In Philadelphia when they were seven runs to the good and we had no chance to win, both Barry and Collins dove into Schaefer and tried to put him out. And Collins did get Stanage and put him out for a week. But we didn't holler. That is baseball. If we get hurt, we take our medicine and don't go around crying over it. Collins is all right. He tried to block me off Tuesday but I dumped him. He didn't say a word because he knew that I was right. He goes into the bases the same way that I do and he's hurt as many men as I have.

It's true; Cobb and Collins played the game the same way, always thinking, running recklessly at times, keeping infielders edgy and off-balance, claiming the baselines, forcing errors. In a June 1911 article in *Pearson's* magazine, Collins wrote, "I think there should be a penalty for blocking a baserunner coming into the bag. The only punishment now is to go into such a player spikes first."

Umpire Billy Evans compared Collins to "an automobile with the engine running, always swinging his hands and body, in motion." Collins, like Cobb, sometimes ran in what seemed a stupid situation to steal a base, like on a 3-0 count with nobody out. Like Cobb, he was doing the unexpected to plant seeds of uncertainty, unpredictability, in the minds of pitchers, catchers, and infielders. Other players played that way too. Cobb and Collins were just better at it than anybody else.

Detroit manager Hughie Jennings accused Mack of looking for somebody to blame when his team fell down, as he had done when "he charged umpire Silk O'Loughlin with crookedness" in 1907.

Neither Baker nor Collins backed their manager's assertions at the time, despite some reports quoting Baker as saying he was deliberately cut. They knew it was nearly impossible to make a so-called routine play against Cobb. "I had no set way of handling Cobb at third base," Baker said. "He was so clever at sliding he kept the infielders off balance. You never knew how he would slide. He could change direction in midair."

Years later, sitting in many a duck blind on cold, wet mornings, Frank Baker and Bill Werber would talk about Cobb and Collins and other oldtimers. "Frank never said that Cobb ever slid into him or cut him deliberately," Werber recalled.

Baker was not the most graceful infielder at applying a tag on a sliding runner while avoiding being spiked. Once Hal Chase slid into third head first and Baker was cut on the hand when Chase brought his feet up under him as he slid across the bag. In the dugout Mack looked at Baker's bleeding hand and said, "What did he spike you with, Bake, his fingernails?"

Collins never said a disparaging word about Cobb, then or later. "Only players opposed to him knew what it meant to have Cobb in the game," he wrote. "Few were the infields he did not turn upside down and many of them he completely wrecked."

Long after their playing days had ended, Collins wrote, "I want to correct the erroneous impression that Cobb deliberately went out of his way to spike opposing players. It just wasn't so. . . . I can truthfully say I remember no time that he went out of his way to cut down another player. . . . His spikes left their marks on countless players, but that was because he was such an aggressive, victory-hungry player. If anyone blocked his way a collision was inevitable. . . . He was an elusive slider who frequently slid away from a tag rather than adopt football tactics."

Was Collins indulging in a sentimental whitewashing of Cobb? Had time dimmed his memory? Not really. He and Baker and Barry all spoke the same of Cobb at the time the incidents occurred. None ever accused Ty of intentionally cutting them. They also knew that Cobb wore his own share of scars on his legs and never complained about them. As an outfielder, he could only have gotten them from infielders' spikes.

The Detroit papers defended Cobb; most of the Philadelphia papers did too. Only one, the rabble-rousing *Record*, fueled the anti-Cobb frenzy among Philadelphia fans. Hate mail and death threats flowed from Quaker City pens. There was no love for Brother Cobb.

Connie Mack always appreciated Cobb's style. It was the way Mack's Pittsburgh teams had played, drawing writers' charges of "dirty tactics." One day he overheard a few of his players comment about some "lucky hits" Cobb had made against them. "Cobb makes his luck," Mack told them. "Cobb fights for everything he gets. You have to hand it to him. I don't know where there is one like him."

So why did he sound off the way he did on this occasion?

One motive could have been to fire up his own team after a disheartening loss. Not that they needed it. He may have misread them. Hughie Jennings suspected this was the case, saying "Mack's grandstand plays injure rather than help his team's chances."

Detroit writer Paul Bruske agreed. "Mack made a tactical error. He put it into his players' minds that they are in danger of bodily injury in the heat of such a series."

It's more likely that Mack hoped to crimp Cobb's style, to make him less aggressive for fear he might be fined or, worse, suspended, for his rough play. If that was his aim, he was helped by an immediate warning from Ban Johnson, who said, "There has been altogether too much of this sort of game with Detroit. Somebody is going to be made a shining example of it if I hear of another such affray. Cobb seems to be the chief offender and a word of advice should go a long way. He must stop that sort of playing or he will have to quit the game. Steps will be taken to overcome the possibility of spiking players."

The *Sporting News* also accused Cobb of using his spikes "to injure and intimidate infielders. . . . The list of his victims is too long to attribute the injury of all to accident or to the awkwardness of the victims."

Every manager makes dozens of decisions before, during, and after a game. Some of them work and some don't. This one, whatever Mack's reasons might have been, didn't work. The furor failed to help the Athletics. Bill Donovan, who had relieved in the first game, beat Plank the next day, 4–3, and George Mullin completed the sweep with a 4-hit, 6–0 win, as the A's made 6 errors, 4 by a jittery Eddie Collins.

If Connie Mack thought Ban Johnson's warnings would hobble Cobb or make him more cautious, he really wasn't "very well acquainted with the young man." None of it deterred Cobb, even before Ban Johnson declared that a photograph of the spiking of Baker, which appeared in the September 11 *Sporting Life*, vindicated Cobb. Over a two-week span, sparking a Detroit 14-game winning streak, Cobb batted .640 and averaged better than one stolen base a game. He passed Collins in the batting race and wound up leading the league in batting, slugging, hits, home runs, runs scored and batted in, and stolen bases. To placate Mack, Johnson issued a vague statement on the subject at the next league meeting, and that was the end of it.

The Detroit lead varied between 2 and 5 games into September. One more opportunity arose to sideline Cobb, but it had nothing to do with his spikes. As Cobb told it, on Saturday night, September 4, in Cleveland, he and some of his teammates went to a theater. When Cobb returned alone to the Euclid Hotel, he got into an argument, then a fight, with the night watchman, who, Cobb said, started it by hitting him on the head from behind. Cobb "turned around and sailed into him." They wrestled on the floor. Cobb pulled a knife and slashed the watchman across the hand. The watchman pulled out a gun. That ended the fight. Cobb went to his room. (The fight probably happened on Friday night; the Tigers left for St. Louis after the Saturday game.)

The watchman, George Stanfield, swore out a warrant for Cobb's arrest for assault with intent to kill. Tigers president Frank Navin persuaded the hotel manager to arrange for any further legal action to be postponed until after the season. Cobb lost no playing time.

The A's kept pace with Detroit but gained no ground. Mack brought Joe Jackson back from Savannah, but the Shoeless One made no better impression on Mack than he had before. At home against New York on September 7, Jackson misplayed 2 singles into a home run and a triple, costing 4 runs in an 8–6 loss.

They swapped 1–0 decisions with Boston, Plank beating Cicotte in the opener and Krause losing to Joe Wood in the second, before a crowd of 31,112, then came to another showdown series with Detroit, four games beginning Thursday, September 16. The Tigers had a 4-game lead. The *Record* continued to whip up the "get Cobb" crowd. Police escorted Cobb to and from Shibe Park and ringed the outfield in front of the roped-off spectators. The A's stopped the sale of bottled soft drinks for the series.

Cobb drew plenty of boos but an equal amount of cheers. The crowd stood and applauded when Cobb, on reaching third base during the game, shook hands with Baker. The only belligerent action occurred in the bleachers and grandstand, where rowdies jostled any gentleman caught violating the post–Labor Day taboo on wearing straw hats. They seized the toppers and skimmed them about the crowd until only remnants remained.

Despite showers that fell before and during the first game, a crowd of almost twenty-five thousand filled the seats. The Phillies, who had a day off, and a visiting Irish cricket team were among them. Eddie Plank kept them all on edge. He was in frequent trouble, twice striking out Cobb to escape. Detroit errors helped the A's eke out a 2–1 win.

On Friday another overflow crowd counted on Harry Krause to continue his mastery over the Bengals. Harry's control was shaky, his mind somewhere else. Between his failure to hold runners close to bases and Ira Thomas's slowness getting rid of the ball, the Tigers pulled 3 double steals in the last 2 innings. Three walks and a hit batter all scored in the visitors' 5–3 win.

Now Connie Mack's boys had to win two to stay alive. On Saturday it seemed as if anybody who had any interest in baseball was determined to be at the game. But the pennant race fever was not confined to the cities where the teams played. By now the names and images of Ty Cobb and Connie Mack and other baseball stars were known throughout the forty-six states and the territories. Relying solely on newspapers, magazines, and telegraph reports posted in the windows of newspaper offices, baseball fans who would never see a big league game eagerly followed the action. Newspapers as far away as the Pacific Coast printed the box scores.

There was no way to count the thousands of people still clamoring to get in when the Shibe Park gates closed at two. The announced total of 35,409 set a major league attendance record. Some of them may have been there to root for the hometown boy, Bill Donovan, who was having a mediocre year but always seemed to be at his best in Philadelphia. But the vast majority were cheering on their youthful Athletics to dethrone the arrogant, hated Tigers.

Mack's preseason psychological pinprick of Bender's pride when he told the press he was not counting on Bender to be an important part of the team seems to have worked. Bender had won 15 and lost 7, almost all complete games. During that morning's meeting Mack appealed to the ego that makes a champion when he turned to Bender and said, "Albert, this is the most important game of the year for us. I'm counting on you to win it."

Bender was not an overpowering pitcher. He changed speeds, threw strikes, and relied on his knowledge of hitters' strengths and weaknesses. And he was cool, unflappable. That afternoon he and Paddy Livingston shut down the Tigers' running game. He gave up 3 singles. Donovan allowed only 4 hits, but they were good for the only 2 runs.

Who knows how many customers a Sunday game might have attracted? As it was, a Monday throng of 27,275 filled the park. Despite a chronic breakdown in trolley service, the four-day total of 117,000 comprised almost 20 percent of the season's total attendance. The majority of them paid twenty-five cents; receipts came to about $42,000. The visitors' one-third share gave them a healthy check to take home.

Mack gave the ball to Plank again. The A's scored quickly off Ed Summers, Baker singling in 2 in the first. Detroit scored 1 in the third. In the top of the fourth, a fuse was lit that might have exploded the palpable tension and simmering antagonism toward Ty Cobb. Moving about in the batter's box, Cobb worked Plank for a base on balls. To hold Cobb close, Plank stood facing the runner, staring at him, varying the length of time he stared before throwing a pitch. Everybody knew that Cobb was going. Plank pitched to Crawford. Cobb took off. Livingston threw to Barry at second. Barry caught the ball, his left leg blocking the bag, as Cobb began his slide. Spikes ripped through stockings and flesh. Down went Barry. The umpire called Cobb out. The crowd roared, an ugly, menacing sound. Cobb stood up and trotted off the field. Hugh Jennings walked over and stopped him. He pointed to the players gathered around Barry and told Cobb to go back and show some concern and regret for the accident. Cobb went out to second base. The calm scene, the lack of any show of anger or hostility by the Athletics toward Cobb, silenced the crowd. The players knew that Barry's carelessness, putting his leg in harm's way, was to blame. Barry left the game.

Once play resumed, 3 hits, an error, and a passed ball gave the A's a 4–1 lead. In the sixth an error by McInnis, Barry's replacement, and hits by Cobb and Moriarty, made it 4–3, leaving the seat of Mr. Mack's trousers a little more threadbare as he squirmed on the bench. The A's held on to win; the Detroit lead was cut to 2 games.

Connie Mack made no public statement about Ty Cobb.

The scarred legs of many players of the time resembled railroad maps, Cobb's as well as those of the infielders and catchers he encountered. For the rest of Barry's life, that ten-inch scar on his left leg was the ugliest combat decoration on his body. Almost fifty years later, at an old timers' gathering in Philadelphia, Barry was visiting with some friends in the hotel lobby. Ty Cobb came up to him, put his arm around Barry's shoulder, and said, "Gentlemen, this is one man I was sorry I spiked."

The loss of Jack Barry disrupted the infield. In their first full season together, Barry and Collins had taken infield play to a new level. Now Eddie Collins tried to do everything himself, especially after errors by McInnis led to two losses. For the rest of the season, the Athletics' performance was ragged, full of mental and physical errors. The day after Barry's injury they made 4 errors in losing to a makeshift St. Louis lineup that had two outfielders in the infield and three rookies in the outfield. Even the dependable Harry Davis made a base-running mistake that cost them a chance to win a game. When they won two from Cleveland, 5–0 and 3–0, on Saturday, September 25, the *Record* accused Cleveland of laying down to help the A's overtake Detroit. It charged Ben Shibe with being involved in the conspiracy. The usually mild-mannered Uncle Ben was hurt. He issued a lengthy defense of his honor, which wasn't necessary. Nobody in Philadelphia put any stock in the accusations. The Athletics reacted by banning the *Record*'s writers from Shibe Park and cutting off the telegraph service to the paper's Chestnut Street office bulletin board, where play-by-play accounts of the games were posted.

The Tigers clinched the pennant on September 30. The Athletics finished second, 3½ games back. It had simply been too much Cobb and Donie Bush. No pair of youngsters under twenty-three has ever matched their combined 361 hits and 129 stolen bases. The twenty-two-year-old Collins had 198 hits and 67 stolen bases, but it wasn't quite enough.

In the last few games, Mack experimented with new "kindergartners," among them a second baseman from New Jersey named Jim Curry. At age sixteen years, six months and twenty-two days, Curry remains the youngest player ever to appear in an American League game. He had 1 hit off Walter Johnson and scored a run.

"So ended one of the grandest struggles for a pennant in local history," wrote Chandler Richter. And so it was. Mack's boys had almost pulled it off, winning 95 games. They won the season series against Detroit, 14-8. Their pitching led the league with 27 shutouts, allowing a league-low 408 runs, 85 fewer than Detroit. Bender worked 250 innings, the most since his rookie year, winning 18 with 8 losses. He earned all his incentive pay. Krause won 18, Plank 19, Cy Morgan 16. Collins, Baker, and Murphy carried the offense.

When a team falls short of a championship by only a few games, any one of a number of factors can be cited: Danny Murphy's occasional slumps; late-season injuries to Thomas and Livingston; this game-turning error or that one. But the most devastating blow had been the loss of Jack Barry for the last two weeks.

Ed Walsh once commented, "People did not realize how invaluable Barry is to the Athletics' success."

The Athletics knew it. Connie Mack knew it. Even Hugh Jennings knew it, saying, "Give me Barry at shortstop and I'd never lose a pennant with my team."

Disappointed as he was, Connie Mack never dwelt long in the land of might-have-been. He looked ahead, always ahead, always with optimism. His no-name boys had played like champions and made believers out of skeptics. The debut of Shibe Park had been a huge success. Only the New York Giants surpassed the Athletics' 674,915 attendance, a record for the city, and nearly double the Phillies' numbers.

Those figures didn't include family. Anybody—nephews, nieces, in-laws—and their friends could walk through the press gate, where George Flood presided and knew them all. Priests and other clergy went in through the press gate too. Although baseball was replete with Irish stars and managers, the Philadelphia Athletics had become the anointed among the cathedrals and parish churches of the nation. Once a Philadelphia reporter was sent to interview an archbishop who had just returned from Rome. The starchy clergyman proved to be a dull interview. The only time he became animated was when he heard a newsboy yelling, "Baseball Extra," and he asked the reporter if the Athletics had won.

A devoted American Leaguer from the league's birth to the end of his life, Connie Mack went to the World Series in Pittsburgh and Detroit rooting for the Tigers, who lost for the third year in a row. (In the 1930s Mack took his daughter Ruth to a World Series in New York. By then the Yankees had become the A's toughest rivals. Ruth sat behind her father, rooting loudly for the National Leaguers to beat the hated Yankees. "Dad stood it as long as he could," she said years later. "He turned around and said, 'Girlie, you're an American Leaguer and don't you forget it.' I still haven't.")

Two days after the World Series ended, Mack was in Chicago to begin a cross-country, two-month barnstorming tour with a team of his Athletics, supplemented by other American Leaguers, and a squad of National All-Stars. The players put up $200 each and shared in the receipts. The two teams went as far as Colorado, then went separate ways. The A's went north to Seattle, down to Los Angeles, east through Arizona and Texas, and finished in New Orleans. Eddie Collins's mother and the wives of Bender and Ira Thomas joined them along the way. Frank Baker's fiancee, Ottillie Rosa Tschantre, had moved from Maryland to California. They were married in San Francisco on November 13, then went to Mexico on their honeymoon.

The barnstormers ran into bad weather and played before some puny gatherings. In one town each player's share of the gate was thirty cents. But they broke even on the trip and received their $200 back. "The boys had the time of their lives," Mack said, "and are in tiptop shape for next season."

Romance kept Eddie Collins in Philadelphia when they returned in December. He was engaged to Mabel Doane. He worked in the sporting goods department at Snellenberg's, played indoor baseball, and wrote columns for the *Evening Bulletin*, airing his opinions on a variety of subjects.

Even after seven months of Pullman berths and hotel beds during the season, the restless Connie Mack had enjoyed the trip. "I like to get out of a rut," he said. Whether he said it with a smile of irony was not reported. Maybe, to him, the rut was visiting the same seven cities three times a year. Then, in an apparent reference to scenery that summed up his philosophy of business, baseball, and life, he added, "Wherever I can see the benefit of a change, I only too quickly grasp the opportunity."

37 | WORLD CHAMPIONS

America was a superstitious society in the early twentieth century. The influx of immigrants brought with it the demons and devils, evil eyes, and charms to seduce good luck and scare away the bad. Baseball players of whatever background were the most hex-conscious, far more so than today. Batters doomed to fail seven or eight times out of every ten times at bat seized on anything they believed might give them an edge. It didn't matter if the laws of physics decreed that there was no relation between how you tied your shoelaces or drew an "X" in the dirt with your bat and whether you hit Walter Johnson's fastball. In a business that bred insecurity, believing helped.

Every hitter knew that finding a hairpin or seeing a wagonful of empty barrels resulted in hits, but not as many as rubbing a black mascot's head or a hunchback's hump before going up to bat. Witnessing a funeral procession guaranteed the collar that day. Being stared at by a cross-eyed person was a sure jinx, to be countered only by quickly spitting in a hat.

Lists of items carried by players as good luck charms included an old detective's badge, short piece of trolley wire, peach pit, shred of ribbon from a WCTU banner, horse chestnut, minute hand of a watch, rook from a chess set, hotel key, and mandolin pick.

Striking out the first batter in a game boded ill for a pitcher. Some pitchers thought pitching a shutout brought bad luck; if they had a comfortable lead, they'd let the other team score a run to ward it off.

Education or intelligence had nothing to do with it. Some of the brainiest players carried the oddest quirks. The Athletics were no exceptions.

Chief Bender refused to warm up at the start of an inning with anyone but the game catcher. If the catcher was on base when an inning ended, Bender stood and waited in the pitcher's box rather than throw to a backup catcher. He refused to throw to the first or third baseman.

Umpires used a broom to sweep the dirt off home plate and leaned it against the grandstand when not in use. On September 22, 1909, Stuffy McInnis, never a slugger, tapped the broom with his bat on his way to the plate, then hit an inside-the-park home run off Jack Gilligan. After that, the only sensible thing to do was to tap the broom with his bat before every at bat. He didn't hit another home run until 1911, but that didn't matter.

Eddie Collins was hopping mad if anybody touched his glove lying in the field. When he stepped into the batter's box, he stuck his chewing gum on the button atop his cap until he had two strikes on him. Then he stuck it in his mouth. As long as he was hitting, he'd wear the same shirt. He had a lot of hot streaks; a shirt could get pretty dirty before he'd change it. Bits of paper strewn on the dugout steps agitated him. Later, as a manager, every time his team won, he would get dressed after a game the same way, putting on every piece of clothing, including his hat, before stepping into his trousers.

There were no bat racks. Bats were lined up neatly in a row on the ground in front of the bench. To get a rally going, or to celebrate one, the A's would pick up an armful of bats and fling them in the air. Otherwise, they'd better not be out of line.

Connie Mack had his superstitions too. When the A's were going well, he used the same pencil to keep score until it was worn to the nub. According to Ira Thomas, road secretary Joe Ohl borrowed it before a doubleheader one day and didn't bring it back. After the A's lost the first game, Mack sent somebody looking for Ohl without success. The A's lost the second game too. When Mack saw Ohl at the hotel that evening, he snapped, "Don't you ever borrow a pencil from me again. Bring your own."

Maybe it happened. It could have.

So it was not surprising when Rube Oldring showed up at Shibe Park on Saturday, October 2, the last day of the 1909 season, with a short, stocky, pale-faced, humpbacked lad of fifteen and asked Connie Mack if the misshapen boy could mind the bats during the doubleheader against Washington. The A's had just lost 3 in a row to the White Sox, enabling Detroit to clinch the pennant. Mack could point to several turns of bad luck that had sunk them during the season. He could use a good luck charm.

"Sure," he said.

The boy kept the bats in order, retrieving and replacing them as they were used. He wobbled a little under Frank Baker's 52-ounce lumber but performed his chores with agility and a smile. And the Athletics won both games.

Thus did Louis Van Zelst become part of the Athletics family. Born in 1894, Louie had been a straight and healthy youngster living in West Philadelphia. When he was eight, a fall twisted his spine and left him unable to walk for two years. A hump developed on the left side of his back, forcing his shoulders up to ear level. A bright, quick-witted boy, Louie never let his confinement or deformity sour his disposition, though he tired easily and suffered chronic painful back spasms. When he could walk again, he spent time at the nearby campus of the University of Pennsylvania. He was soon adopted by Penn athletic teams as a good luck mascot. Some of the Athletics who lived in the neighborhood got to know him. Rube Oldring was one of them.

Impressed by Louie's attitude and efficiency and the two wins over Washington, Connie Mack invited him to be the A's batboy and mascot for the 1910 season, ordered a uniform for him, and put him on the payroll. Suddenly little Louie became a big man among his classmates at the Newton School. For the next five years, Louie was a familiar sight to the fans at Shibe Park as he crouched stonily in the same spot between the bench and home plate during each at bat. He did his job with alacrity and enthusiasm, and the players enjoyed his humor and sunny disposition. On the field before games he warmed up with the players. For two years he was Rube Oldring's regular partner. An accomplished mimic, he broke up the players and Mack with his perfect imitation of Eddie Plank's actions in the pitcher's box. Louie was equally friendly with visiting players, who greeted him warmly.

Beginning in 1911, Little Van, as the players called him, made at least one road trip with the A's and went to spring training beginning in 1912. He traveled with them to every World Series they played in. When the A's hosted a banquet for the Base Ball Writers' Association in New York on December 12, 1911, he received an invitation. He was a guest at Eddie Collins's wedding. The Athletics were his friends, his life. He was not robust and had to conserve his energy. The players looked after him on the road. His idol, Jack Coombs, saw that he was settled in his Pullman berth or hotel room each evening. Jack Barry took him to Mass on Sundays. One day Connie Mack let him go out to the first base coach's box during a game in New York. Umpire Tom Connolly was not amused and ordered Mack to call him back to the dugout.

Louie was well aware of the players' superstitions toward his deformity and felt no shyness or sensitivity about it. When a hitter was in a slump, he'd suggest in his thin voice, "Better rub me for a hit." They did. And Louie brought them luck.

Not everybody saw Louie's role in the same light. A Cleveland writer once criticized Connie Mack for offending fans by exhibiting the boy's twisted body at ballparks around the league. That ignited the kindling in Mack's temper. "I was so mad," he recalled to Fred Lieb, "I walked all the way out to the ballpark so I could cool off and not say something I might regret. When I got there I was pleased to run into Ed Bang, the veteran Cleveland writer. He, too, had read the story, and felt about it exactly as I did."

With the opening of new ballparks and two exciting pennant races, major league attendance had boomed in 1909. Throughout the nation, baseball was becoming more popular. Fifty minor leagues operated in 1910. Every town had an amateur or semipro team. One estimate put fifty semipro, amateur, college, and school leagues in Chicago alone. Equipping them all accounted for $2 million in sales.

Seas of ink were consumed by broadsheet sporting sections of news-papers. Wire services, telegraphers, beat writers, and columnists became major expenses of the press. Competition among a dozen daily papers in major cities expanded the column inches devoted to baseball. It was good for the clubs and good for circulation. Writers looked for angles and scoops and had rich veins of lore to mine among the colorful players and man-agers of the time. They rode with the players, roomed with them, even practiced with them on the field during spring training. Jargon-coining was rampant among the scribes: $10,000 lemons or beauties, sky child, baseball bugs, beating the air, beatific hitting, brushing the plate, fanning, playing by the book, crowding the plate, hassocks, hitsmiths. Some of it stuck, some of it evaporated.

Player salaries were not officially released. They were guessed, occasionally accurately. Once in a while a legal action revealed some specifics. Phillies manager Billy Murray testified that his 1910 salary was $7,500 when the club fired him and he sued.

The first decade of the new century had been good for the baseball business. New York writer Sam Crane estimated average salaries of $3,000 and team payrolls of $75,000. He calculated a team's total expenses at $158,000, receipts of $372,000, for an average profit of over $200,000. Averages conceal extremes. Some clubs did better; some did worse. A *Sporting Life* summary of the Cleveland club's profits disclosed a range from $44,580 in 1904 to $104,958 in 1908.

Baseball was also catching on to creative accounting. In Chicago the Board of Review allowed the White Sox to classify players as merchandise. In a statement filed with the assessors, Charles Comiskey listed their value at $1,981—for the entire team. Added to $105 worth of furniture and $461 in accounts receivable, he declared the club's net worth to be $2,547. Comiskey's stadium and grounds were held by a separate corporation.

Canny investors looking for new fields of profits took notice. There was talk of putting together a new rival twelve-club major league. The players noticed too. The pie had grown, and they wanted a bigger slice of it. They considered starting another, stronger players' union. And once again there were cries of outrage over players' greed. The *Sporting News* editorialized that players "do nothing but talk money on and off the field." Wage earners were still working six-day weeks and ten-hour days for the $500 a year considered necessary for a decent standard of living. It took them almost two years' income to buy a Model T Ford.

To increase revenue, the National League wanted to expand the 1910 schedule to 168 games. The American suggested cutting back to 140 and starting the season later to avoid the April showers. Eventually they agreed to keep the 154-game format. Charlie Ebbets urged the National to extend its season to October 15 to harvest an extra holiday, Columbus Day. A Cleveland writer commented, "Beginning a baseball season before the ice is off the ponds and continuing it until chestnuts are ripe doesn't seem to be very good business policy." But Ebbets got his wish. Philadelphia remained the only city with a twenty-five-cent general admission. The other American League clubs pressured the Athletics to raise it to fifty cents. Ben Shibe and Connie Mack refused.

The nation's most prolific chronicler of baseball, Hugh Fullerton, was already tearful with nostalgia for the good old days. He decried the lack of players with speed, brains, and character. Apparently, Connie Mack had cornered the market. The team he had built was the result of years of creating a scouting network. He lost Sam Kennedy, who went to Cleveland, but he still had Al Maul, Tom O'Brien, and Pop Kelchner. He sent veteran players who were sidelined with injuries on hunting expeditions or special assignments. And he had agents everywhere who might not have been called scouts, but they filled the same role for him. He kept up a voluminous correspondence, sowing good will among minor league and semipro club operators. An example is this letter he typed one spring to Mr. A. J. Heinemann, secretary of the New Orleans club:

My Dear Mr. Heinemann:

Am in receipt of your new Base Ball Score-book. And I want to compliment you on your getting out such an elegant book for the patrons
of your game. Consider this book one of the best that has ever been
produced, by the Base Ball Profession, and great credit is due you for
the able manner in which you have taken care of this, so important a
thing to Base Ball.

> Trusting your season will be a
> very successful one, I remain,
> Yours truly,
> /s/Connie Mack

Every town in the country was an incubator for ballplayers, and Mack
seemed to have somebody in all of them to tip him off to a budding star. Of
course, most of them never bloomed, but he gave plenty of them the thrill
of going to a big league training camp or playing in one big league game.
"Out of twenty, if I get one or two good men I'm satisfied," he said.

No application for a tryout went unanswered. In the spring of 1910 Art
Nehf was a seventeen-year-old semipro pitcher in Terre Haute, Indiana.
His father wrote to every major league manager asking for a tryout for
his son. Connie Mack was the only one who replied. He invited Nehf to
come to Chicago when the A's were there in June. In the meantime, though,
Nehf signed with the Terre Haute club, which later sold him to the Boston
Braves. Nehf, who went on to win 184 games in a fifteen-year career, never
forgot Mack's invitation. Five years later they met for the first time, and
Nehf thanked him for his interest. Chances are, in the years that followed,
when Art Nehf saw a young sandlotter with a humming fastball, he would
think of Mr. Mack.

In November Jack Dunn bought the Baltimore Orioles from Ned
Hanlon for about $35,000. He didn't say how he raised the money; there
is some evidence that it was a loan from Connie Mack. Mack, John Shibe,
and Dunn were close friends. Dunn, Shibe, and Eddie Collins often went
hunting together. Collins became a part-owner and director of the Orioles.
During the 1910 season Mack would send Dunn a half dozen players. His
relationship with Dunn was not unusual for Mack. He did favors, sometimes financial, for many minor league operators. He had strings on so

many players he was always in a position to help out a manager in need of a quick replacement. *Inquirer* writer James Isaminger claimed that Mack carried notes in his pocket that listed five teams' worth of lineups. If he received a wire from a manager somewhere pleading for a catcher, Mack sent a catcher his way. Dozens of grateful managers thought of him first when they saw a promising prospect or had a prize young player to sell. If any player anywhere had a good season, Mack was likely to know about it, scouts or no scouts.

Mack also had his own book on minor league managers and owners. Cross him up or do him wrong and you were off his list forever. Isaminger told of one manager who promised Mack delivery of a promising young catcher at the end of the season. One day Mack read that the catcher had been sold to another team. He wired for an explanation and received this reply: "Had to sell player to Detroit. Will send letter."

Mack shot back, "Never mind the letter," and had nothing more to do with him.

Minor league managers begged Mack for a chance to borrow Stuffy McInnis for a season to develop him. According to Isaminger, one manager pleaded, "Give him to me and I'll make a regular out of him."

"You couldn't make a regular out of anyone," Mack snapped.

McInnis wasn't going anywhere. His schooling wasn't finished. Mack preferred to keep him under his tutelage, even if it meant less playing time, than trust him to any minor league teacher.

On March 1 Harry Davis took the veterans to Hot Springs, Virginia, for ten days of conditioning: running, hiking, golfing. Jack Coombs proved to be the best on the links. They didn't pick up a baseball the whole time. Connie Mack didn't prescribe a strict regimen for them. He trusted them to know how to get themselves ready for the long season at their own pace and in their own way.

Mack took the rookies and prospects and younger players to Atlanta. He devoted his full attention to them, especially the pitchers, the Johnny Foremans and Norwood Hankees who blossomed and faded as fast as peonies in the spring. Maybe one in a hundred would make it, but while they were there, Connie Mack made each one feel as though he was counting on him to become the next Bender or Plank.

Mack's son Earle was in camp. It being politic to praise the boss's son, everybody pronounced the twenty-year-old catcher a "real comer" and predicted "a brilliant future" for him. Earle went to Utica, where he batted .135. He would make token appearances in five late-season games over three years with the A's, and in 1913 he would begin a long career as a minor league player-manager before joining the Athletics as a coach in 1924.

The A's also had a new trainer. Martin Lawler moved to the St. Louis Browns and was replaced by James Chadwick.

Connie Mack wanted a happy ship. Baseball was a game, played for the entertainment of the spectators, and it should be fun for everybody. He enjoyed every minute of it. He ate well and slept well and wanted his boys to do the same.

In the spring of 1910 he saw no shadows on his bright outlook. Once his team was all together in Atlanta, he looked over what he had assembled, and it pleased him. If he couldn't win with these players, he said, he couldn't win with anybody.

Connie Mack had created a different kind of team, one with a close personal bond between players and manager, unlike any team before. It didn't come from mixing with the players socially; they seldom saw him outside the ballpark except on trains and in hotels on the road. It was forged by a combination of Mack's natural head-of-the-family style of authority, rather than that of boss or employer, and the age of his players, most of whom were young enough to be his sons. More than one player was quoted as saying, "We don't look on Connie as a manager or anything of that kind. We look on him as a father." He had few rules, no curfews, no bed checks. He wasn't interested in prowling hotel corridors, putting matchsticks or toothpicks atop doors to catch carousers coming in late. But he knew he had a bunch of hot-blooded young men, no monks, in his charge. In his morning talks he sometimes told them, "If you can't do what you want to do by midnight, you might as well give up." He reminded them often that any player dogging it or getting too much booze and not enough sleep was hurting not only himself but the rest of the team. Sometimes the players took it from there and straightened out the wanderer.

Connie Mack didn't miss much, as those who tested him learned. He might say to a suspected night crawler, "Our train leaves at seven thirty in the morning. Do you think you'll be in on time tonight to make it?" Or he'd be sitting in the hotel lobby in the evening when a player came in, called out an ostentatious "Good night" to him, and got on the elevator. Mr. Mack would get up and walk around to the rear entrance, where the freight elevator opened. When the player emerged and saw him, Mack didn't have to say a word.

There was another element that Connie Mack considered essential to the makeup of a winning player—enthusiasm. He knew when it was genuine and when it was fake. He had a keen eye, not only for talent, but for the degree of eagerness with which a man approached the day, the morning practice, the skull session, the game, the inning-by-inning challenges. He had no use for a loafer or sulker.

That was one of the things that discouraged him about Joe Jackson. He recognized Jackson's ability as a hitter, but the attitude he wanted to see wasn't there. To Jackson, the morning meetings meant nothing. Sometimes he didn't show up at all. He may have said, as he has been quoted, "It don't take school stuff to help a fella play ball." If he never said it, he demonstrated it. Over the winter Mack had offered to provide tutoring in reading and writing for Joe and his wife. They turned it down. To Mack, Jackson was the kind of player Hughie Jennings once described: "If that guy's brains were made of nitroglycerin and they exploded, the bust wouldn't muss his hair."

If Joe Jackson had taken some hazing when he first joined the Athletics, Mack would have noticed how he handled it. Plenty of rookies were teased, especially the few southerners in the big leagues, none more roughly than Ty Cobb. Cobb reacted with an "I'll show you all" vengeance. Jackson shrank inside himself, drank alone in his room, took attempts to help him as ridicule, and was likely to pack his Black Betsy and go home. He didn't fit in, didn't harmonize, with Mack's smart, polished team.

As good a ballplayer as Jackson may be, Mack decided he had a team that could win without Joe. Jackson wanted to go back down south. Mack asked waivers on him. Brooklyn claimed him, then withdrew the claim a week later. Mack sent Jackson to New Orleans with a string he knew was safe in the hands of his friend, Pelicans manager Charlie Frank.

Mack considered his infield set. He suggested that Frank Baker might generate more power by holding his bat down at the end instead of choking up. Baker tried it. He couldn't control his heavy bat as well and went back to choking up. Mack never mentioned it again. Realizing that this would probably be Harry Davis's last season, he bought Ben Houser, twenty-six, from Toronto. Mack gave up on Si Nicholls, once highly regarded by him, and traded Nicholls to Cleveland for a dispensable outfielder, Wilbur Good. Morrie Rath from Reading and Stuffy McInnis were his utility infielders.

The pitching staff looked in top form. Chief Bender had spent the winter indoors at Allinger's Billiard Parlor instead of on the outdoor skeet shooting circuit. He was heavier and stronger than at any time in 1909. During the trip to California, Jack Coombs had worked on cutting down his speed to improve his control and developed a drop ball. Unlike his curve, which broke sharply away from a right-handed batter, the drop headed for the middle of the plate, then fell a foot or two straight down. They didn't call it a splitfinger fastball, but that's the way it acted. Mack expected great things from 18-game winner Harry Krause.

He was satisfied with his catchers, but the outfield remained uncertain among Murphy, Hartsel, Heitmuller, Strunk, and Oldring.

The family atmosphere that Mack encouraged among his players extended to his partners and park employees. The Shibes were his warm friends. Neither Ben nor Tom Shibe had drawn a cent of salary since the club's beginning; Ben Shibe never would. Tom was doing well enough from the sporting goods business to buy a fifty-three-foot oceangoing yacht, the *Josephine II.*

Tom Shibe's wife, Ida, had always wanted to go to spring training. But her husband considered the early camps no place for a lady. Now that the facilities were first class, Ida Shibe accompanied her husband to Atlanta. It may have been because it was her first, or maybe it was the impression she got from the collegiate gentlemen on the team, but she always called the 1910 team her favorite. She soon became known to the players as Aunt Ida. An avid fan who collected elephants made of all sorts of materials, Ida Shibe missed only one wartime spring training from 1910 until she died in 1952.

To the end, Aunt Ida bristled when reporters referred to her as "a grand old lady."

"I'm not old," she insisted. "I'm very young in spirit."

In that regard, she was very much like Connie Mack.

The young colts and their headmaster took the morning meetings to new heights. With a year's experience behind them, they began refining what they had learned and invented. In the process they rewrote the book on baseball and did things the old book said not to do.

Jack Barry and Eddie Collins worked out a strategy to break up the running game, especially the double steal. The eight teams averaged over 200 stolen bases a year. The Tigers' Donie Bush and Ty Cobb had wrecked the A's with this potent weapon. Collins had a weaker arm than Barry. When he covered second with men on first and third, he couldn't make a strong enough throw to the plate to catch a fast runner. So they plotted. Regardless of which side the batter swung from, if the man on first broke for second, Collins would move into a line between the pitcher and second base. Barry covered second. If the runner on third stayed put, Collins would let the throw go through to Barry at second. If the man on third started for home, he would cut off the throw and return it to the catcher to nab the man trying to score. Day after day they practiced the play.

They decided they were ready to use it when Detroit made its first visit to Shibe Park in May. Bush and Cobb soon gave them the chance. With Bush on third and Cobb on first and 1 out, Cobb headed for second on the first pitch. Collins cut in behind the pitcher. Bush didn't move off third. Collins opened his hands and let the ball go by. But Barry was also watching Bush. The ball hit him in the stomach. Cobb slid into second and came up laughing. Barry never made that mistake again.

They questioned the wisdom of pitching to a hitter's weakness. If he liked to pull an inside fastball, they reasoned, why not pitch to his strength, let him pull it, and play him to pull it. Trying to fool the batter could lead to unpredictable results. The more predictable the hitter, the easier it would be to position the defense. This was the basis for Connie Mack's waving his scorecard to move his outfielders. (It was often a decoy; somebody else on the bench or the field was sending the messages.) For the free swingers like Cobb, who moved about in the batter's box, they played straight away. Of course, the pitchers had to have confidence in the men behind them and the manager's use of unorthodox alignments against certain hitters, and they had to have the ability to throw a pitch where they were expected to put it. Bender, Coombs, and Plank all had that confidence. Control was not measured by walks allowed. They would sooner miss with four pitches outside if they were supposed to throw outside than aim one away from where the fielders expected it to go.

Did it work? Anecdotal evidence—and the season's results—suggest it did. Beat writer Edgar A. Wolfe said, "So successful was this method that many times I sat in the press box in Shibe Park and heard visiting newspapermen remark, 'Luckiest team in the world. We hit 'em right on the nose and they were right at somebody.'"

Connie Mack went over the opponent's batting order before every game with the pitcher and catcher, but he never called pitches from the bench and never second-guessed them. The catchers might call the pitches, but Mack made it clear that the pitcher was the final judge of what to throw. Infielders were expected to study the hitters as intently as the battery.

Nor did Mack get on just the catchers for allowing stolen bases. He considered the pitcher more responsible than the catcher. Allow a base runner too big a jump, and no catcher could throw him out.

Everybody studied opposing pitchers. The A's were often accused of stealing catchers' signs, but most of the time they were reading the pitchers. Frustrated catchers might change their signals during a game and find it didn't help. Bender, Coombs, Davis, and Hartsel were the most adept at tipping off hitters. When they weren't playing, they manned the coaching boxes. The third base coach hollered the key words to signal what was coming.

Sometimes they picked up a clue during a game and didn't wait for a meeting to put it to use. Detroit knuckleballer Ed Summers had given them fits for two years. He liked to work fast. One day he was working with a rookie catcher against the A's. The catcher took his time getting the ball back to Summers, sometimes walking it out to the pitcher. Rube Oldring was at the plate and heard Summers snap peevishly at the catcher, "Fire the ball back to me quickly."

"Rube started stalling," Eddie Collins wrote. "Dirt in his eyes, rub his hands with dirt between pitches, delaying stepping into the box. Summers walked him. When Oldring told us what he had discovered, we all did the same. We had less of a problem with Summers after that."

All this intelligence didn't necessarily lead to an easy victory. Once they noticed New York pitcher Jim Vaughn was giving the signs, not the catcher. Even though they quickly deciphered what was coming, Vaughn still held them to 2 runs.

Unlike a year ago, when the A's had been ridiculed and relegated to the second division by the preseason seers, they were regarded as strong contenders by all but Hughie Jennings, who wishfully called them too old, with "too many veterans" to be as strong as they were in 1909. He saw them no better than fourth. "Their outfield has no class," he said.

"We will be the team to beat," Connie Mack declared. He considered New York his biggest threat. The Highlanders' pitching staff, he said, was the best they'd ever had.

The prospect of another contest between the perennial contenders prompted the *Boston Globe* to write what would become a perennial complaint for the next hundred years: "The two major league races are fast growing to be one-sided propositions. The strong teams are growing stronger while the weak ones are having a heap of trouble in building up."

By now most American League club owners were businessmen for whom baseball was a sideline. Clark Griffith's fears of the bushwhackers taking over had become reality. And for the first time there were no playing managers in the leagues when the 1910 season opened on April 14. Another first occurred in Washington, where the Athletics opened the season. President William Howard Taft, Mrs. Taft, Vice-President James Sherman, and Secretary of the Senate Charley Bennett occupied box seats on the first base side. It's unclear whether Nationals president Tom Noyes arranged for Taft to throw out the first ball or it was an impromptu suggestion by umpire Billy Evans, who handed the ball to Taft to do the honors. The 300-pound Taft, a pitcher at Yale in his slimmer days, obliged, to the loud applause of the overflow crowd of twelve thousand. Walter Johnson caught it. The next day Johnson sent the ball to the White House with a request that the president sign it. When it came back, Johnson proudly showed it to the players of both teams. Taft reportedly wrote on it: "For Walter Johnson with the hope that he may continue to be as formidable as in yesterday's game. William H. Taft."

In his first of fourteen Washington openers, Walter Johnson was indeed formidable. He gave up only one hit, a routine fly ball off the bat of Frank Baker that eluded the grasp of right fielder Doc Gessler as he tried to push through the fans in the outfield. The A's hardest hit ball all day was a line drive foul by Baker that the vice-president ducked. It clipped Charley Bennett on the head.

The rain and cold that would force the postponement of eighty-five games in the first two months put off the A's home opener for two days. When they did get to play on a dreary Wednesday, Bender shut out New York, 6–0.

The Athletics sprinted to the front with a 20-5 start, including 13 wins in a row. Bender, stronger and healthier than at any time since 1905, threw a no-hitter against Cleveland on May 12. He faced 27 batters; Terry Turner walked and was caught stealing. Bender didn't lose until May 23, Krause until May 19. They swept 4 from the White Sox, with Harry Davis running the team while Connie Mack was down with a stomach bug. Each morning Davis conferred with Mack, who told him to use mainly right-handers against the righty-swinging Sox. Chicago scored 6 runs in the four games. The A's won 17 of 21 on the home stand, but that didn't stop the fans from giving them a thorough roasting during a horrendous 14–2 loss to the Tigers, in which the Barry-Collins double steal strategy was introduced and Barry wasn't paying attention.

But Jack Coombs got off to a slow start. The cold affected him. He started only four games in the first six weeks and didn't win one until a month into the season. His control was off. Coombs relied on high hard stuff, and it was sailing out of the strike zone too often. Then somebody decided the problem was his catcher. When Coombs was a rookie, Monte Cross had suggested that he use a part of the catcher's body as a target. Coombs focused on the left shoulder. Ira Thomas was six inches taller than Jack Lapp. When Lapp caught him, Coombs's control was better.

"I don't look at the batter when I'm pitching," Coombs told the *Philadelphia Evening Times*. "I gauge my chucks by Lapp's left shoulder. When I want to cut loose a high fast one I look at that shoulder and let it go. With Ira Thomas working with me, I can't do this. He is so much taller that when I look at his shoulder the ball is sky high. It gets me in bad."

Lapp became Coombs's regular catcher. When he needed a rest, Pat Donahue, picked up for cash from Boston, or Paddy Livingston, another five-foot-eight fireplug, filled in. Thomas caught only one more Coombs start all season.

In early June, Baker and Murphy pulled up lame. Ira Thomas broke his thumb. Paddy Livingston had a strained tendon. The inexperienced Jack Lapp, Mack's most reliable pinch hitter, was pressed into doing all the catching. Then Baker was called home because of his wife's siege of typhoid fever.

In past years such injuries and slumps had crippled the Athletics enough to knock them out of pennant races. But this year was different. Mack's young utility corps of McInnis, Morrie Rath, and Amos Strunk filled in admirably. Bender, Plank, and Coombs were steady. Swept in Detroit, they lost the lead to New York on June 5. They limped out of the west in second place but snapped back to win 4 out of 6 in New York and regain the lead.

The only thing Mack might have agreed about with Hughie Jennings was his outfield. He knew it was not first class. Topsy Hartsel at thirty-six was about finished. He was platooning in left field with Heinie Heitmuller. When Amos Strunk banged up his knee, Mack looked for reinforcements. The *Cleveland Plain Dealer* reported that Mack called Charlie Frank in New Orleans and asked him to send Joe Jackson. Frank allegedly protested that Jackson was the reason the Pelicans were in first place; if he lost Jackson, the pennant would go with him.

Cleveland scout Bob Gilks had been urging the Naps to buy Joe Jackson since spring training. But neither Charles Somers nor Frank would do anything to jeopardize Connie Mack's claim to the player. An unsigned column in the *New Orleans Daily States* of August 21, 1915, related a story of Frank's once turning down a $10,000 offer from Cubs owner Charles Murphy for Jackson because he didn't have Mack's okay to sell the outfielder at the time.

The Naps arrived in Philadelphia on Friday, July 22, for a series including three doubleheaders. Club secretary Ernest Barnard was with them. Barnard, the chief financial officer of the club since 1904, was authorized to make player deals over manager Jim McGuire's head. (Charles Somers was in the process of buying out his partner, A. J. Kilfoyle. When he became sole owner of the Naps, Barnard became vice-president.) Barnard's mission was to persuade Connie Mack to cut his strings to Joe Jackson.

That afternoon Mack watched the A's lose the first game, 7–6, then settle for a 15-inning 1–1 tie. More important, he watched Hartsel and Heitmuller misjudge fly balls and lob poor throws to the infield, while Cleveland outfielder Bris Lord threw out three of Mack's men at the plate. The next day Mack told Barnard, "Give me Bris Lord for Morris Rath and I'll surrender my rights to Jackson." (According to a New Orleans version of the story, Charlie Frank took credit for persuading Somers to trade Lord to the Athletics and Mack to free up Jackson.)

In doing so, Mack broke one of his early rules against reacquiring anyone he had once let go. During his three years in Philadelphia, Bris Lord had failed to show any improvement in his hitting. Mack sent him to New Orleans, where he batted .314 in 1908, and the Naps bought him. With Cleveland his batting average had climbed to .269 in 1909. He was back down to .219 at the time of the trade. But he was ten years younger than Hartsel and had a much stronger arm.

On its own merits, the Lord-Rath trade made sense for Cleveland. Lord wasn't playing regularly, and the club was looking to improve at third base. Rath was twenty-three and had hit .300 in the minor leagues. Some accounts of the trade show Lord being traded for Joe Jackson. There was a connection, but it wasn't a swap. At the time of the Rath trade, there were stories that as part of the deal, Mack promised to sell Jackson to Charles Somers for $5,000. Not so. By cutting his strings to Jackson, Connie Mack merely freed Charlie Frank to sell him. Somers still had to deal with Frank.

On Saturday, July 30, Charlie Frank announced the sale of Joe Jackson to Cleveland for delivery at the end of the Southern Association season. No price was given. The Atlanta Constitution called it "semi-officially" $7,000. Other papers put it "in the neighborhood of $6,000." Published figures ranged from $5,000 to $10,000. Whatever the amount, the money went to the

New Orleans Pelicans, not the Athletics. Somers, impressed by his dealings with Charlie Frank, eventually bought control of the New Orleans club.

Not everybody considered the sale of Jackson a big deal at the time. One press box expert commented, "A man who can't read or write simply can't expect to meet the requirements of big league baseball as it is played today." No doubt Jackson could wallop minor league pitching, but he had only 8 hits in 10 major league games at the time.

It proved to be a key trade for the Athletics. Connie Mack moved Oldring to left field and put Bris Lord's speed and strong arm in center. The outfield took on a whole new look. The A's gradually built a 5-game lead that grew to 6, 8, 10 games. When Harry Davis was sidelined with back and shoulder pains, his heir apparent, Ben Houser, came through with clutch hits. At thirty-five, Plank needed more rest than the other pitchers. When Bender went down with stomach flu and Harry Krause with a sore arm, they kept winning with Coombs and Morgan and Coombs and Plank and Coombs and Coombs and Coombs. According to Lyle Spatz, chair of the SABR Records Committee, Coombs's 10 wins in the month of July (he also lost one) equaled Rube Waddell's 1902 record. All 10 of his starts were complete games. The players who had questioned his courage four years ago were somewhere else, dining on crow.

The big, strapping Coombs had a fluid overhand delivery. He threw a heavy ball—"like catching a brick," Jack Lapp said—and could throw as hard after 16 or 18 innings as he did in the first. He still had some wild streaks. But he had become a winning pitcher. He was toughest when he fell behind early in a game. When he had a comfortable lead, he let up. Winning was all that counted.

Coombs loved to hit and sometimes pinch hit for Mack. But Mack didn't want his pitchers wearing themselves out on the bases. When they went up to bat early in the game on a hot day, he'd remind them, "Don't run." He didn't want them risking injury sliding, either.

On July 1 in Philadelphia both the temperature and humidity were over 90. Between innings of a doubleheader against New York, batboys stood in front of the pitchers, waving towels to fan them. In the fourth inning of the first game, the A's led, 1–0. With 1 out and 2 on, Coombs was the batter. Mack ordered him to strike out. New York manager George Stallings ordered Russ Ford to walk him.

The crowd witnessed the spectacle of a batter trying to strike out and a pitcher trying to walk him. Ford threw three wide ones; Coombs swung and missed three times. He walked back to the bench and grumbled, "That second one was near enough to have stepped into it and killed it."

Mack said nothing. Coombs won the game, 2–0.

Coombs could relieve one day, pitch a complete game the next day, and do it all again two days later. The more he pitched, the stronger he grew. In July he won 3 games in six days. In September he pitched 53 consecutive scoreless innings. From July 12 to September 30—half a season—he won 20 and lost 3. One of the losses came on September 25; after pitching 6 scoreless innings in relief in the first game of a doubleheader, he started the second game but didn't have enough left in his tank.

Forget about his 1-hitter on June 16 that put the A's back in the lead, or what he later called his greatest game, a 16-inning 0–0 battle with Ed Walsh, in which he pitched 9 consecutive no-hit innings, gave up a total of 3 hits, struck out 18, walked 6 and hit 1—all in three hours and twenty-eight minutes.

More than any of these, the game that stuck in his mind most vividly for the rest of his life was one he lost, his first start of the year on April 16. On that date in 1936 a reporter approached Coombs on the campus of Duke University, where he was the baseball coach, and asked if he remembered it.

"Remember it, you ask," Coombs said. "You're blamed right I remember it. That's the kind you try but can never forget."

Coombs recalled how "that old weak-eyed scoundrel," umpire Billy Evans, missed a call. The A's led, 3–1, at Washington, with 1 out in the last of the ninth. Four hits tied the score and left men on second and third. Connie Mack ordered Gabby Street walked to load the bases. Then Wade Killefer pinch hit for the pitcher.

"I had Killefer three and two," Coombs related, "and I threw a curve ball to Ira Thomas that cut off over one-third of the plate and Billy stood there and called it a ball. So, I put my glove in my pocket and walked over to the dugout, for the ball game was over and there is no use arguing with the ump. I didn't do it then and I don't do it now.

"Doggone old Billy's hide, that ball really cut the plate. But don't ask me anything more. It's been twenty-six years and I'm still trying to forget it."

Clarence "Lefty" Russell was one of the most sought-after minor leaguers that summer after winning 24 games for Baltimore. Mack outbid several other clubs, paying Jack Dunn $12,000—"an enormous figure," Mack called it in a letter to a friend—for the twenty-year-old southpaw. Russell made his debut on October 1 and shut out Boston, 3–0, for the Athletics' hundredth win, the first AL club to reach that mark. A week later Russell turned down a $2,100 contract for 1911, demanded $3,000, didn't get it, and was an 0-5 lemon over the next two years. He never won another major league game.

The A's finished with 102 wins and a 14½-game lead over New York for Connie Mack's third pennant. They topped the league in batting, fielding, and pitching. It would be thirty-eight years before another AL team was so dominant in all departments. Eddie Collins set a stolen base record with 81.

Jack Coombs pitched 353 innings and won 31 and lost 9, with 13 shutouts—still the league record—and 12 starts in which he allowed only 1 run. Nobody hit a home run off him all year. Bender, who was 23-5, was tagged for 1 homer. Morgan won 18, Plank 16, but Harry Krause's arm trouble cut his workload in half. Still, except for Lefty Russell's one start, Connie Mack had used only seven pitchers all year.

Topsy Hartsel and Harry Davis were the only players who seemed to be slowing down. Davis, at thirty-seven, was racked by lumbago and rheumatism. The four-time home run king hit only 1 in 1910. Mack was peeved by newspaper reports that he was looking to sell or trade Davis. "I am sick and tired of reading that stuff," he fumed. "If Harry Davis ever leaves the Athletics it will be for reasons of Harry's own. Harry stays with the Athletics as long as he wants. This is the last time I'm going to dignify this sort of rot with an answer."

Once the pennant was clinched, Mack's boys chipped in and surprised him with the gift of a new automobile. A *North American* writer commented, "In 1905 they gave Connie Mack a player piano. This year they gave him an automobile. At this rate they'll have to come across with a skyscraper if they win again in 1911."

In the National League, the Cubs won their fourth pennant in five years, finishing 13 games ahead of the Giants. Led by their fiery first baseman-manager, Frank Chance, the Cubs were as dominant in their time as later Yankee dynasties would be. They averaged 103 wins a year for five years and must be rated among the greatest teams of all time. After their upset loss to the White Sox in the 1906 World Series, they had lost only one game while drubbing the Detroit Tigers the next two years. In 1910 they added a 20-4 rookie, King Cole, to the veterans Mordecai "Three Finger" Brown, Orval Overall, Jack Pfeister, and Ed Reulbach.

The heart of the Athletics—Bender, Plank, Davis, Murphy—were well known, but the sparkplugs—Baker, Collins, Barry, Coombs—were new kids in the national spotlight. The entire interested world knew all about the fabled Tinker and Evers. And who could compare second-rate outfielders like Lord and Oldring to the likes of Wildfire Schulte and Circus Solly Hofman? Nor could catchers named Lapp and Livingston and Thomas hold a candle to the great Johnny Kling.

Published unofficial salary lists for the two leagues showed the Cubs with the highest payroll—$120,000—and the A's next to last at $50,000. A bunch of low-paid nobodies were no match for high-priced stars. The Cubs were overwhelming favorites. Betting was light.

The Cubs were in Philadelphia for four games in mid-September. The A's finished a home stand on September 13 and had the next day off before heading to Detroit. The Cubs and Phillies played a doubleheader on the fourteenth. Connie Mack sent his sharpest pitcher-readers to the games. One sat behind first base, one behind third, and one behind the plate. In addition to pitchers Ed Reulbach and Orval Overall, they studied the Cubs' hitters. When the A's departed the next day, Bender stayed home and observed Three-Finger Brown. King Cole didn't work in that series.

Frank Chance said he had no intention of sending any players to look over the Athletics. In 1906 his Cubs scouted the White Sox for a week, he said, and it didn't do them any good. There was no point in trying to steal signs, he added, since these would no doubt be changed for the Series. But there was a Chicago scout following the A's. His report concluded that the Cubs would have little trouble defeating their young challengers, an opinion shared by most baseball people. Only Cincinnati manager Clark Griffith predicted the Cubs' pitching weakness would cost them the Series.

The Athletics played their last game on October 6. The Cubs had another week to go. Connie Mack was not happy with the prospect of an idle week. With Ban Johnson's help, he recruited a squad of players for five exhibition games. The receipts would be split among the players. And what a lineup of sparring partners it was: Ty Cobb, Tris Speaker, Clyde Milan, Gabby Street, Billy Sullivan, Kid Elberfeld, Ed Walsh, Walter Johnson, Doc White. The All-Stars won 4 of the 5. The A's also lost Rube Oldring, who had finally begun to show some confidence at the plate, batting .308 for the year. Oldring wrenched his knee and was out of the World Series. (The Cubs would be without Johnny Evers, who broke an ankle sliding at the plate on October 1.)

In appreciation of their help, each of the All-Stars received a gold watch from the Athletics. The A's had coasted through the last few weeks. The stiff competition the All-Stars gave them sharpened them, brought them back to their game. But that was lost on their critics, who pointed to the four losses and concluded that the A's didn't have what it took to be world champions.

Philadelphians didn't care what the experts said. Slowtown was in a celebrating mood. Interest was so high even the *Morgen Gazette*, the city's leading German newspaper, gave the Series front page coverage. About eight o'clock on a balmy Sunday night, the line began forming at Shibe Park for the fifty-cent general admission tickets. By midnight more than a thousand people were camped out in a nearby park. Cartons of a special fifty-three-page World Series program with biographies of all the players and a white elephant on the cover were delivered for sale the next day at ten cents. Tom Mack, his partner George McKenna, and his wife and daughter were in town for the games. The two men and A's scout Tom O'Brien would go with the team to Chicago. So would the lucky mascot, Louis Van Zelst.

On Monday morning, October 17, Connie Mack had a dilemma. He was anxious about something, but at the same time he thought it was foolish to mention it to his boys. He knew them, the young ones especially; they didn't have to be told. Still, he decided, it wouldn't hurt to bring it up.

Mack opened the meeting with a reminder that the American League champion Detroit Tigers had lost each of the last three World Series. "There were stories," he said, "that they had dissipated and hadn't played their best. If those stories were true, that was poor business, with 60 percent of the players' pool going to the winners and 40 percent to the losers.

"I don't want any such reports flying around about the Athletics. It would be bad enough to lose the championship, without having a bundle of regrets to pester you. It's hard enough losing to a better club, but to beat yourselves. . . ." He left it at that.

Mack asked each man in the room to say whether he was sure he could go without touching any alcohol throughout the Series. If anyone wasn't dead sure, he was to say so, and it wouldn't be held against him.

They all took the pledge.

Mack then said, "Keep Chicago crossed, boys; do the unexpected. Outguessing them will win."

In other words, play their game the same as they had all year, aggressive from the first pitch. He would manage the same way. Mack had no doubt about his pitching plans. With Evers out of the lineup, the Cubs were all right-handed batters except for Jimmy Sheckard and Frank Schulte. They would see plenty of Bender and Coombs. Bender was well rested; he hadn't started since September 7.

Were Mack's young infielders nervous? As is often the case, their answers to that question varied over the years. Probably the closest to the truth is the response players have been giving to that question for a hundred years. "Once the game started I didn't know it was a bit different from any other game," said Eddie Collins. Jack Barry admitted, "The tension was nerve-racking" until he had a ball hit to him. The farmer Frank Baker said simply, "My only idea was that we could lick those fellows and do it good."

Bender, who had been there before, was the coolest man on the field. Joe Tinker had seen Bender pitch for Harrisburg in 1902. He wanted to say something to distract the pitcher. He walked out to the coach's box before Bender came out to start the game.

"When he passed me," Tinker recalled, "I said, 'Big Indian, this is where you get yours good and plenty.' Bender stopped and looked at me for a second. With one of those cold grins he said, 'My word, do you think so?' and walked on. I let him alone from then on."

Not even a dispute at home plate before the game fazed the Chief. For the first time, motion picture cameras were present at a World Series along with the newspaper photographers. Having paid the National Commission for the movie rights, the cameramen had Ban Johnson's permission to remain on the field during the games. The National League banned photographers from the field during the season. The American didn't. Umpire Hank O'Day and Frank Chance wanted them all to clear off. Bender stood calmly waiting for the argument to finish. Finally, under Johnson's impatient eyes, the umpires said the movie cameras could stay but not the newsmen. They lugged their equipment up to the Shibe Park press box, already crowded with more than two hundred writers and forty-six Western Union operators, plus Ty Cobb, the injured Johnny Evers, and other players.

It didn't take the A's long to start crossing the Cubs. The first time Schulte, the Cubs' fastest man, was on first, Ira Thomas guessed he was running, called for a pitchout, and easily nabbed him at second. When Danny Murphy was on first, he took a very short lead. Cubs catcher Johnny Kling guessed he wasn't going anywhere. Murphy took off and stole second. After 3 innings the A's had a 3–0 lead and the Cubs' starter, Overall, was gone.

Bender sailed through the Cubs' lineup with ease. In addition to the hometown crowd of 26,891, he had something else to inspire him. The last time the A's were in St. Louis, Bender read a story that included this line: "The Cubs will triumph over the Athletics and will have no trouble beating Bender." Albert clipped it from the newspaper and stuck it in his pocket. "I read that clipping just before I went to the box . . . and had it in my hip pocket while I was on the mound," he told a Philadelphia writers' dinner in 1942. "The fellow who wrote that story had no idea how much it helped me get set to win."

But Bender didn't need any help. He knew exactly where he was going to throw each pitch and, if it was hit, where it would go. He moved his defense around more than Connie Mack did that day. As a result they had no difficult chances in the 4–1 win. The Cubs scored their lone run in the ninth; their 3 hits equaled Frank Baker's production for the day. The Cubs' scout had reported that Bender's curve was second rate and that they could run on Thomas. Bender crossed them up by throwing curves on 3-2 counts; 3 of his 8 strikeouts came on curves the batters took. Twice Thomas threw out Schulte at second. Frank Chance had new reasons to be skeptical of scouting reports.

The next day Connie Mack gave Louis Van Zelst the honor of taking the lineup to home plate for umpire Cy Rigler to announce. The crowd was a little smaller; the spectators on the rooftops along Twentieth Street were a little more numerous. The Athletics asked the police to patrol the street to curb the neighborhood seating, with little success. Downtown, the *Inquirer*'s huge display board reproducing the action drew thousands of viewers on Market Street and in nearby office windows.

From the start of Game 2, Jack Coombs's fastball was all over the place, and he had to rely on curves and changeups. The long layoff affected him, and he was pitching to Ira Thomas instead of his usual target, Jack Lapp. But Mack wanted Thomas's experience behind the plate. In the first inning Coombs walked 2. Chance legged out an infield hit. A sacrifice fly scored 1 run, but that's all the Cubs got in that inning. When his boys came into the dugout, Mack said to Coombs, "The only way you can lose is for you to beat yourself. I am satisfied they can't hit you effectively."

Colby Jack did his best to beat himself. In the fifth he booted two bunts that helped load the bases. Chance hit a fly to Murphy, whose throw to the plate nailed Brown, and the Cubs failed to score. For the day Coombs walked 9 and gave up 8 hits, throwing 153 pitches. But he had Eddie Collins and Jack Barry behind him.

Collins was everywhere, handling 10 chances. The Cubs were unaware that Jack Barry often covered second base and took throws from Baker as the pivot man on double plays. They had never seen a shortstop who could do that. This enabled Collins to play closer to first than most second basemen. In the first inning, with Sheckard on first, Schulte hit a hard grounder past Davis headed for right field. Collins got to it and threw to Barry for the force on Sheckard. In the second, Tinker was on first with Kling, a left-field pull hitter, at bat. Tinker figured that Collins had to cover second on a steal attempt. He signaled Kling that he would be going with the pitch; Kling should hit it through the hole left by Collins. Eddie guessed the play and motioned Barry to cover second. Tinker ran. Kling lined the ball right at Collins, who threw to first for an easy double play.

In the press box, Johnny Evers shook his head, marveling at the speed of the execution. "Collins is the greatest second baseman I ever saw," he told Chicago writer W. A. Phelon. "Darned if I can explain why he is, but he is, just the same." Having Jack Barry to work with was a big part of the reason.

Collins also drove the Cubs' catcher nuts. He made so many fake starts when he was on base that Kling didn't know what to do. Once, with Collins on first, the catcher called for three pitchouts in a row. Eddie didn't budge. On the next pitch, a strike, he stole second. It was as if the Athletics knew every pitch that was coming. The Cubs changed their signs every day, but it didn't make any difference. Ty Cobb realized the A's were reading the pitchers, not Kling's signs. He was doing it too. Writers sitting near him heard him calling the pitches accurately.

In the seventh the A's pounded the tiring Three Finger Brown for 6 runs to put the game away, 9–3. As Mack had sensed, the Cubs couldn't come up with the clutch hits off Coombs; they stranded 14. One of Coombs's 5 strikeouts was the last major league at bat for pinch hitter Ginger Beaumont, whose first professional at bat Connie Mack had seen after signing him in Milwaukee in 1898.

That night on the train to Chicago everybody, including Eddie Plank, expected Plank to pitch the third game. When reporters asked Connie Mack, he said, "I think I'll use Jawn again." One writer expressed his surprise that Mack would start Coombs on one day's rest spent riding the rails.

"Coombs will pitch," Mack repeated stiffly.

One of the Philadelphia fans on the train had a crate of pineapples among his baggage. It seems that during the season one of the players had enjoyed a good day at the plate after eating some pineapple at lunch. Naturally he then equated pineapple with hits. What player wouldn't? True or not, the story had appeared in one of the Philadelphia papers. At the LaSalle Hotel in Chicago, the crate was delivered to the kitchen with orders to serve the Athletics pineapple every day.

Under a dark sky that spit raindrops all day Thursday, Mack stayed with Coombs through 2 walks and 3 hits, good for 3 runs in the first 2 innings. After that, Coombs allowed only 3 more hits. Meanwhile, the A's chased Ed Reulbach after 2 innings and jumped on Chance's relievers for 5 in the third. Danny Murphy hit a 3-run blast over the heads of the outfield spectators. It hit a sign on the right-field fence. Umpire Tom Connolly called it a home run. A frustrated Frank Chance argued long enough to be ejected. The A's hit everything, no matter where it was thrown, in the 12–5 rout, while Evers muttered, "How can you beat a team that makes doubles and triples and home runs off wild pitches?"

The rain poured down all day Friday.

With a chance at a sweep, the A's went flat on Saturday. Maybe the day of rain took the edge off them. Maybe the lack of big game atmosphere made for a more lackluster Bender. Maybe it was because King Cole, the Cubs' rookie sensation, was the only pitcher they hadn't scouted. They had 10 hits, but they left 10 stranded. They didn't even steal a base. With it all, they still led, 3–2, in the eighth, when they loaded the bases with 1 out and Ira Thomas the batter.

Mack, itching to pad the lead and dispatch the Cubs in four, told Topsy Hartsel to grab a bat and hit for Thomas. Hartsel had a heavy cold, but Mack wasn't counting on him to swing the bat. The keen-eyed little veteran was hard to pitch to. He had led the league five times in drawing walks. Mack hoped he could coax one more from Cole. Then Bender would probably be good for a fly ball to drive in another run.

Thomas was stung. "Connie, let me bat," he said. "I'll start the runners on a hit and run play and push one through the hole. I know I can do it."

Thomas was so worked up that Mack relented and told Hartsel to sit down. Sitting on the bench, Eddie Collins anticipated a squeeze play from Thomas, a good bunter. But Thomas gave no signs to the base runners for any plays. He swung away and hit a tapper back to Cole, who started a home to first double play and was out of the inning.

Mack vowed "then and there, never again to let sentiment interfere with my judgment."

In the last of the ninth an umpire's call that seemed to benefit the A's backfired. With Schulte on third and 1 out, Bender hit Chance with a pitch. Umpire Tom Connolly ruled that Chance had made no effort to avoid the pitch and kept him in the batter's box. Chance then tripled in the tying run. But Chance was left on third when Collins made a brilliant catch in short center field and Baker leaned into the box seats in left field to snare a foul ball. The crowd, augmented by White Sox fans cheering for the American Leaguers, roared its approval on every play.

The Cubs won it in the tenth when Archer doubled and Sheckard singled him home.

That evening, disappointed at having a sweep in his grasp and letting it slip away, Mack called a meeting in his suite. Before the meeting, Topsy Hartsel spoke to Mack alone.

"Connie, I'm a sick man," he said hoarsely, barely above a whisper. "If I don't take something to brace me up, I'll be in bed tomorrow."

"You mean you want to take a drink?

Hartsel nodded.

"All right, go ahead," Mack said. "Do as you think best. But, by golly, if it was me I'd die before I took a drink."

Hartsel pondered for a minute, then looked Mack in the eye. "No drink for me, Connie," he said.

Connie Mack had something more in mind than preaching temperance to Topsy. He was thinking of starting Hartsel in left field and having him lead off the next day instead of Amos Strunk. Hartsel's only duty so far had been coaching at third, where he had been calling the Cubs' pitches. Mack figured the veteran would do well, cold and all, against Brown, the Cubs' probable starter on Sunday. A hangover would dull his mind more than a cold.

For all his vows renouncing sentiment, Mack was also tempted to give Eddie Plank a start. Then he thought again. Plank had had a little soreness in his arm lately, but that wasn't the reason Mack hesitated. On the contrary, when Eddie felt good, he was less likely to pitch well. Plank did his best work when he complained about something. Mack decided to use him only if he said he was sick or hurting.

So when Plank told Mack he felt fine, a shiver of superstition skipped up Connie Mack's spine. "I just had a hunch that something would go wrong," he said. Later Mack said he held Plank in reserve in case the A's lost another game. If the Series had gone to a sixth game, he intended to give the Cubs a different look with Plank's sweeping sidearm deliveries. Maybe.

Mack announced his lineup changes in the morning. Lord would move to center field and Hartsel would play left. Some of the players voiced their support for Strunk, who had had 2 hits off Brown in the second game. They didn't change the manager's mind. He also told them Coombs would pitch again. He had had two days rest this time, plenty for him. And Jack Lapp, who had caught most of Coombs's starts that season, would replace Thomas.

It was a cold day at West Side Park, but that didn't keep a Chicago World Series record crowd of twenty-seven thousand from turning out for the last home game of the year. Mack's hunch—or was it shrewd analysis?—about Hartsel paid off immediately. In the first inning, Hartsel singled, stole second, and scored on Collins's single. In the fifth, Jack Lapp drove in the run that broke a 1–1 tie.

Brown weakened as the game went on; Coombs grew stronger. Unlike his previous starts, when he had relied on his changeup and curve, Coombs threw mostly fastballs with a lively hop to them. In the fourth, when the Cubs loaded the bases with 1 out, Coombs set up Tinker and Archer with high fastballs, then struck them out with crossfire curves that had them bailing out.

In the eighth, Hartsel stole second again and scored the first run of a wild 5-run rally in which Baker scored from second and Davis all the way from first when Zimmerman uncorked a high throw to the plate.

When Jack Barry fielded a grounder and stepped on second to force a runner and end the 7–2 game, Collins chased him to the dugout asking for the ball. He didn't get it. Whoever held the ball when the last out was made in each victory was entitled to it. Barry claimed two of them and turned down an offer of $200 for the last one.

The Cubs made 9 hits, but Coombs walked only 1. His third complete game in six days was his best. Mack had used only Coombs and Bender in the box, twelve players in all, in winning his first world championship. The speed, hustle, brains, and brilliance of the youthful Athletics made it clear that they were on their way up. The Cub machine had broken down and would soon be scrapped.

There was some talk about an experimental ball being used in the Series. In 1941 Hugh Fullerton wrote that the Cubs claimed something was wrong with it the first time they handled it. Pitchers said they couldn't control it. Infielders said it felt funny and darted in the air. The Athletics voiced no complaints.

"We finally obtained two of the balls," Fullerton wrote. "I took them to the hotel and cut them in half, discovering for the first time the now famous cork center. The National League was in ignorance of the fact that the American League had been using the new experimental ball. We never found out whether or not the Athletics knew of it."

This thirty-years-after-the-fact account has some anomalies. If the American League had been knowingly using the ball, there would be no question raised as to whether the Athletics knew of it. If they didn't, then it's reasonable to conclude that the American was as much in ignorance of the fact as the National League clubs. Other accounts suggested that the ball had been introduced in both leagues for the 1910 season, since A. J. Reach was making all the balls used by both leagues under different brand names.

The new ball had not been used during the season. Reach's son, George, when he was eighty-one, told the *Philadelphia Bulletin*, "We used our newly patented cork center ball for the first time in the 1910 World Series. Nobody knew about it except a few people in the factory. Not even Ban Johnson or Connie Mack knew about the different ball."

The cork center was designed to increase the durability of the ball, to protect against its splitting and softening. Perfect vulcanization was beyond the range of the technology of the time, and rubber centers had a tendency to explode. The cork center didn't make the ball any easier to hit safely. It just made it go farther, and because it kept its shape and solidity, it went farther longer into the game.

(To further confuse the issue, in a July 1949 article in *Baseball Digest*, George Reach said, "The resiliency of the ball is governed by the way the wool yarn is wrapped around the core rather than the texture of the core.")

"The next year [1911] the ball was the liveliest it has ever been," Reach said. "In fact we had to tone it down. It was making infielders out of outfielders."

Within six months the cries for changes in the rules to increase offense became a clamor to make the ball less lively. But the purists who considered high-scoring games to be bad baseball were shouted down by surveys of fans that showed they favored keeping the new ball. As the *Philadelphia Telegraph* pointed out, it made for "more wonderful running catches than there used to be. . . . Infielders have to get a quicker jump on hard-hit ground balls now, too."

The Deadball Era seems to have died in 1911.

In any event, both teams had used the same ball in the World Series. The

Athletics simply outplayed, outthought, and outmaneuvered the Cubs in every department. The Cubs were convinced that Eddie Collins's constant kicking at pebbles and scratching in the dirt before every pitch was his way of relaying the signs to the outfielders. It was a ruse. Eddie was sending the intelligence with his right arm behind his back. Jack Lapp made no effort to conceal his wigwagging fingers, knowing the Cubs were watching. Let them look all they wanted. His signs were usually meaningless. Sometimes the A's pitchers were giving the signs, sometimes the catcher. The Cubs never knew which to watch or what to look for. The A's outscored the Cubs, 35–15, batting a record .316. Collins hit .429, Baker .409, Coombs .385. The infield of Collins, Barry, and Baker became famous overnight throughout the nation. Old man Harry Davis had directed the entire performance while batting .353. Yet the Cubs maintained that Jack Barry, because of the way he played his position, was the one most responsible for defeating them.

"They're a grand bunch of boys," Connie Mack told the press. "I'm proud of them. They never quit. The first four games we used only ten men. That speaks well of the way the boys work together and not until today did we make any changes."

The *Reach American League* 1911 *Guide* summed up the Athletics as "a steady concert of action which made the whole team appear to be working like a well-oiled piece of machinery. . . . Harry Davis's clever captaining deserves a word of praise, and last, but not least, is to be commended Manager Mack's skillful handling of the machine he had built—and it is not every manager who can direct as well as construct."

Euripides had put it more succinctly 2,300 years earlier: "Much effort, much prosperity."

Minutes after the final out, the presses were rolling at the *Philadelphia Evening Times*. The city's only Sunday afternoon paper had the market all to itself. Three hundred thousand copies carrying the full story and box score hit the streets before the thousands gathered in front of electric scoreboards had all dispersed.

In the kitchen of the Bellevue-Stratford Hotel, the cooks began planning a menu for a banquet to welcome the conquering heroes. When the train carrying the team arrived Monday afternoon shortly after five, Broad Street Station and all the streets for blocks around were packed with humanity. A glimpse of any player making his way to a chain of waiting automobiles sent the mob into an uproar. The procession inched its way to the hotel, where the entrance was engulfed by a human sea. After the sumptuous meal and all the paeans to the Mackian deities had rung through the dining room, Connie Mack rose to speak. The wave of cheers, whistles, and applause kept him standing a full five minutes before the tide subsided into silence.

Given to brief after-dinner comments, Mack was unusually expansive. It was, after all, the first world championship for all of them. He began by recalling all the dire predictions of the fate that awaited his club when it faced the mighty Cubs. The experts so impressed him, he said, it was difficult to see any prospect of victory for his boys. He then described how each game had gone, the cheers at the mention of climactic moments echoing off the walls. Then, like a chairman not wishing to overlook any members of his hardworking committee, Mack named each of his players and praised his contributions. He saved Harry Davis for last.

"There was not a move made on the field that was not directed by Davis. He has not been appreciated to the extent his work merited by the Philadelphia baseball public."

Mack suggested that a Harry Davis Day would be appropriate next season. After twice being rained out, it would take place on June 12. About $5,000 in gate receipts was added to numerous gifts for the popular captain.

The revelry continued at Keith's Theater, where the actors hastily put together a special show for the occasion. The next morning the Athletics gathered at Shibe Park to divide the World Series money. They voted a full share to everyone, even Claud Derrick, surely the luckiest man in baseball that year. Recommended by Lave Cross, Derrick had been bought from Greenville. He reported to the A's in late August. The twenty-six-year-old infielder replaced Jack Barry late in one game and had one hitless time at bat. For that he earned a month's salary and a World Series check for $2,062.74, the same as every other member of the team. When Eddie Collins backed out of a Cuban barnstorming tour, Derrick took his place and picked up another $375.

On Thursday, October 27, the A's threw a dinner and entertainment for the players and writers at the Hotel Majestic. Dinners and celebrations went on to November 5, when the Cubs, the two New York teams, and members of the nineteenth-century champion Athletics were invited to take part in a three-hour parade that pushed the banquet back to nearly 11 p.m.

The Nadja Caramel Company of St. Louis issued a set of eighteen cards of the world champions. Connie Mack is shown in a high-wing starched collar, his hair still parted in the middle. Over the next four years, the Athletics would be featured on cards accompanying Fatima Cigarettes, Honest Long Cut Smoking or Chewing Tobacco, and Recruit Little Cigars.

In the weeks that followed, parades and banquets honored players in their home towns. In December most of the A's went to Cuba, where Cincinnati business manager Frank Bancroft had lined up exhibition games, one against the Tigers, the rest against Cuban teams. The A's lost all but one game, a 2–1 Bender win over Cuban pitcher Eustaquio Pedroso. They had a grand time, playing before large crowds of baseball fanatics. Some of the A's and their wives relaxed on the Florida beaches before returning home.

Connie Mack was not present for any of these events.

Connie Mack had been a widower for almost eighteen years. He would soon turn forty-eight. During all that time, Mack had been wed to base-ball. There is no evidence of any serious romantic interest, certainly none strong enough to keep him in Philadelphia during the winters.

Mack led an active social life, beyond the football games and prize fights he attended with John Shibe. He went often to the theater, probably accom-panied by a woman. One of them was Margaret Holahan (or Hoolahan, depending on which census roll or story you accept).

The Hoolahans lived in a rented house at 311 North Thirty-ninth Street in West Philadelphia. Irish-born Frank and his wife Margaret had eleven children; nine survived infancy—four boys and five girls. Of the girls, Rose was the oldest, followed by Catherine, thirty-three, Margaret, thirty, and Annie, twenty-seven, who was known as Nan. Frank owned a saloon, which enabled him to satisfy his prodigious thirst at wholesale prices.

Two of the sisters worked at the Tribune Laundry on Fox Street in Germantown. One of them was Catherine, who preferred to be known as Katherine Hallahan, to the disgust of her sister Nan. Katherine was the bookkeeper, a tall, smart, strong-willed woman with a knack for figures. One day an adding machine salesman called on the laundry owner and lost a sale when Katherine demonstrated that she could add a column of numbers faster than the machine.

By any standard, Connie Mack was a good catch. He was prosperous. The Athletics had shown a profit every year. His income from his share of the club and his salary put him, if not among the Main Line elite, in the upper levels of the middle class. He was famous and respected in his field. He was always fastidiously dressed. He was a gentleman and not a drinker.

His children, Roy, twenty-two, and Peggy, eighteen, still lived at home.

That and the presence of his mother, a hardy, feisty, sixty-nine-year-old who ran his household, might have put off some women. But financially and socially, being Mrs. Connie Mack offered a pleasant prospect.

According to bits of family lore gleaned from various sources, one evening in the spring of 1910 Connie Mack called at the Hoolahan home to escort one of the sisters, probably Margaret, to a show. Katherine greeted him at the door. Her sister was ill or otherwise unable to go with him, whereupon Mack said, "I have two tickets. Would you like to have them?"

Katherine said, "Who would I take?"

Mack said, "Why don't I invite you?"

"One thing is certain," their daughter Ruth said, "they didn't know each other long" before they started making wedding plans. One newspaper account said they had "been acquainted" for five years. That's doubtful, but they may have met during the time Mack was escorting Katherine's sister Margaret.

Connie Mack acceded to Katherine's wishes and introduced her as Miss Hallahan. When they were seen together regularly during the summer of 1910, rumors of a romance began to spread. Reporters from the *North American* staked out Katherine's house. One day the couple was stopped as they approached and asked about their plans.

"As to my engagement," said Mack, "I tell you that any such announcement is quite premature. I do not mind publicity in a baseball way, but really, you know, Miss Hallahan and I may never become engaged. If friends of mine have spread the report abroad that I am to marry Miss Hallahan in October, I can only repeat that it may never take place."

Katherine, described as a "tall, slender brunette of striking appearance," added, "No, we are not engaged and may never be."

But the players' comments indicated to the baseball writers that congratulations were in order. It was no longer much of a secret. After the A's clinched the pennant in Cleveland on September 20, Mack confirmed his engagement. He gave the wedding date as November 2.

It was a decoy.

Connie Mack never liked anybody making a fuss over or around him. He didn't want a big wedding. In fact, he told Katherine, he didn't want any kind of ceremony that might draw a crowd and turn into a public spectacle. If he had his way, he wouldn't tell anybody the date, not even their families. He wanted "to pull the wedding off quietly," as he later told a reporter. He preferred to elope, if you could call quietly going around the corner to the parish church eloping.

Katherine agreed. She left all the planning to him.

Three days after the World Series ended, on Wednesday, October 26, Connie Mack went to City Hall and took out a marriage license. When reporters heard about it, he told them he just thought he'd take care of it early. There was no time limit on it. He didn't know when he might use it. Meanwhile, Katherine's mother was busy preparing for the November 2 nuptials.

But the wily Mack had already booked their passage on the steamship *Cincinnati*'s November 3 sailing out of New York, bound for Genoa. He had obtained a dispensation from his parish priest, Fr. Thomas Moore, from the posting of banns, which normally preceded a wedding by three weeks. And he had arranged for Katherine's parish priest to be available on the morning of October 27 at St. James's Church at Thirty-eighth and Chestnut.

Depending on who's telling it, either Miss Hallahan or Mr. Mack slipped out of the house and got into a taxi at eight thirty that morning and went round to the other's house to pick up the spouse-to-be. But some of Mack's signs had been read by Athletics' fans. When the couple, the bride wearing a blue jacket suit, arrived at St. James's, the usually busy thoroughfare was blocked by a small crowd outside the church. One look at the scene and Mack told the driver to keep going. Anticipating that his taking out the license might draw the canny curious, Mack had a backup plan: his own parish church, Our Lady of the Holy Souls, at Nineteenth and Tioga. No crowd greeted the couple there, just Fr. Moore and two church workers, Patrick Coogan and Esther Phillips, who stood by as witnesses while "Cornelius McGillicuddy" and "Catarina Hallahan" were swiftly joined in matrimony and returned to the waiting taxi. They rode to Mack's home and informed his mother and daughter that the deed was done, then went to the bride's home, where her mother, cleaning house and planning the gala reception a week hence, allowed that she was "surprised out of my seven senses" by the news. But, she assured a reporter, "he's a fine fellow."

Without so much as a toast, the newlyweds were off to the station to catch the noon train to New York. They sailed for Italy at ten on the morning of November 3. For the next three months they traveled in Italy, France, Switzerland, England, and Ireland. Mack found no signs of interest in baseball except at the American College in Rome, where he entertained the 150 students with an account of the final game of the World Series.

"In the middle of my story," he told a reporter in Rome, "a grave prelate in flowing robes broke in with, 'Oh, Mr. Mack, why didn't you put Plank in as pitcher?' I replied that I felt the Chicago team could hit left-handers."

The highlight of the trip came early, when the Macks had an audience with Pope Pius X. "He is a wonderful personality," Mack said, "at once natural and dignified, and without effort carries with him an atmosphere that is not of this world. My visit to the Vatican will always remain a red letter day in my life."

In Paris, while strolling arm in arm, Mr. and Mrs. Mack were shocked when streetwalkers came right up to him and solicited his business. In Ireland they kissed the Blarney stone. They boarded the *Mauretania* for home on January 21, 1911, and were met in New York by John Shibe and sportswriters Billy Weart and Gordon Mackay on Friday the twenty-seventh, exactly three months after their wedding day. It was the longest that Connie Mack had been away from baseball since his managing career began in 1894. Mary McGillicuddy had a reception waiting for her son and daughter-in-law, who was three months pregnant.

The next day the well-rested bridegroom, appearing hearty and several pounds heavier, told a reporter for the *Press*:

I had no trouble with the language spoken in the countries I visited. Only once, in France, I tried to get two taxi drivers to understand that Mrs. Mack and I wanted to go from the theater to our hotel. They could not get me. So I went across the street and the first fellow I struck understood me immediately. We found they had a man who could speak English in every hotel we visited. The thing that amazed me most was the cheapness of taxis. I honestly feel we could have ridden in one all day for a dollar. The prices at the hotels are the same as here, however. The boys on our club would certainly be surprised if they could see all the people in the hotel lined up when you start to leave, and every one expects to get a tip.

The reporter noted that Mack said the trip did him much good. "He is glad that he saw Europe, but, he says, never again."

He never went back.

A $5,000 wedding present from the Athletics awaited them. Mack also received an unofficial World Series trophy: a large porcelain white elephant with upraised trunk, made in Austria. Hanging around its neck was a gold, heart-shaped medallion engraved with the score of each game. How the trophy wound up in a bar in Worcester is a tale told by Bill McNamee of that city.

"Connie Mack would come up while scouting players from Holy Cross. He developed a friendship with my great-grandfather, Bill Ferriss, who owned a bar on Cambridge Street, what is now Ferriss Square [not far from the cemetery where Mack's parents and first wife are buried]. Mack would stop in Ferriss's tavern for a beer. As a token of friendship Mack gave Ferriss the white elephant, which stood on display until the tavern closed in the 1920s and it was put away for fifty years in the attic of a home owned by Ferriss's daughter."

The trophy went on loan to the National Baseball Hall of Fame in Cooperstown.

Katherine Mack brought a large family with her when she married into the vast McGillicuddy clan. In the years to come, her sisters, Margaret and Nan, would spend the winter months in the Macks' home with the children while Con, as his wife called him, and Katherine were at spring training. The children adored their aunts and looked forward to their stays.

Connie Mack was a devoted family man. His home was always open to visitors. His brother Tom visited with his wife and family. Mack's cousins from his mother's side, the Dempseys, were frequent visitors from Worcester. His favorite cousin, Nora, a nurse, was always welcome and lived with the Macks for a while.

There were other branches of the family he seldom saw but who were proud of their connection to him. That fall Cornelius Roach ran for secretary of state in Missouri. He told voters there were thirteen reasons they should vote for him: he was the father of twelve children, and Connie Mack was his cousin.

Mack went to family gatherings whenever his schedule permitted, spent time at relatives' homes, wrote letters, and kept up with everybody's lives. And did so until the day he died.

Wedding bells had rung for other Athletics that winter. On November 3 Eddie Collins married Mabel Doane, whose father, Charles, was a boyhood friend of Connie Mack's in East Brookfield and now managed the Kent Mills in Philadelphia. Connie Mack had introduced them. The newlyweds built a $6,000 house in suburban Lansdowne.

In January Jack Barry married Margaret McDonough in Worcester. Collins sent him a telegram: "Congratulations. Best play you ever made."

Before going to Cuba, Jack Coombs married Mary Russ in Palestine, Texas.

Connie Mack was pleased with these developments. He believed in the stabilizing effects of marriage on established players. He encouraged the presence of wives at spring training. When the 1911 season opened, only Rube Oldring, Amos Strunk, and Eddie Plank were single among the regulars.

Mack left the scouting of 1911 spring training sites to Jack Shibe and Harry Davis. Back in his office, his first priority was sending out contracts. He quickly signed Eddie Collins to a three-year deal at $6,000 a year. He faced an exhausting round of fetes on the rubber chicken circuit. At the league meeting in Chicago on February 14, the Athletics hosted a dinner that lasted longer than the two hours it took to dispose of league business. Then it was back home for a long day and evening in Mahanoy City, Pennsylvania, to celebrate with a group of fifty residents who had followed the team to Chicago in October. In the afternoon Mack and a half dozen players toured a coal mine and stopped in at the Elks and Eagles Clubs. Dinner was followed by a production of *Madame Sherry*, performed by a company brought in from New York for the occasion. Mack was presented with a baseball made of coal, which sat on his desk for many years.

Two days after the annual writers' dinner, Mack and Phillies manager Red Dooin were guests of honor at the County Cork Men's Sixth Annual Ball.

On March 1 Mack saw his veterans off to Hot Springs, Virginia, for two weeks of conditioning. Three days later he shepherded his collection of youngsters to Savannah. He was ready to escape the social ramble and get back to baseball.

39 | THE $100,000 INFIELD

Despite a 15 percent drop in attendance in 1910, the American League looked back on its first decade of operation with justifiable pride and ahead with confidence. The cold, wet spring and lack of a closely contested pennant race after June were blamed for the slower turnstile counts. For the Athletics, in their second season in Shibe Park, Connie Mack had his first experience of a winning team playing to smaller crowds. Attendance dropped 10 percent to about six hundred thousand.

None of that deterred the league's directors from giving Ban Johnson a twenty-year contract and a raise to $25,000. Always looking to improve their product, they called for each team to employ a megaphone man to stand on the field and announce the starting batteries and lineup changes during the game, relieving the umpires of that duty and the fans of the need to comprehend the umps' unintelligible announcements. (In 1913 Comiskey would introduce electric enunciators with sixty-three speakers throughout his ballpark.)

Gambling had not abated, but the public believed in the honesty of the game. The improved reputation of the players was aided by the growing number of collegians. There was less drinking. More players realized that staying in shape and playing their best could increase their income and lengthen their careers. Carousers and curfew-breakers remained but were fewer. A $10 fine had an impact. Some managers in the thick of a pennant race had enough confidence in their players' judgment to relax the rules as the strain and pressure built down the stretch.

The professional baseball industry was sounder than ever. The average franchise was estimated to be worth $400,000. The Phillies had been sold to a group headed by former sports editor Horace Fogel for $225,000. The New York Giants were said to be worth $2 million. In the American League, only Boston and New York continued to use leased grounds. The rest had made substantial investments in real estate and stadiums. The minor leagues prospered, taking in $10 million at the gate. The flow of prospects coming off the thousands of sandlots and semipro teams promised an endless supply of low-cost talent.

Travel accommodations improved. Hotel managers who a decade ago had barred ballplayers from their premises now eagerly solicited the business. Teams spent $3 a day per man for room and board at top-flight spring training hotels that charged tourists at least $5. Rooms had bathtubs, sometimes showers. During the season they stayed at the best hotels, two to a room—not to a bed. They ate in the hotel dining room, signing the checks. That way the club could keep track of what they spent and what they ate. Sometimes a player might find his paycheck lighter because he had ordered two steaks or lobsters for dinner. A player who was supposed to be losing weight might arrange with the waiter to bring him pie and call it salad on the check. If they took their meals together at a large table, the manager or captain sat at the head with the rookies at the other end.

On game days players ate a hearty breakfast and light lunch. In between there was morning practice and, for the Athletics, the daily meeting. Games began at three, three thirty, or four o'clock. The nation ate an early supper, and sometimes the players were the last to get to the hotel dining room, where the waiters might be fresher than the food. Some players had never heard of tipping before they reached the big leagues. Some never went beyond a nickel, no matter how much they ate. City and college boys took the farmhands in tow and tried to acclimate them to city ways. They didn't always succeed.

The days of the Sullivan Sleeper were over. Clubs had their own private railroad cars for the long jumps. The reporters traveled with them. Stars slept in the lower berths in the middle of the car. Rookies still rode the uppers and over the wheels. A player who could sleep anywhere might sell his lower for a half dollar. The manager occupied a private compartment.

To while away the hours they played dominoes, checkers, chess, cribbage, and low-stakes card games—rummy, poker, whist, hearts, Seven Up, and pinochle. Cubs manager Frank Chance claimed he could take the measure of a man best by watching him play poker. Some players read. Players who trod the vaudeville boards in the off-season entertained by singing and dancing in the aisles. They all talked baseball. By eleven the car would be silent and dark; the card games moved to the restrooms.

Players wore jackets and ties and caps as long as they were in public view. Once on the train, with the heat and the cinders from the coal-burning locomotives blowing in through the open windows, jackets and ties came off. A low collar instead of a high one might be a fashion concession to the heat. The average fan in the stands was also well dressed by today's standards. Photographs of crowds from the time show a sea of caps, derbies, fedoras, straw hats—depending on the month—suits and ties, and an occasional bared shirtsleeve. Women wore bright dresses, gloves, hats. Some reporters took up the cause of banning women's hats. The elaborate headgear, spiked with colorful plumes, blocked the view of those sitting in back, inspiring some ungentlemanly language.

Away from home, some players slept long hours. Musicals and vaudeville, silent movies, and billiard parlors were popular. Recognized from photographs and drawings in newspapers and magazines, star players were trailed by gangs of kids, adoring women, and male worshipers. Free drinks, cigars, and meals were pressed on them by sports in every city, in exchange for nothing but bragging rights to having "passed the evening" with a well-known baseball player. But most of them headed for the hotel lobby after dinner. Cigarette and cigar smoke billowed out from behind newspapers being read. Some talked baseball. Some just sat and watched in silence, never saying a word all evening.

Connie Mack's tall, slim, unmistakable physique, his age, and his dependable high collar and dark suit made him stand out among his boys. Mack never shut himself away from the public. At train stops he would step down to the platform to stretch his legs or walk out to the balcony at the end of the last car and talk baseball with fans who had been alerted by station masters along the way to which train was carrying the Athletics. An early riser, he would stroll the platforms at early morning stops and chin with anybody who spoke to him.

Mack spent hours in hotel lobbies, as he had on the bench outside the Republican House in Milwaukee before he became famous. Strangers and old friends, strangers claiming to be old friends, men and women and children—all who approached him were greeted warmly and made to feel as though Mr. Mack had been eagerly awaiting them and would have been disappointed if he had missed seeing them. Men who came up to him and said, "Remember me? We sat together at the Rotary Club in Kansas City," departed convinced that Mack did indeed remember both the man and the occasion. "He had the knack," one writer said, "of making people feel that he was so pleased to meet them and that there was nothing he wanted more than to have a good chat with them."

Connie Mack's team appeared to need nothing. The lineup that would open the city series in April was the same that had won the World Series. He made the obligatory preseason comments: "Can't let up. . . other teams improved . . . lucky to escape injury last year. . . ." But he and his boys knew they were the team to beat.

While giving his players free rein to get themselves into condition at their own pace, he cautioned them not to rush to reach midseason form by opening day. "The race is so long," he said, "no matter how carefully they may work, players individually and collectively are certain to go stale at some stage of the campaign."

He was especially keen on his older pitchers' going slow in the south. He had seen the effects on their muscles of stretching them out in the hot sun, then going north into the cold dampness. He was also aware that pitchers were more likely than others to tire and fall into late-season slumps, particularly the older ones. He preferred to give the bulk of the early season work to his younger hurlers until the sun was kinder to older arms. It wouldn't bother him if the A's got off to a poor start, not with the horses he had. "By June some of the early hot teams will lose their pepper and fall behind," he told reporters, "while the A's will find their stride."

Only three rookies were given a chance to make the team: outfielder Bill Hogan, acquired from Oakland; Allan Collamore, a right-hander from Worcester; and Lefty Russell, the expensive purchase from Baltimore who had thrown a late-season shutout in his only start. Russell was the Broadway Charlie Wagner of his time. He showed up in Savannah with a trunk containing nine suits and wore a different one every day.

Ben Houser was expected to replace Harry Davis, whose rheumatic joints were unlikely to last another full season.

In the Washington camp, Walter Johnson was a holdout. He had won 25 games for the seventh-place Senators while earning $4,500. Now he wanted $9,000, as much as Ty Cobb was rumored to be making. Washington manager Jimmy McAleer went as high as $6,500—more than the highest paid university professors—and told Johnson to sign or go home to Kansas. Johnson went home. Like sharks attracted to raw meat, other teams, including the A's, swarmed around McAleer with offers for the pitcher. Johnson eventually settled for a three-year contract at around $7,000 a year.

The deal offered by Connie Mack was said to include Bill Hogan, Ben Houser, and either Russell or Collamore for Johnson. If accurate, this seemingly paltry package of rookies indicates that Mack was unwilling to part with any of the proven young cogs of the machine he had built, even for a pitcher of Johnson's stature. It also indicates that he was not as sold on Houser to replace Davis as the ten Philadelphia beat writers assumed him to be.

Just when or how or even whose idea it was to make a first baseman out of Stuffy McInnis depends on what you read. For two years Mack had been studying where to play the Gloucester lad, now twenty and still, Mack maintained, the greatest natural player he had yet seen. The only looming opening in the Athletics' lineup was at first base. Some accounts have McInnis coming to the same conclusion and buying himself a first baseman's mitt. In his biography, Fred Lieb has Mack suggesting that Jack, as he called McInnis, get a mitt in Savannah and work out at the bag.

A story probably written by Henry P. Edwards of the *Cleveland Plain Dealer* at the close of the 1911 season credits Harry Davis with persuading Mack to give the job to McInnis over six-foot-one Houser or the six-foot Claud Derrick.

"He's too short," Mack told Davis.

Davis said the five-foot-nine McInnis "will get any high throws that any first baseman would get, and anyway our infielders will not make many high throws. All that I am worrying about is whether he will get the low ones. I don't know whether or not he can scoop up the ones that go in the dirt."

Mack knew that McInnis would outhit Houser or Derrick. And Stuffy was baseball smart. Sitting on the bench beside his tutor, he was already demonstrating that he could anticipate other teams' ploys and plays as uncannily as Collins or Barry or Davis.

When Houser saw McInnis with a first baseman's mitt and realized what was happening, he didn't like it. "It was funny," Mack told Lieb, "how Ben took it. Every time Stuffy would go to the bag, Houser would come out from the bench and try to shove him away. Ben was much taller and had a good reach, and at times when both were around the bag Houser would outreach Jack for thrown balls."

But at the time none of this was mentioned in dispatches from Savannah to Philadelphia papers. If anybody in camp was seen as a potential backup first baseman, it was the utility infielder Claud Derrick. Isaminger speculated that to get Stuffy's bat and brains in the lineup, Mack might shift Baker to the outfield and put McInnis on third.

Mack signed two other college first basemen but denied that he had any plans to replace Davis, who was looking as spry as somebody ten years younger.

There was another young catcher in camp besides Earle Mack, a hustling nineteen-year-old, Steve O'Neill, from Pennsylvania. Drafted from Elmira, O'Neill showed up with shoes too big for him and a floppy, unwieldy mitt. "Connie Mack looked at my shoes and catcher's mitt and said, 'Young man, you need a catcher's glove and a pair of shoes.' He immediately wired to Philadelphia to the A. J. Reach factory who sent me my first real catcher's glove and real baseball shoes. He would see that young players had the proper material to work with."

After a few pleasant days in Savannah, a cold wind began to blow and seldom let up. The players couldn't even work up a sweat. Enduring one windy day after another, Mack decided to look elsewhere for next spring, some place where it was hot and dry. He wanted his green pitchers to have the time and conditions to be ready to go on opening day. He looked to Texas again. By May he would close a deal to go to San Antonio.

It rained for three days before Mack and the Yannigans headed north on March 28, Houser playing first every day, McInnis shortstop, Steve O'Neill doing the catching, Earle Mack in left field. They were unbeatable wherever they played. Perhaps it was during this trip that Mack told McInnis to work out at first base, out of sight of the writers, who avoided the one-day stops in the small towns. On the way, Mack dropped Earle off at Scranton and sent O'Neill to Worcester, much to the Pennsylvanian's chagrin. Scranton would have been closer to home for him. When it looked likely that Harry Davis would become the Cleveland manager in 1912, Mack sold O'Neill to the Naps to help Davis and Charles Somers.

They arrived home Friday night, April 7, amid a freezing rain. Mack decided that Ben Houser was not his future first baseman and asked waivers on him. The Boston Braves claimed him. "I'm letting Houser go," Mack said, "because Davis will be good for two or three years more. . . . And if Davis was hurt I could switch some of my other men to his place. Davis is playing excellent ball and I have no intention of removing him."

Philadelphia writers continued their guessing game. A May 18 story commented, "They also say that Mack is grooming Stuffy as a first baseman when Harry Davis retires. That may or may not be true." Some of the players were reported expecting Claud Derrick to take over at first base.

Another paper declared, "It is believed that Connie Mack has decided in due time to make an outfielder of McInnis." They didn't say who believed it. It wasn't Connie Mack.

The Athletics opened at home and lost 3 in a row to New York. The *Evening Telegraph* had urged its readers to contribute to buy a car for Eddie Collins Appreciation Day. When the car was presented to him on opening day, Connie Mack frowned. He had just finished preaching to his boys to refrain from "automobiling" during the season. Mack considered it harmful to "sight and nerves," a prophetic vision. He advised Collins to stay out of the motorcar until the season was over. It was good advice. After the game Eddie and his wife went out to the street and found that somebody had driven a nail into a tire. They pushed the car into the garage under Shibe Park, where the punctured tire was replaced at a cost of $7.50. Frank Baker heard about it and decided to wait until after the season to buy himself an automobile.

The only thing predictable about April weather was that it would be lousy. There weren't a half dozen pleasant afternoons in the first three weeks of the season. Mack's first concern was the disappointing showing of his two young pitchers, Russell and Collamore. Their poor work derailed his plan to rely on the youngsters in the early weeks. Two innings in which Collamore gave up 8 runs was all Mack had to see to send him down. It didn't take much longer for Mack to sour on Russell. He admitted that he had been stung by the $12,000 beauty, whose wardrobe was worth more than his left arm, which was later pronounced dead, strangled by "corded" muscles.

"The best way of ruining a promising ballplayer is to pay a big price for him," Mack declared with peccable logic. "Never again." He vowed to stick to drafting players from then on, a vow that carried a short shelf life. Mack would be stung more than once, proving his adage that "the highest priced players don't make good." In time, he would also prove just as many exceptions to his rule. Otherwise, Mack jokingly ascribed the team's slow start to "too many bridegrooms. Being one myself, I don't know how to handle the case."

Eddie Plank earned their only 2 wins in the first 8 games, before Jack Coombs pitched a 3-hitter at home against Washington on the day they unfurled their 1910 American League pennant. Connie Mack, Ban Johnson, and Governor John K. Tener all had a hand on the rope that raised it up the flagpole.

The Detroit Tigers threatened to wash out all hopes of a close pennant race, getting off to a 21-2 start while the A's were 9-9. Mack remained unperturbed. The Tigers would fade. His boys would hit their stride. Jack Barry sprained an ankle; McInnis replaced him and had 5 hits off the 7 pitches he saw. When Barry came back, Collins turned an ankle, then Barry reinjured his. Through May, Barry and Collins were rarely in the lineup at the same time. Some days the middle of the infield was Derrick and McInnis. Stuffy's bat was so hot he was leading the league at .455 in mid-May. But Jack could play only one position at a time. When he was injured, the world champions' infield was really in tatters. They went west, lost 4 in Chicago, split 4 in Detroit. They had 19 hits in a game in Detroit, but errors cost them a 9–8 loss. The next day they won with no pitching, 14–12. They went into Cleveland and won by scores of 9–3, 9–1, 9–1, and 12–6. They were blasting the cork-center ball, McInnis and Collins over .400 and Murphy near it. But except for Plank, who didn't lose his second game until June, the pitching was erratic. Jack Coombs went down with malaria. Bender had a lame back and didn't start for a month.

Before the A's reached Cleveland, Charles Somers fired his manager, Jim McGuire. Somers asked Mack to release Davis to take over the Naps. Mack said no; he had nobody to replace Davis. McInnis was playing a lot of shortstop. Davis had managing ambitions, but he wanted to finish out the season in Philadelphia. If Somers wanted him, he would have to wait. (On August 4 a Cleveland scout disclosed that Davis had signed a contract at that time to manage Cleveland in 1912 for $12,000, but there would be no announcement until the season was over.)

After a month on the road, the Mackmen were greeted by a throng of thirty thousand, who jammed Shibe Park for a doubleheader against New York on Saturday, May 27. Eddie Plank scattered 10 hits to win the opener, but Jack Coombs pitched poorly in the 8–3 nightcap loss. To atone, he came back on Monday and beat them, 4–1.

On Thursday, June 1, the A's opened a series against Cleveland. In the last of the seventh they led, 12–3. Harry Davis walked. McInnis ran for him, then replaced him at first base in the eighth. It marked the first time the infield of McInnis, Collins, Barry, and Baker appeared in a game. It made no headlines; it wasn't even permanent. The next day Davis was back on first. But he was hitting .219, McInnis .444. Getting Stuffy's bat in the lineup every day was becoming more imperative; the position he would play was becoming more obvious.

Connie Mack remained stoic while his world was in turmoil in early June, symbolized by the world championship banner being raised upside down at Shibe Park on June 2. On Saturday night they boarded a train to Cleveland for a Sunday game, arrived in a rainstorm, got back on the train and came home, and were rained out on Monday. The red-hot Tigers didn't cool off; they arrived in Philadelphia with a 6½-game lead on June 6—and it rained all day. That morning Mack was notified that his brother Dennis had died in the early hours from uremic poisoning at his home at 1732 North Twenty-seventh Street. "God in His mercy saw fit to take him," said Annie, who was left with six children ages five to twenty-one. Hazel worked as a telephone operator for $3.75 a week. Mack paid for Mary to attend Pierce Business School; she became an executive with a pharmaceutical company. Mack quietly provided for Annie until she died in 1942.

The A's won 2 of the 3 Detroit games. Ty Cobb continued to give Frank Baker fits. On June 7 he tripled and kept on running when Baker bobbled the throw to third, scoring before Bake could recover and throw home. The next day Cobb was thrown out trying to steal third in the fifth inning. Sliding with both feet flailing, he tried to kick the ball out of Baker's grip. Baker grabbed an ankle and twisted it. Cobb got up and trotted off the field without retaliating—then. In the eighth Cobb was on third. He took his usual long lead. When Plank threw over, Baker tried to block Cobb off the bag. Their legs tangled like a clumsy four-footed critter. When it looked like they would start swinging, Hughie Jennings and umpire John Sheridan got between them. After the game Cobb left the field with a police escort. The newspapers refrained from making a big deal out of it, so there were no outbursts from the fans the next day. The A's won, 5–4, on Barry's eighth-inning steal of home and Collins's sparkling game-ending grab of Cobb's grounder with 2 on base.

The turn of the tide expected by Mack had begun. After losing 6 in a row, the A's were 24-3 from May 20 through June 22, cutting the Tigers' lead to 1½ games. Mack predicted his boys would be on top by July 1. He was off by three days.

July 4, 1911, was a rare day in Philadelphia baseball history, so rare it happened only one other time. That night both the Phillies and Athletics went to sleep in first place. While Detroit was splitting at Chicago, the A's took 2 in New York, the second game by 11–9, as Mack used 5 pitchers, the Yankees

4, and both teams used 32 players. The A's led Detroit by ½ game. The Phils led the Cubs by the same margin.

It didn't last. Two days later both teams were back in second.

Ban Johnson was tired of fielding complaints about the length of the games. An early season 7–4 A's win had taken an outrageous two hours and forty minutes. Johnson, for whom satisfying the customers was a top priority, decided to do something about it. He calculated that twenty minutes per game was wasted by pitchers taking warmup tosses before the start of each half inning. His solution was to limit them to as many as they could throw until the first batter stepped into the batter's box. "How many he throws," the order read, "depends on how long it takes for the batter to get into position." If a pitcher was on base or made the last out in an inning, he could take at least three warmup tosses regardless of how quickly the first batter was ready.

The rule also allowed that if 2 men were out, the pitcher on the batting team could go some place where he didn't block the fans' view and throw to a catcher. Some teams put a practice plate in an out-of-the-way spot for such warmups. This may have been the start of the widespread use of what became known as the bullpen. Practice plates in front of the grandstand were reserved for pregame warmups, not between innings.

The rule lasted only a few weeks. On June 27 in Boston, the Athletics led, 6–3, after 7 innings. Stuffy McInnis was due to lead off the top of the eighth. When the bottom of the seventh ended, McInnis ran to the dugout from first base, grabbed a bat, and hustled to the plate. Boston outfielders Duffy Lewis and Harry Hooper were ambling toward their positions. Center fielder Tris Speaker had paused to speak to Eddie Collins near first base. Right-hander Ed Karger lobbed the ball to catcher Les Nunamaker. McInnis swung and hit it into center field, where the ball rolled and rolled and rolled. Nobody chased it. Stuffy raced around the bases. When umpire John Egan ruled it a home run, the Bostons let out a howl. Manager Patsy Donovan claimed that two of the Athletics were still on the field when McInnis swung. Connie Mack enjoyed it all thoroughly. That was the kind of headwork he prized. Donovan protested the game. Ban Johnson overruled the protest, then overruled himself and revoked the rule.

The importance of Eddie Collins to the Athletics was demonstrated after he and Danny Murphy collided chasing a short fly ball in Washington on July 1. A dislocated left elbow kept Eddie sidelined for four weeks. The A's were simply not the same team without him. They went to Detroit and looked like anything but champs, dropping 4 in a row. Claud Derrick was inadequate at second base. He and McInnis were hitless in the first two games. Mack put Davis back on first and brought Murphy in to play second. Amos Strunk went to right field, where he uncorked a wild throw and misjudged a few fly balls, contributing to two losses. Mack benched him and played Topsy Hartsel.

Cobb was in his glory. In the first inning of the second game he walked, stole second, third, and home off Krause and Thomas. Twice he scored from second on sacrifice flies. In the third game he scored the winning run from first on a single by Delahanty, running right through Jennings's stop sign at third. He slid wide of the plate, then scrambled back to touch it before Thomas could tag him. Suddenly the Tigers were up by 5½ games.

Mack didn't hesitate to throw rookie pitchers into the breech in the midst of a pennant battle. Lefty Dave Danforth, signed out of Baylor on the recommendation of Hyman Pearlstone, relieved effectively in three of the Detroit games. Harold Martin won 1 game and Elmer Leonard 2. Danforth was the only one who went on to a substantial major league career.

Eddie Collins returned to the lineup in time for another of those perennial crucial series with Detroit at home. Cobb's forces came in on July 28 for five games with a 3½-game lead. A Friday doubleheader drew an overflow crowd of thirty-three thousand. And what a time they had. In the first game, Bender and Summers threw shutouts through 10 innings. Summers gave up 1 hit through 9; Cobb canceled 3 hits with spectacular catches. In the eleventh Eddie Collins drove in the winning run. Detroit led the second game, 5–4, with 2 out in the eighth. Murphy and McInnis singled. Davy Jones dropped Lapp's fly ball, and 2 runs scored to give Jack Coombs a 6–5 win over Bill Donovan.

On Saturday a crowd of twenty-eight thousand watched Plank cruise to an 11–3 win. The teams were in a virtual tie, but after the day of rest the Tigers recouped and took the next 2. Again it was Cobb who smote the crushing blows when Detroit battered Coombs for 9 hits in less than 2 innings. He singled, tripled, stole two bases, and hit a home run before leaving in the fifth inning "on account of illness," unspecified. It was the Athletics who were sick of Cobb.

The A's then won 3 out of 4 from St. Louis, while Boston was roughing up the Tigers. On August 4 the Mackmen went back into first place, this time to stay. (The Phillies didn't; they finished fourth.) Since mid-June,

Bender had won 5 in a row, then, after a few losses, reeled off another 5 in a row. It seemed that as the Chief went, so went the A's.

"When Bender is fit," Isaminger wrote, "the Athletics are as invincible as a battleship attacked by a ferry boat loaded with pea shooters."

But the race was far from over. The Athletics led by 2½ games when they began their last western trip on August 17. Sporting editor George M. Graham of the *North American* decided to cover the grueling two-week test, leaving Isaminger to cover the Phillies.

The pennant race was not the only topic of conversation on the train to Chicago. In mid-July there had been rumors that a pitcher for St. Paul in the American Association, Marty O'Toole, and his catcher, Bill Kelly, were on the market for $20,000. O'Toole, a twenty-two-year-old right-hander, had been tried and turned loose by the Red Sox and Cincinnati Reds. St. Paul club owner Mike Kelley bought him and farmed him out to Sioux City in 1910. Now O'Toole had won 15 games for a sub-.500 team, racking up 199 strikeouts in 204 innings. The rumors were not taken seriously; the highest price anybody had ever paid for a minor league—or major league—player was Connie Mack's $12,000 for Lefty Russell, and everybody knew how *that* had turned out.

So it shocked the baseball world when it was announced on July 22 that Barney Dreyfuss had paid $22,500 just for Marty O'Toole. He then paid another $7,500 for Kelly, but that deal was ignored amid the hilarity and catcalls that followed the O'Toole purchase. Why, $22,500 was twice as much as the New York Giants had supposedly paid for a National League *batting champion*, Cy Seymour, in 1906. The ridicule of Dreyfuss and his extravagance rivaled that of Seward's Folly in the purchase of Alaska. It intensified as weeks went by without O'Toole's appearing in a game for the Pirates.

Reports of the price tags of players are at best unreliable. Different sources show different amounts. They were often just guesses. Sometimes club owners encouraged inflated estimates to impress their customers with their willingness to spend to bring them a winner. Connie Mack preferred not to announce any numbers. Barney Dreyfuss never confirmed or denied the $22,500 O'Toole price. But it was generally accepted.

George Graham was among those poking fun at Dreyfuss and O'Toole. Every Sunday in his column, "Under the Spotlight," he hurled some gibe at the deal. On July 30 he wrote, "Eleven thousand dollar Marquard took three years before he pitched good ball. On this line of argument, 22,500 O'Toole won't be worth shucks to Barney Dreyfuss until six years."

He noted the inflationary effects of the sale: "The market for minor league players has had a violent upward tendency."

The O'Toole purchase also led to the coining of one of baseball's most celebrated appellations: the $100,000 infield.

Connie Mack was heartened by winning 9 of the last 13 games of the home stand before the A's headed west. His infield was executing every kind of play without doubt or hesitation. "It's only been in the last two weeks that the team has been showing form worthy of it," he told Graham in Chicago. "I've been waiting all this year for the right combination of hitting, fielding, pitching, and intelligent work on the bases. In the previous stages of the season one or the other has always been lacking." Mack singled out the "hitting and dashing all-around work of McInnis," his newly installed everyday first baseman, as "the thing that has atoned for the uncertain quality of our pitching."

They opened the trip by sweeping a Thursday doubleheader from the White Sox, Jack Coombs pitching his best game of the year, a 3–1 five-hitter, followed by Bender's 7-hit, 5–1 win. The next day Cy Morgan's wildness cost them a 7–5 loss. On Saturday Eddie Plank had an uncharacteristic tantrum in the sixth inning, throwing his glove in disgust at the umpire's ball and strike calls and earning the first ejection of his career. A disappointed Mack rushed Morgan in to replace him. This time Cy turned in 7 good innings for a 3–1, 13-inning victory.

That night Mack let Plank know that his childish behavior had let the team down. The penitent Plank asked for the ball again the next day in St. Louis and pitched a 2-hitter against the Browns, 6–1.

In those four days in August, the infield of legend was born. With the acrobatic Stuffy McInnis at first base, the inner quartet's brilliance in the field and unstoppable versatility at bat made them the sensation of the baseball world.

Graham's account of the 6–1 win in St. Louis reads: "The Mackmen gave another scintillating exhibition of fielding. The $100,000 infield quartet—this is about what they would bring in the open market at the present day ballplayer quotations—seethed with fire and pepper. It was Baker's day to shine and he cut off at least three hits by sensational stops. McInnis speared a couple of throws with a gloved hand, an everyday event now, and Collins cheated Black out of a safety by diving at a ball, batting it down, throwing to Barry in time to get Stevens on a force play."

On August 27, when Marty O'Toole still hadn't started a game for

Pittsburgh, Graham wrote a variation on his new theme: "O'Toole has a $100,000 sweat every time Fred Clarke suggests it is about time for him to jump into a box score."

A week later, after the Athletics wound up a 10-5 road trip and widened their lead to 5½ games, James Isaminger credited Graham with the origin of one of baseball's most famous labels. "Philadelphia points with pride to the stunning work of the Mackian inner works, which George M. Graham has dubbed the $100,000 infield."

In his column, "Tips from the Sporting Ticker," Isaminger described the way the quartet had grabbed the national spotlight:

The fielding of these four defenders has been nothing short of phenomenal. In every city visited by the Athletics their smart, enthralling plays have captivated the fans. Particularly brilliant has been the first base play of Jack McInnis, who in one season has developed from a bench warmer into the acknowledged superior of Hal Chase. It is said of McInnis that he is making plays today that no other first sacker in baseball can match. He has a natural scent for the ball and seems always to be to the front of ground balls that are batted his direction. With his clean-up batting to take into consideration, McInnis is one of the most valuable players in the American League.

McInnis was catching throws one-handed, barehanded, falling to the ground, or already stretched out prone on the turf while one foot remained anchored to the bag. Connie Mack looked for him to be "the greatest first baseman in the country in a year or two, barring none." The first time John McGraw saw him in action, he said, "Base ball never had a first baseman in the class of McInnis." Stuffy went on to set fielding records while compiling a .308 career batting average. Why Stuffy McInnis is not in baseball's Hall of Fame is a mystery.

Of Eddie Collins, Isaminger wrote:

[He] has been praised so often that any flattering comment on his ability seems superfluous. He is admittedly the best second baseman in the world. If Collins hit .200 he would be the sensation of the league for his dazzling skill on defense. Collins covers more ground than any other second baseman in America. His nearest rival is Lajoie and he has it on Larry in enthusiasm, youth and dash. But Collins doesn't stop at doing miracles in the field. At the bat he is probably the most dangerous hitter in the American League excepting Cobb. The opponents can't play for Collins for he hits to any field. Pitchers seldom fathom what he's going to do. He is an expert bunter yet when he swings the ball travels far.

But the best description of Collins came from Ty Cobb. They were two of a kind: brainy, innovative, intimidating base runners. Cobb's salute to Collins in 1914 reads like many that were written about himself:

Probably the most dangerous base runner in our league is Eddie Collins because he takes chances and does the unexpected. Collins developed a trick a season or two back that got many outfielders for an extra base. He would drill the ball for two bags easy and take his turn at second, slowing up as if to stop, but still being a few feet over the bag toward third.

The outfielder would raise his arm to lob the ball to the second baseman, and Collins would be at full speed in five strides on his way to third. By the time the outfielder could pull his arm back again and change the direction of the heave, Collins would be sliding into the bag. Then the man was hurried, being taken by surprise, and half the time the throw would go wild.

Collins also worked this when on the base, frequently making an extra base in this way if the following batter got a hit. After he had put this over on our club two or three times, Jennings hopped on the outfielders.

"Don't any of you guys throw to the base that Collins is occupying after this," he ordered. "Always make your throws one base ahead. That boy has never stopped even if you think he has."

The praises of Jack Barry are the least sung of the four, especially by historians relying solely on cold, soulless columns of numbers. The public looks at batting averages and appreciates or discounts a player's value accordingly. Players don't. As Pittsburgh veteran Tommy Leach told F. C. Lane, "[A] player who bats many points less may be a more dangerous and a better hitter. Players realize these things and form their opinions of other players on what they see them do, not on what the records claim they do."

Many baseball men of the time considered Barry the most valuable of the foursome. Isaminger wrote:

In 1910 Jack Barry was easily the best shortstop in the American League. He has been rather slow getting the recognition due him. Barry has the reputation of being one of the few shortstops who is always in front of the ball when he stops it, no matter whether the ball is over the bag or it is hit to the left side of the shortstop patch, which puts him in a natural position for a throw. . . . Barry compares with the best ground coverers at shortstop in the last few decades. He has a steel throwing arm and can zing the ball across the infield like a rifle shot. The Holy Cross diploma holder is also one of Mack's pacemakers on the inside. He never has a high average in batting, and the fact is a mystery to the fans, for Jack appears to be in every rally. He is one of the most dangerous sticksmiths on the team at the bat when there are men on bases. In going from first to third there are few players who show more speed or use better judgment. On ordinary singles to left he is able to make third base from first, although most players stop at second. Barry's quick wit broke up the last game in Chicago that ran extra innings. With Baker on third and McInnis on first, Barry went to the bat and made a wild swing at the ball and missed it. He spun around as if he would have driven the ball into the next county had he been able to hit it. White, the Sox pitcher, and the Sox players fell into the trap that Barry set for them. They laid back expecting that he would put his weight against the ball. Instead, as soon as he stepped into the batsman's box, he signed for the squeeze. He bunted past White who, after stopping the ball, was surprised to see Baker crossing the plate. He was so stunned that he didn't make a throw to first. A second later McInnis and Barry came home on Thomas's two-bagger.

There's a reason his teams won pennants in six of his nine full seasons and finished second twice and third once. If Hall of Fame credentials counted brains and defense and knowing how to win, Jack Barry would be there.

Frank Baker was another story.

Isaminger wrote:

It didn't take Baker long to become the leader of his position in the American League. He is a great fielder and covers as much ground as the best of them. Baker is perhaps better known for his terrific clubbing. He hits the ball as hard as anybody in the game. His favorite direction is right field. Although the opposing infield and outfield are dressed for him every time he goes to the plate, he gets enough hits to hit high above the .300 mark. There is no pitcher in the American League who does not shudder at the sight of Baker, who is at any time likely to break up a game. He is just as good hitting portsiders as the righthanders.

Baker is often marked down for fielding deficiencies, but Connie Mack rated him among the best at his position. "I get a little impatient with persons who think Frank was an awkward fellow around the third-base bag. He was really a great third baseman. Look it up in the records; year after year he handled more chances than any other third baseman in the league. He had to move around to get all those total chances."

There was another element that contributed to this infield's popularity. After batting practice, each team had ten minutes of infield drills. The Athletics made such an entertaining show out of it that thousands of fans turned out early so they wouldn't miss it. The foursome did their routine with enthusiasm and obvious, infectious enjoyment. They flipped the ball behind their backs and over their heads, spun and dove and tumbled making stops. McInnis exhorted the others to throw the ball over his head, in the dirt, to his left or right. It was practice for him and a spectacular performance for the onlookers. He had to steel himself for Baker's throws, which were heavy as shot puts, and adjust for Collins, who threw a feather ball.

In September the A's gradually pulled away, gaining a game a week, then 2, then 3, coasting to a final 13½-game margin. For the first time in two years, the last two Detroit series had none of the usual intensity about them.

After Coombs pitched the clincher, 11–5, over Detroit on September 26, in which Baker hit 2 doubles and 2 home runs, Mack rested his regulars and gave some newcomers a look. One was a teacher from Cleveland, Howard Armstrong. With a makeshift lineup behind him, the right-hander worked 3 innings, gave up no earned runs, but took the 4–3 loss. Mr. Mack suggested he go back to the classroom. Another, Carroll Brown, also lost his only start but was invited back for next year. Dave Danforth won in relief over New York, 5–4, on October 6 for the team's 101st win. Wet grounds canceled the last game of the season, denying the A's a chance to tie their 1910 victory total.

It had all gone according to Connie Mack's blueprint. Back in March he had said, "A team that starts on edge is bound to go stale during the long season. I prefer to have my players make a slow start and gradually get up speed." Mack wanted his pitchers to peak at the end of September, and they did. Bender had recovered from an early September bout of grippe. Coombs, who threw 336 innings and won 28 games, was 7-0 after September 1. He also batted .319 and scored 31 runs, a modern record for a pitcher. Plank was 23-8, which may have given him second thoughts about retiring after one more year. Bender won 17, Cy Morgan 15. Harry Krause had come back from arm trouble to win 11.

For the past two years, Jack Coombs had been the equal of Walter Johnson. Forget the earned run averages. They didn't matter to pitchers. They weren't even accepted as worth recording by all baseball writers. Ban Johnson wanted them included in box scores. Older official scorers agreed; younger ones refused. The writers couldn't even agree on what constituted an earned or unearned run.

Treated to a big lead, pitchers like Coombs and Mathewson eased up. Winning and finishing games were their top priorities, not the other stats. Not even strikeouts. Use your head and save your arm, that was their watchword. Sometimes letting up could be hazardous, as Coombs learned in a game at St. Louis on May 12. The A's built a 12–3 lead after 4 innings. Coombs decided to take it easy. So what if the Browns scored a few runs? He threw at a leisurely pace and got by with it while the lead grew to 15–3. Then the Browns scored 2 in the sixth and 3 in the seventh. When they hit him hard in the eighth, he decided to "pull myself together." But he couldn't. Connie Mack yanked him with 2 outs, and by the time Cy Morgan got the last out, the score was 16–13. After the A's scored 1 more in the ninth, Chief Bender held the Browns scoreless.

Bris Lord had played the best left field of his life. He was quick and had the best arm in the league. Danny Murphy had developed into a smart gardener in right and a heavy hitter. Mack considered him the fastest man on the team from third to home. Oldring, who needed some days off because of the knee injury that had kept him out of the 1910 World Series, and Strunk gave the A's the best center-field platoon in the business.

Ira Thomas caught a career-high 103 games. Mack gave him the credit for the pitchers' good work. Jack Lapp hit a surprising .353.

Umpire John Sheridan, later a *Sporting News* columnist, looked back in 1919 and called Mack's 1911 team "not only one of the greatest of teams, it was one of the best joined, best put-together, best-looking, most attractive teams I have ever seen. All young, all of one size [within a few pounds of 170, except for Barry, Collins, and Hartsel, who were a little under or over 150, and Ira Thomas, the biggest at almost 200], all fast, all clever, it was a beautiful team to put on a baseball field. Organizing, training, finishing that team, leading it to a championship was a masterpiece of baseball joinery, and a triumph of good scouting."

During the season, when Connie Mack had refused Charles Somers's request for Harry Davis, a New York paper reported that Mack would move up as president of the Athletics and name Davis to replace him as manager after the season. At the time, Mack snorted, "Somebody's smoking. I will be manager of the Athletics as long as I am actively identified with baseball."

The reports started again once the pennant was clinched. Mack had suffered a few colds during the year. His wife thought the rigorous travel was affecting his health. Hoping to stifle any further speculation, Mack expanded on his present situation and his future. "I am working for a living and managing a baseball team is my work. I am not the rich man many say I am. Every cent I have is tied up in the Athletics baseball club and plant. And I hope to continue as manager until the stockholders fire me. Even if I were a rich man I would not voluntarily retire from the management, for I love the job. I would not feel at ease in any other position."

There is a line in the Shaker hymn, "Simple Gifts": "'Tis a gift to come down where you ought to be."

Connie Mack had come down where he ought to be. In business with the most amiable, upright partner anyone could hope for, free of interference in his running of the team, with four pennants and one world championship to his credit, a profitable business, a new wife and daughter (Mary, born July 27), his health and wits intact, Mack was twice blessed. He was doing what he most wanted to be doing with his life, and he had gained success, fame, prosperity, and the respect of his peers and the public while doing it.

The modern World Series, born in 1903, came of age in 1911. It grew into the biggest national sporting event of the year. The presence of a New York team for the first time in six years was an important factor. The city of 4 million was the nation's largest market.

John McGraw had put an end to the Chicago dominance of the National League. Greatly aided by the coaching of Wilbert Robinson, who was asked by McGraw to make lemonade out of the $11,000 lemon, Rube Marquard, the Giants won by 7½ games. The Athletics had been rooting for the Giants, not to avenge their 1905 defeat—half the team was new since then—but because the newly rebuilt Polo Grounds held larger crowds, swelling the players' pool. A winner's share could equal a year's salary, even more for many players. During the season some games in New York were reported as drawing fifty thousand fans. Those attendance figures had been exaggerated by a Giants official, but the players didn't know that. So when they saw no empty seats at the first game at the Polo Grounds, they concluded, not unreasonably, that there must be fifty thousand paying customers. When the official attendance was announced as 38,281, they yelled fraud and accused the owners of cheating them. It took some explaining to mollify them.

For the first time, hundreds of newspapermen, cartoonists, and photographers applied for press credentials. They came from every newspaper except three in the eleven major league cities and from Denver, New Orleans, San Francisco, Canada, and Cuba. Special dispatches went over the wires to Tokyo.

Enterprising syndicators signed up both managers and several players from the A's and Giants, as well as other players and managers, as commentators on the daily action. Ghostwritten words of wisdom appeared under the bylines of Ty Cobb, Hughie Jennings, George Mullin, Red Dooin, Cap Anson, and Hal Chase.

The modern media circus was also born that fall. The 1910 World Series had been the first to be filmed by motion picture cameras. The players didn't have a union, but their thinking was the same as that of their diamond descendants generations later. When they read that the National Commission had sold the movie rights for $3,500, the players wanted a share of it. They were the ones doing the posing and providing the action. The A's picked Harry Davis to speak for them; the Giants chose catcher Chief Meyers. Davis and Meyers asked the commission for 60 percent of the money for the players' pool. They were turned down.

Hordes of still photographers swarmed over the field before each game, raising hackles of annoyance among the players. When Christy Mathewson tried to warm up before Game 4 in Philadelphia, he was pestered by photographers, shouting for him to look their way and pose in mid-windup.

"Who am I working for, the Giants or the photographers?" the idol of millions growled audibly enough for college student Lloyd Lewis to hear twenty feet away in the first row of the right-field bleachers.

"I was let down for a minute," recalled Lewis, a Matty worshiper who became a sportswriter for the *Philadelphia Daily News*. "He didn't speak like a demi-god, but as I stared, he looked it, all the same."

More than a hundred writers—the Philadelphia chapter of the three-year-old Base Ball Writers' Association of America (BBWAA) had thirty-five members, the New York thirty-four—overflowed the press box facilities in New York. The Giants provided four rows of seats beyond the grandstand in right field. Only those in the first two rows had writing surfaces; the rest had to work with notebooks and typewriters on their knees.

In Philadelphia, where the facilities had been equally inadequate for the 1910 Series, John Shibe and writers Joe McCready and Billy Weart went all out to cater to the press and the fifty Western Union telegraphers. They leased a fleet of automobiles and drivers to carry them between Shibe Park and press headquarters at the Bellevue-Stratford. Every writer had a desk-top to work on. There were well-stocked hospitality rooms at the hotel and ballpark and typewriters for anyone needing one.

George Flood, the veteran guardian of the press gate, kept the traffic flowing smoothly. Flood would be missed by the A's when he left after the Series to become secretary of the Cleveland club. Connie Mack's brother Michael replaced him.

The writers were delighted with the unprecedented arrangements in Philadelphia. No longer was Sleepytown ridiculed, not even by the sophisticates of Broadway. Damon Runyon publicly commended the Athletics and the local writers for their elaborate facilities and generous spreads of food and beverage.

The entire nation was caught up in the second meeting of the great McGraw and the widely admired Connie Mack. Thousands gathered in theaters, on Main Streets, in parks, and along sidewalks in front of saloons to follow the action depicted on a variety of electrical, mechanical, and rope-and-ball devices. Judges presiding in courtrooms, up to the Supreme Court, had their bailiffs and clerks slip them inning-by-inning updates. Proceedings in Congress were interrupted with reports of the scoring.

The impact of baseball on the country's psyche as a unifying denominator was illustrated in a *New York Times* editorial: "Baseball makes the whole world kin. Before the closing of the market recently, crowds in the brokerage offices left the stock ticker to drone along by itself while they gathered around the news tickers. In one of the biggest banking offices, where discipline is rarely suspended, two of the partners were seen bending over the shoulders of the office boys during the last two innings, and in the informal discussion that was going on, the boys proved the instructors and their employers the pupils."

The demand for tickets, priced from $1 to $3, swamped the teams' offices. The Athletics hired temporary clerks to deal with the flood of mail. Connie Mack was determined to honor city residents' requests first and drew irate criticism from fans outside Philadelphia; more than $100,000 had to be returned to disappointed applicants. With the teams only ninety miles apart, the National Commission scheduled alternate sites for the games. The A's lost the coin toss, and the opener went to New York, the second and fourth games to be played at Shibe Park.

This was the first World Series played in two steel and concrete ballparks. It was also the first battle of the lucky charms. The Giants had picked up an adult mascot, Charles "Victory" Faust, for their human rabbit's foot. A would-be pitcher, Faust traveled with the team and was given a chance to pitch a few innings. The Giants also had a young batboy/mascot, Danny Hennessey. The Athletics brought Louis Van Zelst to New York. He and Hennessey posed shaking hands before the first game like a pair of prizefighters before a bout.

To accommodate Charlie Ebbets, the National League had again extended its season to Columbus Day. The A's lined up an All-Star team for four practice games. It helped them to stay sharp batting against Walter Johnson and George Mullin, whose style and delivery closely resembled that of Christy Mathewson. Stuffy McInnis, hit on the wrist by a pitch on September 25, played 3 innings in one game after that and found the wrist too sore to continue. Harry Davis would play first in the Series.

The A's had won 101 games, made the fewest errors, scored the most runs and given up the fewest, and led the league in batting and slugging, but some of the experts thought they were not the same team that had defeated the Cubs. The Giants, they predicted, would be too much for them. The betting line was practically even money.

While Mack's pitching and infield were widely acclaimed, his outfield was not. True, Lord, Oldring, and Murphy weren't sensational, but they were steady and covered a lot of real estate. They made the fewest errors of any outfield trio in the league. Most of those were muffed fly balls, common errors in the days when gloves were no bigger than a hand and had no webbing or rawhide binding the fingers together. Bris Lord was shorter than Socks Seybold and almost as heavy, but he moved deceptively quickly and was a good judge of where a ball was headed. He had the best arm and the instinct to charge ground base hits and come up throwing, an aptitude Mack found frustratingly lacking in most outfielders. In the second game Lord would throw out a surprised Fred Snodgrass at second base on a ball hit down the foul line, where doubles usually go. Rube Oldring was fleet of foot and sure of hand, with the highest fielding average of any outfielder in the league. Danny Murphy swung the strongest bat of the three. A pure guess hitter, he made up his mind if he was going to swing—if it was anywhere near the plate—before the pitcher let the ball go. In a time of chop-and-slash hitters, Murphy was a slugger, often among the leaders in extra base hits.

The Athletics had something else that didn't show up in the numbers. When Mack's boys had taken 3 from the Yankees in September by scores of 12–5, 10–1, and 2–0, Joe Vila of the *New York Sun* warned New Yorkers that Philadelphia would be no pushover for McGraw's forces.

"The Athletics are made up of young men who like to play ball," he wrote. "There isn't a lazy player on the team. . . . From the moment Mack's men put on their uniform they display energy. In practice they show ginger and speed. In championship games they never say die. . . . On the bench they talk baseball. When mistakes are made there is no ill feeling. Great plays prompt enthusiasm and words of praise. Lack of jealousy and friction is one of the reasons for the success of the Athletics. . . . Mack knows baseball and how to handle players of all natures and temperaments."

Now, on the eve of the World Series, Vila reminded his readers, "Everything is done apparently with a system. In short, you might say the Athletics combine brains, brawn, speed, and skill, with a master hand at the wheel."

The running game was at its peak, and the Giants were its paragons. They had swiped 347 bases, still the record. But Connie Mack was unconcerned. "You simply cannot get [Ira Thomas] rattled," he said. "He has no nerves, and the tighter the pinch the better he likes it."

Mack predicted the Athletics would win in five or six games, because "world championships are won in the pitcher's box and that is where we're going to show the advantage."

The A's knew they'd have to beat Christy Mathewson to win. In his eleven full seasons, Matty had pitched 3,560 innings. He reportedly had lost a little zip on his fastball and was relying more on an assortment of curves and the fadeaway. But the A's took no comfort from that. He had won 26 and lost 13 in 1911. And as Ogden Nash wrote, Matty still "had an extra brain in his arm."

They began talking about Matty in their morning meetings in September, when it looked as if they'd be facing the Giants. They had been hitting the curves and fastballs of the best in the American League with great success. In the 1910 Series they had scored 35 runs in 5 games against the Cubs' pitching. So they weren't concerned about hitting Matty's curves and fastballs. The fadeaway was something else. Most of them had never seen it. It had been six years since Davis, Hartsel, Lord, and Murphy had faced him. Those four had been 7 for 45 in the 3 games Matty pitched. They discussed what they could remember about him.

As for scouting, one report said that Mack had sent Eddie Collins and Jack Coombs to Chicago to check out the Giants in late September. If true, they traveled on the twenty-ninth, saw the Giants win the next two days, then returned October 2. They saw Marquard shut out the Cubs but didn't see Mathewson pitch. On October 3 the Giants were in Philadelphia for one game. Mack watched Doc Crandall beat the Phillies, while most of his regulars were playing two in Washington that day.

The A's booked rooms at the Hotel Somerset at 150 West Forty-seventh Street, near Broadway. Except for the night before the first game, they didn't sleep there. National League clubs had visitors' dressing rooms—the American wouldn't require them until 1912—but the A's decided to change at the hotel and ride in a fleet of taxicabs to the Polo Grounds. After the games they returned to the hotel and changed before catching the train to Philadelphia.

On the morning of Saturday, October 14, they met in Connie Mack's suite. The subject was: who should pitch the opening game that afternoon against Mathewson? When Connie Mack refused to announce his pitching plans the night before, the writers predicted Jack Coombs would start. The strongest workhorse on the staff, he would then be available to start two more games if needed.

As usual, Mack encouraged everybody to voice an opinion, while he sat and listened. Some figured if Matty was in top form, they might as well use Krause or Morgan and save their best pitchers. Others pointed out that playing at home gave the Giants the advantage anyhow. Besides, if they got to Mathewson, even one of their second-line pitchers could stop the Giants. Why not save Bender, Plank, and Coombs for the next games?

Connie Mack heard them out, then declared that in his opinion, they should take their best shot at beating Mathewson right out of the gate. His choice was Albert Bender. The possibility that they might have to go into the second game without Bender and one game down may have made some of the players uneasy, but it didn't shake their leader's confidence.

A line began to form at the Polo Grounds on the afternoon before the first game. By the time the sun rose in the morning, the line extended more than a mile. Bleacher, lower grandstand, and standing room tickets went on sale the morning of each game. Despite the enlarged capacity of the park, many of those in line found the ticket window closed by the time they reached it. Outside the grounds vendors hawked souvenirs, including copies of Christy Mathewson's first $90-a-month contract with Norfolk in 1900, supplied by the enterprising Norfolk club owner, Alex Hannam, who held on to the original.

John McGraw, no less superstitious than anybody else in baseball, clad his knights once again in the black outfits they had worn in 1905, when they had handily dispatched the Athletics in 5 games.

Just before game time, the first official World Series announcer, E. Lawrence Phillips, a one-armed megaphone man from Washington, stood near home plate and boomed out the starting lineups for the benefit of the limited few who could hear him in the elongated horseshoe grandstand.

Mathewson was familiar with only half the Athletics' lineup. Baker, Collins, Barry, and the catchers were new to him. He did his scouting by asking for tips from friendly American League pitchers.

Chief Bender could throw a pitch as fast as anybody. John McGraw was aware of Bender's lack of stamina and the exertion it took to pour in his fastball inning after inning in a tight game. He told his men to take a lot of pitches, wait out the Indian, wear him down. While they waited, Bender threw enough strikes past the patient hitters to whiff 11 of them. He wound up throwing about 140 pitches.

Matty relied on changing speeds and pinpoint control, enticing the A's to put the ball in play with as little wear on his arm as possible. He delivered about 95 pitches in 9 innings.

The A's broke through with a run in the second, breaking a string of 28 shutout innings at Matty's hands. The Giants tied it in the fourth on an error by Collins on a hit-and-run grounder. In the end, Bender was unable to outlast Mathewson. A double and single in the seventh gave the Giants the final 2–1 margin of victory. Mathewson finished strong, retiring the last 12 batters on 34 pitches.

It seemed to the Athletics that the Giants were out to get Frank Baker from the start. McGraw, coaching at third, rode Baker all day. "You're a quitter," he barked. "Jennings and the whole Detroit club told us so." McGraw and Jennings had been teammates on the 1890s Baltimore Orioles and were still buddies. In the sixth inning Snodgrass slid into third on the front end of a double steal. Thomas's throw beat him. Baker blocked the bag. Sno's spikes scraped Baker's arms and kicked the ball out of his grasp.

The Athletics took something else away from that game, something more valuable than a victory might have been. All eyes on the bench studied Mathewson's every move throughout the game. By the end of the day they had discovered that Matty tipped off his fadeaway by a little step he took before he threw it. That wasn't all. Most of the time the pitch was out of the strike zone. They decided to watch for the pitch and take it every time he threw it. They also observed that Matty went to his curve in the pinches and pitched his fadeaway mostly to left-handed batters.

The Giants were convinced the A's were picking up their catcher's signs from the coaching box and when they had a runner on second base. They even speculated that the mascot, Louis Van Zelst, might be peeking between Chief Meyers's knees while picking up the extra bat discarded by the next hitter as he stepped into the batter's box. The mascot then relayed it to the third base coach. American League clubs already realized that the A's were sitting on the bench studying the pitchers' habits, not catchers' signs. But the Giants were spooked enough to change their signs often and sometimes have the pitchers give them. Mathewson and Meyers worked out their own code to throw the A's off. And that was the whole idea. The A's didn't care who gave the signs or if they changed with every batter. It was all a bluff. When they had a man on second, he'd go through a lot of motions that meant nothing. Danny Murphy explained, "Teams changing signs and using a lot of them get mixed up and distracted, weakening themselves."

A crowd of 26,285 spilled over into the outfield at Shibe Park for Game 2 on Monday. Thousands more crammed neighborhood windows and rooftops. There was ample evidence that Ban Johnson's efforts to stamp out gambling on baseball had gone nowhere. A local betting pool sold twenty thousand tickets. A huge banner, "MAKE YOUR BETS," which hung between telephone poles above six houses on Twentieth Street, was clearly visible from the grandstand. Inexplicable bursts of cheering erupted in sections of the right-field seats following routine fly balls or singles. Raids by police carted off a few gamblers from time to time. But it was like trying to empty the Susquehanna River with a teacup.

The Giants' lineup had only two left-handed batters, Doyle and Devore. McGraw expected to see Jack Coombs in the box for the A's and had his right-handers pitch batting practice. Mack, expecting Rube Marquard to pitch for New York, used Harry Krause for BP. McGraw and many of the assembled experts were surprised when Eddie Plank walked out to warm up a few minutes before game time. Mack figured that Eddie would give them a look they hadn't seen. No lefty in the National League used the crossfire delivery and frustrating fidgets that Plank inflicted on batters. It didn't matter to him which side of the plate they swung from.

Or was there more to Mack's decision than that?

As a syndicated columnist covering the Series, Ty Cobb took his role seriously. He sat in the press box and wrote or dictated his opinions without relying on a ghost to reword them. The animosity and heated exchanges between him and Connie Mack just two years earlier were forgotten or ignored as he lauded Mack's masterful strategy in starting Plank:

Think of the situations and how craftily manager Mack analyzed every little detail. Think of the different angles and the thought which he put into the problem.

First, Plank is a pitcher of a nervous temperament, every action showing high tension, and to pitch him on his home grounds before a home crowd was the one thing to do. Next, with Marquard, a left-handed thrower for the Giants, Thomas, a right-handed batter as catcher for Plank, would be added batting strength.

If Marquard would have had a left-handed batter [Coombs] and as Jack cannot work successfully with anyone but Lapp, also a left-handed batsman, catching, it can be easily seen that Marquard would have had the chances in his favor with that battery.

That would have necessitated Plank pitching tomorrow against Mathewson, and that would have necessitated Thomas, the right-handed batsman, catching, and he would have proved easier prey for Mathewson. Here manager Mack was planning two days ahead in selecting Coombs . . . and his exclusive catcher, both good left-handed hitters, and Coombs rested for this one task, to oppose Matty, who had pitched a hard game last Saturday.

After a further spinning of the left-handed/right-handed batsmen permutations, Cobb concluded, "It looks to me as if manager Mack has spent quite a while analyzing this situation and he has checkmated manager McGraw by taking a chance and pitching Plank today against Marquard."

Both southpaws were outstanding. Neither walked a batter. Plank fanned 8, including Josh Devore 4 times. The Giants had an attack of first-inning nerves. Red Murray bobbled Lord's leadoff single, and Lord made it to second. Oldring sacrificed him to third. Then Marquard uncorked a wild pitch and the A's had a 1–0 lead.

The Giants scored in the second when Oldring, carefully placed in center field by Mack's waving scorecard, started in on a line drive by Buck Herzog that sailed over his head for a double. Meyers then drove him in.

It stayed at 1–1 until the sixth. With 2 outs, Collins doubled down the left-field line. Baker took a ball and a strike, then took a mighty cut and hit it over the right-field wall. Delirium erupted within Shibe Park, in the windows and along the rooftops of Twentieth Street, and downtown on Broad Street, where the action was being recreated.

"The scene that followed beggared description," wrote F. C. Richter. The howling, stomping, whistling, and cheering had begun at 3:20 and went on for a full five minutes. Fans sitting behind the visitors' dugout banged on its tin roof with canes and bottles and feet.

That was all Plank needed for a 3–1 win.

A lot of stories have been written about the pitch that Baker hit, including memoirs by the ghostwriters for Marquard and Mathewson. As time edited memories, the variations of what happened strayed into fiction. Eyewitnesses reported it as everything from a low curve to a fastball hit off the end of the bat. As for Frank Baker, all he said was that it was a fastball inside without saying whether it was high or low.

Christy Mathewson was one of the $500 player-scribes for the Series. The way his ghostwriter, John N. Wheeler, remembered it in his memoirs, that night on the train to New York, Matty told him Marquard had violated the instructions given by John McGraw in the pregame clubhouse meeting. Wheeler recalled that Matty's column the next day charged, "Rube was especially warned not to pitch low to Baker. Rube pitched just what Baker likes."

But that was not what had appeared under Matheson's byline the next day. Instead, Mathewson/Wheeler wrote, "Rube evidently thought that Baker would not be looking for a fast ball at that time." Matty speculated that either Eddie Collins read the catcher's signs from second base and tipped him off or Baker simply outguessed Marquard. Whichever it was, "Baker was up there all set and waiting for it." The column made no mention of Marquard disobeying McGraw's orders.

In *My Thirty Years in Baseball*, McGraw said, "I had instructed Marquard not to pitch a high fastball to Baker, but he forgot. He put one just in that spot and Baker 'whammed' it into the stands."

McGraw's memory was more accurate, except that Marquard had not forgotten. He had deliberately disobeyed instructions. In his own column the next morning, ghostwritten by Frank G. Menke, a young reporter just breaking in with *International News Service*, Marquard said he had struck out Baker on three curves in the first inning. "In the fourth he caught the first pitch, a high out[curve], and pushed a weak grounder to Doyle. When he came up in the sixth, I fully intended to follow instructions and give him curve balls. After I had one strike on him and he refused to bite on another outcurve which was a little too wide, I thought to cross him by sending in a fast high straight ball, the kind I know he likes. Myers had called for a curve but I could not see it and signaled for a high fastball. Either he knew the signal from Collins who was on second or he outguessed me, for he was waiting for that fast one and sent it over the fence."

That's why John McGraw told his players, "Let me do all the thinking."

It was particularly ill timed and imprudent for Mathewson to take his teammate to task publicly for making a mistake. Marquard had pitched well; he walked nobody and gave up only 2 hits in the first and 2 in the sixth. It also exposed to all the world the contrast in the attitudes of the two teams. Mathewson in particular was never reluctant to criticize teammates in print, then or later, which some writers believed caused resentment among the other Giants. With the Athletics, as Joe Vila had pointed out, "when mistakes are made there is no ill feeling." That difference would be in evidence again before the Series ended.

Mathewson also insinuated that Connie Mack was nothing but a bush leaguer. It had rained on Sunday, and the infield dirt was damp. But Matty, possibly playing some mind games, made an accusation against the Athletics:

> [They resorted to] a trick in preparing their field that reminded me of the bushes. They'd evidently wet down the baselines within a radius of about 20 feet of all the bags so as to slow our men up. In this way they conceded that they fear our baserunners and that they believe their catching department has been weak. They practically acknowledged that we had a faster team and that, in a way, was a comfort.
>
> The doctoring of the field did us little damage, except when Snodgrass made a hit to left field in the sixth inning and tried to get two bases on it. He slipped in the wet turf making the turn around first base and was caught easily at second.
>
> Of course because it rained here on yesterday, they had a good chance to soak the field around the bases today.

(The next spring, when Matty's book, *Pitching in a Pinch*, came out, it repeated the claim.)

Connie Mack didn't respond, but his groundskeepers, Joe Schroeder and Joe Smith, angrily denied the accusation.

"Mathewson is saying what is not true," said Schroeder, "and he is doing it to find some excuse for the Giants losing the game. If we had attempted to wet the base lines any more than the rain did, they would have been plain mud. After the rain we put black sand on the base lines, and that is what made it look muddy. The black sand absorbs the moisture. It is one of the best remedies we have found for wet grounds."

Eddie Collins had made a similar double with no problems just before Baker's home run.

"Snodgrass had no more trouble on base lines than Eddie," Schroeder said, "but he got a poor start from home."

Ty Cobb credited Bris Lord's quick pickup of Sno's hit and "wonderful throw to second" for catching the surprised Giants speedster by a mile. Commenting on the outcome of Mack's surprise starting of Plank, he wrote, "He has surely turned the tide of battle for before today's game the Giants' followers could see nothing but easy victories for their favorites. Think [my] little analysis over, sum up the percentage of strong hitting batteries opposed as Mack has figured out, and don't you think he has worked out a mighty successful-looking plan?"

Plank pitched brilliantly, but it was Baker, not Thomas, who had done the damage.

Speaking of Game 3 in New York, Connie Mack told Fred Lieb, "That's one game I'll never forget if I live to be 100. I think I lived a lifetime during it."

The more than thirty-seven thousand who packed the Polo Grounds (the Giants sold no outfield standing room) were also limp after two hours and twenty-five minutes of nonstop excitement. The game began in a light drizzle from a dark and glowering sky that never cleared. Bill Klem wore gloves and an overcoat while umpiring at first base. Before the game, a little-noticed brief ceremony took place in front of the clubhouse entrance in deep center field. Ty Cobb, named the American League's Most Valuable Player by a panel of eight writers—one from each city—was presented a Chalmers automobile. John McGraw had refused to let the car be driven across the field to home plate for the occasion.

This time there was no doubt that Jack Coombs would chuck for the A's. Mack made the first change in his starting lineup except for pitchers: Lapp catching in place of Thomas.

McGraw had the veteran lefty Hooks Wiltse and right-handers Doc Crandall and Red Ames all well rested. But he considered Mathewson with two days' rest a better bet than anybody else with any amount of rest. Connie Mack had been accurate in sizing up his advantage over McGraw: more pitching depth.

The Athletics had Mathewson pitching in a pinch all afternoon. He didn't walk anybody, but he gave up 9 hits, and his infielders made 5 errors. The A's had their chances. Bris Lord hit a sharp line drive that was turned into a double play. Harry Davis hit a rope headed for two bases, but the ball hit umpire Tom Connolly, limiting Davis to a single and preventing a run from scoring.

Coombs walked 4 but was stingy with the hits, the Giants making only 3. Two came in the second inning; a fumbled ball by Barry allowed a run to score on a force at second that could have been a double play.

Jack Lapp, abetted, the Giants claimed, by second base umpire Tom Connolly, shut down the Giants' running game. Five times they attempted larceny. Five times Lapp nabbed them. The Giants squawked so heatedly on some of the close calls that Fred Merkle was fined $100 and McGraw, shouting accusations of collusion at Ban Johnson (seated in a third base box), drew a reprimand from the National Commission. But both Lapp and Ira Thomas were containing the Giants with their heads as much as their arms. They noticed that the Giants faked a lot of false starts on the bases. By watching the footwork, they figured out when the runners were faking and when they intended to go.

The lone Giants' run stood up through 8 innings, as Matty's mastery of the A's continued. They had hit him hard, but his control was perfect. Of his eventual 136 pitches, all but 28 were strikes. Coombs, mixing his high fastball with sharp curves, had kept New York's batters guessing.

The crowd was tasting victory after Eddie Collins, first up in the ninth, grounded out to third. Baker stepped in. He had read Matty's comments about Marquard. He had seen almost no fastballs from Matty, who had been getting him out on curves all day. Baker took a fadeaway for a strike, then two low curves. The count was 2-1. Baker was looking for another curve. Mathewson wound up and threw.

Sitting behind home plate, Detroit pitcher George Mullin, who had faced the A's many times, had a perfect view of Matty's slants. When he saw where the pitch was headed, he reflexively muttered, "Look out," to himself. He knew it was the kind of pitch Bake loved to jump on. Baker jumped and crushed it into the right-field seats. The stunned crowd, pent up and ready to burst out cheering their hero and head for the exits, sat in stony silence, as if a huge hand had been suddenly clamped across thirty-seven thousand mouths. Fred Lieb claimed that the Polo Grounds was so still, he could hear Baker putting his footprints in the dirt as he rounded the bases. The blow only tied the game, but the crowd and the Giants had believed it won, in the bag. Their high spirits were snuffed out as abruptly as a pinched candle wick.

Not so in the streets of Philadelphia, where the display-board watchers went wild with glee, or the dugout of the Athletics, where whooping players grabbed bats and threw them wildly in the air. When Jack Barry jumped up to toss one, he hit his head on the dugout roof and was stunned. "I was afraid he might have to quit the game," Mack said, "but he insisted on taking the field in the tenth. He told me everything was blurred and he saw black specks in front of him."

Mack had second thoughts after Barry went out to his position and sent Ira Thomas out to make sure Barry was okay. "Spectators probably thought Thomas went out on some sly and secret mission," Mack said. Barry stayed in the game.

Neither team scored in the tenth, but it was anything but dull. Fred Snodgrass, leading off, leaned into an inside pitch, and it hit him. Umpire Bill Brennan said he had failed to try to avoid it. Snodgrass then drew a base on balls. Red Murray sacrificed him to second. As Coombs pitched to Merkle, Snodgrass took long leads off second, acting, Mathewson wrote, "like a madman. He jumps way off the ground and prances about like a dervish." Coombs threw a curve that broke in the dirt and bounced a short distance away from Lapp. Snodgrass, leaning toward second, spun and headed for third. Lapp retrieved the ball and threw to Baker, who was blocking the bag. The throw beat Sno easily, but he jumped in the air and flew, spikes first, straight at Baker. Baker held onto the ball as the spikes ripped his uniform from crotch to knee, taking the skin off his right thigh. It couldn't have been more deliberate. Even the New York rooters booed Snodgrass this time, while the game was delayed to enable Baker to be patched up and secure a new pair of trousers.

In the eleventh the Athletics put together singles by Collins, Baker, and Davis, a wild throw by Herzog, and a booted grounder by Art Fletcher to score 2 runs. But Mr. Mack's one-game lifetime wasn't over yet. Herzog opened the last of the eleventh with a double, only the third hit off Coombs. After Fletcher flied out to Lord, Chief Meyers lined a fastball toward the left-field stands. Calm as he may have looked on the outside, Connie Mack's heart must have been racing as he watched the ball curve foul at the last second. Meyers then grounded out to Collins. Mack's innards probably flipped when pinch hitter Beals Becker hit a grounder to Collins and Eddie couldn't find the handle while Herzog scored. Lapp then cut down Becker trying to steal second for the final out. The streets of Philadelphia erupted with joy. Traffic outside newspaper offices was deadlocked. All business in the city stopped. Connie Mack could breathe again.

A fleet of taxis took the Athletics back to the Somerset. After their opening day loss, the ride to the hotel had been uneventful. Now that they led the Giants, 2 games to 1, angry Giants fans, who had seen the go-ahead game snatched from them by the hated Baker, lined the route armed with eggs and tomatoes. "Our taxicabs were tomato-smeared by the time we got to the hotel," Eddie Collins said. "After that we had a policeman in the front seat of each cab, but as we rolled through Harlem we heard some colorful and uncomplimentary remarks."

Frank Menke later maintained that he went looking for Marquard after the game, eager to write something clever at Mathewson's expense. Some versions of the story say he couldn't find his client and went ahead on his own with the piece for the morning papers. Menke claimed he had seen Rube, who "was just interested in the money he was getting" and gave the go-ahead to snipe back at Mathewson. Menke, who became a prolific compiler of sports encyclopedias, supposedly wrote under Marquard's name, "What happened, Matty? What did Baker hit? It couldn't be that you grew careless, or did you?"

Good story, but no such language appeared in Marquard's column. Here's what Menke wrote: "When [Matty] came back to the bench, after Barry had been thrown out in the ninth inning, I asked him what [the pitch] was.

"'The same thing you did, Rube,' said Matty. 'I gave Baker a high, fast one. I have been in the business for a long time and have no excuse.'"

A few paragraphs later, Marquard detailed the pitch. "[With a 2-1 count] Matty decided to try the trick I tried in Philadelphia—to cross him on his favorite ball, and he gave him a high fast ball over the inside corner. Baker eats this kind, and he ambled home."

John Wheeler wrote in his memoirs that the embarrassed Mathewson decided he had no choice but to admit he too had pitched wrong to Baker.

McGraw went along with this, writing that "Mathewson, who rarely forgot anything in his life," had made the same mistake as Rube. "After maneuvering around a while, he handed Baker a high fast one in an effort to cross him."

The problem with these accounts is that Mathewson's next-day explanation contradicts all of them. Before he got around to his own mistake, Matty pinned the blame for the loss squarely on the poor base running of Fred Snodgrass in the tenth inning. "That play cost us the game." Then he criticized his teammates for their "overanxiety" at bat and in the field. It took him twelve paragraphs to get around to talking about his own role in the loss. "In the seventh I pitched a fadeaway to [Baker], and he hit the ball almost to the right-field wall, where Murray caught it. I made a mental note, and decided to feed him curves.

"When he came to the bat in the ninth I pitched him two curved balls. He missed one, and the other was wide. The next I delivered was a curve over the outside corner knee high, just where I wanted it, but Brennan called it a ball. I thought that he missed a strike, and it put me in the hole. The next one was a curve, and I didn't want to take any chances on not putting it over, because it would get me in a three-and-one hole, so I laid it up better than I meant to, and he caught it on the end of his bat and drove the ball into the stand."

No forgotten instructions. No high fast one trying to cross up Baker. Just a misplaced curve.

The newspapers in both cities were filled with shots fired back and forth over pitching strategy and mistakes. Frank Hough commented philosophically, "The fact that Baker homered off Matty . . . only emphasizes Disraeli's contention that 'it is easier to be critical than correct.'"

Through it all, nobody considered that maybe it wasn't just pitchers' mistakes; maybe some credit was due Baker for his hitting ability. After all, he had batted .324 with 115 runs batted in for the season. His 198 hits included 40 doubles and a league-leading 11 home runs. And he had made 2 hits off Mathewson in the first game.

So Gordon Mackay of Philadelphia's *Evening Times* wrote a lengthy rebuttal, quoting Baker, who probably never spoke that many words on one subject at one time in his life: "If you believe what Marquard and Mathewson are saying, I can't hit the ball only in one spot. Taking it all in all, I'm a lucky guy to be in the league at all, after they get done telling where I hit 'em and where I miss 'em. You want to know the kind of balls I hit for those two homers? Marquard gave me a fast one on the inside. Matty handed me a curve about knee high. It didn't look a bit different than the other curves that he handed me all through the series."

As a result of his two dramatic home runs, Baker's given name, Frank, became Home Run, and Home Run Baker became a national hero—west of the Hudson River. Telegrams and night letters poured in:

From Clarksburg, wv: "Baker I love you. You got to Matty. S. D. Hall."

"Good boy Baker do it again tomorrow and the world is all yours. Alexandria Louisiana Fans."

"Give us one more home run tomorrow navajo blanket will follow. Dr. D. C. Brown and five other guys from Winslow Arizona."

From someone who was clearly not the Chamber of Commerce of an unnamed city: "Should it ever be your misfortune to pass through our city kindly notify us ahead of time in order that we may be lined up at the station. Wishing and predicting for you the most ultimate success in the 1911 World Series we are, Star Trading Company General Merchandise John H. Garner vice-president, Wiley Daniels, Sec-Treas., R. F. Davis, pres."

And from fans in Rising Star, Texas, who had their money on the Athletics: "In you we have great hopes. We have lost on cotton but we are going to make it back on the Athletics. We hope you will bat Ames off his feet and put Matty and Marquard to flight."

There was even advice on how to deal with Fred Snodgrass:

"Put battery in trousers when spikes come in contact electrocute. Harpers Ferry wv Fans"

And of course there were stage offers and pleas for personal appearances:

"Can arrange six weeks for you in vaudeville at finish of series just to talk for ten minutes twice a day have arranged monologue. M. B. Haas, Hotel Metropole."

"Will pay your expenses and 25 percent of the gate receipts if you will play one Sunday game for the benefit of the charity hospital for sweet charity's sake answer. New Orleans Baseball Association, C. J. Heineman, Secretary."

"Will give you $100 to referee lady motorcycle races Ohio Sunday. Answer my expense."

Baker turned them all down. None of it was more interesting to him than duck hunting and watching his asparagus grow.

Immediately after the last out had been made that afternoon, different groups of fans hired bands to greet the team at North Philadelphia station that evening. Three bands showed up with a cheering mob of men and women and a blue flag with a white elephant waving alongside an American flag.

A more hostile reception committee awaited the Giants when they arrived at the Reading terminal at 10:25 that night and headed for taxis to take them to the Majestic. Fred Snodgrass drew the most boos and hecklers. He stopped once and faced the group, but further nastiness was averted when Josh Devore grabbed his arm and pulled him away. "Tomorrow's another day," said a cheerful John McGraw when asked if he still had his hopes up.

It rained that afternoon in Philadelphia. The next day it rained even harder. The Giants got back on the train when the game was called. They made the same quick round trip the next day. For five days the rain never let up.

With nothing else to write about, the scribes and player/columnists dwelt on Snodgrass's spiking of Baker. Half the writers ripped him; the rest excused him. In the absence of instant replays, everyone had to rely on vaguely remembered first impressions. Papers in both cities expounded at length on the subject. The division of opinion was not provincial. Some of the New Yorkers denounced Snodgrass. Connie Mack thought it was intentional; Sno had come in with his spikes too high for any other purpose. But he didn't make a fuss about it, shrugging it off as the "fortunes of war." Unlike similar incidents involving Ty Cobb, some of the Athletics thought this one was deliberate.

Snodgrass denied it. The Giants maintained that only one National League player had been spiked while they were stealing 347 bases, and it wasn't Snodgrass who did it. McGraw said that Baker had an awkward way of taking a throw at third base. Mathewson wrote that Baker put himself in harm's way by sprawling all over the bag while applying a tag. "If Baker played in the [National] League with Fred Clarke, he would be cut to pieces, because Clarke rides high when he comes into the bag." He agreed with Ty Cobb: the baseline belongs to the runner.

Baker did block the bag, and he may not have been the most agile at applying a tag and getting out of the way, but he couldn't have been all that "awkward" or "sprawling." Cobb was the only American League player to cut him all year.

The rain turned Shibe Park into a swamp. Mack and the umpires conferred each day. Mack walked onto the muddy field while the umps kept to the cinder path. The outfield was saturated. Mack refused to consider burning gas or oil on the grass when the rain stopped. "As everyone knows, one burning ruins grass forever," he said. "It would mean $4,000 or $5,000 damage to the field and we will not allow that."

Connie Mack was still fuming about Mathewson's "bush league" comments. Neither of these gentlemen had completely forgotten Matty's contract-jumping episode of 1901. On a day when it looked like it would not rain, Mack considered the field was still too dangerous. "I expect with this rest Mathewson will pitch the next game," he said. "I want the field to be perfectly dry so he will have no excuse to offer."

Mack scoffed at critics who accused him of wanting to delay the resumption of play as long as possible, a ludicrous suggestion. He had nothing to gain. The A's had the pitching depth the Giants lacked. They had the momentum after Baker's heroics. "Now, however, [the Giants] have had a chance to rest up and get back their badly shattered nerves," Mack said.

Baker was the only one who welcomed a respite, giving his lacerated arm and leg a chance to heal.

The sun came out on Monday, October 23. The grounds crew burned off the infield dirt. The outfield remained soggy. There were no tickets sold for standing room on the grass. Both pitching staffs were as ready as they had been when the Series began. So the A's faced Christy Mathewson for the third time. Connie Mack confidently gave the ball to Bender.

The crowd was hardly settled before Josh Devore beat out an infield hit and Larry Doyle hit a fly ball that Rube Oldring could have caught if he had any footing. By the time he splashed and skidded to it, Devore scored and Doyle was standing on third. A sacrifice fly brought him home. When Mathewson struck out Lord and Oldring and, after Collins singled, fanned the mighty Home Run Baker, it looked like "Here we go again" time. A 2–0 lead was usually enough for Matty against the A's. Another foreboding omen came in the second, when Jack Barry was unable to get down a squeeze bunt with Murphy on third, a rare failure for the shortstop that discomfited the hometown rooters.

But from then on, the old Bender was very much in control, and the old Mathewson was not. Players and writers sitting behind home plate and in the press box said Matty had nothing. Maybe so. But seeing him for the third time in ten days, the Athletics were confident they could pick up his fadeaway giveaway. And given his uncanny control, they decided to jump on his first pitch, invariably a strike. They teed off on him in the fourth. Baker, Murphy, and Davis doubled, and the A's took a 3–2 lead. In the fifth Baker doubled again, driving in Collins. It was Baker's sixth hit off Mathewson in 3 games; was Matty throwing "mistakes" every time, or was Baker too good a hitter for him?

Meanwhile, Bender was throwing peas. "Who can hit a pea when it goes by with the speed of lightning?" Josh Devore lamented. Bender and Ira Thomas kept New York base runners off balance all day, with nary a theft by any of the 10 men to reach base.

The Athletics completely outplayed McGraw's men. In the sixth inning Barry and Collins duped the Giants' captain and most adept base runner, Larry Doyle. Doyle was on first with one out when Murray hit a high popup in foul ground just outside third base. Doyle was running with the swing. While the first base coach hollered, "Come back," Doyle saw Barry leaning down as if to scoop up a grounder and Eddie Collins rushing toward second base yelling, "Throw it here." Doyle charged toward second. Baker caught the ball and tossed to Davis for the easy double play.

The 4–2 win put the Athletics within one victory of repeating as world champions. The Giants looked beaten. Out-of-town writers went to New York not expecting to return to the Quaker City.

Amid the cheerful, chattering crowd leaving Shibe Park, the lonely Matty worshiper, Lloyd Lewis, trudged solemnly. In need of a drink to drown his sorrows, he went into a saloon and ordered a nickel stein of beer, his first ever. He took one swallow and learned a lesson: it didn't help.

Back in New York for Game 5, Jack Coombs and Rube Marquard were in the box. Marquard, undercut in the third when Doyle dropped a throw at second base on a ready-made double play ball, then gave up a 3-run homer to Rube Oldring. McGraw brought in Red Ames, belatedly in the opinion of some observers, to start the fourth. Ames held the A's scoreless on 2 hits for the next 4 innings.

Meanwhile, Jack Coombs was baffling the Giants, mixing a variety of curves with his fastball. Out-of-town writers began making their travel plans to go home. Then, in the sixth inning, Coombs pushed off the slab to throw a pitch to Art Fletcher. The spikes in his right shoe caught between the dirt and the edge of the rubber. He landed awkwardly. Something wrenched in his side and groin. Connie Mack could see that he was in pain. Jack Lapp walked out to him. Harry Davis came over. Mack sent Ira Thomas out to see if Coombs was all right. Colby Jack assured everybody that he was fine.

But he wasn't. In the seventh he was clearly hurting every time he threw a pitch. He was relying on his arm alone, and it affected his control. He walked the first batter, Merkle. Herzog hit a double play ball to Barry, who flipped to Collins, who dropped the ball. Fletcher hit a ground ball to Davis, who threw to second to force Herzog. Meyers scored Merkle with a sacrifice fly. When Ames hit a grounder wide of first, Davis went to his right and picked it up. Coombs hustled to cover first as if he didn't have an ache or care in the world to end the inning.

When Doyle opened the bottom of the eighth with a single, Mack sent Bender out to join the entire infield around Coombs. Eddie Plank was throwing on the sidelines. They tried to persuade Coombs to come out, but he insisted he could get them out. And he did, fielding a sacrifice bunt by Snodgrass, then retiring Murray and Merkle.

Doc Crandall had relieved Ames in the eighth and continued to hold the A's. Coombs had a 3–1 lead as Herzog opened the ninth with a line drive right at Barry for the first out. Fletcher hit a soft fly to left that fell just beyond Lord's reach for a double. Meyers grounded out to Barry. One out to go. The New York fans began moving toward the exits. Writers typed out their leads and checked the railroad schedules. Doc Crandall, a solid hitter often used as a pinch hitter, lofted a fly over Oldring's head in center field and pulled into second, scoring Fletcher. The score was now 3–2.

Ira Thomas went out and convened another conference. The batter was little Josh Devore, the left-handed swinger Plank had fanned 4 times in the second game. Devore had done nothing against Coombs all day. By now Coombs was hopping on one leg after each pitch to cut the pain. Nevertheless he told Thomas, "Tell Connie I can take care of the little guy."

Mack made no move. He knew his man. Coombs had gutted it out this far, and Mack would not deny him the chance to nail down the final out and close out the Series.

Devore hit the first pitch to left for a single. The score was tied. The bedlam that broke out in the Polo Grounds surpassed the din in Shibe Park when Baker had hit his home run off Marquard. It echoed in the elevated railway station outside center field like a thunderclap, sending fans who hoped to beat the crowd scurrying back inside to see what was happening.

Lapp threw out Devore trying to steal second to end the inning.

Why didn't Connie Mack take out Coombs and send in Plank earlier? Or at least use Plank against Devore in the ninth? It seems totally incomprehensible today, when the complete game is meaningless, when matchups dictate managers' moves, when the concept of "it's his game to win or lose" is unknown.

Years later Jack Coombs said it was the players who talked him into continuing each time there was a meeting. That's unlikely. Seeing him in excruciating pain, Thomas and Davis and Bender would not have urged him to keep going. Jack Coombs was gruff and stubborn and gritty as gravel. There was an honor to pitching a World Series clincher. He had closed out the Cubs in 1910 and was set on doing it again. "In the excitement I thought the pain would go away," he said after the game. "So I determined to stick it out." Champion athletes have the mental capacity to suppress pain and perform as if it didn't exist. Concentrating on what pitch to throw and fielding a bunt or covering first drove the pain from his mind. It was only when he landed after each pitch or a play was completed that it pierced him like a hot knife.

That was Jack Coombs. What of Connie Mack? For all his hardheaded business acumen, Connie Mack was a players' manager, considerate of his men's feelings ahead of winning or losing. For all his protestations about never letting sentiment overrule his judgment again, he remained as sentimental as any son of Ireland. The proud bull moose of a man from Maine hated to come out of a close game at any time. If Jawn was stubbornly determined to make it to the end, Connie Mack was just as stubbornly determined to let him. The Athletics led the Series, 3 games to 1. Even if they lost today, it wouldn't dent his or his players' confidence that they could beat the Giants tomorrow. Except for Collins's error, the Giants wouldn't have scored at all in the seventh. They had made only 1 hit off Coombs in the eighth. The score was still tied. The game was not yet lost.

So Mack let Coombs, a good hitter, bat with one out in the tenth. Coombs topped a swinging bunt down the third base line and churned toward first oblivious to any pain while Meyers pounced on it and threw. Coombs beat the throw. Once he stopped running, his face was so distorted in agony that there was no more conversation. Mack sent Amos Strunk in to run for him. Strunk was left stranded at first.

Eddie Plank went in, and Doyle greeted him with a double to left. When Snodgrass bunted, Plank elected to throw to third—too late. First and third, nobody out. Murray hit a short fly to right, too shallow to score Doyle. Merkle then hit a fly down the right-field line. Murphy caught it and made a strong, true throw home as Doyle tagged up. Doyle beat the throw and slid around Lapp, wide of the plate. He got up and ran to the bench as the Giants mobbed him and ecstatic fans poured out of the stands and engulfed the players. Lapp hesitated, glanced at Mack, who seemed not to notice him, then joined the rest of the A's as they fought their way through the swarm of jubilant New Yorkers. Umpire Bill Klem stood amid the throng, still behind home plate, until all the players had left the field.

From the umpire's view, from the infield, from both benches, from the press seats behind home plate, it was obvious that Larry Doyle never touched home plate. Had Lapp tagged Doyle before they were both engulfed by the onrushing crowd, Bill Klem would have called him out. Klem had waited for an appeal that never came.

The captain, Harry Davis, whose place it was to make an appeal, said he knew Doyle hadn't touched the plate. But before he could get to Klem, thousands of people were pouring onto the field. The play had detonated a delirium that Fred Lieb called the loudest he ever heard in the Polo Grounds. In that state of exhilaration that can madden mobs, who knows what mayhem might have followed had the Athletics forced the umpire to nullify the winning run while surrounded by a sea of celebrating home-town fans? Harry Davis glanced at Connie Mack on the bench. Seeing no sign from Mack, he did nothing.

Mack backed Davis's decision without reservation. During those tumultuous seconds, a scene from three years earlier had flashed through his mind: the Polo Grounds, teeming with angry fans when the Cubs had dodged a loss on a technicality. Mack told a reporter that if anyone had tried to tell the Giants they had not won this World Series game, "I believe they would have torn down the place."

That evening on the train to Philadelphia, Mack talked about the play and his players' reactions:

It was the most pleasing moment of my life when not one of them tried to take advantage of a cheap technicality. Lapp looked around at the bench to see if I had noticed. I could see him from the corner of my eyes. I did not give him a tumble and he rushed off the field with the rest. Now, I couldn't swear that Doyle missed the plate, but if he did, what difference did it make? He had plenty of time to scuttle along and in my mind the Giants were fully entitled to it. I'm glad that none of my men forced Klem to make a ruling that would have been a rank injustice to New York, probably precipitating a riot and taking a hard-earned victory from the true winners and perhaps given base-ball a black eye. I'm mighty pleased that my team showed themselves true sportsmen.

John McGraw complimented Davis and Mack for "their prudence and sportsmanship."

Twisted in pain, Jack Coombs had to be carried to the train. The next day Connie Mack arranged for play-by-play bulletins to be transmitted to him as he lay in a hospital bed. When the players went to see him, Jack's tearful wife Mary was by his side. It wasn't the injury that made her cry but the letters and telegrams from A's fans accusing him of having deliberately "blown up" and sold out to the Giants.

The Athletics' superior pitching depth came to the fore. Eddie Plank had faced only 4 batters in the loss and was rested and ready. McGraw couldn't use the thirty-one-year-old Mathewson on one day's rest. He chose Red Ames, despite Ames's having worked 4 innings in Game 5, over the little-used left-hander, Hooks Wiltse. Wiltse and Marquard pitched batting practice in anticipation of Plank's starting for the A's.

While Plank was warming up, Chief Bender began to play catch. Gordon Mackay and James Isaminger told slightly different versions of what happened next. According to Mackay, Bender walked over to Mack and said, "I'm going to pitch and win the World Series for you."

"All right, Albert," Mack replied. "You'll pitch and I know you'll deliver."

Isaminger reported that when the umpires came to the bench to get the lineup from Mack, Bender came over and said, "Get a new ball out of the bag for me, Connie," and Mack silently handed him a new ball, then told the umps that Bender would pitch.

It didn't matter that Bender had pitched a complete game two days earlier. He had a full day's rest and would soon have four months off. "It's only once in a century a chap gets a chance to clinch a world championship," he said. He didn't want to take a chance on someone else getting the glory this time.

Connie Mack may well have set up the whole scene. Plank was the bait. Bender wanted the ball, and Mack knew it. More than any of his pitchers, Bender had the ego to shine in the biggest spotlight. If Albert asked for the ball, he would be unbeatable. That's why he considered Bender the greatest one-game pitcher he ever encountered. In 1929 Mack told writer Frederick S. Hovey, "I would say to him, 'Now, Chief, ten days from today we begin the season's most vital series. I must win the first game for its effect on the morale of our boys and not overlooking the enemy's. So I want you to prepare yourself to win that game.' He never failed to accomplish the task I set for him."

Once again John McGraw ordered his men to make Bender throw a lot of pitches to wear him down. Bender knew what they were up to and quickly got ahead of every batter with 0-1 and 0-2 counts. When McGraw saw what was happening, he told his men to start swinging early, whereupon Bender began cutting the corners.

The Giants took a 1-run lead in the first when Danny Murphy dropped a fly ball. When the A's came in to the bench, he apologized to Bender. "All I ask," Bender said, "is to get the run back. The Giants may be able to tie us, but they never can win today."

The A's got the run back and 12 more, pounding Ames and Wiltse, while Bender held the Giants to 4 hits and 1 more unearned run in the ninth. Not even a bruised and bleeding finger from a third-inning line drive that clipped his pitching hand could stop him. His arm may have been weary, but his head was not. He directed the entire performance on the field. "Never," wrote one writer, "did Bender pitch a brainier game. . . . As he threw on the outside to left-handed batters he motioned his outfielders to left field. Now, he would call them in—now he would wave them to the right. . . . It was a mighty exhibition of mechanical skill, backed up by studious thought and gameness."

This time there was no tension, no squirming on the bench, no abraded threads on the seat of Mr. Mack's dark blue trousers. Jack Barry made an uncharacteristic 3 errors, but Collins, Baker, and Davis sparkled in the field. The Giants unraveled in the A's 7-run seventh, highlighted by 2 runs that scored on a squeeze bunt by Barry, who was safe at first when Ames's throw hit him in the head.

"Nice headwork," a fan yelled.

"For the first time during the series I laughed," Christy Mathewson wrote. "So did all the other men on our bench. We felt we were jokes." John McGraw probably did not share in the mirth.

Connie Mack had built a team in the truest sense of the word. His boys played, worked, thought, and rooted for each other as a team. Nobody blamed Jack Lapp for the failure to tag Larry Doyle. Nobody complained when there was no appeal. The closeness, the lack of jealousy and friction Joe Vila had observed, was highlighted in the closing innings of the final game. Stuffy McInnis, just turned twenty-one, had been a high school shortstop two years ago. When Harry Davis, crippled with rheumatism, faltered during the season, McInnis filled in for him and batted .321. A sore wrist had deprived him of the chance to play in his first World Series. Now, with the game in the bag after the seventh inning, Davis and Mack were thinking the same thing. Davis wanted McInnis to go in for him in the eighth. Mack said not yet. He waited until there were 2 out in the ninth, then sent Stuffy out to play first base.

The last ball hit in the Series belonged to the man who made the putout. All the Athletics wanted McInnis to have it this time.

"The most trying minute of the last game was the last batter," Bender said. The right-handed batter was catcher Art Wilson, who was batting for the first time since replacing Chief Meyers. "As he was a comparative stranger to me, I put everything I had on the ball that would cause him to make an infield rap, so that McInnis would stand a good chance of getting the putout. Wilson pulled one toward Baker who fielded the ball nicely and looked over at McInnis and then around at Harry Davis [before throwing to first]. I was satisfied there was something more in baseball than the winning of a world's championship."

John McGraw was the first to reach the A's dugout to congratulate Connie Mack. "You have one of the greatest teams I've ever seen," he told Mack. "It must be. I have a great team, too, but you beat us."

The strained relations of the past between Mack and McGraw were forgotten. McGraw and Christy Mathewson both followed Mack to the A's business office, which was crowded with officials of both leagues and other clubs. Both the Giants heaped more praise on Mack and his men, Matty singling out Harry Davis for his outstanding job.

Then Mack, Hough, Jones, and all the Shibes went into the clubhouse. Mack shook hands with his field leader, Harry Davis. Smiling but uncomfortable with the kudos aimed at him, Mack said:

Mr. Davis and the others deserve all the credit in the world, particularly Bender for having pitched three games, the second and third with only a day in between.

Counting that my team began the American League race twelve games behind Detroit, lost the first game of the world's series, a tradition always taken to mean defeat, and started in three of our four winning games in the present series in the hole, New York scoring first, I hope we have killed for all time that old foolish story about our not being game.

I have been in baseball for twenty-five years, and have never in that time played with, managed or even seen a gamer, braver set of boys than mine, and I am proud of every man of them, from the greatest star down to the lowest substitute.

It is their triumph and to them goes the glory.

Had there been a World Series MVP, Frank Baker would have won the honor. His two dramatic home runs were only part of his .375 batting average. Jack Barry hit .368. Harry Davis matched Baker's 5 runs batted in on only 5 hits and played a flawless—sometimes brilliant—first base.

Using the same strategy of pitching to hitters' strengths that had worked all season, the A's held the Giants to 13 runs and 33 hits in 6 games. Fred Merkle, 3 for 20, admitted, "Bender, Coombs and Plank dished me up the sort of balls of which I like to take a wallop, but I couldn't connect. They didn't pitch to our weaknesses at all. They gave us the best they had, paid no attention to any of our supposed batting deficiencies."

The *New York Sun* hailed the Athletics' victory as "a signal triumph for clean baseball," adding, in a knock on McGraw and the Giants, "Mack's players convinced thousands of critics and fans that a championship could be won without finding fault with the umpires' decisions."

Connie Mack had reached the pinnacle of the baseball world. All across the country, where millions of fans knew of big league baseball and its stars only through newspapers and magazines, the Athletics had become America's team, and Connie Mack the most respected, admired, even beloved, of baseball managers. When veteran baseball writer W. A. Phelon wrote a brief profile of each major league magnate a year later, all he said about Connie Mack was, "No need to write anything about Connie—his characteristics are too widely known for additional applause."

Henry Killilea, Mack's onetime boss in Milwaukee, called him the "greatest baseball man of the century. . . . He is all the more remarkable when you stop to consider that he never had a university education as some of us have had.

"He has handled men under him, both university men and otherwise, in a manner that has been surprising, and still his players have not been as high-priced as others. He held their respect at all times and any of them would go out of their way to help him. His management of the business end of baseball, where he handles nearly $1,000,000 a year, would do credit to an expert accountant."

In the years to come, Connie Mack would often be quoted as calling his

1912 team his best. But thirty-five years later, when Arthur Daley of the *New York Times* asked him which was his favorite, Mack replied, "By golly, it was the 1911 team." Sitting on a bench in spring training in West Palm Beach, the eighty-three-year-old Mack then rattled off the lineup and their batting averages with, Daley wrote, amazing accuracy.

It was indeed the World Series that stayed with Connie Mack for a lifetime.

41 | COASTING DOWN TO THIRD PLACE

A happy band of Athletics met at Shibe Park on Friday morning, October 27, to divvy up the World Series winners' pot. As they had done in 1910, they voted no partial shares. Twenty-one players received $3,654.58 each. They chipped in for generous bonuses for trainer James Chadwick and batboy Louis Van Zelst. Six of the players, having abstained from purchasing pernicious automobiles during the season, now joined the motorists' ranks: Baker, Hartsel, Barry, Plank, Morgan, and Lord. Baker also bought his father's farm in Trappe and another 200 acres across the road from his home. Pitcher Harold Martin, who had appeared in 11 games, used his windfall to cover his tuition at Tufts Medical School. Rookie Dave Danforth did the same to attend dental school at the University of Maryland.

The Giants and A's each banked $90,000 from the Series.

The National Commission presented the players, Mack, the Shibes, and secretary Joe Ohl gold watch fobs on a black silk background with a half-carat diamond in the center of a baseball diamond and "World's Champion 1911" around it. The recipient's name and "Philadelphia Athletics" were on the back.

Then the banquet circuit began. Everybody in Philadelphia and Baltimore wanted to hear Frank Baker talk about the two famous home runs that changed his name. The players even made the guest list of the Poor Richard Club, the most exclusive clique in Philadelphia, for their annual gala. The Athletics threw their own party for players, writers, and friends of the club. An orchestra played during dinner. Song sheets at every table encouraged the guests to sing along on the popular tunes of the day: "Down by the Old Mill Stream," "I Want a Girl," "The Whiffenpoof Song." Moet Chandon champagne flowed. Every guest received a metal white elephant hanging from a blue ribbon. The menu, featuring photos of the players, began with pepper pot soup and ended with after-dinner cigars. Jack Coombs, Chief Bender, and Harry Davis spoke for the players. Connie Mack missed this one; his three-month-old daughter, Mary, was taken suddenly ill, and he stayed at her bedside.

A vaudeville skit starring Bender, Coombs, and Cy Morgan opened in Atlantic City to favorable reviews and full houses. When the show opened at Keith's in Philadelphia, the Macks were there and entertained the cast and their wives at home after the show. Mack diplomatically opined that the show must be a good one, as it was playing to sold-out houses twice a day.

Mr. and Mrs. Mack and Mary went to Atlantic City for a rest. They stayed at a small side street hotel owned by John Burke, one of the legions of friends of Connie Mack. The cook at the hotel was Maggie Page, who would soon become the longtime beloved cook for the Mack household.

At the December league meetings in New York, the Athletics put on a feast for the writers and magnates at the Hotel Astor. The A's were already being picked to repeat in 1912. In his after-dinner remarks, Connie Mack played down his team's chances, praising everybody else in the league. Whereupon Garry Herrmann stood up and said that if Mack was not satisfied with his players, he'd be glad to ask waivers on his entire Cincinnati team and swap it for the Athletics.

Ban Johnson proudly announced that every team in the league had shown a profit, helped by new parks and the debut of Sunday baseball in Cleveland. New or modernized plants in Washington, Detroit, and Boston promised continued prosperity in 1912. Embarrassed by the Mathewson-Marquard sniping in the nation's newspapers during the World Series, the National Commission considered banning ghostwritten commentaries. Nor did it look kindly on players appearing on the stage during the winter. Neither activity was seen as enhancing baseball's new, shining big-business image.

Connie Mack disagreed. He didn't think the commission had the authority to impose such bans, and, besides, he didn't see any harm in any of it. With keener public relations insight than his peers, he observed, "It only brings the stars more in touch with the people, and anything which will bring about this result is good for the game."

A *Boston Globe* writer commented, "Connie Mack has made just as much of a study of the public and writers as he has of the players, and herein lies his all around success."

Assured by Connie Mack that he could stay with the A's as long as he wanted, as a coach and sometime player, Harry Davis was ready to try his hand at managing. He turned down an offer from the Browns and was skeptical that he would find the conditions to his liking in Cleveland, but he gave in to Charles Somers's persuasion. His assessment of the situation was accurate. Disgruntled players, who didn't want to see the popular George Stovall leave the Naps, were ready to undermine anybody who replaced him. The self-discipline that characterized the Athletics was absent among the Naps, and Davis's efforts to impose discipline drew more resentment than cooperation. He didn't get the autonomy he expected from the front office. Davis would resign in August and return to Philadelphia.

With Davis's departure, Mack had to choose a new field captain. During the 1911 season, when Davis was not in the lineup, Eddie Collins had assumed the captain's duties. The writers and players expected Collins to be the new captain. Instead, Mack chose Danny Murphy in recognition of his long and loyal service. Murphy and Eddie Plank were the only players left from Mack's first pennant winner in 1902. Murphy was a popular choice with the players.

Topsy Hartsel's playing days were over. He had given Mack ten years of yeoman service as a leadoff man, five times leading the league in walks. Charles Somers needed a manager for his Toledo club. Mack recommended Hartsel. The money Somers paid for Hartsel's release was given by Mack to Topsy.

The ranks of managers and coaches who had played for Connie Mack were growing. Monte Cross, after managing Scranton, signed with the St. Louis Browns as assistant manager, perhaps the first to be hired specifically as what is now called a bench coach. (Cross resigned in midseason.) Jack Barry returned to Holy Cross to coach the team before leaving for spring training. When his playing days ended, Barry became the school's full-time coach for forty years.

Improvements to Shibe Park included digging up the ground outside the foul lines, putting in French drains covered with cinders, and grading the field so heavy rains would drain better than they had during the six-day delay that had interrupted the 1911 World Series.

Sitting in his tower office, Connie Mack studied the 1912 schedule. He noted with envy the Sunday dates of the four western clubs. The National League, blaming its two latest World Series defeats on its prolonged seasons, abandoned its stretch to Columbus Day. The AL schedule put the Athletics on the road for almost four weeks in September. A red flag went up in Mack's mind. It would be imperative to build a lead by mid-August in order to hold off the rest of the pack through that lengthy road trip. Last year he had held back his older pitchers, letting the team start off slowly and build toward a strong finish. This year he'd concentrate on getting his veteran pitchers in shape for a fast start.

Mack also wrestled with the starting times for home games. The press, pointing out that western clubs began at three, had been after him since last year to move up the first pitch by at least thirty minutes. When a game took more than two hours, a 3:45 start meant cold suppers for his customers. But moving it up a half hour would cut into some fans' work schedules. The Phillies were switching to 3:15. No matter what he did, Mack could satisfy only half his followers in the city that had grown to 1.5 million people. He decided to leave it at 3:45.

In the middle of January 1912, Connie Mack's mother took to her bed. She was probably seventy-one. Her strength had been waning for about a year. Mack spent many hours by her bedside that winter. As a boy, he had been guided along her path, which diverged sharply from his father's. His nature, his toughness, his endurance, and his faith had come from her. He had depended on her when his first wife died and left him with three babies. Her years of running his household in Philadelphia had been the easiest time of her life: no worries about money, all the help she needed, sobriety in the home. Mary McKillop McGillicuddy died on February 1. The funeral mass was celebrated at Mack's parish church of Our Lady of Holy Souls. The casket was put on the night train to Worcester, where Mary was buried beside her husband in St. John's Cemetery.

Connie Mack returned home and prepared to leave for San Antonio. For the first time, he was accompanied to spring training by his wife, whose unmarried sister Annie—Aunt Nan to his children—began an annual stay with the family while the Macks were in the south. The rookies and newly signed prospects left three weeks ahead of the veterans. The Macks led the advance party, which included the Reverend Fr. J. B. McCloskey, an amateur player from Atlantic City who worked out with the rookies and umpired their games with scout James Whiting; the spry, eighty-one-year-old Sam Erwin; and the A's largest fan, C. Emory Titman.

Connie Mack attracted a wide variety of friends, hangers-on, and personal followers. They included clergy of all faiths, university professors, doctors, businessmen, writers, judges, nuns. Some of them traveled with the team at least once a year. All were volunteer scouts. His friendships lasted a lifetime, and he seems never to have lost one. He corresponded by handwritten notes with many of them until his last days. His letters always expressed concern for their families and hopes that they would see each other soon.

Some of them he never met. On October 15, 1929, a nun in Billings, Montana, sent him clippings from her local newspaper about the Athletics' World Series victory and her prayers for his continued success. Connie Mack replied, as he did to everyone who wrote to him. They corresponded regularly until she died fourteen years later.

What attracted and held them was more than his celebrity, more than the ego-boosting status of considering themselves personal friends of a great baseball manager, more than his willingness to leave box seat tickets for them whenever they were in town. They liked him. He was good natured and even tempered. He read the newspapers thoroughly, enjoyed the theater and concerts and other sporting events, and of course never tired of talking baseball. And they never tired of listening and learning. He enjoyed telling stories of his days as a player, of the characters he had played with and against and those he had managed. His letters contain concise, candid comments about his current teams and other baseball matters.

Beyond that, Connie Mack was a gracious, considerate, generous host. When people were his guests, they were the center of his attention. He was a welcome, comfortable, undemanding guest in their homes. He genuinely enjoyed their company as much as they did his. A man of innate kindness, he was as courteous to the cop on the beat or a Shibe Park employee as he would be to the president of the United States.

Probably the oddest of all the friends of Connie Mack was Emory Titman. Sometimes identified as the world's heaviest man, the twenty-four-year-old Titman dented the scales between 550 and 600 pounds. He inherited $250,000 (about $4.5 million today) and spent it all in the next six years on high living, a brief marriage to a chorus girl, and traveling with the Athletics. In spring training he occasionally worked out with the outfielders, wearing a uniform Mack must have had made for him by a tentmaker. During the Great War, he would try to enlist as a flier, but no airplane in existence was capable of lifting him off the ground. He went on a diet, lost 300 pounds and his health. Broke, he did odd jobs and remained an avid Athletics fan and unofficial mascot until he died in 1928 at thirty-nine. At his death he reportedly weighed 587. It took twelve men to bear his coffin to its resting place.

The journey to San Antonio took three days, delayed by a blizzard in St.

Louis. They arrived on Thursday morning, February 15, to a clear sky, cold wind, and warm civic reception. At the welcome luncheon, Mack declared that his team was there to work hard. "We will not spend $15,000 to $20,000 on a training trip just to have a good time." He predicted that Boston would give his team the most trouble in the pennant race. He declared the hotel facilities satisfactory: Turkish baths, sulphur pools, rooms with real bathtubs, clear drinking water. There was plenty of entertainment in the evenings at the Grand Opera House and several vaudeville theaters.

On that same morning the league, meeting in Chicago, passed a rule requiring all clubs to provide visitors' dressing rooms by June 1. This seemingly innocuous rule provoked some controversy. Hugh Jennings feared it would loosen control of managers over their men. Left to themselves, players would arrive late and stop in saloons and get into all kinds of trouble if they no longer traveled together. One side effect was no more club-provided taxis and buses between hotels and ballparks. The players would have to pay their own fare or walk. Some players welcomed it, though. Using hotels as dressing rooms kept them out of some of the better hotels, where the management didn't care for players walking among their fashionably dressed guests in dirty, sweaty uniforms after games.

Mack designed his workouts around extended batting practice; he was less concerned with fielding drills. Those could wait until the morning sessions at Shibe Park. Frank Baker demonstrated that he could get out of bed in the middle of winter and go 2 for 4. On the first day he dispatched a brand new ball high over the right-field fence and a house across the street.

The weather was not as hot and dry as Mack had hoped. Most of the time it was too cold and wet and windy for pitchers to get into shape. Mack tried to arrange a few games against the Giants, who were having the same problem in Marlin. Garry Herrmann, denying a report that there was a National Commission rule against World Series opponents playing spring exhibition games, wondered aloud why Connie Mack was willing to "take a chance on being defeated." But it was McGraw and his players who didn't want the games.

When it came time to head north, Mack left Bender, Plank, Coombs, and Morgan behind to work into better condition. He was disappointed in the dozen fledgling pitchers in camp, including two twenty-one-year-olds, Byron Houck, acquired from Spokane, and Bob Shawkey, drafted from Harrisburg by Baltimore, possibly at Mack's request. He was also carrying a contrite Lefty Russell, who had shown up at Shibe Park in December asking for another chance. *North American* sports editor George Graham called them "a poor lot. Mack will have to look to his veterans to repeat."

Long-term planning was an integral part of Connie Mack's management style. He looked far beyond the coming season. He believed his infield was the best that had ever played in the major leagues. It was a machine that worked perfectly in every respect. Barring accident, he saw their youth, dispositions, and physical strength keeping them working at the same level for three, four, maybe five years. But he had also seen championship clubs break apart in less time than that. The more a team won, the more vulnerable it became to inflated egos and salary demands, complacency, personality clashes, and dissatisfaction with the manager. The time would come, sooner or later, when his machine would need replacement parts. It was not too soon to find one or two fuzzy-cheeked teenagers to enroll in his bench school of baseball for a few years. He sent Al Maul to California in search of new raw material. Maul returned empty-handed. Mack looked over a slew of youngsters in his rookie camp in Austin, including a high school first baseman named Chase, who didn't turn out to be another Hal. He found none of them worth taking home with him.

But for this year Mack was confident. His team was set at every position. He didn't see how it could lose. He was wrong.

"It taught me a lesson," he said. "It's dangerous to ever believe you have a league stopped, no matter how well you did the year before."

Not that he gave his boys or the public the impression that they were invincible. Whatever he thought privately, to reporters he said, "We may win again but it won't do for our players to grow overconfident, believing they are going to have a walkover. They'll have the hardest fight of their lives on their hands next year and they'll have to get in and hustle for every game."

Unlike previous years, Mack saw no need to travel north with the Yannigans. He wasn't building a team, and he had seen enough of the rookies to know there wasn't much there. They began the trek home on March 19. Thirty-five miles out of San Antonio, a train wreck ahead of them stranded them for sixteen hours with no food. The hops between towns never started or arrived on time. The weather was wet and cold. Mack cooled on Texas as a training site. He had tried ten places in the past ten years and hadn't found the ideal location yet. Sitting in a side-tracked railroad car, he concluded that no manager should take his team farther than a thirty-six-hour train ride from home. He had signed a two-year contract to train in San Antonio, so he was stuck for another year. He looked ahead to 1914 and back to where he had taken his first Philadelphia team—Jacksonville, Florida. Before another spring came, he signed a five-year lease with Jacksonville on the condition that the city build a new clubhouse suitable for forty players.

They arrived in Baltimore on a wet day to play Jack Dunn's Orioles. As usual the players put their money and jewelry into a satchel, which Danny Murphy brought to the bench and kept an eye on. Emory Titman, who, like other devoted fans of Mack and the A's, was treated as part of the family, also stowed some of his valuables for safekeeping. Some time during the game the bag disappeared, along with the batboy, Edwin LeRoy Warnick. The next day the police found it stashed in his older brother's bedroom. Warnick was committed to St. Mary's Industrial School, where he undoubtedly became acquainted with another lad, George Herman Ruth.

The A's opened at home against Washington on Thursday, April 11. Mack looked forward to renewed contact with Clark Griffith, his comrade in the trenches since the launching of the American League. Griffith had been the first manager of the White Sox and the first to lead the New York Highlanders. After three years in Cincinnati, he was now the Nationals' skipper. Given an opportunity to buy a 10 percent stake in the club for $29,000, he was turned down by Ban Johnson for a loan, although Johnson had provided similar loans for several other club owners. Griffith's admiration for Johnson eroded a little as a result. He mortgaged his ranch in Craig, Montana, to raise the money and eventually became the club's sole owner. Griffith and Mack visited often in each other's homes and offices for the rest of their lives, which would end four months apart.

Jack Coombs launched the season by holding Washington hitless for 7 innings in a 4–2 win over Walter Johnson. The next day Cy Morgan gave up 1 hit in a 3–1 victory. The A's then lost a big Saturday gate on primary election day, which closed all the saloons, when rain left the grounds too wet to play. Without Sunday baseball, they counted on holidays and Saturdays for their biggest attendance. When these were rained out, the financial setback was significant.

The Red Sox followed the Nationals. Mack decided to use left-handers to counter their top hitters, Tris Speaker and Larry Gardner. Eddie Plank justified the strategy, winning 4–1. But Krause and Danforth were hammered in a 9–2 rout.

They went to Washington and watched it rain for two days before Walter Johnson had a chance to shut them down, 6–0. The next day they won a game but lost Jack Coombs. Delivering a pitch in the sixth inning, he "took too long a stride" and tore a muscle in his side. They carried him off the field. Unrelated to his World Series injury, it was considered less serious. He'd miss a few weeks at most, the doctors said. He was out for a month.

The Athletics stumbled along, winning one, losing two. They couldn't win a series. But they'd gotten off to slow starts before. They went to Boston and lost 3 out of 4, Plank salvaging the only victory. They lost one game, 7–6, even though Morgan and Russell gave up only 4 hits. When Bender had a sore arm, Mack depended on Krause, who had gained twenty pounds during the winter to improve his stamina. It didn't improve his pitching. Krause's arm was sound and he still had plenty of stuff. Too much stuff, Jack Lapp said. "If he tried to throw a curve it was always two feet away from the plate when it reached the batter. . . . He finally lost confidence in himself." Mack stayed with him until June 1 and sent him outright to Toledo. When he started winning, Harry Davis traded for him, but Krause lasted in Cleveland just long enough to get his laundry done before he was sent back to Toledo, never to return to the majors. (Krause found a home in the Pacific Coast League, winning 249 games in seventeen years.)

One day they made 7 errors. Another game was lost on errors by Collins, Barry, and Baker. Mack's tolerance for bonehead plays frayed. Watching Baker chase a runner across the plate while Jack Lapp stood there yelling for the ball, Mack startled everybody on the bench when he jumped up and shouted, "Lock the gates or he'll chase him out of the park." On May 3 they had an 18–5 lead over New York in the ninth inning. Then Roger Salmon and Lefty Russell were pounded for 10 runs before Plank went in and ended the carnage. Princeton grad Salmon, once touted as "another Rube Waddell," walked 4 and gave up 2 hits. Press box wags suggested that Mack try using him only on Fridays. When Mack sent him down to Wilmington, they made a point of writing that they wouldn't write that Salmon was canned.

On Cleveland's first visit to Philadelphia, Harry Davis drew a warm reception from the crowd of sixteen thousand. The A's invited their long-time captain to join Danny Murphy in raising the 1911 world championship flag and presented him with a silver service. Cy Morgan's wildness cost them an 11–3 loss. The next day the arm-weary Plank took a 5–2 lead against Chicago into the ninth and was battered for 7 runs. (Three of Plank's 6 losses came in the ninth inning against Chicago.)

Mack's pitching staff was shattered. He had no dependable starters. Rookies Dave Danforth and Bob Shawkey were in Baltimore, trying to learn to throw strikes. Bender was useless for three weeks. His bouts of "lame arm" were part rheumatism and part elbow-bending. He and his room-mate, Rube Oldring, taxed Mack's patience with their tumbles from the water wagon. A rumor made the rounds that Mack offered them to New York for pitcher Russ Ford and outfielder Birdie Cree. Mack denied it.

In desperation Mack summoned Doc Martin back from Tufts, tried college boys from Santa Clara and Baylor, and gave Lefty Russell one more chance. None of them won a game. Calling Russell his biggest mistake, Mack sold him outright to Atlanta, which took one look at him and sent him back.

Then Connie Mack found what appeared to be another schoolboy gem in his backyard—tall, slender, eighteen-year-old left-hander Herb Pennock. Born into the fox hunting set in Kennett Square, Pennock attended Cedarcroft Prep and Wenonah Military Academy. He reportedly struck out 22 collegians in one game and pitched a 7-inning no-hitter against a black team from St. Louis in Atlantic City. Earle Mack played second base in that game and may have tipped off his father to the youngster. When school was out, Mack signed Pennock, assuring the lad that he wouldn't pitch but just sit on the bench, watching and learning.

Three days later, on May 14, Jack Coombs, strapped in a harness designed by team physician Frank MacFarland, started against Chicago. He tired in the fifth inning. Trailing 6–0, Mack looked down his bench, saw nobody he could send in, and turned to Pennock. "Young fellow, how about you going down and warming up," Mack said. "I may need you."

"I was so excited," Pennock said, "I picked up the right-hand glove of the fellow next to me and ran down to the bullpen. I started to warm up and I'd thrown only about 15 balls when Connie Mack looked down to the bullpen and pointed to me. I'll never forget that feeling. I know now how it feels to walk that last mile. The pitcher's box seemed a million miles away from the bullpen. My legs felt like lead."

"Mack Springs Another 'Boy Wonder,'" the *Chicago Tribune* headlined the next day. Pennock pitched the last 4 innings, gave up 1 hit, walked 2, and hit a batter who scored on an infield out. He appeared in 16 more games that year, picked up a win in relief, and started twice. Pennock was not overpowering; he never topped 160 pounds on his six-foot frame. He depended on a variety of overhand and sidearm curves. He spent hours in front of a mirror perfecting the stylish windup and delivery that would carry him into the Hall of Fame.

Whenever the Tigers came to Philadelphia, strange things seemed to happen. But nothing like the events of Saturday, May 18. Three days earlier in New York, Ty Cobb had become fed up with a loudmouthed heckler spewing "fightin' words" at him. Throwing a few epithets of his own, he leaped into the seats behind third base and started throwing punches. Cobb's teammates didn't like him, but they sympathized with him in this case. They had been subjected to vituperative volleys of "filthy billingsgate" from the same and other taunters of visiting players.

Ban Johnson happened to be a witness to the fracas. The umpires immediately ejected Cobb. After the game, Johnson suspended him indefinitely.

Like him or not, the Tigers knew they needed the .400-hitting hothead in the lineup. Some penalty was in order, they agreed as they rode the train to Philadelphia that evening. But an indefinite suspension? What did that mean?

It rained on Thursday, giving the Detroiters more time to wax their indignation. They set to work composing a protest to the league president. On Friday the sun came out, and they beat the A's, 6–3, with Hank Perry subbing for Cobb. Then they sent a telegram informing Ban Johnson they refused to play another game until Cobb's penalty was reconsidered. The trolley workers were not the only ones with a strike on their minds in Philadelphia that day.

Ban Johnson replied that the suspension stood. The Tigers said, "We won't play." A Saturday game against Detroit always drew a big gate. Connie Mack had no interest in seeing it cancelled. Neither did Hughie Jennings and Tigers president Frank Navin, who faced a $5,000 fine if they didn't field a team. Jennings and his coaches, Deacon McGuire and Joe Sugden, with help from Mack, set out to round up enough sandlotters and semi-pros to put on Tiger uniforms and play if necessary. McGuire, forty-eight, and Sugden, forty-one, said they'd play too. There are different stories of how the standby subs were recruited. One account was given years later to columnist Red Smith by the Reverend Fr. Aloysius Travers, the pitcher for the recruits that day. Travers was a twenty-year-old student at St. Joseph's College and an outfielder on the Park Sparrows, who played at Fairmount Park. On Friday evening, Travers said, a sports editor named John Nolan tipped him off to what might happen at Shibe Park and suggested he bring his friends to the ballpark on Saturday. If they played, Nolan said, they would be paid; the pitcher would be paid double.

Nolan told Jennings that local players would be there if he needed them. In other versions, Jennings and the coaches combed the streets for players and held an audition at the hotel. Maybe they did that too.

Travers and his friends were in the grandstand on Saturday when the Tigers, having dressed at the Aldine Hotel, walked onto the field about two thirty, Cobb among them. When umpire Bill Dinneen ordered Cobb off the field, they all walked off. The recruits were summoned to the clubhouse. Four of them were students younger than Travers. Jennings signed them all to proper contracts, and the Detroit players literally gave them the shirts off their backs.

The game was a farce. The A's won, 24–2. A few disgusted fans demanded their money back, but most stayed and enjoyed the spectacle. The game counted in the standings. So did Collins's 5 hits and 4 stolen bases. Jack Coombs pitched 3 innings and picked up the easy victory. (There were no minimum standards to be the winning pitcher in those days.)

Cobb's replacement in center field was Bill Leinhauser, whose name in some box scores was contracted to L'n'h's'r, which inspired humorist Bugs Baer to write, "When Ban Johnson got the result of the game . . . and heard that four apostrophes were playing center field for Cobb he called himself out on that strike."

Johnson came to town on Sunday and called off the Monday game while everybody looked for a way out of the standoff. Given nothing more than a promise to reconsider Cobb's suspension and with Cobb's urging, the players agreed to play in Washington the next day. Johnson then fined them each $100 and Cobb $50 and commuted the indefinite to ten days.

Before starting a four-week, seven-city road trip on May 24, Mack still sang a confident song: "When Bender, Plank, Coombs, and Morgan are in form, we'll be hard to beat." But when would that be? Mack blamed the rest of the team's letdown on the swelled heads of the two-time champions. "Our players are just getting over their victory in the World Series. They've grown tired of motor cars and other luxuries and are ready to climb the ladder." He predicted that the first-place White Sox, 9 games ahead of the A's, would crack by June 15, and the A's would pass them by July 10.

It's difficult today to appreciate the novelty of the automobile and the radical changes it brought to people's lives at that time. Players now had more mobility to enjoy a wider range of night life. Just the thrill of getting out on the road and barreling along at twenty-five miles an hour was a dangerous enticement. "Too much automobile has played havoc with my club," Mack said. "It rendered Morgan useless and greatly diminished Bender's effectiveness. A love of the whiz wagon has not helped some of the other boys."

Mack was not alone in viewing players' infatuation with their new toys as a distraction. All of baseball was affected by the auto virus. White Sox pitcher Ed Walsh said, "A man can't keep his mind on pitching and his car at the same time." He left his at home for the season.

The *Philadelphia Record* commented:

Automobiling is a fine pastime, but it is not a good sport for ballplayers during the playing season, particularly when it savors of "joy-riding." The number of ballplayers who own or habitually use automobiles is far greater than most people have any idea, and some of the players even park the cars around the country with them when on the road so as to have use of them mornings and evenings in the cities in which they play. Beneficial when taken in reasonable doses, there is a strain on the nerves when automobiling is indulged in to excess that has cost many a base hit and has been a partial cause of many a fumble on the ball field. Some of the managers have learned to recognize the dangers of the auto allurement, and have counseled their players to class "joy-riding" with card playing for money, drinking and other nerve-racking pastimes that should be cut out during the playing season. It would have been a good thing for the local teams had this rule been enforced here.

The Athletics left their autos at home and went west and won 11 out of 16, and optimism broke out like a sunny interval on a cloudy day. Coombs won 3 in a week; as of June 13 he was 9-2, Plank 8-1. But Bender had contributed only 4 wins. They were in fourth place, 4 games back of the league-leading Red Sox. Mack's prediction that the White Sox would crack proved accurate. So did his earlier pick of the Red Sox as the strongest contenders.

Traveling the same circuit as the Athletics, Clark Griffith's Nationals won 16 in a row and climbed into second place. By mid-June Walter Johnson and Boston's Smoky Joe Wood had each won 12. Both pitchers ran up 16-game winning streaks and finished with over 30 wins. Washington won its seventeenth in a row against the A's at home on Tuesday, June 18, before invading Shibe Park for six games. President Taft cheered on the home team's 5–4 ninth-inning victory while the battle over his renomination raged in

Chicago. The next day Coombs ended the streak in a 2–1, 10-inning thriller. The A's were down 1–0 in the ninth, when Frank Baker hit a home run to tie it. In the tenth Jack Barry scored from first on a single by Lapp.

The A's swept two doubleheaders in two days from Washington and leapfrogged into second place. But on Friday neither Morgan nor Pennock survived the first inning, and on Saturday Coombs was shelled in a 7-run sixth, and they were back in fourth, 6 games out. The A's also lost Jack Barry on Friday, when he broke his collarbone diving for a grounder.

All in all, it was a typical week for the 1912 Athletics. They played well some days, made the clutch hits some days, and pitchers blew up some days. Each time the A's showed their championship form, they soon lapsed back into mediocrity. The pitching and catching were inconsistent. Danny Murphy's knee problems sidelined him for most of the year. Amos Strunk was the only healthy outfielder who could hit. All four infielders were solid hitters, but there were too many days when their acclaimed fielding prowess was missing in action.

Eddie Collins played as if he had a sore arm. He couldn't get the ball to first after going to his right and failed to make double plays as the pivot man. Barry's shoulder remained sore. His replacement, Claud Derrick, had a charley horse.

The Athletics had gone into the season expecting to coast, and even when they got off to a slow start, they were nonchalant about the losses. Their attitude was, "We'll pass them all when we get going." But the Red Sox didn't falter. And now, when it was time to turn it up, they found that all the cylinders wouldn't work together. The machine sputtered along, not dying, but not picking up any speed. Mack could only hope that maybe they had gotten the glory out of their systems and would launch a hot streak and charge into the lead.

Connie Mack didn't rant or chew them out. He prodded, cajoled, let them know quietly that he was disappointed in them, that they were better than this, and it was time they woke up and showed it. Above all, he tried to preserve harmony, unity of purpose, even a happy atmosphere. In one of the morning meetings, Mack said, "I want to see all you fellows smile this week. No grouches. Smile, and you'll play better ball."

To the public, Connie Mack continued to sing the same song: wait, just wait.

They didn't have to wait long to be tested. On July 3 the red hot Red Sox came in for six games in four days. The A's had to win at least four to cut into the Boston 6-game lead. Five of the six games were decided in the last three innings, but the A's pitchers did the blowing up. Plank and Coombs picked up the only two wins they could manage, and the Red Sox left town with an 8-game lead.

On many days the Athletics played before acres of empty seats, but for big games the expanded capacity still wasn't enough. Four days hosting the surging Nationals and the four-day Boston series drew a total of two hundred thousand, almost 40 percent of the year's attendance.

The farming out of players with unofficial strings to trustworthy minor league clubs had become common practice. Trust was essential, because players were generally sent outright, not on options. Sometimes they remained with the minor league club for more than a year. That was taking a chance, because they might be drafted by a higher club, or a change in ownership might take place. These were literally "gentlemen's agreements," understandings between individuals, not clubs. If Mack's man sold his interest or lost control of his club, the agreement went with him. The system worked; it provided a source of players for the minor league clubs and a place to send a kid in need of experience while retaining a hold on him.

But sometimes a knot developed.

Mack had a close relationship with Jack Dunn in Baltimore. He supplied the Orioles with plenty of players, so many that one writer quipped, "Baltimore has a population of 555,485, most of them being former members of the Athletic team." Dunn was not about to jeopardize this bond by cutting Mack's strings on anyone.

So Mack was taken aback when, to shore up his pitching, he asked Dunn to return Bob Shawkey to the A's in July and Dunn refused. He was not cutting the string, just holding Mack to the practice of not recalling players until the minor league club's season was over. Dunn was hoping to win the pennant but finished fourth.

And sometimes the string was cut by changing circumstances.

That's what happened with Stanley Coveleski. Stan, twenty-three, started the season with Lancaster in the Tri-State League. The team folded, and the franchise moved to Atlantic City. Between the two, Coveleski won 20 and lost 13. On July 23 he pitched a 16-inning 3–1 win over Wilmington, and Mack bought him on probation. After the Tri-State season ended, Coveleski won 2 games for the A's. Mack's "gentleman" in Spokane was club president Joseph P. Cohn. Mack had obtained Byron Houck from Cohn, but the man he farmed out to replace Houck, Elmer Leonard, had turned out to be a big dud. Mack intended to take Coveleski to spring training in 1913, but he felt an obligation to Cohn and agreed in December to farm Coveleski out to him. The Spokane club was losing money, and in June, Cohn sold his interest to a railway company, which installed its own man as president. The new gentlemen had no obligation to Mack. They traded Coveleski to Portland, where Cleveland had first claim on players, and Mack's string was cut.

The A's were in third place, 10 games behind Boston, when they headed west in late July. The writers had given up on them; only one, George Carroll of the *Evening Times*, traveled with them. But Connie Mack wasn't ready to concede.

"My catching staff has fallen far below expectations," he said. "Reliable Ira Thomas has been in poor condition all year. Despite his wonderful arm, Lapp has thrown poorly, while Ben Egan has not shown his real form. Injury that put Murphy out of the game for the entire season has deprived me of my cleanup man. Reversal of form by Barry and Collins and a slump in hitting by my outfield are just a few of the reasons why the Athletics are not out in front."

Those were reasons enough. And he hadn't even mentioned the pitching or the swelled heads with which they'd started the year or the times a few of them were "out of condition."

"But please don't count my boys as through," Mack added. "Baseball is a mighty uncertain pastime, and on the uncertainty of the game I am largely basing my hopes for success. The season is only two-thirds gone and a lot of things can happen in fifty games. I know a lot of people are ready to inter the world's champions but I hope to fool them."

Those uncertainties that Mack was counting on were late-season collapses by Boston and Washington. They didn't happen.

Meanwhile, Mack took action to improve his pitching and outfield.

The Baltimore Orioles had the two best outfielders in the International League: Eddie Murphy, a Villanova lad Mack had signed and farmed out, and Irish-born Jimmy Walsh. Murphy, a left-handed hitting leadoff man, had scored 108 runs and was batting .361. Walsh was hitting .354. Mack had strings on Murphy but not Walsh. Both Mack and Dunn knew that after the August 25 pre-draft deadline for player sales, one of these hot commodities would certainly be snapped up for the $2,500 draft price. Dunn wanted to sell them before then. The rules prohibited the sale of a minor league player to another minor league club within twenty days of the deadline. That didn't apply to a sale to a major league club.

There were reports that Dunn asked Mack for five players. Mack agreed to send Bris Lord and Claud Derrick immediately, Ben Egan in 1913, and $5,000. Dunn accepted the deal on August 22. Walsh sprained an ankle shortly after joining the A's, but Murphy became an instant crowd pleaser, putting much-needed ginger into the top of the order.

Mack had sometimes waved his scorecard to move his outfielders. In the past few years he had relied more on his captain and the men on the field to position themselves according to the pitcher and batter. Now, with new men patrolling the pastures, he employed the scorecard more often. Sometimes he had to stand and wave it vigorously to get their attention. The fans became more aware of it. The writers played it up, and it became a prominent part of Connie Mack's managing style and image.

Just before the draft began, he acquired one more minor league pitcher: Leslie Bush, a sturdy nineteen-year-old right-hander who had pitched Missoula to the Union Association pennant with a 29-12 record. The Missoula president called him Joe. Local papers dubbed him Bullet Bush. As he had with Coveleski, Mack bought him under a new National Agreement provision for forty-five-day probationary contracts. Bush started once, on September 30 against New York. He was battered for 8 runs and 14 hits, but Mack said he saw "another Bender" in the Brainerd, Minnesota, teenager.

Hoping to launch one last drive for first place, Mack held back his veteran pitchers for a series in Boston August 29–31. Casting his nets far and wide, he pulled in a dozen or more sandlot and minor league pitchers, most of whom never threw a pitch in the major leagues. Somehow they scraped out a 10-4 record at home against the west before heading to Boston.

But Bender, Plank, and Coombs failed to stop the Red Sox, and Mack, the eternal optimist, abandoned all hope. On September 1 they were in third place, 13½ games behind the Red Sox. After a series in Washington, they headed for New York. Bender and Rube Oldring got off the train in Wilmington, picked up Bender's car, and went joy-riding the rest of the way. Bender took Oldring to his home in New York and arrived at the hotel about three in the morning. Somehow Connie Mack heard all about the escapade. That afternoon he told the two players to go home for the rest of the year. (Both returned for the last weekend.) Thirty-nine years later, in telling the story to Frank Yeutter of the *Bulletin*, Oldring made it sound as if Mack had cost the A's the pennant because he and Bender "had a couple of beers." But they were well out of the running by then.

Attendance dwindled as the season wound down. Mack did little experimenting, playing his regulars to the end. Their goal was to overtake Washington for second place, though there was no financial reward in it. The Nationals came to Shibe Park for three days beginning September 25 for a series that produced the most remarkable game of the year for both teams.

Rain idled them on Wednesday. They tried to play two on Thursday. Down 3–0 in the seventh, the A's rallied. Walter Johnson came in with 2 runs in, 2 on, and 1 out. The tying run scored when Johnson threw a fastball that sped past the catcher and almost beaned umpire Billy Evans. The shaken umpire called the game two innings later on account of darkness, although only two hours had elapsed.

So they scheduled a doubleheader for Friday. The A's hit starter Bob Groom all over the lot, but outstanding defensive work kept them from scoring more than once through 8 innings. Aided by a passed ball and wild pitch, Washington scored 4 in the first 2 innings off Eddie Plank. By now Mack's teams were known for late-inning rallies, and they did it again, tying the score in a 3-run ninth. Baker's double off the right-field wall was the big blow. Johnson came in in the tenth, and he and Plank matched goose eggs through the eighteenth. In the top of the nineteenth the Nats scored without a ball hit out of the infield. A walk, a bunt single by Johnson, a fielder's choice at third base, then a double play ball that Eddie Collins threw over the first baseman's head made it 5–4.

The second game was never played. Mack tried to persuade Clark Griffith to play a doubleheader on October 2, an open day, but Griffith refused.

At thirty-seven, Eddie Plank wasn't pitching like a man ready to retire. He won 26 and lost 6. But Plank had expanded his farm and held mortgages on several of his neighbors' places. He did some guiding of tourists around the Gettysburg battlefield and said he was ready to stay home.

The year was disappointing but not exactly a disaster for the Athletics. They won 90 games, hardly a swan dive. The Red Sox never faded, winning a league record 105 and finishing 14 ahead of Washington, 15 over the A's. Connie Mack went into the clubhouse after the last game. "Pointing to each of us," Eddie Collins said, "with a note of true sincerity he said, 'You may not have won the pennant, but I want all of you to know I believe you were the best team of the lot.'"

Looking back on that season with Bob Paul, sports editor of the *Philadelphia Daily News*, Mack said, "Something was lacking. There wasn't anything I could do about it, either."

Before the World Series between the Red Sox and Giants, Boston manager Jake Stahl asked Mack to talk to his players and give them some tips on how to beat the Giants. Mack agreed. He discussed the Giants' weaknesses and strong points as he remembered them. Boston shortstop Heinie Wagner said, "He told us more in ten minutes than all our scouts discovered watching them for several weeks, or what we could have learned about them in a year. I doubt if we would have beaten New York without the knowledge that Mack put into us."

Boston won the 8-game set—there was one tie—in which Joe Wood won 3 and Christy Mathewson lost twice.

Connie Mack knew baseball. More important, he knew just how much he and everybody else in the game didn't know and could never know. Asked how long it would take to rebuild his pitching staff to its 1910–1911 strength, he said, "Well, that's a tough question. It may take years. Then again, Houck, Brown, Crabb, and Coveleski might develop fast enough to round us out right next season. Baseball is an uncertain game, and pitchers its most uncertain accessories. In fact, you do not know if a young pitcher will be an asset or a liability until you start a season."

42 | SPEAKING OF MONEY

The house at 2119 West Ontario was a busy place in the fall of 1912. There were now two babies; Connie Mack Jr. was born on November 2. His sister, Mary, was fifteen months old. Three more children would follow, for a total of eight from Mack's two marriages. Earle, twenty-two, was single and lived at home during the off-season. Marguerite was nearing twenty. Connie Mack's brothers, Michael and Eugene, worked at the White Elephant and dropped in frequently. Dennis's widow, Annie, and her daughters were regular Sunday dinner guests. And Connie Mack's cousin, Nora McGillicuddy, was living with them. Nora was seven years younger than Connie, the daughter of his Uncle Thomas. There was speculation among some relatives that if Connie and Nora had not been cousins, they would have married. A tall, slender, registered nurse, Nora never married. She became a favorite of Mack's children as well, but not of Katherine Mack, who considered her a thorn in the garden of domestic bliss.

Roy was no longer living at home. Unlike Earle, he lacked the tools or the drive for a professional baseball career. He had been working for the American Thread Company and enjoying the night life with his cousin, Dennis's son Harold. Then he decided to learn the hotel business. He went to Worcester to apprentice with his Uncle Tom, who now owned two hotels, the Franklin in downtown Worcester and the Peninsula, a summer resort in South Boston.

Tom's daughter Helen remembered Roy as someone who "needed to be straightened out a little. He was not a playboy, but he was very fussy about his looks and his clothes. He changed his shirt five times a day even if he wasn't going anywhere. It took my dad a while, but he got [Roy] down to three."

Roy didn't take to the hotel business, at least not starting out at the bottom. In Tom's opinion, he needed more "finishing." At Tom's suggestion,

Connie Mack enrolled Roy in Worcester Academy on September 11, 1912. Roy had ostensibly graduated from Central High School in Philadelphia, and he had just turned twenty-four. But the academy was a secondary school, not a college. Not a diligent student, Roy earned mostly Cs and Ds and graduated in June 1915 with a "scientific" diploma at the age of twenty-seven.

Marguerite Mack took after her mother: petite—under five feet tall—and frail, with thick, wavy brown hair, blue eyes, and a round, smiling face. Never in robust health but bursting with personality, she was very popular among her cousins.

"We called her Peggy," said cousin Helen Mack. "She was vivacious, full of fun. She was crazy about my father and we were just as crazy about her. She spent the summers with us at our place on a lake in Paxton, near Worcester." Despite twelve years' difference in their ages, "Pegs," as she signed her letters, and Helen were great pals.

"Peggy was a frail little thing," Helen said. "At home in Philadelphia she'd sit on the radiator all bundled up to get warm. She'd show up for the summer with a fur coat in her big steamer trunk. She'd bring material for my mother's dressmaker to make her clothes, and bonbons—she was crazy about bonbons—all different kinds. She stayed all summer and we had a great time."

Whenever the Athletics had a day off in Boston, Connie Mack visited for the day. Peggy would holler, "Helen Mack, you want to go swimming?" and they'd splash into the cold water of the lake, while Connie Mack watched, relaxing, always in shirt and tie. He never went near the water, never picked up a fishing pole, occasionally picked up a bat and took some swings as Tom tossed them in. Tom had a big, open Packard roadster driven by a chauffeur (neither he nor Connie liked to drive). They sometimes took a Sunday drive to East Brookfield to revisit the lakes and fields where they had grown up.

Tom and Connie were the closest of the brothers. They could talk baseball for hours. A large framed photograph of the 1905 American League champions hung in the kitchen in Tom's house. But their personalities were different. Tom told Irish dialect jokes and laughed heartily. Connie had an "Irish wit," Helen said, "but he was very serious." He responded to Tom's jokes with a smile and a gentle chuckle.

During the Athletics' early years, whenever they were in Boston, Nora and her father drove from Worcester to see them. Helen and her mother took the train. Mack greeted some relatives with a handshake, but he always had a hug and a kiss on the cheek for Tom's wife and daughter. After the game Mack would invite them to dinner at the team's hotel—the Brunswick and (later) the Copley-Plaza.

As a teenager, Helen Mack took the train to Boston by herself. Those visits were among her fondest memories for the rest of her life. "When you were in his presence," she said, "he was so gracious; you came first, you were his guest. He would sometimes have a light supper of just corn flakes and milk, but he told me to order anything I wanted. When he hugged me, he always gave me a little pat, and when he put me on the train after the game and dinner, he put a hundred dollar bill in my hand. Like my dad, Uncle Connie was a kind, loving, warm person."

Connie Mack strongly discouraged his daughters and niece from becoming romantically involved with ballplayers. If they were dining with him in a hotel and a player came over to talk to him, Mack would never introduce them. Katherine Mack told her daughters she prayed every night that none of them would marry a ballplayer. They were told not even to date players, an order they didn't always obey.

According to Helen, during the summer of 1912 Peggy "fell desperately in love" with a ballplayer named O'Brien. This was probably Red Sox pitcher Buck O'Brien, a 20-game winner for the pennant winners, whom she might have seen pitch against the Athletics at the new Fenway Park. Tom found out about it and let his brother know.

"How [Uncle Connie] did it I don't know," Helen said, "but he broke it up and she was brokenhearted." O'Brien was sold to the White Sox in the middle of 1913.

Mack's attitude toward ballplayers as sons-in-law never changed. When he was nearly eighty, he discovered that his youngest daughter, Betty, then a teenager, had telephoned one of his married players.

"When he talked to me about it," Betty recalled, "he went around the thing, but went around it well enough that I knew what he was talking about. He didn't come out and say, 'No more phone calls' or anything like that, more like 'I've never been disappointed in you before, girlie, and I hope I'll never be disappointed in you.' You could see by the expression on his face, he was serious. He never raised his voice. And I never forgot it. He handled it well."

Mack's daughter Ruth managed a few dates with a young A's pitcher, Hank McDonald, in 1933, when she was nineteen. Once McDonald was invited to dinner at the Mack home. "But he ate peas off his knife and he never came back," Ruth said. Such invitations were rare; Connie Mack may have known the young man's behavior would be the end of it. To be sure, he sold McDonald to the St. Louis Browns soon afterward.

So when Helen Mack grew up and had a crush on A's pitcher Dave Keefe, she knew there wasn't a chance in the world of getting an introduction.

As for the heartbroken Peggy, she got over Buck O'Brien when her father introduced her to Robert McCambridge, a handsome, ambitious Chicagoan who, at twenty, was already on his way to becoming the head of the bond sales department at the Sheridan Trust and Savings Bank. They were married November 2, 1914.

With a 15 percent drop in attendance, to 517,653—the lowest since Shibe Park had opened in 1909—and the higher salaries that came with winning pennants, the Athletics had barely broken even in 1912. They lost another $6,000 on a trip to Cuba, where the A's won all but one game so easily that the fans stayed away. Those who showed up booed and hissed them.

As a result of rising expenses and renovations to the grounds, the club had not paid a dividend for several years. In October the two sportswriters, Frank Hough and Sam Jones, decided it was time to sell. Possibly in anticipation of this step, their names first appeared in the shareholders' register as of November 29, 1911, when 247 of the 250 shares held by A's attorney W. J. Turner in trust were transferred to a holding company, the Tioga Company, for Mack, and individual certificates for one share each were registered to Mack, Hough, and Jones. Here again, the numbers mean nothing; the writers held a 25 percent interest in the club.

Hough had been in poor health for a few years; he had less than a year to live. Jones and Hough had given the A's the benefit of their experience, influence, and standing among their peers; these had been instrumental in the early acceptance and success of the franchise.

They first offered their shares to the Shibes. John and Tom Shibe were interested, but their father vetoed the deal. Ben Shibe stuck to his original position that the Shibes should own no more than 50 percent, and he had subdivided some of his half-interest into his sons' names. Jones and Hough then turned to Connie Mack, who wanted the stock but didn't have the money. Ben Shibe agreed to lend it to him.

Selling prices of major league clubs had more than doubled in the past decade. The Phillies had last sold for a price approaching $400,000.

"It didn't take long for us to come to an agreement as to what their shares were worth," Mack said. The price was $113,000. The pair of scribes had invested nothing. Their reward was the equivalent of $2 million today.

The transaction thus valued the team and real estate at $452,000. On October 22 the writers' holdings were transferred to Cornelius McGillicuddy, who gave five shares each to his sons Roy and Earle. They replaced Jones and Hough as directors. Each family now held three of the six seats on the board of the Athletics Grounds Company. Ben Shibe continued as president, Tom Shibe vice-president, Connie Mack treasurer, John Shibe secretary and assistant treasurer, and Joseph C. Ohl assistant secretary. The team doctor, Frank MacFarland, was Ben Shibe's son-in-law. MacFarland's son, Benny, later became the traveling secretary.

By January 2, 1914, a corporate reorganization resulted in the dissolution of the Grounds company, with everybody's shares being transferred into the American Base Ball Club of Philadelphia. A $150,000 mortgage remained on the grounds. Ninety-four of the 100 shares of the Grounds company were transferred to the Philadelphia American League Baseball Club, the other six shares to the six directors.

The stability of the hierarchy and the equal division of authority belied a New York report that Mack and the Shibes were at odds, forcing Mack to buy the writers' shares to protect his position. The fact that Ben Shibe advanced the money for him to buy out Hough and Jones further pokes that story in the eye. Other tales had the Shibes pressuring Hough and Jones to sell to Mack to keep the manager from accepting an offer to manage the Yankees. The contradictions between the two stories didn't prevent both of them from being repeated through the years. Mack had been approached in the past by other club owners and could have had any number of managing jobs at this point in his career if he had chosen to leave Philadelphia. Which he didn't.

Connie Mack shrugged off most such newspaper fiction. He understood that writers had space to fill and made things up or printed rumors and speculation, sometimes parading as facts, to fill it. He preferred to ignore most of it, issuing a curt "Nothing to it" in response. Nor did he try to tell them what to write. "You fellows have your stories to write," he would say. "That's your business. Running the Athletics is my business."

He had been roasted by critics as far back as his days in Pittsburgh and Milwaukee. He rarely replied to them; to argue or attempt to rebut what they wrote only made things worse. You could never have the last word against those who owned the printing presses. In the 1930s, when he would be savagely trashed for selling some of his best players and allegedly pocketing the money, his daughter Ruth became so incensed that she wanted to write to the papers and set them straight. Mack stopped her. "Girlie, that's not a good idea."

By now he knew which writers had their own agendas and disregard for accuracy and which of the hometown writers he could trust. To these he might give some details of a transaction, but always off the record. "I'll tell you this," he'd say, "but you can't use it."

He could be closemouthed, even taciturn when he didn't want to talk about something. That was enough for some writers to characterize him as less than cooperative. He was especially mum when it came to contemplated player transactions, telling one inquiring reporter that he had been so frequently misquoted as to his intentions that he had decided it was best to say nothing about them.

Perhaps that's what led to this assessment by Sid C. Keener of the *St. Louis Times* of how Mack treated the press during his championship years:

"When Mack was the monarch of the field he was anything but an agreeable chap. Probably he had but one thought—that was baseball. To his friends and to the newspaper boys he was abrupt and short. He was sarcastic and sharp. He didn't care for the company of others. He wanted to be alone, and he didn't want to break into print with interviews."

Mack's articles in the *Saturday Evening Post* and other nonsports magazines showed no aversion to "breaking into print." Beat writers and columnists in cities around the league often commented on Mack's accessibility and hospitality. He didn't always tell them all they wanted to know, but he had enough public relations savvy to provide them with plenty of quotes. He wasn't garrulous, no Stengelese storyteller. But he enjoyed reminiscing about the Rube and Schreck and his own playing days.

Mack could be "sarcastic and sharp" with newspapermen at times. (That's true of ballplayers and managers to this day.) He was especially perturbed—and was not alone in this among managers and club owners—at speculation over players' salaries and the riches that club owners were said to be draining from the game. During the 1910 World Series, a Chicago paper printed two boxes showing the alleged salaries paid by clubs in both leagues. The Athletics had the lowest payroll and the Cubs the highest. A writer showed it to Mack, who said if he had the difference between the salaries the paper had his players receiving and what they were actually paid, he would be willing to quit baseball for life. An exaggeration, sure, but Mack always scoffed at the numbers, high or low, that were tossed about in print.

(As further evidence of newspaper exaggerations of baseball salaries and wealth, in 1914 John McGraw testified in a lawsuit filed against him for unpaid taxes that his salary was only $18,000, not the $30,000 "princely sum" generally awarded him by the press. McGraw added that he was deeply in debt due to unspecified business failures.)

Mack didn't think a club's financial business was any more the business of the public than were the affairs of any other privately owned corporation. He considered inquiries into a man's salary or net worth, his or his players', an invasion of privacy. So his cordiality iced over whenever reporters pressed him on those subjects.

Mack bristled at the widespread belief, fostered by the press, that club owners were taking huge fortunes out of the game. There were a few very profitable franchises, but the overwhelming majority were not the gold mines they were purported to be. During the 1911 World Series, a group of reporters collected around Mack in the lobby of the Astor Hotel in New York. "The discussion of baseball turned to the financial end of the game," Mack said, "and one of them intimated that I had made a fortune. I said, 'Boys, I hope I won't die tomorrow because people would say what did he do with his money?' That is the truth."

Mack was well paid for his work as manager, general manager, and treasurer of the Athletics. He was in the $20,000 range. In 1913 he picked up his first commercial endorsement. His picture in coat and tie and straw hat appeared in newspaper ads for Coca-Cola with this ringing endorsement: "I drink Coca-Cola myself and advise all the team to drink it. I think it is good for them." The copy in the ad for the "5c Everywhere" drink read: "Would he advise the team to drink it unless he knew how good it is? Not on his record—and theirs."

Mack's personal overhead had grown since his days as a single father. In addition to supporting his new family and two of his three older children, he was subsidizing Dennis's widow and children, as well as doling out rent and food and coal money to people of no relation to him. He did it all quietly and ungrudgingly, yet his generosity was widely acknowledged at the time. "He is extremely charitable," Marion Parker wrote in the *St. Louis Globe-Democrat*, "and spends much money this way without saying anything about it."

An unsigned 1914 item in the *Pittsburgh Sun* said:

"Someone associated with Connie Mack for many years says Mack has no money at all. Contrary to the reputation of being close with money he is liberal-hearted, gives away all he makes to old players and to support dozens of dependent relatives. 'At least three cases I happen to know,' he said, 'that friends had to step in and stop Connie or he would have been flat broke. He is not a spender in the sense of giving dinners and having a good time. But as far as I know he has never been one to refuse a request for aid from one in need.'"

Yet the stories of the miserly Connie Mack "lining his pockets" and "draining the club" have lived on like tree ferns, supported by nothing but air.

Connie Mack was always sensitive about talk of money. He exaggerated when he used terms like "broke" and "poverty" when talking about his personal finances to make the legitimate point that he was not taking as much out of the game as was sometimes depicted. But, as Marion Parker noted, "Unlike Comiskey, who lives a Baronial life, Mack was only assumed by writers to have a pile stowed away, based on his salary and half ownership in the Athletics. None of them had any real idea of his worth, nor that most of it was tied up in the club."

The subject was uncomfortable to Connie Mack, not because he had anything to hide. He was the product of a flinty New England upbringing. His standards, attitudes, and conduct had been molded in the Victorian age, when money, like digestive disturbances, was not a seemly topic of social conversation, nor anybody's business outside the family.

Connie Mack's attitude toward the press came closest to Keener's description whenever he was quoted as saying something he never said. When Ed Pollock was breaking in as a baseball writer for the *Philadelphia Press*, he went up to Mack's tower office to introduce himself. After some general baseball talk, Mack said, "I think we're going to get along just fine, but there's something I want to ask you to do for me. When you want to know anything about my ball club or the players, ask me. I'll tell you whatever I possibly can. I promise you that. But please don't make me say something in your paper that I haven't really said."

Covering the Athletics and Connie Mack for the next thirty-seven years, Ed Pollock never forgot those ground rules.

Sid Keener's contention that Mack was "abrupt and short" to his friends, "didn't care for the company of others," and "wanted to be alone" might come as a surprise to Emory Titman, Sam Erwin, Hyman Pearlstone, Henry Beach Needham, and others who were invited to sit on the bench during games and travel with the team or to the thousands of strangers he graciously received who would approach him over the years in hotel lobbies and train stations and restaurants and—as the author did—on spring training fields.

43 | CAPTAIN HOOK

Connie Mack made his first venture into ownership of a minor league club in 1912. He did it more to help a struggling league than with any ideas of starting a farm system.

For several years he had a strong working arrangement with Reading in the Tri-State League. When the United States League, an independent group aspiring to big league status, put a team in Reading, the Tri-State club folded. The new league lasted about a month, its Reading club bowing out on June 6. When Altoona dropped out at the same time, the Tri-State wanted to move back into Reading. But it couldn't find a backer. It appealed to Mack, who agreed to buy the franchise in partnership with Bert Leopold of Altoona. At the end of the season, Reading needed money to renovate its rundown grounds. The A's needed the money more for their own renovations to Shibe Park. Mack sold his half-interest to Leopold and the business manager.

To accommodate the occasional sellouts and stop the practice of crowding the outfield with customers, Mack and the Shibes decided to expand Shibe Park. Even though the stands might be half-empty on weekdays, they expected to be perennial contenders and frequent World Series participants. Their biggest-drawing rivals usually filled the park, especially on Saturdays. And who knows, maybe someday the preachers and politicians might permit Sunday baseball.

They built new bleachers in left field from the foul line to the center-field flagpole, cutting the left-field distance from 380 to 334 feet, with a six-foot wall topped by a two-foot wire screen, and increasing the seating capacity by five thousand. This necessitated moving the scoreboard from the left-field corner to just to the right of center field. It was also enlarged, adding a section for the same lineup and score-by-innings information for Phillies games. For all its modernity, the operation of the scoreboard was still nineteenth century. The operator stood beneath it on the field and climbed a ladder, leaning against it to insert the numbers and lineup changes.

From their first year in business, Mack and Shibe had held the line on ticket prices. Shibe Park had more twenty-five-cent bleacher seats than any other big league park. Its bleachers were also the closest to home plate. Visiting clubs had been complaining that though the A's were among the leaders in attendance, the total gate receipts were small. Fearing a backlash from their customers, the Athletics had resisted the pressure to raise their prices. Now, to keep up with rising expenses, they saw no alternative.

They put a steel roof on the bleachers, installed opera chairs, and raised the price to fifty cents. Grandstand seats went to seventy-five cents. Box seats remained $1.00. They had no idea how their customers would react to the higher prices.

It's difficult to say how much of the club owners' handwringing over rising expenses was aimed at discouraging potential competitors from entering the baseball business. The United States League had come and gone in 1912. There was talk of another group of big league aspirants launching a league in 1913. Frank Navin in Detroit declared that "never again would baseball yield such high profits as in the past." Connie Mack told Billy Weart of the *Evening Telegraph*, "The cost of baseball has reached the point where it has forced the club owners to sit up and think. The cost of building new plants, the large increase in salaries of players, and the other expenses have grown to such proportions that it has become a serious question with the magnates as to what is to be done if they are to get even a fair interest on their investments."

(Ninety years later a general manager would be quoted, "Baseball is now in the new age of being as much about business as things on the field." It always had been.)

Average player salaries were now in the $3,000–$5,000 range. Top stars earned about $9,000. Managers who had been in the $5,000–$8,000 range were now earning $10,000–$20,000.

Complaints about greedy, overpaid players who no longer hustled or were corrupted into drinking and other unsavory habits by "the unusual flow of yellow coin," were once again heard throughout the land. *Leslie's Weekly* lamented, "Perhaps the trouble today is that the stars of the game are tremendously overpaid. Many of the baseball peers of today who are receiving yearly stipends that would tickle many a bank president, were lucky to get their beer and beans regularly before they broke into professional company."

Calculations of how much star players were paid per hit began to appear. Ty Cobb was the highest at $40.24 per hit for the past three years. When Walter Johnson threw 170 pitches in a game on April 15, 1911, it was estimated that he earned $1 every time he threw the ball, based on a $7,000 salary.

The average factory worker still earned about $500 a year.

The league's winter meetings were quiet. Garry Herrmann again trumpeted his interleague plan of 112 games followed by home-and-home series against every team in the other league. The idea again went nowhere. The American League passed a rule that teams must dress in clubhouses, not hotels. More meeting time was spent on ways to speed up the games. Umpire Tom Connolly blamed longer games on the pitchers' new habit of throwing to first base to try to catch runners. "This practice wastes a lot of time," he complained. Ban Johnson's concern was not so much the length of the games as the interludes between the action caused by players taking their time going on and off the field or dawdling on the way to the batter's box, pitchers fussing about in the box, and catchers or captains visiting pitchers—complaints that still echo around the game. Johnson put up a $200 prize for the umpire whose games averaged the shortest time during the 1912 season. Bill Dinneen won it with a one hour and fifty-five minute average. There was only three minutes' difference between the slowest and fastest average times.

The Yankees moved into the Polo Grounds as tenants of the Giants for one year, which became ten.

The biggest wrangle took place among the baseball writers over the "Cincinnati base hit," so named because Jack Ryder of the *Cincinnati Enquirer* was its main champion. The situation arose when a ground ball was fielded and thrown to catch a base runner other than the batter and failed to get anybody out. Today it's universally scored as a fielder's choice. At that time some were calling it a hit. Others scored it as a sacrifice. After committees of writers and officials—Mack among them—discussed the issue, Ban Johnson declared that such plays should be scored as hits. (He repealed that decision after one year.)

The writers also pleaded for the establishment of a standard for assigning winning and losing pitchers, and they railed against the varying heights of pitchers' mounds among the parks of both leagues. Shibe Park's was suspected of exceeding the fifteen-inch limit. But nobody filed an official complaint.

Back in Philadelphia, the mails brought a steady flow of signed contracts from all but two of the A's—Chief Bender and Eddie Plank. Upon returning from Cuba, Bender stayed in the south, hunting in Georgia and South Carolina. When Mack had sent the bibulous Bender and Oldring home in September, the *North American* commented, "Cornelius Mack is suave and of long memory, [and] will have the last giggle on the bottled-in-bond boys around contract time."

Mack wasn't giggling, but he slashed Bender's salary, sending a contract for $1,200 to an Atlanta address. He heard nothing through December and January. On Saturday morning, February 1, 1913, Bender showed up at Shibe Park with the unsigned contract. Mack assured him that if he stayed in condition and did the job he was capable of, the contract would be torn up and Albert would be rewarded accordingly. Mack had made the same deal with him in 1909 and had kept his word. Bender was also aware that after the 1911 season, Eddie Collins had been dissatisfied with the amount of his raise. "Eddie," Mack had said, "I can't afford to give you any more now, but if we have a good year [in 1912] I will take care of you in October." They didn't have a good year, but when Collins received his last paycheck it included an extra $500, an amount that players would fight for in those days. So Bender didn't hesitate to sign the $1,200 contract. He and the rest of the Athletics—and the public—knew that Connie Mack "played square," in the lexicon of the time, with his boys.

Marion Parker of the *St. Louis Globe-Democrat* wrote, "Probably Mack's greatest asset in a baseball way is his fairness and honesty. To question this in the presence of his players is to commit a capital crime, and those who have traveled with the Athletics for years and know the inside workings of the club, will tell you that Connie has never broken his word or violated a promise made to a ball player, or for that matter, to any one else. Furthermore, Mack never stands on the letter of a contract, but will go even further if he thinks fairness demands it."

Eddie Plank's last declaration before heading for his Gettysburg farm had been that his retirement was on. It took a long distance phone call—still a novel, expensive act in those days—to persuade the reluctant left-hander to postpone his retirement. Mack told him the team's hopes for regaining the pennant depended on him. Eddie said okay, one more year.

Before leaving for San Antonio on Monday, February 24, Mack told James Isaminger the Athletics would win in 1913. He had fixed the weaknesses of the 1912 team and believed in the reformation of Bender and Oldring. "For the first time in many years I have an outfield [Strunk, Oldring, Murphy, Walsh, and Tom Daley, a .332 hitter from Los Angeles] in which I can place confidence. Bender, Plank, and Coombs will be winners with Brown, Houck, and Pennock." Cy Morgan was sold to Kansas City. Morgan refused to report and sought a new career on the stage and in the movies. Mack had already seen his young pitchers in action in 1912, except for John Wyckoff, a just-turned-twenty-one right-hander from Bucknell. Wyckoff had not done well at Wilmington; he couldn't throw a curve worth a hoot. Mack put Ira Thomas to work with him.

As for the infield, Isaminger wrote, "Connie is worrying as much about his infield as J. Pierpont Morgan is worrying about his next meal." Mack believed his three-year search for a solid utility infielder had ended with the acquisition of Billy Orr, a light-hitting gloveman from Sacramento who turned out to be no field as well as no hit.

His catching corps of Lapp, Thomas, and Ben Egan was set. Mack also had a highly touted rookie from Buffalo he had snatched from the Phillies and Bisons manager George Stallings. Wally Schang, twenty-three, was rated the best catching prospect in the minor leagues. Every team coveted him. The Phils' Horace Fogel thought he had a gentleman's agreement with Stallings for first claim on Schang, but he didn't act on it. Mack drafted him for $2,500, and the National Commission ruled that no private agreement could make Schang immune from the draft.

Mack considered his team's old-fashioned boxy white caps with black stripes a good luck piece. They hadn't won while wearing them in 1912, but he blamed that on injuries, overconfidence, and a few out-of-condition players. Every other team had gone to flat caps, and the A's took a ribbing from bench jockeys and writers for their continued use of the pillboxes.

With little need for experimenting, Mack shortened their stay in San Antonio to one week for the rookies, two for the veterans. They shared the field with the local team, working from nine thirty to eleven in the morning, at which time the local Texas League club took over until two. All the pitchers threw batting practice. In the afternoons they played practice games. Mack was everywhere: behind second base, among the outfielders, watching Ira Thomas catching the youngsters, umpiring intrasquad games. He left the veterans alone and spent his time deciding which rookies to take north, whom to farm out, whom to send home. Minor league managers stopped by to see him, eager to secure any prospects he might send out with or without strings attached.

Asked by a writer why he ignored his older players, Mack said, "Because they know what's expected of them, and each one knows better how he can attain that point of physical proficiency than I do. Consequently, I do not try to lay down any set of rules or routines of work for them to follow. As long as they are ready April 15 I am satisfied."

Frank Baker didn't need any regimen from Mack. Reporting a few days late, he put on his work clothes and rapped out 3 hits in his first game.

The atmosphere among the players was one of intense dedication to reclaiming the title and World Series money they knew they had frittered away. Mack's farewell words at the end of the season still rang in their minds. His quiet expression of confidence in them had made a deeper impression than if he had ripped into them. On their way north, the regulars won 18 straight exhibition games before floods stranded them for two days in Louisville and washed out the rest of their itinerary.

Mack, Sam Erwin, and Joe Ohl traveled with the rookies, but they were hampered by rain and cold, idling them for days at a time. Disgusted with the weather and long train delays, Mack said enough of this. Next year they'd go straight home from Jacksonville. He sent his young pitchers ahead to work in the city series under Danny Murphy's direction. Wyckoff pitched a shutout against the Phillies and, coming from Bucknell, was immediately hailed as another Christy Mathewson. Bush and Pennock gave up one run each in their starts. But Mack was irritated to learn that Murphy had allowed Carroll Brown to pitch the entire 18 innings of a 2–2 tie. Brown said it didn't bother him at the time, but later he blamed it for a career-shortening sore arm.

Mack's longtime scout, Tom O'Brien, who had been in baseball since 1876, tired of traveling and retired to Worcester to go into business. His leaving coincided with—or maybe hastened—Mack's reassessment of his scouting system and its results. He still had his many volunteer eyes: minor league and semipro managers, college coaches, former players, priests and nuns, friends like Hyman Pearlstone in Texas, his brother Tom, and now Roy, who sent his friends at Worcester Academy for tryouts. But Mack had been disappointed in the hordes of youngsters with "can't miss" labels who didn't have what he thought it took. He was spoiled by the early lode of gold nuggets found by his tipsters—Bender, Plank, Barry, McInnis, Krause, and Coombs. Nobody had found him a dependable utility infielder.

Al Maul covered thousands of miles and found nobody worth even the train fare for a look. "Surprising how few good young players are being turned out this year," Mack wrote a friend, S. B. Huston in Portland, Oregon, during the 1913 season. "Seems that there are less than ever. All the reports I get are about players who have had some experience in fast company." He wasn't interested in them.

Having spent more than $10,000 a year on scouting with little to show for it, Mack decided to do without sending scouts on the road. He trusted the judgment of Thomas, Davis, and Murphy. He might send Eddie Collins or Bender to check out a youngster in the area. Whenever the A's had a day off, he routinely went to college and semipro games. Between the draft and conditional purchases, he would try out as many as possible during the last few weeks of the season and quickly return those he didn't want. Sometimes he put on a catcher's mitt to get a firsthand look at a young pitcher's stuff and make an instant decision on whether to sign him.

Billy Weart reported from San Antonio:

Hereafter all promising young players recommended to Connie Mack will be sent for during the season and put through their paces under Ira Thomas while Mack watches from the sidelines.

The work of minor league players will be followed closely from the office. Papers will be subscribed to and the box scores minutely scrutinized daily. Enthusiasm of the scribes will be allowed for and toward the end of the season members of the Mack clan will make side trips to minor league towns to see the young stars in action.

Mack feels he will get better players ultimately and still be in a position at any time to fill positions left vacant by accident.

The Athletics opened in Boston on a cold, wet, and windy day. Sparked by Amos Strunk's 3-run triple and steal of home, they scored 10 runs. But it almost wasn't enough. Bender and Coombs were hit hard. Plank pitched the last 3 innings and salvaged a 10–9 win. After a day of rain Mack sent Coombs to the box again. This time the Iron Man faced five batters and retired just one. Mack rushed Pennock in to give Plank time to warm up. After Pennock walked 2, Mack pulled him. Plank saved the day again, blanking the defending champions the rest of the way while the A's pulled it out, 5–4.

They went to Washington, where a steady rain washed out the entire series. The doubleheaders were already piling up. Connie Mack sat in his hotel suite and pondered the situation. Jack Coombs was not himself. He came down with a cold, then a fever. He was sick; nobody knew how sick. Predictions of his being out a few weeks turned into months. The cold turned into typhoid, which settled in his spine. Mack kept him on the payroll all year. When Coombs tried to come back in September and collapsed, Mack put him on the disabled list, a new category enabling a team to carry an injured player above the thirty-five-man roster.

But in April nobody knew how long Jack Coombs would be out. The uncertainty over his illness was enough for fans and writers to write off the Athletics as contenders. Except for Plank and Bender, the rest of the pitchers were young and green, some wholly untested.

Mack sensed the doubts clouding the minds of his players. He didn't want them worrying about anything—family, money, slumps, other players' injuries. Worry distracted a player; distraction crippled ability. So it wouldn't do for his boys to see any signs of worry from him, whatever his thoughts might be. Connie Mack was by nature an optimist—a clearheaded optimist. But there was more to it than that. He was a leader, and an essential element of leadership was to convey an aura of confidence and determination to his men. To them and the press he appeared unruffled. "We've got pitchers enough," he said. "We'll be all right."

Privately he knew the young pitchers needed experience. He could move two of them into the starting rotation and see what happened. But it was likely that somewhere along the way they would take some beatings that might shake their confidence. He confided to his brain trust of Harry Davis, Ira Thomas, Danny Murphy, and Eddie Collins, "An untried pitcher will learn more and gain more confidence by being in one inning nine separate games, where the situation is apt to be different on each occasion, than he will if he were to pitch nine consecutive innings and maybe get a good beating besides."

This was a sharp departure from his practice of taking a look at a recruit by starting him in a game, sometimes leaving him in to take just such a "good beating." That was okay when there was nothing at stake late in the season and he was looking at a parade of prospects. But this was April, and his boys were determined to avenge themselves for their own 1912 letdown. Hoping to get off to a strong start, Mack may have been rationalizing the radical system he was about to employ or just adapting to the material he had to work with.

On the morning of their home opener, April 17, the players learned of their manager's new strategy. Directing his remarks at the young pitchers,

Mack said, "Now, I don't want any of you to feel bad, or to think I am not satisfied with your work in the box, if I suddenly take you out and put in another man. What I want you all to bear in mind is that we have a lot of capable pitchers right here, and I want each one of you to go at top speed and give us all you've got when you are in the box. If it is only for three innings, or only one, or even to one man, pitch your hardest. When you feel yourself slipping, remember that we've got someone else as good who can take your place."

The players didn't know what to make of it. There had been few relief specialists in the past, so few the term itself was not yet in general use. John McGraw had used Doc Crandall in that role in 1909. The Cubs' Fred Toney and Jack Quinn of the Yankees had been used primarily in relief in 1911. Top starters were accustomed to being called on when needed, anywhere from a half dozen to twenty times a year. But they also started 25 to 40 games. Most contenders still racked up 90 to well over 100 complete games a year.

Mack let his pitchers know he wouldn't hesitate to bring in a lefty, usually Herb Pennock, to pitch to a left-handed batter with men on base, or call on Chief Bender to nail down the last out of a game. Today this is by the book. In 1913 it was revolutionary.

It didn't take long to put the new plan into action. That afternoon Bender was shelled in a 5-run third. Bush relieved him and blanked Boston the rest of the way, as the A's rallied for a 6–5 win. The next day Brown held Boston hitless until the fifth, then gave way to Houck in the seventh. Mack called on Bender to hold a 5–4 lead in the eighth. But Boston clobbered him with 3 doubles and 2 singles in the ninth to hand the A's their first loss.

On Saturday Plank gave up 5 runs in 3 innings. Wyckoff came in and loaded the bases with no outs in the fifth. Mack sent Pennock to the rescue. He got out of it and finished the 7–5 win.

By this time the pitching merry-go-round had become a source of humor. John Shibe joked that he'd buy a three-piece suit for the first pitcher to go the route. Byron Houck almost won it on Monday. He had a 6–4 lead with 2 men on and 2 out in the ninth. Mack was taking no chances. He called on Eddie Plank to get the right-handed batter Heinie Wagner, and it worked.

On April 22 Carroll Brown, showing no effects of his 18-inning preseason outing, won the suit by pitching a complete game 7–4 win over New York.

In sixteen World Series games Connie Mack had made only one pitching change, and that was because of an injury. In the first six games of the 1913 season, he made ten pitching changes. But they won five of them.

After one month they were 16-4. Their hitting carried them. Eddie Collins was batting about .500. They won 4 out of 5 from Washington, losing only to Walter Johnson. In one game in New York Russ Ford held them hitless for 8 innings; they rallied in the ninth to win, 3–2.

Cleveland and Washington replaced Detroit as the A's most heated rivals, both in the standings and in the ill-will department. The Naps resented the accusations the Athletics had made about their undermining of Harry Davis during his brief tenure as the Cleveland manager in 1912. They were now the sentimental favorites around the country; fans rooted for Larry Lajoie to have a chance to play in a World Series.

The Nationals were frustrated by the Athletics' hex over them. Since Clark Griffith had built them into contenders, they had had a hard time winning a series from Philadelphia. Feelings were further strained after an incident in their first series of the year. Stuffy McInnis tagged up on a fly ball to Milan. Catcher Eddie Ainsmith came up the line and plunked his 180-pound bulk in the basepath long before the throw reached him. McInnis ran into him. Ainsmith sat on him until he got the ball and tagged the flattened Stuffy. Umpire Bill Dinneen said, "Out."

The A's claimed interference. Dinneen said no, the catcher had not touched the runner with his hands. After the game, Mack told Dinneen he would have said nothing if the A's had lost, lest it sound like an excuse. But since they had won, he felt free to tell the ump he had made a bum call. A few of the Athletics sounded off to the writers about the need for the league to take action against the rule-breaking, bone-breaking tactics of the Ainsmiths of the league. And the Nats didn't like it.

The A's and won 15 in a row, and Connie Mack had the fast start he wanted, a sizzling 42-13, .764 pace. But Cleveland stayed on their heels, 3 games back—until the Naps came into Shibe Park in the middle of June and lost 3 out of 4 and fell 5½ games back.

Then the A's began to loaf, playing break-even ball. Other teams began climbing, and the A's started looking over their shoulders. Mack saw it and dealt with it.

"I told my players we had only to win the one game we were after," he said. "Chicago, Cleveland, Detroit, or Boston might carry off a series, but the power of doing it would so weaken them that they would lose the next series." And that's the way it went.

Despite his shaky start, Chief Bender stayed on the wagon and became Mack's most dependable late-inning stopper. Mack coaxed 21 wins out of him, 6 in relief. Bender needed time to warm up and usually three days' rest between starts. When trouble erupted suddenly in a close game, Mack handed him a ball and said, "Here, Albert, you better go down and limber up a little." If Bender had pitched within the past few days, Mack would ask him, "How do you feel, Albert?" Albert always nodded and got up before Mack could add, "Well, then, stroll down and throw a couple."

In July, Herb Pennock was out a few weeks with a fever. Jack Dunn finally released Bob Shawkey to Mack in exchange for four players. The Cubs were said to have offered $12,000 for Shawkey, but Jack Dunn was not one to cut a Connie Mack string on a player. Shawkey had been working on his control for two years and succeeded in bringing his walks average from almost 4 per 9 innings to under 3.

Mack kept a close eye on the Tri-State League, a circuit surrounding Philadelphia. He perused the box scores and sent Davis, Murphy, or Thomas out to look over promising youngsters. That's how he decided to pay $2,000 to Harrisburg for an eighteen-year-old left-hander, Rube Bressler. A local lad, Bressler was 15-13 and played the outfield, batting .290.

From August 1 to the end of the season, the Athletics played only .500 ball. But they won when they had to. After watching 3 games melt off their lead in a week, they took 3 out of 4 from Cleveland. Shawkey pitched a 2-hit 7–1 win in the first game. Baker was a one-man wrecking crew: 9 for 16, a game-winning home run one day, 3 runs scored and 3 RBI in another. The lead went back to 8 games and stayed there.

Then the A's settled Washington's hopes by sweeping a Labor Day doubleheader. In the afternoon contest they demonstrated that they were still the hottest late-inning team in the league. They were down 5–4 to Walter Johnson in the tenth, with 2 outs and daylight dimming. Most of the fans were headed home for supper. As Eddie Murphy strode to the plate, Eddie Collins decided it was voodoo time. He picked up an armful of bats and scattered them every which way in front of the dugout.

Murphy swung and missed. Strike one. He probably never saw the next fastball. Umpire Billy Evans called strike two. Evans later wrote, "I never saw Walter Johnson have more stuff. There did not seem a chance for the A's to win with two out and two strikes on the batter."

Murphy swung at the next pitch and lined a single to left.

"Rube Oldring gave the hit and run sign," Evans said. "Murphy was running. Oldring swung and lined it to left center. It got by Clyde Milan and rolled to the bleachers. Murphy scored. Oldring had a double. Collins found a bat among the many he had scattered. He hit the second pitch for a single to right field and Oldring by a magnificent burst of speed and head-first slide managed to beat the almost perfect throw of Mueller to the plate. ... The players gave much credit to the scattering of the bats."

On September 17 the Browns came to town. Branch Rickey, the club secretary, made his debut as the St. Louis manager. The Browns lost and sank into the cellar, narrowly edging Frank Chance's Yankees for the honor. The A's clinched the pennant by taking 2 from Detroit on September 22. It was Connie Mack's fifth in thirteen years in Philadelphia.

For the first time, the Athletics didn't win with pitching. They gave up more runs than three other teams in the league. Their 3.19 earned run average (ERA) was sixth in the league. Byron Houck was 14-6 despite the highest ERA among all regular pitchers: 4.14. They walked more batters than any other staff. Fifteen of those passes were handed out by Carroll Brown in 7 innings on July 12 in Detroit. The Tigers had 10 hits but scored only 1 run in those 7 innings and left 17 on base while losing, 16–9.

That evening in the hotel lobby a stranger asked Connie Mack, "Why did you wait until the eighth inning before you took Brown out? I never would have believed you'd let a pitcher stay in long enough to give 15 bases on balls."

Mack replied that Brown made the pitches he had to make to get out of the jams, until "I noticed that he was slowing up in the eighth. Any time you see a pitcher ease up in order to get the ball over the plate it's time he got out. It's no wonder, though, Brownie was slowing up; he pitched about four games out there this afternoon."

Connie Mack was the American League's original Captain Hook, using his ace starters primarily as relievers. Bender, Houck, Bush, and Wyckoff relieved in more games than they started, and Plank almost as many (22 vs. 29 starts). The A's 69 complete games was a record low for the American League and remained the major league record for a pennant winner for another ten years. Mack made 122 pitching changes during the season, prompting this postseason *Sporting News* headline: "It is a Wonder Connie Mack didn't strain his back using the Derrick."

To Mack, one sign of a tired pitcher was a sudden outbreak of wildness. When he saw it, he didn't wait. He also believed that when a pitcher was being hit hard, it was often the catcher who should be changed, not the pitcher. But he had more pitchers than catchers.

Only 30 of the A's first 77 games, during which they won 57 and built a

9-game lead, were complete games. Mack's use of his pitchers was so radical a departure from the past that *St. Louis Post-Dispatch* columnist J. Ed Wray wrote a July 2 column with these prophetic words:

COMING: THE 5-INNING PITCHER

That keen old blade, Connie Mack, has cut a Gordian knot that baseball managers have long sought to untie. How to obtain top speed pitching for nine innings has addled many a leader's noodle. Only exceptional individuals have been able to deliver it.

Mack has solved the problem. Necessity and a weakened pitching staff early in the season reduced the Athletics' leader to the plan of using at least two pitchers in each game, against strong opponents. At the slightest sign of waning efficiency, out came the hurler and in went a new and fresh flinger.

The majority of Philadelphia games this season has seen so-called relief pitchers sent in. As a matter of fact, Mack has now taken to the plan of relieving his flingers in the middle of the contest whether or not they appear particularly hard pressed.

In one sense it may be said that the A's won the 1913 pennant because of Mack's use of his pitchers. But they also outscored the second-place Nationals by almost 200 runs. The two Eddies, Collins and Murphy, were among the leaders in drawing walks. Baker, McInnis, and Barry—a .275 hitter—were among the top five in runs batted in. They combined slugging and base running and tight defense. They pulled off the double squeeze eight times that year, always with Barry at bat.

Connie Mack told his regulars to go home, do whatever they wanted, don't even think about baseball, and report back for the final series of the year. That was all the tuneup they'd need before facing the New York Giants again in the World Series. Meanwhile, unknown names like McAvoy, Fritz, Lavan, Cruthers, and Daley populated the Athletics' lineup.

44 THE SECOND BEATING OF JOHN MCGRAW

For the third time, Connie Mack and John McGraw matched wits in the World Series. The Giants were the same all-around NL champions they had been in 1911 and 1912. But they hadn't won a world title since their 1905 triumph over the A's.

The games alternated between the two cities, opening in New York. The Athletics did away with the headaches of mail order ticket sales and sold strips of tickets for games 2, 4, and 6. There would be no standing room in the outfield. With an increase in prices, the gate could reach $50,000 in Philadelphia, $75,000 in the Polo Grounds. The $2 top price was high for the times; a good breakfast in a New York restaurant set you back twenty-five cents. A dollar bought a fried oyster dinner or a balcony seat at a Broadway theater. The Commercial Moving Picture Company bought the rights to film the action, but the players didn't try to share in the money.

Not everybody was pleased with the "big show" the World Series had become. The next *Reach Guide* denounced the commercialization, the failure to more evenly distribute the receipts among more teams, and the "postseason demoralization [of] most of the unduly-enriched participants."

The modern designated hitter dilemma in interleague play is not the first time different rules applied in the two leagues. In 1913 there were two differences. In the National, the infield fly rule allowed base runners to advance without tagging up if the ball was dropped. In the American, base runners could not leave the base until the ball was caught or touched the ground or a fielder. In the National, if a pitcher dropped the ball while in the act of pitching or throwing to a base, it was a balk. In the American, it wasn't. (That winter they resolved their differences. The NL adopted the AL infield fly rule, and the AL took the NL balk rule.)

The fuss over players' ghostwritten commentaries continued. The National

Commission wanted to avoid the in-print feuding that had accompanied past World Series. Ban Johnson sent a letter to the Giants and Athletics informing them that players whose names appeared in bylines would not be permitted to play. Connie Mack responded that if Baker and Collins couldn't play, he'd just have to find substitutes for them. He wasn't about to interfere with their writing activities. Marquard and Mathewson also had contracts. A few days later Johnson backed down. They could play if they showed they were capable of writing their own stuff.

Johnson had solid grounds for that stance but scant hope of enforcing it. Players like Cobb and Collins and Mathewson were capable of writing or dictating their own copy. Others clearly were not. Giants pitcher Jeff Tesreau had been assigned to a ghost for the 1912 Series. His penman said that after one of Tesreau's losses he went to the native of the Ozarks for some material. All Tesreau said was, "We oughter beat them there birds today." Tesreau had a deal with a New York paper for the 1913 Series. After he was knocked out in Game 3, his ghost went to him for some words of wisdom he could use.

"When I came in he was rubbing his thumb," the writer related. "Jeff looked at me and looked at his thumb. He thought for a minute or so and finally said, 'I hurt muh thumb.' And that was all he said."

There was plenty of confusion. The National Commission threatened to hold up players' shares until the player-scribes produced contracts dated before September 27 for approval. Those who couldn't faced unspecified penalties. In the end nobody was penalized. The connection between some players' thoughts and what their ghosts wrote remained pretty flimsy.

Most of the experts picked the Giants, despite Fred Merkle's gimpy leg and sprained ankle and Fred Snodgrass's charley horse. Their pitching was a known quality: Mathewson, Marquard, Jeff Tesreau, 13-4 rookie Al Demaree, and the veteran Doc Crandall, now primarily a relief pitcher.

Philadelphia's pitching was questionable. Plank had shown signs of arm weariness late in the season. Behind him and Bender, the loss of Jack Coombs left a huge gap until you came to Brown, Houck, Bush, and Shawkey. Mack's strategy was expected to be Bender and Plank and pray for rain.

The betting odds were about even, though support for the A's temporarily dried up when a rumor spread that New York gamblers had paid Bender $25,000 to "lay down" against the Giants. Bender called the story "laughable. Those gamblers would have better sense than that and they would never dare try such a game on me. You can say for me that I emphatically deny the story."

The Athletics went into the Series believing they couldn't lose. This was not the overconfidence of 1912. It was a general feeling that they knew how to beat the Giants. And it showed.

According to Christy Mathewson, on the eve of the opener, a New York newspaperman with whom he was friendly went to the Athletics' hotel. He found the players as relaxed as if they were on vacation. At ten o'clock Baker yawned and went to bed. The rest soon followed. The writer then visited the Giants' hotel, where, around midnight, he spotted third baseman Buck Herzog nervously shuffling about the lobby.

"Hello, Herzie," he said. "I thought you'd be in bed."

"I'm not a bit sleepy," Herzog said. "I could stay up all night."

Mathewson contrasted the "cold nerve" of the A's with the tense, highstrung Giants. Claiming the Giants were always uptight before big games, he all but accused his teammates of choking, though that term wasn't used. That's why, he said, they had lost the last two World Series.

In August Mathewson had compared the Athletics to a college team. "There is never any dissension. . . . They are all whooping it up for one another. No politics mars the workings of the club and you never hear one member of the team knocking some fellow player. Seldom are there murmurs of dissatisfaction because of the treatment a player has received, and few are the men who hold out for salary increases. The players are generally satisfied, and this helps their game. This is all Connie Mack. He is a marvel at handling men, for it is well known that the salaries paid on the Philadelphia club are not nearly so high as on other teams which are much lower in the standing as a rule."

Fred Lieb confirmed Matty's observation, writing in the *New York Press*, "There is more of a college spirit to that team than to any club in baseball. When a fellow makes a good hit or a good play, his comrades slap him on the back, shake his hand, dance a jig, or whisper soothing language into his ear. When Merkle made his home run in Philadelphia [Game 4] driving in two runs ahead of him in the World Series, not a Giant made a move to congratulate him. If he had gone out on a fly to the outfield, as much fuss would have been made over him."

Connie Mack shared his players' confidence. His optimism was more than just his usual serene outlook. Even though the club treasury gained nothing unless the Series went past four games, he was thinking sweep, something that had never been done. In the meeting on the morning of October 7, he told his boys to set their sights on being the first to win in four games.

"Think of more than the money. Look to the honor. Long after what you win in this series is gone, you will be remembered as heroes who triumphed—or as the team that should have won but lost. Your grandchildren will make their boasts if you win. Each of you will be known to fame as one of the world's champions."

From Ben Shibe to Louis Van Zelst, they set out determined to sweep the Giants. Connie Mack intended to move to the Alamac Hotel at Broadway and Seventy-first Street, away from the noise and bustle of the theater district. But the players wanted to stay at the same hotel they had used during the 1911 World Series, and Mack was never one to go against players' well-founded superstitions. So they booked forty rooms at the Somerset on Forty-seventh Street and returned to New York in the evening after each home game. Once again they turned down the use of the Polo Grounds dressing room. To avoid scratching the marble floor in the lobby, they carried their shoes outside and put them on on the sidewalk, cheered on by a contingent of Philadelphia fans that included fifteen Catholic priests.

At Mack's request, the wives of Baker, Barry, Collins, Davis, and Bender waited until the morning of the opener to go to New York. Mary Coombs and other wives went to Shibe Park, where play-by-play reports were transmitted. Mrs. Coombs telephoned the action to Colby Jack, who lay in University Hospital with thirty-eight-pound weights attached to his feet to keep his spine from moving.

Everybody knew that Bender would start for the Athletics. Before leaving Philadelphia, Connie Mack called him into his office. "Albert," he said, "I am depending on you to win this series. By the way, how much do you owe on the mortgage on your house?"

Bender thought that was a personal question.

"All right," Mack shrugged. "We'll talk about it later."

Mack counted on two wins from Bender, one from Plank, and one from somebody else. His first choice for the "somebody else" was Joe Bush. He knew his pitchers' temperaments. The twenty-year-old Bush had no nerves. He was not the type to tighten up if he was told in advance when he would pitch. Even though Mack had Shawkey, Wyckoff, and Bush warming up before Game 3, starting Bush was no last-minute hunch. He told Bush before the opener that he would start the third game no matter how the first two went.

The Second Beating of John McGraw 589

McGraw chose Rube Marquard to pitch the opener. Mathewson watched the 23-game winner warm up. Rube, he observed, "had everything. His curves never broke sharper and his speed was terrific."

Rube left it all in front of the grandstand. Once on the field he had nothing but frayed nerves. In his story the next day he admitted that he was nervous and lacked the control he needed. Baker and Collins had 3 hits each. Baker lined an RBI single in the 3-run fourth, then came up in the fifth with Collins on second. The plan was to pitch Baker low and outside. Marquard missed. As soon as he saw the ball headed knee-high toward the inside corner—"just where Baker likes them"—he "looked for Baker to give it a ride."

Down in Washington, members of the House of Representatives were locked in the chamber while officials rounded up a quorum for a vote. They had no news of the game. The Republican floor leader, Rep. James Mann of Chicago, rose to ask a parliamentary question: "I wish to ask if the chair had made arrangements to inform the House of the progress of the game in New York?"

"That is not a parliamentary question," the chair ruled.

They waited in silence. A messenger arrived and whispered something to Mann, who rose and said, "Would it be proper for me to announce that the score is now 5 to 1 in favor of Philadelphia in the fifth inning?"

"Out of order," ruled the speaker.

"That being out of order," Mann said, "I ask if it would be in order to announce that Baker of Philadelphia has just hit a home run?"

The cheers drowned out the speaker's ruling.

Bender was not his sharpest either. He issued no walks but gave up 11 hits. The Giants scored 3 in the fifth before Albert shut them down and won, 6–4.

That evening on the train to Philadelphia, Bender sat in the parlor car reading a magazine while the car rocked with boisterous singing and chattering. Writer Gordon Mackay sat down beside him and asked how he felt. Bender reached into his pocket, took out his wallet, and removed a frayed piece of newspaper.

"Remember when I got that?"

Mackay nodded. It was the clipping from a St. Louis newspaper prior to the 1910 World Series, in which the writer predicted the Cubs would find Bender and the Athletics easy pickings. "I couldn't let the Cubs beat me after that, could I," Bender said.

He then pulled out a newer clipping, smoothed it out, and pointed to an underlined sentence: "McGraw knows that he can beat Bender and hopes that Mack will start with the Indian."

"A friend of mine sent me that a week ago. And after I read it I knew there couldn't be a chance for me to lose today. So when I got in the box I thought of the clipping and that was enough."

Bender enjoyed telling this story often when he appeared as a speaker for the next thirty years.

Writer Bill Phelon thought both teams looked lousy, acting like "boiled Mongolians" who "boobed on the basepaths." One of the ragged plays to which he referred occurred in the sixth inning. Fred Merkle was at bat with 2 out. He had opened the third and fifth with singles, so Bender pitched cautiously to him. On a full count, Bender threw a sharp curve low and outside to the right-handed batter. Wally Schang got his glove on the ball and dropped it as Merkle took a half swing. Schang tagged Merkle and rolled the ball toward the mound. But umpire Bill Klem didn't yell, "Strike three." Merkle decided he had drawn a walk and started for first base as the Athletics were running off the field. Merkle kept on running toward second, which mystified Jack Barry, who picked up the ball and ran back to second base before Merkle reached it. Collins and McInnis followed him and Merkle was eventually tagged out in a rundown. Klem conferred with umpire John Egan, then walked back to home plate and called Merkle out on a third strike.

Phelon also blasted McGraw for "[crabbing] the works by keeping Marquard in when it was obvious he couldn't win."

Despite a steady drizzle, more than a thousand people camped out overnight around Shibe Park before the gates opened on Wednesday. Peanut, sausage, and sandwich vendors did a brisk business. Thousands more ignored building inspectors' orders to stay off the rooftops. Before the game, Walter Johnson took possession of a new Chalmers as the MVP. He had won 36 games, 40 percent of the second-place Nationals' 90 victories.

The veterans Plank and Mathewson were in top form. There were stories that Matty had lost something off his fastball and become a curveball pitcher, relying on the hook and fadeaway for his 25 wins. His control helped; he walked 21 in 306 innings. Mathewson was aware of the reports on his fading fastball. So he threw almost all fastballs all day while they kept looking for the breaking ball. He drove Eddie Collins crazy. For starters, Matty worked too fast for him. Eddie's usual routine was a game

The Second Beating of John McGraw 591

delayer: adjust his cap, hitch up his belt, tap the plate. "Matty didn't give me a chance," he wrote. "Before I knew it the ball was in the catcher's mitt. I was forced to do all my motions before I got in." Matty started him off with fastballs. Then, "when I looked for a fastball he broke a curve over for a strike."

Plank was just as cagey. Both teams managed nothing but singles. Nobody crossed home plate before the Athletics came up in the last of the ninth. Amos Strunk led off with a single. Jack Lapp jumped up from the bench and grabbed a bat. "Put your man down to second," he told Mack, "and I'll win the game for you." Barry hit a soft grounder to the right side. Doyle raced in, picked it up and threw it past Hooks Wiltse, the Giants' best-fielding pitcher, who was subbing for the hobbled Merkle at first base. Suddenly there were men on second and third, nobody out. Shibe Park vibrated under the stomping of forty-thousand feet. Atop the residential roofs the improvised bleachers were close to collapsing.

Connie Mack's mind was racing, sorting out everything that had happened during the past two hours. He scanned his scorecard. In the entire game only four fly balls had been hit off Mathewson, three of them too short to score a run. Lapp had struck out the first time at bat, hit a sharp grounder to second, then laced a clean single in the seventh. Each time at bat was better than the one before. He saw no reason to pinch hit for Lapp.

The left-handed batter pulled the ball down to first. Wiltse fielded it and threw home. The throw just beat the streaking Strunk. Barry moved to third.

Now it was Plank's turn. The grandstand, rooftop, and press box managers knew that all it took was a fly ball to score the winning run. Surely Walsh or Schang or Danny Murphy was more likely to deliver a fly ball than the pitcher. But the sore-kneed Danny Murphy was the only available pinch hitter in whom Connie Mack had any confidence.

"Do you feel you can go in and hit for Plank?" he asked Murphy.

"No," Murphy said, glancing at his bum knee. "I do not feel that I could do myself justice. I couldn't even stand right."

Plank had hit the ball harder than anybody but Baker that day: a fast grounder to Doyle, a single, and a line drive caught by the shortstop. So Mack gave Eddie the go-ahead. Plank hit a ground ball to Wiltse, whose throw beat Barry to the plate. Eddie Murphy then hit a comebacker to Mathewson for the third out as the crowd groaned.

It didn't take the Giants long to let the rest of the air out of the deflated crowd. Ironically, the pitcher drove in the first of three runs in the tenth. Mathewson then retired Oldring, Collins, and Baker to end the 3–0 game.

Connie Mack said he never hesitated in his decision to let Plank hit though he knew he'd be criticized if they didn't score. And he was.

The atmosphere in the press box hummed with indignation. No pinch hitter for Lapp or Plank? What was Mack thinking? One writer confronted Mack: "Why in blazes didn't you put in someone to bat for Plank? It looked like throwing the game."

Mack bristled. "That's your job. That's what your paper pays you for, to criticize these games. Now go ahead and do it, and don't ask me to help you."

When Mack walked into the club's business offices, everybody there wanted to know the same thing: "Why didn't you put in a pinch hitter?" Mack recalled:

That night while I was eating my dinner, I was called to the telephone by a baseball writer who told me that I had been severely criticized by the fans for allowing Lapp and Plank to hit instead of pinch hitters. I said, "I have nothing to say and if you want to criticize me that is your privilege."

In justice to this reporter, I will say that he was one of the few who didn't put me on the grill for my tactics. Before the next game started I must have received more than a hundred telegrams from fans advising me to resign as manager because I was no longer capable of handling a ball team. Most of these messages came collect.

Some writers hinted in print that the A's manager didn't care if he lost a game or two in order to prolong the Series for the extra revenue. They charged him with "hippodroming," deliberately losing the game. Some of the telegrams he received made the same accusation.

Asked about that game many times over the years, Mack always insisted that he would do the same thing again. "That night I slept as well as after any game in the series."

But he was concerned with what his players thought of his actions. If they had any doubts, he wanted to know about it. To lose their respect was to lose everything. The next morning he told his boys, "I don't care what the newspapers say and I don't care how much they roast me for keeping in Plank, but I do care what you fellows think. What about it? Did I do right or wrong? I want each of you to give me your honest opinion."

His players knew they could speak up without fear of repercussions. They also knew that Plank had been no easy out for Mathewson all day, and they said so.

Connie Mack could take criticism and second guessing and brush it off. It came with the job. But not when it came to a slur on his honesty or the integrity of the game.

A few months later, still seething over the insinuations, Mack aired his views in a *Saturday Evening Post* article:

"Good honest criticism is to be taken in the spirit it is given. But to accuse us of cheating—playing for the 'gate'—is an entirely different matter. For I want everyone at all interested in baseball to know that I should consider playing for the gate receipts—'throwing' a game or even failing to put forth the team's very best efforts to win—as nothing short of dishonest."

Mack explained that he had been reluctant to even discuss the incident, but he felt it "necessary for the good of the national game" to confront "those who ignorantly attack the grand game to which I have given thirty years of my life."

Yet the slant that he would deliberately undermine his team's chances of winning—a game, a pennant, a World Series—to line his own pockets has been promulgated and parroted into an image as permanently etched as Mount Rushmore. With no basis. Before this World Series was over, Connie Mack would disprove it again.

The Giants went into Game 3 with renewed confidence. Their scouts said the A's were weak against the spitter, and their big right-hander, Jeff Tesreau, doped the ball with the best of them. Most spitballs came in with less speed than a fastball before diving erratically. Tesreau threw his as hard as his fastball. The Athletics were going with a kid who had been pitching in Missoula a year ago.

The A's had problems with Ed Walsh's spitter, but they quickly found Tesreau was no Walsh. They also caught on that he moved his fingers from side to side on the ball if he was going to throw a spitter. They let his fastball go by and clobbered his overloaded spitters, staking Bush to a 3-run lead in the top of the first. A double steal that led to 2 runs was the turning point, McGraw said. "Mack caught us by surprise"

McGraw and Wilbert Robinson, manning the coaching lines, started riding Bullet Joe Bush with his first pitch and never let up. Eddie Collins, the only noisemaker in the A's infield, kept up a counterpatter: "Don't be afraid of the Giants. . . . You got everything today boy." Bush seemed unnerved when, with 1 out, Doyle singled off his glove and he hit Fletcher with a pitch. But Burns lined to Collins, who tossed to Barry to double up Doyle. Bush came off the field smiling. "That's the boy, Leslie," Mack said. "Nothing to it now."

McGraw kept expecting Bush to blow up under the steady taunting. It never happened. Bush retired the next 7 batters. The A's scored 2 more in the second and cruised to an 8–2 victory. The first four A's in the lineup had 9 of the team's 12 hits. Collins had 3 and 3 RBIS, Baker 2 and 2 RBIS. With Wally Schang handling him like a veteran, Bush was just wild enough, walking 5 and hitting 1, to keep the Giants on edge at the plate. Mack had Carroll Brown warming up just in case but never called on him.

After the game the Athletics hopped into taxis for the ride to the hotel. Disappointed Giants fans were waiting for them along Seventh Avenue. They opened fire with bricks, flatirons, cabbages, and other produce. Eddie Collins told Mathewson, "Four of us rode for twenty blocks crouched down, not daring to look up. There was not a whole window in any of the cabs when we reached the hotel. After that game we took Riverside Drive to the hotel. Policemen along the line laughed at the volley we got."

The Athletics kept it up the next day at home. Mathewson, now thirty-three, could no longer work every other day in October after pitching 300-plus innings. McGraw passed over Marquard and started Al Demaree, a twenty-nine-year-old rookie. He expected Mack to use another young pitcher and give Bender another day of rest. But Mack considered two days off enough for Albert, who pronounced himself ready and eager.

This time Demaree held Collins and Baker hitless, but the light-hitting Barry and Schang combined for 5 hits and 5 RBI. The Giants couldn't do anything with Bender for 6 innings as the A's built a 6–0 lead. Then, in the seventh, Burns beat out an infield hit. Murray doubled on an 0-2 pitch. Merkle hit a line drive that bounced into the left-field bleachers for a 3-run homer.

Things got hairier in the eighth, when Herzog singled. Bender's bad throw on a dribbler cost them a double play. With 2 out, Burns doubled and Shafer tripled. Suddenly it was 6–5. Connie Mack squirmed on the bench. He wasn't the only one getting anxious. "Was there any strain?" Eddie Collins said. "Can a duck swim?"

Mack sent Danny Murphy out to ask Bender if he had anything left.

If Albert said he was okay, that's all there was to it. He'd stay in. He told Murphy he was fine. It would take a broken limb for him to come out. "It was a disgrace to get knocked out of a game," Bender believed. "[Whenever] it happened, I felt like crawling into a cave to hide."

Murray hit a sharp grounder to Collins, and the tying run was left on third.

McGraw used two pinch hitters in the ninth, but Bender was back in charge.

In the shower, Bender told a relieved Collins he had gotten a little careless. "I pitched bad to Murray in the seventh inning. I had him two strikes and nothing and I got the ball right in the groove."

Mack told Bender to stay home and relax on Saturday instead of going to New York. If there was to be a game on Monday, he would pitch.

Game 5 on Saturday, October 11, was extraordinary on several counts. Fred Merkle was embroiled in another "boner," less remembered than his fateful 1908 base running mistake. Christy Mathewson made his eleventh and last World Series start and pitched a record tenth complete game. And Connie Mack broke a National Commission rule to make a point.

The sting from the accusations following the loss of the second game still angered Mack. Now the papers in New York and other cities were insinuating—some outright predicting—that the Giants were a sure thing to win on Saturday. There was upwards of $50,000 sitting in the Athletics' safe from the sale of tickets for Game 6. If the A's won on Saturday, it would all have to be refunded. The players already had their shares put away; this money belonged to the club owners, who would do anything to avoid giving it back. Or so the wink-nudge stories went.

Mack's boys had a comfortable 3 games to 1 lead. Their chance for a sweep was gone. Once more they were up against Mathewson, who had shut them out for 10 innings on Wednesday. Even with an all-out effort, beating Matty was no picnic. The players read the papers too. But they knew their manager and the Shibes better than anybody else did. In their minds, there was no chance they'd be asked to toss the game to the Giants or that Connie Mack would deliberately manage in order to lose it.

But they didn't expect what they heard from Connie Mack that morning. He told them the club would give them its share of the day's receipts—over $30,000 after the league's 25 percent cut—if they won that day. That was more than $1,000 a man, on top of the $3,000-plus winners' shares. The National Commission prohibited such bonuses, but Mack didn't care. It meant more to him and the Shibes to prove the wise ones wrong in their certainty that the Athletics would choose to lose that day.

At the time of the meeting, Mack was unaware that his starting pitcher, Eddie Plank, had been up most of the night while the trainer applied hot towels to his aching left arm. And Plank never told him. Some of the players knew—"Just the old rheumatiz," he told them—but their concerns were eased by their experience with him. If Bunny, as the players called Plank, said he felt fine, they worried. If he complained about his arm, he'd throw a great game.

Still, during batting practice, Eddie Collins kept an eye on Plank. Neither one said anything about it, but Plank knew what Collins was thinking. "Gee, I hate to warm up," Plank told him as he started to throw. "But after I get started I guess I'll be all right."

Plank took a long twenty-five minutes to get ready. Then, relying entirely on fastballs, he held the Giants to 2 hits and would have shut them out but for his own error.

Mathewson was almost as masterful. Later he called it the hardest game he ever pitched, "not because it took as much out of my arm as the long one against the Boston Red Sox, but because I desired to win it more than any other battle I ever entered. I realized it might be the last game in a World Series in which I would get an opportunity to show. Therefore I was anxious to close out with a victory."

Reversing his Game 2 plan, Matty threw one curve after another all day. Collins said he saw only one fastball the entire game. Once again Frank Baker did the most damage, if a sacrifice fly and dubious hit could be called damage.

Eddie Murphy hit the game's first pitch for a single. After Oldring's bunt forced Murphy at second, Collins singled Oldring to third. Baker's fly to left scored Oldring.

In the third Murphy again led off with a single. Oldring hit a grounder to second, too hot for Doyle to handle. Collins bunted them to second and third. Baker topped a dribbler down the first base line. Merkle raced in and picked it up. Baker started toward first, then stopped. Murphy started for home, then stopped. Merkle held the ball. The action froze like a *tableau vivant*. Murphy inched back toward third, then suddenly dashed for the plate. By the time Merkle threw home, it was too late. Baker sprinted past Merkle to first and was credited by the official scorers with a Cincinnati base hit. (It was the last such hit; the following spring the writers abolished it and officially encoded the definition of a fielder's choice.) McInnis then hit a fly ball to Burns to score Oldring.

Some players and writers blamed Merkle; others defended him. Brooklyn first baseman Jake Daubert first said Merkle was not to blame, then inexplicably described Merkle's mistake: he should have chased Baker back toward home plate and tagged him, forcing Murphy to hold at third.

The A's now led, 3–0, but it was far from over. McGraw and Robinson had been harassing Plank all afternoon, trying to rattle him. They got on him for his fussing about in the box. They complained to home plate umpire Bill Klem that Plank's delivery, with his windmill arms, was illegal. Klem had seen Plank pitch in the 1911 Series, but except for two-thirds of an inning, he had not worked behind the plate with Eddie pitching. In the second inning he went out to talk to Plank. According to J. G. Taylor Spink, one of the official scorers, Plank said to Klem, "Seeing as how I've pitched this way for thirteen seasons, I hope you're not going to make me change in the last big league game of my life."

Klem said, "Go ahead and pitch," and walked back behind the plate.

With one out in the fifth, Tilly Shafer drew Plank's only walk of the day. On a hit and run, Red Murray hit a high popup in the middle of the diamond. Baker and Collins raced in. Plank stood directly under it. Shafer stood watching, transfixed, on second base, ignoring the shouts of the coaches to get back to first. Plank reached up to catch it just as Baker did the same. They bumped. The ball fell out of Plank's hands and hit the ground. At that the outwardly calm Connie Mack leaped up, banging his head on the concrete roof of the dugout. Fred Lieb related that story many times. In the first version, Mack "saw so many stars and planets he couldn't tell if Plank had caught the ball."

Eddie Collins wrote that after banging his head, Mack "sat down as though nothing had happened."

But neither Lieb nor Collins was on the bench at the time. Billy Orr, who was out of action with a broken hand, was sitting next to Mack. Orr said nothing about Mack banging his head. All he said was, "I thought Connie was going to faint when Baker and Plank came together. He almost fell off the bench as it was."

Larry McLean then singled, scoring Shafer and further jangling Mack's nerves. The score was now 3–1. Eddie Collins walked to the pitcher's box and said, "Are you sure you can handle things, Bunny?"

"Give me that ball and get out of here," Plank said.

When Fred Merkle hit into an inning-ending 4–6–3 double play, it "was like a dash of cold water in [Mack's] face," Orr said.

Connie Mack was composed enough to remind his players not to mention the mixup on the pop fly. "Not a word now about that slip-up," he yelled down the bench. When the players reached the dugout he said, "That's the way, Bunny, to get out of a hole. Keep her going. They can't get you now."

And they didn't. Mathewson singled in the sixth; another double play ended that threat. And that was it for the Giants.

Christy Mathewson was a star and acted the part. Spick Hall of the *Philadelphia Evening Times* wrote, "Those who saw the World Series game in New York know how Christy Mathewson was always the last man on the field, walking along while the fans shook the stands with their cheers."

After striking out Wally Schang to end the top of the ninth, Matty did not return to the dugout. He knew a pinch hitter would bat for him. He had thrown his last pitch in this World Series. He turned and trotted to the clubhouse in center field.

In the last of the ninth Plank easily disposed of Doc Crandall and Buck Herzog. Larry Doyle hit a short fly to right. Half the team—Barry, Collins, McInnis, Strunk, Murphy—converged on it. The superstitious Collins shuddered when he heard Strunk yell to Murphy, "No Snodgrass now, Mike (referring to Snodgrass's muff of a fly ball in the 1912 Series). There's $30,000 hanging on it."

Mike, as they called Eddie Murphy, squeezed it for the final out. The gathering in right field celebrated, while the fans swarmed out of the stands and engulfed them. The players fought their way through the mob to the clubhouse and exits, pummeled by rolled-up newspapers and back-slapping supporters and besieged for autographs. Harry Davis signed the names of Baker, Barry, and Oldring on scorecards thrust at him by fans mistaking him for those players.

John McGraw was the first to congratulate Connie Mack, who introduced him to Mrs. Mack sitting behind the dugout. Not even his stoicism could stifle the joy and excitement Mack felt from the exoneration his boys had given him. But the last thing he wanted was to be hoisted onto anybody's shoulders and given precarious, undignified carriage off the premises. He waited in the dugout until the field was empty before he and Mrs. Mack made their way out.

"The Athletics are what baseball men call 'money players,'" Matty wrote.

"They played that series with the zest of college boys. They seemed to enjoy every minute of it, while the Giants made labor of it."

Once again Frank Baker swung the biggest bat, hitting .450. Collins was close behind at .421. Between them they had 17 hits in 39 at bats and drove in 10 of the A's 23 runs. John McGraw told Mack that Collins was the best ballplayer and the A's infield the most perfect he had ever seen. Wally Schang drove in 6 runs with his 5 hits.

Mack had reversed his season-long pattern of frequent pitching changes. In 21 postseason games so far, he had still made only one pitching change.

That evening the Athletics returned to Philadelphia and went directly to Shibe Park, where bands and fireworks kept the neighborhood awake until well past midnight. Meanwhile, sporting editor George M. Graham was writing an editorial for the *North American* that concluded:

"It is to be hoped that now a lot of small-minded scandalmongers who have sought in speaking whispers to asperse the reputation of the man who has made Philadelphia's base ball fame, will now be as active in apologizing, explaining and humbly striving to correct everywhere the misrepresentation they spread, as they were to give it currency. The Athletics victory was an unanswerable demonstration for base ball honesty."

The Athletics, in their postgame comments, expressed their pride and satisfaction in having proven the integrity of the game and their leader. But not, it seems, to writers like Robert Smith, whose *Illustrated History of Baseball* sixty years later perpetuated the conventional myth that "Connie Mack was more devoted to the dollar, it seemed, than he was to victory."

Addressing the thousands of rooters in Shibe Park before the fireworks exploded, Connie Mack said that "never in my thirty years as player and manager have I felt so happy as tonight."

Three Washington players—Walter Johnson, George McBride, and Germany Schaefer—were also happy. They reportedly had pooled their money to bet on the Athletics and collected $5,000.

When National Commission secretary John E. Bruce handed out the winners' checks for $3,243.94 at the Bellevue-Stratford Hotel, Rube Oldring thanked him and said, "See you again next year." At Shibe Park they picked up their promised bonuses from the club's $34,054 share of the Game 5 receipts. The *Sporting Life* correspondent reported that "no less than nine of the Mackmen have invested their World's Series loot in buzz-wagons, which does not speak well for their good sense."

And Connie Mack handed Albert Bender a check for $2,500, the amount of the mortgage on his house.

On Monday morning, October 13, while the refunds for Game 6 tickets were being paid out at Gimbel's department store, a sudden shroud of sadness halted the planning of parades and banquets. Early that morning Harry Davis Jr., the thirteen-year-old son of the A's coach, died at his home. Just days earlier he and his younger brother Ted had been on the field at Shibe Park as usual, playing catch and shagging flies. He had been there on Saturday, watching the reports of the game in New York, apparently in good health. Doctors could only guess at the cause of death.

The entire team mourned. Junior was popular, and his father was revered. Wives of players and club officials came to the Davis family's support. Eddie Collins had lived with the family before his marriage; Eddie Plank and infielder Bill Orr lived there during the season and had not left yet. Plank and Bender and the four infielders served as pallbearers at the funeral, conducted by the Athletics chaplain, Rev. Thomas W. Davis, a Methodist minister.

"Every one connected with the club sacrificed their own personal interest and pleasures at that time to stand by us," Mrs. Davis told Spick Hall of the *Evening Times*. "That is one great reason why the Athletics win pennants. On and off the field, in happiness or sorrow, they are banded together by ties of friendship which, at times, are stronger than ties of blood relationship."

Ben Shibe and Connie Mack called on the mayor at City Hall and persuaded him to postpone the official celebration until October 28. Then the exhausted Mack and his wife and two babies went to Atlantic City for two weeks, where Maggie Page's cooking helped restore the fourteen pounds Mack had lost during the season. When they returned on the twenty-eighth, Mack took out his rarely worn tuxedo and showed up, as Chandler Richter described him, "in the full, dazzling makeup of a professional diner-out."

One day soon afterward, Henry Beach Needham appeared at Connie Mack's home carrying an envelope. After lunch he said, "Connie, I want you to read this baseball story. It's what I learned under you, used as the basis for fiction." He asked Mack to let him know if he had described the technicalities of the game correctly. The book of four short stories was published in 1915 as *The Double Squeeze*. (Needham became a war correspondent during World War I. One day he talked his way into riding as an observer in a military airplane that crashed, killing him and the pilot.)

Mack made the rounds of the winter fetes, enduring lengthy, repetitive praises, then standing and passing all the credit to his players. On November

3 he went to Worcester for a dinner honoring Jack Barry. He showed up at the Stetson Hat Company to present a trophy to the company champions from the shipping department. The next day he was in Gettysburg for an Eddie Plank dinner. Plank was a shy, self-effacing farmer who didn't want the attention. But he couldn't stop his friends and neighbors from throwing a party for him. After everyone who ever knew him stood up and spoke, Eddie said, "Thanks to you all," and sat down.

Everywhere he went, Mack defended the integrity of the game on the field. He said he would welcome a four-game sweep by any team to demonstrate the honesty of the game. He managed to maintain a constant weight through it all, gaining at most a half pound, which would melt in spring training.

Ira Thomas usually accompanied Mack on the banquet circuit. Always loquacious in his praises, Thomas characterized Mack as the head of a great, all-but-worshipful family. "The players do not look upon Mr. Mack as a manager, but rather as a father." For all the heavy gilding of the nutshell, the kernel within bore some truth. They were a harmonious family. They were also a group of baseball players with varied backgrounds, educations, ambitions, and temperaments. Some, like Eddie Collins and Herb Pennock, became close, lifelong friends. Some hunted together every fall. Others, together out of necessity for seven months of the year, went their separate ways for the winter. They were teammates but not brothers.

On November 19 Mack spoke to more than a thousand members of the Holy Name Society of St. Edward's Church, after movies of the World Series highlights were shown. A week later he was in Harrisburg, where the Athletics filed reincorporation papers, reflecting the change in ownership. The new corporation consisted of fifty shares, twenty each held by Ben Shibe and Mack, the rest by their sons. That evening Mack spoke at a Board of Trade dinner. From there he went to New York for the Army-Navy football game and was listed among the notables, who included President Woodrow Wilson, occupying box seats at the Polo Grounds as Army won, 22–9.

Joe Bush and Wally Schang considered a vaudeville offer, but the manager of Keith's Theater, Harry D. Jordan, talked them out of it. They were too young, he said, and there were too many "temptations. Forget about vaudeville," Jordan told them. "Go home and spend the offseason quietly and report in the spring in the best of condition."

They did, but they went home driving new "evil automobiles."

45 | ANOTHER BASEBALL WAR

Success breeds competition. Investors are attracted to profitable industries. A July 1912 *McClure's* article described the New York Giants' profits as ranging between $100,000 and $300,000 a year. Frank Chance reportedly bought a 10 percent stake in the Chicago Cubs with an IOU for $10,000 and received a $9,950 dividend the first year. Magnificent new baseball palaces indicated a level of prosperity that whetted the appetites of capitalists. Unlike steel or railroads, it was a simple game to get into with a low-cost entry level. Build or renovate playing grounds, hire some players—who were plentiful—and open for business.

Promoters of new independent leagues with great expectations and ambitions had taken harmless air-gun shots at organized baseball in the past few years. In 1912 two were launched, the United States League in the east and the Columbian in the Midwest. The former lasted a month. The latter never played a game. In 1913 the United States League tried again. This time it lasted two days. But the new Federal League, with six clubs in the Midwest signing only free agents, made it through the season.

The Federal organizers had higher aims and deeper pockets than the others. History taught them that Ban Johnson had fought a war against the National League monopoly on nerve, a shoestring, and a lot of legal talent—and he had won. The Feds owners had plenty of money. Their ranks included lawyers, hotel owners, and magnates of the coal, ice, real estate, baking, and restaurant businesses. Eventually twelve millionaires with resources of $50 million became involved. They were undaunted by the prospect of fielding a third team in cities like Chicago and St. Louis or competing against strong minor league teams. They were prepared to lose money for a few years, confident they could outlast the enemy.

When in August 1913 the Federal League owners declared their major league intentions, Ban Johnson and Garry Herrmann brushed them off like a swarm of gnats. Herrmann said the major leagues would do nothing to stop them from operating an independent league as long as they honored the National Commission's reserve clause binding major league players.

But the Federal League, like the American League a dozen years earlier, dared to challenge the shaky legal standing of the reserve clause. Nap Lajoie was still around as a reminder to younger players that they could—if they dared—ignore the reserve clause and sell their services to the highest bidder.

Charles Somers was one of the few who took the Feds seriously from the start. True, they were going up against two prosperous, united big leagues instead of the fractious, bumbling National League that Ban Johnson had defeated. Still, he warned, "We'd better give them real consideration right now, before this matter goes to a point where we'll be forced into some ugly position."

The Federal League preferred a peaceful accommodation. It offered to purchase surplus players from major league clubs to fill its rosters. Not surprisingly, it was turned down. It then announced that it would honor all player contracts already signed for 1914 but not the reserve clause. Anyone unsigned for 1914 was fair game. The Feds would use the same weapons that Johnson's forces had used: money—horse-choking rolls of it—and denunciations of the reserve and ten-day release clauses in language that could have come straight from the legal briefs filed by the American League thirteen years earlier.

As far back as 1910 the National Commission had anticipated legal attacks on its contracts. It had removed the reserve clause and replaced it with a general provision that players "must abide by the rules of the National Commission." One of those rules, of course, bound them by the reserve list of their team as compiled by the commission. By 1912 the contracts specified that 25 percent of a player's salary was considered payment for the privilege of reserving his services for the following season. That, said a friendly judge, would make it stand up in any court. Still uncertain, the lawyers tweaked the language again, changing the "reserve" to an "option" and stipulating a specific dollar amount for the right to exercise that option.

To paraphrase a future New York governor, Al Smith, no matter how they sliced it, it was still baloney. Despite occasional favorable court decisions, organized baseball's contracts remained as indefensible as they had been in 1901. At least the National League was consistent; it never changed legal sides. The American League had abandoned its original righteousness for expediency.

When conciliation talks failed, the first shot was fired on November 2, 1913. George Stovall, ousted as manager of the Browns in September but reserved as a player, signed a three-year contract to manage the Kansas City Packers.

The Brooklyn Dodgers bought Joe Tinker from Cincinnati for $25,000. Tinker was supposed to get $10,000 of it. The Reds' directors didn't want to give it to him. Charles Murphy butted in and said he'd buy Tinker for Chicago and give him the money. Ebbets demanded the Brooklyn deal be honored. Tinker may have been unhappy with the $7,500 salary Ebbets was willing to pay. While everybody was squabbling over him, Tinker slipped away and signed to manage the Chicago Chifeds for $12,000 a year and stock in the club. His teammate, Three Finger Brown, soon followed him.

While all this was going on, two All-Star teams, led by Charles Comiskey and John McGraw, were on a round-the-world tour. Tinker, now the chief recruiter for the Federal League, fired off telegrams to the traveling stars, urging them to hold off signing 1914 contracts until they heard what the Feds were offering. Prospects of double and triple salaries buzzed among the tourists. Tris Speaker displayed a cablegram promising him $20,000 a year. When the troupe arrived in New York harbor aboard the *Lusitania* on a snowy day in March, it was met by agents from both sides trying to out-maneuver each other amid a horde of reporters.

There were other sources of agitation in the fall of 1913. Dave Fultz, Mack's original center fielder in 1901, now a lawyer, had organized the Base Ball Players' Fraternity. In the light of a new threat to the established leagues, Fultz saw an opportunity to improve the players' lot. He presented a list of seventeen demands to the National Commission. Among them: teams to provide players with two free uniforms (the American League already did; the National charged $30 for two, with no refunds if a player was traded and had to buy new ones); travel costs to spring training; copies of contracts to be provided to players (copies were given if asked for, but 90 percent of the players preferred not to antagonize their employers by asking); free agency after ten years' service; written notice of release; and plain green, advertising-free backgrounds on center-field fences.

Most of the demands were rejected. The most important to be granted were free agency, transportation to spring training (some clubs already provided that), written notice of release, and improved hitters' backgrounds. None of these affected the Athletics. Shibe Park had no outfield signs. Mack already allowed his ten-year veterans the freedom to go elsewhere if they wanted to.

Ira Thomas was the A's player rep to the fraternity. Thomas was given to making public statements that were inimical to the militancy of his union brothers. He declared that the Athletics would subscribe to no demands that might make it look like they had any grievances against Connie Mack. "Mr. Mack is more than fair with us and we look upon him not as a manager but more as a father. Connie does not hold his players by signed contracts. He holds them because he is eminently fair and gives us practically all we ask for. He does not stick to hard and fast rules."

The A's were the only team that did not sign the list of demands. Fultz brushed that off as due to their "preoccupation" with the World Series. But the Giants were not too preoccupied to sign it. Fultz went out of his way to paper over any cracks in the fraternity's unanimity, thereby lending credence to the claim of contentment among Mack's players.

"Mr. Mack has already expressed himself in favor of many of our requests," Fultz said, "and I am quite sure he doesn't look upon the petition as antagonistic to him in any sense. It is therefore quite apparent that his players could have no cause to do so."

Fultz's tune soon changed. He decided that Thomas was too much of a company man and that "Mr. Mack is against us and will beat us if he can." He accused Thomas of being a spy planted by Mack and Ban Johnson to thwart the aims of the fraternity. A year later Fultz kicked Thomas off the board of directors for trying to lure the American League players into a separate, more docile association. Thomas admitted that he favored a separate organization for each league.

The hard feelings against the Athletics spilled over into the 1914 season. The Washington players complained to Fultz that the scoreboard in Shibe Park interfered with hitters' vision, especially against lefty pitchers. They also protested against the unsanitary conditions in the visitors' clubhouse at Shibe Park. Fultz demanded the scoreboard be moved.

Connie Mack said no. The scoreboard was embedded in a concrete foundation. A large chunk of the outfield would have to be torn up to remove it. Besides, nobody else in the league complained about it. As for the dressing rooms, Shibe Park had the most modern accommodations for players and umpires in the league.

It was all just harassment, and Mack didn't budge.

Carrying satchels full of cash, Federal League president James Gilmore and Joe Tinker set up shop in Chicago in December. Armed with players' winter addresses from Dave Fultz's files, they invited players to come to Chicago at the Federal League's expense and sign up. Even if they didn't sign, their expenses would be paid. National and American club owners camped out at another hotel. Many a player picked up train fare from the Feds, said he wanted to think it over, went around to his old club's camp, signed a contract, and collected the train fare again.

The Feds faced some of the same obstacles the upstart American League had overcome. The threat of a blacklisting by organized baseball deterred some players from jumping. The possibility that the Federal might go the way of the short-lived Players' League haunted those who knew a little history. A bonus in hand was spendable, but promises of three years' salary might become worthless if the league folded.

Connie Mack found himself embroiled in his third baseball war. He had been an enthusiastic supporter of the players' rebellion of 1890. In 1901 he was Ban Johnson's chief lieutenant, flying the banner of "Down with the Un-American Reserve Clause" in the front lines, raiding National teams, and inflating salaries by placing bushels of green before the likes of Larry Lajoie and Cy Young.

Now he was on the other side. There was room for two major leagues, but he believed there was no room for three. He had gone down in the Red Sea of ink that had threatened to drown everybody in 1890 and had helped inflict multimillion dollar losses on the National League in 1901 and 1902. He knew the financial reefs that lay ahead could wreck his business. Everything he owned and owed was tied up in the Athletics. Mack knew their 1913 profits—$50,000 or more, depending on your source—could be wiped out in the first year of combat.

Connie Mack didn't scramble to lock up all his stars with multiyear contracts before the 1913 season ended. He had confidence in the loyalty and satisfaction of his boys—up to a point. That didn't mean he could afford to be complacent. Even without the Federal League, Mack knew his payroll would be higher in 1914. Winning players expected raises. Mack once told a cousin, Art Dempsey, "The best thing for a team financially is to be in the running and finish second. If you win, the players all expect raises." This is often taken as evidence that Connie Mack liked money more than winning and would rather not win a pennant to avoid paying higher salaries. That's nonsense. His entire life was devoted to building championship teams. He was stating, not a preference, but an elementary fact of economic life, something every club owner knew and every winning club experienced.

Mack decided to secure some of his players and protect himself against further salary inflation by signing them for two or three years. On January 6, 1914, he traveled 125 miles to Frank Baker's home in Trappe, Maryland. Baker was an arrow-straight, bluff, honest farmer who could hit a baseball. He knew what he was worth, wanted every penny of it but no more, and didn't think he should have to ask for it.

Mack asked him to sign a three-year contract. Baker said no. He told Mack not to worry about him; he wasn't going to jump to the Federal League. It wasn't about money. He said he would always be willing to work for Mack for less money than he might make anywhere else. He just didn't want to sign for more than one year. He was looking ahead. Conditions might change, he told Mack. And if he had a bad year, he'd take a pay cut and not complain.

Connie Mack knew only too well how conditions might change. The Feds might have a successful year. Baker might have another sensational year. The entire salary scale might take another giant leap. They were both thinking the same thing.

Mack persevered. Baker, probably tiring of the conversation, finally gave in and signed a three-year contract for $20,000—total. He was not the kind of man who would ask to renegotiate his contract if conditions did change in his favor. But, he made clear, he reserved the right to quit baseball at the end of the 1914 season, contract or no contract.

Mack readily agreed. He didn't take that threat seriously. With his salary, World Series share, and fees for his ghosted articles, Baker had earned $10,000 last year—far more, Mrs. Baker reminded her husband, than he could make farming. Besides, Baker talked about quitting every year. It had become a running joke among baseball people. A March 1914 *Sporting Life* feature, "Some Standard Headlines," included: "J. Franklin Baker Says This Is His Last Year in Baseball."

In August 1913 the Feds had made a big deal out of announcing that they would not approach any players with the White Sox or Athletics, supposedly because Comiskey and Mack had been major factors in defeating the National League in 1901. That charade was soon exposed. In December it pursued Eddie Collins, who turned down $45,000 for three years, the money to be deposited up front in a bank account from which he could draw $1,250 a month. With interest it would total $50,000. Collins said he would not desert Connie Mack, to whom he owed everything he had become in baseball.

At the same time, the players welcomed the new league. Call it greed or opportunism or simply the free market at work; it was a chance to cash in on a situation that probably wouldn't last long. Either peace would come, bringing with it tumbling salaries, as it had in 1903, or the Federal would go under and salaries would drop. For the moment, the players had the upper hand, playing their employers against the Federal's agents. The law of supply and demand prevailed. Inflation was a by-product of all wars. Some players took advances to jump, then jumped back. Clark Griffith hadn't helped his chances of keeping Walter Johnson when he said in July that Johnson was worth twice as much as Ty Cobb. Johnson was finishing a three-year contract at $7,000 a year. Cobb's salary was believed to be $12,000. Now a nervous Griffith had to go to $10,000 plus a $2,000 bonus for 1914. Mack signed Eddie Collins for three years at $8,333 a year.

Other players were rewarded with multiyear contracts at substantial raises. The Feds also raided the higher minor leagues, forcing major league clubs to come up with $2 million in subsidies to keep them afloat.

For the Mackmen, the war evoked conflicting emotions. Publicly they pledged their loyalty to Connie Mack, whom they genuinely respected. "There is only one reason the Athletics don't jump to the Feds," Eddie Collins told a banquet audience, "Connie Mack." They had won it all in 1913 and were likely to win again in 1914. They were treated with respect and considered themselves fairly paid. More than once Baker and Collins maintained publicly that they would take less money in order to play for Connie Mack, which seemed to hand Mack an advantage at contract time. It also indicates that they didn't think of themselves as victims of tight-fisted, petty cost-cutting and ill treatment at the hands of Connie Mack and the Shibes.

That didn't stop Collins from openly rooting for the Federal League to succeed. "Personally, I would like to see the undertaking a success," he wrote in a February 10 column, "as I think it would aid the player in the long run. Whatever happens, the player has everything to gain and nothing to lose." The advance money the Federal was handing out was real. Collins discounted the threats of lifetime bans on jumpers.

The Connie Mack of 1890 would have said, "Hear, hear!" But not now. Nor could he have been pleased when he read the rest of Collins's views:

"In spite of their denial, you cannot make me believe that the managers and club owners of organized baseball clubs have not been worried. It is not to be wondered at that their attitude should be one of apparent disdain and indifference, but in more cases than a few their actions have been quite the contrary. If they were not afraid of inroads being made on their club rosters, why were they so particular to see that emissaries from their own clubs or they themselves saw their players in person, and had them affix their signatures to 1914 contracts, rather than entrust the same to the mails?"

Collins didn't hesitate to give the Federal League's owners some free advice and point out where they were going wrong. They were going into too many minor league cities instead of big markets like Cincinnati and New York. They were spread out from Brooklyn to Kansas City, and their travel expenses would be too high. He wished to see them succeed for the sake of the players, but he had his doubts. "I cannot see how the new league can possibly live financially," he wrote. "The jumps are too long, the cities are not the most desirable ones, and the major league players refuse to desert their present clubs in sufficient numbers to give the new league first class ball."

To Connie Mack, that might have sounded like giving counsel to the enemy. But Collins was a prolific commentator on many subjects, not just baseball. He said what he thought, whatever the consequences. And to him and the rest of the players, the Federal League was no enemy.

To the public, Connie Mack seemed unaffected by it all. On January 26 the *Cleveland News* ran a cartoon of a smiling Mack, headed: "Connie Mack Is the Most Contented Man in Baseball These Warlike Days."

Mack may have been contented that "there isn't a chance for any member of a championship outfit to desert to the outlaws." He had practically every one of his boys signed for 1914. In February Jack Coombs's signed contract arrived in the mail. Coombs had finally shed his back brace, but it would be midseason at least before he could throw a pitch.

Two of the Athletics did go with the Federal League that winter. Utility infielder Harry Fritz, hitless in his 13 at bats in 1913, signed with Chicago. And Danny Murphy jumped—or was pushed.

Connie Mack had the most extensive coaching staff of any club. The Christmas cards Eugene Mack sent out with best wishes from the White Elephant Café featured photos of Connie Mack, Harry Davis, and Danny Murphy. Davis, Murphy, and Ira Thomas were the equivalent of pitching, catching, infield, and bench coaches. Chief Bender also worked with the young pitchers. Mack might have thought he had more coaches than he needed. He might have marked Murphy's judgment down a notch after Danny had left Carroll Brown in to pitch that 18-inning game against the Phillies on a raw day in April. Billy Weart speculated that Mack had soured on Murphy for begging off pinch hitting for Plank in the second game of the World Series. Danny was still popular with the players and fans. And Mack liked him, later naming him the A's all-time best right fielder. But both he and Mack knew that his playing days were over.

Whenever Connie Mack was ready to release a veteran player, he tried to line up another baseball job for him first. He had done that for Lave and Monte Cross, Topsy Hartsel, and Socks Seybold. He thought he would do the same for Danny Murphy. In December Mack asked waivers on him. The Browns were interested but were leery of Danny's arm and knee problems. Mack told Danny if the Browns claimed him, the waiver money would be turned over to him. He also told Murphy that he had found a place for him in Baltimore. The Athletics would supplement his Orioles salary, giving him the same $3,000 he had earned in 1913. Murphy said he'd rather go to Baltimore than St. Louis, but he was negotiating the sale of his White Elephant Café in Norwich and preferred nothing be said about it until the sale was completed. So Mack asked the Philadelphia writers to sit on the story.

When Murphy signed with the Brookfeds (also known as the Tip Tops) instead, Mack expressed surprise and disbelief. He wired Murphy asking if it was true. Murphy replied, "Yes." Mack displayed no hard feelings, not even when Murphy publicly accused him of "railroading" him out of the major leagues. Justified or not, Mack did not believe that Murphy had been square with him. He showed reporters all the correspondence between him and Murphy to back up his version of the incident.

Later, through the refracting filters of memory, Mack said he encouraged Murphy to accept a generous offer from the Federal League, which was looking for players with name recognition to sprinkle among its minor leaguers and semipros. It wound up with 59 players with major league experience, but no stars in their prime, for 1914.

The entrenched major leagues were aided by the newspapers, which referred to the Federal League as an "Outlaw League," although the businessmen behind the venture were at least as respectable as those who sought to preserve their monopoly. A third major league would just ruin everything for everybody, warned the sporting press. Some didn't even carry the league's box scores or credit the players' stats as major league caliber. But it wasn't unanimous. Some writers voiced the same kind of support for the Feds that the American League champions of free labor had enjoyed in 1901.

"It's a mystery to me," Irving Sanborn wrote in *Everybody's Magazine*, "why any man who can win pennants or hit .425 or win 25 games is not free to manage or bat or pitch where he pleases."

Like some cosmic cycle, it seemed that every twelve years baseball writers were forced to become war, courthouse, and financial correspondents. Players with whom the writers traveled, roomed, even worked out on the field, suddenly became greedy, disloyal, contract-jumping scoundrels. Player grievances and contract numbers drew more attention than batting averages. And as always, everybody involved was denounced for ignoring the fans' best interests.

The Bill Killefer case, the test case that everyone believed would be decisive, was finally heard on April 4. Phillies catcher Bill Killefer had signed with the Federal League on January 8, then jumped back to the Phillies, signing on January 20 at double his 1913 salary of $3,200. The Feds sought an injunction in federal court in Grand Rapids to stop him from playing for Philadelphia. The baseball world awaited the decision. When it came, it muddied instead of clarifying the picture. The judge ruled against the Federal because it did not come into court with clean hands. The way it had obtained the contract with Killefer was not equitable. The judge also held that any form of reserve clause, by whatever name, and the ten-day release clause were invalid.

Nobody was sure what the decision meant, so both sides declared it a victory.

The judge's rejection of the release clause sent every club scurrying to get new contracts signed with the clause deleted. According to Frank Baker, some of the Athletics, including Collins and McInnis, held up Connie Mack for more money before they'd agree to sign the new contracts. "I knew the trouble he was having with some of the players," Baker said, "and I felt sorry for him." When Baker's turn came, he told Mack to do whatever he wanted in rewriting the contract. He wasn't going to make any demands. That wasn't Frank Baker's way. Jack Barry gave Mack no trouble either. The dropping of the clause didn't mean much for the top players, who weren't likely to be released anyhow. For other, more marginal players with three-year contracts, it meant the clubs would have a harder time getting rid of them.

The legal picture never developed clearly. In June a Cook County, Illinois, judge said he saw nothing wrong with the old contracts. An appeals court reversed him, clearing the way for a Cincinnati jumper, Chief Johnson, to pitch for the Kansas City Packers.

Connie Mack wished all this nonbaseball nonsense were behind him. He looked forward to the new season with well-founded confidence. His perfect baseball machine had won three world championships in four years. His standing in his adopted city had never been higher. He was a member of the executive council of the Boy Scouts and the board of directors of the Tioga Trust Company. He owned an interest in the Athletic Building and Loan Association, Ira Thomas, president.

The Federal League's raiders had approached many of his players with little success. Only Eddie Plank remained on the fence. Another perennial retiree, Plank rejected the same $5,000 he had earned in 1913. He was flirting with the Feds, but all he said was maybe he'd just rather stay on the farm. For the rest, World Series payoffs with the Athletics were more certain than the life expectancy of the "Outlaws."

Publicly Connie Mack didn't claim the 1914 pennant was in the bag. He praised every other team and hedged only because of "the uncertainty of baseball. . . . There might be new conditions next season to trip over even as great a team as the Athletics. Could be another Walter Johnson at Washington, another Cobb." At the same time, Mack called his A's "my ideal team, the combination I have tried for years to form. It is entitled to the greatest respect from the fans. I haven't quit on the kings of the diamond. I am only trying to hint at the uncertainties."

Most sportswriters were ready to hand the A's the flag, though *Baseball Magazine* in January sounded a tocsin: "Writers seem to forget Connie Mack does not have the pitchers he had two years ago. . . . Plank is not the man he was two years ago. He pitched wonderful ball in the World Series. Bender did too, but these two can not pull them for next season."

Despite that qualification, Connie Mack was right; the Athletics were a great team. Once they got started they were capable of winning with ease on the field, even with unease off it.

46 | THE ATHLETICS WIN ANOTHER PENNANT— HO HUM

Before heading south in the spring of 1914, Connie Mack filed his first income tax return. The new tax, authorized by ratification of the Sixteenth Amendment in 1913, began at 1 percent of income over $3,000 ($4,000 for married couples). The 1040 form consisted of three pages and was due on March 15, 1914. Only 357,598 people earned enough to file a return that year. They included all the Athletics, whose $3,200 World Series share put them over the minimum. The March 15 deadline was inconvenient for ballplayers, coming as it did in the middle of spring training. When the team returned to Philadelphia in April, six of the players faced penalties for not sending in the forms on time. Baker, Barry, Lapp, Shawkey, Oldring, and Eddie Murphy hustled to the IRS office in the Federal Building, where they pleaded for leniency.

A year later many people were still not habituated to what would become the annual tax-time ordeal. Nor was the three-page form 1040, simple as it was, fathomable to the public. On March 2, 1915, Connie Mack, in his role of shepherd and adviser to his players, typed the following letter, as reproduced here, to his attorney, Ormond Rambo:

> Dear Sir:
>
> Am enclosing you herewith blank "Income return" which I wish you would fill out in lead pencil as a form for me to follow in making the returns for the Players who have neglected to do so. I am a little mixed on just where to put the amounts. The reason that I am troubling you with this. The only source of income these Players have are from the salary paid them by our Club and their share of "The World Series Money." What will these Players say in the Income Tax Return to the

Government showing that tax has been deducted at the source, where it has been necessary for our Club to deduct?

Will take for example Edward Murphy, who received a salary of $3,000. From our club and on which we deducted the sum of $30. Wish you would fill out his return as a form, also including his share of "World Series Money" amounting to $2,200.

Thanking you for an early reply
in this matter, I remain,
Sincerely, yours,
/s/ Connie Mack

It was snowing all the way up the east coast on February 24, 1914, when the Athletics went to New York to board a steamship bound for Charleston, South Carolina. From there it was a short train ride to Jacksonville. Connie Mack and a few friends took a train directly to Jacksonville. Mrs. Mack remained at home awaiting the birth of their third child. At the last minute Eddie Plank, still unsigned, showed up at the station and joined them. On the train, Plank told Mack he had received offers from the Federal League and was waiting to see what other players did. If any of the Athletics jumped, he would go too. When it appeared that none of them was going anywhere, he decided to stay put.

This was small comfort to Connie Mack. He was shocked at how willingly one of his longtime stalwarts had turned "a receptive ear to the blandishments of the Federal League sirens." He sniffed the poison of discontent in the air. There was no place on the Athletics for a discontented player. And he didn't want to go through this with Plank again next year. Win or lose, Feds or no Feds, Mack decided then and there that this was Eddie Plank's last year with the Athletics.

Mack knew his boys would be subjected to more overtures as the season went on. There would be divisive talk about big paydays, loyalty, opportunity, who would go and who would stay. It would distract them from the job at hand—the day's game. For the first time since he had come to Philadelphia, there was a sourness to the taste of a new and promising season.

After a few days in Jacksonville, Plank still hadn't signed. Mack, peeved at Eddie's stalling as if he was still waiting for someone to join him in jumping, told him to accept the $5,000 contract on the table or go home. Plank signed.

The Jacksonville facilities were top-notch: sodded field, hot and cold water in the clubhouse. Trolley service between the field and the hotel was unreliable, but Emory Titman and his chauffeur provided limousine service for them. Frank Baker and Jack Barry reported late. Barry had been hit in the mouth by a foul tip while working out with the Holy Cross team. Baker's wife had given birth to twin girls, who died a week later. The only training camp injury occurred when a wild pitch bounced up and splattered Mack's nose as he sat on the bench.

The rookie crop did not impress the manager. He was still looking for a dependable utility infielder and didn't see what he needed among the Yannigans. And he was perturbed by what he took to be indifference to hard work on the part of two of his young pitchers, Herb Pennock and Carroll Brown.

Brown had won 17 games in 1913 but ended the season with a sore arm, which he blamed on the 18-inning city series game in April. He was still hurting but didn't say anything about it. In fact, his arm was dead. He won only 1 and lost 6 before Mack sold him to the Yankees.

Herb Pennock was smart and talented. He and Eddie Collins had taken to each other immediately, a friendship that would last all their lives and make them literally family when Eddie Collins Jr. married Herb Pennock's daughter. But Pennock seemed to Mack to lack the drive to succeed. Grace can be mistaken for nonchalance. Larry Lajoie's critics had been guilty of that misjudgment. Mack watched and waited.

Chief Bender took Bob Shawkey in hand and taught him how to throw an assortment of curves and changeups. "I was throwing too much with my arm," Shawkey said, "and Bender showed me how to get my body into it more, and how to be better balanced on my follow-through so I could field a bunt."

Mack assigned Bender to room with the young left-hander, Rube Bressler. He was not concerned with the veteran leading the rookie astray. If Albert fell "out of condition," he wouldn't take the youngster with him. He was a teacher who could pass on some wisdom, as Bressler related (with a few errant details) in *The Glory of Their Times*:

You never could tell whether Bender won or lost. One day in Washington Walter Johnson beat me, 1–0, and as Bender and I went up to the room that evening I said, "Gee, that was a tough one to lose."

"Are you talking about today's game?" Bender asked me.

"Of course," I said.

"Did you hear the boys yelling when we came into the hotel?"

"What boys?"

"The newsboys," he said.

"Oh, I guess so."

"What were they saying?"

"They were saying Washington wins, 1–0," I said.

"That's right," he said. "It's a matter of record now. Forget about that game. Win the next one." That's all he said.

On Thursday, March 19, Katherine Mack gave birth to a baby girl they named Ruth. The next day Mack's daughter, Peggy, was stricken with appendicitis and operated on at Jewish Hospital. Mack got on a train and went home to be with them.

The Athletics arrived in Wilmington, Delaware, on March 25 for a game against the Baltimore Orioles. Mack may have stopped there before heading down to Raleigh to rejoin his colts. Jack Dunn started his new young pitcher, Babe Ruth, against the A's, but not, as is sometimes said, to showcase him for Mack. Dunn didn't sign Ruth with the intention of selling him right away. He had a powerful team favored to win the International League pennant and was never in a hurry to dispose of promising young players. Ruth gave up 13 hits that afternoon, 4 of them to Baker, but he won, 6–2. Three days later Dunn, eager to show off his ballyhooed prospect in his home town, started Ruth against the A's in Baltimore. The crowd of five thousand could hear the hammers being wielded as the new Federal League ballpark went up across the street, a sound that would echo like an auctioneer's gavel before the season was half over. Ruth didn't fare as well this time: 4 runs in 4 innings of a 12–5 loss.

Connie Mack joined the Yannigans in Raleigh, where his son Earle was coaching the University of North Carolina (UNC) team before the Carolina League season started. About this time, a bizarre item about Earle Mack appeared in the UNC "Alumni Review": "His father, Connie Mack, wishes his son to stop baseball and study violin in Europe. There were perhaps few more appreciative musicians in the audience that heard Kubelik than Carolina's baseball coach." The reference is apparently to a concert given by violinist Rafael Kubelik. The *St. Louis Post-Dispatch* picked up the story with a March 18 dateline out of Raleigh and embroidered it a bit: "The elder baseball man believes baseball will ruin the fingers that will make another Kubelik. Earle Mack will study here, however."

UNC library assistant Jill Sahl could find no other mention of Earle Mack, who was an amateur violinist. Earle continued to study baseball in Raleigh that summer.

In the future, whenever Connie Mack spoke of the fissures dividing the 1914 Athletics, the Federal League was always cited as the underlying fault-line. It was one, but not the only, factor.

In 1912 Gordon Mackay of the *Ledger* had written that the Athletics' infield would be good for six or seven years "unless somebody threw a bomb into the clubhouse and blew them all into small scattered pieces."

Connie Mack unwittingly threw the first bomb himself.

With the departure of Danny Murphy, he had to appoint a new captain. To the surprise of the players, Mack appointed Ira Thomas to replace Murphy. This didn't set well. Nobody was as popular as Mike the Murph, but Ira Thomas was just plain disliked. Seventy-three years later, outfielder Shag Thompson singled out Thomas as the only member of the team he didn't like. He called Thomas "standoffish."

The players preferred an active player, though Murphy had seen little action except as a pinch hitter in his last year. Mack himself was on the record as saying, "On the field any necessary help should come from the team captain." So it seemed incongruous for him to pick a man who was not expected to play regularly. By now Ira Thomas had become Mack's bench/pitching/first base coach, chief scout, family friend, and banquet circuit sidekick. Some baseball people thought he talked too much, was too full of himself, his knowledge of the game somewhat less than he presented. But Thomas had his boosters as well. The *North American* lauded him as deserving much credit for the team's success. "Recognizing Thomas's grasp of baseball and generalship, Connie Mack allows him to outline plans and take initiative. Thomas has charge of the pitchers. While less has been written about Thomas than any other man on the team, it is not justified by the facts."

Many of the players, probably including Eddie Collins, considered the second baseman the ideal captain. Ty Cobb and John McGraw called Collins the smartest player in baseball. Jack Coombs said of him, "Most of the success of the Athletics pitching staff was due to the ability of Collins to ferret out the weakness of opposing batsmen, and retain this information. . . . The Philadelphia club had a pitching staff that was rated as fairly smart but we would nearly always turn to Collins in a crisis."

Nor was Collins the quiet type. Just the opposite; nobody made more noise in the infield, a constant patter of encouragement emanating from him throughout the game.

But Collins was not everybody's favorite teammate. In 1910 he had written about the A's sign-stealing methods and the foibles of opposing players that they noticed and used to win pennants. Some of the players, including Thomas, let him know they thought he was out of line spilling their secrets in public. Connie Mack had to step in and ask him to refrain from writing about it.

Connie Mack knew all that. He also had reason to be wary of Collins's allegiance. Both Collins and Barry made no bones about their confidence that the Federal League would survive and become as permanent as the American. Mack may have been uncertain whether his star's outspoken rooting for the Federal League's success might lead to itchy feet. He didn't need a captain who could turn into a Pied Piper.

He knew he could trust Ira Thomas.

If Mack didn't want to limit his choice to an active player, he had an alternative. His men would have been happy with Harry Davis as their captain. Davis was universally respected. And Mack could have no reason to question his former captain's loyalty.

How did Davis react to the naming of Thomas? With silence, as anyone who knew him would expect. Yet a clue to his feelings may be found in a column written after the season by N. B. Beasley in the *Detroit Journal*:

Like many other championship teams, internal troubles form the foundation of managerial worries. Perhaps the dissension started when Mack appointed Ira Thomas as captain. He was not popular among the A's or other players. During the series with the Braves the story came out that after the first game Davis was asked if he had any idea of Mack's plans for the following contest. He answered, "I can't tell because I know nothing of Connie's arrangements. Remember this, I am not Connie Mack's lieutenant, as some person has so styled me. I am only the third base coach. Thomas is his lieutenant." There wasn't any bitterness in Harry's voice but he made the situation so plain it was evidently a distasteful subject.

Thomas's appointment struck Mack's harmonious chorus like a soprano hitting a flat high C. The club split into two factions, pro- and anti-Thomas.

One Philadelphia paper described the dissidents as "most of those stars who have made Mack and his team famous in baseball history during the past five years. And those veterans were also supported by several of the youngsters. In favor of Thomas were but three or four of the old-timers and most of the youngsters."

Since 1909 the Athletics had carried a reputation throughout baseball for a lack of jealousy and friction. No more. There were reports that the veterans were urging the youngsters to ignore Ira Thomas's orders. Some players continued to go to Davis for advice, which put him in an awkward position as seeming to override or usurp Thomas's authority.

The A's got off to a slow start—7-6 with 2 ties. On May 5 the Tigers were 13-5 and in the National League the Pirates were 13-2, when Mack pecked out a letter to a friend, S. B. Huston, in Portland, Oregon: "The team at the present time are very much out of condition. Have not played any ball that is worthwhile up to this time. Looks right now as though the Tigers and the Pirates might be doing the world series act this fall."

Then they started winning; they were good enough to win in their sleep—and that's what they looked like to Mack: a bunch of sleepwalkers. But they weren't running away from anybody. They were 21-13 through the end of May but only about 6 games ahead of the seventh-place White Sox. The young pitchers were wild and unimpressive. Byron Houck couldn't locate home plate. Mack sent him to Baltimore, but he couldn't find that either and wound up in Brooklyn with the Tip Tops. Injuries began early. Bob Shawkey dislocated a thumb in batting practice. Jack Barry was cut up in a spiking at second base—not by Ty Cobb. Rube Oldring pulled a muscle. Amos Strunk had a heavy cold. Bender went almost four weeks without starting a game.

Aggravating the sore spots was the constant appearance of agents of the Federal League, Danny Murphy among them. Their main targets were said to be the entire infield, plus Bender and Plank. But the whole team was fair game. Clubhouse chatter dealt more with bankrolls than base hits. Rumors of salaries two and three times what the A's were earning floated like sea nettles. Some players were ready to jump after the season. Others ignored the talk, out of either loyalty to Connie Mack or fear of repercussions if the Feds folded.

Ira Thomas asked Mack to call a meeting to address the situation. Mack bided his time and did nothing.

The A's were in Chicago in the middle of June. Walter Ward, son of the

Brooklyn Tip Tops' president, took Eddie Collins out to dinner. Collins returned to the hotel noticeably later than usual. When reporters asked him where he had been, he readily admitted that he had been listening to a "tremendous offer" for 1915 and beyond. He wouldn't specify the terms but hinted that it was not less than the $25,000 a year and $25,000 bonus that the Brooklyns were reported to have offered Walter Johnson.

He was bluffing. He later admitted the offer was under $60,000 for three years and said he never seriously considered jumping anyhow. It was all leverage to pry a big raise out of Connie Mack, who was after him to tear up his contract and sign a long-term one. On July 6 Collins signed a "new form" five-year contract, for $11,500 a year, with no ten-day release clause and a no-trade, no-sale without his permission clause.

The rumors continued into July. There were furtive contacts with Federal agents, huddles of whispering players planning circuitous routes to secret meetings, traversing back alleys to avoid being followed. Mack hated to see his team turning fractious, breaking up into cliques—those who were listening to the siren songs of the "theatrical" salaries and those who weren't or hadn't been serenaded. He watched the life being sucked out of his prized creation. They were not playing well, and it was obvious they were not having fun. Nor was he.

Joe Vila reported in the *New York Sun* that Mack had gone as far as he would go with his stars. "Mack is prepared to supplant his famous stars with young players if necessary. 'I'm not going to give up Shibe Park to save part or all of the $100,000 infield,' Mack is said to have told a friend recently."

It was a roundabout, third-hand source for a quote, but the sentiments it expressed were accurate. Connie Mack was sore as a boil under his high starched collar. His language was stronger than his usual "dern it." He was angry at the players he felt were holding him up and were ungrateful for the World Series checks that lined their pockets thanks to the machine he had built. The efforts to undermine his captain didn't escape him either. He had seen other championship teams begin to crack when the players thought they knew more about managing than the manager. Mack had no stomach for managing a bunch of stars who were not "for the team" the whole way. To him, it wasn't like watching *a* family being torn apart by feuds and grudges and fractured loyalty. It was *his* family breaking up.

His bitterness eventually melted. He later acknowledged that his players had done the same thing that National Leaguers had done when he was an enemy agent inducing the Lajoies and Flicks and Cy Youngs and dozens of others to desert to the new American League. He no longer blamed the players for using the competition as leverage to get what they could out of it. Some of those 1914 A's returned as coaches for him. All remained his friends and admirers. In fact, it may have been some consolation to him that so few of his boys ultimately did jump.

But he didn't feel that way at the time. He and his boys were supposed to be concentrating on winning a pennant between April and October. The machine should have been purring along without a hiccup. And it wasn't.

It reminded Mack of 1912, when his two-time world champions had taken their losses lightly until it was too late. Once again his overconfident players believed they were good enough to wake up any time they felt like it and take charge, and they seemed in no hurry to wake up.

"That's not a good thing," Mack told reporters, "with so many clubs striving for the pennant. Competition is becoming keener each year."

Indeed it was. On June 7 the Athletics were third, behind Washington and Detroit, with three other clubs right behind them.

Meanwhile, Connie Mack's friend Jack Dunn was struggling in Baltimore. Not on the field; the Orioles were far out in front of the International League. But major league baseball, however ersatz, was in business across the street in Terrapin Park. To protect his own stars from the Federal League, Dunn had signed them to multiyear contracts. Now he found he couldn't compete at the gate. He wasn't taking in enough money to meet his payroll. Ned Hanlon, the popular manager of the 1890s Orioles, was involved in the operation of the Terrapins and had the local newspapers behind him. The Terrapins drew 5,000 on opening day while the Orioles played an exhibition game against the Giants before 1,500. The Terrapins maintained that 5,000 average. After the Orioles won 12 in a row, only 150 fans showed up to watch them win number 13. One day they played before 26 paying customers.

Dunn had already borrowed money from Connie Mack and new Red Sox owner Joe Lannin, who was helping keep the entire International League afloat. Dunn's only assets were his players. He didn't want to sell them. He tried to move to Richmond, but the Virginia League wanted $45,000 compensation, and the International wouldn't pay it. Then Dunn applied to the National Commission for an exemption from the draft, so he could wait until his young players had put up a record for the season and he could get full value for them. The commission turned him down.

With no alternative in sight, Dunn began his fire sale on July 7. In three days he sold six players and two more a week later. The sales brought in between $50,000 and $75,000. The press and public understood Dunn's predicament. Nobody accused him of lining his pockets from the liquidation sale or caring more about money than winning. It was the only way he could stay in business.

Some critics of Connie Mack have ridiculed him for turning down Babe Ruth, Ernie Shore, and Ben Egan when Dunn offered them to him for, according to some erroneous accounts, "a paltry $8,500." Many reports at the time put the final price tag for the trio at $25,000–$30,000.

Part of Mack's reluctance to be a buyer was the same that prevented other club owners from offering even higher prices for the nineteen-year-old left-hander Ruth and the more experienced twenty-three-year-old Ernie Shore. (The catcher, Ben Egan, had been tried by Mack in 1912 and found wanting.) In the midst of the Federal League raids, most club owners were hesitant to spend a lot of money for players who might jump at the end of the year. Like Mack, many of them had been forced to raise salaries before and during the season, contracts they were bound to honor even if the Feds folded.

There was another factor. The bullet that started the Great War had been fired just ten days earlier, a shot that was truly heard round the world. Already the sounds of sabers rattling were louder than bats hitting baseballs. Dunn's clearance sale came at a time when attendance was slumping almost everywhere and talk of war dominated barroom chatter. Only three American League teams—Boston, Detroit, and New York—would narrowly avoid a drop at the gate. Cleveland attendance was off about 60 percent. In the National League, only Boston and St. Louis were showing gains.

So Connie Mack was not alone in turning down Dunn's deal. It was a buyer's market for baseball flesh, and most teams were not buying. "No magnate in organized ball is letting go of a cent this season unless he actually has to," wrote C. Starr Matthews in the Baltimore Sun. Only a few teams showed any interest. Phillies manager Red Dooin was eager to buy Shore and Baltimore shortstop Claud Derrick for $19,000 with Ruth thrown in, but club owner William Baker told him, "I wouldn't give $19,000 for the whole International League." Charles Comiskey wasn't interested in any of them.

Connie Mack already knew the Athletics would lose money, perhaps a lot of money. It was too early to tell how much. He was still haggling with Collins and Barry at the time and didn't know what his final payroll would come to, only that it would be the highest he'd ever had and the highest in the league. There was no reason for anyone to count on a resurgence of attendance in 1915; further erosion was more likely. The Federal League and the war clouds in Europe showed no signs of going away soon.

Nor did Mack need any immediate help to strengthen his team. He just needed it to wake up. He had plenty of young pitchers who were demonstrating that they could win in the big leagues: Bush, Wyckoff, Shawkey, Pennock, Rube Bressler—all between nineteen and twenty-three. He didn't need another one, not even one who could hit. He had one of those in Bressler, a .290 hitter in Harrisburg in 1913, who went on to bat .301 over nineteen years, and another in Jack Coombs, if big Jawn ever regained his health. Babe Ruth was batting .231 at Baltimore and had yet to hit his first professional home run. Ruth's future was not visible to anyone. Nobody looked at him as a slugger at the time. He was just another green but promising young southpaw.

Mack's preference for college men was well established. He believed that college coaches—some of them current big league players—provided more and better individual instruction than the average minor league manager. That spring he told J. H. Sheridan of the *Post-Dispatch*,

My reasons for favoring the collegians are:
1. His mind is developed. He has been trained to think.
2. The fact that he has got an education is, on its face, evidence that he wants to learn and, above all, that he can be taught. This last quality is of the utmost importance.

The college boy is educated, mannerly, tractable, teachable. He has learned how to learn. It is not what he knows, but what he can be taught that makes him valuable.

This attitude, philosophy, prejudice—call it what you will—didn't prevent Mack from seeing the potential of a Frank Baker or Stuffy McInnis or Rube Waddell. But it had been solidified by his experience with Collins, Barry, Coombs, and Krause. If it caused him to lose some raw prospects who turned out to be stars, he could live with that. The lack of those qualities he looked for had contributed to his letting go of Joe Jackson. Ernie Shore possessed them; Babe Ruth did not.

Coincidentally, another of Mack's collegians, Lloyd Davies, a pitcher-outfielder from Amherst, reported at that time. On July 11 he started for the A's at home against the Browns. Davies was losing, 4–3, in the eighth inning. The A's had 2 men on base with 2 outs when his turn came to bat.

With a pitcher warming up, Mack called for a pinch hitter. Davies, eager to bat, said in a half-whisper, "I wish he had let me go up. I can hit that long string out there." Mack heard the remark. He told Davies to go up and hit. Davies doubled in 2 runs and won his game, 6–4.

To Connie Mack, this twenty-two-year-old left-hander looked at that moment as promising as Babe Ruth. Davies didn't live up to Mack's expectations. He was gone after the 1915 season (he reappeared as a relief pitcher with the 1926 Giants). That's not the point. It's easy to look back now and say, boy, was Connie Mack ever wrong. But sitting on the bench in Shibe Park on that July afternoon, who among the all-knowing hindsighters would have disagreed with Mack?

Jack Dunn found a buyer in Joe Lannin, who, like Tom Yawkey twenty years later, had plenty of money and no experience with losing it in baseball. The Red Sox needed pitching to stay in the pennant race. Lannin, while not announcing the purchase price, said it was more than $25,000. Maybe. Maybe not.

Historians who try to parse the price of each part of the package assign too much of the total to Ruth. Ernie Shore was clearly the top prize of the bunch at the time. He started 17 games the rest of the year for the Red Sox; Ruth started 3. Ben Egan never caught an inning for them.

Dunn's timing was bad, but he was desperate. He "is selling his men dirt cheap," wrote Matthews in the *Sun*. "It really seems shameful when one thinks of the players Dunn has parted with bringing such small sums of money. . . . Dispatches from Boston state that Dunn was paid more than $25,000, but it is extremely doubtful if so much money was involved. For Dunn's sake the writer hopes the report is true, but from the manner in which the magnates of the organized major leagues have been holding onto their money, it is hard to believe."

Take all these things into consideration and it's easier to understand why Connie Mack considered it an unwise business or baseball decision to spend whatever the price was at that moment on those players. Mack's alleged cheapness in not spending the money for what turned out to be the biggest bargain of the century looks different in the context of the time.

So here they were in the middle of the season in a close pennant race that Connie Mack believed his Athletics should be leading by at least 10 games. On July 4, after breaking even in three doubleheaders in three days, they led the Tigers by 1½, the sixth-place Browns by only 5½.

When the Tigers arrived in town on Tuesday, July 7, they trailed by 3 games, with Washington just 3½ back. The grounds were too wet to play that day. The next day Plank gave the A's a little breathing room with a 3-hit shutout. On Thursday Detroit roughed up Shawkey and Wyckoff and took a doubleheader. The lead was down to 2. For the series finale Mack called on his young lefty, Herb Pennock, to hold off the Tigers. And he did—for 7 innings. In the eighth the A's 5–0 lead disappeared in a 6-run debacle of hits and errors. The whole team acted as if it didn't know or didn't care how to play the game. Routine fly balls dropped untouched. Detroit's lead grew to 8–5 in the ninth off Wyckoff. In the last of the ninth, the A's tied it on Harry Davis's 2-run single. Darkness ended the 8–8 tie after 11 innings, a game they should have won.

Connie Mack was not assuaged by his team's ninth-inning rally. It was time to wake up his boys. They were going through the motions the way they had done two years ago. Any of five other teams could take this one away from them too. It was time to remind them that despite all the distractions around them, the business at hand was winning now, today, every day. A World Series payoff depended on it.

The next morning, before a doubleheader against the Browns, Mack delivered his wakeup call. In a 1938 *Saturday Evening Post* article, he recalled saying "something like this" in the meeting:

"Inside this clubhouse are two factions. One is pulling against the other. If you don't stop this tug of war you will never see this World Series, unless you have the price of admission. I know some of you have been hearing and thinking about big money next year. Maybe you care more about dreaming about the big money you may get next year than collecting the thousands you will get in hand this year if you win the pennant and the series."

Whether Mack's pep talk had any more influence than the rooster's crowing has on the sun rising, the record shows that from that day through September 1 the Athletics won 39 and lost 7. At one point the pitchers threw 10 consecutive complete games. Chief Bender went on to win 14 in a row and finish with a 17-3 record. They opened a 13-game lead that ended the pennant race in August, prompting Walter Trumbull to write in the *New York World,*

> The Mackmen inconsiderately
> Have hit upon such a pace
> That they've changed to a procession
> What was scheduled as a race.

Connie Mack believed that baseball should be fun. He took each game seriously but didn't consider a little sideshow to be a mockery or travesty of the game. Even in his eighties he readily went along with Bill Veeck's stunts when they involved the A's. They were coasting along in late August when the Browns came to town. In the first game of a doubleheader on August 25, Rube Bressler led, 7–0, in the eighth inning. In his biography of Branch Rickey, Arthur Mann described the Browns manager scanning his bench in vain for a pinch hitter.

Ira Thomas, who had played with Rickey in New York, hollered across the field, "Why don't you hit, Rick?"

The St. Louis players egged on the old catcher. The relaxed Mack joined in the chorus from the A's dugout. Rickey agreed to bat, providing the young left-hander promised not to throw any curves. Connie Mack signaled Bressler accordingly.

In spite of that condition, Rickey told Mann, "I was sure they'd curve me to death, so I wasn't set for the first pitch, which was a fastball strike one. Well, I thought they did that to build up my complacency. I just knew the next one would bend over. The second fastball went by me for a strike. Now I really got ready for the curve and was utterly amazed to see a third fastball go by for a called strike three. My last turn at bat taught me that nothing is gained by distrusting your fellow man."

It was Branch Rickey's last appearance in a major league game.

On August 1 war was declared in Europe. An exciting pennant race could crowd tariff debates, even presidential elections, off the Philadelphia front pages. Without one, the big black headlines of war dampened the public's enthusiasm for baseball. It's easy to scoff at the notion that the Athletics were so good that people tired of going to games where the outcome was taken for granted. But the numbers, even if slightly inaccurate, cannot be denied. Attendance at home and on the road plummeted, off by 225,000—40 percent—at Shibe Park. The 346,641 was the lowest since Connie Mack had opened for business in 1901. In 1910 and 1911 the exciting young pennant winners had drawn more home fans through the turnstiles than any other team in the league. This year the same superior baseball machine fell to fifth in home attendance.

There is some merit in the claims that the Athletics lacked the color, the eccentric characters, of their past champions. Not one of them was a prime source of material for feature stories outside the sports pages. They did their jobs to perfection, went about their business and lived clean, scandal-free lives. They were truly a machine. It didn't help that there were no longer any Charles Drydens among the local writers to spin tall tales and true about them.

Jack Coombs told James Sinnott of the *New York Evening Mail*, "We were never drawing cards. I don't know why it was, unless because we didn't wrangle with the umpires or swear at the opposing players. I guess we were too businesslike. But that is the way Connie wants his men to play."

Even their uniforms were blamed for turning away people on the road. The brownish outfits seemed to be always in need of washing, even when they were clean. Walter Hapgood of the *Boston Herald* called them the most "hideous suits that ever adorned ball players. . . . We often have thought that these sartorial prizes had something to do with the astonishing lack of drawing power of the Mackmen." Writers and fans in other cities echoed this fashion critique.

Mack was unmoved. The uniform had a history. After they had gone 22-55 on the road in 1908, Mack suggested to John Shibe that they change their traveling outfits. They picked out the dirty-looking brown shade and played .600 ball on the road ever since. Mack wasn't about to make any changes as long as his team was winning.

Attendance was also hurt when the *Philadelphia Record* erected a scoreboard recreating the action for both home and away games across from City Hall. On some days more people stood on Broad Street watching than sat in Shibe Park. The *Evening Telegraph* was planning to put up a similar display.

Mack and Ben Shibe appealed to the paper to stop the accounts of home games. The paper refused. The A's retaliated by barring the *Record*'s beat writer, William Brandt, from using the press gate. Brandt bought a ticket and was ejected from the "scorers box," as the press box was called. The *Record* complained to the Baseball Writers' Association. The matter went to the group's president, who arranged a compromise. Mack and Shibe lifted the ban on Brandt, and the *Record* discontinued the scoreboard for home games.

Meanwhile, in the National League John McGraw's Giants rode a comfortable lead. Nobody outside of Boston took much notice of the Braves' 3–2 win over Cincinnati on July 19 that lifted them into seventh place. Well, almost nobody. Years later Chief Bender told this story:

> Early in July, Grantland Rice, a broker named Oswald Kirksey and I were having lunch at the Englewood Golf Club.
> During the meal, Kirksey said, "Chief, I'll lay you $25 to $75 that the Braves will win the pennant and the World's Series."

Both Rice and I looked at him quizzically. "You're crazy," we said. "Why, the Braves are in last place."

Kirksey merely smiled. "I'll still take your money," he declared.

"I'll take the bet, but I'll not take your money," I said, "because you're nuts."

The day the Series was over I wrote him out a check for $75. I often wondered what got into his mind that day.

A week later the Braves were fourth, still 12 games back of the Giants. In mid-August they swept the Giants in New York and cut the lead to 3½. On September 2 they passed the Giants. Winning 34 of their last 45 with 3 ties, they finished 10½ games in front.

Connie Mack blamed the Giants' late-season collapse on "the easy life and overconfidence . . . a fault that usually affects every champion after a long run of success. I'm told the Giants are very fond of motoring. Most of the players have invested in cars. Even some of McGraw's bushers. That is a bad sign. When a team gets its mind occupied with luxuries it is not very apt to center attention on the happenings of the diamond, even while the game is under way."

The Braves woke up at the same time as the Athletics, going 35-10 from July 11 to September 3. But the Braves got all the publicity because of their spectacular rise in the standings. The A's revival was taken as a matter of course. They were so much better than everybody else, they won seemingly without trying. They outscored, outhit, and outfielded the rest of the league by wide margins. In the first week of September they lost 4 straight to second-place Boston, and it didn't faze them because their lead was so secure. Then they relaxed, went 16-15 the last five weeks, toward the end using lineups loaded with rookies, including Earle Mack in his last major league appearance.

The oddsmakers were calling the World Series a "cakewalk" for the Athletics. One newspaper wag wrote, "The A's are worrying these days, if it rains it will take them more than four days to win the World Series. Ha ha."

Connie Mack was still unable to shake off the blows to his pride and integrity cast by the writers in the 1913 World Series.

"I guess we'll be expected to win in four games," Mack told James Isaminger. "Personally I hope we will be able to do this. If we're going to lose I trust that we will be the worst beaten team on earth and the Braves lick us in four straight. Either result will allay any suspicion of the skeptics of a frame-up and that the series will be lengthened on purpose."

47 | SWEPT

The 1914 World Series was an upset only because the pundits said it was. If ninety-nine out of a hundred of them had picked the Athletics to win and they were wrong, that made it an upset. Most of them were following the habit of favoring the team that had won the year before. Cincinnati writer W. A. Phelon was one of the few who predicted a Boston victory. But many nonexpert fans gave the psychological edge to the Braves, citing their hunger and aggressiveness and the world champions' complacency.

Damon Runyon, having watched with a stunned nation as the Braves vaulted over the entire National League in less than six weeks, said only that he would not be surprised at anything they accomplished in the World Series. Without alluding to any dissension, Runyon compared the 1914 Athletics to the 1911 A's and concluded that the new blood was good but not as good as the old blood that was now three years older. "There has been a very perceptible falling off in the Mackmen not individually perhaps but as a club," he shrewdly observed.

The result was no upset in the minds of either Connie Mack or Braves manager George Stallings. Neither foresaw a sweep; both believed the Athletics could be beaten. Mack said, "I didn't consider [the Braves] an outstanding team when we entered the series, yet I knew very well we wouldn't win . . . because of the hatred that existed between one player and his neighbor on our club."

The role of underdogs suited the Braves fine. Written off for most of the season, they had caught the Giants on Labor Day and kept on rolling. From July 17 to the end they won 61 and lost 16, an astounding .792 pace. Their pitching trio of Dick Rudolph, George "Lefty" Tyler, and Bill James was 44-9 during that stretch. Bill James, who had won 19 out of 20 after a slow start, was a spitball specialist. Dick Rudolph, considered by some baseball men as smarter than Mathewson, relied on exceptional control and an assortment of curves; his spitter, said catcher Hank Gowdy, was wet, and that was the most you could say for it. Between them, James and Rudolph had won 53 games and pitched 668 innings.

Unlike the A's, who relaxed after clinching, Stallings drove his men hard to the last day. "I don't want them to get in the habit of losing," he said. They played 20 games—including eight doubleheaders—in the last two weeks, won 14, lost 4, with 2 ties. All the ginger, pep, and confidence rode with these onrushing one-year wonders, while the Athletics rusted mentally and physically. Only Hank Gowdy, his hands "bunged up" by foul tips, was given much rest. Butch Schmidt and Johnny Evers took a few days off.

Connie Mack was right about one thing: the Braves were not an outstanding team. They were castoffs and leavings for the most part. Stallings platooned outfielders Les Mann and Herbie Moran in right, Joe Connolly and Ted Cather in left. Moran had been with four teams. Cather and center fielder Possum Whitted had been picked up from the Cardinals in June.

Catcher Hank Gowdy and right-hander Dick Rudolph had started out with the Giants and been turned loose by John McGraw. First baseman Butch Schmidt had been Highlanders property five years earlier and was playing his first full season. Third baseman Red Smith was obtained from Brooklyn in August and broke his leg on the last day of the season. His replacement, Charlie Deal, had been waived out of the American League.

Johnny Evers had been headed to the Federal League when he was saved for the National League by Boston president James Gaffney, who gave him a reported signing bonus of $25,000, a $10,000 salary, and a bonus based on where the team finished. Evers hit the jackpot for over $40,000 in his last full season.

A green Rabbit Maranville, twenty-two, in his second full season, had a lot to learn and learned it from Evers. Pitchers Bill James, who turned out to be a one-year star, and Lefty Tyler had not played for any other major league club.

The club's average age was twenty-five. Only Evers, Moran, and pitcher Otto Hess were thirty or older.

George Stallings knew what he had to work with too. He was quoted as saying the 1914 Braves consisted of "one .300 hitter, the worst outfield that ever flirted with sudden death, three pitchers, and a good working combination around second base."

It was an accurate appraisal, perhaps, but an understatement in regard to the keystone combination. Stallings may have held the ignition key, but

Evers and Maranville, who finished one-two in the Chalmers MVP voting, were the sparkplugs that fired up the club. Maranville took care of everything hit into the air between second base and the grandstand. Everything. "His spikes picked up more dirt around third base than mine did," Red Smith recalled. The veteran Evers took the young Rabbit in hand. "Evers taught me how to play the shortstop position," Maranville said. "He showed me how to play the hitters. He wouldn't let the pitcher throw the ball til I was where he wanted me to be." Evers taught him other tricks. With a man on first and a ball hit safely to the outfield, Maranville stood idly watching the throw headed for third. If the batter made too wide a turn at first or headed for second, Rabbit cut off the throw at the last instant and whirled and threw to second or first.

For that one week in October, the Boston middle infielders were the equals of Eddie Collins and Jack Barry. Maranville credited Evers with making the play that saved their 1–0 win in Game 2, even though Evers never touched the ball. In the last of the ninth the A's had Barry on second and Walsh on first with 1 out. Eddie Murphy was the batter.

"Come over here," Evers yelled at Maranville, who moved closer to second.

"Come over; what's the matter, you deaf?" Evers hollered.

"By that time," Maranville said, "I was almost at second base. Charlie Deal on third moved over too, til he was practically playing shortstop."

"All right," said Evers, "now stay there."

Murphy hit James's pitch right back through the pitcher's legs. "If it had not been for Evers, it would have been a base hit over second," Maranville said. "I stepped on second and threw to first for a double play and the game was over. As we were running off the field, I said, 'Thanks, John,' and he said, 'Thanks nothing. If you hadn't got that ball I would have killed you.'

"I believe he would have, at that."

As the captain, Evers sarcastically berated his teammates to keep them on their toes. Pull a skuller and they heard about it with both barrels. He ran them ragged and took it personally when one of them let him down.

"Evers would make you want to punch him," Maranville said, "but he only thought of the team."

And then there was Stallings himself. Like the Athletics, the Braves were made in their manager's image. Like Mack, Stallings was confined to the bench, where he wore a gray suit, white shirt, bow tie, and fedora. He was a master psychologist, a smart baseball man who knew his personnel and his opponents. The forty-six-year-old Stallings had adopted some of his older rival's innovations. He conducted daily meetings, going over the mistakes of the previous game and the strategy for the next. He used subtle signs: mouth open meant something, a smile something else. His infielders constantly telegraphed each other, passing along the catcher's signs and relaying them to the outfielders—not a common practice at the time.

Both managers sat in the same spot throughout a game. Mack was not immobile. He slid side to side, squirming when things got tight, and occasionally stood up, which was sometimes interpreted as a sign of worry. When Henry P. Edwards of the *Cleveland Plain Dealer* asked him if this was true, Mack replied, "Say, the fans get up and stretch during the seventh inning, don't they? Well, try sitting on the bench in the dugout for a doubleheader and see if you think the wood there is any softer than the seats in the grandstand."

When it came to superstition, Stallings was at another level. He sat rigid, not moving a muscle, when his team began a rally. If they blew a lead in the late innings, he'd blame his players; somebody must have moved and jinxed them. He abhorred scraps of paper around the dugout. This well-known phobia resulted in anti-Braves fans and opposing players deliberately decorating the area in front of the bench with shreds of paper.

Connie Mack could shoot sarcastic barbs at a player; Stallings drove his men like a teamster trying to motivate a team of mules. As a tuxedo-clad host at his Georgia plantation, the vmi graduate and one-time medical student was a suave Southern gentleman. But on the job he was transformed into a fire-eating, fidgety bundle of nerves. He lashed his players with language so caustic, profane, and unrelenting that he blew smoke rings around McGraw. Players on the bench gave him plenty of room if the game was going against them. Damon Runyon once described Stallings's conduct as he sat with one leg crossed over the other, one hand hanging beside the knee, throughout a game: "He harried them with verbal goad even as they were winning. He spoke rudely of their personalities. He abused their ancestry. Invective fell from his tongue in a searing stream as he crouched there conning the field before him, his strong fingers folding and unfolding against his palms as if grasping the throat of an enemy."

Will Wedge of the *New York Sun* wrote, "He was called the miracle man because it was a miracle how he ever thought up all the scorching phrases that encrusted his vocabulary. He could swear his way from one end of the bench to the other. He cussed his own players, the opposition, the umpires, sparrows in the air and bits of paper that blew near the dugout."

Eddie Collins remembered watching him when Stallings was managing the Highlanders. "He gave vent to his nervousness by sitting with his legs crossed and kept one of his feet moving at the rate of about a thousand vibrations a second."

For all that, Stallings rode the men he knew he could ride and patted the backs of those who needed a gentler touch. And he carried psychological warfare to new heights—or depths—with his bench jockeying. He didn't invent it; the A's were used to some riding, especially by Hugh Jennings and his crew. But this was studied, deliberate contempt on the scale of a barrage from a battery of heavy artillery. The Braves had what is now labeled "an attitude," calculated to harass, irritate, discomfit, distract. And it succeeded.

The campaign began as soon as the Braves clinched the pennant. Stallings ordered his players not to speak to the Athletics unless it was to insult them. They were to ignore them or say only nasty and demeaning things. For Johnny Evers, such orders were redundant. He was crabby anyhow. In one game a Philadelphia base runner was on second. "You fellows have done a great job," said the Mack gentleman to Evers. "You deserve credit."

Evers spat on the ground. "We don't take praise from yellow dogs," he snarled.

Maranville was a receptive pupil and joined in the invective from the bench or the first base coaching box. But the Braves were a chorus, not a trio. Stallings had picked up a pair of utility infielders more for their mouths than their mitts: Bill Martin, who appeared in only one game in the big leagues but was as adept with the needle as a quilter, and Oscar Dugey, who had a dead arm and couldn't hit but kept a book on the temperamental weaknesses of every player.

Red Smith told broadcaster Ernie Harwell thirty years later, "Our boys did a neat verbal lashing. . . . Stallings, Evers, Maranville, and the others were all expert needlers and they showed Mack's men no mercy. The Athletics hadn't joined the baseball fraternity, and refused to go along with a strike vote called by Dave Fultz during the season. That gave the Braves plenty of material. They barbered the Philadelphians relentlessly and then outplayed 'em all the way."

Syndicator John Wheeler and Eddie Collins had been college chums at Columbia. Wheeler tried to sign Collins for a World Series column. Collins signed with another syndicator for more money. Wheeler then approached Evers. According to Wheeler, Evers asked if Collins was writing for him.

"No, he got a better proposition than we made him."

That was loaded into the Braves' howitzers. "We kept yelling, 'So you'd throw down an old pal for fifty bucks, you cheapskate,'" Evers said. "We had that Collins so up in the air he couldn't spit and hit the ground."

J. W. McConaughy commented in the *New York American*:

Several of the Athletics who have not been in the series told the writer that the boys had been subjected to the most persistent and unscrupulous system of abuse, so gross that it had even angered Eddie Collins and Chief Bender. They say that some of the Braves even made constant references of an amazingly ingenuous and venomous kind to the marital troubles of Rube Oldring. [Oldring was appearing in municipal court on charges of desertion and nonsupport of his wife, Helen.] And the most careful expurgation and transcription can give no idea of the line of remarks that was aimed at Bender and Collins.

"This fellow Stallings was talking the other day about sportsmanship," said one of the team. "Our boys can stand a lot of riding. We are used to it, because everybody knows that Connie's system is to play baseball and win the games with better ball playing. We don't ride anybody, but we don't mind a team getting after us ordinarily. The Giants tried it every year, but there was a limit to even what McGraw would stand for. But there is no limit to what these fellows have pulled off on the field. It's one way to win ball games and it's no alibi for yourself if you lose on that account. . . . If the fans in Boston could be told some of the stuff these fellows have pulled they wouldn't have a friend even in their home town."

The fans in Boston didn't have to be told; the howling from the bench and coaching lines during the third game in Boston could be heard even in the rooftop press box at Fenway Park, where the games were played to accommodate larger crowds. It was "quite offensive . . . altogether out of keeping with such a great and dignified interleague event," sniffed the *Reach Guide*. Six years later the *Reach* editor was still calling the language "the worst" of any series. Its like would not be heard again until the 1930s.

George Stallings had more of an incentive than winning a World Series. He had a personal score to settle with Ban Johnson. It went back to the Western League, when Stallings managed Detroit and Ban Johnson was the league president. Neither Mack nor Johnson cared for Stallings's style, which was that of a profane, tantrum-throwing umpire baiter. Johnson had put up with him through the launching of the American League, then looked for a way to be rid of him. When Johnson suspected Stallings of trying to move the Tigers into the National League after the 1901 season, he found a buyer for the team and forced Stallings to sell his interest in the club. Back in the minor leagues, Stallings continued to earn suspensions for swinging and kicking at umpires. When Frank Farrell, unknown to Johnson, gave Stallings a two-year contract to manage the Highlanders in 1910, Johnson fumed but could do nothing about it except to make sure the contract wasn't renewed.

Stallings went back to the minors for two more years before James Gaffney brought him to Boston. This was Stallings's first—and, it turned out, only—opportunity to take revenge against Ban Johnson. That kind of motivation was worth as much as a .300 hitter in the lineup.

Stallings trained his sights on Connie Mack before the series began. After a season-ending doubleheader in Brooklyn, the Braves arrived in Philadelphia on Tuesday night, October 6, and checked into the Majestic Hotel. They planned to practice at the Phillies' park Wednesday morning, then watch the A's finale against the Yankees that afternoon.

Before the game Stallings appeared in Mack's office and asked to use Shibe Park on Thursday afternoon, the day before the series opener. Mack was taken aback by the request. He had never asked John McGraw or Frank Chance to use their fields before a World Series, nor had they ever made such a request of Mack. They had always used the Phillies' grounds. When he saw Stallings was serious, he said, okay, you can use it any time except between two and three, when the Athletics had been told to report for a final workout. By some accounts, Stallings said that wouldn't do; he wanted the grounds at two o'clock. Mack later claimed that Stallings made no protest at the time. He instructed the groundskeeper to let the Braves use the field Thursday morning if they wanted it.

The next morning Mack almost choked on his oatmeal when he read that Stallings had blasted him, calling him unsportsmanlike and a few other things, for refusing the Braves permission to practice at Shibe Park. When he reached his office, Mack called the Majestic and had Stallings paged to a telephone in the lobby. He asked Stallings if he had been quoted correctly.

Stallings said yes.

"Why didn't you say that at my office?" Mack asked.

"I started to think about it later on and felt differently then."

Mack blew up, "and one word led to another until we both spoke things we should not have said," he told reporters. It culminated in Stallings's threatening to punch Mack in the nose if he showed his face at the hotel. "If Stallings wants to fight let him lick one of the porters at the Majestic," Mack said.

Some reports had Jim Gaffney standing at Stallings's side, egging him on. Others reported that Stallings deliberately spoke in a loud voice so the reporters in the lobby could hear him, his choice of words unrestrained by an audience. Those who didn't hear it were quickly informed of the exchange by Stallings. An Athletics fan heard it all and heckled Stallings, drawing a punch that set off a brief brawl.

Still another version of the episode, told by Mrs. Stallings, has Stallings faking an indignant call to Connie Mack and speaking loud enough for onlookers to overhear it, then denouncing the Athletics' manager to the press.

The Braves didn't practice at Shibe Park, but Stallings didn't care. He had gotten Connie Mack's goat. That was the point. He was a warrior on a mission, a quest for revenge. He was practically frothing at the mouth. After the first game, Johnny Evers wrote, "I have seen many managers but I have never seen a man in action as Stallings was this afternoon. He has been crazy to win this series and he had been on edge for days. Today he drove, drove, drove all the way. 'Get in there and beat that big Indian,' he kept shouting. 'You can do it. Wait and pickle that fast one.'

"Up and down the bench he slid and showed his teeth until he had every man on the club fighting with the crazy frenzy they say a soldier shows when he goes into battle and once gets a taste of it."

Whatever the sound and fury and the insults and invective signified, in the end the Braves defeated the Athletics at their own game: preparation. They hired Phillies coach Pat Moran to scout the A's for the last few weeks of the season. With a day off in New York on Sunday, October 4, they held a team meeting all afternoon, going over Moran's reports on every aspect of the Athletics' offensive and defensive tendencies. They had other help. On Monday evening Christy Mathewson spoke to them about the strengths and weaknesses of Mack's batters. John McGraw gave them pointers on defending against the A's.

There were others, not named but alluded to by Johnny Evers as "certain friends," who were helpful. A few weeks after the Series ended, a debate broke out in the press over the ethics of a former A's star who, "according to evidence," had been paid to coach the Boston pitchers as to the weaknesses of the Philadelphia hitters. W. A. Phelon wrote in the *Cincinnati Times-Star,* "He is defended by people who maintain he had a perfect right after leaving the club to get the money. But sentimental ones say no. They point out how Connie Mack took this man when another club had dismissed him, how Mack made him rich through fat wages and World Series coin. Connie carried him in recent years. They speak of these things, and they ask if even the right to get the money should outweigh the days that have been, and the kindness and protection of the past."

The only player who matched that description was Danny Murphy.

Stallings was aware of the Athletics' reputation for stealing signs. He devised an entirely new system for giving pitchers signs. The catcher gave three signs, then indicated which of the three was on. The pitchers were told to concentrate on covering up their deliveries and grips on the ball to conceal them from the eyes of Bender and Davis. Coupled with the A's lack of familiarity with Tyler, Rudolph, and James—only Collins had seen Rudolph pitch, when they were teammates at Rutland, Vermont, in 1906—it took the A's out of their usual game.

On the other hand, Red Smith claimed the Braves had the A's signs "down pat."

Stallings had another man who was the equal of anyone among Mack's brain trust, coach Fred Mitchell. Mitchell began his career as a pitcher—had pitched for the Athletics in 1902—and finished it as a catcher. After every pregame team meeting, he met with the pitchers and catchers and went over the hitters as thoroughly as today's pitching coaches. He conferred with catcher Hank Gowdy before and after each game, reviewing the pitches thrown, what worked, and what didn't. Without the aid of videos, they kept it all in their heads. Harry Davis said, "Fred Mitchell beat us. Our club had been playing ball on a system no other ball club ever had used, and Mitchell found it out. He simply kept crossing us up. There's your miracle man."

The results: Frank Baker batted .250, Eddie Collins .214, Eddie Murphy .188, Wally Schang .167, Jack McInnis .143, Jack Barry .071, and Rube Oldring .067.

And what of the Athletics' scouting? They were at home while the Braves were in New York for the last week of the season. We'll never know for sure who did what, but it wasn't much. The most repeated tale, one that circulated at the time, was that Mack ordered Chief Bender to go to New York to look them over. A few hours later Mack sees Bender in Philadelphia.

"I thought you were in New York to look over the Braves," Mack says.

"I didn't bother," Bender replies. "What's the use of looking at that bunch of bush leaguers?"

With the usual variations, that's the way Philadelphia and New York papers reported it. That's the way Ban Johnson related it to reporters a few days after the opener. Whether he had read it in the papers or heard it from Mack is unknown.

Outfielder Shag Thompson's memory placed the confrontation in the team meeting the day before the first game. "Mack asked Bender what he thought about the Braves. Bender said, 'I didn't go.' Connie flared up. 'You didn't go? Why not?' Bender said, 'They're just a bunch of misfits. I won't have any trouble with them.' And Connie said, 'I hope you don't.'"

In his 1938 *Saturday Evening Post* article, Connie Mack spread the blame, saying he sent "several of our smartest players" to scout the Braves for the pre-series meeting. "Then I learned that the players to whom I had given the scouting assignment had never left Philadelphia. . . . I called no meeting. . . . We met the Braves without a single piece of advance information."

Mack may have had Bender in mind when he wrote what he did but preferred not to single him out.

Bender had his own perfect recall, and it was the opposite of Mack's. In a 1948 Taylor Spink column, Bender is quoted as saying they had advance information but it was all wrong. "The [unspecified] man who scouted the Braves for us came back with the wrong reports. . . . We pitched wrong to them."

(Bender also said, "Not one of us had been approached by the Federal League" before the Series. Maybe not *just* before the Series, but they had certainly been approached during the season.)

Apparently *somebody* did go to New York. An October 6 dispatch in the *Sporting News* reported that some of the A's "spent a few afternoons at the Polo Grounds watching Boston play the Giants."

Tom Meany, in *Baseball's Greatest Teams*, has Harry Davis at the Polo Grounds during the Braves' series, supposedly congratulating outfielder Herbie Moran, who had broken in with the A's briefly in 1908. "You fellows did a great job," Davis says, "and I expect we'll have a great series."

To which Moran replies, "I don't think you fellows will win a single game."

Whichever story making the rounds at the time was closest to the facts, Billy Weart commented in *Sporting Life*, "It about sizes up what the Athletics thought of the Boston Braves before the first game was played."

They believed they could win just by walking on the field. They were plodding along a familiar track for the fourth time in five years. They'd beaten the powerful Chicago Cubs and John McGraw's mighty Giants twice. The Braves were fluke winners in a weak league.

They failed to appreciate the difference this time. Their opponents were riding into the Series on a hot streak, with a whip-wielding jockey on their backs.

On a damp, chilly Friday morning Chief Bender arrived at Shibe Park about fifteen minutes before game time for the Series opener. He missed the presentation of a new automobile to Eddie Collins, the Chalmers MVP. He was feeling ill, he said, with "vertigo and trouble with my gall bladder and stomach."

Shag Thompson called Bender's illness a hangover. He had heard that Bender and Rube Oldring had been out drinking the night before. He wasn't the only one who heard it.

Bender said he told Mr. Mack he didn't feel well, but Mack assured him he could "beat these fellows."

"When I warmed up I didn't have anything. I told him again, but he brushed my complaints aside. I went in and got my licking. I really didn't have much and it didn't take them long to find out. My control was bad. I was frequently in the hole with three and two and on the next pitch—wham!"

George Stallings said there was another reason they teed off on Bender. According to a story by Jack Kofoed, Stallings had managed catcher Wally Schang at Buffalo in 1912. Schang had a habit of setting up about six inches off the plate for a curve. Before the Series Stallings sent Dick Rudolph and Fred Mitchell to scout Schang. They reported that he still did the same thing. But Schang caught the next three games too, and the Braves didn't "tee off" on any other A's pitchers.

When the Braves knocked out Bender during a 3-run sixth inning, Thompson was sitting near Mack on the bench. "Bender comes in. Mack waits a minute and turns to him. 'Well, Albert, pretty good bunch of misfits,' he says. 'You can go take a shower.'"

Mack was disgusted, disappointed. Albert, "the greatest money pitcher the game has ever known," had failed him. Bender had lost World Series games before, but he had never pitched poorly in the postseason. In 79 innings he had given up 26 runs before today. It was the first time in 22 World Series games that Connie Mack used a relief pitcher, except for an injury. Mack made up his mind that Albert Bender would not pitch again for the Athletics, even if the Series went seven games.

Dick Rudolph pitched the opener for Boston. The Fordham student from the Bronx was no stranger to Mack. In 1909 Mack had sold Al Kellogg to Toronto for $500 and his choice of any Toronto player for $2,000—except the one he wanted most, Dick Rudolph. Rudolph pitched more with his head than his arm. Early in the game his pattern was to waste the first two pitches. When the A's hitters started looking for that, he began to throw quick strikes, then worked them with curves and changeups away. He kept them off balance all day. Rudolph's imminent fatherhood never fazed him; his wife went into labor during the game, a lengthy labor that ended the next morning with the birth of a 10-pound girl.

The thousands who lined the surrounding porch roofs and rooftops and those who watched the recreations on scoreboards outside newspaper buildings and in theaters were disappointed by the 7–1 loss. But the capacity crowd inside Shibe Park felt firsthand the stunning effects of their team's lackluster performance. The gloom was more palpable there than elsewhere. The Athletics seemed to be in a trance at the plate. They were gingerless in the field—except for Jack Barry. The highlight of the day was an outstanding play by Black Jack. In the sixth inning Herb Moran hit a foul pop fly near the stands. Jack Barry, running hard, reached out his right hand at the edge of the grandstand and made a barehanded catch as his momentum carried him up the steps. One writer called it the greatest play ever seen in a World Series. "It took the fans by storm while the Braves looked on in amazement."

James Isaminger pulled out all the verbs: "Boston beat, whipped, licked, tormented, maltreated, belabored, walloped, smashed, gashed, bruised, mangled and wrecked us." Hank Gowdy led the mayhem with a single, double, and triple.

Connie Mack took it in stride. He had lost World Series openers before.

The outcome of Game 2 was decided by the breaks. Spitballer Bill James and Eddie Plank matched goose eggs for 8 innings. In the sixth Schang doubled with 1 out. On a short passed ball he lit out for third. Gowdy retrieved the ball and threw. Schang slid into third, photos later showed, before the ball reached Deal. Umpire Bill Byron called him out. Plank's grounder to short would have scored him. A scratch hit by Collins was the only other hit the Athletics managed.

In the ninth Amos Strunk turned the wrong way on a fly ball hit by Deal, who wound up on second. Either Charlie Deal was as clever as Ty Cobb or he just caught a break on a blunder. Two blunders, really. Picked off first early in the game, he crossed up the A's by heading for second while McInnis swiped at the air on the bag. Now he took an extra step lead off second. Schang snapped a throw to Barry. Instead of trying to get back, Deal raced for third. Although some eyewitness reports have him beating Barry's throw to third on a close play, others say Barry made no throw. Whether Barry held the ball because Deal was in line with Baker and the ball might have hit him and bounced away, or because Baker, taken by surprise, was not covering third, depends on whose game account you read. Whatever. Deal was on third when Les Mann looped a Texas Leaguer into short right field, which Eddie Collins desperately pursued, only to see it tick off the tip of his glove as Deal scored. A's scout Al Maul called the Collins effort as close to making an impossible play as he had ever seen.

"Collins turned his back, ran as I have never seen a man do, and then, if he had measured the distance and had electric timers, could not have turned and leaped into the air, yes, leaped backwards, at a more exact instant. His glove just tipped the ball. It looked like Collins had come up out of a cellar in the ball park, so unexpected was his appearance. For one fraction of a second I thought that he had the ball, then I saw him tumble to the earth and Deal shot over the plate. . . . I never expect to see any living man come so close to the impossible."

The A's drew two walks in the last of the ninth, then Rabbit Maranville started the game-ending double play that he credited Johnny Evers with setting up. Eddie Plank had thrown 129 pitches in losing to a shutout for the third time in a World Series.

Nobody spoke in the home clubhouse after the game. Plank sat on a stool, head in his hands, while the others silently showered, dressed, and left.

Writers called Game 3 at Fenway Park the most bitterly contested in the fall event's brief history. Connie Mack told Chicago columnist John Carmichael it was the pivotal game. "If we had won it we would have won the series," he maintained.

Joe Bush and Lefty Tyler were tied 2–2 after 9 innings. The A's loaded the bases in the tenth with 2 outs. Baker hit a hard shot at Evers—"the meanest ball I ever handled," Evers called it. "It almost got away from me as Schang scored." But then, inexplicably, as if frozen, Evers held the ball while Murphy also crossed the plate. "What did I do but stand there plumb dumb. . . . I wish the ground had swallowed me."

The 4–2 lead didn't last long. It was more Gowdy, Gowdy, Gowdy. Had there been a Series MVP, the regular-season .243 hitter would have won it unanimously. Gowdy bounced a leadoff home run over the center-field fence. After Devore, pinch hitting for Tyler, struck out, Rabbit Maranville went down to the first base coach's box and began to ride Bush. He waved his arms and pranced up and down the line, yelling anything he thought might rattle the pitcher. Bush walked Moran. Evers singled him to third. Joe Connolly sent a fly ball to Walsh in center field that scored Moran with the tying run. Maranville turned somersaults, and the crowd went crazy.

Two innings later Gowdy doubled. Les Mann ran for him. Mack ordered pinch hitter Larry Gilbert walked. Moran bunted. Bush fielded it in plenty of time to get Mann at third and threw the ball past Baker, and the winning run scored as the thirty-five thousand fans swarmed onto the field and mobbed their hometown heroes.

The A's were done. Dick Rudolph subdued them handily the next day. Everybody expected to see Bender again, but Mack gave the start to young Bob Shawkey. Heywood Broun of the *New York Tribune* reported that after Evers's 2-run single in the fifth broke a 1–1 tie, Ira Thomas suggested that Mack send Bender in to pitch. Mack shook his head and said he was sending Pennock in. "Why?" asked Thomas. "The experience will help him when he goes up against these fellows next year," Mack replied. There was no further scoring.

As Isaminger noted, the Athletics were flat and "didn't exhibit any more enthusiasm than a missionary being led up to a cannibal king's soup pot," while "the Braves fought harder than the Belgians at Liège."

The players made their way through the bedlam on the field to the Braves' bench and congratulated them. Connie Mack did not. Too many harsh words had been said too recently by the two managers for either one to face the other. To Mack, Stallings "had never been on the square." To Stallings, Mack was a sorehead.

"I am more than pleased we beat the Athletics four straight games," he told Boston writers, "for, of all the poor sports in the world, Connie Mack is the worst."

Their intense dislike for each other never melted and had further repercussions that would rock the baseball world.

Damon Runyon, a New York writer who had no need or reason to kowtow to Connie Mack, disagreed with Stallings's sour opinion of Mack:

The world seems to rejoice that [Mack] has been ignominiously beaten. But he has been and is a great character in baseball. He has always been a baseball man, has given his life to baseball. New York fans have no reason to love him but they always respected him and his team. He fought many a hard battle with McGraw and they always quit with a hearty handshake of mutual respect. Every dollar Connie Mack has made out of baseball and every dollar he owns—and they are not as numerous as some people think—is invested in it. As a magnate he is no carpetbagger with an eye to side issues. He is in and of baseball and the money he has put in and taken from baseball is clean and without taint. It would be a good thing for baseball if all stockholders of all clubs could say as much. Connie has always been a good winner and good loser. It is a great thing to be a good loser, but a greater thing to be a good winner.

Strange, isn't it—not a word about the miserly, penny-pinching, pocket-lining Connie Mack who supposedly treated his players so miserably. Was Damon Runyon blind or so easily fooled? Or are the myth makers and their acolytes?

When reporters caught up with Mack, elbowing his way through the dense crowd, he told them, "We lost the series and that is all there is to it. The Braves played better ball. We couldn't get going right."

There was more truth in this initial on-the-spot explanation of the outcome than in all of Mack's subsequent observations about the effects of the Federal League's undermining of his team. "The Braves played better ball" said it all.

Later he added:

I haven't enough vanity to think that I'm going through my baseball career without ever losing. McGraw, Chance, Clarke and other great managers have their years of adversity. I am no exception. I'm thankful for the fact that we won the pennant and played in the series, so the season was not exactly misspent. Don't misunderstand me. The Braves were entitled to the laurels. They won every game on sheer merit. We played our best but our best wasn't good enough to defeat the Braves. I have some feeling against Stallings for the way he misrepresented and personally attacked me, but that doesn't apply to the Boston players. They have my warmest congratulations for their wonderful triumph.

Chief Bender said the Braves had done their advance scouting well. "We had great batters, but all of them . . . were inside hitters—pull hitters. Rudolph and James never gave them one ball on the inside to hit. They pitched away from our men, were always in front, and made us hit what they wanted, rather than what we wanted."

Bender said that both pitchers covered up their deliveries so well the A's never had a good read on them, then added, "But it was the Braves' spirit . . . that carried them through. . . . It wasn't mere combativeness. It was confidence and determination mixed. And that is a hard nut to crack."

Heywood Broun summarized the Athletics' pitching as "very good" except for Bender's stint. "It failed to bring victory simply because it was pitted against pitching that was extraordinary. Pennock was not scored upon when he finished up the last game for Shawkey. Bush was not defeated until 12 desperate innings had been played. And Wyckoff gave a very good account of himself in the first game when he succeeded Bender. Plank of course was exceedingly effective."

Less than two years later, *St. Louis Times* sporting editor Sid C. Keener wrote, "The Braves won in 1914 because they had pitching and confidence." He called them "one of the gamest clubs in the history of the game" for their bulldog tenacity in holding on to a one-run lead. In the last half of the season they had won 22 of 29 one-run games.

Connie Mack told his boys to forget it, put it behind them, relax for the winter, and come back in the spring ready to win again.

On the overnight train from Boston, they tried to forget it, put it behind them. They played cards and tried to not talk about it. No bands and few fans awaited them when they arrived the next morning at North Philadelphia station. The few writers who showed up were brushed aside. Nobody felt like talking. They walked to Shibe Park to collect their $2,216.34 losers' shares. Shag Thompson had picked up an additional $24 by selling his allotted tickets to Ty Cobb for $3 apiece. Then Jimmy Walsh, Harry Davis, Frank Baker, and their wives escorted Joe Bush to St. Columbia's Catholic church in time for his noon wedding to Miss Sylvia McMahon.

There were no parades, no banquets for the dethroned world champions. Mack and Ben Shibe persuaded the mayor to forget any celebrations for the American League pennant winners.

The World Series itself came under more criticism than the performance of the Athletics. The short Series of the last two years had produced few financial benefits to the clubs involved or the leagues. Some owners considered abolishing the World Series. They saw it as one of the causes of the Federal League's formation, as inexperienced outsiders looked at the big crowds and concluded that baseball must be a highly profitable business. Some writers blamed it for causing dissension among the envious players on the less successful clubs.

The Braves' startling sweep was the first but not the only such unexpected sweep in baseball history. In 1954 the Cleveland Indians, winners of a league-record 111 games behind pitching aces Bob Lemon, Bob Feller, Early Wynn, and Mike Garcia, would be swept by the weaker New York Giants. In 1966 Don Drysdale and Sandy Koufax couldn't prevent the Baltimore Orioles from winning four straight over the Dodgers. There were consecutive sweeps in 2004 and 2005. Those things happen in a short series.

Among the many ridiculous myths that dangle from history's thread of repetition is the rumor that Connie Mack suspected his boys of throwing the 1914 World Series. The sole alleged evidence for this is a purported letter of unknown date written by Connie Mack to an unidentified friend in which Mack supposedly voiced his suspicions. The letter is said to be in the archives at Notre Dame University. Nobody there can locate it, nor has anyone ever seen it.

The story would be revived whenever future gambling or game-fixing scandals erupted. Mack grew tired of putting the lie to it, as he did with Rube Waddell's alleged sellout in 1905. In his 1938 *Saturday Evening Post* article he briefly touched on the rumors. Describing the discord in the A's clubhouse as a major factor in their failure to play at their best, he noted, "That doesn't mean the club threw the series to the Braves. Our players were simply more bitter against one another than interested in the series."

Some historians believe that if a story appears in two places, it must be true. Others, more demanding, won't accept its validity unless it has appeared in three or more sources, regardless of whether it began life as speculation or pure fiction.

Wilfrid Sheed, who must have been snacking on sour apples while writing his contribution to *The Ultimate Baseball Book*, characterized the 1914 A's as "easily raffish enough to throw a Series," without producing any evidence to support this, and screeded at length about "hearsay reason to believe that Mack suspected his heroes of dumping the Series. . . . Mack was fussy about his integrity . . . and perhaps this legend of integrity began with the break-up of the 1914 team, not for excellence but for naughtiness."

Bilge.

Sheed started with the premise that Mack "looked like a minister who would cheat his own flock at bingo" and skewed everything he wrote to conform to that bias, with inverted causes and effects and the disdain for substantiation common to the prejudiced.

Even respected researchers have perpetuated the myth. Relying solely on the rumored existence of the Notre Dame letter, one wrote in the fifth edition of *Total Baseball*, "Suspicion of corrupt play in the 1914 World Series had been hinted." That line was deleted in subsequent editions. But other authors and columnists continue to repeat it, each one adding another patch to the quilt of fabrication, as in "There were hints that Mack decimated his great team because he suspected a fix . . ." and similar baseless allusions.

In fact, there were no hints of anything "queer" at the time. Unlike the 1919 Series, which smelled rotten to a lot of people before it even started, there was not the faintest suggestion of anything out of line in any of the contemporary coverage. Betting on the Series was unusually light. A week before it opened, J. C. O'Leary reported in the *Boston Globe* that New York scorecard impresario Harry Stevens tried to bet $1,500 on the Braves at 2 to 1 odds, but the best he could find was 10 to 7 or 10 to 8. Las Vegas gambling regulators look for sudden shifts and volatility in the betting odds as a sign of a fix. There were none.

If the fix was in, nobody told Arnold Rothstein, the alleged kingpin behind the fixing of the 1919 World Series. The *New York Tribune* reported that he had lost a bundle when the Giants failed to win the pennant and "plunged heavily on the Athletics offering odds of 8 to 5" to recoup his losses. One member of the sporting crowd was said to have listened to Rothstein explaining why the Braves couldn't win, then won $25,000 betting on them. There were other big winners and losers among the Wall Street and theatrical crowds, but nobody questioned the honesty of the outcome. Nobody.

It would have been impossible to fix that World Series without reaching the $100,000 infield. Anyone who believes that Baker, Barry, Collins, and McInnis—individually or collectively—would conspire to throw the Series knows nothing of each man's character. No quartet of arrows ever flew straighter. Not the faintest whiff of scandal ever touched any of them then or throughout their baseball careers or personal lives. Though Mack later had his problems with Baker, they had nothing to do with suspicions of dishonesty. Mack expected Baker to be playing for him in 1915. Jack Barry, longtime coach at Holy Cross, remained a close friend and admirer of Mack's. Eddie Collins returned to the A's as a player and coach. Ted Williams said that Mack was one of three people in baseball Collins always spoke of with reverence. Stuffy McInnis remained with the A's for another three years and later had a distinguished career as a coach at Harvard.

Rube Oldring had gone 1 for 15. Amos Strunk misjudged a fly ball. Had Mack suspected them of dishonesty, they would have been gone in a hurry. Both played for Mack the next year and in future years.

As for Connie Mack "decimating" his team because of his "suspicions," the fact is that Eddie Collins was the only player Mack sold before the 1915 season began. The only one. And that had nothing to do with the outcome of the World Series.

48 | THE END OF THE BEGINNING

"In previous years," Connie Mack said, "at the end of the season or the World's Series, there was always hearty partings between player and manager. It was pleasant to shake hands with a valuable player and wish him an enjoyable rest and express the hope that he would be back the next spring better than ever.

"No compliments were exchanged at the end of the World's Series of 1914. It was a most chilling and mournful parting."

Mack used such terms as "disgusted," "disappointed," and "disillusioned" to describe his mood. The entire pennant-winning year had been unpleasant, with its schisms, the renegotiating of contracts, the sight and sounds of Federal League agents infiltrating the clubhouse and entertaining his players, the antagonism toward Ira Thomas, and the undermining of Thomas's (and by inference his own) authority. He was proud of creating what Grantland Rice called "in the main a body of serious-minded, clean living young fellows, who behaved themselves, let umpires alone, started no trouble of any sort, played baseball—and let it go at that."

This superb machine that he had built, every piece carefully selected and nurtured, trained, and taught by him, regarded as his sons—all that was torn apart by "me" superseding "team" and, yes, by too much success achieved too easily. And the last act, sad but not surprising to Mack: his boys going down to defeat with quiescent bats and solemn faces, the sweep he had wished for to silence the cynics small consolation.

An unaccustomed blues hung over Shibe Park. The heaviness of the atmosphere was epitomized by an incident shortly after the last game. Mack arrived at Shibe Park one morning just as Eddie Plank was leaving after cleaning out his locker. What happened next, as usual, varies with the telling. Recalling it when Plank died in 1926, Mack said he walked right by Eddie without speaking. "Maybe I should have stopped," he mused, "but I was too upset by what I knew was going on."

Five years later Mack remembered it as a mortified Plank putting down his gear and mumbling, "Hello."

"So Eddie's off to the Federal League," Mack said.

"Well, you don't care," said Plank. He picked up his gear and walked away.

Either way, it was an awkward, uncomfortable moment for the longtime friends and comrades in arms.

Long before the loss to the Braves, Mack had made up his mind that the time had come to part with Bender, Plank, and Coombs. Bender had been with him for twelve years, Plank for fourteen. They had been the steady-beating heart of the pitching staff, a combined 440-236 since 1903, still the winningest pitching pair in modern baseball history.

But they were the past, glorious as it was, not the future. The last time Mack's team had grown old, he had waited too long to rebuild. He believed that may have cost him the 1907 pennant.

Mack considered Bender an old thirty—"fragile as Dresden china," one writer said—afflicted by rheumatism, digestive ailments, chronic respiratory problems, and periodic tumbles from the water wagon. Johnny Evers wrote, "It is no secret of the profession that Bender has had to have his arm treated with electricity after every game he pitched during the [1914] season and for several days afterwards to put life back into it."

As far back as 1911, James Isaminger had called Bender "always the most carefully nursed and watched pitcher in the fast set."

Connie Mack considered Albert's extended interludes on the sidelines no longer worth what it would cost to keep him—more important, to keep him happy. And, to Mack, an unhappy player had no place on a winning team.

Plank was now thirty-nine. He had talked about quitting for years, might actually do it this time, although he was actively being pursued by the Feds, as was Bender. Mack knew they were both being offered salaries he couldn't match and wouldn't even if he could. If a player was free to shop his services, a club owner was equally free to refrain from the bidding. He acknowledged that either man could win a game for any team on any given day. But Mack didn't expect either one to work as much as in the past. Plank had slipped below 200 innings pitched for the first time in 1914. He completed just over half his starts, par for the league but not for Eddie, who had completed more than 80 percent before then.

Before departing for West Virginia on his honeymoon, Bob Shawkey gave an interview to a Butler, Pennsylvania, reporter. He was quoted as saying that Bender and Plank had rheumatism in their arms and Mack had "nursed them along" for two years "to be very successful against opponents chosen for them."

Bender reacted with an angry denunciation of his pitching pupil:

I did not think one ballplayer would hand it to another that way, particularly when he is indebted to a ballplayer for a large part of his success. I worked harder with Shawkey than I ever have with a young pitcher. . . . I taught him his curve ball, his change of pace, slow curve ball and rehearsed with him time and again little weaknesses of batsmen and gave him hints that I have always found invaluable. It is hard to believe that he would pan Plank and me the way he has after all we have done for young pitchers. . . . I thought Shawkey was going to be a great pitcher. He might, at that, but it requires brains to last long and I am now convinced that he hasn't any, or any sense of appreciation. . . . I will be pitching major league ball as long as Bob Shawkey.

(Bender pitched another three years, Shawkey another thirteen.)

Shawkey hastened back to Philadelphia to deny that he had said any of the things he said. To Connie Mack, bickering within the family was bad enough. When it became public, it was like a loud family argument with the windows open and the neighbors getting an earful. It was everything Mack had worked so hard to eliminate and succeeded in doing so until this year.

The neighbors were noticing.

Ed Bang of the *Cleveland News* commented, "In every ball club there are petty jealousies and invariably a couple of knockers. The Mackmen are known as a club that was practically free from this little disturbance until the past season. That there is something wrong is evident in the way certain players do not mind knocking each other in public."

Shawkey's comments were not without basis, and it had nothing to do with Mack's using Bender and Plank only against weaker teams. He was simply doing what he and other managers long before him had done, and he would continue to do as long as he managed—creating pitching matchups.

For years Mack had ignored the dictates of a fixed pitching rotation. If a team had a particular type of hitters, not just heavily lefty or righty lineups, he saw to it that pitchers who might be more effective against that type of lineup started against them more often. Those who didn't stack up well against a team seldom faced them. Thus in the last two years Bender had started only once each against a strong Boston and weaker Detroit team. He made the most starts—11—against the seventh-place Yankees, 7 of them in 1914. Plank made 6 starts each year against Detroit and faced Cleveland twice, Washington only once, and the Yankees not at all in 1914.

Jack Coombs was a different story. Mack had no reason to think that Colby Jack was headed for the Federal League. He also had no assurance that Coombs would ever regain his health sufficiently to be the pitcher he had been. For the first time in over a year Coombs had worked in exhibition games in Atlantic City in May, Syracuse in July, and Grand Rapids in August. Once the pennant was won, Mack gave him 2 starts, a 3-inning outing on September 28, in which he gave up 1 run and took the loss, and 5 innings against Washington on October 3, when he gave up 3 runs in the fifth but was not involved in the decision. Otherwise, Mack carried him on the payroll for two years and won two pennants without his pitching to a single batter.

As Mack put it, "One cannot pitch for me, another is going back, and the third has an offer from the Federal League."

What's more, the Athletics had a stable of strong young healthy arms: Bush, Wyckoff, Pennock, Bressler, Shawkey—a combined 64-35 in 1914. At twenty-four, Shawkey was the oldest. Mack considered his pitching staff as good as any in the league except the Red Sox, whom he considered the team to beat in 1915.

So at the end of October, Mack asked waivers on Bender, Plank, and Coombs. Asking waivers didn't mean the players would be sold at the waiver price to the first club to claim them. Waivers could be withdrawn and the players sold at a higher price. It was a way to see who might be interested in them. If an American League club claimed a player, he couldn't be sold to a National League club. That's why Mack later said he asked waivers "to give some other club in my own league a chance to secure them." If he couldn't sell them, he was prepared to release them outright.

Asking waivers was considered a confidential matter. Under the rules, written or unwritten, no club was supposed to make public either that waivers had been asked or a claim entered. Thus if the waivers were withdrawn, neither the players nor the public would be aware of it. The secrecy of the waiver list—and, in 1914, the draft selections—had been heightened by the desire to avoid tipping off the Federal League as to players who might be traded or released.

When Detroit president Frank Navin saw Plank's name on the list, he put in a claim and notified manager Hughie Jennings, who was appearing on the vaudeville circuit in Atlantic City. Jennings told somebody about it who told somebody else, and it wound up in the Atlantic City newspaper. Bender and Coombs were also mentioned.

Connie Mack had a fit. "I had hoped this would not become public because it hurts my plans," he told Chandler Richter of *Sporting Life*. He called Jennings "a baseball manager six months of the year and a vaudeville actor the other six. I don't expect him to know the rules. . . . Probably Jennings was so surprised when Navin tipped him off that he could not keep it to himself."

Jennings apologized to Mack for his indiscretion, but Mack remained sore about the leak. When player transactions were involved, he preferred to hold his cards close to his navy blue vest until he was ready to show his hand. He expected other clubs to exercise similar confidentiality. The need to explain himself or deny rumors, even if they were on the right track, irritated him.

Philadelphia fans were stunned, even angered by the news. They could understand Jack Coombs's illness making him expendable, but letting their old heroes Plank and Bender go? Why, they'd sooner part with Billy Penn's statue atop City Hall.

But out-of-town writers doffed their hats to Mack for realizing it was time to rebuild, even if the three pitchers might have another good year in them. Better to act too soon than too late and go with the youngsters now instead of waiting for the veterans to crack. "The Federals can have Eddie Plank," wrote *St. Louis Times* sporting editor Sid C. Keener. "They can have Bender and Coombs, too, if they wish. But with such material they will never be in the major league class."

On Saturday morning, October 31, in his office in the tower of Shibe Park, Connie Mack sought a quiet refuge from the bustle at home, where preparations were under way for his daughter Marguerite's wedding reception the following Monday. His solitude was interrupted by a covey of curious reporters with a long list of questions.

The first questioner asked if Mack thought that Bender and Plank were at the end of the line. Described as wearing the same bland smile he showed when accepting congratulations, he replied, "I believe they are as good as they ever were. I have no doubt that Jack Coombs can come back and pitch good as ever. This may sound funny for a man to say after the action I took, but it is a fact nevertheless."

"Then why do you want to get rid of them?"

"Because one of them [Plank] is negotiating with the Federal League. I wanted to protect organized baseball and give others a chance to bid for their services. I refuse to pay salaries all out of proportion to the value of the player." Then he added enigmatically, "In addition, I had other reasons." The reasons, he said, were different in each case.

Mack would have been better off if he hadn't added the "in addition." It invited more questions about his reasons.

"What are they?"

"I can't tell them just at present."

"Did the reports that Bender had broken training rules the night before the start of the world's series have anything to do with your action?"

"Absolutely not. I think those reports were false. Bender told me he didn't touch a drop of booze during the big games and I believe him. He's never lied to me."

[Maybe not "during," but the night before the first game?]

"Isn't it unusual to release pitchers of Bender's and Plank's caliber?"

"It is."

"Then why did you do it?"

"Because I am through with them and that's all there is to it. I don't mind saying now that there are more surprises for the fans. I know that I may be criticized but I am going to shake up the team."

Mack was then asked if a "certain outfielder" who figured in a scandal was among those to be traded. The question referred to Rube Oldring's domestic problems.

"Stop right there," Mack snapped. "I don't want to mention names and eliminate this player and that player. I'm not yet prepared to mention the other changes that I have in mind. That will come out later."

"But isn't it odd that a manager would shake up a team that for many seasons has been the best in baseball? Even though the Braves defeated the Athletics, many still insist that your team is superior to them. Then why make a lot of changes?"

"We are doing it for the best interests of the club. I'm willing to start all over again and develop a new team. I did it once and can do it again."

And who was there to doubt him? He had done it not once but twice in the last fourteen years and won six pennants.

In closing, Mack threw another log on the fire of speculation. "I don't want one man on the team who is not for the club. That goes for the whole bunch."

What did "not for the club" mean? Breaking training to the detriment of the team? Sowing dissension by fomenting opposition to the manager's choice of a captain? Talking about jumping to the Federal League? Nobody present asked. Mack didn't say.

It certainly wasn't aimed at Coombs, who never assumed any astral airs. It may have been aimed at Bender or some of the anti-Thomas clique. It was clear that Mack was disturbed by the fracture in the harmony he valued so highly.

(Two generations later Mack's concept of the value of team harmony was still recognized. In March 1972, union leader Marvin Miller conducted a meeting in the Dodgers' clubhouse to authorize a players' strike. The vote was 21–4 in favor. Later that day Walter O'Malley asked Miller for the names of the four who voted not to strike. Miller, puzzled because he knew O'Malley could not be pro-strike, refused to name them. He asked O'Malley why he wanted to know. "I don't want those four on my ball club," was the reply. "A team is a team. Team spirit and harmony and sticking together are essential.")

The *Evening Bulletin* reporter came away from the session concluding that Mack had no intention of trying to sell Bender, Plank, or Coombs. He needed waivers in order to release them. "Had he offered to sell them he could get a small fortune for them."

Maybe, maybe not. No club was going to pay a high price for a player without the certainty that they could agree on salary and not lose him to the Federal League.

Mack later attempted to clarify the waiver rules and his thinking, telling the *Public Ledger*, "Before releasing a player unconditionally, all the clubs in the American League must ask waivers on said player. While I have no intention of retaining the three players, I would not have asked for waivers on the players at this time if not for the fact that one of the three has told me he was talking business with the Federal League. He told me he had been offered big money and did not suppose that we wanted to meet the offer. I suggested to this player that perhaps some of the other clubs in the league would meet the demand. I want it strictly understood that I am for the American league in victory or defeat."

Explanatory vacuums are filled by rumors and speculation. What were Mack's "different reasons in each case"? Coombs's physical condition was certainly one. Plank's apparent readiness to jump was another. As for Bender, if there was a reason different from Plank's, it may have been his frail physical constitution or drinking habits.

James Isaminger cast Mack's decisions entirely in terms of money. And there was plenty of basis for that conclusion. The sharp drop in income coinciding with a rising payroll caught Mack by surprise. He did not anticipate that his perfect baseball machine would bore his customers to the extent of a one-third drop in receipts. Attendance at Shibe Park that year seldom topped three thousand to watch "the best team in the world," except for Saturdays and holidays. Guesses of the Athletics' loss for the year ranged from $12,000 to $60,000. (The Athletics Grounds Company had been dissolved on January 2, 1914, and all its assets, primarily Shibe Park, transferred to the American Base Ball Club of Philadelphia, so there are no accountants' records for the year from that source.)

Other clubs were in the same straits. League attendance had fallen 20 percent, the National's by 40 percent. Phillies attendance plummeted 70 percent. Only a few clubs had made money: the Giants, White Sox, and Tigers. So Mack was not alone in paring payroll and resisting still higher salary demands. Even the Federal League, for all its bluster and talk of moving into New York City, was retrenching. Its pitch to players was no longer, "Name your price, and we'll pay it."

Nobody made an offer for Bender or Plank. Everybody figured it would take too much to keep them from going with the Federal League. And what if club owners did take a chance and match the Feds' offers and peace was declared or the outlaw league folded, leaving them stuck with long-term contracts at inflated wartime salaries for aging pitchers? There was no reason for anyone to expect a better year in 1915. Headlines danced with talk of peace with the Federal League, but there was no peace in the air over Europe. Names like Ypres, Verdun, Antwerp, Metz, and Cracow filled big black headlines on front pages. The prospect of operating a baseball club for another season just to cover expenses, if they were lucky—and a winner was no guarantee of that—had some club owners considering whether they should invest in some other business instead.

Looking back from his prefabricated tower of bias, Wilfrid Sheed made a big deal out of ridiculing the notion that fans would stay away from Shibe

Park because the A's were too good for the competition. But at the time, writers in other cities, who held no brief for Connie Mack, saw it for themselves. Nobody at the time was skeptical of Mack's situation.

Even the faraway *San Jose Mercury Herald* picked up the story: "Philadelphia had seen one organization too long. Its $100,000 infield had become a matter of course. It reached the stage where its drawing power, with all its value and ability, was less than a novice big league infield would bring in at the box office."

Marty McHale, a pitcher for the Yankees, recalled a few years later, "The way the Philadelphia fans supported the famous A's was nothing if not criminal. . . . I've seen days in that ball orchard when a very [soft] chorus boy armed with a lip stick would be able to frighten the whole mob of cash customers so badly that 'both of them' would run far enough to find a new street. . . . Can you wonder that Connie scrapped his wonderful machine? No one in Philadelphia cared to see it, so why have it there?"

The problem extended beyond their home park. The A's didn't draw on the road either. Grantland Rice observed in the *New York Tribune*, "They never had enough glow . . . to light up a thimble. They lacked the drawing quality at the gate. . . . Their efficiency was beyond debate, but when they appeared in a hostile town there was little of that fan yearning to storm the turnstiles and watch them play. They lacked the personal appeal. They were more like machines than human beings."

Unlike John McGraw's Giants or later Yankee machines, nobody hated the A's enough to come out and boo them.

Since the end of the World Series, Connie Mack seemed to spend more time denying rumors than anything else. He could have just hung a sign on his office door, "No comment," and played golf. Among the stories:

- The Yankees would be sold and Mack would move to New York as manager and part owner;
- Ira Thomas would manage the Yankees;
- Eddie Collins would manage the Yankees;
- There was friction in the A's front office; tired of losing money, Ben Shibe would retire, Mack would move up as president, and Jack Dunn would become the new manager;
- The Federal League was broke and in debt to the railroads for 1914 travel bills;

- Chifeds owner Charles Weeghman would buy the Cubs; the Ward baking brothers, owners of the Brooklyn Tip Tops, would buy the Phillies or the Yankees or the Dodgers or maybe all three of them;
- Frank Baker would be the next to go.

There were more. Connie Mack pronounced them "all bunk," and they were. "If the reporters and fans keep on guessing they are certain to hit on something right." Weary of it all, he pleaded, "I hope they lay off me for a while."

With that, Mack took the afternoon off on Monday, November 2, to give his daughter, Marguerite Veronica, in marriage to Robert McCambridge in a small, private ceremony at the Church of the Holy Souls, followed by a quiet reception at the Mack home at 2119 West Ontario Street. Nine months later, on August 4, 1915, Connie Mack would become a grandfather for the first time when Robert Jr. was born in Chicago.

The day after the wedding, Mack and John Shibe headed for Chicago and the league meetings, where the rumor mill ground on. High on Ban Johnson's agenda was improving his New York club to compete with the Giants in the largest market in the nation. Since narrowly losing the 1904 and 1906 pennants, the club had had only one winning season, finishing seventh or eighth for the last three years, while the Giants were winning two pennants. Johnson was looking for new owners with deep pockets. He thought he had landed them in brewing millionaire Col. Jacob Ruppert and engineer Cap Huston. But Ruppert wanted promises of help in the form of players from other clubs and a well-known manager before he'd go ahead with the deal. A neophyte in baseball, he naively asked first for John McGraw, then Connie Mack.

On November 20 Johnson showed up in Philadelphia. He conferred with Governor (for another six weeks) and National League president (for another four years) John K. Tener about possible peace feelers from the Feds and was seen dining with Ben Shibe and Connie Mack. He may have sounded out both men about Mack's interest in moving to the Yankees. If he did, he received a definite no. Mack then went off to Atlantic City with his family for a week, denying more rumors as he left town.

On Friday, November 27, Chief Bender visited Eddie Plank at his home in Gettysburg. They talked about more than hunting. The following Wednesday Plank had another visitor, Henry Goldman, secretary of the Baltimore Terrapins. Acting for the Federal League, Goldman offered him a two-year contract to pitch for the St. Louis Terriers. Plank signed. Three days later Goldman secured Bender's autograph on a two-year contract with a promise that he would be assigned to either Baltimore or Newark so he could remain close to his home and expanding sporting goods business.

"Best move I ever made in my life," Bender told reporters. Bender's nose was out of joint. He didn't think "the summary way I was treated [by Mack] the right kind of treatment for my years of labor." But, he said, he bore no grudge against Connie Mack, with whom he parted "the best of friends." He refused to be drawn into any discussion of the Athletics' internal turmoil.

Reached by telephone that night, Mack was told that Bender had jumped. "I don't care," he told Isaminger. "I have no more to say." And he hung up.

Henry Goldman also had Frank Baker on his list, but the Federal's lawyers advised him to forget about Baker. His contract with the Athletics, which had two more years to go, was binding.

Receiving no offers for Jack Coombs, Mack gave him his release on December 9.

Plank won 21 games for St. Louis in 1915 and worked 268 innings. He then pitched two more years for the Browns. His last game was typical of his career, a 1–0, 11-inning loss to Walter Johnson.

Bender, vowing that he had ten more good years in his arm, turned in an embarrassing 4-16 record and 3.99 earned run average for the third-place Terrapins, who were so unhappy with him they tried to break his contract. He then put in two years with the Phillies, where his workload declined sharply each year.

Jack Coombs signed with Wilbert Robinson in Brooklyn, turned in two good years, including a World Series win in 1916, followed by two losing years, in which he tried to get by with his head and a fastball that wouldn't leave a bruise if it hit a batter. He began a thirty-five-year coaching career in 1921.

Connie Mack had intended to lead an American League All-Star team on a cross-country, cross-ocean tour to Hawaii with a National league squad. But after the World Series he decided he had more important business to deal with, and he wanted to be home for his daughter's wedding. So he put Ira Thomas in charge of the AL team. The tour was a financial success; each player netted over $1,300. They spent three weeks in California in

November before boarding the steamer *Nanona* for the week-long cruise to Honolulu, where they stayed for two weeks.

Sometime during their stay in California or during the voyage or in Hawaii, Ira Thomas gave an interview to a writer for a Los Angeles paper. It was picked up by the Philadelphia papers and ran on the morning of Friday, December 4. That same day Ban Johnson and Charles Comiskey were on a train to Philadelphia, and Joe Tinker was on his way back to Chicago from Coffeyville, Kansas, with Walter Johnson's signature on a Federal League contract to pitch for the Chicago Whales.

Clark Griffith subsequently hurried out to Kansas and convinced his star pitcher that he was legally bound by his Washington option clause. So Walter Johnson reneged on his Federal contract and returned to the fold with a healthy raise.

But that was yet to happen. On that Friday morning, all Comiskey knew was that he suddenly faced stiffer competition for the Chicago baseball dollar. His Sox had finished sixth, Tinker's Whales second in 1914. Attendance was down almost 30 percent.

Ira Thomas's interview was a broadside fired at Eddie Collins. His attack on the almost unanimous MVP, the brainiest, and (to some experts) the best player in the game shocked the baseball nation. "The players blame Collins," Thomas was quoted, "for the loss of the world's series to the Boston Braves because of the series of articles he wrote before and during those games."

There was more, much more:

In writing his articles Collins has tipped off many things that he should have kept to himself. He did not give away signs or tell so much about the inside workings of our club. He did something which is just as bad. For years our players have been grabbing the signs of other clubs, peculiarities of the different players, and their weaknesses. Very little of this was gathered by Collins, but naturally, along with the rest of the players, everything was told to him. Eddie's used this information in his articles, telling just how we knew what was coming from a certain pitcher because he always did a peculiar windup when he was going to throw a curveball. Naturally the rival players heard about this and started to remedy their defects. Certain signs that have been used a long time by other clubs have changed. With the information we had at our disposal we would have been able to win pennants for the next six years. But all this was changed because Collins wanted to grab all the money in sight and thus spoiled the work of several years by a few of us. The other clubs now watch us keenly and we won't have the big edge over visiting teams in future.

Collins did write a daily detailed analysis of each game during the Series for the *Evening Ledger*, with some pointed comments about the play of some of his teammates. He also took a shot at Bill Klem, referring to "his majesty, the so-called 'best' umpire in the National League," for some of his pitch calls in Game 3. He analyzed how the Boston pitchers, especially Rudolph and James, were effectively tying up Philadelphia batters.

Why did Thomas rip Collins? Much of it was old news. Everybody knew after the 1910 season that the world champions were experts at swiping signs and reading pitchers. Thomas and other players had clashed with Collins then about his writing on the subject. At the time Christy Mathewson defended Collins, claiming that everybody in the game had already caught on to the same tip-offs by the time Collins wrote about them. That was four years ago.

Did Thomas rake up this old stuff with Mack's permission, knowledge, direction? Nobody knew. Connie Mack didn't say. To him, it was a matter of no importance.

The writers who knew Mack best made much of his silence. Isaminger wrote:

It proved beyond question that Thomas knew he had the inside track with the manager, or he would never have dared to make such bold statements. . To those who have followed the Athletics, it is known that Connie Mack hitherto has always frowned on any inside information regarding the club reaching the public through the players.

And especially had he put his foot down against his players telling of any internal troubles that might be used to injure the champions in the eyes of the public. Under those conditions and with Mack remaining quiescent after Thomas's interview, it showed that Connie at least held a partial brief for the statements himself.

If the interview with Thomas is correct, the meaning is clear: Collins will leave the team. Thomas would scarcely authorize such an interview unless he had advance information.

Fans and writers hoped that Thomas had been misquoted. They wanted to believe that he possessed better judgment than to attack "a man of character like Collins," even if a coolness had developed between them when Thomas was named the Athletics' captain. At the least, it was "bad taste" and a mystery why a club official would revive old disputes at this time.

Collins questioned the accuracy of the interview. "I do not believe that Thomas criticized me. We got along well together and I would not believe it unless Ira told me so with his own lips."

Ira Thomas never claimed he was misquoted, nor recanted nor apologized for anything.

Publicly Connie Mack sloughed it all off. But he had to be upset over this latest family spat. This was more than a crack; it was a shredding of the fabric of harmony and unity that was so important to him. And it gave further credence to his stated intention to shake up his team.

At the time, Mack called it "too picayune a matter" to have anything to do with what followed. That was true. Mack had already made it known that Eddie Collins might be available. Comiskey was interested. So was Col. Ruppert. The *Chicago Tribune* quoted Ban Johnson as having intended Collins for New York, "but unforeseen happenings altered the original plans." The unforeseen happenings were that Ruppert was now balking at the $450,000 asking price for the Yankees because the big-name manager he was promised had not materialized. There might not be any deep pockets there after all. That's why Ban Johnson and Comiskey were on their way to Philadelphia even before the Thomas story appeared in the Philadelphia papers.

Comiskey's franchise was one of the few consistent moneymakers in baseball. For all his skinflint reputation, he had never hesitated to spend money buying highly touted but inexperienced minor league stars who flopped. He'd had enough of that. Now he was prepared to spend whatever it took to buy the best player in the land and to sign him.

Eddie Collins was at home reading at five o'clock on the evening of Sunday, December 6. The telephone rang. Collins was used to getting calls from fans, cranks, practical jokers. His wife screened his calls. Mabel Collins picked up the phone.

She heard, "This is President Johnson of the American League."

"Oh, it is, is it?" she said. "We've had practical jokers call us up before." She hung up.

A few minutes later, the phone rang again. "This is Mr. Comiskey of the

Chicago club. I'm anxious to speak to Mr. Collins. Please get him on the phone."

"I guess Mr. Johnson's voice has failed him," Mabel snapped and hung up.

Eddie continued reading. The phone rang. The exasperated Mabel picked it up, prepared to give the caller an earful.

"This is Connie Mack."

She recognized the voice. Mack assured her that the two previous calls had not been fakes and asked to speak to Eddie. The embarrassed Mabel handed the phone to her husband. "I want you to come to the Bellevue-Stratford immediately on private business," Mack told him and gave him Ban Johnson's room number.

Collins grabbed his hat and coat and drove downtown.

His first words to the three men were apologies for his wife's greetings. They assured him there was no harm done. Then Comiskey and Johnson explained their business.

"They asked me whether I would object to playing in Chicago," Collins told reporters. "The question almost knocked me off my feet. I mumbled that I would never leave Philadelphia."

Comiskey discussed the possibility of a long-term contract at a substantial increase in salary. There was no mention of Collins's managing the team. Collins asked for time to think it over.

"We're on our way to New York," Comiskey said. "Will you come up tomorrow and meet us at the Belmont Hotel?"

Collins said he would. Before he left, Connie Mack took him aside and told him if he didn't want to go, that would be the end of it. His contract with the Athletics would continue.

Collins didn't want to go anywhere. He'd been happy in Philadelphia for eight years. He had a home in Lansdowne and a baby boy, Paul. His friends were here. His family lived not far away, just north of New York City. He was satisfied with his salary, the outlook for the A's, and his writing sideline. And he didn't have to go; he had a no-trade clause in his contract.

Collins had been rumored in the press as going to New York, as either a player or manager. If he went anywhere, he preferred New York to Chicago. He knew, too, that Ban Johnson was pulling all the strings in the possible sale of the Yankees. When he mentioned that possibility to Johnson the next day in New York, Johnson told him the sale of the Yankees was still unsettled, which was true, and he would get a better deal from Comiskey, which was also true.

Faced with Eddie's reluctance to move to the Midwest, Comiskey raised his offer: a five-year no-trade contract at $15,000 a year, putting him among the highest-paid players in the game. If there was a signing bonus, it was never recorded. Comiskey was looking for a new manager, but he was not considering Collins for the job.

Again Collins asked for time to think it over.

In a 1950 version of his life story in the *Sporting News*, Collins revealed that rather than go to Chicago, he "went to Mr. Mack and obtained his permission to try to make another deal, one that would keep me in the east.

"I induced Joe Lannin, then owner of the Red Sox, to see if he couldn't make a deal for me with Mr. Mack. Lannin's attempt to get me for the Boston club was foredoomed to failure."

Collins offered no explanation for this supposed foredoomedness, other than blaming Ban Johnson for refusing to "sanction any deal which would send me anywhere but Chicago. . . . So it was with reluctance that I accepted the dictum to report to Chicago."

Joe Lannin was at the meeting. Collins may have approached him sometime that day or evening. Lannin may have told him something like, "Yes, I'd like to buy you, but Ban Johnson wouldn't let it go through." Maybe. We'll never know. But Collins was not obligated to obey any "dictum" from Ban Johnson. He could have rejected the offer and stayed in Philadelphia.

The next morning Collins agreed to the deal and signed a White Sox contract in Ban Johnson's room. He conceded that the money involved was so big that anybody who turned it down would be considered eligible for commitment.

Comiskey announced the sale that afternoon, proudly declaring, "I paid the highest price any ballplayer ever fetched," and immediately named Collins team captain. The announced sale price was $50,000. Comiskey offered to throw in a couple of players, but Mack was not interested in any of the choices presented to him.

The experts immediately concluded the White Sox had bought the 1915 pennant.

New York writer Joe Vila described Connie Mack as "visibly disappointed" that he had not sold Collins to the Yankees. Why Mack should have been disappointed and what form Mack's supposed "visible disappointment" took are unknown. Did he frown, shake his head, raise his arms to the heavens in despair? If Mack was disappointed, it may have been because he knew Collins would rather go to New York than Chicago, and he always tried to fulfill a player's wishes when parting with him.

Collins met the press informally in the hotel lobby that afternoon. "Mr. Mack and I part the best of friends," he said. "There was talk of friction on the team last season but it wasn't true. I count every member of the Athletic club as a friend. I see where there is a report that Ira Thomas had the hammer after me. But I don't believe he ever gave out that interview. I certainly will miss playing alongside Barry and McInnis, but in baseball sentiment cuts little figure."

Collins was the best, but far from the most popular, player among his teammates or the public. Rube Oldring and Stuffy McInnis led in citywide popularity polls. Collins was the highest paid among the A's by a wide margin. His nickname, Cocky, fit him. He was aloof, abrupt in his manner. He was not part of the hunting cliques. Once he went duck hunting with Frank Baker near Trappe on a winter morning, didn't like the dawn's icy wind or sticking his hands in the cold water, and was not invited back. He preferred the company of the fox-hunting set in Kennett Square.

What Isaminger called "the most amazing transaction in the history of baseball" shared front page space with the Kaiser in Philadelphia papers. But it caused less of a public reaction than the release of Bender and Plank had stirred. It did not come as a surprise.

The headline about the Collins sale in the *New York Times* shared equal billing with:

Connie Mack May Manage Yankees

Maker of World's Champion Teams Ready to Quit Philadelphia

Dismantles Club of Stars

Shibes, After Poor Season Last Year, Start Financial Retrenchment—
To Run Cheaper Club

The *Times* was not immune to fanciful reporting in 1914.

The story quoted George Stallings, "You can bet all you like that Mack will manage New York next year."

"[Ruppert's] designs upon John J. McGraw, it is said, were appeased by an offer of Connie Mack as a substitute," the paper said. Just who made the "offer" was unspecified, but Ban Johnson was doing all the wheeling and dealing, and he knew Connie Mack wasn't going anywhere.

Nevertheless, the *Times* went on, "Connie, who controls the Philadelphia Americans, is not so popular as he once was there.

"The sale of Eddie Collins to the Chicago Americans is reported to be in keeping with the prospective switch of Connie Mack to this city. The Shibes were eager to recoup their losses. . . . Jack Dunn . . . is supposed to be in line as Mack's successor in the Quaker City. That Mack was seriously considered as a prospective asset of Col. Ruppert in the local enterprise was the general gossip of well-posted baseball men yesterday afternoon, when the premature announcement of the sale of the New Yorks was made."

It was all but a done deal, the New York papers said.

So much for the reliability of "well-posted baseball men" as a source.

Philadelphia papers ran headlines: CONNIE MACK IS LIKELY TO MANAGE NEW YORK YANKEES

To which Mr. Mack replied simply, "I would not accept the managership of the New York Americans if it were offered to me, and it hasn't been offered."

The sale of the Yankees dragged on for another two weeks before it was completed. During that time, Mack was offered part ownership and the managing job with the Yankees. A few months later he admitted, "I turned down propositions from the two biggest baseball cities in the country in order to remain with the Athletics, and I would have been independently wealthy if I had accepted either."

One was the Yankees. The other was probably Chicago. Both the White Sox and Cubs were in search of new managers. Comiskey didn't need any partners, but the National League was trying to get rid of Cubs owner Charles Murphy.

Where there is a need to say something at a time when one would rather say nothing, whatever is said may be taken with some skepticism. Mack's vague and empty explanations following the sale of Eddie Collins only invited further conjecture. His hinting at undisclosed reasons left the guessers with an open field to run, knowing there would be no denials of anything they wrote. A simple "We had to cut expenses" or "We refused to match the Feds' extravagant offers" or "I sold Collins to enable American League fans to continue watching this superb second baseman"—any or all of them would have rung with enough truth to fend off further speculation and close the subject.

Back in Philadelphia, Mack brought up the Ira Thomas interview only to deny that it had anything to do with the sale. If that had been the trigger, it would make the deal look like an impetuous act. And it wasn't.

It was generally supposed that the motive was to cut the payroll and replenish the club's finances, anticipating that, as Mack said, his team "as constituted, could not win in 1915." It was now evident that the war in Europe would not be over by Christmas, as the British jingoes had so cheerily promised. Baseball attendance was likely to sink even more, and if the Athletics couldn't show a profit with the world's greatest team in 1914, they weren't likely to do so with the same team for another year.

Collins opined that only financial losses and high overhead were the reasons for his sale. "Had the series with the Braves lasted six games," he wrote, "I have always believed . . . that he would have refused the offer for me."

True, had the World Series gone to six or seven games, that would have relieved some of the financial pressure on the Athletics. But those "other reasons" remained.

All Connie Mack said was, "The sale of Collins is a matter which I must say that it speaks for itself."

That left it wide open for anyone to decide what it was saying and what they were hearing when it spoke for itself.

Then Mack said, "I sold Collins for reasons entirely my own and I would not have sold him if I didn't think that it was the right and proper thing for me to do so."

And that left it open still wider for speculators to guess what Mack's reasons were. Some ignored the "best of friends" happy talk and pinned it squarely on the friction between Thomas and Collins that had split the team, as in:

"Followers of the Athletics believe that lay at the bottom of the entire affair. They believe that Eddie's purchase . . . is another move by the thin tactician to rid his team of all opponents to Thomas, and all critics of the captain's regime."

And:

"In fact Mack's players themselves feel there will be a general house-cleaning and that others are to go."

This theory was given a boost when the *New York Times* ran a story with a Philadelphia dateline of December 8 and no byline:

Connie Mack denies that Eddie Collins' sale has any bearing on friction between the second baseman and Ira Thomas. Despite this denial one of the most prominent members of Mack's team declared today that it has been the selection of Thomas as Captain that has wrecked the once-great world champions. This player declares that the manager must have seen how Thomas was causing dissension, but the tall manager has stood by his Captain. This member of the Athletics, who knows the game and policy of the club, recited the internal strife in a verbal statement. He is an opponent of Thomas.

The Athletic baseball club has never been the same since Thomas was made Captain. To begin with he was not a regular player, and the other fellows always like to see one of the regulars in the Captain's position. Again the older fellows on the club and many of the new ones were against Thomas because they believed that he was responsible for forcing Danny Murphy out of the Athletics. He had Connie's ear all through last winter and there is not any question [that] what Ira said had a great deal of influence with the manager. For that reason and from several things that were dropped, most of the boys felt that Thomas had got rid of Murphy and that made him unpopular. When he was made captain he began to call down many players who knew more baseball than Ira Thomas will ever know. There shouldn't be any doubt in anybody's mind that Jack Barry is almost as fine a shortstop and as great an all-around ballplayer as anybody would want. Everybody knows too that he is as game as they come. What do you think of Thomas telling Barry that he was quitting, and 'get in there and do something.' That happened in one of the world's series at Boston.

Ed Bang of the *Cleveland News* had considered the rumors about the A's all bunk, but he changed his mind after reading the Bob Shawkey and Ira Thomas interviews. "Each day something else crops up which shows that Connie Mack was unquestionably right in his decision to shake up the club."

Tommy Rice of the *Brooklyn Eagle* quoted one unnamed manager, "Mack had to decide whether he was going to run the team, or the team was going to run him."

Christy Mathewson chimed in with comments hinting that Collins had "trouble" with Connie Mack, to which Collins replied, "Matty did not know whereof he wrote," an opinion of Mathewson's commentaries shared by more than one newspaperman.

That there was dissension is indisputable. Over the years Mack would maintain that the Federal League broke up his club. But it was more than that, and Eddie Collins was at the center of it, either as protagonist or symbol of the anti-Thomas cause. Had Mack replaced Danny Murphy with Harry Davis, there would have been no dissent, even though Davis was no longer an active player either.

It's equally undeniable that money was a factor. Nobody at the time was skeptical of Mack's lack of support by the fans. The numbers were there. Visiting beat writers saw it for themselves. Columnists conceded that Philadelphia attendance had fallen because it was taken for granted that other teams couldn't give the A's a good enough battle to warrant going to watch them. Nor did anyone criticize Mack for cutting expenses and replenishing the club's bank account under the conditions that existed. They were seen as prudent moves. In Detroit Henry Ford was promising a $5-a-day wage—double the $750 a year for a six-day week that most manufacturing jobs paid. Fans in the bleachers couldn't relate to sums like $10,000—$12,000—$15,000—just for signing a contract, before a day's work was done. They had no sympathy for men earning $4,000, much less $15,000, to play ball for six months—and complaining about it. It didn't occur to them to call the Macks and Griffiths and Comiskeys skinflints and misers for refusing to match Federal League foolishness. Indeed, when Walter Johnson said during the season that Washington meant nothing to him and he would go with anybody if the money was right, the fans' hostility was aimed at the star pitcher, not Clark Griffith. Their only outlet was through letters to the newspapers, and they wrote plenty of them.

The sale of Collins made sense to many writers as a baseball and business move. They didn't castigate Mack. Sam Crane in New York hailed the sale as "a brilliant stroke of business policy and [it] reflects credit of those who conceived the idea. It is not mere spite against Philadelphia fans, but will allow retrenchment in the club's expenses and revive interest in Philadelphia fans. The A's were so superior to other teams they had the leanest year in 1914. Fans thought no club had a chance against them."

W. A. Phelon wrote in *Baseball Magazine*:

The Collins deal, when you consider all angles . . . was the neatest, smoothest, nicest thing that both Mack and Comiskey could have done.

[It] can be boiled down like this: it reduces the Athletics' payroll, brings the needed cash, yet will not hurt the gate. Hence it's a great thing for the Mackmen. It gives the White Sox the strength they needed, and thereby insures enough added coin to fully repay the sum invested, besides hurting the Federal competition.

It gives Collins big, big money, and a change of scenery, thus saving him from "getting in a rut."

All things considered, the deal is a great thing for everybody.

Connie Mack could have said all those things. But he didn't.

Transactions for salary considerations are as old as professional baseball. Connie Mack was not the first nor would he be the last to act on that basis. Nobody has repealed the law of economics: if expenses exceed income, you won't be in business long. Three generations later major league general managers would still be saying, "Payroll in general plays a part in just about everything anyone does." Connie Mack was doing the same thing in 1914—refusing to meet salary demands he considered unwarranted or unaffordable at the time, cutting payroll to survive.

But he couldn't bring himself to admit it to the press. There seemed to be a conflict within him between the baseball side of the business and the business side of baseball. Making baseball decisions—on players, strategies, how to bat and field and throw—this was his life, his joy. Not money.

To small groups and in private he was more open about the economic aspect of his actions. Speaking to students at a school in Pottstown on February 15, 1915, he invited questions. Asked about the shakeup of his team, he attributed the changes to high salaries pitched by the Federal League that major league teams could not match. Players, he told them, received 90 percent of the profits as it was. Collins was a high-salaried player who had asked too much to stay.

In a letter to Frank Baker written a week before his Pottstown talk, Mack wrote, "As you probably are aware, I disposed of Collins for the reason that we could not handle his salary."

Yet five months later, after further sales, Mack gave a lengthy interview in which he said economics had nothing to do with it. (He was more criticized for giving it to a New York newspaper for syndication instead of a Philadelphia paper than for anything he said.) He denied that he "broke up my team for the sake of economy. In fact you cannot convince some people that I did not, so I do not bother trying. The Federal League wrecked my club by completely changing the spirit of the players. After that change came, there was nothing for me to do but protect myself and the club."

That seems to say that Mack would not have sold Collins or released the pitchers if the Federal League had not existed. He would have kept his machine intact, except for the matter of the dissension with Collins at its core. In that sense he didn't do it for "the sake of economy." But the Federal League did exist, and its effects did turn it in part into a matter of economy. The matter of "protecting myself and the club" could be taken as explanation for either reason.

Mack also said, "There was no chance of my holding any of the players I let go." This was true of Plank and Bender, with whom he was ready to part anyhow, but not of Eddie Collins, who, despite the Feds' overtures, had no plans to jump. But Mack couldn't afford Collins's salary for the next two years, and he knew Eddie could earn more elsewhere. In that sense, there was no way for him to hold a contented Collins.

For all of Mack's optimism, there was no doubt that Eddie Collins, strategist, hitter, base runner, fielder—the equal and, to some, the superior of Ty Cobb at outguessing his opponents and coming through in a pinch—was irreplaceable. One of the four famous infielders was gone, a reduction to some observers of more than 25 percent. Without an adequate replacement—if such a man existed—the A's were written out of the 1915 pennant race.

The *Chicago Tribune* welcomed Collins the second baseman, but not Collins the journalist. Citing his writing activities as a cause of discord in Philadelphia, it urged the White Sox to curtail his sideline and predicted that harm would come to the team if he continued. "The *Tribune* does not believe the White Sox need authors."

For the next five years, Collins's batting average would be well below his production with the Athletics. This came as no surprise to Jack Coombs, who attributed it to the same factor that enabled the White Sox pitchers to stay at or near the top of the league every year, whether the club finished first or sixth, and accounted for the team's light hitting: "Too many signboards. Comiskey's park is so congested with advertisements as to leave only a small background against which the batter can see the ball coming up to the plate. The batsman is handicapped when looking into the face of a red and white breakfast food sign. The background of green on the center field fence back of the pitcher's box was so small, that a foxy pitcher like Eddie Plank, by using his crossfire, could start the ball from one side of this, and the ball would seem to float up from the middle of a beer sign."

Shibe Park still had no outfield signs.

After the sale of Collins, Mack indicated that he had no more player transactions in mind. Contrary to reports that Frank Baker was headed for the Feds, the Trappe farmer said on December 13, "Connie and I parted the best of friends. All my interests are centered in the Athletics and I will be back next spring and try to help them win another championship."

Three-fourths of the famed infield, all the outfielders and catchers, and a corps of strong, experienced young pitchers would be back next spring. Words like wrecked, dismembered, decimated, torn apart, broke up—these and other terms of destruction were applied to the Athletics that winter and handed down forevermore thereafter. But plenty of managers at the time would have gladly swapped their entire rosters for what remained of the Philadelphia Athletics and considered it the best Christmas present they ever received.

EPILOGUE

The 1915 season began with high hopes that quickly disintegrated. By late May the Athletics were in last place to stay—for seven years. Over the next several years Connie Mack gradually sold off the remaining parts of his championship machine and set about building a new one.

It took him fifteen years and a complete change in his team-building methods to return to the top. When he did, he had put together the greatest team in baseball history, the American League champions of 1929–1931, world champions in 1929–1930.

Connie Mack was sixty-eight when he won his last pennant in 1931. He managed the Athletics for another nineteen years—fifty in all, "one year too long," by his own admission.

Years of losing teams; discord among his sons, who succeeded him in running the business; and the ascendance of their Shibe Park tenants, the Phillies, left the business with no resources to continue. Fifty-four years after Connie Mack started the American Base Ball Club of Philadelphia, the Athletics were sold out of the family and out of the city, moving first to Kansas City, then to Oakland. The white elephant symbol went with them.

But that's another story, yet to be written.

Connie Mack was among the first group of baseball immortals inducted into the National Baseball Hall of Fame in 1937. He died at ninety-three on February 8, 1956.

A WORD ABOUT SOURCES

During more than three decades of wandering through baseball's laby-
rinths of lore and legend, I've accumulated scraps of notes jotted down
on ticket stubs, paper napkins, hotel laundry lists—you name it. Stories
and anecdotes have stuck in my mind like lint on a blue serge suit. I can no
more tell you when or where I picked them up than I can tell you the kinds
of trees that gave their lives to make the paper they were printed on.

As I began to research the life of Connie Mack in earnest twenty-two
years ago, I still was not the kind of diligent source-noter who warms the
hearts of academic PhD thesis advisers. So I cannot cite date, page, and
column whence cometh all the raw material of this book. Nor do I think
most readers care.

Suffice it, then, for me to tell you that in addition to those sources mentioned in the acknowledgments, the National Archives in Washington DC
provided military records; the Athletic Department of the College of the
Holy Cross in Worcester, MA, the scrapbooks of Jack Barry; the National
Baseball Hall of Fame Library, files of clippings on numerous players. I left
my eyeprints on antiquated microfilm readers in the Library of Congress
and libraries in cities from coast to coast, perusing newspapers in Los
Angeles, San Francisco, Philadelphia, Milwaukee, Chicago, Pittsburgh,
Cincinnati, Boston, East Brookfield (MA), Elmira (NY), Spencer (MA),
Springfield (MA), Worcester, Hartford, New Haven, Meriden (CT), St. Louis,
Jacksonville, Cleveland, New Orleans, Detroit, Washington, New York,
Buffalo, Gettysburg, Grand Rapids (MI), Atlanta, Augusta (GA), and Dallas,
as well as *Sporting Life, The Sporting News*, the *National Police Gazette*,
and the following magazines: *Baseball Magazine, Saturday Evening Post,
Collier's, Harper's Weekly, Everybody's, Leslie's Weekly, McClure's, Literary
Digest, St. Nicholas, Atlantic Monthly,* and *Pearson's.*

I used few books, preferring to rely on contemporary reports. Background on Philadelphia came from *The Shame of the Cities*, by Lincoln Steffens (1904), and *Philadelphia: Holy Experiment*, by Maxwell Burt Struthers (Garden City, NY: Doubleday, Doran, 1945). Useful were *Connie Mack*, by Fred Lieb (New York: G. P. Putnam's Sons, 1945), and *Baseball: The Early Years* and *The Golden Age*, by Harold Seymour (New York: Oxford University Press, 1960 and 1971). *My 66 Years in the Big Leagues*, ghostwritten for Connie Mack (Philadelphia: John C. Winston, 1950), contained nothing reliable.

INDEX

advertisers and baseball, 437, 490–91

Ainsmith, Eddie, 582

alcohol abuse: by baseball players, 34, 58, 59, 64, 75, 88, 91, 112, 140, 159, 430–31, 469, 481; by Dennis Mack, 132, 334; by Michael McGillicuddy, 30

Altrock, Nick, 349

American Association, the: demise of, 91, 133, 161; resurrection of, 162, 167–69; teams, 24, 34, 51, 61, 78, 83, 89, 146. *See also* American League, the

American Federation of Labor, 170

American League, the: Benjamin Shibe and, 198–202; conflicts over players with the National League, 184–90, 227–31, 237, 248–52, 289–91; Connie Mack's loyalty to, 460–61; early success of, 184–90; the Federal League and, 604–5; financial investment in, 259–61; first year success of, 259; 1901 inaugural season managers, 232–34; media coverage of, 222–23; New York ballpark built by, 308–11; operating expenses, 379–80; owners, 473–74; pennants, 292; raiding of the National League, 209–19; rules committee, 216–18, 575, 586–87; salaries in, 216, 221, 325, 326–27; salary negotiations with the National League, 303–7.

Ames, Red, 528, 536–37

Anderson, John, 169, 171

Anderson, William Y. C., 203, 228

Angus, Samuel F., 260, 306, 325

Anson, Cap, 518; and the Chicago White Stockings, 23–24; and the National League, 51, 61, 73; and the New York Giants, 79; and the Pittsburgh Pirates, 87; playing against Connie Mack, 58, 99; retirement of, 152; William Terry and, 140

Arbuckle's Coffee Company, 82

Armour, Bill, 272, 274

Ashbridge, Samuel, 236

Atlanta Constitution, 362

Atlantic Monthly, 401

attendance at baseball games, 325, 460, 465; drops in, 498, 567, 627–28; Philadelphia Athletics and, 290–92, 358, 390, 395–96, 402, 434–35

Atz, Jake, 450

Augusta Chronicle, 373

Auten, Phil L., 105

automobiles, 160, 545, 556–57, 602

Baer, Bugs, 556

Bair Funeral Home, Oliver H., 1–5

Baker, Charles, 240

Baker, Frank "Home Run," 3, 416, 463, 480, 624, 665, 670; automobile purchased by, 504, 545; banquets

Baker, Frank "Home Run" (*cont.*)
attended by, 545–46; character of,
647–48; fans of, 532–34; games, 428–
32, 445, 454, 455, 460–61, 474, 483,
505–6, 558, 562, 578, 585, 638; income
taxes paid by, 614; 1911 World Series
and, 523–26, 529–36, 541–43; 1913
World Series and, 590, 597–600; 1914
World Series and, 645; the press on,
513–14, 658, 672; salary of, 608, 612;
spring training, 549, 616
Baker, John Franklin, 416
Baker, William, 623
Baldwin, Charles, 77
Baldwin, Mark, 88
Ballard, George M., 45
Baltimore Orioles, the, 95–96, 102–3,
119, 206, 255, 265, 279, 617; financial
troubles of, 622–23; Hughie Jennings
and, 248–49; Jack Dunn and, 467–
68, 552, 559; Ned Hanlon and, 99,
105, 138, 160, 622; players recruited
by, 209, 211
Baltimore Sun, 124, 125, 623, 625
Bancroft, Frank, 491
Bang, Ed, 394, 465, 651, 668
Barnard, Ernest, 476
Barr, Hyder, 414
Barrow, Ed, 87, 323
Barry, Jack, 464, 480, 490, 602, 632;
automobile purchased by, 545; character of, 647–48; Eddie Collins and,
471–72; games, 412, 418, 427, 430,
432–33, 440, 443, 458–59, 483–84, 489,
585, 638; income taxes paid by, 614;
injuries of, 505, 558, 620; marriage of,
496; 1911 World Series and, 529–30,
535–37, 541, 543; 1913 World Series
and, 591; 1914 World Series and, 641;
the press on, 512–13, 668; recruitment of, 402–3; salary of, 612; spring
training, 616

Barry, Matt, 36
Bartley, Bill, 375, 391, 393–94
Barton, Harry, 339, 345
baseball: batboys, 463–64, 477, 519;
black players in, 46, 152, 257,
294–95; Board of Control, 84–86; in
Brookfield MA, 20, 21, 22–24, 25–28;
cards, 59, 149; competition from
vaudeville, 75; corruption in, 50–51,
133, 154; effect of war on, 150; equipment, 44–45, 76, 95, 159, 442, 488,
503; farming system, 136–37, 191–92;
gambling on, 321, 355, 524, 587–88,
600, 647; game attendance, 290–92,
325, 358, 390, 395–96, 402, 434–35,
460, 465, 498, 567, 627–28; mascots, 519; minor league, 42, 130, 146,
156, 165, 465, 510, 559–60; motion
picture cameras and, 482; operating
expenses, 379–80; popularity of, 186,
233–34; profits, 74–76, 79–80, 144–45,
180, 259, 279, 287, 465–66, 498–99,
545, 546, 596–97, 603; rules, 95–96,
141, 216–19, 260–61, 305–7, 364–65,
488–89, 507, 575, 586–87; salaries, 22,
23–24, 31, 36, 38, 45, 67–69, 80–81,
138–39, 140, 146, 148–49, 158, 172,
210–11, 216, 221, 266, 272, 295–96, 298,
307, 325, 326–27, 371, 428–29, 465, 501,
569–70, 607–8; stadium investment,
498–99; stock, 45–46, 295; ticket
prices, 519, 574; umpires, 49, 56, 76,
103, 111, 113, 117–18, 124–25, 141–42,
236, 250, 256, 319, 327–28, 345, 395,
463, 506, 641; writers, 337–38. *See also*
players, baseball
baseball cards, 59, 149
Baseball Digest, 488
Baseball Magazine, 201, 222, 372, 413,
423, 613, 669
Base Ball Players' Fraternity, 605–6

baseballs, rules regarding, 487–89
Baseball's Greatest Teams, 639
Baseball Writers' Association of
America, 464, 518, 628
batboys, 463–64, 477, 519
batting cages, 382
batting skills of Connie Mack, 36–37,
46–47, 55, 64, 66, 70–71, 92, 101,
104–5
Bealle, Morris, 47
Beasley, N. B., 619
Beaumont, Ginger, 151–52, 154–57, 295
Beaven, Fr. Thomas, 61
Beck, Emil, 207
Becker, Beals, 530
Beckley, Jake, 87, 102–3, 104, 111, 125–26,
129, 243
Beecher, Ed, 77, 82
Bender, Charles Albert "Chief," 374,
375, 470, 509, 587, 600, 611, 638; on
the Boston Braves, 645; fans of, 351;
the Federal League and, 620; games,
298, 314–15, 316, 317–18, 319, 323, 327,
331, 334, 341, 350, 365–66, 382, 386,
388, 393, 394, 417, 445–47, 458, 460,
473, 482, 485, 515, 553, 557, 561–62,
579, 584, 651–52; housing, 427; illnesses and injuries of, 337, 347, 366,
401, 407, 553, 582–83, 650–51, 652–56;
leaves the Philadelphia Athletics,
658–59; 1905 World Series, 356; 1911
World Series and, 522–23, 535, 538,
540–41, 543; 1913 World Series and,
589–91, 596; 1914 World Series and,
640–41, 650; salary of, 428–29, 576;
scouting by, 639; speaking engagements, 546; spring training, 550–51,
616; superstitions of, 462; vaudeville
acting by, 546; waiver rules and,
652–56
Bender, Chief, 224

Bennett, Charley, 474
Bergen, Bill, 166
Bergen, Marty, 166
Berger, Charles, 415
Beringer, Col., 86
Bernhard, Bill: baseball games, 206, 212,
237, 241, 251, 263; Col. John Rogers
and, 272; lawsuit by the Philadelphia
Phillies and, 220, 227, 243, 266,
268–69, 272; signed by Connie Mack,
218, 219
Berry, David, 298–99, 300
Betts, William, 118
Bierbauer, Lou, 84, 85, 86, 87, 101, 102,
126, 171
Billings, J. B., 224
birth of Connie Mack, 12
black baseball players, 46, 152, 257,
294–95
Blaine, James G., 38, 39
Blau, Maurice, 321
Blue, Bird, 418
Boardman, Albert, 30, 31, 33, 35
Board of Control, 84–86
Bollard, Frederick, 95
Bonds, Barry, 242
Bone, Scott C., 325
Bones Battery, Hartford baseball club,
40–49
Bonner, Frank, 274, 279
Boston Beaneaters, the: Arthur Soden
and, 190, 215–16; Frank Selee and, 91;
John Morrill and, 69; Kid Nichols
and, 100–101; players signed by, 84;
players stolen from, 210; Vic Willis
and, 224; Wiley Piatt and, 303
Boston Braves, the, 503, 629, 630–35,
640–48
Boston Globe, 118, 189–90, 326, 352, 473,
546, 647
Boston Herald, 387, 447, 628

Boston MA: Connie Mack's first visit to, 25; Irish immigrants to, 5

Boston Reds, the, 75. *See also* Boston Beaneaters, the

Boston Red Sox, the, 625, 664; games, 445–46, 509, 510, 552, 557, 558–59, 562; and the 1912 World Series, 563

Botkin, Benjamin A.: *Treasury of New England Folklore*, 2

Boudreau, Lou, 376

Bowerman, Frank, 289, 304, 305

bowling alleys owned by Connie Mack, 333, 335

Boyce, Fr. J., 10

Bradley, Bill, 210

Brandt, William, 628

Brennan, Bill, 530

Bresnahan, Roger, 355, 384

Bressler, Rube, 583, 616, 624, 627

Brewerytown Chronicle, 204

Bromley, C. S., 421

Brookfield Manufacturing Company, 15

Brookfield Times, 22, 27, 39, 60

Brooklyn Eagle, 668

Brooklyn Tip Tops, 621, 658

Brotherhood of Professional Base Ball Players, 67–69, 71–72, 73, 74, 80, 82–83, 91

Broun, Heywood, 643, 645

Brouthers, Art, 362, 366

Brouthers, Dan, 197

Brown, Carroll, 514, 578, 581, 584, 595, 611; spring training, 616

Brown, Mordecai "Three Finger," 479, 484, 487, 605

Browning, Pete, 86, 87, 88

Bruce, John E., 305, 600

Bruce, Lou, 328

Brunell, Frank, 79, 81

Brush, John T., 171, 182, 190, 250, 262,

324, 332; the Cincinnati Reds and, 136, 214, 221, 291; the New York Giants and, 291, 304, 308–9

Bruske, Paul, 455

Bryan, William Jennings, 419

Buckenberger, Al, 89, 90–91, 96, 107, 111–12, 126

Buckley, Davis, 9

Budner, Larry, 381

Buelow, Fritz, 284

Buffalo Bisons, the, 72, 75, 76–83

Buffalo Express, 75

Burke, John, 546

Burns, Tommy, 90, 91

Burt, George, 20, 30–31

Burt Shoe Company, 20, 29, 30–31

Bush, "Bullet" Joseph: games, 224, 452, 471–72, 561, 581, 584, 587, 589, 594, 602, 624, 642, 652; marriage of, 645

Byrnes, Jimmy, 370

Byron, Bill, 641

cages, batting, 382

Callahan, Nixey, 210, 325

Cambria (ship), 8

Campana, John, 32, 33, 38

Cantillon, Joe, 409, 428, 445

cards, baseball. *See* baseball cards

Carmichael, John, 642

Carnegie, Andrew, 91, 110, 196

Carney, Pat, 403

Carr, Charlie, 234, 237

Carroll, Cliff, 49, 68

Carroll, Fred, 87

Carroll, George, 560

Carron, C. J., 246

Carruthers, Bobby, 319

Carter, Nick, 406, 407–8

Cartin, Rev. John A., 5

Cassidy, Joe, 339, 359

Castro, Fidel, 8

Castro, Lou, 266, 274, 280, 294
catching skills of Connie Mack, 41–42, 55, 56–57, 70, 97–100
Cather, Ted, 631
Caylor, O. P., 23, 114, 118
Central Massachusetts Amateur Base Ball Association, 26, 28
Cephalonia (ship), 8
Chadwick, Henry, 21, 68–69, 305, 329, 358
Chadwick, James, 469, 545
Chance, Frank, 479–80, 482–86, 499, 584, 603, 636
Chariot of Fame (ship), 8
Chase, Hal, 361, 454, 511, 518
Chech, Charlie, 161, 171
Chesbro, Jack, 252, 289–90, 331, 341
Chicago American, 400
Chicago Colts, the, 84, 152
Chicago Cubs, the, 425, 479–90, 569–70, 603, 640
Chicago Daily Journal, 242
Chicago Orphans, the, 151, 153, 165, 169, 180, 210, 233, 252, 262
Chicago Pirates, the, 78
Chicago Tribune, 85, 150, 242, 554, 662, 671
Chicago Whales, the, 660
Chicago White Stockings/Sox, the, 357–58, 417, 670, 671; Buck O'Brien of, 566; the Federal League and, 608–9; game attendance, 325, 345, 368; games, 23, 65, 167, 170–71, 178, 242, 286, 303, 349, 388, 409, 442, 474, 479, 485–86, 557; players classified as merchandise, 466
children of Connie Mack, 167, 427, 492; births of, 12, 16, 65, 76, 90, 564, 615, 617; and the death of Margaret Mack, 93–94; education of, 131; moved to Philadelphia, 333–34;

playing baseball, 468–69, 617–18; raised by Mary McGillicuddy, 131–32; romances of, 564–67
Childs, Samuel, 40
Cicotte, Ed, 445, 457
Cincinnati (ship), 494
Cincinnati Commercial-Gazette, 162
Cincinnati Enquirer, 22, 34, 76, 88, 575
Cincinnati Reds, the, 136, 150, 162–63, 214, 221, 291, 325, 383, 509
Cincinnati Times-Star, 75, 638
Civil War, the, 11, 12, 14
Clark, Spider, 70
Clarke, Bill, 171
Clarke, Boileryard, 210
Clarke, Fred, 173–74, 178–80, 511, 534
Clarke, Josh, 449
Clarkson, Arthur, 140
Clement, Marie, 331
Cleveland, Grover, 38, 39
Cleveland Indians, the, 646
Cleveland Naps, the, 379, 547, 582
Cleveland News, 394, 610, 651, 668
Cleveland Plain Dealer, 475, 502, 633
Cleveland Press, 448–49
Cleveland Spiders, the, 87, 102
Clingman, Billy, 108
Clymer, Otis, 332
Coakley, Andy, 365, 369, 374, 375; games, 297, 316, 319, 321, 331, 340, 341, 342, 347–48, 350; and 1905 World Series, 356
Cobb, Ty, 470, 482, 518, 534, 642, 645, 671; on Bris Lord, 528; as a columnist, 524–25; Connie Mack and, 453–59, 524–25; on Eddie Collins, 512, 618; Eddie Collins on, 451; fighting by, 555–56; games, 365, 396–98, 401, 407, 412, 414, 415, 447, 450, 452–59, 471–72, 480, 506; salary of, 501, 575, 609

Coca-Cola, 570
Cochrane, Mickey, 4
Coe, Judge Levi L., 38
Coghlan, Rose, 111
Cohan, George M., 20, 342, 375
Cohn, H. H., 149, 150–51, 167
Cohn, Joseph P., 559–60
Colcolough, Tom, 108, 110, 112, 113
Cole, King, 480, 485
Coleman, Joe, 3
Collamore, Allan, 501–2, 504
Collier's, 377
Collins, Eddie, 429, 430, 461, 467, 480,
    490, 601, 632; as captain, 547, 580,
    618–19; character of, 647–48; Connie
    Mack and, 666–70; fans of, 504; the
    Federal League and, 608–10, 621;
    friendship with Connie Mack, 602;
    games, 3, 369–73, 388–90, 393, 431,
    440–41, 443, 447–48, 479, 485, 489,
    507–8, 562, 582–84, 585, 638; housing,
    427; injuries, 407, 418, 505, 558; Ira
    Thomas and, 618, 660–62; Jack Barry
    and, 471–72; John McGraw on, 600;
    John Wheeler and, 634–35; leaves
    the Philadelphia Athletics, 662–70;
    marriage of, 496; 1911 World Series
    and, 525–31; 1913 World Series and,
    591–92, 594–98; 1914 World Series
    and, 640, 642; the press on, 511–12,
    657, 669–70; on Rube Oldring, 473;
    salary of, 497, 609, 612; scouting by,
    521, 579; superstitions of, 463; train-
    ing of, 407–8, 410, 411; Ty Cobb and,
    451, 453–55, 512
Collins, Eddie, Jr., 616
Collins, Jimmy, 209, 210, 232, 273, 386,
    394, 439
Collins, Michael, 238
Columbia Park, Philadelphia PA, 204–8,
    238, 244, 263–64, 294–95, 379

Comfort, C. D., 50
Comiskey, Charles, 259, 427, 571, 605;
    and the American Association, 61,
    83, 167, 182–83; American League
    rules committee, 216–17; Ban
    Johnson and, 162–63, 188, 357–58,
    660, 662–63; on baseball fans,
    340; and the Chicago grandstand,
    183, 184; and the Chicago White
    Stockings, 167, 170–71; on John
    McGraw, 250; negotiations with
    the National League, 303–7; and
    the Players' League, 75; purchase of
    Eddie Collins and, 664–66; value of
    players estimated by, 466; and the
    Western League, 150, 153
Compiler, 241
conflicts between the National League
    and American League over players,
    184–90, 237, 248–52, 289–91; lawsuit
    and, 227–31, 243, 265–66, 271
Connecticut State League, 29, 36, 40, 42
Connolly, Tom: games, 250, 256, 395,
    398, 464, 485–86; 1911 World Series
    and, 528
Conroy, Wid, 164, 169, 171, 289, 305
Considine, Bob, 4
Coogan, Danny, 117
Coogan, Patrick, 494
Coombs, Jack, 587, 610, 624, 671; on
    Eddie Collins, 618; games, 224,
    366–69, 370, 382, 385, 391–94, 408,
    415, 417, 441, 445, 446, 464, 473,
    474–75, 477–79, 483, 485–87, 504,
    508, 510, 514, 553, 557–58, 579, 652;
    housing, 427; illnesses and injuries
    of, 505, 579–80, 652–56; leaves the
    Philadelphia Athletics, 659; marriage
    of, 496; 1911 World Series and, 524,
    528–29, 536–38, 540, 543; 1914 World
    Series and, 650; and the press, 628;

scouting by, 521; speaking engage-
ments, 546; spring training, 468,
550–51; vaudeville acting by, 546;
waiver rules and, 652–56
Corbett, Jim, 137–38
Corbett, Young, 276
Corcoran, Larry, 24
Corey, William, 300
Corrigan, William, 36
corruption in baseball, 50–51, 133, 154
Coughlin, Charlie, 20, 298
Courier, 81, 82
Coveleski, Stanley, 559–60, 563
Craig, George, 392, 394
Crandall, Doc, 521, 528, 537, 581, 587, 599
Crane, Sam, 465, 669
Crawford, Sam, 171, 214, 290, 305, 395,
398, 450, 458
Cree, Birdie, 554
Criger, Lou, 210
Crisham, Pat, 160, 234
criticisms of Connie Mack, 172–73,
418–19, 535, 594
Cromwell, Oliver, 8
Cross, Lave, 327, 341, 366, 416, 490;
baseball games, 210, 234, 242, 249,
255, 274, 275, 282, 283, 289; as captain,
295–96, 359–60; fighting by, 321; and
the 1905 World Series, 355; salary
of, 315
Cross, Monte, 309, 327, 339, 359–60, 374,
382, 611; as batboy, 294; games, 108,
122, 262, 265, 269, 282–83, 285, 352,
387, 390, 399, 475; honored, 406–7; as
manager, 547
Cuban X Giants, 257
Cummings, Candy, 22
Cunningham, Frank, 449
Cunningham, Mody, 375
Cuppy, Nig, 210

Curry, Jim, 459
Cushman, Ed, 43

Dahlen, Bill, 255
Dale, Richard, 228, 230, 231
Daley, Annie, 17
Daley, Arthur, 312, 432, 544, 585
Daley, Simon, 17, 166
Daley, Tom, 577
Dallas News, 381
Daly, Tom, 70, 143
Danforth, Dave, 508, 514, 545, 554
Daniels, Charles F., 46, 47, 48
Daniels, Wiley, 533
Daubert, Jake, 598
Davies, Lloyd, 624–25
Davis, Al "Lefty," 220, 289, 598
Davis, George, 118, 305
Davis, Harry, 320, 322, 323, 324, 327,
331, 369, 384, 404, 490, 580, 638, 639,
669; as captain, 359–60, 363, 619;
Eddie Collins and, 372–73; games,
127, 243, 255, 257, 275, 283–84, 288,
293–94, 309, 317, 328, 343, 352, 357,
366, 382, 386–87, 394, 397, 408, 441,
443, 447, 473, 474, 489, 626; housing,
427; illnesses and injuries of, 328–29,
339, 418, 479, 501–3, 541–42; on John
Wesley Coombs, 368; as manager,
546–47, 553, 582; 1911 World Series
and, 520, 521, 528, 538, 539, 542, 543;
1913 World Series and, 599; 1914
World Series and, 645; as players'
spokesmen, 518; scouting by, 359,
497; speaking engagements, 546
Davis, Harry, Jr., 601
Davis, Rev. Thomas W., 601
Davis, R. F., 533
Davis, Ted, 601
Day, John, 74, 79, 81
Deal, Charlie, 631–32, 642

Dealey, Pat, 54, 64
Delahanty, Ed, 197, 213, 270, 305, 508
Delahanty, Jim, 452
Demaree, Al, 587, 595
Dempsey, May, 5, 30
Dempsey family, 10
Derrick, Claud, 490, 502, 508, 558, 561, 623
Detroit Journal, 619
Detroit News, 314, 400
Detroit Tigers, the: games, 250, 260, 287, 302, 330, 393–401, 410, 412, 419, 440, 505, 507–8, 625–26; Ty Cobb and, 446–59, 471–72, 506, 555–56, 609
Detroit Wolverines, the, 75, 139
Devery, Bill, 308–9, 419
Devore, Josh, 525, 534, 535, 536, 643
Diggins, Mama, 171
Dinneen, Bill, 292, 556, 575, 582
Doane, Charles, 9
Doane, Mabel, 461, 496
Dolan, Joe, 231, 242
Donahue, Pat, 475
Donlin, Mike, 250
Donovan, Bill, 305, 396–98, 457
Donovan, Patsy, 90, 97, 113, 128, 373, 507
Dooin, Red, 497, 518, 623
Double Squeeze, The (Needham), 377, 601
Dougherty, Hughie, 424
Dougherty, Pat, 328
Dowd, Tommy, 171
Dowling, Pete, 168, 171, 172, 177
Doyle, Larry, 535–36, 539, 541, 592, 599
Doyle, Pat, 26
draft prices for players, 164–65
Drake, Eddie, 14, 19, 40, 166
dressing rooms, 380, 522, 575
Drexel Biddle Press, 296
Dreyfuss, Barney, 149, 157, 164, 168, 209, 251–52, 289, 302, 304, 315, 380, 509;

Rube Waddell and, 174, 178, 179; the World Series and, 324
Dryden, Charles, 207, 236, 628; on Connie Mack, 279; on Doc Powers, 288; on Ed Kenna, 273–74; on foul balls, 364; on Larry Lajoie, 230; and the New York Giants, 238; and the 1905 World Series, 356; on Rube Waddell, 279, 312–14, 318, 337
Drysdale, Don, 646
Duff, Margaret, 61, 76
Duffy, Hugh, 100–101, 189, 210, 232, 256, 358
Duggleby, Bill, 262, 264, 265, 269, 271
Dunlap, Fred, 69
Dunn, Jack, 467–68, 478, 552, 559–61, 617, 622–23, 625, 657, 666
Dutton, Patrick, 33
Dygert, Jimmy, 347, 382, 387, 391–92, 393, 394, 396, 401–2, 408
Dykes, Jimmy, 2, 3

East Brookfield MA, 10; baseball team, 22–24, 25–28; cotton mill, 15; early baseball in, 20, 21, 22–24; liquor sales in, 60; post–civil war boom in, 18–19; prominent businessmen in, 18–19; railroads and, 18, 19; secession issue and, 19; show business in, 20; social life in, 20–21; telephones in, 19
Eastern League, 42–43, 45, 153
Ebbets, Charles, 210, 249, 253, 288, 373, 427, 466, 519–20, 605
Ebright, Hi, 70
education of Connie Mack, 13–14, 16
Edwards, Henry P., 502, 633
Egan, Ben, 419, 561, 577, 623
Ehret, Red, 90, 103, 108
Ehrlich, George, 50
Elberfeld, Kid, 163, 290, 305, 321, 360–61, 369, 480

Elmira Daily Advertiser, 299–300
Ely, Bones, 122, 128, 252, 257
Emslie, Bob, 103, 111, 250
Engel, Theodore, 149
Ensworth, George H., 346
Ensworth, H., 26
equipment, baseball, 44–45, 76, 95, 159, 442, 488, 503
Erringer, Charles, 199, 253
Erwin, Sam, 338, 344, 351, 431, 548, 571, 578
Esper, Duke, 138, 140, 160
Evans, Billy, 440, 474, 478, 562, 583
Evers, Johnny, 480, 481–82, 484, 631–35, 637, 642, 650
Ewing, Buck, 43, 57, 69, 75, 243
exhibition games set up by Connie Mack, 143–44
Exposition Park, 87
extended family of Connie Mack, 9, 496, 506, 564–65

Faatz, Jay, 78
Fain, Ferris, 121
Falkenberg, Cy, 351
fans of Connie Mack, 50, 239, 548–49
farming system, the, 136–37, 191–92
Farrell, Frank, 308–9, 419–20, 636
Fatima Cigarettes, 491
Faust, Charles, 519
Federal League, the: Connie Mack on, 669–72; establishment of, 603–11; the media and, 657; the Philadelphia Athletics and, 618, 619, 620; recruitment of American and National League players by, 623, 650, 655, 656
Feller, Bob, 646
Ferriss, Bill, 496
Ferson, Alex, 70
Fetzer, Willy, 375
Fields, W. C., 195, 196, 242

Fitzgerald, Charles R., 73, 76
Fitzgerald, Ed, 48
Fitzgerald, Jim, 423
Fitzgerald, John "Honey Fitz," 326
Fitzpatrick, William A., 346
Fitzsimmons, Bob, 137–38, 357
Fleischmann brothers, 291, 315
Fletcher, Art, 530, 536, 595
Flick, Elmer, 197, 213–14, 231, 262, 265, 269, 271, 281, 288, 316, 319, 364
Flint, Silver, 23
Flood, George, 438, 439, 518
Fogel, Horace, 388, 394, 419, 498, 577
Fohl, Lee, 444
football team, Athletics, 298–301
Forbes, Eli, 19
Forbes, George E., 18–19
Forbes family, 18–19
Ford, Henry, 669
Ford, Russ, 477, 554
Ford, Tris, 377
Foreman, Brownie, 108
Foreman, Frank, 240
Foreman, Johnny, 468
Foster, James, 288, 309, 316, 319
Foster, John B., 254, 302
foul balls, 364–65
Foutz, Dave, 88, 243
Fox, Jack, 408, 449
Frank, Charlie, 384, 470, 475, 476
Franklin, Benjamin, 10, 209
Franklin, James, 192
Fraser, Chick: baseball games, 242, 252, 266; Col. John Rogers and, 271–72; injuries of, 237; lawsuit by the Philadelphia Phillies and, 219, 220, 227, 243, 268–69; popularity of, 236; salary of, 212
Frazee, Harry, 326
Freedman, Andrew, 221–24, 238, 262, 291, 308–9

Freeman, Buck, 210, 317
Friend, Danny, 159
friends of Connie Mack, 548–49, 601–2; childhood, 9, 14–15, 346
Fritz, Harry, 610
Frysinger, Jesse, 298, 339
Fullerton, Hugh, Sr., 99, 212, 278, 466, 487–88
Fultz, Dave, 364, 370, 634; baseball games, 234, 237, 242, 249, 257, 274, 282, 288, 295, 316, 361; Base Ball Players' Fraternity and, 605–7; disputes over, 305; recruited by Connie Mack, 169; refusal to work on Sundays, 171
funeral of Connie Mack, 1–5

Gaffney, James, 631, 637
Gaffney, John, 49–51, 56, 57, 61, 68
gambling on baseball, 321, 355, 524, 587–88, 600, 647
Ganley, Bob, 445
Gannon, Gussie, 113
Garcia, Mike, 646
Gardner, Jim, 115
Gardner, Larry, 403, 552
Garner, John H., 533
Garvin, Ned, 210
Geier, Phil, 234, 242
Gessler, Doc, 474
Gettysburg Compiler, 241
Gifford, Jim, 43
Gilbert, Frank, 79
Gilbert, Larry, 643
Gilks, Bob, 475
Gilliam, A. M., 402
Gilligan, Barney, 55
Gilligan, Jack, 463
Gilmore, Frank, 41, 45, 58, 335; and the Bones Battery, 42–43; injuries of, 53–54, 65; marriage of, 68; and the

Washington Nationals/Statesmen, 47–49
Gilmore, James, 607
Glasscock, Jack, 108
Gleason, Kid, 284, 355
Glory of Their Times, The (Ritter), 616–17
Goldman, Henry, 658–59
Goldsmith, Fred, 24
Gompers, Samuel, 170
Good, Wilbur, 470
Goodfellow, Charles, 199, 253
Goodwin, Charles D., 37
Goodwin, W., 81
Gordon, Joseph W., 308
Gore, George, 23
Gowdy, Hank, 631, 638, 641, 643
Graham, George M., 311, 509, 510–11, 551, 600
Grand Rapids Democrat, 144
Grand Rapids Gold Bugs, the, 136, 144
Grant, Ulysses S., 20
Graves, Frank, 141
Green and Twichell, 19
Grey, Bill, 157
Griffin, Mike, 113
Griffith, Clark, 364, 370, 377, 473, 669; family of, 335; the Federal League and, 609; friendship with Connie Mack, 552, 562; as manager of the New York Highlanders, 308, 331, 343, 361, 365, 419–20; and the 1905 World Series, 355; playing skills of, 187–88, 210, 233, 242, 250, 256, 259, 275, 288; Walter Johnson and, 660; Washington Nationals and, 557
Grillo, J. Edward, 430, 448
Groom, Bob, 562
Gross, Fred C., 135, 163, 164, 260
Gruber, Henry, 77
Gruber, J. H., 125

Guest, Bernie, 3
Gumbert, Ad, 96, 114

Haas, Mule, 2
Haddock, George, 78
Hall, Spick, 601
Hallahan, Katherine, 492–94. *See also* Mack, Katherine
Hamilton, Billy, 166, 197
Hankee, Norwood, 468
Hanlon, Ned, 232, 243; and the Baltimore Orioles, 99, 105, 138, 160; and the Brooklyn Superbas, 160; as manager, 622; and the National League rules committee, 217; and the Pittsburgh Alleghenys, 71; and the Pittsburgh Burghers, 82–83; and the Pittsburgh Pirates, 86–89; and the Players' League, 74, 75
Harper, Jack, 270
Harris, Joe, 368
Hart, Bill, 108, 111, 112, 122, 151, 157
Hart, James, 153, 165, 167–68, 185, 252, 254, 292, 303, 305, 311
Hartford club, the, 40–49
Hartford Courant, 41, 43, 48
Hartman, Fred, 108, 138
Hartsel, Topsy, 611; automobile purchased by, 545; disciplined assaulting an umpire, 319; games, 282, 294–95, 350, 382, 386, 390, 401, 473, 475; illnesses and injuries of, 322, 479, 485; 1911 World Series and, 521; retirement of, 547
Harvey, Ervin, 242
Harwell, Ernie, 634
Haskell, John, 236, 256
Hastings, Charlie, 128
Hawley, Emerson, 108, 110, 112, 116, 122, 123–24
Hayden, Jack, 234, 237, 251

Hayes, Frank, 245–46
Haymarket Square riots, 68
Hedges, Robert L., 260, 304, 306
Heidrick, Emmett, 270
Heineman, C. J., 533
Heinemann, A. J., 466–67
Heinz, H. J., 110
Heitmuller, Heinie, 406, 431, 441, 475
Henley, Weldon, 316, 319, 330, 343, 346, 365
Hennessey, Danny, 519
Henry, John, 48, 55
Herrmann, August A. "Garry," 315, 373, 546, 575; Ban Johnson and, 303, 304; the Cincinnati Reds and, 291, 292, 325; the Federal League and, 603–4; rules negotiations by, 336–37
Herzog, Buck, 416, 525, 530, 537, 588, 595, 599
Hess, Otto, 631
Hewett, Robert C., 47, 61, 65, 69–70
Hewett, Walter, 47
Heydler, John, 53–54, 56
Hickey, John, 297
Higley, Charles, 228
Hill, Jephan, 206
Hines, Paul, 49, 70
Hodgkins, David, 93
Hoffer, Bill, 125
Hoffman, Danny, 329, 331, 343, 344, 346, 364
Hoffmeister, John G., 203
Hofman, Circus Solly, 480
Hogan, Bill, 501–2
Hogan, Jack: and the Brookfield baseball team, 14, 25–27; and the Meriden club, 31–33
Hogan, John, 76
Hogan, Margaret: early years, 26–27, 40, 44; marriage to Connie Mack, 60–61. *See also* Mack, Margaret

Hogan, Will: and the Brookfield baseball team, 14, 25–27; death of, 37, 44; and the Meriden club, 29–32, 35, 36, 37
Holahan, Annie, 492
Holahan, Frank, 492
Holahan, Margaret (daughter of Frank and Margaret Holahan), 492–93, 496
Holahan, Margaret, 492
Holahan, Nan, 492, 496, 548
Holahan, Rose, 492
Holmes, Ducky, 357
Holmes, Jim, 373, 374
Honest Long Cut Smoking or Chewing Tobacco, 491
Hooper, Harry, 507
Hope, Sam, 392
Houck, Byron, 550–51, 559, 563, 581, 584, 587
Hough, Frank L.: on Claude Rossman, 452; as owner of the Philadelphia Athletics, 182–83, 188, 190–92, 201, 203, 213, 219, 532, 567–68; Philadelphia Athletics sold by, 567–69; sued by the Philadelphia Phillies, 227–31, 268
Houser, Ben, 501–3
housing and traveling conditions: of baseball players, 49, 52–53, 62–63, 76, 86–87, 109–10, 461, 499–500, 551–52; of Connie Mack, 132, 427; improvements in, 499
Howe, Harry, 89
Howe, John M., 95
Howell, Harry, 210
How to Play Baseball (Mack), 296
Hoy, Ellsworth, 62–63, 64, 76–77, 79, 82, 125, 168
Hughes, Tom, 415
Hughey, Jim, 122
Hulbert, William A., 67

Hulswitt, Rudy, 305
Hurst, Tim, 365, 450
Husting, Pete, 161, 172, 173, 181, 273–75, 285, 286, 295
Huston, Cap, 658
Huston, S. B., 579, 620
Hutt, Louis, 322, 422
Hyperion (balloon), 21

Illustrated History of Baseball (Smith), 600
immigrants to the United States, 5–10, 134, 194–95, 234, 462
income taxes, 614–15
Indiana League, 170
Indianapolis Hoosiers, the, 65
injuries of Connie Mack, 53, 101, 102, 103
insurance on baseball players, 379
interleague play, 336–37
International Association, 75
International News Service, 526
Irish immigration to the United States, 5–10
Irwin, Arthur, 23, 49, 70, 71, 74, 82, 189
Isaminger, James, 468, 511–12, 540, 576–77, 629, 630, 650, 665, 656; on Ira Thomas, 661

Jackson, George W., 203
Jackson, Joe, 413–16, 431–32, 456, 470, 475–77, 624
Jackson, Travis, 354
James, Bill, 630, 632, 641, 645
Jennings, Hughie, 518, 523, 653; games, 89, 116, 190, 210, 237, 251, 460, 475; on Joe Jackson, 470; John McGraw and, 248–50; as manager, 390–91, 473, 506, 549, 556
Johnson, Albert L., 71, 74, 146
Johnson, Ban, 239, 254, 257, 264, 390, 437, 482, 504, 606; baseball rules

and, 365, 507, 575; Charles Comiskey and, 162–63, 188, 357–58, 660, 662–63; Clark Griffith and, 552; dissolution of the Western League and, 164–65; Eddie Collins and, 662; Federal League and, 603–4; first year of the American League and, 184–90; on gambling, 321, 524; George Stallings and, 635–36; John McGraw and, 249–50, 280; lawsuit by the Philadelphia Phillies against the Athletics and, 227–31, 237, 264–69; leadership of, 168–69, 181–82, 191–92, 201, 209, 228, 232, 385, 400, 546, 555, 587; the media and, 186–87, 238; the Milwaukee Brewers and, 256; negotiations with the National League, 303–7; and the 1905 World Series, 355; the Philadelphia Athletics and, 234–35; raiding of National League players and, 209–11; salary of, 259; success of major league baseball and, 308–9; success of the Western League and, 162, 167–68; on Ty Cobb, 456

Johnson, Charles, 57

Johnson, Chief, 613

Johnson, John G., 227–31, 267–68

Johnson, Randy, 324

Johnson, Walter: and the Chicago Whales, 660; the Federal League and, 609, 621; gambling by, 600; games, 393, 441, 452, 459, 462, 474, 480, 562, 582; Jack Coombs and, 515; 1911 World Series and, 520, 552–53; 1913 World Series and, 591; salary of, 501

Jones, Bert, 144

Jones, Davy, 397–98, 419

Jones, Fielder, 210, 390

Jones, Jack, 36

Jones, Samuel H., 182, 191, 203, 279, 385, 426, 567–69

Jones, Tom, 452

Jordan, Harry, 107, 115–16, 602

Joss, Addie, 319, 329, 452

Joyce, Bill, 117, 124, 159

Kansas City Cowboys, the, 50–51

Kansas City Packers, 605

Karger, Ed, 507

Keefe, Dave, 567

Keefe, George Washington, 77, 78

Keefe, Tim, 43, 76, 77

Keeler, Willie, 89, 116, 290, 364, 369

Keener, Sid C., 569, 570–71, 645

Kelchner, Pop, 466

Kelley, Joe, 90, 104–5, 288

Kelley, Mike, 509

Kellogg, Al, 641

Kelly, Bill, 509

Kelly, John, 24

Kelly, Michael "King," 23–24, 57–58, 75

Kendle, Sam, 235–36

Kenna, Ed, 273–74

Kennedy, Brickyard, 113

Kennedy, John F., 326

Kennedy, Sam, 367, 414, 466

Kerr, William W., 82, 89–94, 96, 156, 420; and Connie Mack as manager of the Pirates, 104, 105–6, 116, 119, 123, 126–28; and the farming system, 137; fires Connie Mack, 128–29

Ketchum, Fred, 237

Kieran, John, 404

Kilfoyle, A. J., 303, 306, 425, 476

Killefer, Bill, 612

Killefer, Wade, 451

Killen, Frank, 102, 108–9, 110, 112, 124, 128; fighting by, 114; injuries, 104, 122; joins the Pittsburgh Pirates, 96

Killilea, Henry: Ban Johnson and, 256; Boston club sold by, 326; Charles Comiskey and, 184; on Connie Mack, 543; Connie Mack and, 129, 131, 135–36; financial investment in clubs by, 260; negotiations with the National League, 303; the Western League and, 158, 163, 165, 167, 181–83; the World Series and, 324

Killilea, Matthew: Connie Mack and, 135–36, 147, 153, 154; as president of the Milwaukee Brewers, 249, 260; and the Western League, 158, 163, 164, 167, 182, 192

Kilroy, Matt, 51

King, Roger W., 33

King, Silver, 86, 87

King James I, 8

Kinslow, Tom, 114

Kirksey, Oswald, 628–29

Kittridge, Mal, 365

Kleinow, Red, 331

Klem, Bill, 539, 591, 598, 661

Kletzch, Charles, 132

Kling, Johnny, 480

Knight, Jack: baseball games, 339, 344, 352, 360, 366, 369, 382, 387–89, 394, 439; traded to the Red Sox, 389

Koelsch, William F. H., 191

Kofoed, Jack, 640

Koufax, Sandy, 324, 646

Krank and His Language, The (Loftin), 186

Krause, Harry, 624; games, 406, 417, 429, 441, 445, 447, 450–51, 457, 460, 508, 515; health of, 553; injuries, 477

Krauthoff, L. C., 85

Krieg, Bill, 48, 49, 54, 55

Kubelik, Rafael, 617

LaChance, Candy, 318

Lajoie, Napolean, 197, 218, 219, 220, 234, 242, 251, 305, 319, 390, 582, 604, 616; Col. John Rogers and, 272–73, 281; Connie Mack on, 255; Connie Mack recruits, 212–14; lawsuit between the Philadelphia Phillies and Athletics and, 227–31, 243, 265–66, 271; National League attempts to recruit, 263, 291; New York Giants and, 263, 272; press accounts of, 257; salary of, 607; signs with Cleveland, 270

Lake, Fred, 142

Lally, Daniel, 141

Lane, F. C., 413, 512

Langervine, Alexander, 147

Langway, H. E., 26

Lannin, Joe, 622, 625, 664

Lapp, Jack, 577; games, 247, 418, 475, 477, 480, 483, 489, 508, 560; on Harry Krause, 553; income taxes paid by, 614; 1911 World Series games, 529, 530, 539, 541; 1913 World Series and, 592–93

Lardner, Ring, 312–14

Latham, Arlie, 226

Lawler, Martin P., 380–81, 423, 436, 438, 469

Leach, Tommy, 289, 305, 512

Leahy, Tom, 251

Leever, Sam, 252

Leinhauser, Bill, 556

Lelivelt, Jack, 416

Lemon, Bob, 646

Leonard, Elmer, 508, 560

Leopold, Bert, 573

Leslie's Weekly, 574

Lester, William R., 96

Levin, Harris: The Ultimate Baseball Book, 646

Levy, Sam, 163

Lewee, Ed, 149
Lewis, Duffy, 507
Lewis, Lloyd, 518
Lieb, Fred: on Christy Mathewson,
   588; on Connie Mack, 29, 43, 47, 111,
   201, 399, 502, 598; Connie Mack's
   conversations with, 27, 72, 101, 145,
   279, 397, 415, 465, 502, 528; on Frank
   Baker, 529; John Heydler and, 53–54;
   on Margaret Mack, 93; on Mary
   McGillicuddy, 131–32; on the 1911
   World Series, 539
Liebhardt, Glenn, 390
Livingston, Paddy, 440, 460, 475, 480
Lobert, Hans, 3
Lochhead, Harry, 237, 242
Lofton, Thomas W.: *The Krank and His
   Language*, 186
Loftus, Tom, 153, 162, 169, 260, 293,
   305–6
Long, Herman, 101
Long Island club, the, 45
Loos, Pete, 237
Lord, Bris, 561; automobile purchased
   by, 545; games, 339, 343, 382, 387, 476,
   477, 480, 515; 1911 World Series and,
   520, 521, 525; Ty Cobb on, 528
Los Angeles Times, 276
Louisville Colonels, the, 149, 151
Louisville Courier-Journal, 155
Lush, Billy, 370–71
Lusitania (ship), 605
Lynch, Jack, 43
Lynch, Tom, 98
Lynn, George H., 35, 38
Lyons, Denny, 84, 96, 98, 108, 122, 125,
   128
Lyons, Walter, 147

MacFarland, Benny, 568
MacFarland, Frank, 554, 568

Mack, Alice, 402
Mack, Annie, 66, 132, 206, 245, 335, 506,
   564
Mack, Betty, 566
Mack, Connie: Albert Bender and,
   314–15; and the American League
   rules committee, 216–17; ancestors and distant relatives of, 5–10;
   appointed captain of the Buffalo
   Bisons, 79; attacked by the press,
   154–58; automobiles and, 160; on
   baseball cards, 59; baseball school,
   409–12; batting skills of, 36–37, 46–
   47, 55, 64, 66, 70–71, 92, 101, 104–5;
   on being fired by William Kerr,
   128; Benjamin Shibe and, 197–203;
   birth of, 12; bitterness over loss
   of players, 621–22; and the Bones
   Battery team, 41–43, 45, 47; bowling alleys owned by, 333, 335; and
   the Brookfield baseball team, 22–24,
   25–28; and the Buffalo Bisons, 72, 75,
   76–83; catching skills of, 41–42, 55,
   56–57, 70, 97–100; on Chattanooga,
   Tennessee, 109; children of, 12, 16,
   65, 76, 90, 93–94, 131–32, 167, 333–34,
   427, 468–69, 492, 564–67, 615, 617;
   Christy Mathewson and, 220–25;
   concern over stability of baseball,
   44–45; conflicts over players with
   other managers, 248–54; criticisms
   of, 172–73, 418–19, 535, 568–71, 594;
   death of, 673; disappointment over
   the 1914 World Series, 649; early
   baseball playing by, 22; early jobs
   of, 15–16, 18–20; on Eddie Collins,
   670–72; Eddie Collins and, 666–70;
   Eddie Plank and, 239–42; education
   of, 13–14, 16; exhibition games set
   up by, 143–44; extended family of, 9,
   496, 506, 564–65; fans of, 50,

Mack, Connie (*cont.*)
239, 548–49; on the Federal League,
669–72; first book deal, 296; and the
first year of the American League,
184–90; football team organized
by, 298–301; and formation of the
Philadelphia Athletics, 204–8; Fred
Lieb and, 27, 72, 101, 145, 279, 397,
415, 465, 502, 528, 598; friends of, 9,
14–15, 346, 548–49, 601–2; funeral of,
1–5; George Stallings and, 636–37,
643–44, 665; in the Hall of Fame,
673; on Harry Jordan, 115–16; and
the Hartford club, 45–49; *How
to Play Baseball*, 296; Hyman
Pearlstone and, 381–82; income taxes
paid by, 614; injuries, 53, 101, 102, 103;
investments of, 378–79, 426–27, 613;
John McGraw and, 280–81; lawsuit
by the Philadelphia Phillies against,
227–31, 237, 264–69; management
style of, 137, 141–42, 161; as manager of the Milwaukee Brewers, 129,
131–33, 135–36; as manager of the
Pittsburgh Pirates, 104–7, 108–19,
122–28; manner of dress of, 24–25;
marriages of, 60–61, 493–97; minor
league club owned by, 573; moves to
the big leagues, 49–51; *My 66 Years
in the Big Leagues*, 94; name shortened from McGillicuddy, 22–23; on
Napoleon Lajoie, 274; negotiations
in Philadelphia, 185–93; personality of, 94, 117, 130, 145, 239, 283,
336, 500–501, 548–49, 627; physical appearance of, 24, 57, 121, 122,
500; as a Pittsburgh Pirates player,
86–91, 125–26; on players leaving the
Philadelphia Athletics, 659; political
interests of, 39; press accounts of,
47–48, 50, 59, 60, 62, 75, 88, 97–98,
121, 128, 154, 161, 256–57, 262, 329–30,
332–33, 377, 401–2, 441, 448–49,
568–70, 576, 585, 657–58, 665, 666;
recruitment of players by, 137–39,
142, 146–49, 169–70, 209–16, 220–26,
239–42, 257, 273–75, 279–80, 297–98,
316, 332, 339–40, 360–62, 366–69,
369–73, 392, 402–3, 406, 412–18,
501–4, 550–51, 554; and resurrection
of the American Association, 162,
167–68; Rube Waddell and, 173–80,
311–14, 317–23, 337, 348–49, 351–53,
376–77, 403–5; salaries of, 31, 36, 38,
45, 51, 158, 259, 295, 378, 570; serious-
ness about baseball, 58–59; shares
in the Philadelphia Athletics, 203;
Shibe Park and, 421–27; similarities
with John McGraw, 353–54; simple
lifestyle of, 378; superstitions of,
463; tryouts for professional teams,
29–30; Ty Cobb and, 453–59, 524–25;
versatility in playing different positions, 45; visit to Europe, 494–95. *See
also* management style of Connie
Mack
Mack, Connie, Jr., 564
Mack, Dennis, 93, 166, 206, 378, 437;
alcoholism of, 132, 334; attacked
by Thomas Murphy, 244–46, 248,
253–54; childhood of, 13, 17; children
of, 72, 570; death of, 506; marriage
of, 66; as witness at Connie Mack's
wedding, 61; working life of, 30, 39
Mack, Earle Thaddeus, 76, 94, 131–32,
167, 333–34, 468–69, 564; baseball
played by, 503, 629; coaching the
UNC team, 617–18; ownership of the
Philadelphia Athletics by, 568
Mack, Ella, 378
Mack, Eugene, 16, 17, 30, 40, 93, 166,
170, 333, 378, 564

Mack, Harold, 378, 564

Mack, Hazel, 506

Mack, Helen, 333, 402, 427, 564–67

Mack, Katherine: children of, 546, 564–66, 615, 617; honeymoon with Connie Mack, 494–96; 1913 World Series and, 599; travels to spring training with Connie Mack, 548. *See also* Hallahan, Katherine

Mack, Margaret, 61, 62; children of, 12, 16, 65, 72, 76, 90, 93, 131, 167, 333–34; death of, 93–94. *See also* Hogan, Margaret

Mack, Marguerite Veronica, 131, 333, 427, 492, 564–66, 617; childhood, 93, 95; marriage of, 653, 658

Mack, Mary. *See* McGillicuddy, Mary McKillop (mother of Connie Mack)

Mack, Mary (daughter of Connie Mack), 546, 564

Mack, Mary (daughter of Dennis Mack), 334, 506

Mack, Michael, 9, 16, 17, 30, 39, 61, 92–93, 378, 518, 564

Mack, Michael, Jr., 93; childhood of, 11–13, 15, 16, 17; on Connie's acceptance into professional baseball, 30; marriage of, 61; working life, 17, 39

Mack, Neil (son of Dennis Mack), 334, 437

Mack, Norman, 419

Mack, Roy, 65, 94, 131–32, 333–34, 427, 492, 564–65; ownership of the Philadelphia Athletics by, 568

Mack, Ruth, 493, 566–67, 569, 617

Mack, Thomas, 333, 496, 564–66; early years, 9, 15, 16, 17, 30, 95; scouting by, 297, 366, 402

Mackay, Gordon, 495, 532, 540, 590, 618

Madden, Billy, 413

Magee, Sherry, 432

Maine (battleship), 150

management style of Connie Mack: in the American League, 232–34; documented in books, 296; in handling players' personal lives and behavior, 111–15, 120–21, 145, 285–86, 337, 354, 404–5, 469–70, 497, 558; and his baseball school, 409–12, 577–78; long-range planning and, 296–97, 433, 516, 551; playing strategies and, 104–7, 108–19, 122–28, 137, 141–42, 161, 242–44, 282–85, 293–94, 393–99, 436, 442–45, 477–78, 501, 514–15, 522, 538, 580–81, 584–85, 592–93; scheduling of games and, 395. *See also* Mack, Connie

Manassau, Al, 256

Mann, Arthur, 627

Mann, Fred, 346

Mann, James, 590

Mann, Les, 631, 642–43

Manning, Jimmy, 183, 210, 232, 250, 260

Manning, Tom, 150, 156

Manush, Frank, 408

Manush, Heinie, 408

Maranville, Rabbit, 631–32, 643

Marquard, Rube, 517, 521, 526, 531, 536, 587, 590, 595

marriage of Connie Mack: to Katherine Hallahan, 493–97; to Margaret Hogan, 60–61

Martin, Bill, 634

Martin, Doc, 554

Martin, Harold, 508, 545

Martin, Luther, 190

mascots, team, 519

Massachusetts State Association, 35

Mathewson, Christy, 578, 587, 588, 637; baseball games, 220–25, 237, 239, 257, 260, 264, 289, 349, 515, 563; on Connie Mack, 527; disputes over,

Mathewson, Christy (*cont.*)
304, 305; on Eddie Collins, 668; football games, 299; and the 1905 World Series, 354, 355–56; 1911 World Series and, 521–32, 535, 541; 1913 World Series and, 591–92, 596–99; photographers and, 518; *Pitching in a Pinch*, 527; Waddell matchup, 383–85
Matthews, C. Starr, 623, 625
Mattimore, Mike, 338
Maul, Al, 335, 392, 413, 466, 551, 578–79, 642
Mauretania (ship), 495
McAleer, Jimmy, 184, 209, 233, 417, 501
McAllister, Jack, 298
McBride, George, 600
McCambridge, Robert, 567
McCarthy, Joe, 239
McCarty, Fr., 342
McCarty, Joseph and Mary, 10, 11, 12
McCloskey, Rev. Fr. J. B., 548
McClure's, 371, 374, 603
McClurg, William A., 110
McConaughy, J. W., 635
McCool, James, 437
McCormack, John, 395
McCormack, Pete, 406
McCready, Joe, 518
McDaniel, Charles, 205
McDevitt, Harry S., 39
McDonald, Hank, 566–67
McDonald, Patrick, 12
McDonough, Margaret, 496
McFadden, George, 434, 436
McGillicuddy, Cornelius (son of Michael and Mary McGillicuddy). *See* Mack, Connie
McGillicuddy, Cornelius, Jr. (son of Cornelius and Ellen Joy), 9
McGillicuddy, Cornelius and Ellen Joy, 9

McGillicuddy, Daniel, 11
McGillicuddy, Dennis. *See* Mack, Dennis
McGillicuddy, Eduardo, 9
McGillicuddy, Ellen, 333
McGillicuddy, Eugene. *See* Mack, Eugene
McGillicuddy, Harold, 132, 245
McGillicuddy, Hazel, 132
McGillicuddy, James, 11
McGillicuddy, Mary (daughter of Michael and Mary McGillicuddy), 15–16
McGillicuddy, Mary Agnes, 9
McGillicuddy, Mary McKillop (mother of Connie Mack), 10–11, 15–16, 30, 92–93, 495; Connie Mack's children and, 95, 131–32, 166–67, 333, 427, 493; death of, 548
McGillicuddy, Michael. *See* Mack, Michael
McGillicuddy, Michael, Jr. *See* Mack, Michael, Jr.
McGillicuddy, Nellie, 11, 13, 15
McGillicuddy, Nora, 564
McGillicuddy, Patrick, 9, 11, 333
McGillicuddy, Thomas. *See* Mack, Thomas
McGinley, Johnny, 3
McGinnity, Joe, 210, 256, 356
McGovern, Terry, 276
McGraw, John, 255, 288, 324, 405, 605, 657, 658, 665; and the American League, 167, 183, 192, 233, 332; the Boston Braves and, 637; and the Baltimore Orioles, 89, 102, 116, 117, 162, 209, 211; Connie Mack and, 280–81, 353–54; Doc Crandall and, 581; on Eddie Collins, 618; Frank Nohowel and, 429; in the Hall of Fame, 232; Hughie Jennings and, 248–50; *My*

Thirty Years in Baseball, 526; the
New York Giants and, 280, 292, 383,
640; 1905 World Series, 353, 354, 355,
356; 1911 World Series and, 356, 522,
534, 540–42; 1913 World Series and,
589–91, 594–96, 599; Rube Marquard
and, 526; salary of, 259, 570
McGuire, Jim "Deacon," 55, 476, 505,
555
McGunnigle, Bill, 89
McHale, Marty, 657
McInnis, John "Stuffy," 624; character
of, 647–48; childhood of, 412–13,
430–31; games, 436, 438, 439, 440,
475, 502, 504–5, 507, 582, 585; injuries,
520; 1911 World Series and, 541–42;
1914 World Series and, 638, 642; pop-
ularity of, 665; the press on, 513–14;
salary of, 612
McIntyre, Matty, 251, 257
McKenna, George, 481
McKillop, John, 10, 11
McKillop, Mary, 10–11
McKillop, Michael, 9–10
McKillop, Nancy, 10
McKillop, Sarah, 10
McKillup, Michael. *See* McKillop,
Michael
McKinley, William, 254
McLean, Larry, 598
McMahon, Jess, 361
McMahon, Sylvia, 645
McNally, James R., 309
McNamara, Joseph, 271
McNamee, Bill, 496
Meany, Tom, 639
Menefee, Jock, 104–5
Menke, Frank G., 526, 531
Mercer, Win, 124
Meriden baseball team, the: Connie
Mack leaves the, 38; Connie Mack's

rookie season with, 30–38; Connie
Mack's tryout for, 29–30; demise
of, 42; management, 35–36; money
troubles, 35–36, 38
Meriden Republican, 31, 32, 33–34
Merkle, Fred, 529, 530, 537, 587, 588, 591,
596, 597–98, 599
Merrimac (ship), 11
Merritt, Bill, 104, 115
Mertes, Sam, 210, 305
Merwin, A. G., 50
Meyers, Chief, 518, 523–24, 530
Milan, Clyde, 480, 583
Miller, Bing, 2–3
Miller, Doggie, 87
Miller, Marvin, 655
Milligan, Harry, 241
Milwaukee Brewers, the: accused of
breaking rules, 154–58; Connie
Mack hired to manage, 129; 1898
season, 146–58; 1899 season, 159–65;
failures of, 150–51; financial backing,
260; financial difficulties, 136; Matt
Killilea and, 249, 260; 1900 season,
170–80; players recruited to, 137–39,
142, 146–49, 160, 169–70; Rube
Waddell and, 173–80; spring training
by, 149–50; success under Connie
Mack's management, 131–33, 135–36,
144–45, 151–52
Milwaukee Journal: on the American
League, 184; on Arthur Clarkson,
140; on Bert Myers, 139; on the
Brewers' fans, 136; on Connie Mack,
121, 137, 141, 143, 147, 148, 154, 161; on
Jim Corbett, 144; on the Western
League, 163
Milwaukee Sentinel, 136, 155–56, 159, 172;
on Rube Waddell, 179
Milwaukee wi, 133–35
Minneapolis Millers, the, 160

minor league baseball, 42, 130, 146, 156, 165, 510, 559–60; clubs owned by Connie Mack, 573; college players in, 297–98; expansion of, 465; rules, 305

Mitchell, Fred, 273–74, 638, 640

Monahan, Annie, 66, 132

Moore, Fr. Thomas, 494

Moore, Michael J., 190

Moran, Herbie, 408, 631, 639, 643

Moran, Pat, 637

Morgan, Cy, 577; automobile purchased by, 545, 557; games, 445–46, 452, 460, 510, 515, 552, 558; spring training, 550–51; vaudeville acting by, 546

Morgan, John D., 346

Morgan, J. P., 196, 216, 577

Morgen Gazette, 481

Moriarty, Catherine, 285

Moriarty, George, 395, 400–401

Morning Republican, 54, 55, 65

Morrill, John, 58, 69

Moses Wheeler (ship), 8

motion picture cameras, 482, 518

Mountain, Frank, 23

Mulligan, Swats, 14

Mullin, George, 284, 450, 518, 520, 529

Murnane, Tim, 118, 189, 352

Murphy, Charles, 425, 476, 605, 666

Murphy, Danny, 419, 445, 553, 577, 610–11, 618, 669; as captain, 547, 578, 580; the Federal League and, 620; Francis C. Richter on, 411–12; games, 279–80, 282–83, 286, 297, 334, 368, 374, 375, 382, 387, 408, 414, 438, 441, 446, 460, 483, 515, 552; injuries, 475, 507, 558; 1911 World Series and, 520–21, 524, 535, 541; 1913 World Series and, 592, 595–96; 1914 World Series and, 638; the press on, 668

Murphy, Eddie: games, 560, 583, 585, 592, 597–98, 638; income taxes paid by, 614–15

Murphy, Morg, 242

Murphy, Sadie, 389

Murphy, Thomas, 206, 244–46, 254

Murray, Billy, 380

Murray, Jeremiah, 64, 113, 118

Murray, Red, 525, 598

Musselman, Maurice, 240

Mutrie, Jim, 51, 62, 70

Myers, Al, 66

Myers, Bert, 138, 142, 148–49, 151

Myers, Joe, 352

My 66 Years in the Big Leagues (Mack), 94

My Thirty Years in Baseball (McGraw), 526

Nadja Caramel Company, 490

Nash, Frank, 35–36

Nash, Ogden, 521

National Association, 107

National Baseball Hall of Fame, the, 232, 295, 496, 555

National Commission, 604, 605, 622

National Football League, 299

National League, the, 47, 57, 59, 66, 138, 547; absorption of American Association teams by, 89, 91, 161; Ban Johnson and, 153–54; and the Brotherhood of Professional Base Ball Players, 68, 74, 80; conflicts over players with the American League, 227–31, 237, 248–52, 289–91; Connie Mack's reputation in, 129; corruption in, 21–22; creation of, 21; financial losses, 73; and the first year of the American League, 184–90; lawsuit against the American League, 227–31; National Association and, 107; and the Players' National League of Base Ball Clubs, 71–72, 74–75, 81–82; and the Players' Protective Association, 187–88; raided by the American League, 209–19; and resurrection of the American Association, 162, 167–69; rules committee, 217, 586–87; salaries in, 303; salary negotiations with the American League, 303–7; secretiveness in, 262–63; strength of, 51; top players in, 23–24; weaknesses in, 153–54; and the Western League, 153, 161–64

National Police Gazette, 171

Navin, Frank, 574, 653

Needham, Henry Beach, 130, 374–75, 444, 571, 601; *The Double Squeeze*, 377, 601

Nehf, Art, 467

New England League, 40

Newhouse, Frank, 338, 362–63

New Orleans Baseball Association, 533

New Orleans Daily States, 338, 475

New York American, 635

New York Evening Mail, 628

New York Evening Telegram, 254, 504

New York Giants, the: Bill Bernhard and, 272; Cap Anson and, 152; Charles Dryden and, 238; Christy Mathewson and, 221; early years of, 51, 52, 57, 62, 67, 70; financial troubles, 79; financial worth, 498; game attendance, 460; games, 383–85, 477–79, 628–29; John McGraw and, 280, 292; John T. Brush and, 291; Napoleon Lajoie and, 263, 272; and the 1905 World Series, 352–57; and the 1911 World Series, 517–42; and the 1912 World Series, 563; and the 1913 World Series, 586–99; players recruited by, 509

New York Herald, 23, 80, 114, 118

New York Highlanders, the, 360–61, 369, 387, 408, 439; managers of, 308, 419–20; salaries, 326

New York Mets, the, 42–43, 44

New York National Guard, 186

New York Press, 588

New York Sun, 73, 280, 437, 520, 543, 621, 633

New York Telegraph, 379

New York Times: on baseball games, 21, 43, 118–19, 312, 361, 404, 429, 432; on Connie Mack, 544, 666; on Eddie Collins, 665, 667–68; on the World Series, 519

New York Tribune, 643, 647, 657

New York World, 74, 442, 626

New York Yankees, the, 575, 657–58, 658, 666

Nicholls, Si, 382, 387, 390, 398, 408, 412, 440, 449

Nichols, Kid, 100, 166

Nicholson, Bill, 242

Nicol, George, 139, 142

Nicol, Hugh, 24

Niles, Hezekiah, 190, 207

Nohowel, Frank, 429

Nolan, John, 555–56

Nolen, Jim, 121

North, Sheree, 121

Noyes, Thomas C., 325, 474

Nunamaker, Les, 507

O'Brien, Billy, 55

O'Brien, Buck, 360, 466, 481, 566, 567, 578

O'Brien, John, 127

O'Connor, Jack, 115–16, 289, 291

O'Day, Hank, 55–56, 64, 69, 118–19, 482

Odenbrett, George, 160

O'Donnell, Harry, 4

Ohl, Joseph C., 406–7, 429, 545, 568, 578
Okrent, Daniel: *The Ultimate Baseball Book*, 646
Oldring, Rube, 480, 497, 554, 576–77, 648; batboy recruited by, 463–64; games, 360–63, 387, 390, 393, 441, 446, 473, 561–62, 583, 638; illnesses and injuries of, 407, 515, 620; income taxes paid by, 614; 1911 World Series and, 525, 535–36; 1913 World Series and, 600; 1914 World Series and, 640; popularity of, 665
O'Leary, Charley, 397
O'Leary, J. C., 647
O'Loughlin, Silk, 345, 369, 391, 394, 395, 398, 399–402
O'Malley, Walter, 655
O'Neill, Cap, 431
O'Neill, J. Palmer, 85, 86, 88–89
O'Neill, Steve, 503
operating expenses, baseball, 379–80
Orr, Billy, 598, 601
Orth, Al, 270
Orthwein, Max, 260, 303
O'Sullivan More family, 8
O'Toole, Marty, 509, 510–11
Overall, Orval, 479–80, 482
Overfield, Joe, 77, 79
Owen, Frank, 349

Pabst, Fred, 134
Pabst Brewery, 134
Padden, Dick, 126, 178
Page, Maggie, 546, 601
Parker, Marion, 571, 576
Parsons, W. E., 28
Paul, Bob, 128, 563
Payne, Fred, 397–98
Pearce, C. J., 221
Pearlstone, Hyman, 381–82, 508, 571, 578

Pedroso, Eustaquio, 491
Pen and Pencil Club, 182
Penn, William, 183, 195
Pennock, Herb, 554, 558, 579, 581, 624, 626, 643, 645, 652; friendship with Connie Mack, 602; spring training, 616
Perry, Hank, 555
personality of Connie Mack, 94, 117, 130, 145, 239, 283, 336, 500–501, 548–49, 627
Pettit, Bob, 30, 32, 38, 40
Pfeffer, Fred, 73
Pfeister, Jack, 479
Phelon, W. A., 242, 305, 484, 591, 630, 638, 669–70
Philadelphia Athletics, the: advertisers and, 437, 490–91; allegations of fixing the 1914 World Series by, 646–48; Ben Shibe and, 198–204, 206; celebrations for, 294; Columbia Park built for, 204–8; Connie Mack's separation from, 673; disputes with the National League, 218–19, 248–54; Eddie Collins leaves, 662–70; fans, 545–46; the Federal League and, 608–9; financial restructuring in 1914, 567–69; financial troubles, 623–24; first season, 234–39; football team, 298–301; game attendance, 290–92, 358, 390, 395–96, 402, 434–35, 498, 627–28; incorporation of, 203; lawsuit by the Philadelphia Phillies, 227–31, 237, 264–69, 270–71; moves to Kansas City and Oakland, 673; 1901 season, 292–98; 1905 games against the New York Giants, 383–85; the 1905 World Series and, 354–57; 1910 World Series and, 489–91; 1911 World Series and, 517–45; 1913 World Series and, 586–99; 1914 World Series

and, 640–48; peace between the
Phillies and, 315–16; players leaving,
658–59, 663–70; players recruited to,
209–16, 220–26, 239–42, 257, 273–75,
297–98, 316, 332, 339–40, 360–62,
366–69, 369–73, 392, 402–3, 406, 412–
18, 501–4, 550–51, 554; salaries, 266,
272, 288, 289–90, 295–96, 298, 371,
406, 497; the press on, 208, 211, 220,
221, 223, 236, 238, 241, 284, 288, 292,
509–14, 515–16, 600; spring training,
220–22, 309–11, 327, 338–40, 407, 429,
468, 497, 548–49, 615–17; uniforms,
628. *See also* Shibe Park
Philadelphia Bulletin, 201, 488
Philadelphia Daily News, 128, 518, 563
Philadelphia Evening Bulletin, 461, 655
Philadelphia Evening Telegraph, 246,
379–80, 488, 574
Philadelphia Evening Times, 475, 489,
532, 560, 601
Philadelphia Inquirer, 483; Ben Shibe
and, 423; on Columbia Park, 235;
Connie Mack and, 93–94, 330, 349,
362, 467; on Connie Mack's death, 1;
on Dennis Mack, 245; Frank Hough
and, 182, 202, 213; and the 1905
World Series, 355
Philadelphia North American, 251;
on baseball's decline, 311; on
Connie Mack, 262, 479; on Dennis
McGillucuddy, 245, 246; Harry
Davis in, 359–60; on Ira Thomas,
618; and the 1905 World Series, 355,
356; on the Philadelphia Athletics,
208, 211, 220, 221, 223, 236, 238, 241,
284, 288, 292, 509, 600; on players'
salaries, 576
Philadelphia pa: American League
negotiations with, 188–90, 197–200;
baseball teams in, 196–97; Benjamin

Shibe and, 197–203; Columbia Park,
204–8, 238, 244, 263–64; Connie
Mack in, 185–93, 193, 204–5; found-
ing and development of, 182–83,
194–97; newspaper writers in, 380;
Shibe Park, 421–27
Philadelphia Phillies, the, 198, 210–11,
506–7; game attendance, 291–92;
Horace Fogel and, 498; lawsuit
against the Philadelphia Athletics,
227–31, 237, 264–69, 270–71; owner-
ship change, 315; peace between the
Athletics and, 315–16
Philadelphia Press, 570
Philadelphia Public Ledger, 242
Philadelphia Record, 378, 387, 402, 459,
557, 628
Philadelphia Sporting Writers
Association, 380
Philadelphia Times, 242
Phillippe, Deacon, 151, 252
Phillips, E. Lawrence, 522
Phillips, Esther, 494
physical appearance of Connie Mack,
24, 57, 121, 122, 500
Piatt, Wiley, 212, 219, 241, 251, 303
Pickering, Ollie, 316, 328–29
Pinkerton Detective Agency, 276
Pinnance, Ed, 323
Pitching in a Pinch (Mathewson), 527
Pittsburgh Alleghenys, the, 71,
82–85; merger with the Pittsburgh
Burghers, 86
Pittsburgh Burghers, the, 82–83; merger
with the Pittsburgh Alleghenys, 86
Pittsburgh Pirates, the, 23; Connie
Mack as manager of, 104–7, 108–19;
creation, 86; 1892 season, 86–91; 1893
season, 96–101; 1894 season, 101–7;
Jack O'Connor and, 291–92; under
Ned Hanlon, 86–89; newspaper

Pittsburgh Pirates (*cont.*)
accounts of, 106–7; 1900 season, 173–74; under William C. Temple, 89–94

Pittsburgh Post, 96, 97, 106, 111, 114, 124

Pittsburgh Press, 85, 125, 128, 138, 156

Pittsburgh Sun, 571

Pius X, Pope, 495

Plank, Eddie, 319, 374, 375, 381, 497, 506, 510, 601, 611; automobile purchased by, 545; the Federal League and, 620, 650; games, 224, 246–48, 251–52, 257, 263–64, 272, 275, 279, 283, 287, 295, 317–18, 330–31, 345, 350, 366, 382, 388, 391–97, 401, 407, 411, 417, 441, 445–46, 450–52, 457, 484, 486–87, 504, 552–53, 561–62, 581, 626; housing, 427; illnesses and injuries of, 651, 652–56; leaves the Philadelphia Athletics, 658–59; 1911 World Series and, 356, 524–25, 537–40, 543; 1913 World Series and, 589, 591–94, 597–99; 1914 World Series and, 642, 649–50; recruited by Connie Mack, 239–42; salary of, 576, 613; spring training, 550–51, 615; waiver rules and, 652–56

players, baseball: alcohol use by, 34, 58, 59, 64, 75, 88, 91, 112, 140, 159, 430–31, 469, 481; black, 46, 152, 257, 294–95; Brotherhood of Professional, 67–69, 71–72; conflicts between the National League and American League over, 227–31, 237, 248–52; draft prices for, 164–65; farming system, 136–37, 191–92; housing and traveling conditions, 49, 52–53, 62–63, 76, 86–87, 109–10, 132, 427, 461; injuries, 53, 101, 102, 103, 161, 171; insurance, 379; Protective Association of Professional, 180; recruited by Charles Somers, 272–73, 516; recruited by Connie Mack, 137–39, 142, 146–49, 160, 169–70, 209–16, 220–26, 239–42, 257, 273–75, 279–80, 297–98, 316, 332, 339–40, 360–62, 366–69, 369–73, 392, 402–3, 406, 412–18, 501–4, 550–51, 554; rowdy behavior by, 30, 34–35, 120–21, 142, 233–34, 244–46, 248, 253–54, 506; salaries, 22, 31, 36, 38, 45, 51, 67–69, 80–81, 138–39, 140, 146, 148–49, 158, 172, 210–11, 221, 266, 272, 295–96, 298, 307, 326–27, 371, 379–80, 428–29, 465, 501, 607–8; sold by the Baltimore Orioles, 622–25; superstitions among, 462–63

Players' National League of Base Ball Clubs: administration of, 74; disbandment, 82–83; field captains, 75; financial troubles, 81–82; incorporation of, 71–72; profit sharing, 74; umpires, 76

Pollock, Ed, 201, 337

popularity of baseball, 186, 233–34

Populist Party, 186

Porter, Odie Oscar, 275

Postal, Fred C., 260, 304, 306

Potter, James, 315

Povich, Shirley, 63

Powers, Doc, 436; death of, 438–39, 440; games, 242, 253, 274, 294, 322, 343, 374, 381, 382, 418, 438; illnesses, 407; and the 1905 World Series, 357;

Powers, Florence, 438–39

Pratt, Al, 78, 86

press, the: on the American League, 217, 222–23; on the Atlanta Braves, 633, 635; on automobiling, 557; Ban Johnson and, 186–87; Connie Mack on, 568–71, 657–58; on Connie Mack's career, 50, 59, 75, 88, 97–98, 128, 142, 329–30, 332–33, 377, 401–2, 418, 441, 448–49, 568–70, 576, 585,

665, 666; on Connie Mack's death, 1–2; on Connie Mack's life, 47–48, 60, 62, 121; coverage of the 1905 World Series, 354; coverage of the 1911 World Series, 517–19, 520–21; criticisms of Connie Mack, 172–73, 568–71; on early baseball, 21–22, 23, 27; on Eddie Collins, 511–12, 657, 669–70; on Ellsworth Hoy, 63; on football, 299–300; Henry Beach Needham and, 374–75; on Margaret Mack's death, 93; on the Meriden club, 31, 32, 33–34; on the Milwaukee Brewers, 136, 137, 139, 154–56, 161; motion picture cameras and, 482, 518; on the New York Mets, 43; on the Philadelphia Athletics, 509–14, 515–16, 600; on the Pittsburgh Pirates, 106; on the Players' League, 74; on the Players' Protective Association, 187–88; on politics, 39; relationships between Philadelphia teams and, 380; on salaries in baseball, 574; on the Washington Nationals/Statesmen/Senators, 55, 58, 62, 63, 64–65; on the Western League, 161, 165. See also *North American; and individual newspapers*

Prince, George A., 84

profits, baseball, 74–76, 79–80, 144–45, 180, 259, 279, 287, 465–66, 498–99, 545, 546, 596–97, 603

Prohibition, 60

Protective Association of Professional Baseball Players, 180, 187–88

Providence Grays, the, 89

Pulliam, Harry, 151, 157, 164, 209, 295, 304

Queen Victoria, 191

Quinn, Clarence, 297

Quinn, Jack, 581

Radbourn, Hoss, 55

Rambo, Ormond, 614–15

Rath, Morrie, 475, 476

Rayburn, John E., 385

Reach, Alfred J., 51, 338, 424; baseball supplies manufactured by, 76, 159, 488, 503; the National League rules committee and, 217; the Philadelphia Phillies and, 139, 198–202, 202, 315; *Sporting Life* and, 163

Reach, George, 488

Reach American League Guide, 190, 373, 424, 489, 586, 635

Recruit Little Cigars, 491

Reidy, Bill, 142, 143, 170

Reilly, Charles, 141

Reilly, Josh, 406

Reilly, Thomas, 33, 34

Reitz, Heinie, 169, 171

release clauses and free agency rules, 605–6, 612–13

Remsen, Jack, 40

Rettger, George, 142, 150, 170, 171

Reulbach, Ed, 479–80, 485

Rice, Grantland, 628–29, 649, 657

Rice, Tommy, 668

Richter, Chandler, 460, 601, 653

Richter, Francis C.: the American Association and, 163, 190; on baseball rules, 96; on Connie Mack, 333, 336; on Eddie Collins, 411–12; on Jack Knight, 439; on Lave Cross, 295; on Rube Waddell, 348; on Silk O'Loughlin, 400

Rickert, Joe, 384

Rickey, Branch, 182, 278, 354, 366, 411, 627

Rigler, Cy, 483

Ritter, Lawrence S.: *The Glory of Their Times*, 616–17

Roach, Cornelius, 9, 496

Roach, David, 9

Robinson, Clyde, 263

Robinson, Wilbert, 57, 99, 183, 255, 517, 594, 659

Robison, Frank, 292, 303

Rockefeller, John D., 196

Rogers, Col. John I., 266, 338; on the Board of Control, 85; conflicts with the Western League, 190, 191, 265; Hughie Jennings and, 249; lawsuit by the Philadelphia Phillies and, 74, 266–67; Napoleon Lajoie and, 272–73, 281; the Philadelphia Phillies and, 199, 202, 219, 227, 229, 238, 315, 326; players recruited by, 272

Roosevelt, Teddy, 196, 338

Rossman, Claude, 441–42, 447, 452

Roth, Mark, 420

Rothstein, Arnold, 647

rowdy behavior by baseball players, 30, 34–35, 120–21, 142, 233–34, 244–46, 248, 253–54, 506

Rowe, Jack, 72, 73, 74, 75, 77, 79–80

Rucker, Nap, 373–74, 413

Rudolph, Dick, 370, 630–31, 640–41, 643, 645

rules, baseball, 95–96, 141, 216–19, 260–61, 305–7, 586–87; baseballs and, 487–89; dressing rooms, 380, 575; foul ball, 364–65; free agency, 605–6; interleague play and, 336–37; length of games and, 507; waivers and, 652–56

Runyon, Damon, 519, 630, 633, 643–44

Ruppert, Jacob, 658, 665, 666

Rusie, Amos, 95, 221, 383

Russ, Mary, 496

Russell, Clarence "Lefty," 478–79, 501–2, 504, 553

Ruth, Babe, 247, 617, 623, 624, 625

Ryan, Nolan, 324

Ryder, Jack, 575

Sahl, Jill, 618

salaries, baseball, 36, 38, 379–80, 574, 576; in the American League, 172–73, 210–11, 216, 221, 325, 326–27; of Ban Johnson, 259; and the Brotherhood of Professional Base Ball Players, 67–69; caps on, 307; complaints about, 22, 148–49; of Connie Mack, 31, 45, 51, 158, 259, 295, 378, 570; Connie Mack on, 428–29, 607–8; of John McGraw, 259, 570; in the minor leagues, 45, 138–39, 140; in the National League, 303; Philadelphia Athletics, 266, 272, 288, 289–90, 295–96, 298, 371, 406, 497; in the Players' League, 80–81; press accounts of, 569–70; release clauses and, 612–13; secrecy of, 465; of Ty Cobb, 501, 575, 609; Washington Senators, 501; in the Western League, 146

Salmon, Roger, 553

Salsinger, H. G., 314

Salva, Gus, 419

San Jose Mercury Herald, 657

Saturday Evening Post, 569, 594, 626, 639, 646

Scanlon, Mike, 49

Schaefer, Germany, 395, 398, 452, 600

Schang, Wally, 577, 591, 599, 600, 602, 638, 641, 642

Schlitzer, Vic, 406, 408, 412, 439, 441, 446

Schmidt, Boss, 397–98

Schmidt, Butch, 631

Schmidt, Henry, 297

Schrecongost, Osee, 337, 339, 375, 382, 404; baseball games, 274, 276–77, 286, 294, 313, 322, 323, 334, 343, 345, 390, 417; death of, 405; Harry Davis and, 363; and the 1905 World Series, 357

Schroeder, Joseph, 262, 327, 344–45, 357, 424–25, 527–28
Schroeder, Robert, 262, 327
Schulte, Frank, 480, 482
Schumann, Carl, 375
Schweitzer, Albert, 419
Scioscia, Mike, 57
Selee, Frank, 29, 31, 91, 100, 232, 243
Selter, Ron, 387
Seybold, Ralph, 374, 415, 419, 520, 611; baseball games, 234–35, 241, 266, 274, 282–83, 295, 324, 368, 382, 390, 412; injuries of, 328–29, 407
Seymour, Cy, 384, 509
Shafer, Tilly, 598
Shame of the Cities, The (Steffens), 195
Shannon, Joseph, 40
Shantz, Bobby, 3
Sharsig, Billy, 199–200, 204, 205, 235, 245, 253
Shaughnessy, Frank, 408, 416, 449
Shaw, Al, 386
Shawkey, Bob, 624, 650–51; games, 550–51, 554, 559, 583, 589, 643, 652; income taxes paid by, 614; injuries of, 620; spring training, 616
Shean, Dave, 370, 375
Sheckard, Jimmy, 211–12, 263, 482
Sheed, Wilfred, 418, 646–47, 656–57
Sheerin, Fr. Thomas, 12
Sheridan, John, 249, 250, 275, 506, 515, 624
Sherman, James, 474
Shettsline, Bill, 210–11, 214–15, 230, 231, 265–68, 288, 315, 338; on the press, 349
Shibe, Benjamin F., 238, 262, 281, 293, 301, 363, 385, 420, 589, 628, 645; accused of wrongdoing, 459; on admission prices, 466; formation of the Philadelphia Athletics and, 197–

203, 206, 210, 219; Frank MacFarland and, 568; lawsuit by the Philadelphia Phillies against, 227–31, 265, 266; partnership between Connie Mack and, 296–97; on the pennant races, 402; the press on, 657; real estate investments of, 379; rules committee and, 305–7; Shibe Park and, 421–27, 437; and the success of the American League, 259
Shibe, Ida, 471
Shibe, John, 200, 203, 253, 327, 337, 374, 380, 445, 467, 581, 658; expensive tastes of, 378; football team organized by, 301; friendship with Connie Mack, 492, 495; the media and, 518; and the 1905 World Series, 355, 357; scouting by, 497; Shibe Park and, 422, 424
Shibe, Tom, 200, 203, 424, 568
Shibe Park: building of, 421–27; improvements to, 547, 573–74; motion picture cameras at, 482; opening day, 434–36; success of, 460
Shire, Moses, 73, 79
Shoch, George, 48, 146
Shore, Ernie, 623, 624, 625
Shronk, LeRoy, 239
Sibley, Charles, 23, 28
Sibley, George A., 16
Simmons, Al, 3
Sinnott, James, 628
Skinner, May Wynne, 319
Smith, Al, 604
Smith, Elmer, 90, 110, 124
Smith, Frank, 410
Smith, Harry, 160, 171, 253, 305
Smith, Harvey F., 298
Smith, Joe, 527
Smith, M. J., 245
Smith, Red, 1–2, 224, 555, 632, 638

Smith, Robert: *Illustrated History of Baseball*, 600

Smith, Syd, 406, 412, 418

Snodgrass, Fred, 530, 533, 534, 537, 587, 599

Society for American Baseball Research, 33

Sockalexis, Louis, 139

Soden, Arthur, 190, 216

Somers, Charles W., 209, 210, 289, 475, 476, 503, 505; and the American League, 168–69, 182–85; Arthur Irwin and, 189–90; financial difficulties of, 260; financial investments in baseball, 201, 270; Harry Davis and, 547; Jimmy Manning and, 232; lawsuit against the Philadelphia Athletics and, 228; negotiations with the National League, 303–7; Philadelphia Athletics and, 203; players recruited by, 272–73, 516; Shibe Park and, 425; teams owned by, 192

Sousa, John Philip, 54

Southern League, 150

Southern New England League, 40, 42

Spalding, Albert G., 66, 76, 425; and the American League, 184–85; financial resources of, 51; and the National League, 81–82, 198, 262–63; and the New York Giants, 79; on player salaries, 22

Spalding Guide, 40, 46, 55; on the Pittsburgh Pirates, 106–7; on the Players' League, 74; on the Washington Senators, 64–65

Spanish-American War, 150

Sparks, Tully, 169

Spatz, Lyle, 477

Speaker, Tris, 480, 507, 552, 605

Speer, Kid, 161

Spencer, Tubby, 419

Spencer Leader, 93

Spencer Sun, 20, 23, 28, 60, 61

Spink, Al, 162

Spink, J. G. Taylor, 598

Spink, Taylor, 639

Sport, 48

Sporting Life, 68, 74, 131, 211, 333; on the American League, 191, 192, 217; on Ban Johnson, 163; on baseball profits, 465; on baseball rules, 305; on baseball salaries, 260; Ben Shibe and, 271; Christy Mathewson in, 222; on Connie Mack, 50, 120, 142, 167, 256–57, 424; Connie Mack in, 285; on Eddie Collins, 411–12; on Frank Baker, 608; on Hughie Jennings, 653; on Joe Jackson, 414; on John T. Brush, 136; on J. Palmer O'Neill, 86; on Lave Cross, 295; on the Milwaukee Brewers, 180; on Napoleon Lajoie, 273; on the Philadelphia Athletics, 600, 639; on the Pittsburgh Burghers, 83; on players contracts, 290; on sale of players, 149; on the Western League, 161, 165

Sporting News, 74, 156, 163, 274, 381; on baseball salaries, 466; on the Chicago White Sox, 368; on Chief Bender, 366; on Connie Mack, 329–30, 388, 584; John Sheridan and, 515; on the National League, 263; on negotiations between the National and American Leagues, 307; on the Philadelphia Athletics, 639; on Rube Waddell, 375; on Ty Cobb, 456

spring training, Philadelphia Athletics, 220–22, 309–11, 327, 338–40, 407, 429, 468, 497, 548–49, 615–17

Stafford, Bob, 149, 161

Stagg, Amos Alonzo, 69, 310

Stahl, Chick, 210

Stahl, Jake, 355, 359, 563
The Stain of Guilt, 318, 323
Stallings, George: Ban Johnson and, 635–36; Connie Mack and, 636–37, 643–44, 665; games, 162, 212, 233, 256, 260, 477, 577; 1914 World Series and, 630–34, 640, 643
Stanage, Oscar, 450–51
Standard Oil Company, 196
Stanfield, George, 456
Star Trading Company, 533
Stebbins, Ella, 61
Steele, Joseph M., 426
Steelman, Morris, 253, 257, 274
Steffens, Lincoln: *The Shame of the Cities*, 195
Stengels, Casey, 276
Stenzel, Jake, 90, 168
Sternberger, Agnes, 285
Stetson, Nathan, 245
Stevens, Frank, 135, 647
Stevens, Harry M., 87, 135, 149
St. Louis Browns, the: games, 84–86, 97–98, 122, 138, 289, 304, 405, 408, 447, 509, 584, 625–26; George Stovall and, 547, 605; Harry Davis and, 547; Martin Lawler and, 469; Monte Cross and, 547
St. Louis Cardinals, the, 270
St. Louis Globe-Democrat, 441, 570, 576
St. Louis Maroons, the, 50
St. Louis Post-Dispatch, 585, 617, 624
St. Louis Republic, 75
St. Louis Times, 569, 645, 653
stockholders, baseball, 45–46, 295
Stoddard, Emerson H., 13, 15, 16, 19, 60
Stone, John and Julia, 13, 16
Stouch, Tommy, 413
Stovall, George, 547, 605
Stovey, Harry, 23, 84, 85
Stratton, Scott, 86, 87

Street, Gabby, 478, 480
Strunk, Amos: games, 416–17, 431, 436–38, 475, 486, 497, 648; illnesses of, 620; 1911 World Series and, 558, 577, 579; 1913 World Series and, 599; 1914 World Series and, 641–42
Sudhoff, Willie, 318
Sugden, Joe, 96, 104, 111, 114, 125, 322, 555
Sullivan, Billy, 210, 480
Sullivan, Cornelius, 10
Sullivan, Denny, 386
Sullivan, Eddie, 372, 375
Sullivan, John L., 328
Sullivan, Marty, 58
Sullivan, Ted, 61–65, 69
Summers, Ed, 473, 508
superstitions among baseball players, 462–63

Taft, William Howard, 419, 474, 557
Talcott, Frank, 81
Tannehill, Jesse, 252, 289, 328, 329
Taylor, Harry, 180
Taylor, Jack, 131, 144, 151, 258, 357
Taylor, John I., 326
Tebeau, Pat, 102, 123, 139
Temple, William C., 89–94, 105, 300
Tener, John K., 66, 504, 658
Tenney, Fred, 40
Terry, William, 90, 140, 144, 149
Tesreau, Jeff, 587, 594
Texas League, 150
Theis, Lewis E., 221
Thomas, Ira, 480, 577, 580, 602, 610–11, 613, 666; Base Ball Players' Fraternity and, 606; as captain, 618–20, 668; on Eddie Collins, 618, 660–62; friendship with Connie Mack, 618; games, 430–31, 441–42, 460, 461, 475, 478, 483, 508, 560, 627; as manager, 659–60; 1911 World Series and, 528,

Thomas, Ira (*cont.*)
536, 538; 1914 World Series and, 643,
649; the press on, 657
Thomas, Roy, 211, 216, 261
Thompson, Bill, 112–13
Thompson, Sam, 197
Thompson, Shag, 639, 645
Thoreau, Henry, 289
Thorn, John: *Total Baseball*, 647
Thurman, Allen W., 84, 85
ticket prices, 519, 574
Tilden, Otis, 26
Tinker, Joe, 482, 605, 607, 660
Titman, C. Emory, 548, 549, 552, 571,
616
Titus, Willington, 382
Toney, Fred, 581
Total Baseball (Thorn et al), 647
Travers, Rev. Fr. Aloysius, 555–56
Treasury of New England Folklore
(Botkin), 2
Tri-State League, 573, 583
Truby, Harry, 126
Trumbull, Walter, 626
Tschantre, Ottillie Rosa, 461
Tucker, Tom, 100–101
Tufts, Washington, 12
Turner, Terry, 474
Turner, William Jay, 228, 230, 265–67,
567
Twain, Mark, 314
Tyler, George "Lefty," 630, 642

Uber, George W., 435
Ultimate Baseball Book, The (Okrent
and Levine), 646
umpires, baseball, 56, 103, 111, 141–42,
236, 256, 319, 345, 395, 506, 641;
as columnists, 515; Connie Mack
and, 113, 117–18, 124–25, 250; games
using two, 327–28; as managers, 49;

Players' League, 76; superstitions
among, 463
Unglaub, Bob, 341
Union League, 408

Van Zelst, Louis, 464–65, 481, 483, 519,
523, 545, 589
Vare, William, 196
vaudeville, 75, 111, 121, 137, 218, 546
Vaughn, Jim, 473
Veblen, Thorsten, 283
Veeck, Bill, 627
Vickers, Harry "Rube," 383, 386–87,
407–8, 412, 417–18
Vila, Joe, 348, 520–21, 527, 541, 621, 664
Virginia League, the, 221, 622
Vizard, Henry, 295
Vizard, W. J., 18, 19, 61
von der Ahe, Chris, 162, 316
Vorhees, Cy, 293

Waddell, George Edward "Rube," 624,
646; baseball games, 173–80, 224,
252, 258, 275–79, 282, 283, 286, 288,
293–95, 313, 327–28, 329, 330, 340–44,
345–46, 351, 363, 365, 386–88, 391–92,
401, 417, 429; Connie Mack and,
173–80, 311–14, 317–23, 337, 348–49,
351–53, 376–77, 382–83, 403–5; death
of, 405; Eddie Collins and, 372;
fans of, 292, 338, 340; featured in
books, 296; football games, 299;
health problems of, 343; injuries of,
368; Mathewson matchup, 383–85;
problems of, 317–23, 340–41, 374–75,
392–93, 422
Wagner, Charlie, 501
Wagner, Heinie, 563
Wagners, Honus, 210, 212
Walberg, Rube, 2
Waldron, Irv, 154–56, 161, 170, 171

Wallace, Bobby, 270
Wallace, Charles, 298
Walsh, Ed, 577, 594; on automobiles, 557; games, 375, 408, 416, 441, 443, 460, 480, 632
Walsh, Jimmy, 560, 645
Walsh, Michael, 37
Ward, John Montgomery, 52, 57, 67, 68, 69, 74, 75, 81, 82
Ward, Walter, 620–21
Warnick, Edwin LeRoy, 552
Washington, George, 293
Washington Evening Star, 51, 59, 325
Washington Morning Republican, 54
Washington Nationals/Statesmen, the, 408; Connie Mack joins, 47–51; 1887 season, 54–59; 1888 season, 63–66; 1889 season, 69–72; games, 557, 562, 583; name change, 325–26; travels through the South, 62–65. *See also* Washington Senators, the
Washington Post, 58, 62, 63, 64, 241, 293, 325, 343, 362, 430, 442, 447
The Washington Senators, 47
Washington Senators, the, 64, 117, 325–26, 330; salaries, 501. *See also* Washington Nationals/Statesmen, the
Watkins, W. H., 107, 156
Watson, Thomas, 283
Weart, Billy, 495, 518, 574, 579, 611, 639
Weaver, Earl, 117
Weaver, Farmer, 142, 144, 149
Wedge, Will, 633
Weeghman, Charles, 658
Weidman, George, 124–25
Werber, Bill, 454
Western League, the: Connie Mack on, 158; and the National League, 153, 161–64; teams, 128, 136, 139, 146; uniform dress code, 159

Wheeler, John N., 526, 634
White, Deacon, 72, 73, 74, 75
White, Doc, 480
Whiting, James, 548
Whitney, Jim, 55, 66
Williams, Jimmy, 209
Williams, John Arthur, 22
Williams, Ted, 648
William Steel & Sons, 424
Willis, Vic, 220–24, 237, 260, 264, 305
Wilson, Art, 542
Wilson, Howard, 281
Wilson, Woodrow, 602
Wiltse, Hooks, 528, 540
Wiltse, Snake, 252, 253, 257, 263, 279, 280
Winter, George, 253
Wise, Sam, 76, 82
Wolfe, Edgar, 330, 472
Wolverton, Harry, 270
Wood, Joe, 457, 557, 563
Woodward, Rich, 425
Worcester Evening Gazette, 412
Worcester Ruby Legs, the, 23
World Series, the: allegedly fixed in 1914, 646–48; the Boston Braves and, 629, 630, 640–48; Connie Mack's attendance at, 460–61; first "official," 354–57; lost by the Philadelphia Athletics, 640–48; the New York Giants and, 517–42, 563, 586–99; 1919, 647; press coverage of, 517–19, 520–21, 586–87; team mascots at, 519; ticket prices, 519; won by the Philadelphia Athletics, 489–91, 542–44, 545, 599–600
Wray, J. Ed, 585
Wright, Harry, 51, 336
writers, baseball, 337–38
Wyckoff, John, 577, 578, 581, 584, 589, 624, 645, 652

Wynn, Early, 646

Yawkey, Tom, 625
Yawkey, William, 325
Yeager, George, 169, 171
Yeutter, Frank, 561
Yoekel, Fred C., 437

Young, Cy, 210, 251, 275, 292, 317, 328,
329, 331, 342–44, 348, 385, 412, 607
Young, Nick, 59, 68, 96, 138, 139, 162, 192

Ziegler, Ray, 402
Zimmer, Chief, 179, 180, 315, 383–84
Zimmerman, Heiniè, 487